The Birth of Democracy in South America

South America contains some of the oldest democracies in the world, yet we still know relatively little about how and why democracy arose in the region. Raúl L. Madrid argues that three main developments – the professionalization of the military, the growth of parties, and splits within the ruling party – led to democratization in the early twentieth century. Military professionalization increased the incentives for the opposition to abandon the armed struggle and focus on the electoral path to power. The growth of parties boosted the capacity of the opposition to enact and enforce democratic reforms that would level the electoral playing field. And ruling party splits created the opportunity for the opposition and ruling party dissidents to ally and push through reforms. This persuasive and original book offers important implications for the study of democracy. This title is also available as Open Access on Cambridge Core.

Raúl L. Madrid is the Harold C. and Alice T. Nowlin Regents Professor in Liberal Arts at the University of Texas at Austin. He is the author of *The Rise of Ethnic Politics in Latin America* (2012) as well as numerous other books and articles on Latin American politics.

Cambridge Studies in Comparative Politics

General Editors

Anna Grzymala-Busse, *Stanford University*
Dan Slater, *University of Michigan*

Associate Editors

Lisa Blaydes, *Stanford University*
Catherine Boone, *London School of Economics and Political Science*
Thad Dunning, *University of California, Berkeley*
Anna Grzymala-Busse, *Stanford University*
Torben Iversen, *Harvard University*
Stathis Kalyvas, *University of Oxford*
Melanie Manion, *Duke University*
Prerna Singh, *Brown University*
Dan Slater, *University of Michigan*
Susan Stokes, *Yale University*
Tariq Thachil, *University of Pennsylvania*
Erik Wibbels, *University of Pennsylvania*

Series Founder

Peter Lange, *Duke University*

Editors Emeritus

Margaret Levi, *Stanford University*
Kathleen Thelen, *Massachusetts Institute of Technology*

Other Books in the Series

Luis Schiumerini, *Incumbency Bias: Why Political Office is a Blessing and a Curse in Latin America*
Alexander Reisenbichler, *Through the Roof: Housing, Capitalism, and the State in America and Germany*
Raúl L. Madrid, *The Birth of Democracy in South America*
Nicholas Kuipers, *States against Nations: Meritocracy, Patronage, and the Challenges of Bureaucratic Selection*
Nicholas Barnes, *Inside Criminalized Governance: How and Why Gangs Rule the Streets of Rio de Janeiro*
Isabel M. Perera, *The Welfare Workforce: Why Mental Health Care Varies Across Affluent Democracies*
Graeme Blair, Fotini Christia, and Jeremy M. Weinstein, *Crime, Insecurity, and Community Policing: Experiments on Building Trust*
Georgia Kernell, *Inside Parties: How Party Rules Shape Membership and Responsiveness*
Volha Charnysh, *Uprooted: How post-WWII Population Transfers Remade Europe*

Continued after the index

The Birth of Democracy in South America

RAÚL L. MADRID
The University of Texas at Austin

Shaftesbury Road, Cambridge CB2 8EA, United Kingdom

One Liberty Plaza, 20th Floor, New York, NY 10006, USA

477 Williamstown Road, Port Melbourne, VIC 3207, Australia

314–321, 3rd Floor, Plot 3, Splendor Forum, Jasola District Centre,
New Delhi – 110025, India

103 Penang Road, #05–06/07, Visioncrest Commercial, Singapore 238467

Cambridge University Press is part of Cambridge University Press & Assessment,
a department of the University of Cambridge.

We share the University's mission to contribute to society through the pursuit of
education, learning and research at the highest international levels of excellence.

www.cambridge.org
Information on this title: www.cambridge.org/9781009633819

DOI: 10.1017/9781009633802

© Raúl L. Madrid 2025

This publication is in copyright. Subject to statutory exception and to the provisions
of relevant collective licensing agreements, with the exception of the Creative Commons
version the link for which is provided below, no reproduction of any part may take place
without the written permission of Cambridge University Press & Assessment.

An online version of this work is published at doi.org/10.1017/9781009633802 under a
Creative Commons Open Access license CC-BY-NC 4.0 which permits re-use, distribution
and reproduction in any medium for non-commercial purposes providing appropriate
credit to the original work is given and any changes made are indicated. To view a copy
of this license visit https://creativecommons.org/licenses/by-nc/4.0

When citing this work, please include a reference to the DOI 10.1017/9781009633802

First published 2025

A catalogue record for this publication is available from the British Library

Library of Congress Cataloging-in-Publication Data
NAMES: Madrid, Raúl L. author
TITLE: The birth of democracy in South America / Raúl L. Madrid,
The University of Texas at Austin.
DESCRIPTION: Cambridge ; New York, NY : Cambridge University Press, 2025. | Series:
Cambridge studies in comparative politics | Includes bibliographical references and index
IDENTIFIERS: LCCN 2024059521 | ISBN 9781009633819 hardback |
ISBN 9781009633789 paperback | ISBN 9781009633802 ebook
SUBJECTS: LCSH: Democracy – South America | South America – Politics and government
CLASSIFICATION: LCC JL1866 .M33 2025 | DDC 320.48–dc23/eng/20250508
LC record available at https://lccn.loc.gov/2024059521

ISBN 978-1-009-63381-9 Hardback
ISBN 978-1-009-63378-9 Paperback

Cambridge University Press & Assessment has no responsibility for the persistence
or accuracy of URLs for external or third-party internet websites referred to in this
publication and does not guarantee that any content on such websites is, or will
remain, accurate or appropriate.

The Birth of Democracy in South America

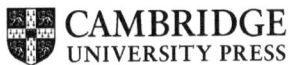

For Paloma

Contents

List of Figures	*page* ix
List of Tables	xi
Acknowledgments	xiii
List of Abbreviations	xvii
Introduction: The Origins of Democracy in South America	1
1 Armies, Parties, and the Birth of Democracy	17
2 Elections and Democracy in South America before 1930	48
3 Military Professionalization and the Decline of Revolts in South America	74
4 The Origins of Strong Parties in South America	98
5 The Roots of Strong Democracies: Chile and Uruguay	123
6 The Roots of Weak Democracies: Argentina and Colombia	175
7 The Roots of Stable Authoritarianism: Brazil, Peru, and Venezuela	224
8 The Roots of Unstable Authoritarianism: Bolivia, Ecuador, and Paraguay	262
Conclusion: Contributions and Implications	302
References	317
Index	349

Figures

1.1 Determinants of regime outcomes in South America before 1930	*page* 38
3.1 The decline of major revolts in South America by decade, 1830–1929	77
3.2 The frequency of major insider and outsider revolts in South America, 1830–1929	79
4.1 Party institutionalization in South America, 1870–1929	102

Tables

I.1	Conceptualization and measurement of key variables	page 11
1.1	Opposition parties and democratic reform	30
1.2	Scoring regime outcomes in South America during the early twentieth century	40
2.1	Comparing databases on democracy in South America before 1930	54
2.2	Suffrage restrictions and voter turnout in South America in the nineteenth century	57
2.3	Competition in presidential elections in South America during the nineteenth century	64
2.4	Ephemeral democratization in nineteenth-century South America	67
2.5	Presidential elections and democracy in South America, 1900–1929	70
3.1	A typology of revolts based on the origins of their leaders	78
3.2	Indicators of military strength and professionalization in South America, 1870–1929	90
3.3	The varying stability of regimes in South America, 1870–1929	91
3.4	Determinants of outsider revolts in South America, 1830–1929	96
4.1	Major political parties in South America, 1870–1930	106
4.2	Liberal and conservative strength in South America, 1700–1850	116
4.3	Geographic fragmentation in South America circa 1900	119
5.1	Major revolts in Chile, 1830–1929	125
5.2	Presidential and legislative elections in Chile, 1831–1924	138
5.3	Major revolts in Uruguay, 1830–1929	150
5.4	Presidential and legislative elections in Uruguay, 1900–1929	160
6.1	Major revolts in Argentina, 1852–1929	178
6.2	Presidential elections in Argentina, 1854–1928	196
6.3	Major revolts in Colombia, 1830–1929	201

6.4	Presidential elections in Colombia, 1819–1930	213
7.1	Major revolts in Venezuela, 1830–1930	228
7.2	Major revolts in Peru, 1830–1929	237
7.3	Major revolts in Brazil, 1830–1929	250
8.1	Major revolts in Bolivia, 1830–1929	265
8.2	Major revolts in Ecuador, 1830–1930	280
8.3	Major revolts in Paraguay, 1830–1929	292
C.1	Democracy in South America, post-1929	306

Acknowledgments

This book has been ten years in the making. It began as a study of the struggle for democratic consolidation in Latin America during the late twentieth and early twenty-first centuries. Early on, however, I realized that the countries with the strongest democracies in the region today (e.g., Chile, Costa Rica, and Uruguay) were also among the first Latin American countries to establish democracy. Thus, to understand why some countries had strong democracies today, it seemed important to examine what led to the emergence of democracy in the early twentieth century. And to understand why democracy arose in some countries in the early twentieth century, it became necessary to explore why nineteenth-century efforts to establish democracy had failed. Thus, through historical regress, I embarked upon a study of the struggle for democracy in the region from independence until 1930.

To make the study more feasible, I decided early on to limit it to South America alone. Nevertheless, it has still seemed an overwhelming task at times. If a graduate student had proposed carrying out a dissertation on ten countries over 100 years of history, I would have summarily thrown them out of my office. But one of the advantages of having tenure is that I cannot be easily thrown out of my office. Tenure makes these ambitious projects possible.

My location at the University of Texas at Austin (UT Austin) also made this book feasible. We are blessed to have the finest Latin American library in the country: the Nettie Lee Benson Collection. Over the last ten years, I have checked out so many library books on this topic that I have come to refer to my office as the Benson Annex. I am also thankful to have had access to the congressional libraries in Argentina, Chile, Colombia, and Uruguay, which are beautiful and fructiferous places to carry out archival research.

UT Austin provided me with a variety of other essential resources, and I hope this book represents some return on its investment in me. The College of the Liberal Arts awarded me two semester-long research leaves, which were necessary to make significant progress on this book. The Harold C. and Alice T. Nowlin Regents Professorship in Liberal Arts, which I have held since 2019, financed the hiring of research assistants. The Teresa Lozano-Long Institute for Latin American Studies funded my field research in Argentina, Chile, Colombia, and Uruguay, as well as trips to various conferences where I presented my ideas. I am also grateful to my current and former department chairs, Dan Brinks and Robert Moser, for many forms of support along the way.

I am fortunate to have brilliant and generous colleagues in the Department of Government at UT Austin. John Gerring and I had many helpful chats about this book while our dogs frolicked. The members of the Latin Americanist Faculty Working Group – Dan Brinks, Zach Elkins, Ken Greene, Wendy Hunter, and Kurt Weyland – provided frank and insightful comments on various chapters of this book, as did John Gerring, Amy Liu, and Xiaobo Lu.

I also owe a debt to several UT Austin graduate students, namely, Danissa Contreras, Jonatan Lemus, Matthew Martin, Alex Norris, and Daisy Ward, who contributed to the elections and revolts data sets that I have used in this study. An army of undergraduate interns helped with the construction of these data sets as well. Special recognition goes to Leonardo Di Bonaventura and Bianca Vicuña who worked with me for multiple semesters and are well on their way to becoming accomplished political scientists.

Various colleagues outside of UT Austin have provided excellent comments on parts of this book, including Diego Abente, Elena Barham, Asli Cansunar, Michael Coppedge, Jennifer Cyr, Michael Hirsch, Alisha Holland, Evelyne Huber, Calla Hummel, Robert Kaufman, Fabrice Lehoucq, Steve Levitsky, Scott Mainwaring, Vincent Mauro, Jana Morgan, Gerardo Munck, Aníbal Pérez-Liñán, Eduardo Posada-Carbó, Luis Schenoni, Dawn Teele, Daniel Treisman, and Samuel Valenzuela. I am especially indebted to Luis Schenoni, who co-authored an earlier version of Chapter 3, in addition to providing helpful comments on the entire book.

Chapter 3 originally appeared in a slightly different form as an article in *International Security* (Vol. 48, No. 3, Winter 2024, https://doi.org/10.1162/isec_a_00479). Parts of Chapters 5 and 6 were published as articles in *Comparative Politics* (Vol. 51, No. 2, 2019) and *Comparative Political Studies* (Vol. 52, No. 10, 2019, https://doi.org/10.1177/0010414019830738) and as a *Kellogg Working Paper* (No. 441. December 2020, https://kellogg.nd.edu/emergence-democracy-colombia). I thank these journals for allowing me to reuse material from these articles.

This study builds on the fantastic work that historians and social scientists have done on democracy, elections, parties, and the military in Latin America before 1930. These scholars are too numerous to name here, but their work is cited extensively throughout this manuscript.

I was lucky to be a Visiting Research Fellow at the Kellogg Institute at the University of Notre Dame during the fall of 2019 where I wrote first drafts of some of the chapters of this book. I benefitted enormously from Kellogg's top-notch facilities, helpful staff, and terrific Latin Americanist faculty and students. There may be no better place to get work done than the Kellogg Institute where my apartment was located fifty feet from my office!

I presented parts of this book at Harvard University, Tulane University, the University of Chicago, the University of Notre Dame, and the University of Wisconsin-Madison, as well as at annual meetings of the American Political Science Association and the Latin American Studies Association. I am grateful to those who attended these talks for their thoughtful questions and comments.

At Cambridge University Press, Rachel Blaifeder did a terrific job of steering the book through the publication process. To her credit, she chose the two best reviewers I could have wished for: Evelyne Huber and Scott Mainwaring. I am grateful not just for their enthusiasm for this manuscript but, even more importantly, for their detailed suggestions, which have significantly improved this book. Carrie Parkinson and Claire Sissen of Cambridge University Press and Vidhya Ramamourthy of Lumina Datamatics Limited efficiently supervised the book through production. Dan Harding of Spartan Eloquence carefully copyedited the manuscript and Doreen Anderson of Arc Indexing compiled its lengthy and thorough index.

I had my first exposure to democratization studies as a graduate student at Stanford University during the 1990s where I was fortunate to take classes on the topic from some of the leading figures in the field, including Terry Karl, Larry Diamond, and Philippe Schmitter, all of whom subsequently served on my dissertation committee. As an undergraduate at Yale University in the 1980s, I also had the opportunity to take a class from the late great James Scott, whose support proved crucial for my subsequent decision to do a PhD in political science. I am thankful to these eminent scholars for planting the seeds that I am still harvesting today.

I also owe a debt to the good people of Pilas de Bejuco, Costa Rica where I served as a Peace Corps volunteer in the early 1990s. Long before I was aware of Winston Churchill's dictum, I learned from my community development work in Costa Rica that democracy is the worst form of government, except for all the others.

My greatest debts are to my family. My parents encouraged my intellectual interests from a young age and have served as role models for me throughout my life. My mother, who is in her eighties, also served as an (unpaid) research assistant for this project, editing the entire manuscript, photographing archival records, coding data on elections, and transcribing consular dispatches. Other members of my family provided emotional support. My children, Nico and Bela, have been a great joy and distraction from the day they set foot on this planet. My wife, Paloma Díaz, has been a source of fun, support, love, and inspiration since that fateful day that we met at *carnaval* in Brazil thirty-two years ago. I am so thankful to have her in my life, and I dedicate this book to her.

Abbreviations

APRA	Alianza Popular Revolucionaria Americana (American Popular Revolutionary Alliance)
CNC	Convención Nacional Constituyente (National Constituent Convention)
GDP	gross domestic product
LAHED	Latin American Historical Elections Database
LARD	Latin American Revolts Database
MBP	Mainwaring, Brinks, and Pérez-Liñán dataset (Democracies and Dictatorships in Latin America, 1900–2010)
PAN	Partido Autonomista Nacional (National Autonomist Party)
PDR	Partido Democrático Reformista (Democratic Reformist Party)
UCR	Unión Cívica Radical (Radical Civic Union)
V-Dem	Varieties of Democracy dataset

Introduction

The Origins of Democracy in South America

For most of the nineteenth century, Colombia, like the rest of South America, was under authoritarian rule. Colombian leaders manipulated elections to maintain their hold on power, and at times governed with an iron hand. Opposition parties rebelled repeatedly, but these revolts only brought further repression. The nadir came with the War of a Thousand Days (1899–1902) in which an estimated 100,000 people perished. In the wake of the war, however, the political situation gradually improved. Opposition revolts came to an end, and in 1910 Colombia enacted important reforms that paved the way for the establishment of relatively free and fair elections.

Similar transformations took place in Argentina, Chile, and Uruguay at about the same time. In each of these countries, opposition parties abandoned the armed struggle during the late nineteenth or early twentieth century, and governments enacted democratic reforms. To be sure, none of the four countries became full democracies during this period since they did not extend the franchise to all adults, nor end all electoral chicanery. Nevertheless, in all four countries, competitive and relatively free and fair elections became increasingly the norm, as did respect for civil liberties.

In other countries in the region, however, governments continued to manipulate elections during the early twentieth century to ensure that they or their allies remained in power. In some of these countries, such as Bolivia, Ecuador, and Paraguay, the opposition continued to seek power through armed rebellions and in some cases overthrew the government. In other countries, such as Brazil, Peru, and Venezuela, the opposition revolts of the nineteenth century largely came to an end but without a transition to democracy.

What explains these remarkably different regime outcomes in the early twentieth century? Why did some South American countries democratize during this period, while others remained under authoritarian rule? And why did some countries stabilize politically, whereas others continued to experience frequent outsider revolts and overthrows of their governments?

There is, perhaps, no question more central to political science than the origins of democracy, but we still lack a persuasive theory about what led democracy to emerge in South America. This lacuna is surprising, given that South America was a democratic pioneer in many respects. After independence, most South American countries enacted constitutions that established representative institutions and laid out significant civil and political rights for the citizenry. The region's governments held elections regularly throughout the nineteenth century, and in some cases, they allowed nearly universal male suffrage at a time when the United States and most European countries imposed significant restrictions on the franchise. Nevertheless, South America's nineteenth-century governments typically looked better on paper than in practice. Presidents often trampled on constitutional rights and bypassed or manipulated the legislature. Voter turnout was generally low, and elections were almost never free and fair since governments intervened regularly to ensure that their preferred candidates won. It was not until the early twentieth century that the region enjoyed lengthy and meaningful experiences with democracy.

The rise of democratic regimes in South America is puzzling from the perspective of traditional theories of democratization. As we shall see, the first wave of democratization in South America did not centrally involve the working classes or the bourgeoisie, which some prominent theories have identified as the main proponents of democracy. Nor did democratization occur exclusively among the most developed countries of the region, as modernization theory would predict.

This book argues that two main actors – the military and political parties – brought about democratization in South America during the early twentieth century. These were not the only actors that played a role in the emergence of democracy in these countries, but they were by far the most important. The professionalization of the military at the turn of the century made democracy feasible by providing the state with a monopoly on violence for the first time, thus bringing an end to the opposition revolts that had plagued the region during the nineteenth century. Once the opposition could no longer seize power by force, it began to focus on the electoral path to power and pushed for democratic reforms to level the playing field. Nevertheless, reforms typically passed only in countries where relatively strong opposition parties arose and where the ruling party split. In the wake of such splits, ruling party dissidents often allied with the opposition to push through democratic reforms.

THE ARGUMENT IN BRIEF

The military has traditionally been viewed as an obstacle to democracy in Latin America and around the world, and for good reason. Militaries in Latin America and elsewhere have often overthrown elected presidents, suspended

The Argument in Brief 3

constitutions, and violated the human and civil rights of the citizenry. Thus, one might expect that the strength of the military would be inversely related to the likelihood of democratization. Indeed, a prominent branch of the theoretical literature has suggested that authoritarian governments are more likely to democratize when the military cannot easily suppress the opposition or when the costs of doing so are too high.

Nevertheless, strong militaries may also enhance the prospects for democracy. Where the military is weak, opposition groups will be tempted to carry out violent uprisings to seize power or achieve other aims. These uprisings subvert the rule of law, undermine political stability, and typically lead to state repression, all of which will deepen authoritarian rule. By contrast, if the military is strong, the opposition will have incentives to avoid armed uprisings on the grounds that such revolts would presumably have large costs and be unlikely to succeed. Instead, the opposition may pursue a peaceful, more democratic path to power.

South American countries followed this latter path to democracy. During the nineteenth century, South American militaries were quite weak, which led the opposition to seek power via force quite frequently. Many of these revolts toppled elected governments, which undermined constitutional rule. Moreover, even when the opposition failed to take power, the rebellions undermined the prospects for democracy by subverting the rule of law and provoking government repression. Beginning in the late nineteenth century, however, South American countries experienced an export boom, which provided them with the resources to strengthen and professionalize their militaries. Not all South American countries invested heavily in their armed forces during this period: The smaller, poorer countries, such as Bolivia, Ecuador, and Paraguay, had fewer resources and were slower to professionalize their militaries. Nevertheless, most South American countries expanded the size of their armies, imported sophisticated weaponry, hired foreign military missions, adopted meritocratic standards for recruitment and promotion, and overhauled military training. These reforms gave the military the capacity to easily suppress rebellions, providing South American governments with a monopoly on violence for the first time. As a result, the opposition in these countries increasingly eschewed revolts and began to focus on the electoral path to power.

Political parties played an equally important role in the emergence of democracy in South America. Scholars have long recognized that political parties may shape the likelihood of democratization, but they have tended to focus on ruling parties. As this study shows, however, ruling parties have strong incentives to oppose democratic reform since such reforms will typically undermine their hold on power. By contrast, opposition parties will tend to support democratic reform, especially if they cannot take power by force. Opposition parties support democratic reforms because such measures will typically level the electoral playing field and increase the likelihood that opposition parties can win elections. The establishment of the secret ballot, for example, makes it more difficult for the government to monitor and sanction people who vote for the opposition. The elimination of suffrage restrictions, meanwhile, often undermines the government's control of elections by diminishing the electoral weight of state employees and by making it more difficult to disqualify opposition supporters.

Strong opposition parties are particularly conducive to democratization. Powerful opposition parties tend to have greater representation in the legislature, which is crucial to proposing and enacting democratic reforms. They can also more easily carry out protests to put pressure on the government to enact reforms. In addition, strong opposition parties can oversee the implementation of reforms more effectively – they have followers and affiliated organizations throughout the country that can monitor the elections and protest infractions. As Enrique Santos, a Colombian Liberal leader, noted in 1915: "fraud became more difficult in the face of an organized opposition party" (cited in Posada-Carbó 1996a, 11).

But what leads to the emergence of strong opposition parties? During the late nineteenth and early twentieth century, strong parties tended to arise in South American countries where the population was concentrated in a relatively small area with no major geographical obstacles dividing it. This made it easier for politicians and party leaders to build national organizations and communicate with the vast majority of the electorate. In addition, strong parties were more likely to emerge in countries that had intense and relatively balanced religious or territorial cleavages – that is, where neither side of a cleavage clearly dominated the other. This was the case in Uruguay, which was divided between residents of the capital and the provinces, and in Colombia and Chile, where conservative supporters of the Catholic Church and liberal critics of the Church were both strong. Intense and balanced cleavages generally gave birth to strong parties on both sides of the main cleavage, which was good for democracy because at least one of the strong parties was typically in the opposition.

Nevertheless, even strong opposition parties typically lacked the votes in the legislature to enact democratic reforms without support from some members of the ruling party. Democratization therefore occurred only when there was a split within the ruling party that led a faction of the governing party to side with the opposition. Ruling party dissidents often supported democratic reform for the same reason that members of opposition parties did – democratic reform leveled the electoral playing field and gave the dissidents a chance to prevail in elections.

Thus, three factors – the professionalization of the military, the rise of strong opposition parties, and splits within the ruling party – led to the initial emergence of democracy in Argentina, Chile, Colombia, and Uruguay. Military professionalization increased the *incentives* for the opposition to abandon the armed struggle and pursue democratic reform. The rise of strong parties boosted the *capacity* of the opposition to enact and enforce democratic reforms. And ruling party splits created the *opportunity* for the opposition and ruling party dissidents to push through reforms.[1]

The combination of these three variables generated very different regime outcomes across the South American countries during the nineteenth and early twentieth century. Where the military remained weak and nonprofessional, the predominant outcome was unstable authoritarianism. Under these conditions, opposition groups frequently resorted to armed uprisings, which undermined constitutional rule, engendered political instability, and led to authoritarian clampdowns. This was the most common regime type in South America during the nineteenth century because of the weakness of the region's militaries. A few South American countries, namely Bolivia, Ecuador, and Paraguay, also remained unstable authoritarian regimes in the early twentieth century in part because they were slow to strengthen their armed forces.

Where the military became strong but opposition parties remained weak, the predominant outcome was stable authoritarianism. The strengthening of the armed forces discouraged the opposition from carrying out armed revolts, but the weakness of opposition parties meant that they had little possibility of enacting democratic reforms or challenging the government in elections. Several South American countries, including Brazil, Peru, and Venezuela, became stable authoritarian regimes during the late nineteenth or early twentieth century once they professionalized their militaries. These regimes were not completely stable, however. Although they generally faced few challenges from the opposition, they sometimes experienced military coups in part because the opposition had incentives to call on the military to intervene since it had little prospect of toppling the government by other means.

Where both the military and opposition parties were strong, the regime outcome depended largely on the degree of unity of the ruling party. If the ruling party was united, the countries tended to remain authoritarian regimes since the opposition did not typically have the strength to enact democratic reforms on its own. However, if the ruling party split, democratization was likely to occur since the ruling party dissidents would join forces with the opposition to push through democratizing measures. This is what occurred in Chile in the late nineteenth century and Argentina, Colombia, and Uruguay in the early twentieth century.

As the Conclusion discusses, the emergence of democracy in some South American countries in the early twentieth century had important long-term consequences. The democratic reforms that the pioneer countries enacted in the late nineteenth or early twentieth century largely remained in force in the decades that followed. Countries that expanded the franchise or established the secret ballot typically maintained these measures in subsequent years

---

[1] I thank Jana Morgan for suggesting this way to summarize my argument.

and, in many cases, they took steps to strengthen the reforms or ensure their enforcement.[2]

The democratic reforms endured in part because they were enshrined in legislation and constitutions, but more importantly because they created vested interests. The beneficiaries of suffrage expansion, for example, opposed efforts to strip them of the right to vote. Legislators who were elected under new electoral rules, such as proportional representation, often resisted efforts to change those rules. Equally important, democratic norms developed over time in the citizenry of these countries as well as in the international community, which made it more difficult to overturn these democratic institutions.

The same variables that helped bring about democratization in the early twentieth century continued to have a mostly positive impact on South American democracies after 1929. Strong militaries, for example, continued to provide South American governments with a monopoly on violence and increased the likelihood that the opposition remained committed to the electoral path to power. As a result, in the mid-twentieth century, South American countries with strong armies had fewer opposition revolts than countries that were slow to strengthen and professionalize their militaries, such as Bolivia, Ecuador, and Paraguay. South American countries with strong militaries were still susceptible to military coups, but countries with strong parties tended to have fewer coups than countries with weak parties post-1929. Strong parties enabled the opposition to effectively compete with and sometimes even defeat the ruling party in elections. Thus, they had fewer incentives to call on the military to intervene. Strong opposition parties were also in a better position to ensure the implementation of democratic reforms, to promote further democratic measures, and to resist efforts by the president to concentrate power.

With the exception of Argentina, the South American countries that established democracy in the first decades of the twentieth century enjoyed more years of democracy after 1929 than did the other South American countries.[3] Nevertheless, the stability of democracy among the democratic pioneers after 1929 should not be exaggerated. All the pioneer countries (as well as the democratic laggards) experienced military interventions after 1929 and, in some instances, the military held on to power for a long time. Post-1929 political developments, such as coups, in South America were shaped by a variety of factors, not just the strength of parties and militaries. International factors, including the worldwide depression of the 1930s and the Cold War,

---

[2] South American countries also enacted other types of democratic reforms during the late nineteenth and early twentieth century, establishing presidential term limits and direct presidential elections. The enactment of these latter reforms did not play a key role in the first wave of democratization in South America, but they strengthened the quality of democracy in the region in the long run.

[3] As Chapter 6 discusses, Argentina suffered from frequent military coups post-1929 in part because it typically had only one strong party at any given time, which made it difficult for the opposition to take power through elections.

destabilized South American governments, as did the rise of labor and populist movements. As a result, even the democratic pioneers encountered democratic setbacks during the mid and late twentieth century.

RESEARCH DESIGN

This study examines the struggle for democracy in ten South American countries from independence to 1929. I focus on South America in part because it offers crucial variation on my dependent variable. Although four South American countries (Argentina, Chile, Colombia, and Uruguay) democratized during this period, the remaining six countries (Bolivia, Brazil, Ecuador, Paraguay, Peru, and Venezuela) did not. Examining countries in a single region also enables me to control for the large number of institutional, cultural, and historical characteristics that they have in common, using a most similar systems design (Gerring 2007; Przeworski and Teune 1970). Note that I only examine the Spanish- and Portuguese-speaking countries of the region. The English-, French-, and Dutch-speaking nations were still colonies during this period.

The first wave of democratization in South America has been a curiously neglected topic. Some important studies have examined the rise and consolidation of democracy in the region after 1929 (Collier and Collier 1991; Mainwaring and Pérez-Liñán 2013; Rueschemeyer, Stephens, and Stephens 1992). There are also some excellent studies that examine the pre-1930 emergence of democracy in Central America (Mahoney 2001; Lehoucq and Molina 2002; Yashar 1997) and in selected South American countries (Botana 2012; Remmer 1984; Scully 1992; Collier 1999; López-Alves 2000; López 2005b; Valenzuela 1998; Castro 2012; Mazzuca and Robinson 2009; Posada-Carbó 2012; Valenzuela 1985; Vanger 2010). Historians have also produced some illuminating studies that have sought to describe the conduct of elections and politics in nineteenth-century Latin America (Annino 1995; Drake 2009; Malamud 2000b; Posada-Carbó 1996b; Posada-Carbó and Valenzuela 2012; Sabato 2018). This, however, is the first book-length study to seek to explain the first wave of democratization in South America as a whole.[4]

In doing so, I enlist both qualitative and quantitative evidence. The research for this book included the compilation of systematic data on elections, parties, revolts, and the military in South America during a period covering more than 100 years, from independence to 1929. I relied on the burgeoning Spanish, English, and Portuguese literature on this period to compile databases and analyze the processes of military professionalization, party development, and democratization. I also used a variety of archival sources,

---

[4] López-Alves (2000) examines state-building and regime formation in five South American countries but ends his study in 1900 before most South American countries enacted the key democratic reforms.

including census data, presidential messages, texts of legislative debates on reforms, contemporary journalistic accounts, and letters and memoirs of the key participants.

As part of this study, I developed two original databases: the Latin American Historical Elections Database (LAHED); and the Latin American Revolts Database (LARD).[5] LAHED, which is discussed in Chapter 2, provides comprehensive data on presidential elections in all ten South American nations between independence and 1929, including the vote totals, information on the contenders, and measures of the competitiveness and fairness of the elections. LARD, which is discussed in Chapter 3, contains data on all revolts in South America from 1830 to 1929, including information on their leaders, participants, aims, battle deaths, and outcomes. Both these databases are currently being extended to the present time and the rest of Latin America with the assistance of various collaborators.

In addition, like some pioneering recent studies on democratic emergence (cf. Mares 2015; Ziblatt 2017), this study tested some of its central arguments by carrying out statistical analyses of the determinants of legislators' support for key democratic reform measures in Argentina and Chile. This required the compilation of original data sets on legislators and their districts.[6]

At its core, however, this is a work of comparative historical analysis. According to Thelen and Mahoney (2015), comparative historical analysis is a largely inductive research approach, which stresses historical process-tracing, comparisons across countries and time, and the careful elucidation of causal mechanisms.[7] It emphasizes getting the cases right, focusing on internal rather than external validity. This approach allows for consideration of a broad range of explanatory variables, not simply those that are available in large-n data sets or that can be easily collected. This study examines both the long-term processes (e.g., opposition party development and the formation of strong militaries) and the short-term factors (e.g., ruling party splits) that led to democracy and democratic reform. In this way, it seeks to strike a balance between distal and proximate causes and minimize the problems associated with both types of explanations, such as the difficulty of identifying the direct impact of distal factors or the myopia that occurs when scholars focus merely on precipitating events (Coppedge 2012, 120–122).

This study relies centrally on process-tracing evidence that directly links the independent variables to the outcomes of interest. It delineates the causal process through which the independent variables brought about (or impeded) democratization in each country. For example, it does not simply show that the countries with strong opposition parties democratized, while countries with weak parties did not. It also demonstrates that strong opposition parties

---

[5] LARD is being developed jointly with Luis Schenoni, Guillermo Kreiman, and Paola Galano Toro.
[6] For a detailed discussion of these analyses, see Madrid (2019a; 2019b).
[7] See also Mahoney and Rueschemeyer (2003, 10–15).

actively promoted democratic reforms and used their legislative influence to enact them. Similarly, in exploring whether ruling party splits played a role in the democratization process in any of the countries, it does not just show that splits immediately preceded democratization in each country. It also demonstrates that the splits directly contributed to democratization since following the split, the ruling party dissidents allied with the opposition to enact democratic reforms.

The proposed causal relationships that I identify in this study are probabilistic rather than deterministic ones, however. Although strong militaries, strong opposition parties, and ruling party splits jointly increased the likelihood of democratic transitions in South America during this period, I do not claim that they were necessary or sufficient conditions for democracy. The literature has identified multiple paths to democracy, and it is quite possible that democracy in the region could have arisen in some other manner. Nevertheless, in the early twentieth century, the only South American countries to democratize all pursued the path discussed here, even though the precise details of the democratization process varied somewhat from country to country.

Although the empirical scope of this study is the first wave of democratization in South America, the theoretical arguments should apply to some extent to any electoral authoritarian regime that allows a degree of political contestation.[8] The arguments, however, would presumably not apply to exclusionary authoritarian regimes since opposition parties in these regimes would have few opportunities to enact democratic reforms, and strong militaries might be used to repress the opposition and impede democratization. It is also quite likely that some factors that played little role in the democratization process in South America during the nineteenth and early twentieth century, such as international pressures, mattered more in other periods and regions. Nevertheless, I would still expect a minimal level of party and military development to be conducive to democratization in other contexts.

CONCEPTUALIZATION AND MEASUREMENT

Any study of democratization must deal with the complex issue of how to measure democracy and identify when it first emerged. In measuring democracy, I follow the minimalist definition advocated by Mainwaring, Brinks, and Pérez-Liñán (2001), which requires: (1) fair and competitive elections; (2) the protection of civil and political rights; and (3) elected government control of major policy decisions and the military. I count countries with no major violations of these three criteria as democratic, even though they may have partial violations

---

[8] According to Schedler (2013, 2), electoral authoritarian regimes "establish the institutions of liberal democracy on paper, yet subvert them in practice through severe, widespread, and systematic manipulation."

and thus not be fully democratic.⁹ I deliberately set a low bar for countries to count as democratic in part because partial violations of these criteria were widespread during this period. Thus, I refer to countries as democratic that would not count as democratic by current standards.

Mainwaring, Brinks, and Pérez-Liñán (2001) make universal suffrage an additional requirement for countries to count as democratic after 1950, but they relax this requirement for regimes prior to 1950. Because this book focuses on the pre-1930 period in South America, I also omit this criterion. To insist upon universal suffrage as a requirement for democracy would obscure the important democratic progress that some South American countries achieved in the first few decades of the twentieth century. As we shall see, Argentina, Chile, Colombia, and Uruguay took important steps in the early twentieth century to establish free and fair elections and maintain civil and political liberties, which made them minimally democratic by my definition even though they retained some suffrage restrictions.¹⁰

The democracies that emerged in this period might be more accurately referred to as limited or partial democracies, given the continuing suffrage restrictions that they maintained. No South American country granted women the right to vote prior to 1929 and some countries that I count as democratic, such as Chile and Colombia, maintained income and/or literacy restrictions during this period. For simplicity, however, I refer to these countries as democratic even though they were clearly not full democracies. Moreover, the elite nature of these democracies should not be exaggerated. Both Argentina and Uruguay allowed virtually universal male suffrage during this period, and even though Chile and Colombia retained some literacy and/or income requirements, these restrictions became less important over time owing to growing incomes and literacy rates in these countries. By the early twentieth century, many members of the lower classes in all four countries could and did vote. Indeed, as Chapter 2 shows, voter turnout rose considerably in all four countries during the early twentieth century.

I define the emergence of democracy in South America as the first ten-year period during which no major violations of democratic criteria took place. I stipulate a ten-year period to ensure that democratic institutions and practices have taken root. By this definition, democracy arose in South America in the first decades of the twentieth century.¹¹ This is not to suggest that the region was entirely authoritarian in the nineteenth century. As various historians have

---

⁹ Mainwaring, Brinks, and Pérez-Liñán (2001) classify countries with partial violations of these criteria, such as Colombia from 1910 to 1948, as semi-democratic, but I eschew the use of this term in part because no South American regime before 1930 was fully democratic.

¹⁰ I would also note that free and fair elections are important even in the absence of universal suffrage, whereas universal suffrage is of little meaning if elections are neither free nor fair.

¹¹ I refer to the emergence of democracy in Chile as taking place in the early twentieth century because it did not complete the required ten-year period of democratic rule until 1906 even though it held its first relatively free and fair presidential election in 1896.

Conceptualization and Measurement

TABLE I.1 *Conceptualization and measurement of key variables*

Concept	Operationalization	Sources of quantitative data
Degree of democracy	1. Free and fair elections 2. Civil and political liberties 3. Elected leaders must be in control of the military and major policy decisions	LAHED; Coppedge et al. (2023); Mainwaring and Pérez-Linán (2013)
Degree of regime stability	1. Number of major outsider revolts 2. Number of executive overthrows	LARD
Military strength	1. The number of military personnel 2. Imports of weaponry 3. Number of military schools 4. Degree of use of meritocratic criteria for promotion	Correlates of War (2020); Toronto (2017); Coppedge et al. (2020)
Party strength	1. Strength of ties to the electorate 2. Degree of party organization	Coppedge et al. (2024b)

shown, many nineteenth-century elections were competitive, and some were probably even free and fair. Nevertheless, these democratic episodes proved short lived, as Chapter 2 discusses.[12] The presidents elected in relatively free and fair elections during the nineteenth century were either overthrown shortly after coming to power or themselves undermined democracy by presiding over unfair elections or engaging in repression. Perhaps most importantly, the brief democratic episodes left no enduring institutions or norms. Indeed, the countries that had democratic episodes during this period did not become more democratic in the long term than the countries that had no such episodes.

Table I.1 provides summary information on how I conceptualize and measure the key variables in this study. (Chapters 2–4 discuss the measurement of these variables in more detail.) In coding the variables, I rely not just on the quantitative indicators in the sources identified in the table but also on qualitative assessments gleaned from the extensive historical literatures on the military, parties, and regimes in South America during the nineteenth and early twentieth century, which are discussed in Chapters 5–8.

I measure the stability of regimes by the degree to which they managed to avoid major outsider revolts and unconstitutional overthrows of their executives.[13] As Chapter 3 discusses, I define a major revolt as one involving at least 500 rebels. Stable regimes generally had few, if any, revolts from outside the state apparatus, and those revolts they did have tended to be relatively small. I define an executive overthrow as an instance where the president or supreme

---

[12] I refer to brief episodes of democracy as ephemeral democratization.
[13] Insider revolts tend to have little impact on political stability unless they succeed in overthrowing the executive.

leader of the nation is removed in an unconstitutional manner, typically by force or the threat of force. In stable regimes, executives are not overthrown or removed via unconstitutional procedures. Stable regimes typically change their leaders at regular intervals through elections, although those elections may not be free and fair. Stable regimes may even have unscheduled leadership changes owing to the death, resignation, or impeachment of their executives, provided that these leadership changes adhere to constitutional rules. Stable regimes may be authoritarian or democratic. I refer to those democracies that are prone to instability in the long run as weak democracies, and those democracies that are relatively stable in the long run as strong democracies.

As Chapter 3 indicates, I count as strong those militaries that had relatively large standing armies, possessed sophisticated weaponry, employed merit-based criteria for the recruitment and promotion of officers, and maintained multiple schools that provided training to officers. The number of military personnel is the traditional, and presumably the most important, measure of military strength, but the other indicators also shape the power capabilities of the military. More professionalized armies tend to be more powerful armies. I focus on the army rather than other branches of the military because in the nineteenth and early twentieth century armies played the most important role in the maintenance or overthrow of regimes.

As Chapter 4 discusses, I count as strong those parties that maintained extensive national organizations and widespread and lasting ties to the electorate. Strong parties had permanent organizational structures throughout much of the country. They also enjoyed the enduring support of significant portions of voters.

It is important to note that these are continuous variables, although I frequently break down the variables into dichotomous categories, such as strong or weak, stable or unstable, and democratic or authoritarian. In making these distinctions, I set a relatively low bar for what counts as strong, stable, and democratic to adapt my categories to the conditions and standards of the nineteenth and early twentieth century. What I classify as a strong party or a strong military during the nineteenth or early twentieth century would certainly not qualify as such by current standards of party or military strength. Similarly, the South American regimes that I count as stable or democratic might not be considered particularly stable or democratic today. Nevertheless, as this book shows, the differences that existed between militaries, parties, and regimes in South America during the nineteenth and early twentieth century were significant and had meaningful consequences in both the short and long term.

PLAN OF THE BOOK

Chapter 1, "Armies, Parties, and the Birth of Democracy," lays out the central theoretical arguments of the book. It argues that three factors played a key role in the emergence of democracy in region: the professionalization of the military, the rise of strong opposition parties, and splits within the ruling party. It analyzes what led to the professionalization of the military and the rise of strong opposition parties and it shows how they led to varying regime outcomes in South America. This chapter also discusses why existing theories of democracy can offer only a partial explanation for the emergence of democracy in the region.

Chapter 2, "Elections and Democracy in South America before 1930," uses an original database on historical elections in South America to examine the dependent variable of this study, exploring when and where democracy first emerged in the region. Scholars traditionally portrayed nineteenth-century elections in Latin America as farces, but in recent years historians have challenged this view. This chapter shows that many South American elections in the nineteenth century involved significant participation and competition, and a few were even free and fair. Nevertheless, authoritarian rule predominated. Most elections were noncompetitive, numerous restrictions on the franchise existed, and voter turnout tended to be low in comparison to Europe and the United States. Moreover, the few democratic episodes in the nineteenth century proved to be quite brief, as the freely elected presidents were either overthrown or subverted democracy to perpetuate themselves or their allies in power. However, in the first three decades of the twentieth century, a great divide occurred. A few South American countries, namely Argentina, Chile, Colombia, and Uruguay, established democratic regimes that lasted a dozen years or more. By contrast, authoritarian rule held fast or deepened in the other six countries of the region.

Chapter 3, "Military Professionalization and the Decline of Revolts in South America," argues that the professionalization of the armed forces played a key role in the emergence of democracy in the region by bringing an end to the opposition revolts that had plagued the region in the nineteenth century. It employs an original database on historical revolts in South America to trace the evolution of political violence in the region and analyze its causes and consequences. The chapter shows that revolts plagued Latin America throughout the nineteenth century, and these revolts undermined the prospects for democracy by overthrowing elected governments and provoking state repression. Most of these revolts were outsider rebellions – that is, they came from opposition groups and other forces outside the state apparatus. In the late nineteenth and early twentieth century, however, most South American countries strengthened and professionalized their armed forces with the assistance of foreign military missions. As a result, the opposition abandoned the armed struggle and began to focus on the electoral path to power, which had positive implications for democracy in the region. Nevertheless, a few countries were slow to modernize their militaries, which led to continued revolts in these countries. Moreover, insider revolts, especially military coups, continued to plague many South American countries. A series of regression analyses show that increases in military strength and professionalization are correlated with a decline in outsider revolts, but not insider revolts, during this period.

Chapter 4, "The Origins of Strong Parties in South America," examines what led to the emergence of the strong parties that played a key role in the democratization process in South America. It shows that during the late nineteenth century and early twentieth century, relatively strong national parties arose in Chile, Colombia, and Uruguay, and, to a lesser extent, in Argentina and Paraguay, but not in the other South American countries. The chapter argues that two main factors shaped party development during this period. First, strong parties emerged in countries that had intense but relatively balanced religious or territorial cleavages, where neither side of a cleavage clearly dominated the other. The religious cleavage, which pitted conservative supporters of the Catholic Church against liberal advocates of church–state separation, generated the strongest attachments and proved most conducive to party building, especially in Chile and Colombia where both liberals and conservatives were numerous. Territorial cleavages only generated powerful parties in Uruguay where the capital city controlled roughly similar levels of economic, political, and military resources as the provinces. In addition, strong parties tended to emerge in countries that had populations concentrated in relatively small areas without major geographic barriers. In these countries, it was easier for politicians to mount national campaigns and for party leaders to develop organizations that penetrated the entire country. These arguments are explored through comparative statistics and brief case studies of party development in all ten South American countries.

Chapter 5, "The Roots of Strong Democracies," shows how the development of strong parties and professional militaries contributed to the emergence of enduring democracies in Chile and Uruguay. Both countries developed strong parties during the late nineteenth century thanks in part to the geographic concentration of the population and the existence of a relatively balanced religious cleavage in Chile and center–periphery cleavage in Uruguay. During the nineteenth century, opposition parties at times resorted to revolts, but once the military professionalized, the opposition began to focus exclusively on the electoral route to power. This occurred in the late nineteenth century in Chile but not until the early twentieth century in Uruguay. In both countries, opposition parties pushed for democratic reforms to enfranchise their supporters and level the electoral playing field. It was not until the ruling party split, however, that the opposition managed to enact major democratic reforms. This took place in Chile in 1890 and in Uruguay in 1917. In both countries, strong opposition parties played a central role, not only in the enactment of the reforms but also in their subsequent enforcement.

Chapter 6, "The Roots of Weak Democracies," examines how parties and the military shaped democracy in Argentina and Colombia. In Argentina, only one strong party arose during the late nineteenth and early twentieth century: the opposition Radical Civic Union (UCR). The Radicals initially sought power through armed revolts as well as elections, but the professionalization of the military at the end of the nineteenth century made armed struggle futile.

Plan of the Book

The Radicals then opted for electoral abstention, declaring they would only participate in elections if democratic reforms were enacted. A split within the ruling National Autonomist Party led to the enactment of democratic reforms in 1912, which paved the way for the Radicals to win the 1916 presidential elections. Once the Radicals took power, however, Argentina lacked a strong opposition party, which undermined democracy in the long run because the opposition could neither compete in elections nor resist efforts by the executive to concentrate power. By contrast, two strong parties arose in Colombia during the nineteenth century thanks to a relatively balanced religious cleavage, which gave birth to numerous liberals as well as conservatives. Whichever party was in the opposition took up arms frequently against the government during the nineteenth century, which led to state repression and undermined constitutional rule. The bloody Thousand Days War (1899–1902), however, pushed Colombia to take steps to professionalize its armed forces, which in turn forced the opposition to abandon the armed struggle and focus on the electoral path to power. Although the opposition initially faced an uneven playing field, a split within the ruling party in the first decade of the twentieth century led ruling party dissidents to form an alliance with the opposition Liberal Party and push through democratic reforms. In the wake of these reforms, Colombian elections became relatively free and fair. Nevertheless, the country's military never managed to acquire a monopoly on force throughout the country, which led to increasing regional violence as time went on, thereby undermining the country's democracy.

Chapter 7, "The Roots of Stable Authoritarianism," explores the reasons why Brazil, Peru, and Venezuela had relatively stable autocracies during the early twentieth century. All three countries professionalized their militaries during this period, which helped bring an end to the frequent revolts that had undermined their prospects for democracy in the nineteenth century. None of the three countries developed strong parties, however. The absence of strong parties impeded democratization in several ways. First, party weakness allowed presidents to concentrate authority and extend their hold on power in some cases. Second, and even more importantly, the weakness of opposition parties meant that the opposition had little chance of winning elections or enacting democratic reforms, particularly in the face of widespread government electoral manipulation. As a result, the opposition frequently abstained from elections, which only deepened authoritarian rule in these countries. In some instances, notably in Peru, the opposition also encouraged the military to intervene to overthrow the president, which undermined otherwise stable regimes.

Chapter 8, "The Roots of Unstable Authoritarianism," examines the failed struggle for democracy in Bolivia, Ecuador, and Paraguay during the late nineteenth and early twentieth century. In contrast to the other South American countries, Bolivia, Ecuador, and Paraguay made relatively little progress in professionalizing their armies in the early twentieth century and were not able to establish a monopoly on violence. As a result, the opposition, especially in Paraguay and Ecuador, continued to seek power via armed revolt, which undermined constitutional rule and encouraged state repression. The weakness of parties in Bolivia and Ecuador also enabled presidents to manipulate elections, resist democratic reforms, and run roughshod over the opposition.

The Conclusion summarizes the main arguments in the book and discusses to what extent the factors that shaped regimes outcomes in the early twentieth century mattered post-1929. It also discusses the broader theoretical implications of the book, analyzes to what extent the arguments work in Mexico and Central America, and lays out an agenda for future research on historical democratization.

1

Armies, Parties, and the Birth of Democracy

Much of the literature on democratization focuses on structural variables, such as the level of economic development, institutions, geography, and culture. This literature has generated important insights that help explain some crucial aspects of the first wave of democratization in South America. Nevertheless, many structural theories, such as modernization theory, do not provide a very comprehensive or thick explanation of the emergence of democracy in the region. Although structural variables may explain cross-national variation in democracy, they cannot typically explain the precise timing of democratization because structural variables usually change only slowly over time. Moreover, structural approaches often do not indicate who the key actors in the democratization process were, why they supported or opposed democratization, and how advocates of democracy managed to prevail.[1]

By contrast, this book develops a thick explanation for the origins of democracy in South America that not only identifies the key actors in the struggle for democracy and explains their preferences but also specifies the structures that constrain or empower them. It aims to illuminate the process of democratization, explaining why and how supporters of democracy prevailed over its opponents. I focus on two main actors – political parties and the military – and show how they shaped regime outcomes in ten South American countries from independence until 1929. I also explain what led to the emergence of strong militaries and parties in some countries of the region.

---

[1] To provide an analogy, a structural theory of malaria might focus on underdevelopment or geography (malaria is prevalent in poor, tropical countries) but omit any discussion of the central role of the Anopheles mosquito, the main actor in malaria transmission. This would be a thin theory indeed.

This chapter is structured as follows. The first section examines the role of the military in democratization. It suggests that the professionalization of the military in South America helped facilitate democracy by bringing an end to the widespread revolts that plagued the region in the nineteenth century. The second section discusses the causes of military professionalization, focusing on the export boom of the late nineteenth and early twentieth century and regional military conflict and competition. The third section explains why opposition parties typically support democratic reforms and ruling parties oppose them. It argues that the existence of strong opposition parties and splits within the ruling party helped bring about democracy in South America by providing the votes necessary to enact democratic reforms. The fourth section analyzes why strong parties emerged in some countries and not others, focusing on two main variables: the geographic concentration of the population and the existence of relatively balanced religious or territorial cleavages. The fifth section summarizes how the different explanatory variables interacted to produce regime outcomes in South America during the early twentieth century. The final section discusses some existing theories of democracy and shows that, while they contribute some important insights, they do not provide a comprehensive explanation of the first wave of democratization in South America.

THE MILITARY AND THE EMERGENCE OF DEMOCRACY

As the Introduction noted, many scholars have viewed the military as an impediment to democracy, especially in Latin America where the armed forces have frequently overthrown democratic governments and engaged in repressive practices that have violated the basic rights of the citizenry. Nevertheless, as we shall see, the military played a constructive role in the first wave of democratization in South America, helping to bring an end to the opposition revolts that had destabilized the region during the nineteenth century. After South American governments strengthened and professionalized their militaries, the opposition in these countries largely abandoned the armed struggle and began to concentrate on the electoral path to power.

Weber (1946, 78, emphasis in original) claims that states must successfully claim a *"monopoly of the legitimate use of physical force* within a given territory," but he does not address what impact the absence of such a monopoly means for democratic rule. This study argues that the failure of states to achieve a monopoly on violence will typically have deleterious effects on their prospects for democracy by encouraging the opposition to carry out armed revolts. I do not claim that a state monopoly on violence is a prerequisite for democracy since some democracies have arisen in the midst of serious challenges to the state's monopoly on violence and a few have even survived civil wars (Mazzuca and Munck 2014). Nevertheless, as the South American experience illustrates, a state monopoly on violence can dramatically improve a country's prospects for democracy by persuading the opposition to focus on the electoral path to power.[2]

Much of the democratization literature has suggested that democracy arises as a mechanism to settle conflicts – the government provides the opposition with a share of power (or a chance to win it) and the opposition, in turn, refrains from revolting (Dahl 1971; Acemoglu and Robinson 2006; Mazzuca and Munck 2014, 1224–1225; Przeworski 2011; Przeworski, Rivero, and Xi 2015; Rustow 1970, 354–355). From this perspective, democracy is facilitated by military weakness: It emerges when the government concludes that it cannot suppress the opposition or that the costs of doing so are too high. Rustow (1970, 352), for example, contends that "the dynamic process of democratization is set off by a prolonged and inconclusive political struggle." Similarly, in *Polyarchy*, Dahl (1971, 49) postulates that "the likelihood that a government will tolerate an opposition increases with a reduction in the capacity of the government to use violence or socioeconomic sanctions to suppress an opposition." He goes on to suggest that democracy arose in Chile, New Zealand, Norway, and Switzerland in part because the geographies of these countries made it impossible for the state to achieve a monopoly on violence (Dahl 1971, 56). The class pressure model discussed in this chapter also rests on the assumption of state military weakness – it contends that the governing elites agree to democratize in order to prevent the masses from overthrowing them by force (Acemoglu and Robinson 2006; Aidt and Franck 2015; 2014; Boix 2003). According to Acemoglu and Robinson (2006, 25), for a real threat from the masses to exist, "the elites – who are controlling the state apparatus – should be unable to use the military to effectively suppress the uprising."

Nevertheless, there is little evidence to suggest that democracy in South America emerged from military weakness or declining government capacity to suppress the masses or the opposition. South American militaries were weak during the nineteenth century and had a difficult time suppressing revolts, but democracy did not arise until the early twentieth century after many of the region's armed forces professionalized and gained a monopoly on violence. Democracy in South America thus emerged not when the government's capacity to suppress the opposition declined but rather when it increased. Moreover, the countries that democratized first in South America had some of the strongest militaries in the region and the greatest ability to suppress the opposition.[3] In three of these countries – Argentina, Colombia,

---

[2] The literature has generated mixed findings on the relationship between state capacity and democracy, but much of that literature has focused on the effect of state capacity on democratic stability, rather than on democratization per se. Moreover, state capacity has been measured in a variety of different ways, many of which have little to do with establishing a monopoly on violence. (See Andersen and Doucette 2022; Mazzuca and Munck 2014; Andersen et al. 2014.)

[3] As we shall see, the countries with the weakest militaries in the region – Bolivia, Ecuador, and Paraguay – failed to democratize during this period.

and Uruguay – democracy arose during a period in which the opposition was demobilized after its resounding military defeat. In Chile, democracy emerged in the wake of a momentous opposition victory in a civil war in which the navy sided with the rebellious parliamentary opposition. In none of the four democratizing countries was there an ongoing armed conflict at the time of democratization; nor was there a high likelihood that the opposition would rebel in the near future.[4] To the contrary, in all four countries, the government had a clear monopoly on violence when it democratized.

Why would military dominance, rather than military weakness, lead to democratization? The answer to this question has to do with the impact of revolts on the prospects for democracy. As the civil war literature has shown, state weakness, especially low coercive capacity, will tend to foster revolts (Fearon 2010; Fearon and Laitin 2003; Hendrix 2010; Cederman and Vogt 1997; 2017). Where the state cannot easily suppress revolts, the opposition has an incentive to engage in them. The opposition may carry out these revolts because it believes it can overthrow the government or because it hopes to win concessions. In authoritarian regimes, these revolts may represent the opposition's best chance of gaining power and influence, given the regimes' control of the electoral process. Indeed, in the past 200 years, power worldwide has changed hands much more frequently through force than through elections (Przeworski, Rivero, and Xi 2015, 235).

Armed revolts, however, typically deepen authoritarian rule, undermining the prospects for democracy. Governments usually respond to such revolts with state repression, clamping down on the media, restricting civil and political liberties, and arresting, exiling, and even killing members of the opposition. These repressive measures often engender further revolts, thereby creating a vicious cycle. Such a cycle is unlikely to be broken if the opposition takes power in a revolt since victorious opposition rebels are typically reluctant to establish democracy. Governments that obtain power by force typically rule by force, concentrating power and repressing their opponents. They use authoritarian measures to concentrate their hold on power, fearing that other parties will seek to come to power in the same manner they did. Opposition parties that gain power by force not only violate the principle of constitutional succession but also encourage other parties to do the same.

By contrast, strengthening the coercive capacity of the state can bring an end to most opposition revolts, thereby terminating the cycle of rebellion and repression. I am not suggesting that strengthening the coercive capacity of the

---

[4] As the Conclusion discusses, military stalemate has led to democratization in some circumstances (e.g., Central America in the early 1990s), but it may be uncommon in part because it requires that both sides recognize that the conflict is at a stalemate. Moreover, the opposition often has little reason to trust that the government will democratize (i.e., carry out free and fair elections) if it lays down its arms. In addition, the opposition may benefit from a military stalemate that allows it to control territory and resources.

state will always be propitious for democratization. Indeed, some studies have suggested that increases in the coercive capacity of the state may undermine the likelihood of democracy by enabling authoritarian regimes to repress dissent (Albertus and Menaldo 2012; Hariri and Wingender 2023). Nevertheless, where opposition revolts have been common, increasing the coercive capacity of the state may have a positive impact on the likelihood of democracy by encouraging the opposition to abandon the armed struggle. The opposition will not typically rebel if it expects any revolt to be quickly suppressed. Where armed struggle is foreclosed, the opposition will have incentives to pursue the electoral path to power. Under these circumstances, the opposition is likely to push for democratic reforms to reduce the government's ability to manipulate elections and improve the opposition's chances of winning. These include measures that establish the secret ballot, expand the franchise, prevent the police or military from intervening in elections, and mandate opposition party representation in the electoral commissions and the legislature.

The opposition, however, cannot always judge the strength of the military, nor can it necessarily assess its own military capabilities with any degree of reliability. As a result, it is difficult for the opposition to know what the costs of rebellion will be and what likelihood it has of prevailing in an armed revolt. Nevertheless, as the international relations literature has shown, warfare provides important information about the capabilities of both sides, which can shape decisions about whether to go to war (Slantchev 2003; Wagner 2000). Recent conflicts can supply intelligence not only on the troops and weaponry both sides can mobilize but also on how effectively they will use these soldiers and equipment and how willing each side is to fight. Opposition groups are therefore likely to use recent experiences with rebellion to assess its costs and their prospects of capturing power through armed struggle.[5] If the opposition has triumphed in rebellions against the government in the recent past, then it is more likely to believe that it can do so again in the future. However, if the opposition has experienced repeated defeats, it is likely to conclude that future rebellions will yield the same outcome. The longer the time that has elapsed since an opposition victory in a rebellion, the more the opposition is likely to conclude that it will not prevail in the future. Similarly, where the opposition has experienced high casualties in recent uprisings, it is likely to believe that it will experience considerable casualties if it rebels again. Thus, repeated opposition defeats in costly rebellions may help to bring about democratization by pushing opposition parties to abandon the armed struggle and focus on the electoral path to power.

As Chapter 3 discusses, the coercive capacity of South American states was initially quite low (Johnson 1964; Lieuwen 1961; Rouquié 1987; Centeno 2002). For much of the nineteenth century, standing armies in the region were

---

[5] Opposition parties may be particularly likely to use past conflicts to assess their prospects in future conflicts if the underlying dynamics of the conflict have not changed much.

small and troops lacked training and sophisticated weaponry. South American armies also typically had poor leadership since political connections, rather than competence or training, determined officer recruitment and advancement. The weakness of the military encouraged the opposition to seek power through armed rebellions. Indeed, opposition revolts and other types of outsider rebellions were extremely common during the nineteenth century – they were much more frequent than insider revolts, such as military coups. These rebellions were occasionally successful, which undermined constitutional rule and encouraged further uprisings. Latin American governments, meanwhile, responded to the revolts by declaring states of siege, censoring the media, and repressing the opposition. These actions had profoundly negative implications for the prospects for democracy in the region.

In the late nineteenth and early twentieth centuries, however, most Latin American governments took steps to strengthen the coercive capacity of the state by professionalizing their militaries with the assistance of foreign missions (Nunn 1983; Resende-Santos 2007). Military professionalization included: the acquisition of sophisticated weaponry such as artillery, repeating rifles, and machine guns; the establishment of military schools, including for noncommissioned officers; the adoption of more rigorous training for officers and soldiers; the enactment of merit-based criteria for advancement within the military; the creation of standardized requirements for military recruitment; and the formation of mass armies and military reserves. These measures made the military a larger, more disciplined, and more effective fighting force.[6]

Military professionalization increased the costs of rebellion and made it less likely that the opposition could prevail in armed uprisings. Opposition rebellions in Argentina, Colombia, and Uruguay repeatedly failed in the late nineteenth and early twentieth centuries, and some of these rebellions, such as the Thousand Days War in Colombia, generated enormous casualties. As a result, opposition parties in these countries, along with Chile, which had developed a strong military even earlier, became reluctant to take up arms and increasingly focused on the electoral path to power. However, where the military remained weak, opposition parties and politicians continued to seek power by force, with negative implications for democracy.

But why didn't authoritarian regimes in South America use their increasingly powerful militaries to repress the opposition and dispense with elections altogether? In a few cases, they did, but not typically for long. Repression was not costless. It could undermine the legitimacy of the regime and antagonize the citizenry who had come to expect elections, legislative representation, and a degree of civil liberties. Members of the ruling elite also frequently opposed any move to dispense with representative institutions since these institutions provided them with positions and patronage. The suppression of elections or

---

[6] In some cases, Latin American governments also made it difficult for rebel leaders to obtain weapons and fighters by banning the import of weaponry and eliminating independent militias.

the repression of the opposition could also lead to rebellions, which were disruptive even if the opposition had little chance of prevailing against a professionalized military. In addition, the military was sometimes reluctant to engage in repression. It was one thing to employ repression temporarily in response to a rebellion, but it was quite another to use it against a peaceful population and to maintain it indefinitely.

Moreover, as the literature on authoritarian regimes has shown, authoritarian leaders benefit in some ways from elections, civil liberties, and representative institutions, which can make the leaders reluctant to eliminate them (Brancati 2014; Gandhi and Lust-Okar 2009). Elections can be used to signal the degree of strength and popular support of an authoritarian regime, which may deter the opposition from challenging it (Magaloni 2008; Simpser 2013). Elections, the media, and legislatures also provide forums for the voicing of discontent, thereby providing useful information to leaders about political problems or disaffected constituencies, which the government can then seek to address (Gandhi 2008; Brownlee 2007; Geddes, Wright, and Frantz 2018). Representative institutions may also be used to share power and to co-opt potential opponents by providing them with posts, patronage, and policies that they prefer (Blaydes 2011; Svolik 2012). Finally, the media, civil liberties, and representative institutions may enable elites to monitor dictators and the dictators to monitor elites, ensuring that neither engages in excessive corruption or undertakes other actions that could undermine the authoritarian regime (Blaydes 2011; Geddes, Wright, and Frantz 2018; Svolik 2012).

For all these reasons, South American countries generally held elections and maintained representative institutions from independence through the early twentieth century.[7] Indeed, even when leaders took power by force during this period, it was common for them to subsequently call elections to consolidate their hold on power. Rather than eliminate elections and representative institutions, South American leaders typically preferred to maintain them and intervene regularly in these institutions to ensure they maintained control. This strategy provided the regimes with a degree of legitimacy as well as the other political benefits mentioned earlier without jeopardizing their hold on power.

---

[7] Under colonial rule, Latin America had limited experience with elections and representative institutions, but in the wake of independence, most Latin American countries declared themselves republics and called for elections and representative institutions. In making these choices, Latin American leaders drew on enlightenment ideas and highly salient constitutional models, such as the US Constitution and the 1812 Spanish (Cádiz) Constitution (Guerra 1994; Posada-Carbó and Valenzuela 2012; Sabato 2018). Without a monarch to provide legitimacy, independence leaders had little alternative to deriving power from the citizenry. Indeed, so powerful was the idea that sovereignty should be vested in the people that no leaders felt they could dispense with elections for long. Even the emperor of Brazil, the supreme dictator of Paraguay, and other autocrats felt obliged to legitimize their rule to some degree through elections and representative institutions.

Elections in South America only became free and fair, however, once democratic reforms were enacted in the early twentieth century. The professionalization of the military helped bring about democratization by encouraging the opposition to desist from armed uprisings and push for democratic reforms. Nevertheless, even professionalized militaries proved to be a threat to democracy in some instances. Although opposition revolts declined dramatically in the twentieth century owing to the professionalization of the military, military coups continued to take place. On balance, however, the strengthening and professionalization of Latin American militaries had a positive impact on the prospects for democracy in the region.

THE ORIGINS OF MILITARY PROFESSIONALIZATION

What leads to military professionalization? Why did many Latin American countries professionalize their armed forces during the late nineteenth and early twentieth centuries?

The strengthening of Latin American militaries in the late nineteenth and early twentieth centuries stemmed from three main developments. First, the export boom brought large inflows of foreign currency to Latin American governments, providing them with the resources to contract foreign military missions, establish military schools, create mass armies, and import sophisticated weaponry. Second, Latin American countries faced considerable regional military conflict during this period, including two major wars and numerous militarized interstate disputes. Regional competition and conflict triggered an arms race of sorts. Once some Latin American countries upgraded their militaries, their neighbors felt considerable pressure to do so as well. Third, the nations that emerged victorious in interstate wars tended to invest more in their militaries than the nations that were defeated. Victory in war typically strengthened state-building forces, whereas losses weakened them (Schenoni 2024).

The development of a strong military and the acquisition of a monopoly on violence is only one aspect of the state-building process, but it is an important one.[8] The literature on state building has long been dominated by the bellicist approach, which argues that war produces state building. European nations, for example, developed systems of taxation to fund the militaries that facilitated conquest and ensured their survival. In Tilly's (1975, 42) famous words, "war made the state, and the state made war." Working from this approach, Centeno (2002) contended that state building in Latin America was

---

[8] There is a growing literature on historical state building in Latin America, which includes important works by Centeno (2002), Centeno and Ferraro (2013), Kurtz (2013), López-Alves (2000), Mazzuca (2021), Saylor (2014), Schenoni (2020, 2021), Soifer (2015), and Thies (2005), among others. These studies have identified a broad range of factors that shape state building in the region, but my focus here is specifically on those variables that led to military professionalization.

The Origins of Military Professionalization

undermined by the relative absence of large-scale interstate wars in the region.[9] As Centeno (2002, 8) points out, no Latin American country disappeared after 1840 as a result of war. Because they did not face the same risk of annihilation as European countries, Latin American countries did not have the same incentives to invest in the military or engage in state building more generally. Although Latin America suffered from numerous internal conflicts during the nineteenth century, Centeno (2002, 127–130) and others argue that internal wars do not promote state building.[10] Internal wars can, under some circumstances, lead to military buildups that strengthen the armed forces, but they do not consistently do so. Indeed, civil wars often destroy the economy, divide the armed forces internally, and deplete scarce resources.

Latin American countries during the nineteenth century experienced a significant degree of international conflict, however. Between 1820 and 1914, Latin American nations fought almost as many interstate wars as European countries did, and these wars lasted much longer and killed a significantly larger percentage of the population than they did in Europe (Schenoni 2021, 408). The late nineteenth century witnessed two particularly lengthy and bloody conflicts in South America: the War of the Triple Alliance (1864–1870), which pitted Paraguay against Argentina, Brazil, and Uruguay; and the War of the Pacific (1879–1883), in which Chile fought Bolivia and Peru. In these conflicts, the losing sides suffered significant casualties and lost large amounts of their territory. In the War of the Triple Alliance, for example, Paraguay lost half of its territory and 60–70 percent of its population, according to some estimates (Whigham 2002; Whigham and Potthast 1999).[11] Although wars became less frequent after the 1880s, countries in the region continued to have numerous border conflicts and militarized disputes.

The wars and militarized conflicts in Latin America during the late nineteenth and early twentieth century provided incentives for countries to strengthen and professionalize their militaries (Resende-Santos 2007; Arancibia Clavel 2002; Fitch 1998; Philip 1985; Wesson 1986; Grauer 2015; Johnson 1964; Lieuwen 1961; Loveman 1999; Nunn 1983; Rouquié 1987; Schenoni 2020). Chile was the first country to professionalize its armed forces, bringing in a German mission in 1885 that dramatically overhauled and strengthened the Chilean military. Beginning with Chile's neighbors, most other South American countries also hired foreign military missions in the decades that followed. Thus, regional conflict provided an impetus for state building in Latin America as well as in Europe (Schenoni 2021; Thies 2005).[12]

---

[9] See also Soifer (2015, ch. 6).
[10] For a contrary view, see Rodríguez-Franco (2016) and Slater (2010).
[11] Reber (2002) and Kleinpenning (2002) provide lower estimates of the number of deaths.
[12] Thies (2005) contends that interstate rivalries, rather than large-scale wars, incentivized state building in South America throughout the twentieth century, as countries increased taxation in response to these conflicts.

War outcomes also shaped military strength and professionalization in South America. As Schenoni (2021; 2024) argues, victory in wars strengthened state-building efforts in nineteenth-century Latin America by empowering those elites who had supported a strong army and state-building efforts. By contrast, loss in war often brought to power peripheral elites who had opposed the war and were not supportive of state building. Moreover, defeat in war could destroy a country's army, as it did to Paraguay during the War of the Triple Alliance, and occupying forces were typically reluctant to allow their subjugated foes to rebuild their military.

Military professionalization and other forms of state building are expensive, however. It is costly to hire foreign military missions, establish military schools, purchase foreign weaponry, and create a permanent mass army. To finance these armies, European countries expanded domestic taxation, which required state building, but it was initially difficult for Latin American states to extract similar levels of resources, given the poor economic performance of the region in the decades that followed independence. Meager economic growth severely constrained tax revenues, which in turn limited government spending. Thus, most Latin American governments could ill afford to spend large sums of money on their armed forces during most of the nineteenth century.[13]

In the late nineteenth and early twentieth century, however, Latin American countries experienced an export boom, which was fueled by technological advances, infrastructure improvements, greater political stability, and growing worldwide demand for Latin American products. The real value of exports increased nearly tenfold between 1870 and 1929, dramatically strengthening the region's economies. Latin America's gross domestic product (GDP) grew from $29.1 billion in 1870 to $194.9 billion in 1929 in constant 1990 dollars (Bértola and Ocampo 2013, 97).

Commodity booms and the expansion of trade financed state building in the region, including the modernization of the military, which involved significant government expenditures (Mazzuca 2021; Saylor 2014). The converse was also true: State building contributed to the expansion of exports and the economy by delivering public goods, such as infrastructure and political stability. The expansion of trade also provided incentives to build up the military since the export boom depended on the ability of Latin American states to pacify the areas where export commodities were produced and transported.[14]

---

[13] During the nineteenth century, the small size of Latin American governments meant that military expenditures typically accounted for a large share of state spending. Centeno (2002, 119–121) shows that before the 1880s military expenditures and debt payments – the latter typically stemmed in part from war debts – almost invariably accounted for more than 50 percent and often more than 70 percent of the budgets of Latin American governments.

[14] Mazzuca (2021) notes that pacification involved not just military subjugation but also the cooptation of rural leaders by allowing them free rein in their domains.

In Latin America, as in other parts of the world, the more developed countries advanced furthest in terms of military professionalization (Toronto 2017). The wealthier Latin American countries, such as Chile and Argentina, could more easily afford to make large investments in their armed forces. Indeed, Chile and Argentina engaged in an arms race of sorts in the late nineteenth and early twentieth century, with both countries importing increasingly sophisticated weaponry. The more developed countries also had higher literacy rates, which facilitated the training of troops and officers. Although the poorer Latin American countries also sought to upgrade their militaries during this period, they had a difficult time matching the investment of the region's military powers and their troops continued to be mostly illiterate and poorly trained.

Thus, interstate wars and conflicts provided the incentives for military professionalization in Latin America, whereas the expansion of the region's trade furnished the wherewithal. Latin American states lacked the revenues to make major investments in their armed forces for much of the nineteenth century, but the export boom of the late nineteenth and early twentieth century made new resources available. The most developed countries made the largest investments in their militaries, but all countries in the region took some steps to upgrade their armed forces.

POLITICAL PARTIES AND DEMOCRATIC REFORM

Although the professionalization of the military paved the way for democratization in the region, political parties, especially opposition parties, played the central role in the enactment and implementation of democratic reforms. Opposition parties typically promoted democratic reforms to level the electoral playing field and improve their chances of winning elections. Ruling parties, by contrast, usually resisted democratic reforms for the same reasons and used their power to block the measures. As a result, meaningful democratic reforms typically only passed where there were relatively strong opposition parties and where the ruling party split. In the wake of splits, ruling party dissidents sometimes sided with the opposition and pushed through reforms that helped create free and fair elections.

Scholars have long argued that political parties are central actors in the establishment of democracy (Collier 1999; LeBas 2011; Capoccia and Ziblatt 2010; Gibson 1996; Middlebrook 2000b; Rokkan 1970; Schattschneider 1942; Ziblatt 2017; Valenzuela 1985; Lehoucq 2000). One branch of the literature has focused on conservative parties. Gibson (1996), Middlebrook (2000b), and Ziblatt (2017), for example, contend that traditional elites were more likely to tolerate democracy in countries that had strong conservative parties because these parties could protect elite interests. As a result, according to Gibson (1996, 26), Latin American countries that developed strong conservative parties before the advent of mass politics experienced more years of democratic rule than countries where conservative parties were slow to emerge.[15]

The arguments about conservative parties tend to focus on the role that these parties play in preserving, rather than creating, democracy. This begs the question of why conservative parties would support the establishment of democracy to begin with, given that the existing authoritarian regimes often represent the interests of conservative elites quite effectively. Bendix (1969, 117) and Rokkan (1970, 32) argue that conservative parties have sometimes supported the enfranchisement of the lower classes (or women) because they have believed that they would vote for conservative parties. Nevertheless, this does not explain why conservatives would support other democratic reforms, such as the secret ballot, proportional representation, or the creation of independent electoral authorities. As we shall see, conservative support for democracy in nineteenth-century South America was contingent: Conservative parties tended to support democratic reform when they were in the opposition but not when they were in power.

Another branch of the literature has identified the ruling party more generally as the main proponent of democratic reform. Schattschneider (1942), Rokkan (1970), and Collier (1999), for example, argue that ruling parties often extended the franchise in order to win votes among sectors of the population who did not yet have strong partisan attachments. According to Collier (1999, 55): "Incumbents extended the suffrage to the working class much less in response to lower-class pressures than in response to their own political needs as they jockeyed for political support." Other studies contend that ruling parties enfranchised women in order to win their political support in the face of growing electoral competition (Przeworski 2009a; Teele 2018, 32). Some scholars maintain that ruling parties are especially likely to democratize when they believe that they can continue to win elections and hold on to power after the return to democracy (Riedl et al. 2020; Miller 2021; Slater and Wong 2013).

The focus on ruling parties is understandable given that they are influential actors who have the power to enact democratic reforms and strengthen (or undermine) democracy. Moreover, strong ruling parties can serve as a check on personalism and executive overreach (Rhodes-Purdy and Madrid 2020). Nevertheless, it is not clear why ruling parties would have supported democratization in Latin America during the nineteenth and early twentieth century. During this period, there were few, if any, international pressures to democratize, and the ruling parties typically controlled elections through a wide range of techniques, including fraud and intimidation, so they did not need to win votes by extending the suffrage. Moreover, suffrage expansion had risks since it could lead to a flood of new voters with uncertain loyalties who could destabilize the existing political system. Indeed, ruling parties often

---

[15] Ziblatt (2017) similarly argues that strong conservative parties led to more stable democracies in western Europe.

dominated elections by relying on the support of state employees and members of the military and/or national guard who typically represented a large share of the electorate before the expansion of the franchise. In addition, eliminating certain suffrage restrictions, such as income and literacy requirements, could make it harder for the ruling parties to disqualify opposition voters since selective application of these criteria was historically used to turn away supporters of the opposition.

Ruling parties had even fewer incentives to enact the other types of democratic reforms that helped bring democracy to Latin America during this period. These included measures that mandated the secret ballot, required the representation of minority parties, created more independent electoral authorities, and banned the police or military from intervening in elections. Ruling parties typically opposed these reforms because they weakened their control of government institutions and reduced their ability to intervene in elections. The creation of independent electoral authorities and the adoption of the secret ballot, for example, made it more difficult for ruling parties to monitor the voting process and to identify and sanction opposition voters. Laws that banned the police or military from intervening in elections hindered government efforts to intimidate voters or coerce state employees to support the ruling party (see Table 1.1).

Even leaders of liberal ruling parties were reluctant to support democratic reforms because they feared that such reforms might jeopardize their hold on power. As one Liberal politician in Brazil quipped: "nothing so much resembles a Conservative as a Liberal in power" (cited in Barman 1988, 229). A desire to hold on to power also stymied the liberal impulses of leaders in other regions. In discussing Catherine the Great's hesitance to enact democratic reforms, Gopnik (2019, 58) observes: "For the catch, of course, with all enlightened despots is that they feel about liberty for their subjects the way the young St. Augustine felt about chastity for himself: they want it, just not quite yet."

This does not mean that ruling parties never supported democratic reforms in Latin America during this period. In some cases, ruling parties supported reforms that they believed would not jeopardize their control over elections. In other cases, ruling parties agreed to reforms because they had little choice, having lost control of the legislature or the constituent assembly. Finally, as we shall see, ruling party dissidents often supported democratic reforms. These ruling party dissidents typically represented a small minority of the members of the ruling party, but in a few cases, they gained control of the legislature (usually with the support of the opposition party) and pushed through democratic reforms to weaken the traditional ruling elites' control of the political system. Nevertheless, for the most part, ruling parties resisted meaningful democratic reforms during this period and used their influence to block or water down proposed measures.[16]

---

[16] Ruling parties may have been more likely to support democratic reforms in recent decades because there has been greater international and domestic pressure for democratization.

TABLE 1.1 *Opposition parties and democratic reform*

Type of reform	Benefits of the reform for the opposition and democracy	Examples of reforms
Elimination of some suffrage restrictions	Leads to an influx of new voters and reduces electoral weight of state employees; makes it harder to disqualify opposition voters	Chile 1874 Colombia 1910 Uruguay 1918
Enactment of obligatory voting and/or registration	Leads to an influx of new voters and reduces electoral weight of state employees; makes it harder to disqualify opposition voters	Argentina 1912 Uruguay 1918
Adoption or strengthening of the secret ballot	Reduces vote buying and government control of the electoral process	Chile 1890 Argentina 1912 Uruguay 1918
Adoption of measures that mandate representation of minority parties	Increases legislative representation of opposition parties	Chile 1874 & 1890 Argentina 1912 Uruguay 1918
Creation of independent electoral authorities	Reduces fraud and weakens the executive's control of the electoral process	Chile 1874 Argentina 1912
Changes to voter registration procedures	Makes it more difficult to disqualify voters; reduces government control	Chile 1890
Participation of parties in the scrutiny of the vote	Reduces fraud and weakens the executive's control of the electoral process	Chile 1890
Ban on military/police participation in elections	Reduces voter intimidation; reduces the electoral weight of state employees	Uruguay 1918
Strengthening of the attributions of Congress	Weakens executive dominance	Colombia 1910

By contrast, opposition parties generally supported democratic reforms in Latin America during the late nineteenth and early twentieth century. In fact, opposition parties were the main proponents of democratic reforms during this period in Latin America since there were no significant international pressures to establish democracy at the time and no other important domestic groups consistently supported democratic reform. Labor unions, for example, were still relatively weak during this period and were dominated by anarcho-syndicalist currents that rejected liberal democracy. The bourgeoisie was not well organized either; nor did it consistently support democratic reforms.

Opposition parties had strong electoral incentives to support democratic reforms. Measures such as the establishment secret ballot, the creation of independent electoral authorities, and prohibitions on police and military involvement in elections improved the opposition's electoral prospects by weakening

Political Parties and Democratic Reform

the government's control of the electoral process. Other reforms, such as the adoption of electoral rules that mandated the representation of minority parties, typically boosted the number of legislative seats held by opposition parties. Even suffrage expansion and obligatory voting measures often benefited the opposition because they made it more difficult to disqualify opposition voters and led to an influx of new voters with unclear loyalties to whom the opposition could appeal.[17]

Opposition parties would typically support democratic reforms only while they were in the opposition, whereas ruling parties would often oppose democratic reforms only while they held power. For example, opposition Liberals in Chile generally supported democratic reform during the mid-nineteenth century, whereas the ruling Conservatives opposed it. However, when the Liberals gained control of the government in the late nineteenth century, they began to resist democratic reform, while the Conservatives who moved into the opposition began to support it.

Although the opposition generally supported democratic reforms, it was difficult for it to enact or enforce these measures during the late nineteenth and early twentieth century, given that the ruling party typically controlled the legislature as well as the executive branch of government. In some countries, however, the opposition developed relatively strong parties, which enhanced the likelihood of democratic reform. These parties had widespread and enduring ties to the electorate and permanent national organizations with broad networks of affiliated local associations.

Strong opposition parties facilitated democratic reform for several reasons.[18] First and most importantly, the more powerful the opposition party, the more likely it was to control significant numbers of seats in the legislature, which made it easier to pass democratizing electoral reforms. In addition, strong opposition parties tended to have higher rates of party discipline, which also increased the likelihood that they could enact democratic reforms. Second, strong opposition parties could coordinate efforts to push for democracy and they could negotiate more effectively with the ruling party. Where opposition parties were strong, they could put greater pressure on the regime and they could make and enforce bargains, which facilitated negotiations over democratic reform. Third, strong opposition parties were more likely to believe that they could triumph in fair elections, which gave them greater incentives to push for democratizing reforms. Fourth and finally, strong opposition parties tended

---

[17] As Table 1.1 indicates, democratic reforms were often enacted in packages that included various complementary measures. As important as these reform packages were, they did not bring an end to the democratization process. Indeed, most Latin American countries enacted further democratic reforms over the course of the twentieth century.

[18] Lebas (2011) contends that strong opposition parties played a central role in the third wave of democratization in Africa, although she focuses on their actions in the street rather than the legislature. She argues that strong opposition parties carried out sustained protests that put pressure on the ruling party to democratize.

to have longer time horizons since they were likely to endure. Thus, they could afford to be patient and to agree to democratic reforms that might not give them access to power immediately but would benefit them in the long run.

Some might object that the relationship between strong opposition parties and democracy is endogenous since democratization might have led to powerful opposition parties rather than vice versa. However, the rise of strong opposition parties clearly predates the emergence of democracy in the region. As Chapter 4 discusses, parties first emerged in Latin America in the middle of the nineteenth century, and by the last quarter of the century some of them had developed into tightly organized national institutions that selected candidates, drafted platforms, maintained memberships, and developed ties to the electorate (Sabato 2018, 62–64). Particularly strong opposition parties emerged in Chile, Colombia, and Uruguay, even though they were governed by authoritarian regimes during this period. It is certainly true that the existence of regular elections in which the opposition could compete was necessary for strong opposition parties to emerge, but all South American countries met this criterion for most of the late nineteenth century.

Nevertheless, even strong opposition parties could not typically enact democratic reforms on their own. Splits within ruling parties, however, sometimes weakened the incumbent parties' control over the legislature and provided opportunities for the opposition. Party splits took place frequently in South America during the late nineteenth and early twentieth century, but the critical splits were those that led key members of the ruling party or coalition to defect and ally with the opposition.[19] Together, the ruling party dissidents and the opposition sometimes controlled enough votes to enact democratic reform.

Various studies have argued that splits within authoritarian regimes played a key role in the third wave of democratization, but splits clearly played a key role in the first wave as well (O'Donnell and Schmitter 1986; Przeworski 1992; Madrid 2019a; 2019b). Ruling party splits represented a serious threat to authoritarian regimes during this period because the dissidents often had considerable resources and political networks. Not only did the ruling party dissidents frequently hold legislative seats but they also often had the financial resources and following necessary to win elections. As Schedler (2009, 306) argues: "if anyone is capable of defeating the incumbent [in competitive autocracies], it is someone from the inner ranks of the ruling elite."

A wide range of factors can lead to ruling party splits, including differences over ideology or policy issues, but in electoral authoritarian regimes, internal leadership struggles are typically the main cause of divisions. Elections create intense competition for key nominations. When prominent politicians do not earn their desired nominations, they sometimes decide that they can

---

[19] The opposition frequently split as well but splits within the opposition did not necessarily undermine the prospects of democratic reform because the various opposition factions all stood to benefit from democratizing measures and so typically supported them.

improve their political prospects by joining the opposition (Ibarra Rueda 2013; Langston 2002). Defections of minor politicians are unlikely to have much impact on the ruling party in electoral authoritarian regimes, but the exit of major leaders can have significant repercussions because they frequently take many of their supporters and allies with them. Moreover, the defections of major leaders can have a snowball effect since other politicians may also be tempted to defect if they see that their party is weakening. Of course, major political figures in electoral authoritarian regimes are often reluctant to defect from the ruling party because they fear that they will not be able to win elections in the face of opposition from the ruling party. Nevertheless, ruling party dissidents who are marginalized within their parties sometimes conclude that defection is the best way to achieve their professional aims and policy goals.

Once dissidents break with the leadership of the ruling party, they, like opposition parties, have strong incentives to enact democratic reforms. Without democratic reforms, ruling party leaders are likely to use their control of the electoral process to try to prevent the dissidents, as well as members of the opposition, from winning elections. Thus, ruling party dissidents will seek to enact democratic reforms to weaken the ruling party leaders' control of the electoral process.

Ruling party splits sometimes bring about democratic reform by leading to divided government. In the wake of splits, dissident members of the ruling party at times leave the governing coalition and join forces with the opposition, providing them with a majority in the legislature. As a result, the dissidents and the opposition sometimes have enough votes to push through democratic reforms over the objections of the ruling party. Under these circumstances, the ruling party may seek to negotiate reforms with the opposition, rather than risk the imposition of such measures. As we shall see, this was the path to democratic reform taken in Chile and Uruguay in the late nineteenth and early twentieth century.

Where the defecting faction is particularly large, the ruling party dissidents may gain control of the executive as well as the legislative branch of government. Even where the dissidents occupy the executive branch, however, they will still have incentives to enact democratic reforms if their hold on power is threatened by the traditional ruling elites. In some countries, particularly those with federal systems, regional or local officials, such as governors and mayors, have a great deal of influence over the electoral authorities and the electoral process. Ruling parties that govern for a long time typically control these regional and local officials and they frequently hang on to this influence even after they lose the presidency. Indeed, many ruling parties build important local-level political machines while in office. Thus, once they gain control of the executive branch, ruling party dissidents may support democratic reforms to weaken the traditional leaders' control of the electoral process. As we shall see, this is what occurred in Argentina and Colombia in the early twentieth century.

Thus, a combination of strong opposition parties and ruling party splits helped lead to democratization in some Latin American countries during the late nineteenth and early twentieth century. Strong opposition parties aggressively promoted democratic reform during this period, but they did not have the votes to enact democratic reforms on their own, given the resistance of ruling parties. Splits, however, weakened the ruling party's control of the legislature in some countries, and provided an opportunity for the opposition to push through reforms with the assistance of ruling party dissidents.

THE ORIGINS OF STRONG PARTIES IN SOUTH AMERICA

What led to the emergence of strong opposition parties in South America during the late nineteenth and early twentieth century? And why did strong parties arise in some countries and not others?

Parties emerged throughout South America during the nineteenth century, but two factors helped shape whether they developed strong organizations. First, strong parties tended to arise in those countries where the population was concentrated in a relatively small area with no major geographical obstacles dividing them. This made it easier for politicians and party leaders to build and manage national organizations and communicate with most of the population. Second, strong parties were more likely to emerge in those countries that had relatively balanced religious or territorial cleavages – that is, where neither side of a cleavage clearly dominated the other. These types of cleavages often gave birth to strong parties on both sides of the cleavage, which was good for democracy because at least one of the parties was typically in the opposition where it would push for democratic reform.

Most South American countries were internally fragmented during the nineteenth century so that there was little communication among people living in different regions. Seven of the ten countries in the region spanned more than 750,000 square kilometers, and Brazil alone covered more than 8.5 million square kilometers. The population of these countries was overwhelmingly rural in the nineteenth century and citizens were frequently located at a great distance from one another. Moreover, the territories of these countries were divided by often impenetrable mountains, forests, and swamplands. In some countries, such as Bolivia, Colombia, and Ecuador, the capital and other major cities were located far inland, which complicated internal travel. To make matters worse, transportation and communications infrastructure was quite primitive in the nineteenth century. Railroads did not penetrate Latin America until the late nineteenth century, and even then, they generally linked together only a small area of the country. As a result, in some countries it could take weeks to travel from one major city to another. Even communication was often difficult because the telegraph also came late to South America and telegraph lines were frequently out of service even where they existed.

The high level of geographic fragmentation of many countries in the region made it difficult to form strong national parties. Politicians could not easily campaign throughout their countries. Nor could party leaders manage branches and affiliated organizations nationwide. In addition, the large, geographically fragmented South American countries tended to be quite culturally diverse, which further complicated efforts to form national parties. Many Latin Americans had stronger attachments to their region than their nation. These attachments led to the emergence of numerous regional parties, but most of these parties failed to transcend their regional bases, creating a plethora of small and weak regional organizations (Gibson 1996). Indeed, Colombia was the only large, geographically fragmented, and culturally diverse country to develop strong national parties during this period.

Nevertheless, a few South American countries, namely Chile, Paraguay, and Uruguay, had relatively low levels of geographic fragmentation, which facilitated party building.[20] In these countries, the bulk of the population was concentrated in relatively small areas that were not divided by major geographic barriers. In Uruguay and Paraguay, most of the population lived within a relatively short distance of the capital. Although Chile was much longer and more mountainous than Paraguay or Uruguay, the vast majority of its population in the nineteenth century resided in the Central Valley, which was easily traversable. The concentration of the population in the three countries made it easier for national politicians and party leaders to campaign and build party organizations in all the major towns and cities during the nineteenth century. The lack of geographic fragmentation also reduced cultural diversity and weakened regional identities, which made it easier to form national party platforms that had broad appeal.[21]

Balanced social cleavages also fostered the emergence of strong parties in Latin America during the nineteenth century. The literature on political parties has long emphasized the role that class, ethnic, religious, and territorial cleavages have played in the formation of party systems (Lipset and Rokkan 1967; Caramani 2004; Bartolini and Mair 1990; Rokkan 1970). Lipset and Rokkan (1967), for example, argue that various international developments, including the Protestant reformation, the French Revolution, the process of state formation, and the Industrial Revolution, generated strong center–periphery, church–state, land–industry, and owner–worker cleavages that formed the basis of party systems in Europe. Caramani (2004), meanwhile,

---

[20] Even today, the smaller, more centralized, and less geographically fragmented countries of Latin America tend to have stronger, and more nationalized and institutionalized, party systems than the larger, more decentralized, and more geographically fragmented countries. See the data in Harbers (2010), Jones and Mainwaring (2003), and Mainwaring (2018).

[21] Argentina represented an intermediate case of geographic fragmentation. It covered a vast territory – the second largest in South America – but it had no major internal geographical barriers and the railroads and the telegraphs penetrated it extensively in the late nineteenth century, facilitating communication, travel, and party building within the country.

shows how the emergence of strong class and church–state cleavages in the nineteenth and early twentieth century helped nationalize European party systems, enabling the most important parties to build support throughout their territories. As many scholars have noted, however, social cleavages do not automatically give birth to parties. Political entrepreneurs must translate the cleavage into the political arena by developing parties that represent voters on each side of a cleavage.

For a cleavage to translate into the political arena, elites with sufficient resources to develop and sustain such parties must be present on both sides of the cleavage. Not all cleavages present in Latin America during the nineteenth century translated themselves into the political arena, in part because they did not have elites in large numbers on both sides. Neither class nor ethnic cleavages, for example, played an important role in the emergence of parties in Latin America during the nineteenth century. Most Latin American nations had significant ethno-racial diversity, but in the nineteenth century only the European-origin population had the resources to create political parties. In many countries, large sectors of the indigenous and Afro-Latino population were not even eligible to vote during the nineteenth century because they were illiterate, did not meet the income requirements, or were not considered independent citizens. Nor could class cleavages easily serve as the basis for strong parties in Latin America because neither the working classes nor the middle classes were well organized. A few working-class parties emerged during the nineteenth century, but none survived for very long. The middle classes participated in some of the parties that formed during this period, but none of the major parties were dominated by members of the middle class or were created to defend middle class interests.[22] Indeed, the only important parties to emerge in the region during the nineteenth century were created by and catered to elites.

The two most intensely felt cleavages that divided South American elites during the nineteenth century were territory and religion. Territorial cleavages did not give birth to national parties in most countries, however, because territorial divisions were numerous and fragmented the electorate. In most countries, various regional parties emerged, but none of these parties could unite large sectors of the electorate. Territorial cleavages only gave birth to strong parties in Uruguay where the population was relatively balanced between people living in or near the capital and those residing in the provinces. In Uruguay, the population surrounding Montevideo was of sufficient size to sustain a major party, and the provinces were sufficiently compact to stitch together a party representing peripheral areas. In most South American countries, however, the population in the provinces far outnumbered the population in the

---

[22] As Chapters 5 and 6 discuss, the Radical parties of Argentina and Chile, which are sometimes described as middle-class parties, were founded by elites and did not become middle-class dominated until the twentieth century.

capital, which made it difficult for a party based in the urban center to compete. Moreover, the provincial areas were so dispersed and heterogenous that it was difficult to forge a party that could unite them.

During the nineteenth century, religious (church–state) cleavages played the most important role in the formation of party systems. Even before independence, Latin American elites were divided between liberals who were critical of the Catholic Church and conservatives who defended it, but their differences deepened over the course of the nineteenth century. Both conservative and liberal politicians created parties to promote their causes and advance their personal ambitions. Conservative parties tended to represent the interests of the Catholic Church in the political arena, whereas liberal parties tended to attack the Church, calling for freedom of religion and the separation of church and state. Conservative and Liberal parties often differed on other issues, such as federalism or free trade, but none of these other issues were able to mobilize their supporters with the same level of passion as did the religious issue. As a result, the religious cleavage came to be reflected in most of the region's party systems.

The parties became strongest where the cleavage was sharp and relatively balanced – that is, where there was a rough parity between conservative and liberal forces and where both sides fought vigorously to advance their goals. This occurred in Chile and Colombia where the Catholic Church was traditionally strong, but where liberals gradually gained power and implemented sweeping reforms, prompting a conservative backlash (Middlebrook 2000a, 10). By contrast, where one side clearly had the upper hand, the parties that emerged from the cleavage tended to be weaker and more ephemeral. In countries where the Church was strong and the liberal impulse was weak, such as Bolivia, Ecuador, and to a lesser extent Peru, conservatives had few incentives to invest in party building because of the absence of a significant liberal threat. Politics in these countries was often more personalistic than programmatic, and parties had shallow roots in part because they failed to establish issue-based linkages to the electorate. In countries where the Church was weak, such as Brazil, Paraguay, Uruguay, and Venezuela, conservative parties also tended to be weak and ephemeral, and the religious cleavage failed to provide the basis for the emergence of a strong and programmatic party system (Middlebrook 2000a, 15–22).[23]

Thus, balanced religious or territorial cleavages, along with the concentration of the population in relatively small areas, contributed to the formation of strong parties in some Latin American countries. Balanced cleavages typically created strong parties on both sides and, as a result, countries that had strong

---

[23] As Chapter 4 discusses, conservatives and the Catholic Church tended to be stronger in rural and inland areas and in regions with large indigenous populations. Liberals tended to be more powerful in cities and coastal areas and in regions where the European-origin or Afro-Latino population predominated.

opposition parties typically had strong ruling parties as well. As we have seen, democratic reforms were typically only enacted when the ruling party split. Under these circumstances, strong opposition parties could take advantage of a moment of ruling party weakness to push through reforms.

REGIME OUTCOMES IN SOUTH AMERICA

As the preceding discussion makes clear, regime outcomes in South America during the nineteenth and early twentieth century were shaped by three main variables: the strength of the military, the strength of opposition parties, and the unity of ruling parties (see Figure 1.1). These three variables did not change in a strict sequence, nor were they closely causally related to each other. The strengthening and professionalization of the military did not cause strong opposition parties to emerge, nor did it necessarily precede the rise of strong opposition parties. In fact, in two of the cases, Colombia and Uruguay, strong opposition parties arose before the professionalization of the military and the establishment of a state monopoly on violence. Similarly, the emergence of strong opposition parties did not necessarily cause or precede ruling party splits, but it did increase the likelihood that such splits brought about democratization.

Each of these variables was driven mostly by exogenous factors. Regional military competition, international conflicts, and export wealth, for example, shaped the likelihood that countries would strengthen and professionalize their militaries, whereas the geographic concentration of the population and the existence of balanced cleavages influenced the strength of parties. Party splits were typically caused by intraparty leadership competition, although ideological and programmatic differences sometimes gave birth to party splits as well. For the sake of simplicity, the figure depicts only the three main variables and their associated outcomes.

Where the military was weak, the most common outcome was unstable authoritarianism, which I define as authoritarian regimes characterized by frequent outsider revolts that occasionally overthrow the government. As Chapter 3 discusses, most South American countries were unstable authoritarian regimes during the nineteenth century and a few countries remained

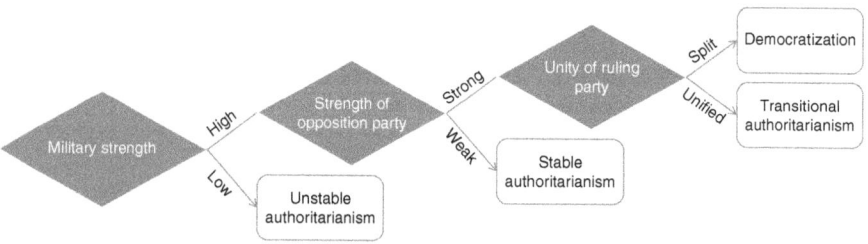

FIGURE 1.1 Determinants of regime outcomes in South America before 1930

in this category during the early twentieth century in large part because they were slow to professionalize their militaries. In these countries, military weakness encouraged the opposition to resort to armed revolts, especially given the meager likelihood of defeating the ruling party at the ballot box. These revolts sometimes succeeded, but even where they did not, they were destabilizing and deepened authoritarian rule. Regimes often responded to the revolts with repression, which created cycles of violence that led to greater political instability and authoritarianism.

Where the military was relatively strong, the regime outcome depended in large part on the strength of opposition parties. If the opposition parties were weak, the most common outcome was stable authoritarianism, which I define as authoritarian rule in which outsider revolts are uncommon and do not typically endanger the government.[24] In these cases, the opposition rarely, if ever, revolted because it had minimal prospects of defeating a strong military, but it sometimes called on the military to overthrow the government. Weak opposition parties also had little chance of prevailing in elections, particularly given government intervention on behalf of the ruling party. As a result, the opposition often chose to abstain from elections, but when it competed, it fared poorly. Thus, authoritarian rule was stable because the opposition did not pose a military or an electoral threat to the regime.

By contrast, if the military was professionalized and the opposition was organized into a strong party, the fate of the regime depended in large part on the unity of the ruling party. As long as the ruling party remained united, it could use its control of the electoral process to tilt the playing field in its favor, ensuring that it gained consistent victories at the polls.[25] The strength of the opposition party would enable it to win some legislative seats, but the prospects for democratic reform remained meager since the opposition had little chance of winning a majority of the legislature or capturing the presidency. Nevertheless, the opposition typically refrained from revolts, given the scarce prospects of defeating a professional military. Although these regimes resemble stable authoritarian regimes, given their absence of revolts, I refer to them as transitional authoritarian regimes because they represent at best a temporary equilibrium since splits within ruling parties were relatively frequent.

If the ruling party split, the prospects for democratization would increase considerably. Under these circumstances, ruling party dissidents would often join forces with the opposition to enact democratic reforms to weaken the ruling party's control of elections. As we shall see, this is what occurred in Chile in 1890, Colombia in 1910, Argentina in 1912 and Uruguay in 1918.

---

[24] As Chapter 3 discusses, these countries may nevertheless experience military coups since a professionalized military does not preclude coups.

[25] The outcomes in these cases resembled those that typically prevail under competitive authoritarianism (Levitsky and Way 2010).

TABLE 1.2 *Scoring regime outcomes in South America during the early twentieth century*

Countries	Military strength	Party strength	Early twentieth-century regime outcome
Chile	High	High	Democracy
Uruguay	Medium	High	Democracy
Argentina	High	Medium	Democracy
Colombia	Medium	High	Democracy
Brazil	High	Low	Stable authoritarian regime
Peru	Medium	Low	Stable authoritarian regime
Venezuela	Medium	Low	Stable authoritarian regime
Bolivia	Low	Low	Unstable authoritarian regime
Ecuador	Low	Low	Unstable authoritarian regime
Paraguay	Low	Medium	Unstable authoritarian regime

Source: Author codings based on the data presented in Chapters 3–8.

Table 1.2 scores the countries on two of the key independent variables – military and party strength – and shows how these two variables influenced regime outcomes in the early twentieth century. (I omit the variable on ruling party splits from the table because it explains the precise timing of democratization, which is not the focus here.) I count as having relatively strong militaries or parties any case that is scored as medium or high in terms of military or party strength. As the table indicates, democracy arose in the early twentieth century in those South American countries that had developed strong militaries and parties by this time, namely Argentina, Chile, Colombia, and Uruguay. By contrast, relatively stable authoritarian regimes emerged in those countries that had strong militaries but had failed to develop strong parties, specifically Brazil, Peru, and Venezuela. Finally, those South American countries that failed to produce strong militaries (Bolivia, Ecuador, and Paraguay) remained unstable authoritarian regimes, regardless of the strength of their parties.

As we shall see, the most robust democracies arose in Chile and Uruguay. Chile was the first South American country to professionalize its armed forces, and by the late nineteenth century it had perhaps the strongest military in the region. As a result, the Chilean opposition largely abandoned the armed struggle after the 1850s and began to focus on the electoral path to power.[26] Strong opposition parties also developed in Chile during the late nineteenth century and these parties began to promote democratic reforms to level the electoral playing field. Thanks in part to splits within the ruling party, the opposition managed to push through electoral reforms in 1874 and 1890 that significantly

---

[26] As Chapter 5 discusses, Chilean opposition parties did take up arms in 1891, but they did so in large part because they obtained the assistance of the navy, which enabled them to prevail in the civil war that year.

expanded the suffrage and established the secret ballot, paving the way for the emergence of democracy in Chile.

Uruguay was slower to professionalize its military than Chile and, as a result, the Uruguayan opposition continued to carry out major armed revolts into the first decade of the twentieth century. At the turn of the century, however, the Uruguayan government took steps to strengthen and professionalize its military, which led to the opposition Blancos' devastating defeat in the 1904 civil war. Subsequently, the main opposition leaders abandoned the armed struggle and concentrated on the electoral path to power, although some members of the opposition participated in a final revolt in 1910. Strong parties arose in Uruguay during the late nineteenth century, but it was not until the second decade of the twentieth century, after the opposition Blanco Party abandoned the armed struggle, that democracy emerged. In 1917–1918, the Blancos took advantage of the split within the ruling Colorados to push through a new constitution that instituted universal male suffrage, established the secret ballot, mandated proportional representation, and set Uruguay on a democratic path.

Democracy also arose in Argentina and Colombia during the early twentieth century, but it proved weaker there than in Chile and Uruguay, although the weakness of the Argentinian and Colombian democracies only became evident after 1929. Argentina, like Chile, strengthened and professionalized its military in the late nineteenth century, which led to a dramatic decline in the revolts that had plagued the country throughout most of the century. After the military easily squashed a final revolt in 1905, the opposition abandoned the armed struggle, although it initially refused to participate in elections to protest continued government electoral manipulation. Parties were slower to develop in Argentina than in Chile and Uruguay, but by the end of the nineteenth century, a strong opposition party, the UCR, had emerged. The Radicals pushed for democratic reforms that would ensure free and fair elections, but these measures were not passed until 1912 after a split within the ruling party led to the election of a dissident faction led by President Roque Sáenz Peña. These reforms, in turn, helped lead to the election of a Radical president, Hipólito Yrigoyen, in the country's first free and fair presidential election in 1916. Once the Radicals took power, however, Argentina lacked a strong opposition party to compete effectively with the ruling party or to prevent it from intervening in elections and concentrating power. This led the opposition to call on the military to intervene in 1930, a process that would be repeated in subsequent years.

Colombia also professionalized its armed forces at the outset of the twentieth century, although to a lesser degree than Argentina and Chile. The strengthening of the Colombian military, along with the bitter memory of the bloody Thousand Days War (1899–1902), discouraged the opposition from carrying out revolts after 1902, and led it to focus increasingly on elections. Colombia, like Chile and Uruguay, had developed strong parties in the nineteenth century, and the opposition Liberal Party used its influence to push for democratic reforms. Nevertheless, as in Argentina, major reforms were not passed until the ruling party split in the early twentieth century and a dissident faction came to power. This faction, which was composed of both Liberals and dissident Conservatives, pushed through constitutional reforms that expanded suffrage rights, strengthened horizontal accountability, and guaranteed minority representation, which helped bring democracy to Colombia. However, the failure of the military to achieve a nationwide monopoly on violence led to periodic outbreaks of regional violence throughout the twentieth century, which undermined the country's democracy.

Relatively stable authoritarian regimes arose in Brazil, Peru, and Venezuela because the countries had strong militaries but weak parties during the early twentieth century. Brazil was the first of these countries to develop a strong military: It modernized its armed forces during the late nineteenth and early twentieth century, which helped reduce the revolts that had plagued Brazil during the early nineteenth century. The weakness of parties in Brazil, however, meant that the opposition had little chance of prevailing in elections, particularly given governmental electoral manipulation. As a result, the opposition often abstained from presidential elections or offered token candidates, enabling the candidates chosen by the ruling elites to win overwhelming victories during the first three decades of the twentieth century.

Venezuela also developed a relatively stable authoritarian regime during this period, but it differed significantly from that of Brazil. In Venezuela, the government of Cipriano Castro, which came to power through armed revolt in 1899, modernized and strengthened the military. This gradually brought an end to the frequent opposition revolts that had plagued Venezuela throughout the nineteenth century. In 1908, Castro's right-hand man, General Juan Vicente Gómez, seized power and then governed with an iron hand until his death in 1935. Because Venezuelan parties were weak, they could offer little opposition to Gómez's regime, enabling him to manipulate elections and consolidate his rule.

A relatively stable authoritarian regime also arose in Peru during this period, although it experienced some instability in the 1910s. With the assistance of a French military mission, Peru modernized its armed forces at the turn of the century, which helped bring an end to the frequent opposition revolts that had plagued it during the nineteenth century. The Civil Party used its control of the electoral authorities to win repeated elections in the early twentieth century, which opposition parties were too weak to resist. An opposition candidate, Guillermo Billinghurst, did manage to gain power in 1912 thanks to the support of urban workers who disrupted the elections in Lima, but he was deposed in a 1914 military coup, and the Civil Party subsequently returned to power. In 1919, however, former President Augusto Leguía seized power with the assistance of the military and the police. Leguía then manipulated Peruvian political institutions to remain in office until 1930.

The three other South American countries – Bolivia, Ecuador, and Paraguay – failed to strengthen their militaries significantly during the early twentieth century and, as a result, they remained plagued by revolts and political instability.

Of the three countries, Bolivia undertook the greatest efforts to professionalize its military during this period, bringing in a French and then a German military mission at the outset of the twentieth century. These missions appeared to have initially made progress in strengthening the army, but the outsider revolts that had disappeared in the first two decades of the twentieth century resumed in the 1920s and the military struggled to suppress them. Indeed, the opposition successfully overthrew the government in 1920. The weakness of Bolivian parties also undermined the prospects for democracy during this period. Opposition parties were too feeble to enact democratic reforms or resist government electoral manipulation, and, as a result, the ruling party consistently won presidential elections by large margins.

Ecuador made even less progress than Bolivia in modernizing its military in the early twentieth century. The small Chilean mission that Ecuador hired during this period failed to make much of an impact and the military remained heavily politicized and underfunded. As a consequence, Ecuador continued to suffer frequent revolts – there were five major outsider revolts as well as two military coups between 1900 and 1929 – and the rebellions in 1906 and 1911 overthrew the government. The weakness of parties in Ecuador also hindered the prospects for democracy since it made it difficult for the opposition to enact democratic reforms or prevent the government from manipulating elections. Thus, the opposition often abstained from elections or offered only token opposition.

Finally, Paraguay also failed to professionalize its military during the early twentieth century, and as a result, its armed forces remained small, highly politicized, and poorly trained and equipped. This encouraged the opposition to seek power through armed rebellions. Paraguay suffered fourteen revolts between 1900 and 1929, and eight of these rebellions overthrew the government. Although the country began to develop strong parties in the early twentieth century, the political opposition viewed armed revolts as the most effective means of gaining power, given government manipulation of elections, so it typically abstained from presidential elections. The one exception was the relatively free and fair 1928 presidential elections, but even in this contest, the opposition candidate was unable to overcome the advantages of the ruling party.

Thus, the strength of the military and parties shaped regime outcomes in South America during the first three decades of the twentieth century. Democracy emerged in some countries and stable or unstable authoritarian regimes in others, depending on their configurations of military and party strength. As the Conclusion discusses, these variables would continue to shape political outcomes in the decades that followed, albeit to a lesser degree.

ALTERNATIVE EXPLANATIONS

Existing theories shed light on certain aspects of the democratization process in South America, but they offer at best a partial explanation for the emergence of democracy in the region. Structural theories, for example, offer explanations for the cross-national variance in democracy, but they struggle to explain the precise timing of democratization. Moreover, neither structural theories nor existing actor-based theories correctly identify the key actors behind democratic reforms in South America or explain why they prevailed over opponents of reform. This study builds on these theories but seeks to offer a thicker and more complete explanation for the birth of democracy in the region.

The most widely known structural explanation for democratization is modernization theory. Modernization theorists have shown that there is a positive correlation between economic development and democracy, but there is little agreement about the precise nature of that relationship or what actors and causal mechanisms, if any, undergird it (Acemoglu et al. 2008; 2009; Boix and Stokes 2003; Mainwaring and Pérez-Liñán 2003; Przeworski and Limongi 1997). Moreover, modernization theory cannot explain the precise timing of democratization in the region since development typically changes only slowly over time.

Most variants of modernization theory would expect democracy to have emerged first in the most developed countries in South America. To a degree, this is what happened. Argentina, Chile, and Uruguay were the wealthiest and most literate countries in the region during the late nineteenth and early twentieth century, with GDPs per capita of more than $2,000 (in constant 1990 dollars) and literacy rates between 44 and 60 percent in 1900 (Bolt et al. 2018; Thorp 1998, 354). Nevertheless, Colombia, another democratic pioneer, ranked only in the middle of the region in terms of wealth and literacy, with a GDP per capita of only $683 and a literacy rate of 34 percent in 1900 (Bolt et al. 2018; Thorp 1998, 354).

This study shows that economic development fostered democratization in the region, but through different mechanisms than modernization theory has traditionally emphasized. As noted, the export boom led to economic development in South America during the late nineteenth and early twentieth century, which facilitated democratization by financing the professionalization of the armed forces. Development also contributed to democratization by enabling investments in infrastructure and reducing barriers to transportation and communication, which helped lead to the emergence of strong national parties that promoted democratic reform. Democracy arose in Colombia despite its relatively low level of development in large part because the country's intense yet balanced religious cleavage helped give birth to relatively strong parties in the late nineteenth century. Moreover, the country took steps to professionalize its military in the wake of the War of a Thousand Days, which led the opposition to abandon the armed struggle and focus on the electoral path to power.

The professionalization of the military and the rise of strong parties in the region also help explain why some South American countries democratized when they did. Nevertheless, ruling party splits can best account for the precise timing of democratization in individual countries of the region since the enactment of democratic reforms typically closely followed these schisms. Thus, my approach offers a thicker, more comprehensive explanation than modernization theory for the birth of democracy in the region.

Another potential structural explanation for the emergence of democracy in the region would focus on each country's ethno-racial composition. Some studies have argued that ethnic diversity may lead to ethnic conflict that is detrimental to democracy (Horowitz 1985; Rabushka and Shepsle 1972). Other studies have argued that where there are high levels of inequality, including ethno-racial inequality, elites are particularly likely to oppose democratization for fear that subordinate groups will take advantage of the suffrage to strip them of their wealth and power (Acemoglu and Robinson 2006; Engerman and Sokoloff 2012). Still other studies have argued that democracy is a European export and, as a result, the countries that had larger European-origin populations were more likely to become democratic (Hariri 2012; Gerring and Apfeld 2018).

This approach, too, sheds light on some aspects of democratization in South America. Most of the countries where democracy emerged first, namely Argentina, Chile, and Uruguay, had majority European-origin populations, which meant that they had little reason to fear that indigenous people or Afro-Latinos could take power via democratic means. Ethno-racial discrimination can also help us understand why some Latin American governments maintained literacy restrictions that disproportionately disenfranchised indigenous and Afro-Latino voters. Indeed, the South American countries that maintained literacy restrictions the longest – Brazil, Ecuador, and Peru – all had large Afro-Latino or indigenous populations. Nevertheless, ethnic composition can only partly explain the first wave of democratization in South America. It does not explain, for example, why ethnically diverse Colombia democratized or why ethnically homogenous Paraguay did not. Nor can ethnicity easily explain the timing of democratization in South America since the ethnic composition of countries only changes slowly over time. Finally, although ethno-racial discrimination may explain why the dominant ethno-racial groups would disenfranchise subordinate groups, it does not explain why they would use democratic methods to allocate power among themselves.

Another explanation for the emergence of democracy in the region would focus on the countries' past experiences with democratic institutions. There is a large literature that suggests that elections in authoritarian regimes promote democratization by diffusing democratic norms and strengthening democratic institutions, such as the media, opposition parties, and the judiciary (Lindberg 2006; 2009; Miller 2013). Some studies have found that countries with previous experiences with democracy are more likely to be democratic today (Pérez-Liñán and Mainwaring 2013; Persson and Tabellini 2009). As we have seen, some of the democratic institutions, such as parties, that some South American countries developed in the nineteenth century played a key role in the emergence of democracy in the twentieth century. Moreover, as the Conclusion discusses, the prolonged experiences with democracy that some South American countries had during the early twentieth century help explain why these countries enjoyed more years of democracy in the decades that followed.

Nevertheless, there is much that a focus on past experiences with democratic institutions cannot explain. Past experiences with elections or other democratic institutions cannot account for the precise timing of democratization in individual South American countries; nor can they easily explain why some South American countries democratized in the early twentieth century while others did not. Indeed, with the notable exception of Colombia, the countries that were the first to democratize in the early twentieth century did not hold more competitive or more free and fair elections in the nineteenth century than the other South American countries, as Chapter 2 shows. Although some South American countries enjoyed brief experiences with free and fair elections during the nineteenth century, these episodes were too ephemeral to contribute to the development of democratic norms.

A final structural explanation would focus on geographic and temporal diffusion. Numerous studies have found that democracy diffuses along regional and temporal lines: Democratization often occurs in waves, and the probability that a country will democratize increases as the number of democratic countries in its region goes up (Brinks and Coppedge 2006; Gleditsch and Ward 2006; Markoff 1996; Wejnert 2014; Weyland 2014). Diffusion-based explanations typically focus on ideational contagion – they suggest that both elites and masses demand democracy when it becomes a regional or worldwide norm.

An explanation based on diffusion also has some merit. Certainly, there was a degree of geographic and temporal clustering during the first wave of democratization in Latin America: All the Southern Cone countries adopted democratic reforms within a few decades of each other. Moreover, it is clear from congressional debates that politicians in Latin America were aware of democratic reforms in other countries and designed their own reforms based partly on these foreign models. Ideational diffusion also helps explain why South American countries embraced elections and representative institutions to begin with and why democratic norms took increasing hold among the public as time went on. Nevertheless, an explanation based on ideational diffusion cannot explain the precise timing of democratization since liberal ideas and democratic reform models were flowing into Latin America throughout the nineteenth century. Nor can it easily explain why most South American countries failed to participate in the first wave of democratization. Finally, diffusion-based explanations tend to be vague on causal mechanisms and key actors: They do not explain precisely how and why democracy diffused.

Other theories of democratization focus on actors, although they also identify the structural factors that shape their behavior. The class pressure model, for example, suggests that democratization is the product of a class struggle. One version argues that the masses or the working classes support democratization because they want to redistribute their country's wealth, and the landed elites resist democracy in order to block redistribution (Acemoglu and

Alternative Explanations 47

Robinson 2006; Przeworski 2009a; Rueschemeyer, Stephens, and Stephens 1992). In these accounts, the struggle for democracy takes place in the streets and often involves violent strikes, protests, and revolts, or at least the threat of violence. Democratization occurs when authoritarian rulers, who represent the landed elites, yield in the face of these threats.

Another version of the class pressure model focuses on the rising bourgeoisie, which is said to demand democratization to advance or protect its economic interests (Ansell and Samuels 2014; Moore 1966; Sidel 2008). Moore contends that capitalist development strengthened the bourgeoisie, which supported democracy, and weakened the landed elites, which opposed it. Hence, "no bourgeois, no democracy," in his memorable phrase (Moore 1966, 418). Ansell and Samuels (2014), meanwhile, argue that emerging financial and industrial elites promoted democratization in order to protect themselves against taxation and confiscation. In both versions of this model, democracy emerged as the result of a struggle between a rising socioeconomic actor that aimed to advance its economic interests and a ruling elite that sought to defend its wealth and prerogatives.

Neither the working classes nor the bourgeoisie played a significant role in the emergence of democracy in South America, however. The bourgeoisie was relatively small during the early twentieth century and lacked political organization. None of the major parties that promoted democratization was predominantly bourgeois in terms of leadership, supporters, or platforms. Although some members of the bourgeoisie supported democratization during this period, others resisted it. The urban working classes were also relatively small and weakly organized at the outset of the twentieth century. Moreover, most of the unions expressed little interest in democracy, owing to their anarcho-syndicalist tendencies. Although organized workers played an important role in subsequent waves of democratization (Rueschemeyer, Stephens, and Stephens 1992; Collier 1999), their contribution to the first wave was modest. Nevertheless, as Rueschemeyer, Stephens, and Stephens (1992, 8) argue, the relative weakness of the working classes in Latin America prior to 1930 may explain why the franchise remained restricted in some of the South American countries that did participate in the first wave of democratization.

Thus, existing theories of democracy offer important insights but cannot explain many aspects of the emergence of democracy in South America. A fuller explanation requires a focus on the military and political parties: the two actors that played a central role in the first wave of democratization in the region. Chapters 3–8 discuss how and when these actors developed and contributed to the emergence of democracy in the region.

2

Elections and Democracy in South America before 1930

When and where did democracy first emerge in Latin America? This chapter uses a plethora of data on elections and suffrage rights in South America to assess the degree of democracy in the region before 1930. As it shows, the first lengthy and meaningful experiences of democracy in the region did not occur until the early twentieth century, although there were brief episodes of democratization in the nineteenth century. Chapters 3–8 show how democracy arose during this period and why in some South American countries and not others.

Throughout the nineteenth century, Latin American countries held regular elections, but there is a significant debate about how democratic these elections were. Scholars traditionally portrayed elections in nineteenth-century Latin America as farces riddled with violence, fraud, and manipulation. In 1919, for example, Seymour and Frary (1919, 267) reported that "it is probably not unfair to say that elections were usually a pure sham" in the region in the greater part of the nineteenth century.[1] More recently, Nohlen (2005a, 4) argued that "[e]lections in Latin America were mostly characterized by fraud and were used more to provide political legitimacy to the incumbents rather than to control their right to govern a country." The main democracy indexes exhibit similar skepticism, portraying Latin American elections during this period as unfree and unfair and the region's regimes as consistently authoritarian.

In recent decades, however, scholars have challenged this view, showing that many nineteenth-century elections involved considerable electoral competition and participation (Annino 1995; Aguilar Rivera, Posada-Carbó, and Zimmermann 2022; Drake 2009; Malamud 2000b; Posada-Carbó 1996a;

---

[1] Cited in Posada-Carbó (2000a, 612).

2000a; Posada-Carbó and Valenzuela 2012; Sabato 2001b; 2018; Valenzuela 1996; 2012). The revisionists acknowledge that there was significant electoral corruption in the nineteenth century and that many countries restricted the franchise, but they argue that democratic practices were much more widespread than the traditional literature recognized.

Until now, we have not had a comprehensive source of data on elections in the region during this period, which has made it difficult to arbitrate between these two conflicting views. Without such data, we cannot assess with any precision the degree of competition, participation, and democracy in elections in nineteenth-century Latin America.

This chapter takes a large step toward filling this gap by presenting and analyzing an original data set on presidential elections in South America from independence to 1929. LAHED is based on both archival research and wide-ranging scrutiny of the growing secondary literature on elections in the region. It contains information on all presidential elections during this period – 263 elections in South America alone – which is far more than existing data sets include.

The analysis of LAHED data in this chapter focuses on electoral competition and participation because they are widely viewed as the cornerstone of democracy, at least since Schumpeter (2008 [1942]) and Dahl (1971). I examine presidential elections in part because of the greater availability of data on these elections, but also because the president was clearly the most powerful actor in Latin American politics during the nineteenth century and had the greatest impact on democracy.

My analysis of LAHED data finds that the revisionist view is accurate in that democratic practices did exist in nineteenth-century Latin America. Some South American countries established broad suffrage rights during the nineteenth century and a few even enacted universal male suffrage. Voters of all social classes participated in elections, and in several countries voter turnout was relatively high. Most presidential elections were contested, some were competitive, and in a few cases the opposition won. A handful of nineteenth-century elections appear even to have been relatively free and fair.

Nevertheless, we must be careful not to exaggerate the degree of democratic practices in nineteenth-century South America. By focusing on the limited democratic trees that existed in the nineteenth century, the revisionist approach risks obscuring the authoritarian forest.[2] Government intervention, fraud, and intimidation marred the vast majority of elections during the nineteenth century. More than 70 percent of presidential elections were uncompetitive and at least one-third were not even contested. Most South American countries also significantly restricted suffrage rights, maintaining literacy and/or economic restrictions throughout most or all of the nineteenth century as well as denying

---

[2] I thank Kurt Weyland for this phrasing.

the vote to women. Even where suffrage rights were broad, voter turnout was often low. Indeed, valid votes typically represented less than three percent of the total population during the nineteenth century. To be sure, corrupt, uncompetitive, and exclusionary elections were also quite common in Europe, North America, and the Antipodes at that time, but, as we shall see, the level of competition and voter turnout was higher on average in these regions than in South America during the nineteenth century.

The few democratic episodes in South America during the nineteenth century proved ephemeral. In some cases, the governments elected in free and fair elections were quickly overthrown by their opponents. In other cases, the democratically elected presidents themselves subverted democracy, intervening in elections and repressing the opposition to ensure that their favored candidates triumphed. Moreover, the brief democratic episodes failed to leave a lasting mark.

It was not until the early twentieth century that South American countries experienced lengthy and meaningful episodes of democracy. At the outset of the twentieth century, a great divergence occurred in the region. A few nations, such as Argentina, Chile, Colombia, and Uruguay, established democratic regimes that would last for a dozen years or more. During this period, these nations regularly held reasonably free and fair elections with relatively broad voter participation. Three of these four countries remained democratic for most of the twentieth century (Argentina being the exception), although they all experienced coups at one point or another. By contrast, most of the other South American countries – Bolivia, Brazil, Ecuador, Paraguay, Peru, and Venezuela – became *more* authoritarian during the early twentieth century. Indeed, in Bolivia, Ecuador, Peru, and Venezuela, elections were less competitive and less democratic in the first three decades of the twentieth century than they had been on average during the late nineteenth century. Moreover, all six of the democratic laggards remained authoritarian for most of the twentieth century.

These findings indicate that democracy, as I defined it in the Introduction, did not emerge in South America until the early twentieth century. The nineteenth-century episodes correspond to what I refer to as ephemeral democratization: brief democratic openings that did not have enduring impact. By contrast, the democratic episodes of the early twentieth century were lengthy and had a lasting impact.

This chapter is organized as follows. The first section of the chapter describes LAHED and compares it to other databases on democracy and elections that cover this period. The second section uses LAHED to examine the evolution of suffrage rights and voter turnout in the region in the nineteenth century. The third section discusses the competitiveness and fairness of South American elections in the nineteenth century. It also describes the few episodes of democracy that occurred in the region during this period and demonstrates that they were short lived. The fourth section shows that sustained episodes of democracy arose in four South American nations during the early twentieth century, whereas the other countries in the region remained authoritarian. The concluding section summarizes the main findings of this chapter.

A NEW DATABASE ON HISTORICAL ELECTIONS

LAHED provides comprehensive coverage of presidential elections in Latin America from independence to 1929. It covers both direct and indirect elections for provisional as well as constitutional presidents, including those elections that were conducted in the legislature or constituent assembly. LAHED provides data on the electoral results, the candidates, suffrage rights, and the freeness and fairness of the elections, among other characteristics. The data were culled from more than 300 sources, including general histories, electoral compendia, and studies of individual elections, as well as archival sources such as newspapers, ambassadorial dispatches, presidential messages, and congressional minutes and reports.

LAHED counts as a presidential election only those elections that involve, directly or indirectly, the citizenry. This includes instances where the legislature, a constituent assembly, or an electoral college elects the president provided that those bodies are elected by the citizenry. LAHED does not count as elections instances where a body whose members were selected by the incumbent president elects the new president. Nor does LAHED cover instances where the resignation, death, forcible removal, or impeachment of the existing president leads to the ascension of the next-in-line for the presidency (e.g., the vice-president or the first designate), even if such ascension requires a vote by the legislature. Finally, LAHED does not cover instances where a plebiscite or legislative vote is held to decide whether a president should remain in office or extend his/her term.

LAHED has identified and coded 263 presidential elections in South America during this period: 182 in the nineteenth century and eighty-one between 1900 and 1929. It contains the actual vote totals for 151 elections in the nineteenth century and sixty-five elections in the first three decades of the twentieth century, including both direct and indirect elections.[3] In addition, it provides estimated results for thirty-four other presidential elections in which the vote totals are unknown but where only one candidate ran and/or the result was reported to be unanimous. Thus, it contains actual data on 82 percent of the presidential elections that took place in South America between independence and 1929 and actual or estimated data on 95 percent of all presidential elections in the region during this period.

---

[3] For most indirect elections, including those that took place through legislatures or constituent assemblies, LAHED only has data on the final round of the presidential elections (the vote by the electors or legislators), but the database includes first-round data where available. Where data on multiple rounds of elections are available, they correspond to the earliest round available.

The presidential elections covered include fifteen elections in Argentina, twenty-nine in Bolivia, eleven in Brazil, twenty-five in Chile, thirty-five in Colombia, thirty-five in Ecuador, twenty-four in Paraguay, thirty in Peru, twenty-five in Uruguay, and thirty-four in Venezuela. Some countries held more presidential elections than others, in part because they had shorter constitutional terms, or because the terms of some presidents were interrupted and new elections were held ahead of schedule. Brazil has the fewest elections in the data set because it did not hold presidential elections for most of the nineteenth century, since it was an empire. Argentina, meanwhile, was fragmented after independence and, with one exception, did not hold presidential elections during the first half of the nineteenth century.

LAHED goes significantly beyond any other source in its coverage of historical elections in the region and the data it provides. The most thorough and reliable source for twentieth-century elections in Latin America is Nohlen (2005a), but it does not include the nineteenth century and its coverage of early twentieth-century elections is spotty.[4] The main democracy databases also lack comprehensive data on elections during this period. Neither Polity, nor Boix, Miller, and Rosato, provide data on elections per se. The Political Institutions and Political Events (PIPE) data set developed by Przeworski (2013) provides data on suffrage rights and other nineteenth-century political institutions, but it does not report the results of the elections or assess their quality.[5] The Varieties of Democracy (V-Dem) project codes some elections during this period, but it omits presidents elected by the legislature or a constituent assembly, which accounted for 39 percent of presidential elections in South America during the nineteenth century and 28 percent in the first three decades of the twentieth century. V-Dem provides the results for only fifty-two presidential elections in South America during the nineteenth century and twenty-seven elections between 1900 and 1929, which represents only 36 percent of the presidential election results contained in LAHED (Coppedge et al. 2022b).[6] V-Dem has even more limited data on the results of legislative elections during this period.

---

[4] Nohlen (2005a) provides data on presidential elections beginning in 1916 in Argentina, in 1951 in Bolivia, in 1894 in Brazil, in 1920 in Chile, in 1914 in Colombia, in 1901 in Ecuador, in 1953 in Paraguay, in 1931 in Peru, in 1926 in Uruguay, and in 1947 in Venezuela.

[5] PIPE has variables measuring voter turnout, but it only has eighteen observations for presidential elections and twenty-two observations for legislative elections in South America during this period.

[6] V-Dem identifies sixty-six presidential elections in the nineteenth century and forty-five in the first three decades of the twentieth century and codes their freeness and fairness. (See the V-Dem variable: v2eltype_6). V-Dem only includes presidential elections that are "direct elections and elections by an electoral college that is elected by the people and has the sole purpose of electing an executive or members of parliament" (Coppedge et al. 2022a, 58). However, in some countries, such as Uruguay, the constitution assigned the legislature the role of electing the president, whereas in other countries, congress or constitutional assemblies elected the president under irregular transitions or other exceptional circumstances.

The most comprehensive source on nineteenth-century presidential elections in Latin America is Vanhanen (2000), but he only provides data on the winner's share of the total vote (competition) and the percentage of the total population that cast votes (participation).[7] Moreover, a significant portion of the data Vanhanen includes is misleading owing to some problematic coding rules.[8]

As Table 2.1 indicates, LAHED's variables measuring the freeness and fairness of elections and the vote share of the winner are only modestly correlated with variables from other databases that measure the level of democracy or the quality of elections in South America before 1930. The strongest correlations are between LAHED's measure of free and fair elections and: (1) V-Dem's measure of free and fair elections (0.58); (2) Boix, Miller, and Rosato's dichotomous measure of democracy (0.57); and (3) Vanhanen's Index of Democratization (0.51).[9] All of these variables, however, were much more weakly correlated in the nineteenth century than in the early twentieth century.[10] LAHED's measure of votes cast as a share of the total population is highly correlated with Vanhanen's equivalent measure of participation (0.82), but this high level of correlation should not be construed as validating Vanhanen's data on participation. The vast majority of Vanhanen's inaccurate data on participation come from indirect elections, but LAHED has very little data on voter turnout in these elections.

---

[7] Vanhanen provides data on 142 presidential elections in South America during the nineteenth century and sixty-six between 1900 and 1929, which represents approximately 80 percent of the data included in LAHED.

[8] In indirect elections, which represented more than 80 percent of all presidential elections in the nineteenth century, Vanhanen (2000, 254) measures voter participation by counting only the votes cast in the final round of the elections by the electors or members of the legislature or constituent assembly, which dramatically understates the overall level of voter participation. In addition, in many elections, Vanhanen incorrectly coded voter participation as zero and the winner as earning 100 percent of the vote, presumably because he lacked data on these elections and assumed they were not contested. For example, in Bolivia, he inaccurately codes the winner as earning 100 percent of the vote in all sixteen presidential elections between 1825 and 1880 when ten of these elections were contested and three were relatively competitive. Vanhanen does not justify these codings other than to report that in this period "Bolivian presidents were *caudillos* [regional leaders] who had nearly always usurped power by force or other unconstitutional means" (see his Bolivia country file: www.prio.org/data/20). This is an exaggeration because even when Bolivian presidents took power by force, they almost always subsequently held elections. In his article introducing the data set, Vanhanen (2000, 254) notes that when executive power is not based on popular elections such as in monarchies and military and revolutionary regimes, then the share of the vote of the executive is assumed to be 100 percent and the degree of voter participation is assumed to be zero, but the vast majority of South American regimes that he codes incorrectly were based on popular elections.

[9] LAHED's measure of the vote share of the winner in presidential elections is most strongly correlated with Vanhanen's measure of competition (−0.48) and V-Dem's measure of free and fair elections (−0.41).

[10] LAHED's measure of free and fair elections in South American countries during the nineteenth century had only a 0.26 correlation with V-Dem's equivalent measure; and LAHED's measure of the winner's share of the vote before 1900 had only a −0.34 correlation with Vanhanen's measure of competition.

TABLE 2.1 *Comparing databases on democracy in South America before 1930*

	Correlation with LAHED's free and fair elections (no. of observations)	Correlation with LAHED's vote share of winner (no. of observations)	Correlation with LAHED's votes cast/total population (no. of observations)
V-Dem variables			
Free and fair elections	0.58 (122)	−0.41 (120)	0.43 (128)
Polyarchy	0.32 (260)	−0.24 (247)	0.38 (165)
Polity variables			
Polity2	0.17 (261)	−0.21 (248)	0.14 (166)
Competitiveness of executive recruitment	0.05 (261)	0.08 (248)	0.04 (166)
Vanhanen variables			
Index of Democratization	0.51 (262)	−0.32 (249)	0.67 (166)
Competition	0.43 (262)	−0.48 (249)	0.28 (166)
Participation	0.30 (262)	−0.04 (249)	0.82 (166)
Boix, Miller, and Rosato			
Democracy	0.57 (261)	−0.24 (248)	0.43 (166)

In sum, LAHED draws on extensive historical research to provide systematic data on South American presidential elections from independence to 1929. It contains considerably more data and many more elections than existing data sets, and the data it provides are only modestly correlated with that in existing databases. It therefore facilitates a more comprehensive and accurate assessment of the degree of democracy in the region during the nineteenth and early twentieth century.

SUFFRAGE RIGHTS AND ELECTORAL PARTICIPATION IN THE NINETEENTH CENTURY

As noted, the traditional view was that elections in the nineteenth century were elite affairs in which only a small sector of the population participated. Indeed, many scholars have referred to Latin American regimes of this period as elite or oligarchic republics because of their limited mass participation. In recent decades, however, historians have challenged this view, emphasizing that elections in Latin America during this period often involved considerably more voter participation than was traditionally believed. They note that the 1812 Spanish constitution, the so-called Cádiz Constitution, provided a model for the extension of broad suffrage rights in Latin America after independence. The Cádiz Constitution extended suffrage to almost all free adult males in the Americas, including indigenous people. It excluded people of African origin, but they could apply for citizenship based on their talents, good behavior, and service to the country (Aguilar Rivera, Posada-Carbó, and Zimmermann 2022, 12–13). The Cádiz Constitution imposed no property or income requirements, and it suspended literacy requirements until 1830, but it barred domestic servants, debtors, the unemployed, and criminals from voting.

My analysis of LAHED data suggests that the revisionists are correct in that nineteenth-century South American suffrage rights were sometimes broad and voter turnout was occasionally high. Half of the South American countries adopted nearly universal male suffrage at some point during the nineteenth century. Moreover, some of the countries that maintained economic restrictions, such as Brazil and Chile, set the requirements to vote at relatively low levels or allowed inflation to erode their real value over time, which reduced the impact of these restrictions. Social and economic progress also gradually increased the share of people who satisfied the economic and literacy requirements. In addition, the restrictions that did exist were not always enforced. For example, in some cases, citizens were asked only to sign their names to demonstrate that they could read or write. At different points, the electoral registries of various countries contained many people from the lower classes, including illiterates, artisans, farmhands, day laborers, and free men of color (Madrid 2019a, 8; República de Chile 1863; 1871; 1879; Gil Fortoul 1942, 272–273; Gilmore 1964, 17; Graham 1990; Klein 1995; Navas Blanco 1993; Sabato 2001a; Sabato and Palti 1990).[11] Artisans not only voted frequently, they also played a key role in campaigns in Chile, Colombia, Peru, and elsewhere (Sanders 2004; Sowell 1992; Wood 2011; García Bryce 2004; Gazmuri 2002; Posada-Carbó 2003; Sobrevilla Perea 2002).

Nevertheless, we should not exaggerate the degree of suffrage rights and voter participation in the nineteenth century. Suffrage restrictions in the region disenfranchised a large majority of the adult population for most of the century. Women were prohibited from voting throughout the nineteenth century in South America as elsewhere – Ecuador in 1929 was the first Latin American country to grant women the right to vote in national elections.[12]

---

[11] For example, only one-third of registered voters were literate in Venezuela in 1846 (Gilmore 1964, 17; Gil Fortoul 1942, 242–243).

[12] During the nineteenth century, women were granted suffrage rights in a few provinces, but these exceptions were isolated. The Colombian province of Vélez, for example, granted women the right to vote in 1853, as did the Argentine province of San Juan in 1862 (Posada-Carbó 2018).

Most South American countries also banned illiterates from voting for the bulk of the nineteenth century, which had a major impact since the vast majority of the population in the region was illiterate. In addition, South American countries imposed a host of economic restrictions on the franchise, from income and property requirements to prohibitions on voting by workers in dependency relationships, such as domestic servants, peons, and day laborers. The economic requirements typically disenfranchised fewer people than the literacy provisions, but they both significantly reduced the size of the electorate.

The economic and literacy restrictions were quite pervasive. One or the other (or both) were in place in 532 of the 768 country-years that South American nations were independent during the nineteenth century, or 69 percent of the time.[13] These data understate the percentage of years in which countries imposed economic or literacy restrictions by excluding the 1816–1853 period in Argentina and the 1853–1863 period in Colombia in which suffrage rules were set at the state or provincial level. (Some states or provinces in Argentina and Colombia imposed economic and literacy restrictions during these periods, but others did not.) Although South American countries did not typically ban members of marginalized ethnic or racial groups from voting, the economic and literacy restrictions disenfranchised most indigenous people and Afro-Latinos during the nineteenth century.

Other restrictions had a smaller impact. Slaves, for example, were prohibited from voting, but the enslaved population in South America declined rapidly over the course of the century.[14] Rank-and-file soldiers and the clergy were also frequently banned from voting, although neither of these groups typically represented a large sector of the population. In addition, Brazil and Ecuador restricted the suffrage to Catholics during parts of the nineteenth century, but it is unclear how strictly these religious restrictions were enforced.

As Table 2.2 indicates, suffrage rights varied considerably across countries and over time. On the whole, Argentina, Paraguay, and Venezuela granted the broadest suffrage rights, followed by Peru, Colombia, and Brazil. By contrast, Bolivia, Chile, Ecuador, and Uruguay had the most restrictions.

The majority of Latin American countries followed what Sabato (2001b, 1297) referred to as a zig-zag path of suffrage rights, alternating between expansion and contraction over the course of the nineteenth century. During

---

[13] A country-year is a unit of analysis in which each year that occurs in a country under study represents a separate observation. If a study examines 10 countries over 100 years, it includes 1,000 country-years.

[14] All South American countries had abolished slavery by 1855, except for Bolivia (1861), Paraguay (1869), and Brazil (1888) (Andrews 2004, 58). Partly as a result, by mid-century, there were few slaves in the region, except in Brazil where enslaved people still constituted 15.8 percent of the population in 1872 (Klein 1969a, 36).

TABLE 2.2 *Suffrage restrictions and voter turnout in South America in the nineteenth century*

Country and type of suffrage restrictions	Votes cast as a % of total population (election years and type)	Registered voters as a % of total population (election years and type)
Argentina		
1816–1853: Voting rights varied by province		
1853–1947: Universal male suffrage	1.4 (1854p–1898p)	
Bolivia		
1825–1839: Economic restrictions		
1839–1952: Economic and literacy restrictions	1.5 (1840p–1896p)	
Brazil		
1824–1880: Economic restrictions	6.9 (1835r and 1872d)	10.6 (1870d–1874d)
1881–1891: Economic and literacy restrictions	0.8 (1881d and 1886d)	1.2 (1881d)
1891–1985: Literacy restrictions	2.5 (1894p and 1898p)	6.8 (1894p & 1898p)
Chile		
1818–1839: Economic restrictions	1.5 (1825d–1837d)	2.0 (1824d–1834d)
1840–1874: Economic and literacy restrictions	1.5 (1840d–1873d)	1.6 (1840d–1873d)
1874–1970: Literacy restrictions	3.1 (1876d–1897d)	6.4 (1876d–1897d)
Colombia		
1819–1853: Economic restrictions		
1853–1863: Universal male suffrage	5.8 (1856p–1860p)	
1863–1886: Voting rights varied by state	3.0 (1864p–1883p)	
1886–1936: Economic and literacy restrictions		
Ecuador		
1830–1834: Economic restrictions	0.5 (1830p)	
1835–1861: Economic and literacy restrictions	0.4 (1835p)	
1861–1978: Literacy restrictions	2.7 (1865p–1899p)	
Paraguay		
1811–1856: Universal male suffrage		
1856–1869: Economic and literacy restrictions		
1870–1961: Universal male suffrage		

(continued)

TABLE 2.2 (continued)

Country and type of suffrage restrictions	Votes cast as a % of total population (election years and type)	Registered voters as a % of total population (election years and type)
Peru		
1821–1828: Economic restrictions		
1828–1834: Universal male suffrage		
1834–1855: Economic restrictions		
1855–1856: Universal male suffrage		
1856–1891: Economic *or* literacy restrictions	13.6 (1858p–1890p)	
1891–1979: Literacy restrictions	1.6 (1899p)	3.0 (1899p)
Uruguay		
1830–1840: Economic restrictions	1.8 (1830s & 1834m)	5.9 (1833d)
1840–1919: Economic and literacy restrictions	1.0 (1862m–1898d)	4.1 (1860g–1896d)
Venezuela		
1830–1856: Economic restrictions	4.7 (1846p)	8.7 (1845 & 1846p)
1856–1936: Universal male suffrage	11.6 (1860p–1897p)	

Source: Latin American Historical Elections Database.
Notes: The table focuses on economic and literacy restrictions only. The restrictions listed refer to the rules governing voting in the first round of elections – the requirements to be an elector or a candidate were often more restrictive. Voter turnout and registration data represent the average for the period listed. The suffix after the year indicates the type of election: c = constituent assembly; d = deputies (lower chamber of legislature); m = mayor; p = president; r = regent; s = senator. Voter turnout data for Uruguay is for the Department of Montevideo only from 1830 to 1898. From 1839 to 1855, Peru imposed a literacy requirement, but it suspended it for indigenous people and, between 1839 and 1851, for *mestizos* (people of mixed race), who constituted the vast majority of illiterates (del Águila Peralta 2013, 185).

the independence and immediate post-independence periods, most South American countries extended relatively broad suffrage rights, imposing economic restrictions but eschewing or suspending literacy restrictions so as not to disenfranchise the many illiterate men who had fought in the wars of independence. Almost all countries subsequently tightened their voting restrictions only to later relax or eliminate them, but the timing of these suffrage contractions and expansions differed significantly from country to country. Bolivia, Chile, Ecuador, and Uruguay imposed literacy restrictions in the 1830s or 1840s and did not lift them until the twentieth century, whereas Brazil, Colombia, and Peru did not significantly tighten their voting restrictions until late in the nineteenth century.

A few South American countries, namely Argentina, Paraguay, and Venezuela, took a different route, institutionalizing virtually universal male suffrage during the mid-nineteenth century.[15] Suffrage rights in these countries went well beyond what most European countries had at the time. Colombia and Peru also instituted virtually universal male suffrage during the nineteenth century, but only for brief periods: Colombia had it between 1853 and 1863, although some provinces continued to maintain it until 1886; Peru adopted it between 1828 and 1834 and again in 1855–1856. Overall, however, universal male suffrage was the exception rather than the norm in the nineteenth century. In total, South American countries maintained universal male suffrage at the national level in 138 country-years during the nineteenth century, which represents 18 percent of the region's 768 independent country-years during this century.[16]

As Przeworski (2009b, 15) has shown, universal male suffrage arrived at about the same time in Latin America and western Europe. According to his estimates, the proportion of the population that was eligible to vote in each region was relatively similar in the first half of the nineteenth century – it was well under 10 percent of the population in both regions. Nevertheless, by 1900, approximately 20 percent of the population had suffrage rights in western Europe, whereas only about 12 percent did in Latin America (Przeworski 2009b, 17).

The economic and literacy restrictions in South America dramatically reduced the size of the electorate since the vast majority of the population was poor and illiterate. In 1870, only 23.5 percent of the population aged fifteen years or older in Argentina could read and write and only 16 percent of this population could do so in Brazil (Thorp 1998, 354). By 1900, literacy rates in South America had risen somewhat, but they still only averaged 35.8 percent for the population over fifteen years of age (Thorp 1998, 354).

There are relatively little data available on the number of people registered to vote in South America during the nineteenth century, but the data that exist suggest that they represented a small percentage of the total population. During the nineteenth century, registered voters constituted only 4.8 percent of the population on average. This proportion grew somewhat over the course of the century but still remained low. In the first half of the nineteenth century, the number of registered voters averaged 4 percent of the

---

[15] I define universal male suffrage as voting laws that enfranchise the overwhelming majority of the adult male population. Countries may still be classified as having universal male suffrage if they maintain restrictions on noncitizens, nonresidents, prisoners, the insane, debtors, vagrants, or small occupational categories, such as the clergy or soldiers. Many of these latter types of restrictions still exist today in countries that are widely considered to be democracies.

[16] These figures would be somewhat higher if we included those years in which some Argentine and Colombian provinces maintained universal male suffrage but others did not. Nevertheless, even including these years, periods of universal male suffrage would still represent less than one quarter of all post-independence country-years in the nineteenth century.

total population, whereas in the second half it averaged 5.1 percent – even in the 1890s, registered voters only represented 6.2 percent of the total population on average.

The number of registered voters in the nineteenth century represented only a fraction of males of voting age, probably less than one-third on average. Precise data on the voting age population are lacking, but it seems reasonable to assume that during the nineteenth century, males of voting age typically represented between 15 and 25 percent of each country's population, depending on the country's demographics and its voting age requirement. For example, men who were at least twenty-five years of age represented only 18.8 percent of the total population in Chile in 1875 (Oficina Central de Estadística 1885, xlii). Latin America's population was quite young in the nineteenth century because fertility rates were high and life expectancy was low. In 1900, for example, life expectancy at birth was only twenty-five years of age in Paraguay, twenty-six in Bolivia, twenty-nine in Brazil and Chile, and thirty-nine in Argentina (Thorp 1998, 356). As a result, the majority of the population in the region was below the minimum voting age.

Suffrage restrictions and the relative youth of the region's population, along with citizen disinterest, limited the number of people who cast ballots. In the ninety-four nineteenth-century elections for which LAHED has data, the number of actual voters constituted 3.4 percent of the total population on average. These data include both presidential and legislative elections – the two types of election had similar levels of turnout.[17] Voter turnout fluctuated considerably over the course of the nineteenth century, but it followed a generally upward trend. During the first half of the nineteenth century, it was relatively low, averaging only 1.7 percent of the total population. In the 1850s, it soared to an average of 5.4 percent, but then declined steadily for several decades, falling to an average of 2.6 percent in the 1880s, before rising again in the 1890s, when it averaged 4.6 percent.

According to LAHED data, a few South American countries, namely Venezuela, Peru, and Brazil, had high levels of voter turnout, although data are available for only a few elections in each of these countries.[18] Voters averaged 10.5 percent of the total population in six elections in Venezuela and 10.6 percent of the population in four elections in Peru during the nineteenth century. In Brazil, the number of votes cast represented an average of only 3.4 percent of the population in six elections in the nineteenth century, but voter turnout was much higher prior to the enactment of the suffrage restrictions of 1881: Voters represented 5.1 percent of the population in the 1835 elections for regent, and 8.6 percent in the 1872 legislative, elections.

---

[17] These data also include a small number of other types of elections, including elections for vice-president, regent, and departmental mayor. Turnout was lower for these other types of elections, but the number of these elections was too small to make any reliable generalizations.

[18] No data on voter turnout are available for Paraguay in the nineteenth century.

Nevertheless, low voter turnout was the norm in most South American countries. Colombia had very high voter turnout in the 1856 elections, when it reached 8.6 percent, but this election, which took place using universal male suffrage, was atypical. On average, voter turnout constituted 3.4 percent of the population in thirteen nineteenth-century elections in Colombia. Voter turnout was even lower in Chile and Ecuador, averaging 2.3 percent of the population in twenty-four nineteenth-century elections in Chile and 2.3 percent in eleven elections in Ecuador during the nineteenth century. In both countries, voter turnout fluctuated considerably in the nineteenth century, but it never exceeded 5 percent of the total population. Bolivia, Argentina, and Uruguay had the lowest levels of voter turnout in the nineteenth century, averaging 1.5 percent in thirteen elections in Bolivia, 1.4 percent of the total population in nine elections in Argentina, and 1.3 percent in seven elections in Uruguay.

Even those countries with relatively high levels of voter turnout saw their turnout levels drop considerably when they enacted suffrage restrictions. Only 0.8 percent of the total population voted in Brazil in 1881 after it implemented a literacy requirement, down from 8.6 percent of the population in 1872 (Castellucci 2014, 194; Carvalho 2012, 27–28; Graham 1990, 202, 332). Similarly, only 1.6 percent of the total population voted in the 1899 presidential elections in Peru after it tightened suffrage requirements, down from 12 percent in 1890 (Aguilar Gil 2002, 25; Chiaramonti 2000, 249; Tuesta Soldevilla 2001, 611). Conversely, the loosening of suffrage requirements could lead to a dramatic expansion in voter turnout, as it did in Venezuela after 1857 and in Colombia, briefly, after 1853. Nevertheless, even maintaining broad suffrage rights was no guarantee of high voter turnout, as the Argentine case attests.

During the nineteenth century, voter turnout in South America was on the whole low in comparison to the more developed Western countries. According to V-Dem data, voters represented an average of 10.4 percent of the population in fifty elections in the United States, 12.4 percent in eight elections in Canada, 4.9 percent in eighteen elections in Australia, and 22.2 percent in fourteen elections in New Zealand during the nineteenth century. Voter turnout was also higher in Europe than in Latin America on average: Voters represented an average of 7 percent of the population in the seventeen European countries for which V-Dem has data on nineteenth-century elections. Nevertheless, there were some notable exceptions: Belgium, Greece, Italy, the Netherlands, Norway, and Sweden all had voter turnout that averaged less than four percent of the population during the nineteenth century.

Thus, a comprehensive analysis of suffrage rights and voter participation in South America during the nineteenth century shows that suffrage restrictions were significant and voter turnout tended to be low, particularly in comparison to more developed countries in other regions. A few South American countries enjoyed universal male suffrage and/or high voter turnout for parts of the nineteenth century, but the norm was to maintain significant economic and/or literacy restrictions as well as gender restrictions, all of which depressed voter turnout.

ELECTORAL COMPETITION AND DEMOCRACY IN THE NINETEENTH CENTURY

How competitive or democratic were elections in South America during the nineteenth century? As revisionist scholars have pointed out, Latin American countries had numerous competitive elections during the nineteenth century. The opposition frequently won representation in the legislature, and on a few occasions even prevailed in presidential elections. Nevertheless, comprehensive data from LAHED indicate that most presidential elections were uncompetitive, and many elections were not even contested. Fraud, intimidation, and government manipulation deprived the opposition of any chance of winning most presidential contests. Although a few elections were relatively democratic, the openings they produced did not last long and left no enduring influence.

Throughout the nineteenth century, governments, parties, and candidates employed numerous strategies to manipulate elections. These included:

Bringing voters from a long distance and in groups to the polls; securing votes through incentives (meals, gifts) or buying votes outright; pitched battles to control voting stations or ballot boxes or to prevent opponents gaining access to them; preventive imprisonment of hostile voters; multiple voting by supporters (either at the same or at different booths); voting by non-registered voters or those legally disqualified (foreigners, transients, minors, the military); voting on behalf of dead or absent people; filling ballot boxes with ballots prepared in advance; falsifying oral voting processes. (Guerra 1994, 21)

It is difficult to assess the true extent of fraud and intimidation because the losing sides often denounced abuses without providing specific evidence of them, but it is clear that abuses were widespread. There was considerable variation in the degree of electoral manipulation, however. Moreover, electoral fraud and intimidation were far from unique to Latin America. Contemporary elections in the United States and Europe suffered from similar problems.

All sides engaged in electoral abuses, but the national government typically had the most opportunities to manipulate elections since it usually controlled the electoral authorities and could direct the military and the police to intervene. In some countries, the executive branch became known as the great elector since it decided the fate of elections. Nevertheless, the opposition was also guilty of electoral abuses. The opposition, for example, sometimes controlled the local electoral authorities or the police, which intervened on its behalf. In addition, the opposition at times resorted to violence to intimidate government supporters or to protest electoral abuses. Indeed, many of Latin America's civil wars in the nineteenth century stemmed at least in part from electoral disputes.

The prevailing electoral regulations and laws facilitated the electoral abuses. In the nineteenth century, Latin American countries, with few exceptions, did not have or did not enforce the secret ballot. This made it easy for the electoral authorities and others to identify, intimidate, and disenfranchise opposition supporters. Similarly, the counting of the ballots at the polling places, and the initial absence of voter registries and party representation at the polls, provided numerous opportunities for cheating (Sabato 2018, 77). In addition, for much of the nineteenth century, Latin American countries used the complete-list electoral system, which awarded all the legislative seats in a district to the party or candidate list that finished first, thereby making it more difficult for the opposition to win legislative representation.

The electoral abuses led the opposition to frequently boycott elections in the nineteenth century. According to LAHED data, 36 percent of all presidential elections during the nineteenth century were uncontested, although in some of these elections more than one candidate pursued the ruling party's nomination. In some cases, opposition candidates initially mounted campaigns but withdrew from the race when they saw that they had no chance of winning. Presidential elections that took place in the legislature or in constituent assemblies were particularly likely to be uncontested, as were elections that occurred after the previously elected constitutional presidents had been overthrown by force. Forty-nine percent of presidential elections that took place in Congress or in a constituent assembly were uncontested, as opposed to only 27 percent that took place via other means (i.e., via a direct popular election or an electoral college). Similarly, 46 percent of elections where the previously elected president had been overthrown were uncontested, as opposed to only 29 percent of other types of elections.[19]

The percentage of elections that were uncontested increased over the course of the nineteenth century: 45 percent of the elections in the last three decades of the nineteenth century were uncontested, as opposed to only 28 percent before 1870. As Table 2.3 indicates, uncontested elections were most common in Paraguay, Uruguay, Venezuela, Chile, Peru, and Bolivia (in descending order). In these countries, uncontested elections represented at least one-third of all presidential elections during the nineteenth century. In Paraguay and Uruguay, they represented a majority of the elections in this period.

Even where elections were contested, they were usually uncompetitive. During the nineteenth century, the winning candidate in South American presidential elections won an average of 81 percent of the vote. These data include both contested and uncontested elections, but if we only count the former, the winner still captured an average of 72 percent of the vote. Direct elections were somewhat more competitive than indirect elections, but the winning candidate nevertheless won an average of 75 percent of the vote in direct presidential

---

[19] Unless otherwise specified, all data mentioned in this section refer to both direct and indirect presidential elections, including elections carried out by the legislature or constituent assemblies.

TABLE 2.3 *Competition in presidential elections in South America during the nineteenth century*

Country	Average share of vote for winner (%)	Average margin of victory (%)	Contested elections/all elections	Competitive elections/all elections	Free and fair elections/all elections
Argentina	79.1	62.6	8/10	4/10	0/10
Bolivia	79.6	64.3	14/21	6/21	2/21
Brazil	75.6	55.1	3/3	1/3	0/3
Chile	84.2	71.8	11/18	4/18	1/18
Colombia	67.8	46.9	24/28	15/28	3/28
Ecuador	78.8	62.6	19/24	7/23	1/23
Paraguay	100.0	100.0	1/13	0/13	0/13
Peru	83.9	72.1	14/21	5/21	1/21
Uruguay	83.1	69.0	8/18	4/18	0/18
Venezuela	85.4	78.6	14/26	5/26	1/26
All South America	81.0	67.6	116/182	51/181	9/181

Source: Latin American Historical Elections Database.

elections during the nineteenth century. Perhaps the least competitive types of election were those that took place after the previously elected president had been overthrown. In these elections, the winning presidential candidates typically won 87 percent of the vote.

The competitiveness of elections varied somewhat across countries and over time. Paraguay had the least competitive elections since all but one of its elections in the nineteenth century were uncontested. It was followed by Venezuela, Chile, Peru, and Uruguay, where the winner averaged between 83 and 86 percent of the vote. Elections in Brazil, Ecuador, Argentina, and Bolivia were not typically competitive either: The winner earned between 75 and 80 percent of the vote on average in these countries during the nineteenth century. Only in Colombia, where the winner averaged 68 percent of the vote, were elections usually competitive, and even there, competitive elections represented a narrow majority of all presidential elections if we define competitiveness as the winner earning less than 70 percent of the vote. The winner's share of the presidential vote fluctuated somewhat from decade to decade, reaching a peak of 89 percent in the 1880s. Elections generally became less competitive as the nineteenth century progressed. During the late nineteenth century, the winner earned an average of 85 percent of the presidential vote, as opposed to 77 percent during the early nineteenth century.

Latin American presidential elections were much less competitive than elections in the more developed Western countries during the nineteenth century. In twenty-five nineteenth-century presidential elections in the United States, the winner earned only 53.9 percent of the vote on average, according to V-Dem data. In Canada, the largest parliamentary party won an average of 41 percent of the vote during the nineteenth century, in Australia it captured a mean of 43 percent, and in New Zealand it captured an average of 55 percent. European parliamentary elections also tended to be much more competitive during the nineteenth century than South American presidential elections. For example, the largest legislative party in Great Britain only won an average of 54.7 percent of the vote in sixteen parliamentary elections in the nineteenth century, and in France, the largest party only won 53.2 percent of the vote.

The lack of competitiveness of most elections in nineteenth-century South America becomes even more clear if we use another measure of competitiveness: the winner's margin of victory. In all nineteenth-century presidential elections, the winner's share of the vote was sixty-eight percentage points more than that of the runner-up on average, and in contested elections, the victor still won by an average of fifty-three percentage points. The winner's margin of victory in South America was lower before 1870 than in the last three decades of the nineteenth century, but in no decade did it drop below an average of seventy percentage points. The winner's margin of victory was also lower in direct elections than in indirect ones, although winners still won by an average of fifty-six percentage points in direct elections.

The winner's average margin of victory was much greater in South America than in the industrializing countries during the nineteenth century. In the United States, for example, the winner's average margin of victory was only 14.5 percentage points in twenty-five nineteenth-century presidential elections, according to V-Dem data.[20] In western Europe, the largest parliamentary party's share of the vote was on average only eighteen percentage points higher than that of the second-largest party.

Although most elections were uncompetitive, a sizable number of elections did involve significant competition. In fifty-one presidential elections in South America during the nineteenth century, the winner won less than 70 percent of the vote. This represents more than one-quarter of the nineteenth-century presidential elections for which we have data. In thirty-four elections, the winner won less than 60 percent of the vote, and in fifteen elections the margin separating the winner and the runner-up was fewer than ten percentage points. Colombia had the largest number of competitive elections: Fifteen out of its twenty-eight elections in the nineteenth century were competitive, meaning that the winner earned less than 70 percent of the vote. Ecuador had the second highest number of competitive elections in the nineteenth century – in seven of its twenty-three elections the winner won less than 70 percent of the vote – followed by Bolivia (six out of twenty-one), Peru (five out of twenty-one), Venezuela (five out of twenty-six), Argentina (four out of ten), Chile (four

---

[20] The vote margin separating the winner and the runner-up in parliamentary elections was only 5.3 percentage points in Canada, 7.9 percentage points in Australia, and 24.3 percentage points in New Zealand during the nineteenth century.

out of eighteen), and Uruguay (four out of eighteen). Brazil had one competitive presidential election in the nineteenth century and Paraguay had none, but Brazil only had three presidential elections during the nineteenth century, whereas Paraguay had thirteen.

Nine presidential elections in the nineteenth century appear to have been relatively free and fair. I coded elections as free and fair when they did not have systematic violations that appeared to have affected the outcome of the election, even if there were some minor irregularities or incidents of fraud or manipulation. The coding scheme considered all aspects of the electoral process, including voter registration, but did not take suffrage rights into account in evaluating whether an election was free or fair. It is not easy to assess how free and fair elections were during this period, given the limited data available and the potential biases of the sources.[21] My assessment is necessarily uncertain, but it is based on a critical scrutiny of the sources available, granting more weight to those sources deemed more reliable.

The elections that appear to meet the criteria for free and fair elections during this period are: the 1834 election in Venezuela; the 1836, 1848, and 1856 elections in Colombia; the 1872 election in Peru; the 1873 and 1884 elections in Bolivia; the 1875 election in Ecuador; and the 1896 elections in Chile.[22] Most of these elections were competitive: on average, the winner won 45.4 percent of the vote in these elections, and a margin of 22.3 percentage points separated the winner from the runner-up. In five of the elections, the winner won by fewer than ten percentage points. More importantly, in four of these nine elections, the opposition candidate managed to defeat the candidate supported by the incumbent president. This is a strong sign that the election was free and fair since the government clearly did not intervene so heavily in favor of the official candidate as to prevent the opposition from winning. In the other five elections, there was no clear official candidate.

Unfortunately, only one of these elections led to an extended period of democracy and to the institutionalization of democratic practices. As Table 2.4 indicates, revolts overthrew presidents who had been elected freely and fairly in Venezuela in 1834, Bolivia in 1873, and Ecuador in 1875. The presidents who were democratically elected in Peru in 1871, and in Colombia in 1836, 1848, and 1856, also faced revolts, but they managed to survive them. However, these leaders responded to the revolts by repressing the opposition and manipulating elections in ways that brought an end to the short-lived democratic openings. In Chile, however, the 1896 election paved the way for a lengthy democratic episode that lasted until 1924. This extended experience

---

[21] Contemporary as well as later observers often supported one side or the other.
[22] There were some other presidential elections, such as the 1833 election in Peru, the 1868 election in Argentina, the 1870 election in Paraguay, and the 1895 election in Ecuador, which had important democratic elements but in my view did not reach the minimum threshold required to be considered free and fair.

TABLE 2.4 *Ephemeral democratization in nineteenth-century South America*

Country and election year	Outcome of free and fair election	How did the democratic episode end?
Venezuela 1834	An opposition candidate, José Vargas, defeated the candidate supported by the incumbent president.	Vargas was overthrown in an 1835 revolt. He was restored to power but then resigned under pressure.
Colombia 1836	An opposition candidate, José Ignacio de Márquez, defeated the candidate supported by the incumbent president.	A civil war broke out in 1839 and the government repressed the opposition in the 1840 presidential elections.
Colombia 1848	The ruling Conservatives split, which enabled the opposition candidate, José Hilario López, to win.	The opposition rebelled in 1851 and abstained from elections in the face of government electoral manipulation.
Colombia 1856	Mariano Ospina, a Conservative, won a narrow victory in an election with high turnout and universal male suffrage.	A revolt by one of the losing candidates overthrew Ospina's successor in 1860.
Peru 1871	An opposition candidate, Manuel Pardo, defeated the candidate supported by the incumbent president.	Pardo survived revolts but intervened in the 1875 elections to ensure that his preferred presidential candidate won.
Bolivia 1873	Adolfo Ballivián won a close election after the incumbent president was assassinated.	The minister of war, General Hilarión Daza, overthrew the president in 1876 after being asked to resign.
Ecuador 1875	An opposition candidate, Antonio Borrero, was elected after the assassination of the former president.	President Borrero was overthrown in an 1876 revolt by General Ignacio de Veintemilla.
Bolivia 1884	Gregorio Pacheco, a mining magnate, won a close election with minimal government interference.	President Pacheco intervened in the 1888 elections to ensure that his preferred candidate won.

with democracy helped to establish democratic practices that would make Chile, along with Uruguay, the most democratic country in South America for most of the twentieth century.

Thus, except for Chile's 1896 election, the few democratic episodes that the South American countries experienced during the nineteenth century proved quite short lived. The governments that were elected democratically were either overthrown or themselves undermined democracy to retain power. As we shall see, it was not until the early twentieth century that some South American countries had prolonged experiences with democracy.

EARLY TWENTIETH-CENTURY DEMOCRATIZATION

A great divide opened in South America during the early twentieth century that would last, with a few interruptions, into the twenty-first century. Some countries, specifically Argentina, Chile, Colombia, and Uruguay, took important steps toward democracy during this period, enacting major reforms that expanded suffrage rights and helped make elections relatively free and fair. The initial democratic episodes in each of these countries lasted at least a dozen years, and they had even longer implications. Beginning in the early twentieth century, democratic rule became the norm in these countries, except for Argentina. Although all four countries experienced democratic breakdowns at some point in the twentieth century, most of the breakdowns in Colombia, Chile, and Uruguay were short lived.[23] Indeed, over the course of the twentieth century, these countries collectively experienced far more years of democracy than of authoritarian rule.

Chile was the first country to experience a prolonged democratic episode in South America, which was facilitated by the enactment of an 1890 law that established safeguards to ensure the secrecy of the ballot. Beginning in 1896, Chile enjoyed a long period of relatively free and fair elections that was only interrupted in 1924. During this period, the executive branch ceased to impose its preferred candidates, although some electoral abuses, especially vote buying, continued to take place, especially at the local level. Elections were quite competitive during this time and an alternation in power occurred on several occasions. The 1896, 1915, and 1920 elections were particularly close, with the winner triumphing by only a few electoral votes. Voter turnout also increased significantly during this period, averaging 5.9 percent of the total population between 1900 and 1929, as opposed to 2.3 percent in the nineteenth century. Although Chile experienced a few military interventions between 1924 and 1932, it subsequently developed into one of the region's most vibrant democracies, with high levels of political participation and contestation.

Uruguay established a strong democracy after the passage of the 1918 constitution, which mandated the secret ballot, universal adult male suffrage, and proportional representation. In the wake of this reform, electoral fraud and manipulation declined significantly, and voter turnout soared, typically exceeding 15 percent of the population, as opposed to 1.3 percent in the nineteenth century. National elections became highly competitive. Between 1919 and 1929, the winner in presidential elections won an

---

[23] The exceptions were the breakdown of democracy in Colombia in 1949–1957, Chile in 1973–1989, and Uruguay in 1973–1984.

average of 55 percent of the vote, as opposed to 83 percent in the nineteenth century. Presidential elections were often decided by a narrow margin: For example, in the 1922 election, the winner won by only 2.1 percent and in the 1926 election the victory margin was only 0.5 percent. More importantly, Uruguay managed to maintain its vibrant democracy for most of the twentieth century.

Colombia democratized in 1910 when it enacted a series of constitutional reforms that ensured the representation of minority parties, expanded suffrage rights, and strengthened the powers of the legislature and the judiciary. For the next few decades, Colombian governments generally conducted electoral processes fairly and respected political and civil rights. Minority parties won significant representation in the legislature and opposition candidates even won the presidency in 1914 and 1930. Voter turnout also rose significantly, averaging 7.1 percent of the population in presidential elections, as opposed to 3.4 percent in the nineteenth century. Not all presidential elections were competitive, but the ones held in 1910, 1918, and 1922 were. To be sure, some electoral manipulation and violence continued, most notably in the 1922 elections. Nevertheless, Colombia after 1910 became one of the more democratic countries in the region, and it remained democratic for most of the twentieth century, although it was plagued by intermittent violence.

Argentina began to democratize in 1912 following the passage of a sweeping electoral reform that established the secret ballot, made voting compulsory, and mandated minority representation. In the wake of this reform, voter turnout soared, averaging 8.6 percent of the population between 1912 and 1929, as opposed to only 1.4 percent in the nineteenth century. Electoral abuses also diminished considerably since political bosses could no longer easily monitor or control voter behavior. Elections became more competitive: Between 1912 and 1929, the winner won only 53 percent of the vote on average in presidential elections, as opposed to 79 percent in the nineteenth century. Minority parties gained greater representation in the legislature, and in 1916, the opposition UCR won control of the presidency for the first time. Democracy, however, proved to be less stable in Argentina than in the other three democratic pioneers. A military coup brought democracy to an end in 1930 and over the next five decades the country was only intermittently democratic. Nevertheless, from 1916 until 1930, Argentina had a vibrant, if imperfect, democracy.

By contrast, authoritarian rule persisted in the other South American countries during the early twentieth century, and elections became less competitive on average. In Bolivia, Ecuador, Peru, and Venezuela, electoral fraud and manipulation worsened in the early twentieth century, and in Brazil and Paraguay, elections showed meager, if any, improvement. Between 1900 and 1929, the winner averaged 92.4 percent of the vote in the six democratic laggards, as opposed to 83.9 percent in the nineteenth century. Although these countries experienced democratic episodes after 1930, until the 1980s the

TABLE 2.5 *Presidential elections and democracy in South America, 1900–1929*

Country	Votes as a % of total population (LAHED)	Winner's share of the valid vote (LAHED)	Free and fair elections/total elections (LAHED)	Years of democracy/ total years (MBP)	Mean Polyarchy score (V-Dem)
Argentina	7.0	67.9	3/5	14	0.43
Chile	5.9	71.3	6/7	26	0.27
Colombia	7.1	65.9	4/7	20	0.22
Uruguay	10.5^a	74.4	3/7	14	0.41
Democratic pioneers	7.6***	69.9***	16/26***	74/120***	0.33***
Bolivia	3.0	88.7	0/8	0	0.17
Brazil	2.4	84.3	0/8	0	0.21
Ecuador	6.5	92.1	0/11	0	0.24
Paraguay	9.9^b	96.0	1/11	0	0.21
Peru	2.5^c	93.5	0/9	6	0.22
Venezuela	NA	100.0	0/8	0	0.02
Democratic laggards	4.9	92.4	1/55	6/180	0.14

Source: Latin American Historical Elections Database; Mainwaring and Pérez-Liñán (2013, 67–68); Coppedge et al. (2023).
*** $p < 0.0001$
Notes: All data represent country averages, except for the data on free and fair elections and years of democracy. The t-tests for difference of means were conducted using elections or country-years as the units of analysis. The table counts as democratic any years that Mainwaring and Pérez-Liñán code as democratic or semi-democratic.
^{a} The data for Uruguay include both presidential and legislative elections because, prior to 1922, the legislature elected the president.
^{b} The data for Paraguay only include the 1917 legislative elections and the 1928 presidential elections. Only partial data, if any, are available for other elections.
^{c} The data for Peru only include the elections for 1903, 1904, 1908, 1915, and 1919 presidential elections. Data for other presidential elections were unavailable.

democratic openings tended to be short lived.[24] Authoritarianism, not democracy, remained the norm in these countries for most of the twentieth century, and even today, these nations typically have shallower and more fragile democracies than the democratic pioneers.

Table 2.5 presents a simple comparison of electoral statistics for the democratic pioneers and the democratic laggards during the first three decades of the twentieth century. As the table indicates, from 1900 to 1929, voter turnout was much higher among the democratic pioneers, averaging 7.6 percent of the population, as opposed to 4.9 percent among the democratic laggards. A similar gap emerged with respect to the competitiveness of presidential elections

---

[24] The two main exceptions were Ecuador, which had a democratic episode that lasted from 1948 to 1962, and Venezuela, which was democratic from 1958 until the end of the century.

during this period. Between 1900 and 1929, the winner of presidential elections in Argentina, Chile, Colombia, and Uruguay captured 69.9 percent of the vote on average, whereas in the democratic laggards, the victor won an average of 92.4 percent of the vote. In addition, the frequency of free and fair elections was much higher in Argentina, Chile, Colombia, and Uruguay than in the other countries during this period: sixteen of the twenty-six presidential elections held between 1900 and 1929 in the pioneer countries were relatively free and fair, as opposed to one out of forty-nine elections in the laggards. A series of t-tests indicate that the difference in the means of the democratic pioneers and laggards is statistically significant for all three variables (voter turnout, the winner's share of the vote, and free and fair elections) at the 0.0001 level. Moreover, the gaps between the democratic pioneers and laggards on these indicators are even greater if we focus on the period after the pioneers enacted key democratic reforms – that is, after 1890 in Chile, 1910 in Colombia, 1912 in Argentina, and 1918 in Uruguay.

By contrast, no such democratic gap existed between the two groups of countries in the nineteenth century. Argentina, Chile, Colombia, and Uruguay did not experience more frequent free and fair presidential elections than the other South American countries during the nineteenth century. Approximately 5 percent of nineteenth-century presidential elections were free and fair in both groups, and a t-test of the differences in the frequency of free and fair elections does not approach statistical significance. The democratic pioneers did have slightly more competitive elections on average in the nineteenth century: The winner's share of the presidential vote averaged 76.8 percent in the democratic pioneers compared with 83.9 percent in the laggards, a difference which is significant at the 0.05 level. However, this is mostly due to Colombia, which had the most competitive presidential elections in the nineteenth century, and Paraguay, which had the least competitive elections during this period. The difference in the means of the two groups loses statistical significance if we omit either Colombia or Paraguay from the sample. There was also a gap with respect to voter turnout in the nineteenth century, but it favored the democratic laggards. Whereas votes represented an average of 4.9 percent of the total population in Bolivia, Brazil, Ecuador, Paraguay, Peru, and Venezuela during the nineteenth century, they constituted only 2.3 percent in Argentina, Chile, Colombia, and Uruguay, a difference that was statistically significant at the 0.01 level.

As Table 2.5 indicates, the leading democracy indexes also show a democratic divide occurring in South America during the early twentieth century. Moreover, the differences in means of the democratic pioneers and democratic laggards are highly statistically significant for both the Mainwaring, Brinks, and Pérez-Liñán (MBP) and the V-Dem indexes. The MBP index does not cover the nineteenth century, but it lists Chile as semi-democratic beginning in 1900, Colombia as semi-democratic starting in 1910, and Argentina and Uruguay as democratic or semi-democratic beginning in 1916 (Mainwaring and Pérez-Liñán 2013, 67–68). By contrast, none of the democratic laggards are listed as becoming democratic or semi-democratic before 1930, except for Peru, which is coded as semi-democratic from 1912 to 1913 and again from 1915 to 1918.[25]

V-Dem reports dramatic increases in the Polyarchy index for Colombia beginning in 1910, Argentina in 1912, and Uruguay as of 1916, but the scores of the remaining countries either stagnate (Chile, Paraguay, and Venezuela) or decline (Bolivia, Brazil, Ecuador, and Peru) between 1900 and 1929 (Coppedge et al. 2023). On average, V-Dem reports significantly higher Polyarchy scores for the democratic pioneers, especially Argentina and Uruguay, than for the democratic laggards during this period. As Table 2.5 make clears, however, Colombia scores slightly lower on V-Dem's Polyarchy index than Ecuador and nearly the same as Brazil, Paraguay, and Peru, all of which I classify as democratic laggards during this period. Colombia's low score on the Polyarchy index during this period presumably stems in part from the country's continued suffrage restrictions. Indeed, Colombia scores well above all the democratic laggards on V-Dem's measure of free and fair elections (v2eltype_6) during this period.

As the Conclusion shows, the gap between the democratic pioneers and the democratic laggards persisted for most of the twentieth century. Although the pioneer countries suffered military coups during the twentieth century, all of them except for Argentina experienced far fewer coups than the democratic laggards. With the exception of Argentina, the pioneer countries also enjoyed many more years of democracy during the twentieth century as a whole.

Thus, South America divided into two groups of countries during the first few decades of the twentieth century: those which democratized and those which did not. This division would persist throughout most of the twentieth century, albeit with some ups and downs. As the ensuing chapters show, the emergence of professionalized militaries and strong parties played a key role in bringing democracy to Argentina, Chile, Colombia, and Uruguay in the early twentieth century. Professionalized militaries helped bring an end to the revolts that undermined constitutional rule, disrupted elections, and

---

[25] The other indexes report a similar divergence in the early twentieth century. Boix, Miller, and Rosato (2013) code all nineteenth-century country-years in South America as nondemocratic, but they list Chile as democratic beginning in 1909, Argentina as of 1912, and Uruguay as of 1919. None of the other South American countries are listed as becoming democratic before 1930. Vanhanen's Index of Democratization records a sharp increase in Argentina beginning in 1916, Colombia starting in 1918, and Uruguay beginning in 1919, but the scores for the other countries remain relatively low (under 2) in the early twentieth century (Vanhanen 2000). Polity ranks Chile, Argentina (after 1912), and Uruguay (beginning in 1910) among the most democratic South American countries during the first three decades of the twentieth century, with Polity2 scores of 2 or 3 (Marshall, Gurr, and Jaggers 2016). However, Colombia has inexplicably low Polity2 scores (−5) throughout this period, whereas Bolivia and Peru receive surprisingly high scores (2).

led to state repression. Strong opposition parties, meanwhile, helped enact, implement, and enforce the electoral reforms that proved crucial to democratic progress. The South American countries that lacked strong parties and/or professionalized militaries, however, continued to struggle with political violence, personalistic rule, government repression, and electoral manipulation.

CONCLUSION

This chapter began by posing the question of when and where democracy first emerged in South America. Traditionally, scholars depicted nineteenth-century Latin American elections as authoritarian regimes with highly fraudulent elections, but in recent decades revisionist historians have pointed out that many democratic practices existed in the region during this period. This chapter, however, has shown that these democratic practices were the exception rather than the norm. Some South American countries adopted broad suffrage rights during the nineteenth century and enjoyed relatively high levels of voter turnout in elections, but the majority of South American countries maintained significant restrictions on the franchise, and voter turnout on the whole tended to be low. Although there were numerous competitive elections during the nineteenth century, most presidential elections during this period were uncompetitive and many were not even contested. Moreover, the few democratic episodes that occurred in the nineteenth century did not last long: The governments that were elected through relatively free and fair elections during this period were either overthrown or subverted democracy to maintain themselves and their allies in power.

It was not until the early twentieth century that South American countries enjoyed sustained periods of democracy, and even then, only some countries in the region democratized. Whereas Chile, Uruguay, Colombia, and Argentina adopted democratic reforms and repeatedly held free and fair elections with high voter turnout between 1900 and 1929, the other South American nations mostly moved in the opposite direction, deepening government intervention in elections, repressing the opposition, and clamping down on civil and political liberties. Except for Argentina, the countries that joined the ranks of democracies in the early twentieth century would remain democratic for most of the century. By contrast, authoritarian rule would remain the norm in the other South American countries until the 1980s.

The remaining chapters explore what led democracy to emerge in some South American countries and not others during the early twentieth century. Why were some countries able to enact democratic reforms and experience long periods of democratic governance after a century of almost uninterrupted authoritarian rule? And why did other countries remain firmly in the grip of authoritarianism?

3

Military Professionalization and the Decline of Revolts in South America

Throughout the nineteenth century, South America suffered not just from fraudulent elections but also from recurrent political violence. The French political scientist Alexis de Tocqueville ([1835] 1945, 251) remarked in 1835 that "the turmoil of revolution is ... the most natural state of the South American Spaniards at the present time." Two decades later, Bolivian President Manuel Belzú summarized the plight of many statesmen in the region when he complained of "[s]uccessive revolutions, revolutions in the south, revolutions in the north, revolutions fomented by my enemies, directed by my friends, put together in my house, arising from my side ... holy God! They condemned me to a state of perpetual war" (cited in Aranzaes 1918, 158). The revolts took a terrible toll. They devastated economies, undermined national unity, and led to the deaths of hundreds of thousands of people.

The widespread revolts in South America also hindered the prospects for democracy in the region. Revolts sometimes led to the overthrow of elected leaders, thus interrupting constitutional rule. Between 1830 and 1899, rebels toppled South American presidents seventy-three times. Moreover, even when the rebels did not directly overthrow the government, they often destabilized it, leading to the eventual resignation and replacement of the president. Revolts also frequently interrupted elections. Opposition groups that sought to overthrow the government often tried to disrupt elections, attacking polling places, destroying ballot boxes, and driving off potential voters.

Revolts typically provoked repression from the state. Latin American governments facing rebellions often declared states of siege and suspended civil and political rights. They shut down or censored the independent media. They disqualified, harassed, and arrested opposition candidates, leaders, and

---

This chapter is based on a co-authored article with Luis L. Schenoni, which appeared in *International Security*, Vol. 48, No. 3 (Winter 2023/24), 129–167.

supporters. Sometimes, they even suspended elections or banned opposition parties altogether. The widespread prevalence of revolts in South America thus led to a deepening of authoritarian rule in the region.

This chapter shows that the nineteenth-century revolts in South America were made possible by the weakness of the region's militaries. The small, untrained, and poorly equipped South American armies of the nineteenth century could neither deter, nor easily suppress, revolts. In the late nineteenth and early twentieth century, however, most South American countries took important steps to strengthen and professionalize their militaries. Governments modernized their armed forces to deal with both external and internal threats, but it was the export boom of the late nineteenth and early twentieth century that provided the resources that made the military professionalization efforts possible. The export boom enabled South American governments to contract foreign military missions, create mass armies, import large numbers of sophisticated weapons, establish new military schools, and overhaul the basic organization, training, and procedures of the armed forces.

The strengthening of the military led to a dramatic reduction in revolts in South America at the outset of the twentieth century. A few countries that were slow to professionalize their militaries, such as Bolivia, Ecuador, and Paraguay, continued to experience frequent rebellions in the early twentieth century, but the other countries enjoyed an unprecedented degree of internal peace. To be sure, not all types of revolts came to an end. Insider revolts, especially military coups, remained prevalent throughout the twentieth century, but the most common type of revolt in the nineteenth century, the elite-led outsider rebellion, declined precipitously.

The decline in revolts brought tremendous benefits to the region. Increased political stability not only stimulated economic growth and investment, it also strengthened the rule of law, reduced state repression, and increased respect for civil and political liberties. As Chapters 5–6 show, the decline of revolts even paved the way for the emergence of democracy in a few countries in the region. Since they could no longer overthrow governments by force, opposition parties began to focus on the electoral path to power, pushing for democratic reforms that would level the electoral playing field.

This chapter is organized as follows. The first section documents the decline in revolts using LARD, an original and comprehensive data set on revolts in the region from independence onward.[1] It also presents a typology of revolts and shows how the frequency of different types of revolts changed over time and across countries. The second section discusses the theoretical literature on civil war and assesses to what extent it can explain trends in revolts. The third and fourth sections examine the evolution of state coercive capacity in South

---

[1] The Latin American Revolts Database is a collaborative project headed by Raúl L. Madrid, Luis Schenoni, Guillermo Kreiman, and Paola Galano Toro, which catalogs all revolts in Latin America from independence to the present.

America from independence to 1929. These sections argue that the weakness of the region's militaries encouraged outsider revolts during the nineteenth century but that the professionalization of the military at the turn of the century dramatically reduced these rebellions. The fifth section presents a statistical test of this argument, showing that indicators of military strength and professionalization are correlated with the number of outsider revolts, but not insider revolts, in South America. The concluding section briefly summarizes the arguments made in this chapter.

THE DECLINE IN REVOLTS IN SOUTH AMERICA

How frequent were revolts in South America during the nineteenth and early twentieth century? How did they vary over time and across countries? Existing studies have lacked the data to answer these questions with any precision. Indeed, the sheer number of revolts has led some scholars to despair of the possibility of counting them all (Centeno 2002, 61; Loveman 1999, 43). To come up with a comprehensive count of revolts for LARD, we drew on more than 250 historical sources that cover rebellions in the region from 1830 to 1929.[2] We define a revolt as *an instance of the use or the credible threat of violence by an identifiable domestic political group that defies the authority of the state.* We use the terms revolts and rebellions interchangeably.

LARD reveals a dramatic decline in major revolts in South America from the nineteenth to the twentieth century, as Figure 3.1 indicates.[3] This chapter focuses on major revolts, defined as those involving at least 500 rebels, because they are the most important types of rebellions. Moreover, data on them are more plentiful, which reduces measurement and identification error. From 1830 to 1899, there were on average forty-five active major revolts per decade, meaning that each country had an almost even chance of facing an important rebellion in any given year. By contrast, in the first three decades of the twentieth century, this average declined to twenty-one, or an approximately one-fifth chance of seeing a major rebellion in any given year. While the decline is partly due to the longer duration of revolts in the nineteenth century, the finding holds when we look at revolt onsets alone: An average of thirty revolts were initiated per decade in the nineteenth century, as opposed to only fifteen per decade in the early twentieth century. Similar trends are apparent if we focus on especially large, lengthy, or impactful rebellions. As Figure 3.1 shows, revolts that involved more than 5,000 rebels, lasted for more than one

---

[2] This chapter focuses on revolts in South America from 1830 to 1929 to omit conflicts associated with the independence struggle. South American states only gradually consolidated their national boundaries over the course of the nineteenth century. We define political conflicts as revolts if they defy the central authorities of states even in the absence of consolidated territorial boundaries.

[3] An analysis of minor revolts shows an even steeper decline and suggests that the trends for major rebellions apply to all rebellions in our dataset.

The Decline in Revolts in South America

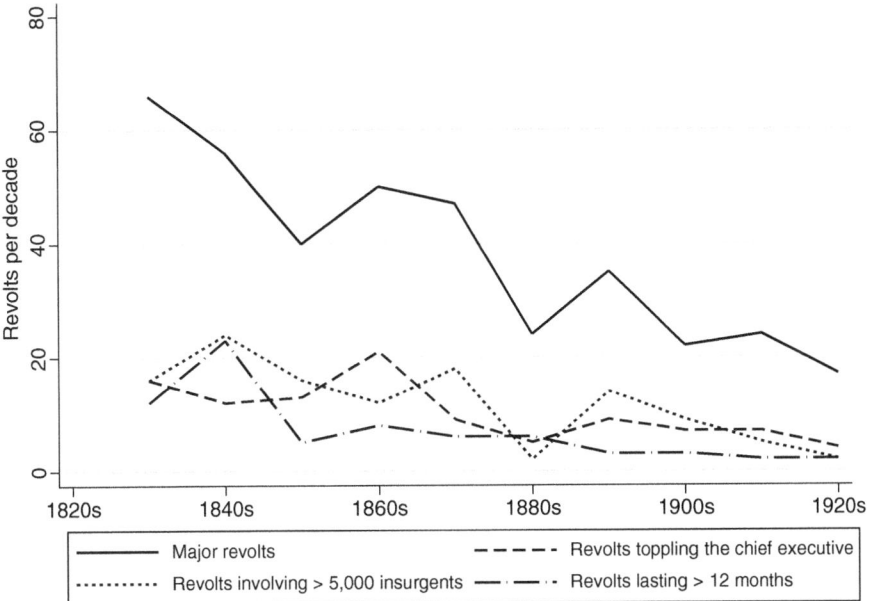

FIGURE 3.1 The decline of major revolts in South America by decade, 1830–1929
Source: Latin American Revolts Database.

year, and led to the overthrow of the chief executive all declined dramatically during the early twentieth century, amounting to only a handful of cases by the 1920s.

The frequency of major revolts varied across countries as well as time. Argentina, with an average of eight major revolts per decade, was the most rebellious country between 1830 and 1899. By contrast, Chile and Paraguay had the fewest major revolts during this period. All South American countries experienced a decline in the number of revolts during the first three decades of the twentieth century, with the sole exceptions of Ecuador and Paraguay.

Not all types of revolts declined at the same rate, however. To explore variation across different types of revolts, we identified four distinct categories based on whether the leader of the revolt came from inside or outside the national state apparatus, and whether the rebel leader hailed from the elites or the masses.[4] Our typology, which is depicted in Table 3.1, is based to a large degree on previously conceptualized revolt types, such as coups, but it also introduces an important additional type of revolt, elite insurrections (i.e.,

---

[4] Some revolts have multiple leaders with different backgrounds, but in classifying them, we focus on the paramount leader of each revolt. Thus, revolts led by opposition elites are categorized as elite insurrections, even if some military units and officers participated.

TABLE 3.1 *A typology of revolts based on the origins of their leaders*

		Position of rebel leaders vis-à-vis the national state apparatus	
		Insiders	Outsiders
Socioeconomic position of rebel leaders	Elites	Coup	Elite insurrection
	Masses	Mutiny	Popular uprising

revolts led by elites based outside the state apparatus), that had not previously been conceptualized by political scientists.[5] Alternative categorizations which focus on the consequences of the revolts cut across our categories. Civil wars, for example, typically refer to revolts by nonstate actors that exceed a battle-death threshold of 1,000 – any of our revolt types may become civil wars if they escalate (Fearon 2004).

In line with extant databases, we define coups as "illegal and overt attempts by the military or other elites within the state apparatus to unseat the sitting executive" (Powell and Thyne 2011, 252). The vast majority of coups originate in the military, although coups may also be undertaken by high-ranking government officials, such as cabinet ministers. We identify sixty-six major coup attempts between 1830 and 1929.

Elite insurrections are revolts led by elites from outside of the state apparatus. They may consist of local elites attempting to secede or opposition parties or politicians taking up arms to overthrow the government. Elite insurrections were by far the most common type of major revolt between 1830 and 1929: We record 152 of them during this period.

Popular uprisings refer to rebellions led by subalterns who are located outside of the state, which would include indigenous revolts, violent labor protests, and slave rebellions. We identify thirty-four major popular uprisings during this period.

Finally, mutinies consist of revolts from within the state by nonelites, such as rank-and-file soldiers or noncommissioned officers. Mutinies typically did not meet our threshold of 500 rebels required to count as major revolts, so we do not discuss them at length.

The leadership of revolts matters for at least two reasons. First, the leaders help determine the likelihood of success of the revolts. Revolts led by insider elites, such as coups, are more likely to succeed because insider elites tend to have greater access to resources, including troops, weaponry, financing, and the media. Between 1830 and 1929, almost 71 percent of coup attempts in South America overthrew the government, as opposed to only 30 percent of elite

---

[5] Somma (2011, 1–8), however, noted that most nineteenth-century insurgencies in Chile, Colombia, Costa Rica, and Uruguay were led by powerful elites.

The Decline in Revolts in South America

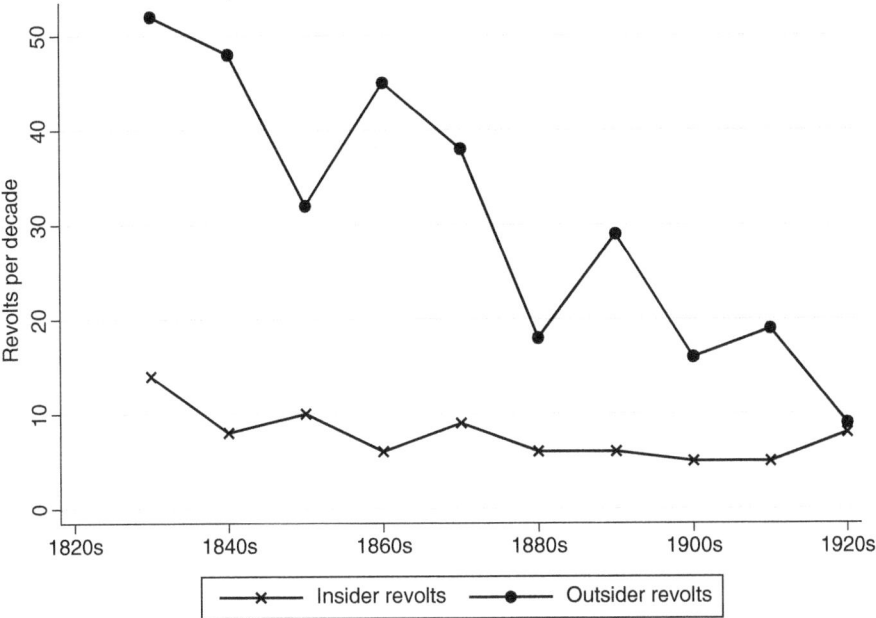

FIGURE 3.2 The frequency of major insider and outsider revolts in South America, 1830–1929
Source: Latin American Revolts Database.

insurrections and 3 percent of popular uprisings.[6] Second, the origins of the rebel leaders also impact the size and costs of the revolts. Whereas insider rebellions tend to be resolved quickly and with minimal bloodshed, outsider revolts are usually more prolonged and more violent. Between 1830 and 1929, 21 percent of popular uprisings and 14 percent of elite insurrections in South America lasted more than one year, as opposed to 6 percent of coups. Similarly, 29 percent of outsider revolts led to more than 1,000 battlefield deaths in comparison to only 10 percent of coups.

Even more important for our purposes, disaggregating revolts by the origins of their leaders helps shed light on the decline in revolts from the nineteenth to the twentieth century. As Figure 3.2 shows, the decline was driven by a sharp drop in the number of *outsider revolts* – that is, revolts from outside the state apparatus. During most of the nineteenth century, there were three times as many outsider rebellions as insider revolts, but by the 1920s their numbers were roughly the same.

In sum, LARD shows that during the early twentieth century there was a sharp decline in revolts in South America, and the large, bloody, and lengthy

---

[6] These figures should be viewed with some caution, however, since some unsuccessful coup attempts may not be reported in the historical literature.

internal conflicts that plagued the region during the nineteenth century mostly came to an end. Outsider revolts drove the decline in political violence – they declined precipitously, whereas insider revolts remained relatively stable. As we shall see, the divergent trends in insider and outsider revolts can be explained by the modernization of South American militaries at the beginning of the twentieth century since the growing strength of the region's armies discouraged outsider revolts but not military coups.

EXPLAINING THE DECLINE IN REVOLTS

The historical literature has stressed that nineteenth-century revolts in South America were complex and had a wide variety of causes, but most of most of this literature focuses on the motivations of the rebels. Scheina (2003, xxiii), for example, argues: "The causes for wars in in Latin America during the nineteenth century are numerous and create a vivid, plaid tapestry ... The most vivid threads have been the race war, the ideology of independence, the controversy of separation versus union, boundary disputes, territorial conquests, caudilloism, intraclass struggles, interventions caused by capitalism, and religious wars." Safford (1992; 2000), meanwhile, identifies five types of explanations for these revolts, including cultural factors, economic structures, fiscal weakness, changing power relations among elite groups, and conflicting ideologies and interests. Various scholars have also shown how electoral fraud, or allegations of it, often triggered revolts. (Malamud 2000c; Posada-Carbó 1996b; Alonso 2000). Indeed, during the nineteenth century, revolts were considered a legitimate response to electoral manipulation and other forms of despotism (Sabato 2018, 112–115; Earle 2000a, 3–4).

Much of the general social science literature on political violence similarly focuses on the motivations of the rebels, or what the literature has sometimes referred to as grievances and greed. The conflict literature, for example, has extensively explored the role that economic factors (Blattman and Miguel 2020, 45; Bell 2016, 1170), ethnic and religious cleavages (Cederman and Girardin 2007; Roessler 2011; Bormann, Cederman, and Vogt 2017; Esteban, Mayoral, and Ray 2012), and regime type (Fearon and Laitin 2003, 84–85; Powell 2012, 1035; Hegre et al. 2001) have played in revolts.

Although rebel motivations are important, they cannot fully explain long-term trends in South American revolts. Rebel motives do not explain why insurgents were able to assemble their armies and fend off or defeat government troops, irrespective of their motivations. Moreover, an emphasis on rebel motivations cannot easily account for the dramatic decline in revolts that occurred at the outset of the twentieth century, since authoritarian regimes, ethnic cleavages, electoral fraud, interstate rivalries, and economic hardships continued to be widespread.

Another approach in the conflict literature focuses on the weakness of the state, rather than the motivations of rebels, as the main cause of revolts

(Fearon and Laitin 2003; Hendrix 2010; Fearon 2010). Stemming in part from the study of revolutions (Skocpol 1979), this approach "has become the dominant explanatory paradigm in the civil war literature" (Cederman and Vogt 2017, 1997). The weak state approach suggests that motivations for rebellion (grievances and greed) are widespread, but they only tend to result in significant revolts where the state lacks the ability to prevent or suppress rebellions. Revolts occur, in the words of one influential study, because "financially, organizationally, and politically weak central governments render insurgency more feasible and attractive due to weak local policing or inept and corrupt counterinsurgency practices" (Fearon and Laitin 2003, 75–76).

Building on this approach, as well as on the work of historians, we focus on a specific dimension of state capacity: military strength. We define military strength as not simply the number of troops but also the degree of its professionalization – that is, the sophistication of the weaponry, training, and leadership that the military possesses. We argue that revolts occurred frequently during the nineteenth century because South American countries had small armies that were poorly equipped, trained, and led. Once these states expanded and professionalized their armed forces in the early twentieth century, the number of revolts in the region declined precipitously. Strong militaries could defeat uprisings before they became major revolts, but, even more importantly, military strength discouraged rebellions. Would-be rebels were unlikely to revolt if they believed that the rebellions would be quickly suppressed by a powerful military.

To be sure, this is not the first study to suggest that military professionalization reduced revolts in South America in the twentieth century.[7] Nevertheless, we go well beyond existing studies in documenting how increased military strength led to the regionwide decline. In addition, we show that increased military strength explains not only why revolts diminished in South America from the nineteenth to the twentieth century but also why this happened more rapidly in some countries than others, since not all states expanded and professionalized their militaries at the same time or to the same degree. Of equal importance, we demonstrate that growing military strength explains why outsider revolts decreased in South America at the outset of the twentieth century while insider revolts did not.

Although military professionalization is supposed to marginalize the military from politics and establish clear civilian control over the military (Huntington 1957), it did not achieve these aims in South America. As Stepan (1973) has

---

[7] Lieuwen (1961, 29–31), for example, argues that the strengthening and professionalization of the military "made it progressively more difficult to launch rebellions without at least some support from the nation's regular armed forces." Safford (1992, 97), meanwhile, suggests that "as trade and government revenues expanded, Spanish American governments increasingly had the fiscal and therefore the military strength to sustain themselves." Neither scholar makes military professionalization or the regional decline of revolts the focus of his analysis, however.

argued, militaries in this region have traditionally been responsible for maintaining internal as well as external security, which provided them with a rationale to intervene in politics.[8] The armed forces overthrew civilian leaders not just to resolve perceived threats to national security but to safeguard their own interests as well as those of allied political elites. According to Rodríguez (1994, xiii), "professionalization had the long-term effect of politicizing the armed forces to defend their corporate interest, which they identified as synonymous with those of the nation." Military professionalization may have even encouraged some coups by enhancing the confidence and autonomy of military officers and persuading some officers that they could do a better job of governing than civilian leaders (Rouquié 1987, 102–104; Fitch 1998, 6–7). Increases in military budgets and personnel also increased the influence of the armed forces and the number of potential coup conspirators, thereby complicating coup-proofing efforts. As a result, insider revolts, in contrast to outsider revolts, did not decline significantly in the wake of the professionalization of South American militaries.

THE WEAK ARMIES OF NINETEENTH-CENTURY SOUTH AMERICA

The weakness of South America's militaries during the nineteenth century stemmed from a variety of factors, including: the small size of the region's armies, their rudimentary weaponry, the paucity of military discipline and training, and the politicization of the officer corps.[9] In addition, South American states decentralized security, creating militias which sometimes turned against the national government. All these shortcomings fostered outsider revolts.

South American governments could not afford to invest in their militaries for most of the nineteenth century because they were starved of funds, especially foreign currency. The wars of independence disrupted trade and destroyed Latin American economies; and political instability, combined with a lack of infrastructure and inefficient policies, slowed economic recovery in the decades that followed. Per capita GDP grew at a rate of less than 0.6 percent annually between 1820 and 1870 in South America (Bértola and Ocampo 2013, 62). The small size of South American economies and their low rates of growth meant that their governments generated little tax revenue and could not afford to spend much on their armed forces.

Even though military expenditures were relatively low, they typically accounted for a large share of state spending, reducing the ability of South American governments to address other needs (Centeno 2002, 119–121). After the wars of independence, South American governments reduced the size of

---

[8] Stepan (1973) focuses on Latin American militaries during the late twentieth century, but the military's involvement in internal security dates to the nineteenth century.

[9] This chapter focuses on South American armies, as opposed to navies, because the former were the principal forces used to suppress revolts.

their militaries to alleviate these fiscal burdens. Most armies remained quite small throughout the remainder of the nineteenth century, particularly compared to their European counterparts. According to Centeno (2002, 224–225), less than 0.5 percent of the population usually participated in the militaries of South American countries. Bolivia's army typically numbered fewer than 2,000 men during the nineteenth century (Dunkerley 2003, 71). The Colombian military never exceeded 4,000 troops before the 1880s and it often had fewer than 2,000 men (López-Alves 2000, 138; Payne 1968, 120).

When a foreign or domestic threat required it, South American militaries usually swelled, but in a rather ad hoc way. During wartime the military would sweep through urban neighborhoods and rural villages, press-ganging whatever able-bodied men they could find. A popular saying of the time was: "If you want more volunteers, send more chains" (cited in Johnson 1964, 54).

As might be expected, the discipline and training of the troops were poor. The troops' wages were miserable, the government sometimes fell into arrears on payments, and soldiers frequently deserted despite severe punishments for doing so (Rouquié 1987, 65). Soldiers came overwhelmingly from the poorest sectors of the population and typically had little, if any, education. Most of the soldiers were illiterate and many were vagrants and even criminals: Colombia reported in 1882 that only 30 percent of its troops could read (Deas 2002a, 92). Moreover, the armed forces provided little military training to the troops. As Resende-Santos (2007, 121) notes: "Prior to the 1880s, none of the regional militaries had a standardized system of enlistment, training, and reserves."

Military officers in South America also lacked proper training and organization during this period. According to Loveman (1999, 30), the nineteenth-century armies "were not organized under an operational general staff, did virtually no planning for diverse military threats, carried out few military exercises, and were unprepared for sustained combat." Army officers rarely attended military schools: In 1893 the Argentine War Ministry reported that only 30 of its approximately 1,400 army officers had received advanced training or graduated from a military academy (Resende-Santos 2007, 122). Some South American governments founded military academies during the nineteenth century, but these typically operated irregularly, and their curriculums were woefully outdated. Political connections, rather than military expertise, determined ascent in the officer ranks (Johnson 1964, 52–53; Resende-Santos 2007, 122; Loveman 1999, 42–43; Philip 1985, ch. 4; Rouquié 1987, 64–65). In many South American countries, widespread promotions led to an excess of officers, particularly at the higher ranks. Bolivia, for example, had one general for every 102 soldiers and one officer for every six soldiers in 1841 (Scheina 2003, 263; Dunkerley 2003, 18). Venezuela's officer ranks were even more bloated: A census of the state of Carabobo in 1873 counted 3,450 commissioned officers, including 627 colonels and 449 generals, out of a population of 22,952 (Philip 1985, 87).

South American militaries also lacked sophisticated weaponry for most of the nineteenth century, relying on pointed weapons, such as the lance, the pike, the sword, and the machete, rather than on firearms (Scheina 2003, 427). Arráiz (1991, 151) writes that during the revolts: "Combat took place in a series of personal encounters in which people attacked each other with lances, swords, bayonets, fists and whatever was at hand."[10] Both sides typically had some firearms, but these were primitive weapons with limited range and accuracy. Even when South American militaries did obtain more sophisticated weapons, they often had problems repairing and servicing them, and sometimes let them slip into the hands of the rebels (Arráiz 1991, 157; Somma 2011, 236; Scheina 2003, 427).

During the nineteenth century, most South American governments reorganized and expanded their civic guards or urban and provincial militias, which had existed since colonial times (Sabato 2018, 90–96). These militias were less expensive to maintain than the regular army, but they did little to enhance the authority of the central state. First, militia members typically had little training or equipment, although there were exceptions, such as in Brazil where the state militias, especially those of São Paulo and Minas Gerais, gradually became better trained and armed than the federal army (Resende-Santos 2007, 124). South American governments usually required members of the militias to provide their own weapons and training, but the members often did not own firearms and drilled rarely if at all. In the Rio de la Plata region, the members of militias only trained one or two days per month during peace time (Rabinovich and Sobrevilla Perea 2019, 784).

Second, militias could not be counted on to support the government. Indeed, they often formed the main base of rebel armies, which was particularly problematic given that in most countries the militia troops vastly outnumbered the army.[11] In Argentina, provincial militias typically supplied both the troops and the weapons that were used in revolts during the nineteenth century (Forte 2002; Gallo 1986, 379), and in Brazil the local militias of southern states sustained a ten-year campaign against the imperial army during the Ragamuffin War (Ribeiro 2011, 271). In some cases, the militias were set up or expanded to counterbalance the regular army. In Uruguay, for example, the Blanco Party built up a civic guard to offset the Colorado Party-dominated army (López Chirico 1985, 29–30; Somma 2011, 150). Despite periodic efforts to centralize control, in most countries the militias remained under the leadership of provincial or local authorities (Sabato 2018, 98–99).[12] In many rural areas, local

---

[10] For a vivid description of nineteenth-century warfare, see Rabinovich and Sobrevilla Perea (2019, 786–791).

[11] In Chile, for example, the regular army had only 3,000 troops, whereas the civic guard reached 60,000 troops in the 1850s, before declining (Wood 2011, 86–88; Somma 2011, 398).

[12] The militias were not a threat to the authority of the central state everywhere in South America: Militias rarely revolted in Chile, and in some countries like Paraguay, they were abolished early.

leaders controlled unofficial militias, which often participated in rebellions and guerrilla warfare (Rabinovich and Sobrevilla Perea 2019, 785).

It is not a coincidence that the two South American countries that had perhaps the highest coercive capacity during much of the nineteenth century (Chile and Paraguay) also had the fewest revolts. Chile did not avoid internal revolts all together – it experienced numerous revolts prior to 1860 and a civil war in 1891, but its military prowess, demonstrated in the War of the Pacific (1879–1883), deterred most domestic rebels in the late nineteenth century. Chile developed a strong military during this period, not by expanding its size, but rather by making early investments in foreign training – the Chilean government sent officers to study in France beginning in the 1840s and hired a small French training mission in 1858 – as well as in tactics and weaponry (Ramírez Necochea 1985, 39–40; Hillmon Jr. 1963, 76; Valenzuela 1985, 182). Early on, Chile also asserted centralized control of its national guard, which played an important role in squashing rebellions as well as turning out votes for the ruling party (Sabato 2018, 107, 110–111; Valenzuela 1996, 228–231). As discussed later in this chapter, the Chilean military grew even stronger after a large German military mission arrived in 1885.

Paraguay also initially enjoyed relative political stability thanks to its considerable military strength. During the mid-nineteenth century, Paraguay developed one of the largest and strongest militaries in the region. The Paraguayan government imported massive quantities of weapons, overhauled the training of the troops, and brought in foreign officers, most notably the Hungarian Lieutenant Colonel Francisco Wisner, to modernize and discipline its army (Williams 1979, 110–111, 179; Whigham 2002, 182; Hanratty and Meditz 1988, 24). It even built up an important domestic arms industry. By 1864–1865, the Paraguayan army had 30,000–38,000 troops, including thirty infantry regiments, twenty-three cavalry regiments, and four artillery regiments, and the military could count on an additional 150,000 men in its reserves (Hanratty and Meditz 1988, 205; Casal 2004, 187). The country's military strength effectively deterred revolts prior to the War of the Triple Alliance (1865–1870). In this war, however, the combined forces of Brazil, Argentina, and Uruguay destroyed the Paraguayan military. Consistent with our theoretical expectations, in the decades that followed, Paraguay was plagued by revolts.

MILITARY STRENGTHENING

In the late nineteenth and early twentieth century, South American nations undertook major efforts to professionalize their militaries, often with the assistance of foreign military missions. They expanded the size of their armies, upgraded their weaponry, established new military schools, adopted meritocratic criteria for officer recruitment and promotion, and banned private arms imports and local militias. As a result, the military strength of South American countries increased and outsider revolts declined significantly, both in number and intensity, during the first few decades of the twentieth century. The only countries that continued to have numerous outsider revolts were those with the weakest militaries.

South American countries expanded and professionalized their militaries during this period for two main reasons: the export boom and the continuing threat of interstate war. The export boom was the permissive condition (i.e., it provided the necessary resources to invest in the military) and the threat of interstate war was the productive condition, because it made military strengthening a pressing necessity.

South American countries experienced a significant amount of international conflict in the nineteenth century, which put pressure on their governments to build up their militaries. The War of the Triple Alliance (1864–1870), with an estimated 290,000 casualties, was the bloodiest interstate war of that period, exceeding even the Crimean War (Clodfelter 2017, 180).[13] The other major South American war of this period, the War of the Pacific (1879–1883), had casualty levels similar to the average European conflict of the time. Although there were no major wars in the region between 1884 and 1929, the region continued to suffer from numerous militarized conflicts (Ligon 2002; Hensel 1994). Mares (2001, 77) reports that between 1884 and 1918 alone, South American countries had thirty-one militarized interstate disputes, in which military force was used, threatened, or displayed. Holsti (1996, 153) notes that in the region, "one sees patterns of peace and war, intervention, territorial predation, alliances, arms-racing, and power-balancing quite similar to those found in eighteenth-century Europe."

These conflicts provided two type of exogenous shocks affecting military strength. First, the threat of war forced every country to expand, modernize, and often mobilize its armed forces. South American countries may not have risked annihilation in international conflicts, but they certainly risked losing territory and lives. For this reason, once one country strengthened its military, its neighbors and rivals felt compelled to do the same. As Resende-Santos (2007, 37) puts it, "[i]ntensifying military competition and war, in turn, prompted a chain reaction of large-scale military emulation," resulting in military modernization that was "of a scale, intensity and duration not previously known in the region."

Second, war outcomes had an independent effect on military strength since defeat in war typically resulted in military downsizing, which was often imposed by the winners. Victory in war, meanwhile, frequently led to military expansion, either for the purposes of manning occupations or because of the newly acquired legitimacy and popularity of the military. Of these two types of shocks, the threat of war had the most important and longest-lasting

---

[13] Civil wars such as the American Civil War and the Taiping Rebellion claimed even more lives but were not international.

Military Strengthening

effects, since the threat of conflict was more pervasive in South America than actual war.

Military strengthening was costly, but the export boom of the late nineteenth and early twentieth century brought new revenues to South American governments.[14] The real value of exports increased almost tenfold, from less than $1.3 billion in the early 1870s to $12.4 billion in the late 1920s in constant 1980 dollars, thanks in part to infrastructure improvements, technological developments, more liberal economic policies, and growing world demand (Bértola and Ocampo 2013, 86, 97; Coatsworth 1998, 39–42). At the same time, foreign investment flowed into the region, climbing from $1.1 billion in 1880 to $11.2 billion in 1929 (Bértola and Ocampo 2013, 124). Foreign investment helped capitalize the export sector and build infrastructure, such as railroads and ports, which made the exports possible. The expansion of foreign trade and investment not only provided the foreign currency to pay for weapons imports and foreign military missions, it also provided incentives to build up the military, since the export boom depended on the ability of South American states to control the areas where export commodities were produced. Export booms also fueled conflict by creating incentives to wrestle land from neighboring states and by bringing miners, farmers, and speculators into disputed areas. The War of the Pacific, for example, originated in a dispute between Bolivia and Chile over nitrate-rich lands in the Atacama Desert.

Military competition was more intense where the threats of war were more pressing and where resources were more readily available (Resende-Santos 2007). Wealthier South American countries, especially those in the midst of export booms, such as Chile and Argentina, could more easily afford to make large investments in their armed forces. Indeed, Chile and Argentina engaged in a formidable arms race in the late nineteenth and early twentieth century, and nearly went to war on several occasions between 1898 and 1902.[15] The victories of Argentina and Chile in foreign wars during the late nineteenth century contributed to the arms race by strengthening their militaries, energizing nationalist sentiments, and stiffening their positions on territorial disputes.

Surrounded by foes, Chile was the first mover in the turn-of-the-century process of military modernization, engaging a German mission headed by Captain Emil Körner in 1885. Argentina responded by hiring military advisers in the 1880s, and in 1899 it, too, engaged a German military mission. Bolivia and Peru, which continued to claim the land Chile had conquered in the War of the Pacific, responded in kind. Peru hired a French mission in 1895, bringing in thirty-three French officers to teach in Peruvian military schools between 1896 and 1914 (Nunn 1983, 114–117; Hidalgo Morey et al. 2005, 349–352).

---

[14] State building, including the strengthening of the military, also contributed to the expansion of exports by delivering public goods, such as infrastructure and political stability.

[15] In the early twentieth century, Argentina and Chile even went so far as to obtain dreadnoughts, the most sophisticated warship of the era.

The Bolivian military also hired various foreign officers to teach in its military schools during the 1890s, and in 1905, its first French military mission arrived, followed by a German mission in 1910. The foreign missions gradually spread outward from Chile and its neighbors to the other South American countries. Some of these countries, such as Brazil, Paraguay, and Uruguay, engaged European missions or advisers, but others, such as Colombia, Ecuador, and Venezuela, hired Chilean military advisers to impart the Prussian model and sent their own military officers to train in Chile (Arancibia Clavel 2002).

With the support of the foreign missions, most South American countries moved to expand the size of their militaries by enacting laws that mandated military service. Chile was the pioneer again, instituting universal obligatory military service in 1900 (Resende-Santos 2007, 135–138). In response, Argentina enacted a similar conscription law in 1901, and by 1910 it could field a standing force of 250,000 men, if needed (Resende-Santos 2007, 201–202; Nunn 1983, 128–129). Meanwhile, Uruguay doubled and Peru and Venezuela tripled the size of their respective armies (Moore 1978, 40; Klarén 1986, 601).

South American militaries also sought to improve the training of officers and troops by opening new military institutes and adopting meritocratic criteria for the promotion of officers. In Chile, Körner revamped military training along Prussian lines: The government created highly selective military academies for junior officers as well as noncommissioned officers in 1887, and subsequently established specialized schools for the infantry, cavalry, and engineers (Sater and Herwig 1999, 44). In addition, 130 Chilean officers were sent to Germany for further training between 1895 and 1913 (Resende-Santos 2007, 138–141). The Argentine military similarly modeled its educational curriculum on Germany's war academy, employing various German officers as instructors and sending between 150 and 175 officers to train in Germany (García Molina 2010, 47–65; Potash 1969, 4; Resende-Santos 2007, 203–206; Schiff 1972). With the support of its Chilean mission, the Colombian government established several institutions to train military officers and adopted meritocratic criteria for promotion (Arancibia Clavel 2002, 385–386; Atehortúa Cruz and Vélez 1994, 60–63; Cardona 2008, 88–91).

Most South American countries also imported a massive amount of foreign weaponry during this period. In the 1890s, for example, Chile undertook a major purchase of Krupp artillery, along with 100,000 Mauser rifles (Resende-Santos 2007, 134). In 1889, Argentina acquired 60,000 German Mauser rifles, and in 1894, when tensions with Chile were high, it purchased so much equipment that, according to one high-ranking military official, it could "burn half of Chile" (Ramírez Jr. 1987, 183; Resende-Santos 2007, 198). During the early 1900s, Brazil also purchased several hundred thousand Mauser rifles as well as Krupp cannons from the Germans (McCann 1984, 746; Nunn 1972, 35; Resende-Santos 2007, 252–253), whereas Uruguay imported Krupp cannons, Colt and Maxim machine guns, and enough Mauser and Remington rifles to arm 50,000 men (Somma 2011, 160; Vanger 1963, 89, 95; López Chirico

1985, 42). Venezuela similarly strengthened its military by purchasing Mauser rifles, Krupp artillery, and Hotchkiss machine guns, among other weapons (Scheina 2003, 248; Straka 2005, 103; Schaposnik 1985, 20).

South American governments also took steps to gain a monopoly on the use of force by restricting the ability of nongovernmental entities to import arms and by asserting control over or eliminating regional and private militias. These measures were also driven in part by international competition, which put pressure on military organizations to become more centralized and cohesive to prevent autonomous forces from being co-opted by foreign foes and used as fifth columns. As part of a process of centralization of the armed forces that started during the War of the Triple Alliance, the Argentine government passed a law in 1880 that prohibited "provincial authorities from forming military forces" (Sabato 2010, 137). It also dissolved the national guard and integrated it into the army as a reserve force, boosting its numbers by 65,000 men (Nunn 1983, 48). Countries that were further away from the intense competition of the Southern Cone were slower to centralize military power, but they would eventually implement similar reforms. The Colombian government initiated a program in the early 1900s to gain control of the many weapons its citizens had stockpiled during the War of a Thousand Days and earlier. By 1909, this program had collected 65,505 guns and 1,138,649 bullets, making it more difficult for potential rebels to arm themselves (Bergquist 1978, 225; Esquivel Triana 2010, 265; Atehortúa Cruz 2009, 21). Similarly, Venezuela restricted the extent of weapons available to private citizens and subnational states in the early twentieth century (McBeth 2008, 6, 79–80), and in 1919 it abolished state militias (Blutstein et al. 1985, 248; Schaposnik 1985, 21).

Table 3.2 displays the ten South American countries' average scores between 1870–1899 and 1900–1929 on three different indicators of military strength and professionalization. These indicators are: the number of military personnel (in thousands), which is from the Correlates of War Project (2020); the number of military academies, which was compiled by Toronto (2017); and a variable from V-Dem that measures the degree to which appointment decisions in the armed forces are based on merit (Coppedge et al. 2020).[16] The data on merit-based promotions and the number of military academies should be viewed with some caution, but they represent the best available quantitative measures on military professionalization for this period.

The indicators show that the strength and degree of professionalization of the military increased appreciably throughout South America from the late nineteenth century to the early twentieth century. Collectively, the data also indicate that by the early twentieth century, Argentina, Brazil, and Chile had the strongest militaries in South America, whereas Bolivia, Ecuador, and Paraguay had

---

[16] This variable (v2stcritapparm) ranges from 0 (none of the appointments are based on skill and merit) to 4 (all of them are).

TABLE 3.2 *Indicators of military strength and professionalization in South America, 1870–1929*

Country	Military size (1870–1899)	Military size (1900–1929)	Military academies (1870–1899)	Military academies (1900–1929)	Merit-based promotions (1870–1899)	Merit-based promotions (1900–1929)
Strong militaries						
Argentina	11.6	29.0	1.93	2.60	3.34	3.34
Brazil	28.3	38.1	2.00	2.37	2.73	2.73
Chile	9.4	24.9	2.00	2.57	1.59	2.92
Middle militaries						
Colombia	3.6	6.3	2.00	2.30	0.76	0.76
Peru	6.5	7.8	0.13	1.63	1.32	1.32
Uruguay	3.2	8.5	1.00	1.90	0.87	1.28
Venezuela	5.3	8.7	2.00	2.33	0.71	0.85
Weak militaries						
Bolivia	2.4	4.2	0.30	1.00	1.25	1.25
Ecuador	2.9	5.6	2.00	2.33	2.01	2.01
Paraguay	1.4	2.7	0.00	0.00	1.23	0.99
Regional average	7.5	13.6	1.34	1.90	1.58	1.75

Source: Correlates of War (2020); Toronto (2017); Coppedge et al. (2020).
Note: Military size refers to the number of soldiers in thousands.

the weakest armed forces.[17] Not surprisingly, the larger and wealthier countries of the region tended to have stronger militaries since they could afford to spend more on their militaries than could smaller and poorer nations.

Although the strengthening of South American militaries was mostly driven by international threats, it discouraged internal revolts because would-be rebels knew that they had little chance of prevailing over strong, professional militaries. In 1911, for example, some leaders of the opposition Blanco Party in Uruguay sought to carry out a revolt, but the party blocked them, stating that the rebels would be at a "notorious disadvantage," given the strength of the military which was evidenced by the disastrous failure of previous revolts (Vanger 1980, 151–152). Similarly, in 1917, the Blanco leader Basilo Muñoz persuaded the party to sign a pact with the government and compete in elections because armed revolt would be futile (Vanger 2010, 232). In Colombia as well, the professionalization of the military at the outset of the twentieth

---

[17] The data on the degree of merit-based promotions suggest that Ecuador should rank in the middle group, whereas Colombia and Peru should be in the bottom group, but this variable should be viewed with caution, given that the scores for some countries do not appear to reflect important changes that took place in military promotion criteria in some countries during the early twentieth century. The data on the number of military academies, which is a rough measure of military professionalization, also appear to contain some errors.

TABLE 3.3 *The varying stability of regimes in South America, 1870–1929*

	Major outsider revolts (1870–1899)	Major outsider revolts (1900–1929)	Executive overthrows (1870–1899)	Executive overthrows (1900–1929)
Strong militaries (1900–1929)				
Argentina	6	1	0	0
Brazil	3	1	2	0
Chile	2	0	1	2
Medium militaries (1900–1929)				
Colombia	6	0	1	1
Peru	4	2	6	2
Uruguay	5	3	2	0
Venezuela	6	2	4	1
Weak militaries (1900–1929)				
Bolivia	9	4	4	2
Ecuador	7	5	3	3
Paraguay	5	7	3	8

Source: Latin American Revolts Database.

century deterred revolts that had been commonplace during the nineteenth century. Many Liberals wanted to rebel in response to the widespread fraud in the 1922 elections, but General Benjamín Herrera, the Liberal leader and presidential candidate that year, dissuaded them in part because the strength of the country's military gave them little hope of success (Maingot 1967, 165–166).

As a result of the strengthening of the military, the number of outsider revolts fell from twenty-two per decade between 1830 and 1899 to nine per decade between 1900 and 1929. Revolts from outside the state apparatus declined in large part because political outsiders recognized they had little chance of defeating professional militaries. Popular uprisings had always been highly unlikely to overthrow governments in South America and none did so between 1900 and 1929, but elite insurrections also became increasingly unlikely to prevail. During the 1900–1929 period, only five elite insurrections succeeded in overthrowing a government, whereas thirty-eight had done so between 1830 and 1899. Moreover, four of the five successful elite insurrections between 1900 and 1929 occurred in the South American countries with the weakest militaries.

As Table 3.3 indicates, the strengthening and professionalization of the military helped bring political stability to many South American countries in the early twentieth century. Between 1900 and 1929, countries with strong militaries experienced fewer outsider revolts and executive overthrows than did countries with militaries of medium strength. And countries with militaries of medium strength experienced far fewer outsider revolts and executive overthrows than did countries with weak militaries.

Outsider revolts almost entirely disappeared in the nations that developed the strongest militaries post-1900. Partly as a result of its military professionalization efforts, Chile experienced no outsider revolts during the first three decades of the twentieth century, although it did have a couple of military coups in the 1920s. Argentina suffered the most revolts of any South American country during the nineteenth century, but its enormous military buildup during and after the War of the Triple Alliance helped deter outsider revolts in the twentieth century. During the first three decades of the twentieth century, it only experienced one elite insurrection, the Radical revolt of 1905, and this was quickly squashed.[18] Outsider revolts also gradually diminished in Brazil in the late nineteenth and early twentieth century as the government gradually strengthened its military. Nevertheless, Brazil's vast size and the ruggedness of its terrain made it difficult to stifle outsider revolts when they did occur. Between 1912 and 1916, for example, the Brazilian military struggled to defeat a popular uprising, dubbed the Contestado War, by poor settlers in the remote frontier area bordering Argentina. This rebellion posed no real threat to the national government, however; nor did the few insider revolts Brazil experienced in the early twentieth century.

The countries with medium-strength militaries also experienced a dramatic decline in outsider revolts during the late nineteenth century. Colombia, for example, suffered no major outsider revolts in the first three decades of the twentieth century, after experiencing six between 1870 and 1899. Nor were there any major outsider revolts in Venezuela after 1903 or in Uruguay after 1910, thanks in large part to their efforts to strengthen their armed forces. Peru also experienced a decline in outsider revolts after 1895 when it began to professionalize its military, although it did experience a successful insurrection by an opposition presidential candidate in 1919 as well as a failed indigenous uprising in 1923–1924. The 1919 revolt resembled a coup in many respects, however, and its success was only made possible by the participation of military and police officers.

As we have seen, the poorest South American countries, namely Bolivia, Ecuador, and Paraguay, failed to develop strong militaries during the early twentieth century. Their armed forces remained small, politicized, poorly trained, and underequipped, and, partly as a result, these countries continued to be plagued by revolts.

---

[18] The Radicals sought military support for their 1905 revolt as they had in previous rebellions, but their failure to obtain sufficient backing from the armed forces doomed the insurrection. Argentina also experienced several major labor protests in the early twentieth century that turned violent, but these were easily repressed by the military as well.

Paraguay suffered the most revolts, experiencing seven elite rebellions and seven military coups between 1900 and 1929, several of which were successful. Overall, the number of revolt onsets and revolt-years more than tripled in Paraguay compared to the nineteenth century. The explanation for this reversal is straightforward: The Paraguayan military was destroyed in the War of the Triple Alliance (1864–1870). Whereas Paraguay had some 40,000 soldiers before the war and mobilized 70,000 troops at the height of hostilities, by the time occupation forces left in 1876, its army had declined to a mere 400 men (Kallsen 1983, 33). The conflagration also affected the country's territory and demographics – some historians estimate it lost half of its territory and up to 60–70 percent of its population (Whigham 2002; Whigham and Potthast 1999). In the decades that followed, the country lacked the will and the resources to rebuild a severely factionalized military. At the outset of the 20th century, Paraguay still had the lowest level of exports in South America (Bértola and Ocampo 2012: 86). Not surprisingly, it also had the region's smallest army, and its officers and troops often lacked even the most basic training and equipment. Paraguay did not take important steps to strengthen its military until the mid-1920s when a growing conflict with Bolivia prompted the Paraguayan government to purchase foreign weapons, reorganize its general staff, and hire first a French and then an Argentine military mission (Bareiro Spaini 2008, 76–77; Lewis 1993, 142).

The Ecuadorian government, meanwhile, downsized its military considerably after its defeat in the Ecuadorian–Colombian War (1863). Only in the 1930s would Ecuador muster a force of 6,000 soldiers, equivalent to the one that preceded the 1863 conflict (Henderson 2008, 85). Ecuador undertook some efforts to professionalize its military at the turn of the century, hiring a Chilean military mission to train Ecuadorian officers – it also created some new military schools and began to send officers to Chile for training (Arancibia Clavel 2002, 190–196). In addition, the Ecuadorian government made military service obligatory, enacted new laws governing promotions and salaries, and purchased military equipment from Chile as well as France and Germany (Moncayo Gallegos 1995, 155; Fitch 1977, 15; Arancibia Clavel 2002, 212). Nevertheless, the reforms took a while to bear fruit, and Arancibia Clavel (2002, 267) and Romero y Cordero (1991, 380–383) suggest that the long-term influence of the Chilean mission was relatively superficial. The Ecuadorian military remained highly politicized and senior Ecuadorian officers continued to be promoted, demoted, and discharged based on their personal and political affiliations (Fitch 1977, 16). Moreover, military budgets were reduced significantly between 1908 and 1913: The size of the standing army was slashed, and military salaries fell behind those of civilian employees (Fitch 1977, 16; Rodríguez 1985, 225). The weakness of the military encouraged the opposition to continue to carry out rebellions and some of these revolts were successful. Rebels overthrew the government in 1906 and 1911, and nearly did so again in the bloody 1911–1912 civil war. The military also had a very difficult time suppressing a rebellion that ravaged the province of Esmeraldas from 1913 to 1916.

Of the three small and poor South American countries, Bolivia took the most important steps to professionalize its military, hiring a small French mission and then a larger German one in the early twentieth century. With the assistance of these missions, the Bolivian government purchased foreign weaponry, created a military conscription system, overhauled the military schools and training system, and tried to establish a professional military career (Bieber 1994; Díaz Arguedas 1971; Dunkerley 2003). These reforms initially appeared to work, and outsider revolts disappeared in the first two decades of the twentieth century. Nevertheless, the transformation of the Bolivian military was largely illusory: The country's armed forces remained small, poorly trained, and heavily politicized. Outsider revolts resumed in the 1920s and the Bolivian military struggled to contain them. Indeed, an opposition revolt overthrew the government in 1920 and major indigenous rebellions destabilized the country in 1921 and 1927. Bolivia's military deteriorated even further after the country's stunning defeat in the 1932–1935 Chaco War, which led to further revolts, culminating in the 1952 Bolivian revolution.

Thus, the poorest South American countries made less progress in strengthening and professionalizing their armed forces. As a result, they remained highly politically unstable. By contrast, the other South American countries significantly strengthened their armed forces in the late nineteenth or early twentieth century, which led to a sharp decline in outsider revolts and executive overthrows in these countries, as Table 3.3 indicates. Nevertheless, the professionalization of the military during this period did not lead to a reduction in insider revolts, such as military coups. Indeed, there were approximately six onsets of insider revolts per decade between 1900 and 1929, down only slightly from an average of seven per decade between 1830 and 1899. Many of these insider revolts succeeded in taking power, which encouraged military officers to continue to undertake them.

A STATISTICAL TEST OF THE ARGUMENT

To further explore the impact of military variables on the number of outsider revolts in a given country year, we carry out a statistical test using panel data from ten South American countries from 1830 to 1929. Because our outcome of interest is a count variable, we use a series of Poisson regressions with two-way fixed effects and clustered standard errors, following established procedures (Angrist and Pischke 2009).

As Table 3.2 indicated, we measure military strength and professionalization using three variables: the number of military personnel (in thousands) from the Correlates of War Project (2020); the number of military academies from Toronto (2017); and a measure of the degree to which appointment decisions in the armed forces are based on merit from V-Dem (Coppedge et al. 2020). The coverage of these variables is limited for most countries between 1830 and 1845, resulting in an unbalanced panel. However, except for Uruguay, all countries enter the panel by 1854, and no observations drop due to attrition after a country enters the sample. When we include additional confounders in Models 2 and 3, we lose only fifteen additional observations.

Model 1 includes only the military variables, uses two-way fixed effects to control for time- and country-invariant confounders, and reports standard errors clustered by country. However, our military variables are related to other variables – such as economic growth and international conflict – which vary over time and across countries and could shape the likelihood of revolts. It is therefore key to control for these confounders, which we do in Model 2. Since export booms can affect the size and quality of the military, as well as the propensity of outsiders to rebel, we include a variable measuring total exports in current US dollars from Federico and Tena-Junguito (2016). Relatedly, the expansion of railroads and telegraphs might have facilitated both economic growth and military recruitment, and increased the reach of state authorities, narrowing opportunities to rebel. We therefore account for the miles of railway track and telegraph lines in each country (Banks and Wilson 2014). To measure the potential impact of international conflict, we include a yearly count of the militarized interstate disputes each state was involved in (Palmer et al. 2022), as well as a dummy variable capturing whether the country lost an international war in the past fifteen years (Schenoni 2021). In addition, we include a series of controls that are common in the political violence literature. To control for the effect of hybrid regimes on political violence we use the Electoral Democracy Index (v2x_polyarchy) from V-Dem (Coppedge et al. 2020) and its squared term. We also use an urbanization rate variable (e_miurbani) and the log of the population from Coppedge et al. (2020), since outsider revolts and many of the aforementioned variables (e.g., military size) would presumably be affected by socioeconomic modernization and population size. Finally, we include the years elapsed since independence – and drop year-fixed effects – in Model 3 to test if revolts declined simply as a function of time.

Unfortunately, the scarcity of data for nineteenth-century Latin America precludes controlling for other potential confounders. For example, there are no comprehensive time-series data on inequality or economic performance for this period. Nor are there reliable time-series data on the time-varying ethno-racial composition of South American countries or the relative strength of liberal and conservative parties during the nineteenth and early twentieth century. Nevertheless, we trust that our use of country-fixed effects should control for most of these unobservable characteristics that change slowly over time. The roughness of the terrain, which is also a prominent confounder in the civil war literature, is one of these time invariant factors. Similarly, we trust that our year-fixed effects will control for international shocks that affected all countries equally, such as global financial crises and changes in commodity

TABLE 3.4 *Determinants of outsider revolts in South America, 1830–1929 (Poisson regressions on number of revolts per year)*

	Model 1	Model 2	Model 3	Model 4
Military personnel (in 10,000)	−0.358*	−0.368*	−0.350*	−0.309*
	(0.16)	(0.17)	(0.16)	(0.13)
Number of military academies	−0.390*	−0.427*	−0.381*	−0.299**
	(0.16)	(0.21)	(0.18)	(0.09)
Military appointments by skills and merit	−0.549*	−0.581**	−0.336*	−0.395
	(0.23)	(0.23)	(0.16)	(0.32)
Urbanization rate		−0.049	0.032	−0.522
		(0.56)	(0.47)	(0.55)
V-Dem Electoral Democracy Index		−0.466	−0.320	−0.534
		(0.38)	(0.44)	(0.38)
V-Dem Electoral Democracy Index^2		0.106	0.092	0.121
		(0.09)	(0.10)	(0.10)
Militarized interstate disputes		0.178	0.178	0.194
		(0.17)	(0.16)	(0.16)
Defeat in international war (15-year period)		−0.106	0.166	−0.137
		(0.26)	(0.42)	(0.29)
Total exports		−0.178	−0.666	−0.150
		(0.33)	(0.54)	(0.31)
Hundreds of miles of telegraph lines		0.279	0.095	0.353
		(0.21)	(0.23)	(0.24)
Hundreds of miles of railway track		−0.052	0.067	−0.091
		(0.12)	(0.15)	(0.13)
Population (log)		−0.005	0.008	0.060
		(0.09)	(0.08)	(0.11)
Years since Independence			−0.010	
			(0.01)	
GDP per capita				−0.000
				(0.00)
Constant	−3.761	−1.317	12.938	−7.160
	(6.34)	(13.99)	(6.96)	(8.62)
Pseudo r-squared	0.2252	0.2344	0.1371	0.2540
Fixed effects	Two-way	Two-way	Country	Two-way
Standard errors	Clustered	Clustered	Clustered	Clustered
No. of observations	800	775	775	695

Notes: Standard errors in parentheses. Country and year dummies not shown.
* p < 0.05; ** p < 0.01.

prices. In Model 4 we make an exception and test the robustness of our results to an important remaining confounder, GDP per capita, which we measure using data in real 2011 dollars (cgdppc) from the Maddison Project (Bolt et al. 2018). GDP per capita is perhaps the most significant predictor of political violence in the literature, but data on this variable are missing for numerous years, so Model 4 should be viewed with some caution.[19]

Table 3.4 presents the results. In almost all models, the size of the military, the number of military academies, and the extent to which appointment decisions in the armed forces are meritocratic have a negative and statistically significant impact on the number of revolts in each year. The only exception is Model 4. When GDP per capita is included in the analysis, the number of military academies ceases to be significant, but this could be explained by the reduced number of observations in this model. Most of the other variables have the expected sign, but do not achieve statistical significance in any of our models. The minimal change in the r-squared statistics when confounders are included in Model 2 suggests that military variables explain most of the variance in the outcome. With observational data, endogeneity issues will inevitably remain a concern, but this should be taken as a strong indication that military strength might be mediating the impact of more structural geopolitical and economic variables. Further model specifications confirm this intuition. For example, when we drop all three military variables, one of the confounders, total exports, becomes significant (at $p < 0.05$). This suggests the effect of export booms runs through military strength.[20]

Overall, this statistical analysis of the determinants of revolts in South America between 1830 and 1929 provides support for the argument that military size and professionalization reduced the prevalence of outsider revolts. Military strength does not have an impact on the likelihood of insider revolts such as coups and mutinies, however. As expected, when we switch the dependent variable from major outsider revolts to major insider revolts, such as coups, the military variables lose statistical significance in most of the models. Although military strength effectively deterred regime outsiders from mounting rebellions in South America pre-1930, it clearly did not have the same impact on regime insiders.

CONCLUSION

This chapter shows that the expansion and professionalization of the military significantly reduced revolts by political outsiders in the region. The importance of this decline is clear: It vastly reduced the number of lives lost to violence, brought greater political stability to the region, and helped pave the way for a lengthy period of economic growth and state building. As we shall see, military professionalization also laid the groundwork for the first wave of democratization in the region by encouraging opposition parties to abandon the armed struggle and focus on the electoral path to power.

---

[19] We interpolated missing years for the GDP per capita variable where feasible, but the number of observations nevertheless declined to 695 in Model 4. Paraguay dropped out of the analysis altogether in this model because it lacks GDP data for the entire 1830–1929 period.

[20] For the result of these models and further information, see the appendix to Madrid and Schenoni (2023/2024).

4

The Origins of Strong Parties in South America

Political parties played a crucial role in the emergence of democracy in South America. Democracy arose first in those South American countries that developed strong parties because such parties placed democratic reform on the agenda and provided the legislative votes required to enact the reforms. Strong parties also had the organizations necessary to monitor and enforce the implementation of the reforms.

This chapter describes the evolution of parties in South America during the nineteenth and early twentieth centuries and analyzes what led to the development of strong parties in some countries but not in others. Political parties first emerged in South America during the nineteenth century, and by the end of the century, these parties had established permanent national organizations and enduring linkages to the electorate in some countries, such as Chile, Colombia, and Uruguay. In other countries, however, party organizations and identities would not consolidate until the twentieth century.

The theoretical literature on parties, which has predominantly focused on Europe and the United States, offers several potential explanations for the emergence of strong parties. Some studies have ascribed the rise of political parties to economic development or to the spread of elections and democracy. Other analyses have attributed the emergence of strong parties to violent struggles or to class and ethnic cleavages. Although most of these factors contributed to the rise of parties in South America, none of them can adequately explain the variance in party development in the region before 1930.

This chapter argues that two main factors shaped party development in South America during the nineteenth and early twentieth century. First, strong parties arose from intense but balanced religious and territorial cleavages. In nineteenth-century Latin America, religious and territorial cleavages often generated fierce passions, and strong parties tended to emerge where both sides of the cleavage were powerful – that is, where each side had numerous proponents and ample resources that they could devote to party building. More specifically, strong parties tended to arise where there were numerous conservative supporters of the Catholic Church as well as numerous liberal critics of the Church, and where both sides enjoyed considerable resources. Alternatively, strong parties might emerge where the capital city and the provinces had roughly similar economic, demographic, political, and military resources. Under these circumstances, neither side could easily dominate the other. Instead, they often fought to a standstill, deepening partisan identities and loyalties. By contrast, where one side of the cleavage was considerably stronger than the other, competition for power tended to take place within a cleavage rather than between different sides of the cleavage. Where this was the case, political competition often revolved around personalities, rather than ideologies or interests, and the parties that emerged typically had weak organizations and ephemeral loyalties.

Second, strong national parties were more likely to arise in countries with few geographic barriers where the bulk of the population lived in relative proximity to each other. Given the lack of communications and transportation infrastructure during the nineteenth century, it was much harder to build national parties in geographically fragmented nations where the population was widely dispersed. In the latter countries, politicians and party leaders could not easily travel to or even communicate with much of the population, which made it difficult to campaign, manage organizations, and build support throughout the nation. Geographically fragmented countries also tended to have strong regional identities, which impeded the construction of national institutions such as parties.

To be sure, these two factors were not the only variables that influenced party development before 1930. Nevertheless, they were the most important ones. It was very difficult for strong parties to emerge in the nineteenth and early twentieth century without at least one of these factors being present, and the presence of both variables significantly increased the likelihood that strong parties would arise. It is also true that religious and center–periphery cleavages overlapped to a degree in the nineteenth century since liberals tended to be stronger in urban areas and conservatives were typically stronger in rural areas.[1] And geographic fragmentation tended to increase the number of territorial cleavages and decrease the likelihood that the center–periphery cleavage was balanced. Nevertheless, the correlation between these variables should not be exaggerated. Geographic concentration was no guarantee that the center–periphery cleavage would be balanced, and conservatives as well as liberals were often strong in both urban and rural areas.

The organization of the chapter is as follows. The first section describes how I measure party strength and examines the variation in party development

---

[1] Gibson (1996, 32), for example, argues that "[i]deological conflicts, such as those revolving around church-state issues, were drawn along these rural-urban alignments."

across South America during the late nineteenth and early twentieth century using data from the V-Dem project as well as the secondary literature. The second section discusses existing theories of party development and assesses to what extent they can explain differences in parties within the region during this period. The third section examines how religious and territorial cleavages shaped the prospects for party building in South America during the nineteenth century, and the fourth section discusses the role played by geographical fragmentation. The concluding section summarizes the main findings of the chapter.

PARTY STRENGTH IN SOUTH AMERICA BEFORE 1930

In the broadest sense of the term, a political party is "any group, however loosely organized, seeking to elect government officeholders under a given label," but parties vary considerably in terms of their strength and organization (Epstein 1980, 9).[2] Conceptualizing and measuring party strength in Latin America before 1930 is difficult because of the incipient nature of parties during this period and the paucity of data available. By current standards, none of the parties operating in Latin America during the nineteenth or early twentieth century would rank as strong because they lacked the extensive bureaucracies, mass memberships, and developed territorial organizations that characterize strong parties today. Nevertheless, as we shall see, there were important differences in party strength across Latin American countries during this period.

I define parties as strong when they have two main characteristics. First, they must have broad and lasting attachments to the electorate. Strong parties should be able to repeatedly gain the support of large swaths of the electorate, even if the electorate represents a relatively small segment of the total population, as it typically did in nineteenth-century Latin America. Second, strong parties must possess enduring national organizations with platforms, rules, and numerous branches or affiliated associations. A strong party will have a permanent organization, rather than one that only exists during election periods, and it will have a presence in various parts of the country, rather than in a single municipality, state, or province. This bipartite definition captures the important differences that existed between the parties of this era, while focusing on characteristics for which there are data.[3]

---

[2] For a similar definition, see Schlesinger (1991). Some scholars only count institutionalized electoral organizations as parties. According to Aldrich (1995, 19): "Political parties can be seen as coalitions of elites to capture and use political office. [But] a political party is more than a coalition. A political party is an institutionalized coalition, one that has adopted rules, norms and procedures."

[3] My definition of party strength differs somewhat from the complex – and difficult to measure – definitions of party institutionalization offered by Dix (1992), Huntington (1968, 12–32), Levitsky (2003), and others.

Political parties first emerged in Latin America in the middle of the nineteenth century, but it was not until the late nineteenth century that some of them developed relatively strong and permanent organizations.[4] In the mid-nineteenth century, politicians and political brokers created electoral clubs or societies that promoted candidates and helped turn out the vote for them (Sabato 2018, 62–63). Politicians initially resisted calling these electoral organizations "parties" because the term had negative connotations. The early parties or electoral clubs tended to be ephemeral and personalistic organizations that functioned only during electoral periods. Nevertheless, some of them gradually developed loyal partisans and permanent organizational structures that reached much of the nation (Drake 2009, 122). According to Sabato (2018, 64), by the last quarter of the nineteenth century, some parties "developed into tightly organized institutions, with prescribed rules and mechanisms to join in, choose authorities, draft platforms and programs, select and put forward candidates for elective office, define and enforce party discipline, and so forth." Even at the end of the nineteenth century, however, most parties in the region remained weak, personalistic, and underinstitutionalized.

Systematic data on party strength is scarce for the nineteenth and early twentieth century. There are no sweeping cross-national analyses of parties in Latin America during this period. Fortunately, the V-Dem project does have data on several party-related variables, which are coded by country experts. V-Dem's party institutionalization index (v2xps_party) adds the indicators for various party-related variables, including party organization (v2psorgs), party branches (v2psprbrch), party linkages (v2psprlnks), distinct party platforms (v2psplats), and legislative party cohesion (v2pscohesv), and then converts the sum to a cumulative dimension function (Coppedge et al. 2024a, 320). According to V-Dem, the regional average of party institutionalization increased relatively steadily over the course of the nineteenth century, reaching a high in the 1890s, before declining slightly in the early twentieth century. As Figure 4.1 shows, Uruguay, Chile, and Colombia stood out as having the most institutionalized parties in the region, both in the late nineteenth century as well as in the first three decades of the twentieth century. Paraguay ranked fifth and Argentina sixth, behind Venezuela, on this index between 1870 and 1899, whereas Argentina ranked fifth and Paraguay sixth, just after Bolivia, between 1900 and 1929, according to V-Dem.

The historical literature on parties in these countries, which is discussed in detail in Chapters 5–8, provides relatively similar evaluations of cross-national variation in party strength during this period. As this literature shows, the first South American countries to develop robust and enduring parties were Chile, Colombia, and Uruguay (Drake 2009, 122–124, 159–161; Fitzgibbon 1957, 10–11). Parties were founded in these countries in the middle of the nineteenth

---

[4] The precursors of parties were loose coalitions of notables who supported each other's campaigns, cooperated in the legislature, and staffed administrations.

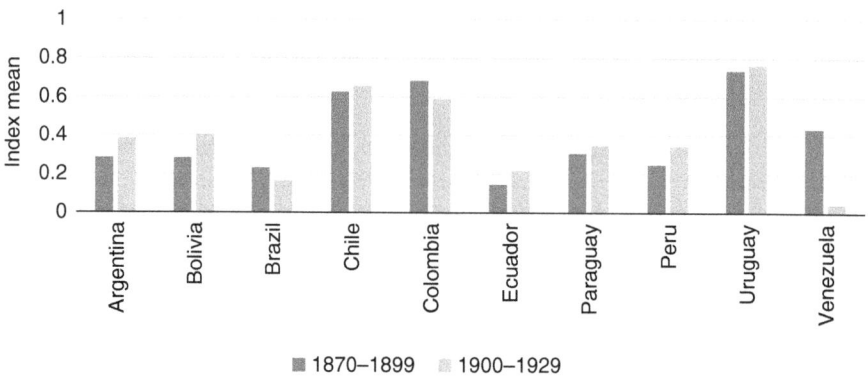

FIGURE 4.1 Party institutionalization in South America, 1870–1929
Source: Based on data from Coppedge et al. (2024b).
Note: The y-axis shows the means of V-Dem's party institutionalization index.

century and, in the decades that followed, they evolved into national institutions with broad networks of branches or affiliated organizations. In all three countries, parties developed strong and enduring ties to the electorate: Many people came to identify with parties and passed on their party loyalties over generations.

As Chapter 5 shows, in Chile four major parties – the Liberal Party, the Conservative Party, the National Party, and the Radical Party – arose and developed widespread and lasting partisan loyalties during the nineteenth century. Two of these parties – the Conservative Party and the Radical Party – also established relatively strong national organizations (Valenzuela 1996, 249; 2000; Guilisasti Tagle 1964, 22–23; Heise 1982, 317–318, 327; Remmer 1984, 15; Snow 1963). Although the Liberal Party and the National Party had weaker organizations and suffered from frequent splits and defections, all four parties proved enduring, dominating Chilean politics throughout the late nineteenth and early twentieth century (Urzúa Valenzuela 1968, 32; Scully 1992, 49; Heise 1982, 291).

In Uruguay only two strong parties, the National or Blanco Party and the Colorado Party, arose during the nineteenth century, as Chapter 5 discusses. Both parties gradually built up deep partisan loyalties and powerful national organizations with branches and affiliated organizations throughout the country (Corbo 2016, 104–106; Hierro López 2015, 168; Fernández and Machín 2017, 144). The Blancos and Colorados occasionally split and periodic efforts were made to unite the two parties or establish third parties, but none of these attempts prospered for long (McLaughlin 1973, 277; López-Alves 2000, 57). People overwhelmingly stuck with the party of their parents, and the two parties dominated the political system throughout the nineteenth and early twentieth centuries.

Colombia also developed a strong two-party system during the nineteenth century, as Chapter 6 discusses. The Conservative and Liberal parties first arose in Colombia during the 1840s and gradually created relatively complex and centralized organizations (Bushnell 1993, 65; Delpar 1981, 3–4; Safford and Palacios 2002, 134–143). Both parties established numerous branches and affiliated organizations, including newspapers, schools, elite clubs, and mass societies such as associations of artisans (Sowell 1992; Sanders 2004, 66–69; Posada-Carbó 2010). By the end of the nineteenth century, the Conservatives and Liberals had achieved an organizational presence nationwide (Delpar 1981, 126–127, 177, 183). Although the two parties underwent frequent splits, which sometimes resulted in the formation of third parties, these splits proved temporary. Both parties proved extraordinarily durable, and much of the population established close ties to the parties, which were passed down from generation to generation.

By contrast, strong parties did not emerge in Argentina and Paraguay until the early twentieth century, and even then, the parties remained weaker than in Chile, Colombia, and Uruguay. According to López (2001b, 58), for most of the nineteenth century, Argentine parties "were extremely weak, both because they consisted of local groups without practically any national articulation, and because they completely lacked organization." As Chapter 6 discusses, the first important party in Argentina, the UCR, developed a strong organization and partisan ties in the city and province of Buenos Aires in the 1890s, but it did not have much of a presence in most other parts of the country until the early twentieth century (Alonso 2000, 162; Rock 2002, 144). Moreover, the UCR was the only strong party to emerge in the country during this period. It dominated Argentine politics between 1916 and 1930.

As Chapter 8 details, two important parties, the Colorado Party and the Liberal Party, were established in Paraguay in 1887, but they did not develop into strong parties until the early twentieth century. The Colorado Party initially dominated the government, but the Liberal Party seized power in a revolt in 1904 and maintained control until the military overthrew it in a 1936 coup. The two parties did not develop strong organizations during this period, but they did establish enduring loyalties in the population, attracting both urban and rural supporters (Lewis 1993, 124; Caballero Aquino and Livieres Banks 1993, 50). Family members typically belonged to the same party and passed down their partisan attachments to their children (Nichols 1970, 47–48).

Parties in the other South American countries lacked strong organizations and enduring support during the nineteenth and early twentieth century. As Chapter 8 discusses, Bolivian parties were largely personalistic vehicles during this period without organizational structures or committed followers (Dunkerley 2003, 62; Klein 1969b, 24–25; Irurozqui 2000, 399–400). In 1908, Manuel Rigoberto Paredes wrote that: "In Bolivia what we call parties are only factions, bands or tendencies of a markedly personal character" (cited in Dunkerley 2003, 136). Several parties emerged in Bolivia during the late nineteenth and early twentieth century, including the Conservative Party, the Liberal Party, the Republican Party, the Socialist Republican Party, and the Nationalist Party, but only the Liberal Party survived the downfall of its founding leader. And even the Liberal Party remained on the margins of power after 1920.

Ecuador also failed to develop strong parties during the nineteenth century and early twentieth century, as Chapter 8 discusses. Several parties, including the Conservative Party, the Progressive Party, and the Liberal Party, were founded in the late nineteenth century and took turns governing, but none of them developed meaningful organizations during this period. According to Rodríguez (1985, 45), nineteenth-century "political parties were only loose collections of small groups that owed primary loyalty to an individual or region." The Conservative and the Liberal parties made some organizational investments beginning in the 1920s and gradually gained mass followings, which enabled them to endure into the twenty-first century, but their level of party development in the early twentieth century remained quite low (Ayala Mora 1989, 23–25; Fitch 1977, 18).

As Chapter 7 details, strong parties did not emerge in Peru either. The most important Peruvian party of the period, the Civil Party, first arose in the 1870s and built a network of regional alliances and a relatively disciplined contingent in the legislature, but it never developed a strong national organization (Mücke 2004; McEvoy 1994). Throughout most of its existence, it lacked a formal membership, a clear platform, bureaucratic rules, or any permanent structures aside from an executive committee (Mücke 2004, 200–201). The other political parties that arose in Peru during the nineteenth and early twentieth century, such as the Constitutional Party, the Democrat Party, and the Liberal Party, were mere personalistic vehicles, lacking organizations, firm ideologies, and internal discipline, not to mention a broad membership and an experienced second generation of leaders (Pike 1969, 218; Klarén 2000, 214). One prominent politician of that time observed that "the total membership of any given political party in Peru could easily fit into one railroad coach" (cited in Stein 1980, 25). The organizational weakness of these parties made it relatively easy for Augusto Leguía, the Peruvian dictator, to co-opt, repress, and dismantle them after he came to power in 1919 (Pike 1969, 218; Stein 1980, 38). Leguía founded his own party, the Democratic Reformist Party (PDR), in 1920, but he stacked it with friends and family members who would blindly support him (Pike 1969, 218; Stein 1980, 47–48). The PDR, like the other personalistic parties, did not survive for long the death of its founding leader.

Strong parties also failed to arise in Brazil during the nineteenth century and early twentieth century, as Chapter 7 discusses. Two parties, the Conservative Party and the Liberal Party, emerged during the 1830s and alternated in power until 1889, except for a brief period between 1853 and 1868 when they jointly governed in a temporary alliance. Neither of these parties developed strong organizational structures or enduring partisan loyalties, however. They depended instead on local political bosses (*coroneis*) to turn out the votes in exchange for patronage (Barman 1988, 226; Graham 1990, 156–159). Factionalism was pervasive in both parties, and partisan loyalty was sorely lacking. According to Graham (1990, 181): "Party labels were put on and taken off almost as easily as a set of clothes." The Liberal and Conservative parties dissolved after the fall of the empire in 1889, but no strong national parties emerged to replace them. A few regional parties governed the country during the First Republic (1889–1930): The Paulista Republican Party captured the presidency six times during this period, whereas the Mineiro Republican Party won it three times (Fausto 1989, 272). Although some Republican parties had strong state organizations that routinely captured a large share of the state vote, they failed to build national organizations (Love 1970, 13; 1980; Wirth 1977). As a result, Brazil continued to suffer from party weakness.

As Chapter 7 details, Venezuelan parties were also underdeveloped in the nineteenth and early twentieth century, leading the Venezuelan novelist and politician Rómulo Gallegos to write in 1909 that political parties "have not yet existed in Venezuela" (cited in Rey 2015, 65). The Conservative Party and the Liberal Party emerged shortly after independence, but these parties were little more than loose collections of notables that lacked permanent structures and centered power in their paramount leaders (Gilmore 1964, 25, 27, 56; Pérez 1996, 49). Both parties split frequently along personalistic lines, and neither party established strong roots in Venezuelan society even though much of the population was eligible to vote. The Conservative Party fell apart after the 1859–1863 Federal War, although Conservative candidates still participated in elections in the years that followed (Pérez 1996, 61; Tarver and Frederick 2005, 68). The Liberal Party, meanwhile, was repressed under the dictatorships of Cipriano Castro and Juan Vicente Gómez. Although Gómez initially brought some Liberals into his regime, he quickly turned against the party's leaders and other traditional politicians, excluding them from his cabinet and exiling, imprisoning, and even killing those who dared oppose him (McBeth 2008, 24–27, 30–31, 63, 318). Gómez and his advisers believed that there was no need for political parties and he sought to "unite Venezuelans without distinction of parties" (McBeth 2008, 372; Rey 2015, 63–64). Venezuelan parties were too weak to survive in this environment.

Table 4.1 presents some basic data on the main parties in South America between 1870 and 1930. I code parties as having a high level of party strength if they had a strong organization *and* widespread support during at least half of the years of this period. If they only had one or the other (i.e., a strong organization *or* widespread support), then they are coded as being of medium strength, and if they had neither, then they are coded as being of low strength. These codings are based on a thorough review of the historical literature on parties in these countries, much of which is cited in Chapters 5–8.

As Table 4.1 indicates, Chile, Colombia, and Uruguay clearly had the strongest parties in the region during this period, followed by Argentina and Paraguay. The strongest parties in Argentina (the UCR), Chile (the

TABLE 4.1 *Major political parties in South America, 1870–1930*

Country	Party name (year founded and dissolved)	Years holding the presidency, 1870–1930	Party strength (1870–1930)
Argentina	Partido Autonomista Nacional (1874–1930)	1874–1910	Low
	Unión Cívica Radical (1891–)	1916–1930	High
	Unión Nacional (1909–1912)	1910–1916	Low
Bolivia	Partido Conservador (1884–1909)	1884–1899	Low
	Partido Liberal (1883–1978)	1899–1920	Medium
	Partido Republicano (1914–1921)	1920–1921	Low
	Partido Republicano Socialista (1921–1946)	1921–1926	Low
	Partido Nacionalista (1926–1930)	1926–1930	Low
Brazil	Partido Liberal (1837–1889)	1878–1885; 1889	Low
	Partido Conservador (1837–1889)	1868–1878; 1885–1889	Low
	Partido Republicano Paulista (1873–1937)	1894–1906; 1918–1919; 1926–1930	Low
	Partido Republicano Mineiro (1888–1937)	1906–1910; 1914–1918; 1922–1926	Low
Chile	Partido Liberal (1849–1966)	1871–1891; 1896–1906; 1910–1915; 1920–1925	Medium
	Partido Conservador (1856–1949)		High
	Partido Nacional (1857–1930)	1906–1910	Low
	Partido Radical (1863–present)		High
	Partido Liberal Democrático (1893–1932)	1915–1920; 1925–1927	Low
Colombia	Partido Liberal Colombiano (1848–)	1870–1886	High
	Partido Conservador Colombiano (1849–)	1900–1910; 1914–1930	High
	Partido Nacional (1869–1902)	1886–1900	Low
	Unión Republicana (1909–1921)	1910–1914	Low
Ecuador	Partido Conservador Ecuatoriano (1883–2002)	1884–1888	Low
	Partido Liberal del Ecuador (1890–2006)	1895–1911; 1921–1952	Medium
	Partido Unión Republicano (1888–1895)	1888–1895	Low
Paraguay	Partido Colorado (1887–)	1882–1904	Medium
	Partido Liberal (1887–)	1904–1936	Medium

TABLE 4.1 (*continued*)

Country	Party name (year founded and dissolved)	Years holding the presidency, 1870–1930	Party strength (1870–1930)
Peru	Partido Civil (1871–1930)	1872–1879; 1881–1883; 1899–1912; 1915–1919	Medium
	Partido Demócrata (1884–1933)	1879–1881; 1895–1903	Low
	Partido Constitucional (1884–1930)	1886–1895	Low
	Partido Democrático Reformista (1920–1930)	1920–1930	Low
Uruguay	Partido Colorado (1836–)	1870–1930	High
	Partido Nacional (1836–)		High
Venezuela	Partido Conservador (1830–1859)	1830–1848	Low
	Partido Liberal (1840–1899)	1848–1858; 1868–1899	Low

Source: Elaborated by the author based on the historical literature.

Conservative Party, the Liberal Party, and the Radical Party), Colombia (the Conservative Party and the Liberal Party), Paraguay (the Colorado Party and the Liberal Party), and Uruguay (the Blanco Party and the Colorado Party) continued to flourished long after the transition to democracy in these countries, racking up large shares of the vote. This suggests that they had robust organizations and/or strong roots in the electorate. By contrast, parties in the other South American countries, with the exception of Ecuador, were much shorter lived, typically dissolving even before these countries democratized

EXISTING EXPLANATIONS FOR PARTY STRENGTH

What explains the variation in party strength in South America during the late nineteenth and early twentieth century? The existing theoretical literature identifies several potential explanations for the emergence of strong parties in any context, including democratization, socioeconomic modernization, and violent conflict. Although these factors all played a role in the development of parties in the region, none of them can provide a convincing explanation for the variance in party strength during this period.

One strand in the literature suggests that parties were a natural outgrowth of democratization. According to Duverger (1972, xxiii), "the development of parties seems bound up with that of democracy, that is to say with the extension of popular suffrage and parliamentary prerogatives."[5] Similarly, LaPalombara and Weiner (1966, 8) note that "it is customary in the West to associate the development of parties with the rise of parliaments and with the

---

[5] According to Epstein (1980, 19): "There is every reason to believe that modern political parties emerged with the extension of the vote to a fairly large proportion of the franchise."

gradual extension of the suffrage." They and others have argued that once the right to vote was extended to a large share of the population, it became necessary to organize parties in order to publicize the candidates' platforms and mobilize citizens to vote (Boix 2007, 500; Aldrich 1995; Epstein 1980, 19–20; Duverger 1972, xxiv). They also suggest that as legislatures became increasingly autonomous and important, like-minded representatives saw a need to coordinate their activities. In addition, a large literature has shown that partisan attachments develop over time through repeated participation in elections (Lupu and Stokes 2010; Converse 1969; Dinas 2014).[6] From this perspective, parties did not produce democracy, but rather democracy created parties. Conversely, repressive authoritarian regimes impeded the emergence of strong parties.

Certainly, the existence of elections, legislatures, and a degree of civil and political liberties were crucial to the emergence and growth of parties in South America. Parties could not arise or survive for long in exclusionary dictatorships where the rulers harshly repressed the opposition, as in Paraguay before 1870. Nevertheless, democratic institutions cannot explain the considerable variance in the strength of parties within the region since, as Chapter 2 discussed, all South American countries had elections and legislatures and a degree of civil and political liberties for much of the nineteenth and early twentieth century. Nor can the expansion of the suffrage or other democratizing measures readily explain the emergence of strong parties. Robust parties emerged during the nineteenth century in some South American countries, such as Chile, Colombia, and Uruguay, before these countries expanded the suffrage or took important steps toward democracy.[7] Moreover, in most countries, parties emerged not just to compete in elections and coordinate legislative activities but also to engage in armed struggles for power. Thus, democratic institutions provide at best a partial explanation for the rise of strong parties in the region.

Another explanation for the emergence of parties in Latin America might attribute it to socioeconomic modernization. Modernization theorists have long argued that socioeconomic development contributes to the growth of intermediary associations, including parties. Lipset (1983, 52), for example, maintains that "the propensity to form such groups seems to be a function of level of income and opportunities for leisure within given nations." LaPalombara and

---

[6] Similarly, Mainwaring and Scully (1995, 460) contend that "no single factor is more propitious for the successful institutionalization of party systems than continuously having elections that are the principal route to state power."

[7] As Chapter 2 discussed, the 1853 constitution in Colombia established universal male suffrage but it proved short-lived. In 1863, a new constitution was adopted, which allowed Colombian states to set their own suffrage restrictions and most enacted literacy or income requirements. Parties in Colombia developed over the course of the nineteenth century – they did not arise suddenly with the 1853 constitution, nor did they disappear when the 1863 constitution was enacted.

Weiner (1966, 21) go so far as to say that "parties will not in fact materialize unless a measure of modernization has already occurred." They argue that the spread of mass education, urbanization, and the development of communication and transportation networks all facilitate the rise of parties by making political organization easier (LaPalombara and Weiner 1966, 19–21). They also suggest that economic development contributes to the growth of the state and that, as the state grows in importance, individuals will form parties to try to gain control of it.

Socioeconomic modernization certainly did foster the development of parties in South America. As we shall see, urbanization, increases in literacy, and the expansion of the media and transportation networks helped strengthen parties by making it easier for party organizers to communicate with and mobilize supporters nationwide. Nevertheless, socioeconomic development cannot readily explain why strong parties emerged in some countries and not others. Although some countries that developed strong parties, such as Chile and Uruguay, were among the wealthier countries in the region in the nineteenth century, others, such as Colombia and Paraguay, were not. Moreover, as noted earlier, Argentina, the wealthiest Latin American country at that time, lagged behind Chile, Colombia, and Uruguay in the development of parties. Thus, although socioeconomic modernization played a role in the emergence of strong parties in the region, it was clearly not a determining factor.

A third approach to understanding the emergence of strong parties focuses on violent conflict. As various scholars have argued, conflict and repression can contribute to party building by mobilizing activists, generating intense partisan attachments, and encouraging an "us versus them" mentality (LeBas 2011; Levitsky, Loxton, and Van Dyck 2016, 14–21; Wood 2003). People who participate in violent struggles not only bear intense antipathies toward the side that they fight, they also frequently develop strong bonds with the people on their own side. Where the conflicts involve the loss of lives, family members of the deceased will frequently come to share these intense attachments and antipathies even though they may not have participated directly in the conflicts themselves. These intense feelings, moreover, are often passed down over generations, thereby leading to the endurance of partisan loyalties over time.

Clearly, interparty civil wars during the nineteenth century played an important role in generating strong partisan ties in some South American countries, such as Colombia and Uruguay (López-Alves 2000; Zeitlin 1984; Somma 2011). Where opposition parties engaged in repeated uprisings that were violently repressed, they gradually developed committed local leaders and strong partisan ties to the population. Moreover, in an era of suffrage restrictions and limited voter turnout, civil wars often engaged more people than elections did, which enabled parties to become mass vehicles (Safford 1974, 74). Nevertheless, violent conflict cannot readily explain the variance in party strength since interparty wars were common throughout the region. Indeed, as Chapters 7 and 8 discuss, some countries that did not develop strong parties during the nineteenth century, such as Bolivia, Ecuador, Peru, and Venezuela, suffered as much internal political violence as the countries that did have strong parties. In addition, Chile developed strong parties in the late nineteenth century even though it suffered less violent conflict during this period than most South American countries.

As we shall see, religious and territorial cleavages and the degree of geographic fragmentation provide a more compelling explanation for variation in party strength in the region than do democratization, development, or violent conflict. Strong parties tended to arise in countries with intense yet balanced religious or territorial cleavages and low levels of geographic fragmentation.

SOCIAL CLEAVAGES AND PARTIES

Scholars have long argued that social cleavages, including class, ethnic, religious, and territorial divisions, have driven party formation in Europe and elsewhere (Lipset and Rokkan 1967; Caramani 2004; Bartolini and Mair 1990; Rokkan 1970). In South America, however, class and ethnic cleavages played virtually no role in the initial emergence of parties in the region, in part because they divided the population into haves and have nots. By contrast, religious and territorial cleavages generated numerous parties in the region during the nineteenth century, in part because wealthy and powerful people and institutions tended to be located on both sides of these cleavages and they could use their resources for party building. Religious and territorial cleavages only led to the emergence of strong parties, however, where they divided the population into two similarly powerful groups, which prevented one side from dominating the other and fostered long-term competition for power.

Lipset and Rokkan (1967, 14) contend that the process of building nation-states created two central cleavages in Europe: the division between the center and periphery (or what they call the dominant culture and the subject cultures); and the conflict between secular forces and the Church. The Industrial Revolution, meanwhile, produced two other important cleavages: the divide between industry and agriculture; and the class cleavage, which pitted employers against workers. In Europe, parties arose to represent people on both sides of these cleavages: workers as well as employers; rural as well as urban interests; conservative Catholics as well as anti-clerical liberals; and ethnolinguistic minorities as well as majorities. Moreover, the party systems that emerged often froze in place – that is, the parties that had arisen from the cleavages continued to dominate even after the cleavages waned in importance (Lipset and Rokkan 1967).[8]

---

[8] Party competition may also shape social cleavages, deepening their societal importance (Bartolini 2000; Mainwaring and Torcal 2003; Bartolini and Mair 1990).

In any society, however, there are numerous cleavages that never become politicized or reflected in the partisan arena and, even if they do, they often fail to translate into strong parties. Cleavages are more likely to give birth to strong parties if they embody issues central to the identity of much of the population or involve strongly held beliefs or important interests. Cleavages that divide the population into large groups that have an important presence throughout a nation's territory are also more likely to produce strong national parties than cleavages that only hive off very small segments of the population or are relevant in only a few areas of a country. As Caramani (2004) has shown, the class cleavage and the church–state cleavage played an important role in nationalizing European party systems because these cleavages were relevant throughout much of the territory of most European countries.

The mere existence of social cleavages, even profound ones that resonate throughout a country's territory, does not guarantee the emergence of parties based on these cleavages, however. Parties do not spring naturally from cleavages; they must be created by individuals or organizations. The most successful and enduring parties are typically established by political entrepreneurs with ample networks and resources. In many instances, societal organizations have played a key role in forming and supporting parties that represented a particular cleavage. Unions, for example, helped create many socialist parties in Europe and provided them with activists, leaders, and supporters as well as financing (Bartolini 2000). Similarly, priests and various associations and individuals affiliated with the Catholic Church provided the base for conservative parties during the nineteenth century and Christian democratic parties in the twentieth century (Kalyvas 1996; Mainwaring and Scully 2003).

Neither ethnic cleavages nor class cleavages produced important political parties in Latin America during the nineteenth and early twentieth century, in large part because members of subordinate classes and ethnic groups lacked the political networks and organizational and financial resources necessary to create parties. Latin American countries had significant ethnic diversity during the nineteenth century, with large populations of indigenous people and Afro-Latinos, but only the European-origin population had the networks and resources to create political parties. Moreover, in many countries, most indigenous and Afro-Latino people were not even eligible to vote during the nineteenth and early twentieth century because they were poor, illiterate, or in relations of dependency.

The development of class-based parties in the nineteenth century and early twentieth century was also stymied by voting restrictions and the unequal distribution of financial and organizational resources. The rural peasantry represented a huge share of the population during this period, but in many countries the majority of peasants could not vote because of income and literacy restrictions. Moreover, peasants were often in the thrall of landowners and lacked the resources to form parties. Voting restrictions and a dearth of financial and organizational resources similarly obstructed party formation among the urban working classes, which were still relatively small during the nineteenth and early twentieth century. Industrialization came much later in Latin America than in Europe and the United States. Labor unions first emerged in Latin America during the late nineteenth century, but these unions initially had tiny memberships and little influence. In addition, many unions had anarcho-syndicalist tendencies during this period and eschewed involvement in political parties and electoral politics. In some countries, leaders founded socialist parties or other parties that sought to represent the workers, but only in Argentina did a socialist party gain a significant following by the early twentieth century, and even there, its support remained confined mostly to the capital (Walter 1977).

The middle classes had greater financial and educational resources and participated in many of the important political parties that emerged during this period. Some major parties of this era, such as the Radical parties of Argentina and Chile, gradually embraced the interests of the middle classes and became middle-class dominated, but this did not typically occur until well into the twentieth century. In the late nineteenth and early twentieth century, the Latin American middle classes were still relatively small, and they did not have significant class consciousness, which impeded the development of parties based in the middle classes.

During the nineteenth century, many parties sprang from territorial cleavages in South America, but in most cases these parties did not develop into strong parties. The first parties in South America typically arose in cities because they had the densest concentration of elites, organizations, and resources, and spatial proximity made it easier for parties to organize and mobilize voters. Capital cities, in particular, fostered parties because of the size and density of their populations and their proximity to the government. These parties, however, generally represented urban interests, which made it difficult for them to win support in rural areas. In addition, as we shall see, geographical barriers impeded travel and communication, making it difficult for urban-based parties to extend their reach into the provinces. Provincial parties faced even more daunting obstacles to party building, given the difficulty of campaigning and building bases of support among dispersed populations in far-flung regions. Moreover, territorial identities and rivalries often made it difficult for a party founded in one province or city to win support in others. As a result, while many parties emerged that represented a single city or province, few of these organizations developed into strong national parties. Some politicians managed to stitch together networks of supporters in various regions, but these alliances tended to be temporary and the parties that emerged from them were typically highly decentralized, weakly institutionalized, and prone to splits (Gibson 1996, 34–36).

Only in Uruguay did territorial cleavages give birth to strong parties.[9] As we shall see, Uruguay's small size and absence of geographical barriers facilitated

---

[9] Territorial cleavages shaped party systems in some other countries, such as Chile and Colombia, but the religious cleavage played the dominant role in structuring their party systems.

Social Cleavages and Parties

the construction of strong national parties. Moreover, the relative balance in resources and population between the capital city, Montevideo, and the countryside facilitated the development of a party system along center–periphery lines. Prolonged warfare between the two regions, including a siege of Montevideo that lasted years, helped strengthen partisan identities in Uruguay and laid the groundwork for the emergence of these parties. As discussed later in this chapter, balanced cleavages contribute to the construction of strong party systems by encouraging enduring political competition along cleavage lines and preventing one side from dominating the other.

Most important parties in South America during the nineteenth century arose from a religious cleavage, namely the cleavage between secular liberals and religious conservatives. Although this cleavage waned in importance in the twentieth century, in some cases the party systems that had emerged based on this cleavage endured. Throughout the nineteenth century, conservative and liberal politicians formed parties to promote their programmatic aims as well as their political ambitions. Conservative parties defended the prerogatives of the Catholic Church, whereas liberal parties favored freedom of religion and the separation of church and state. The liberal critics of the Church drew inspiration in part from Europe and the United States where liberal ideas were increasingly dominant in the wake of the Enlightenment. Although many Latin American liberals were practicing Catholics, they viewed the Church as an obstacle to progress and they resented its wealth and power.[10] Not only was the Church the largest landowner in Latin America, but it controlled numerous institutions, from schools and hospitals to cemeteries and civil registries.

Conservative and liberal parties often differed on a range of other issues as well, including federalism, free trade, and civil and political rights, but these issues did not generate the same degree of passion as religious differences. Moreover, their positions on these other issues tended to vary over time and across countries (Bushnell and Macaulay 1994, 33–35; Safford 1974, 72). For example, liberals often supported and conservatives frequently opposed federalism, free trade, and individual rights, but at times their positions were reversed.

Political parties arose from the religious cleavage in large part because it involved strongly held beliefs. Conservatives believed themselves to be the true defenders of the faith, and liberals viewed themselves as voices of reason, science, and progress. Religious fervor was often widespread among the population, and religious beliefs tended to provoke considerable passion, which politicians used to mobilize their supporters. According to Bushnell and Macaulay (1994, 35), conservatives "quickly discovered that religion was the most effective single cause with which to stir the popular masses into action on their side."

---

[10] Many Latin American liberals also resented the Church's support for the Spanish Crown in the wars of independence.

Conservative supporters of the Church largely dominated Latin American governments during the first decades after independence, but liberals gradually gained control of the governments of many countries in the latter half of the nineteenth century and began to enact secularizing reforms that separated church and state, established freedom of religion, and stripped the Church of some of its property and institutions (Lynch 2012; Mecham 1966). Conservatives objected strenuously to these measures, creating parties and sometimes taking up arms to resist the liberal reforms.

Conservative and liberal parties, like those based in the center and the periphery, typically only evolved into strong parties where the religious cleavage was important and relatively balanced – that is, where both sides had numerous supporters and ample resources, as in Colombia and Chile. Unlike class and ethnic cleavages, powerful figures and organizations with substantial resources were often found on both sides of the religious divide.[11] The founders of successful parties used their networks, constituencies, and resources to form and sustain the parties. Conservatives drew on the resources and networks of the Catholic Church, which was the most powerful national organization in nineteenth-century Latin America. The Church provided manpower as well as ideological support to conservative parties, "with the parish priest often serving as conservative ward boss in elections and even as recruiting officer in times of revolution" (Bushnell and Macaulay 1994, 35). The Church also controlled numerous charitable organizations, hospitals, and schools, all of which could be put at the service of conservative parties. Liberals, meanwhile, typically enjoyed the support of universities and schools, Masonic lodges, associations of firefighters, and literary societies. These institutions provided them with candidates, activists, and platforms for their campaigns.

Only where both sides of the cleavage were relatively strong did political entrepreneurs on each side typically have the incentives and the resources to build powerful parties. Where neither side dominated, each side of a cleavage felt pressure to invest in parties to keep up with or surpass the other. Party building in these countries often had a mutually reinforcing dynamic, with each side copying the other's organizational investments and innovations. Elections were also more likely to be closely contested where the two sides were evenly matched, which contributed to party building since participating regularly in contested elections obliged the parties to engage in frequent organizing and campaigning. Where a cleavage divided the population relatively equally, parties typically made extensive ideological appeals since there

---

[11] The church–state and center–periphery cleavages constituted what Horowitz (1985, 21–24) termed unranked systems. By contrast, ethnic and class cleavages in Latin America created ranked systems since they divided the population into a clear socioeconomic hierarchy. Indigenous people, Afro-Latinos, workers, and peasants were at the bottom of this hierarchy and thus lacked the kind of political connections, experience, and resources that facilitated party building.

were ample members on each side who would be receptive to such appeals. The appeals galvanized their supporters and antagonized members of the other side, thus helping to build partisan loyalties.

By contrast, elections tended to be contested less frequently where only one side of a cleavage was strong, since parties representing the weaker side typically had little chance of winning. As a result, both sides campaigned less frequently, established weaker ties to the electorate, and made fewer investments in parties. Even when contested elections did occur, the fact that the results were largely preordained discouraged both sides from campaigning extensively or building parties. The stronger side often eschewed making significant investments in party building because it did not need a strong party to dominate, whereas the weaker side often viewed party building as futile. The weaker side might run candidates in areas where it was strong, but not throughout the entire country, which prevented it from developing into a national party. In some cases, the weaker side also eschewed party building because it lacked the necessary leaders and resources.

Where cleavages were unbalanced, the leading candidates for national offices tended to come from the dominant side of the cleavage, often representing different factions of the same political party. Under these circumstances, competition tended to take a personalistic form, rather than an ideological one, since the different factions usually represented the same general ideology. These factions typically eschewed investments in organization and frequently did not survive the death or decline of their founding leaders. In some countries where cleavages were unbalanced, parties representing the weaker side failed to emerge or become serious competitors for political power. In other countries with unbalanced cleavages, parties representing the weaker side initially had some influence but became increasingly marginalized over time or disappeared altogether. In both cases, the failure of the weaker side to develop or maintain a strong party discouraged the stronger side from making investments in party building as well.

Where both sides of a cleavage were weak, strong parties also typically failed to emerge. Under these circumstances, neither side typically had the personnel or organizational resources to invest in party building. Moreover, prospects for party building were dim if neither side had many potential supporters to recruit.

Unfortunately, there are no time-series data on the strength of liberals and conservatives in nineteenth-century Latin America, but Mahoney (2003, 78) provides estimates of their strength between 1700 and 1850. Mahoney's estimates have the advantage that they predate the emergence of liberal and conservative parties and thus are presumably exogenous from them. The disadvantage of his estimates is that they do not reflect the changes in the relative power of conservatives and liberals that took place during this period. As Table 4.2 indicates, only three South American countries – Argentina, Chile, and Colombia – had strong conservatives as well as strong liberals. Moreover,

TABLE 4.2 *Liberal and conservative strength in South America, 1700–1850*

	Strength of liberals	Strength of conservatives	Degree of balance between liberals and conservatives
Argentina	Very high	Medium	Balanced
Bolivia	Very low	High	Unbalanced
Brazil	High	Low	Unbalanced
Chile	Very high	Medium	Balanced
Colombia	Very high	Very high	Balanced
Ecuador	Low	High	Unbalanced
Paraguay	Low	High	Unbalanced
Peru	Low	Very high	Unbalanced
Uruguay	Very high	Very low	Unbalanced
Venezuela	Very high	Low	Unbalanced

Source: Mahoney (2003, 78).
Note: I used the following scale in converting Mahoney's (2003, 78) scores. Countries receiving scores of 1.00 and 0.83 were coded as very high; 0.67 as high; 0.50 as medium; 0.33 as low; and 0.17 and 0.00 as very low. I scored Brazil because Mahoney only coded Spanish-American nations.

according to Mahoney, only Colombia had very strong liberals and very strong conservatives. The remaining countries had either strong liberals (Brazil, Uruguay, and Venezuela) or strong conservatives (Bolivia, Ecuador, Paraguay, and Peru) but not both.[12]

What led to the development of strong conservatives and/or strong liberals in some countries and not others? The strength of conservatives was closely tied to the influence of the Catholic Church (Middlebrook 2000a), which in turn was shaped by ethno-racial demographics and human geography. The Catholic Church and conservatives tended to be stronger in inland and rural regions where tradition prevailed and rates of religiosity were high. Areas with large indigenous populations also tended to be a stronghold of conservatives and the Catholic Church. Indeed, the countries where conservatives were strongest – Bolivia, Colombia, Ecuador, Paraguay, and Peru – all had sizable indigenous populations in the nineteenth century. During the colonial era, the Church proselytized extensively in indigenous communities and grew wealthy in part owing to its ability to extract indigenous tribute and exploit indigenous labor. A strong and wealthy Church helped promote conservative ideology.

---

[12] Mahoney (2003, 80) was more interested in the economic than the religious differences between liberals and conservatives, but, as he noted, they typically went together. In coding conservative strength, he considered "the social, political, and economic prominence of those merchant guilds, landlords, and bureaucrats that represented the core of conservative factions," and to score liberal strength he focused on "those free-market merchants, urban professionals, and intellectuals that made up the core of liberal movements" (Mahoney 2003, 95).

By contrast, liberals tended to be stronger in cities and coastal areas. These areas tended to be more open to international influences and to depend on and support free trade, which liberals often espoused. Liberals also tended to be stronger in countries with large European-origin populations. To a significant extent, liberal ideas originated in Europe and were diffused throughout Latin America by European immigrants (Gerring et al. 2022). Countries with large Afro-Latino populations also tended to be a stronghold of liberals, as Table 4.2 shows. During the colonial era, the Church proselytized less in Afro-Latino communities, barred Afro-Latinos from the priesthood, and tolerated and even practiced slavery, all of which undermined the standing of the Church and conservatives among Afro-Latinos. Liberals, by contrast, often opposed slavery and made efforts to win support among the Afro-Latino population. Thus, liberal strength was correlated with the density of the Afro-Latino and European population as well as the percentage of the population that lived on or near the coast.

Nevertheless, we must be careful not to overstate the impact of human geography on the varying strength of conservatives and liberals. Nor should we exaggerate the impact that balanced social cleavages had on party development in the region. Although these variables were important, other factors also helped shape the fate of parties in the region.

GEOGRAPHIC FRAGMENTATION

The prospects for party building in South America during the nineteenth century were also shaped by the level of geographic fragmentation of the countries. I define geographic fragmentation as the degree to which a country's population is dispersed into different geographic zones. Geographic fragmentation matters for party building because it determines the ease with which parties can build national organizations and broad networks of supporters. During the nineteenth century, politicians in geographically fragmented countries had difficulty building national parties because they could not easily travel to or communicate with voters in many areas of their countries; nor could they establish or manage branches or affiliated organizations in these areas. Moreover, national identities tended to be weaker in geographically fragmented countries, and regional voters and politicians often distrusted national party leaders. By contrast, politicians had an easier time developing national organizations and followings in the smaller countries where the population was geographically concentrated.[13]

There are a variety of ways to measure geographic fragmentation. One recent study by the Inter-American Development Bank (IADB) measured

---

[13] Geographically fragmented countries are more likely to be politically decentralized, which may also impede the development of strong national parties (Chhibber and Kollman 2004; Harbers 2010). Nevertheless, some of the geographically fragmented South American countries, such as Bolivia, Ecuador, and Peru, were unitary states throughout the nineteenth century.

geographical fragmentation as the probability that two people taken at random lived in different ecozones (Gallup, Gaviria, and Lora 2003, 11–12). This study found that Latin America was the most geographically fragmented region in the world (Gallup, Gaviria, and Lora 2003, 11). Ecuador, Colombia, Peru, Bolivia, and Brazil had the highest level of geographic fragmentation within South America, whereas Argentina, Chile, Paraguay, and Uruguay had the lowest level of geographic fragmentation (listed in order from the most fragmented to the least).[14] The IADB study measured geographic fragmentation in the late twentieth century, but the level of fragmentation in Latin America was almost certainly worse during the nineteenth century when urbanization rates were quite low.

Unfortunately, given data limitations, it is not possible to produce a similar index for South American countries in the late nineteenth or early twentieth century, but it is clear from the data that do exist that geographically concentrated countries produced much stronger parties than geographically fragmented nations. Of the countries that produced medium or strong parties in the nineteenth or early twentieth century, only Colombia had a high level of geographic fragmentation. Table 4.3 provides several indicators of geographical fragmentation circa 1900. The table shows that countries with fewer geographical barriers, smaller territories, denser populations, and larger cities had stronger parties on average. Railroad track and telegraph lines also covered a greater percentage of the territory in countries with strong parties than in countries with weak parties. In spite of the small number of observations, the differences in means are statistically significant at the 0.5 level (two-tailed t-tests) for all of the variables except territorial size and population per square kilometer. The last two variables are statistically insignificant because both Argentina and Colombia had relatively large territories and low population density in 1900.

Political entrepreneurs in the geographically fragmented South American countries faced daunting obstacles to the creation of national parties during the nineteenth century. As Table 4.3 indicates, most of the countries with weak parties had immense territories.[15] Brazil alone covered 8.5 million square kilometers at the outset of the twentieth century (República de Chile 1907, xiii).[16] All of these countries also had significant internal geographic barriers, such as enormous mountain ranges, swamps, forests, and jungles. The Andes, for example, separated the lowlands and the highlands of Bolivia, Ecuador, and Peru, and made journeys long and often treacherous. Moreover, during the nineteenth century,

---

[14] The study did not score the level of geographic fragmentation in Venezuela.
[15] Ecuador was much smaller than most of the other South American countries, but it was one of the most geographically fragmented countries in the region.
[16] Some South American countries, such as Bolivia, Peru, and Paraguay, lost considerable land owing to their defeat in wars during the late nineteenth century, while other countries, namely, Argentina, Brazil, and Chile, acquired more territory because of their victories.

TABLE 4.3 *Geographic fragmentation in South America circa 1900*

Country	Internal geographic barriers	Largest city/total population (%)	Territory in km²	Population per km²	Railroad track/ territory (%)	Telegraph lines/ territory (%)
Countries with medium to strong parties						
Argentina	Low	17.1	2,806,400	1.6	0.590	2.48
Chile	Low	10.2	757,366	4.3	0.575	3.66
Colombia	High	2.4	1,135,550	4.0	0.056	1.55
Paraguay	Low	9.8	253,100	2.5	0.099	0.96
Uruguay	Low	29.7	186,926	5.2	0.925	6.61
Average	Low	13.8*	1,027,868	3.5	0.449*	3.05*
Countries with weak parties						
Bolivia	High	3.7	1,226,600	1.4	0.043	0.40
Brazil	High	4.0	8,528,218	1.7	0.179	0.40
Ecuador	High	3.9	307,243	4.1	0.163	1.72
Peru	High	4.4	1,769,804	2.6	0.101	0.47
Venezuela	Medium	3.1	942,300	2.7	0.090	1.13
Average	High	3.8*	2,554,833	2.5	0.115*	0.82*

Sources: Largest city populations: Capello (2006, 133); Kleinpenning (1992, 477); Morse (1974, 435–443); and República de Bolivia (1900, 125). Railroad track: Summerhill (2006, 302). Telegraph lines: Banks and Wilson (2014). Territory and population: República de Chile (1907, xiii).
Note: * A t-test comparing means between countries with strong and weak parties is significant at the 0.05 level for these variables.

the population of these countries was typically spread throughout their territories, rather than being concentrated in one region or city. In Peru, for example, the population was relatively evenly divided among the northern, central, and southern departments, according to the 1876 census (Gootenberg 1991, 112–115). In the geographically fragmented countries, the largest city typically accounted for less than 5 percent of the country's population.

To make matters worse, transportation infrastructure was extremely poor during the nineteenth century (Summerhill 2006). Roads were often little more than bridle paths, bridges were scarce, and railroads were absent in most of the region. The weather could also be a major obstacle. During the 1800s, the road from Guayaquil to Quito was often impassable during the six-month rainy season and the trip took 14–21 days in the dry season, involving travel on foot as well as by mule (Henderson 2008, 7; Rodríguez 1985, 16). The capitals of some of these countries, such as Bogotá, La Paz, and Quito, were located far inland, which precluded oceangoing transport, and South America had few navigable rivers connecting major cities. Even where it was possible to use ships to travel from one city to another, the trip was not necessarily an easy one. Indeed, during the nineteenth century, it took more time to travel by boat from some states in northeastern Brazil to Rio de Janeiro than it took to sail from these states to Portugal (Graham 1990, 45).

The infrastructure gradually improved over the course of the nineteenth century. Many South American countries invested in roads. The government of Antonio Guzmán Blanco in Venezuela, for example, built 720 miles of roads during his first administration (1870–1877), more than double the number that had been built during the previous thirty years (Floyd 1982, 103). Governments also invested in telegraph and railroad lines. In 1870, Latin America had only 4,065 kilometers of railroad track, but this rose to 54,151 kilometers in 1900 and 115,786 kilometers in 1930 (Summerhill 2006, 302). The growth in telegraph lines was even more dramatic: South America had only 4,000 miles of telegraph lines in 1870, but by 1900 it had 73,000 miles and by 1930 it had 183,000 miles (Banks and Wilson 2014). Nevertheless, the region still had relatively limited and unreliable communications and transportation networks at the beginning of the twentieth century. The telegraph lines frequently broke down, and the railroads typically only linked together a few major cities – often only those in close proximity to each other. Moreover, the vast majority of the population in South America lived in rural areas during the nineteenth century, and thus had limited access to the telegraph and railroad lines.

Geographical fragmentation impeded the development of national parties in several ways. The obstacles to communication and travel made it difficult for politicians and party leaders to campaign throughout the country, which meant it was hard for them to build up a national following. The barriers to communication and transportation also obstructed the creation of national organizations. Party leaders could not easily establish or manage regional branches or affiliated organizations. Nor could they ensure that regional leaders and affiliates hewed to the party line. In addition, geographical fragmentation strengthened local identities. During the nineteenth century, people in different regions typically identified with their region more than their country. Voters and politicians often distrusted candidates and parties from the capital or other regions, which made it difficult for them to establish a national base of support. Geographical fragmentation did not make it impossible to establish strong parties. Strong parties arose in Colombia even though it was extremely geographically fragmented. Nevertheless, geographical fragmentation represented a significant obstacle to party building.

By contrast, the geographically compact South American countries had significant advantages when it came to party building. In Chile, Paraguay, Uruguay, and to a lesser extent Argentina, the bulk of the population was concentrated in a small area, in or near the capital city. The concentration of the population, along with the lack of internal geographical obstacles and the development of railroad and telegraph lines, made travel and communication between different parts of these nations easier. This, in turn, enabled politicians and parties to develop countrywide followings and to manage national organizations. The geographical concentration of the population also facilitated the construction of party organizations and followings by strengthening national identities. Thus, it is not surprising that these four countries were among the first in South America to establish strong, national parties.[17]

In sum, the level of geographic fragmentation combined with the nature of religious and territorial cleavages to shape party building in South America during the nineteenth and early twentieth century. To be sure, the level of geographic fragmentation and the nature of religious and territorial cleavages were not the only factors to influence party building in South America during this period, but they were the most important ones. The countries that had both balanced religious/territorial cleavages and geographically compact populations, namely Chile and Uruguay, developed parties that ranked among the strongest in the region by the late nineteenth century. Those countries that were geographically compact but lacked balanced cleavages (or vice versa), such as Argentina and Paraguay, were typically slower to develop strong parties, but by the early twentieth century, these countries had developed one or more parties of at least medium strength. The exception was Colombia, which developed two strong parties by the end of the nineteenth century even though it was not geographically compact. Colombia managed to develop strong parties not just because it had a balanced religious cleavage but also because this cleavage generated particularly intense and widely felt passions. Indeed, Colombia was the only country that Mahoney coded as having very high concentrations of both conservatives and liberals. Finally, the countries that had neither balanced cleavages, nor geographically compact populations, had only weak parties during the late nineteenth and early twentieth century. This includes Bolivia, Brazil, Ecuador, Peru, and Venezuela.

CONCLUSION

As we have seen, parties first emerged in South America in the middle of the nineteenth century, but only in some countries did they grow strong before 1930. Religious and territorial cleavages significantly shaped the development of political parties in South America. Strong parties arose in countries, such as Chile, Colombia, and Uruguay, where religious or center–periphery cleavages were intense and relatively balanced. Where both sides of a religious or territorial cleavage were strong, neither could dominate the other and each side had

---

[17] Even today, the smaller, more centralized, and less geographically fragmented countries of South America tend to have stronger, more nationalized, and more institutionalized party systems than the larger, more decentralized, and more geographically fragmented countries. See the data in Harbers (2010), Jones and Mainwaring (2003), and Mainwaring (2018).

incentives to invest in party building in order to prevail in elections. By contrast, where only one side of the cleavage was strong, there were few incentives to invest in party building, and parties tended to be ephemeral, personalistic, and weak.

The fate of parties in nineteenth-century South America was also shaped by human geography. Strong parties arose in countries, such as Chile, Paraguay, and Uruguay, where the bulk of the population was concentrated in a relatively small area with minimal geographical barriers. In these countries, politicians and party leaders could more easily campaign throughout the country, establish and manage regional branches, and develop a national organization and base of support. By contrast, geographically fragmented countries typically gave birth to weak parties. These countries usually had strong regional identities and significant barriers to internal travel and communication, which made it difficult to develop national organizations and ties to a large share of the electorate.

Chapters 5–8 show how the emergence of strong political parties in South America during the nineteenth and early twentieth century facilitated democratization in the region. Strong parties not only helped increase voter turnout and political competition but also played a key role in the enactment of democratic reforms that expanded the suffrage and established free and fair elections. In addition, strong parties facilitated the implementation and enforcement of these democratic reforms and reduced the likelihood of military coups. These positive effects tended to occur where at least one of the strong parties was in the opposition. Moreover, these parties had to be committed to taking power via elections, which typically only occurred once the emergence of a professional military impeded them from taking power via armed revolt.

5

The Roots of Strong Democracies
Chile and Uruguay

For most of the nineteenth century, the governments of Chile and Uruguay routinely intervened in elections to ensure that their preferred candidates won, and the opposition, especially in Uruguay, engaged in periodic armed revolts, which led to state repression. The turn of the century, however, brought dramatic changes to both countries. In the 1890s, Chile began to hold highly competitive and relatively free and fair elections, and the opposition largely respected the outcomes, rather than resorting to armed revolts. A similar transformation took place a couple of decades later in Uruguay. Moreover, both countries managed to remain democratic for most of the twentieth century.

What led to the establishment of democracy in Chile and Uruguay during this period? And why did democracy remain relatively stable in both countries, particularly compared to the rest of the region?

The professionalization of the military, which took place in Chile in the late nineteenth century and in Uruguay in the early twentieth century, represented a crucial first step in the democratization process because it helped the state establish a monopoly on the use of violence. As a result, the opposition in both countries gradually abandoned the armed struggle and began to focus on the electoral path to power. The decline in revolts, in turn, led the state to engage in less repression and to allow for greater civil and political liberties.

The development of organized parties also played a crucial role in the emergence of democracy in the two countries. As we have seen, strong parties arose in Chile and Uruguay in the late nineteenth century thanks both to the geographic concentration of the population as well as the existence of an intense but relatively balanced religious or territorial cleavage. Opposition parties in both countries used their influence to promote democratic reforms in the nineteenth century, but the ruling parties generally blocked or watered down their proposals. The opposition was only able to enact transformative reforms when major splits occurred within the ruling party that gave the opposition temporary control of the relevant law-making bodies. In Chile, the split helped the opposition enact an 1890 reform that established the secret ballot and stripped the government of control of the electoral process. In Uruguay, a split within the ruling party gave the opposition control of the 1917 constituent assembly, which allowed it to push through measures establishing universal male suffrage, the secret ballot, and proportional representation.

In the wake of these reforms, both Chile and Uruguay established relatively strong democracies, which lasted, with only brief interruptions, until the 1970s. Neither country initially became a full democracy because important suffrage restrictions remained and some electoral shenanigans, such as vote buying, continued. Nevertheless, governments scrupulously observed civil and political rights and administered relatively free and fair elections in which the opposition at times defeated the incumbents.

REVOLTS AND MILITARY PROFESSIONALIZATION IN CHILE

Although Chile has traditionally been viewed as a country that enjoyed considerable political stability during the nineteenth century, for much of the century it suffered from frequent revolts. Chile, for example, experienced major civil wars in 1829–1830, 1851, 1859, and 1891, along with numerous smaller revolts and a long-running conflict with the Mapuche indigenous population in the south (see Table 5.1).[1] These revolts, which were encouraged by the initial weakness of the armed forces, deepened authoritarian rule in Chile. It was not until the Chilean government professionalized its military in the late nineteenth century that the opposition revolts subsided and democracy gradually emerged.

Chile had only a weak military in its first decades as a republic. Independence had been won in large part by the Army of the Andes, which was composed of and led mostly by Argentines (Ossa Santa Cruz 2014; Collier and Sater 1996, 37). Although the Chilean General Bernardo O'Higgins subsequently assembled a Chilean army of almost 5,000 soldiers, this army was ill paid and poorly organized and equipped (Terrie 2014, 114–115; Nunn 1976, 23; Hillmon Jr. 1963, 34–35). According to Nunn (1976, 20): "By 1823, when O'Higgins fell, the army's thirteen-year history was one of privation, poor organization, inconsistent support, and generally incompetent leadership. Seven years later the situation was worse." Military officers lacked training and the troops were undisciplined. There were sixteen military mutinies in 1825–1829 alone, most of which were motivated by dissatisfaction with the lack of payment of military salaries (Varas 2017, 88; Maldonado 2019, 24–26).

---

[1] In an 1867 pamphlet, Liberals and Radicals maintained that the military and national guard had suppressed more than 100 conspiracies and mutinies, in addition to the two civil wars, since 1833 (cited in Valenzuela 1985, 142).

TABLE 5.1 *Major revolts in Chile, 1830–1929*

Year	Description of revolt	Type of revolt (outcome)
1829–1830	Conservatives with the assistance of Army of the South overthrew the Liberal government because of an electoral dispute. The rebels mobilized 2,200 troops.	Elite insurrection (took power)
1837	Colonel José Antonio Vidaurre and 1,000 men rebelled against Peru-Bolivia war. The rebels assassinated Minister Diego Portales but they were defeated.	Military coup (suppressed)
1851	Liberals in the Society of Equality rebelled with the support of the Valdivia battalion. The government suppressed the uprising.	Elite insurrection (suppressed)
1851	Opposition presidential candidate, General José de la Cruz, rebelled with support of some troops and Liberals/Radicals. The rebels surrendered.	Elite insurrection (suppressed)
1859	Radicals led by mining millionaire José Pedro Gallo rebelled and assembled a 2,000-men army but were defeated by the military.	Elite insurrection (suppressed)
1859–1881	The Mapuche carried out a series of intermittent revolts in response to settler incursions in the south. The uprisings were brutally repressed.	Popular uprising (suppressed)
1891	The congressional opposition rebelled against President José Manuel Balmaceda. The army remained loyal, but the navy helped the opposition triumph.	Elite insurrection (took power)
1924	A military junta led by General Luis Altamirano took power and sent President Arturo Alessandri into exile.	Military coup (took power)
1925	Military officers arrested Altamirano and a new governing junta with a civilian head invited Alessandri to resume his presidency.	Military coup (took power)

Source: Latin American Revolts Database.

During the 1830s, the government restructured the military and reduced its size to put the government on sounder fiscal footing. An 1834 law fixed the size of the army at 3,000 men and it remained near this number for most of the next several decades (Arancibia Clavel 2007, 132; Somma 2011, 397). As a result of these efforts, military spending began to decline, falling to 37.5 percent of government expenditures in 1835, 32 percent in 1845, and 26 percent in 1855 (Somma 2011, 397). At the same time, however, the government expanded the national guard in order to help suppress internal rebellions and serve as a counterbalance to the military (Nunn 1976, 41; Collier and Sater 1996, 56; Hillmon Jr. 1963, 44).[2] By the 1850s, the national guard exceeded

---

[2] In response to opposition conspiracies in 1832–1833, the Prieto administration also created a secret police, which helped stifle opposition activity and lasted for thirty-two years (Nunn 1976, 43).

60,000 men, but its troops were poorly trained and equipped and it was gradually disbanded in the late nineteenth century (Wood 2011, 86–88; Somma 2011, 398).

The initial weakness of the military encouraged revolts. Opposition revolts were particularly common in the immediate post-independence period. Galdama (1964, 230) reports: "From 1826 to 1830 Chile lived in a state of constant disturbance. Different congresses and supreme directors succeeded each other and executed such measure of organization as they could and soon fell, defeated by revolts and military coups that had no more justification than the caprice of their leaders." One of these revolts led to the Chilean civil war of 1829–1830. In this war, Conservatives, who were angry about the disputed election of the vice-president as well as the fraud that the government had committed in the previous legislative elections, rebelled against the governing Liberals. The weakness and lack of discipline of the military, combined with the support the opposition received from army units in the south, enabled the Conservatives to prevail.[3]

The 1829–1830 civil war ushered in an era of relatively stable Conservative rule in which presidents generally served out their terms, but it did not bring an end to revolts. To the contrary, there were at least twenty attempts to overthrow the government between 1830 and 1837 (Heise González 1978, 207; Terrie 2014, 130). Many of these efforts originated among the Liberal officers and leaders who had been purged after the 1829–1830 civil war. In 1833, Liberals planned two insurrections, known as the Arteaga Conspiracy and the Conspiracy of the Daggers, both of which sought unsuccessfully to topple the government (Wood 2011, 92–95). In 1836, General Ramón Freire, who had led the Liberal army in the 1829–1830 civil war, hatched a plan, with the support of some other Liberal leaders, to invade southern Chile with two warships rented from the Peru–Bolivian Confederation (Arancibia Clavel 2007, 135–136).[4] The invasion failed, but the Chilean government subsequently declared war on the Peru–Bolivian Confederation and assumed emergency powers, shutting down Congress and suspending constitutional rights (Wood 2011, 100–101). In June 1837, Colonel José Antonio Vidaurre, who opposed the war, rebelled with more than 1,000 men and took as a hostage the minister of war, Diego Portales. The rebels called for a return to constitutional government, the toleration of political opposition, and the abrogation of the mass discharges of Liberal officers that had taken place after the 1829–1830 civil

---

[3] The Conservatives had on their side important military leaders, such as General José Joaquín Prieto and Colonel Manuel Bulnes, who commanded army units in the south. In the decisive battle at Lircay, the Conservative army of the south defeated the smaller Liberal or Constitutional army, which consisted principally of the Santiago garrison (Fernández Abara 2017, 55; Collier and Sater 1996, 50; Somma 2011, 357).

[4] The Peru–Bolivian Confederation was an alliance that brought together northern and southern Peru and Bolivia in a single state from 1836 to 1839.

war. The uprising was eventually suppressed with the assistance of 1,800 civic guard troops, but not before the rebels executed Minister Portales.

Chile did not experience another major uprising until 1851. The catalyst of the 1851 rebellion was the election of Manuel Montt, as the handpicked candidate of the incumbent president, General Manuel Bulnes.[5] The Society of Equality, an organization that grouped together liberal intellectuals and artisans in Santiago, opposed Montt, and in April 1851 they enlisted a recently retired army colonel, Pedro Urriola, to carry out an uprising in Santiago that included troops from his Valdivia battalion. The government suppressed the uprising but only after bloody fighting that led to 110–160 deaths, including Colonel Urriola (Wood 2011, 220). Another series of uprisings by Liberals occurred later that year in the northern cities of La Serena and Copiapó, after Montt's disputed election. The most serious threat to the government, however, came from the south where the opposition presidential candidate, General José María de la Cruz, denounced Montt's victory as fraudulent and rebelled at the head of more than 3,000 troops from the southern army. The government assembled an army of similar size and fought the rebels to a standstill at the bloody Battle of Loncomilla on December 8, 1851. Cruz subsequently signed a peace agreement in which he recognized Montt as president in exchange for the government's agreement to allow the rebel soldiers to rejoin the national army with their ranks and pensions intact (Collier 2003, 101).

Another rebellion took place in early 1859 when Radical Liberals opposed to Montt carried out brief uprisings in Santiago and Valparaíso (Collier 2003, 223). The rebels also organized rural guerrilla bands that carried out numerous attacks in both northern and southern Chile before finally being dispersed by government troops. The greatest threat to the government, however, came from the rebel army assembled by a mining millionaire, Pedro León Gallo, in the northern mining town of Atacama.[6] Gallo, who subsequently helped found the Radical Party of Chile, organized an army of more than 1,800 artisans and miners whom he armed with weapons seized from local ships and troops or manufactured in the region's foundries. The rebel army scored some initial victories, but it failed to attract any major defections from the military itself, which sealed its fate (Encina 1949, 304–305).[7] The government sent an army of 3,000 men to the north where they defeated the rebels (Somma 2011, 367–368; Collier 2003, 227).

---

[5] Montt was a former interior minister in Bulnes' cabinet who had managed to alienate many Conservatives as well as Liberals with his authoritarian ways.
[6] Although Gallo had originally been a supporter of Montt, he turned against the government in part because of a disagreement over a concession that his family had purchased to establish a railway (Somma 2011, 336).
[7] President Manuel Montt may have improved the loyalty of the military by taking a hard line on those who revolted in the 1850s (Somma 2011, 366; Collier 2003, 192, 204–205).

The various revolts provoked harsh state repression, leading to the imposition of states of siege and the enactment of laws restricting civil and political liberties. The government, for example, assumed emergency powers in the wake of various rebellions in the 1830s as well as during the 1851 and 1859 rebellions and the 1852 military mutiny (Collier 2003, 192, 228; Arancibia Clavel 2007, 129; Loveman 1993, 335–336, 341–342; Wood 2011, 100–101). Revolts also frequently led the government to arrest, imprison, exile, and even execute members of the opposition. In April 1837, for example, the government convicted three citizens of conspiracy for what Chilean historian Diego Barros Araña described as "conversations that in better times would hardly have been noticed" (cited in Loveman 1993, 336). In the aftermath of the June 1837 rebellion, the government shot eleven of the mutineers, and it executed another twenty-four rebels after the 1851 revolt, and perhaps even more during the 1859 civil war (Collier 2003, 28, 192; Amunátegui Solar 1946, 122).[8]

The opposition abandoned the armed struggle after 1859 in part because it was a costly strategy. Collier (2003, 28) estimates that a total of 4,000 people perished in the civil wars of 1851 and 1859. At least 1,800 soldiers died at Loncomilla alone, and hundreds more perished at the other battles of the 1851 civil war (Somma 2011, 363; Collier 2003, 101).[9] And, of course, the costs of rebellion must also include the many people wounded, arrested, or exiled as a result of these wars.[10] Santos Tornero, the editor of the Chilean newspaper, *El Mercurio*, reported that there were "few families in the country that did not have someone who was killed or wounded, thrown into preventive detention, imprisoned, or persecuted" during the 1859 conflict (cited in Zeitlin 1984, 56).

Perhaps more importantly, the opposition came to realize it had little chance of defeating an increasingly powerful military. According to Somma (2011, 399–400), "from the 1860s onward it became clear that armed insurgency was far from being an effective way of accessing power." As the century progressed, the Chilean government strengthened and professionalized its armed forces, which made it increasingly easy to suppress revolts.[11] Investments in infrastructure, such as telegraph lines, railroads, and shipping, also helped suppress revolts by improving military transport and communications.[12]

---

[8] In 1852, the government passed a law declaring that during conflicts the sentences of war councils would be implemented without appeal, which led to the precipitous executions of many civilians during the 1859 revolt (Amunátegui Solar 1946, 122).

[9] Such was the carnage at Loncomilla that, according to Hillmon Jr. (1963, 112), it "served to kill militarism in Chile."

[10] According to Zeitlin (1984, 56), the Montt administration deported 2,000 people after the war.

[11] Beginning in 1862, the government also sought to ensure military loyalty by rotating army units throughout Chile, which prevented them from establishing ties to the local population (Soifer 2015, 222–223).

[12] One newspaper, *El Ferrocarril*, credited investments in telegraphy with having shortened the 1959 civil war by several months (Hillmon Jr. 1963, 120).

Chile strengthened and professionalized its armed forces largely in response to international conflicts. The country fought major wars against Peru and Bolivia in 1836–1839 and 1879–1883, it fended off attacks from Spain in the 1865–1866 Chincha Islands War, and it had a long-running border dispute with Argentina, which almost led to war in the 1890s. The conflicts spurred massive buildups in troops and military equipment and exposed some of the shortcomings of the Chilean military, which the country sought to address in the aftermath of the wars. Chile's victories in the wars against Bolivia and Peru also helped build up political support for the military by strengthening nationalist forces who sought to maintain the country's regional military preeminence (Schenoni 2020). When the War of the Pacific broke out in 1879, the military quickly mobilized more than 50,000 men, and although it reduced its troop size after the war, the army continued to have twice as many soldiers as it had previously (Arancibia Clavel 2007, 181–183; Sater and Herwig 1999, 36).

The export boom, which occurred earlier in Chile than elsewhere in South America, financed the growing expenditures on infrastructure and the military. Between 1820 and 1870, Chilean exports grew at a rate of 5.1 percent annually, the highest rate in South America (Bértola and Ocampo 2013, 62). The country's exports continued to grow rapidly between 1870 and 1929, albeit at the somewhat reduced rate of 3.6 percent per year (Bértola and Ocampo 2013, 86).

Chile's efforts to professionalize the armed services date to the 1840s, but they gathered force over time. In the 1840s, the government reopened its military academy, established a school for corporals and sergeants, and began sending officers to train in French military schools – it also purchased artillery from France (Arancibia Clavel 2007, 156–158; Hillmon Jr. 1963, 76, 93). In 1858, the Chilean military received a French mission that consisted of four officers who provided training in infantry, cavalry, artillery, and military engineering (Ramírez Necochea 1984, 39–40; Resende-Santos 2007, 126). In the years that followed, the military sought to reorganize its internal structure along French lines, and it continued to acquire French weapons and to send Chilean officers to be trained in France.

During the 1880s, the Chilean government turned toward Germany to lead its military modernization efforts. In 1885, the administration of Domingo Santa María (1881–1886) hired Emil Körner, a German artillery captain and instructor at the Prussian Artillery and Engineering School, to supervise the reform effort. In spite of the resistance of some Chilean officers, Körner revamped military training along Prussian lines, creating a war academy in 1887 for junior officers, which required high scores on an entrance exam: Only 5 percent of applicants were admitted each year (Sater and Herwig 1999, 44). That same year, Körner also established a military school to train noncommissioned officers (Arancibia Clavel 2007, 212–213). In addition, the armed forces sent 130 Chilean officers to Germany for further training between 1895 and 1913 (Resende-Santos 2007, 138–141).

Körner believed that modern militaries had to maintain large standing armies, which required compulsory service. As a result, Chile became the first Latin American country to institute obligatory military service, adopting a conscription system based on the one in Germany. The size of the army expanded considerably, reaching 6,000 troops by 1894 and 9,000 by 1896 (Somma 2011, 397). At the direction of Körner, the Chilean government also spent massively on German weapons, purchases which were financed with German loans. By the late 1890s, the government had signed contracts to import fifteen million German marks of weapons and planned to purchase enough weapons to equip a standing army of 150,000 men (Resende-Santos 2007, 134). The Chilean government also invested heavily in its navy during this period, increasing the size of its naval forces from 17 warships and 2,000 sailors in 1890 to 29 warships and 7,000 sailors in 1902 (Resende-Santos 2007, 134).

The gradual strengthening and professionalization of the Chilean armed forces made it increasingly unlikely that the opposition could prevail in a revolt. As a result, the opposition mostly abandoned the armed struggle after 1859. The only major opposition revolt that occurred after 1859 took place in 1891 and the opposition only revolted in this instance once it obtained the support of the navy. As revolts came to an end, the government began to respect political and civil liberties more consistently. Chilean presidents, for example, did not impose any states of emergency between 1860 and 1890, a period in which there were no opposition revolts (Loveman 1993, 347). Instead of carrying out revolts, opposition leaders began to focus exclusively on the electoral path to power. According to Valenzuela and Valenzuela (1983, 29), after 1859 the opposition "correctly perceived that representative institutions were in their best interests and the only alternative they had once the military solution was precluded."

PARTIES AND DEMOCRATIZATION IN CHILE

Political parties played a key role in the emergence of democracy in Chile. Parties first arose in Chile during the mid-nineteenth century and these parties gradually developed strong organizations and enduring loyalties. The parties participated in elections, but for most of the nineteenth century these elections were far from democratic. Nevertheless, as they grew stronger, opposition parties gained increasing representation in the legislature, which they used to promote democratic reform. In 1890, a split within the ruling party gave the opposition control over the legislature, which enabled the enactment of a reform that helped bring democracy to Chile.

A religious conflict gave birth to political parties in Chile during the mid-nineteenth century. Conservatives who were unhappy with the government of Manuel Montt because of its intervention in Church affairs broke from the government in 1856 and formed a group that became the Conservative Party. Supporters of the government, meanwhile, formed the National Party the following year. The National Party was more personalistic than ideological, but it embraced many liberal positions, including the secularization of the state.

The Liberal Party also took official form in 1857, although some of its members had been collaborating loosely since the 1840s (Scully 1992, 217). It tended to support secular policies, but the party's platform became increasingly amorphous over time because of internal divisions and shifting alliances. Some of the more hardline Liberals eventually split off to form the Radical Party, although other members remained Liberals in name but acted independently from the party. The Radical Party, which did not become a cohesive organization until 1863, embraced anti-clericalism to a greater degree than did the other parties.

Thus, from the outset, the main cleavage that separated the parties, especially the Conservatives and the Radicals, was the church–state issue, and the enactment of secularizing policies by Liberal governments in the late nineteenth century only deepened this religious cleavage. The Conservatives were the strongest supporters of the Church, whereas the Radicals were its most vehement critic.

The four parties did not differ dramatically in terms of their leadership, social composition, or economic interests.[13] As Remmer (1984, 15) argues, the parties all "represented a very narrow upper class and their members shared the same fundamental socioeconomic interests and outlook." Elites sometimes changed parties, but most had loyalties to one party or another.

Over time, the parties developed broad and enduring ties to the electorate, which consisted not just of elites but of people of all social classes.[14] According to Valenzuela (1996, 249), Chilean parties in the nineteenth century "were able to generate loyalties among the populace ... They forged strong organizations binding together sizeable numbers of the more militant and politically engaged individuals that exist in any national society."

Each party had its zone of influence. The Conservative Party, for example, developed particularly high levels of support in devoutly Catholic areas of central and southern Chile (Valenzuela 2000, 192). The Radical Party, meanwhile, was especially strong in the north, especially in the mining

---

[13] The Conservative Party has often been described as the party of the landed elites, but this is somewhat of an exaggeration. Like other parties of this period, its leadership included many prominent landowners, but it also drew its leaders from numerous other sectors as well (Valenzuela 2000, 191–192; Remmer 1984, 72–73). The Radical Party was led mostly by wealthy mining families located in the north of the country, but it also had numerous leaders among the landowning, merchant, and banking elites of southern Chile (Heise 1982, 323–325). The Liberals were a very heterogeneous group, including both landholding elites as well as the new elites in mining, finance, and commerce (Heise 1982, 315). Many of the Nationals had banking interests, but they, too, were a heterogeneous party (Remmer 1984, 15).

[14] By 1877–1878, farmers/agricultural workers and artisans/industrial workers represented the two largest occupational categories in the electoral registry (Madrid 2019a, 8; República de Chile 1879, 316).

towns. Nevertheless, by the end of the nineteenth century, the Conservatives and the Radicals as well as the Liberals had developed significant levels of support in provinces throughout the country (Urzúa Valenzuela 1992, 342–362).

The four parties dominated the Chilean legislature from 1861 to 1890. In some years, they accounted for 100 percent of the legislative seats and in no year in this period did they represent less than 85 percent of the seats (Heise González 1982, 310–335; Obando Camino 2017, 76; Scully 1992, 58). The rise of the Liberal Democratic Party, which represented supporters of the former president José Manuel Balmaceda, reduced the dominance of the four main parties beginning in the 1890s, but they usually maintained control of three-fourths of the seats in the legislature through the 1924 elections.

The Conservatives and the Radicals developed the strongest ideological principles and organizations, and they gradually displaced the Liberals as the largest parties. The Conservative Party celebrated its first national convention in 1878, in which it defined its program and mobilized its cadres. It followed that up with additional national conventions in 1884, 1891, and 1895, and it gradually developed a complex hierarchical and territorial structure (Guilisasti Tagle 1964, 22–23; Heise González 1982, 317–318). At its base, the Conservative Party had Communal Assemblies and Communal Directorates, both of which reported to the Departmental Directorate, which, in turn, took orders from the Provincial Council and the General Directorate. The Communal Assemblies elected the members of the Communal Directorate as well as well as the candidates for the legislature and the councils from lists provided by the leadership (Heise González 1982, 317–318). The General Directorate, which was composed of 500 people, selected the members of the Governing Board and the party's presidential candidate (Heise González 1982, 318).

The Conservatives benefited from a dense Catholic organizational network composed of charitable associations, schools, workers' societies, and religious communities (Valenzuela 2000, 190–191). Priests and other church workers supported the Conservative Party from the pulpit, lent the considerable Church resources to the party, and campaigned on its behalf, even though the Church hierarchy was careful to maintain some distance from the party (Valenzuela 2000, 202–210). The Conservative Party sought to defend the Catholic Church, but it was not controlled by the Church, and it took centrist positions on many issues (Valenzuela 2001, 265–266).

The Radical Party developed a more decentralized, democratic, and participatory organization. In its first couple of decades, it lacked a national party leadership structure, relying instead on autonomous assemblies, which were held in Copiapó in 1863, in La Serena in 1864, and in Santiago and Concepción in 1865 (Scully 1992, 218; Remmer 1984, 17). In 1888, it held its first national convention, which provided it with a national organization for the first time (Snow 1963, 58). At this convention, which was attended by sixty-three departmental delegates representing forty-three assemblies throughout Chile, it developed a detailed party program and party regulations and it elected a party president and a Central Governing Board (Durán Bernales 1958, 24; Palma Zuñiga 1967, 59–60; Snow 1963, 58; Guilisasti Tagle 1964, 134; García Covarrubias 1990, 85–86). By the time the Radicals held their second convention in 1899, they had eighty-five Communal Assemblies (Remmer 1984, 67).

The party established a clear hierarchy that ran from the Governing Board to the Provincial Directorates to the Communal Assemblies (Heise González 1982, 326). Nevertheless, the Communal Assemblies, which gradually diffused throughout the country, continued to play a key role in the party (Gazmuri 2019, 177–179). They met as frequently as once per week and were responsible for designating the party's candidates in elections, electing the governing board, formulating the party's policies, educating members, and recruiting future leaders of the party (Heise González 1982, 327). The Radical Party also received considerable assistance from the Masonry, which established its first grand lodge in Chile in 1862 – by 1872 it had ten lodges in the country (Collier and Sater 1996, 117). Associations of firefighters as well as various clubs, such as the Reform Club, also became important bases of support for the Radical Party (Gazmuri 2019).

By contrast, the Liberal and the National parties had weaker organizations and ideologies. Whereas the Conservatives and the Radicals had "exemplary discipline, abiding rigorously the resolutions of their leadership," both the Liberal Party and the National Party had relatively weak party discipline (Heise González 1982, 291). The Liberal Party lacked firm party principles, and it frequently split between members who supported the government, dubbed the government Liberals, and those who opposed it, called the opposition or loose Liberals (Remmer 1984, 18; Heise González 1982, 309). Scully (1992, 49) argues that the Liberal Party was "the most organizationally fragmented [party] and the one with the weakest ideological underpinnings." Nevertheless, the Liberal Party held the presidency from 1871 until 1891, and it used its control of the electoral authorities to consistently win the largest share of seats in the legislature during this period.[15]

The National Party, by contrast, constituted the smallest of the four main parties. It had a highly personalistic structure and suffered frequent splits and defections throughout the nineteenth century. According to Urzúa Valenzuela (1968, 32), the National Party was "a typical example of a party that owes its birth to the personal influence of certain leaders (personalistic party), [and] whose electoral strength is maintained only as long as those leaders maintain their status and political power."

---

[15] After 1891, the Conservatives and the Radicals had the largest legislative contingents.

Leaders of all four parties established newspapers to communicate with their supporters and help diffuse their ideas, which contributed to the growth of partisanship. According to Remmer (1984, 15):

> By the end of the Liberal Republic two important dailies supported the Nationals: *El Mercurio* of Valparaíso and *La Epoca* of Santiago; the government Liberals' viewpoint was expressed by *La Tribuna* and *La Nación* of Santiago and *El Comercio* of Valparaíso; the Conservatives' by *El Independiente* and *El Estandarte Católico* in the capital and *La Unión* in Valparaíso; the Radicals' by *El Heraldo* in Valparaíso; while *La Libertad Electoral* in Santiago spoke in favor of the opposition or independent Liberals.

Party leaders also established newspapers in smaller towns and cities. The Radicals, for example, not only founded *La Ley* in Santiago and *El Deber* in Valparaíso but also *El Sur* in Concepción and *El Constituyente* and *El Atacama* in Copiapó (Heise González 1982, 328).

As Chapter 4 discussed, the parties, especially the Conservatives and the Radicals, developed relatively strong organizations and partisan loyalties thanks in part to the relative balance between Liberal and Conservative forces in the country. In addition, the concentration of the population in Chile and the absence of internal geographic barriers made it easier to build national parties. Chile was a relatively small nation for most of the nineteenth century, although the subjugation of the Mapuche and Chile's victory in the War of the Pacific enabled it to significantly expand its territory at the end of the century. Even after it expanded its frontiers, the majority of the country's population (55 percent in 1907) was concentrated in the ten provinces that made up the central region, an area that constituted only 12.5 percent of Chile's land and was easily traversable (República de Chile 1907). Chile's extensive coastline also facilitated transport along the length of its territory, as did its significant railway lines. By 1900, Chile already had 2,817 miles of railroad track, and by 1930 it had 5,553 miles, giving it the third highest ratio of railway track to territory in South America (Summerhill 2006, 302).[16]

Chile enjoyed regular elections throughout the nineteenth century, but only a small percentage of the population participated in these elections. Indeed, during the first three-quarters of the century, voter turnout constituted only 1.5 percent of the population, and even in the last quarter century, voters only represented 3.1 percent of the population. A central obstacle to increased voter participation was the 1833 constitution, which restricted suffrage to literate Chilean males over twenty-one years of age (twenty-five if unmarried) who met certain income requirements (or who had property or capital). Although the income restrictions were relaxed beginning in 1874, the literacy requirement

---

[16] Chile also expanded its telegraph lines rapidly in the late nineteenth century, and by 1900 it already had 10,400 miles of lines (Banks and Wilson 2014).

remained. This restriction disenfranchised most adult citizens since a large majority of Chileans were illiterate during the nineteenth century.

Voter participation was also low in the nineteenth century because the results of most of the elections, especially presidential elections, were predetermined. Before 1890, elections were largely controlled by the executive branch, especially the minister of interior, which ensured that candidates supported by the president won the vast majority of races. To be sure, members of the opposition sought to manipulate elections as well, but the government had many more ways of intervening since it controlled the state, the national guard, and the electoral authorities. As one government agent wrote to the Chilean minister of interior in the mid-nineteenth century, "if there should arise an opposition, we have a thousand means to make it fail" (cited in Valenzuela 1996, 242). The minister of interior and his agents compiled lists of preferred candidates, bought votes, distributed pre-marked ballots to supporters, and prevented opposition voters from gaining access to the voting tables. Perhaps most importantly, the executive branch used its control of the voter registration process to disqualify potential opposition voters and to stack the electoral registries with supporters of the government, including national guard troops and state employees.

During the first several decades after independence, the opposition frequently abstained from elections or competed only in selected races because of the dim prospects of winning. According to Collier (2003, 35), "in seven of the eleven legislative elections held between 1833 and 1864 the opposition scarcely bothered to run candidates at all." During this period, the opposition typically won no more than three or four seats in the lower chamber of the legislature (Urzúa Valenzuela 1992; Valenzuela 2012, 60; Donoso 1967).

Once it abandoned the armed struggle, however, the opposition began to compete more systematically in elections. Although the electoral playing field was tilted against them, opposition parties typically won 20 percent or more of the seats in the Chamber of Deputies beginning in 1858 (Urzúa Valenzuela 1992; Valenzuela 2012, 60; Heise González 1982). Chilean presidents permitted opposition candidates to be elected to the legislature during this period in order to keep the social peace or to satisfy powerful interests, as long as the opposition victories did not threaten the government's control of the legislature.[17] As the Conservative leader Abdón Cifuentes (1936a, 148) pointed out: "If one or another congressional candidate of the opposition emerged victorious, it was because the opinion of a Department was so unanimous or energetic that it could not be overcome, without provoking scandalous outrage, or because it was in the government's interest to allow the appearance

---

[17] The executive often included ruling party dissidents on the government's lists of official candidates to appease local notables and increase its chances of winning races (Valenzuela 1996, 236; 2012, 58). These dissidents at times defected to the opposition after the elections.

of freedom."[18] Each party had strongholds where its partisan ties ran deep, which enabled it to sometimes overcome the disadvantages it faced.

As opposition parties grew stronger in the 1860s and increasingly focused on the electoral path to power, they began to promote a variety of democratic reforms, including measures that would expand the suffrage, level the electoral playing field, and strengthen the attributions of Congress. The executive branch used its legislative influence to block these reforms, however. For example, in 1864 a Liberal and a couple of Radical legislators proposed loosening the suffrage requirements, but the government easily voted down their proposal (Heise González 1982, 52–53). A stronger push for electoral reform came in the late 1860s with the founding of the Reform Club (Estelle Méndez 1970). Liberals and Radicals associated with this movement proposed various reforms, but allies of the executive branch blocked most of these proposed reforms, including measures to expand the suffrage and reduce the executive's control over the electoral process (Anonymous 1878, 312–313; Heise González 1982, 52–53). Congress did pass a minor reform in 1869 that made some changes to the administration of the electoral registry and stripped the right to vote from members of the army and navy (Heise González 1982, 50–51; Encina 1950, 504–506; Valenzuela 1985, 102). This reform did not significantly diminish the executive's ability to control elections, however, since national guard troops retained the right to vote, and they were much more numerous than members of the military.

Opposition parties in Chile tended to energetically support democratic reforms because they recognized that such measures would strengthen their position in the legislature and improve their chances of winning elections. Members of the ruling coalition, by contrast, tended to oppose such reforms or seek to water them down to preserve their control of elections and their dominance in the legislature. Thus, when parties left the ruling coalition, they tended to become much more enthusiastic about democratic reform, but when they joined the ruling coalition, their enthusiasm tended to wane. For example, the Conservative Party only became a strong advocate of democratic reform after it left the ruling alliance in mid-1874 and joined the opposition (Valenzuela 2012, 62; Heise González 1982, 313–314; Madrid 2019a, 8). Similarly, the Liberal Party's support for democratic reform waned once it took over the government beginning in 1871.[19] Indeed, Liberal governments, such as those headed by Domingo Santa María and José Manuel Balmaceda, became aggressive practitioners of electoral manipulation.

Although the opposition typically held a significant number of seats in the legislature during the late nineteenth century, it could not enact legislation

---

[18] Valenzuela (1985, 66–67) notes that the opposition was more likely to win if the head of the local national guard unit had close ties to local elites and opted not to intervene in favor of the official candidates.

[19] Some Liberals continued to support reform, effectively joining the opposition.

without the support of members of the ruling coalition. Nevertheless, splits within the ruling coalition were frequent and these splits provided opportunities for the opposition. Because of the fragmentation of the party system, Chilean presidents typically had to govern through coalitions from the 1860s onward, and these coalitions were often unstable.[20] To persuade opposition parties to join the ruling coalition, the executive often had to grant policy concessions. Changes in the minister of interior could also strengthen the opposition because most of the legislators in the ruling coalition owed their seats to the minister who presided over their election. Once this minister was replaced, it was common for some of these legislators to defect to the opposition or at least become a less dependable vote for the ruling coalition.

Splits within the ruling coalition paved the way for the enactment of the two most important democratic reforms that occurred during this period. The first reform was enacted in 1874 following a split that brought the Liberals to power.[21] The opposition proposed a reform that: mandated cumulative voting, which increased the likelihood that the opposition would win legislative representation;[22] allowed literacy to count as sufficient proof that voters satisfied the income requirements on the franchise; and stripped control of the voter registration process away from the municipalities, which the executive dominated, putting it in the hands of the largest taxpayers in each district. Although the president and his ministers objected to these provisions, they had a difficult time blocking them, given the splits that had undermined the government's control of the legislature. In the end, the government agreed to a compromise bill that effectively eliminated the income requirement and weakened the government's control of voter registration but restricted the use of the cumulative vote to lower chamber elections. The 1874 reform significantly expanded and diversified the electorate, leading the number of voters in legislative elections to increase from 25,981 in 1873 to 80,346 in 1876, and 104,041 in 1879 (Valenzuela 1985, 150; Borón 1971, Table 3).[23]

The 1874 reform initially helped reduce electoral intervention by the executive and expand opposition representation in the legislature. The 1876 and

---

[20] As a result of frequent splits within the ruling coalition, the average duration of cabinets declined from more than two years prior to 1861 to less than one year beginning in the 1870s (Scully 1992, 46–47; Heise González 1974, 285–288; Somma 2011, 431–432).
[21] For a detailed discussion of this reform and its enactment, including an analysis of a roll-call vote on a key provision, see Valenzuela (1985) and Madrid (2019a).
[22] Cumulative voting granted citizens as many votes as positions to be filled in a district but allowed them to concentrate their votes on a single candidate, which increased the likelihood that minority parties could win seats.
[23] Valenzuela (2012, 225) estimates that about 30 percent of the adult male population in Chile was registered to vote in 1878. By the late nineteenth century, the electorate included people from all social classes, with farmers and agricultural workers, along with artisans and industrial workers, constituting a large majority of registered voters (República de Chile 1879, 316; 1882, 32).

TABLE 5.2 *Presidential and legislative elections in Chile, 1831–1924*

Election year	Presidential electoral votes (winner vs. runner-up)	Legislative seats (government vs. opposition)	Valid votes (as a % of the population)
1831	207–186	48–4	1.3
1834		55–0	0.6
1836	145–14		
1837		51–0	0.8
1840		43–9	2.1
1841	154–9		
1843			1.1
1846	164–0	50–3	1.8
1849		51–4	1.3
1851	132–29		
1852		51–3	
1855		55–3	
1856	207–0		
1858		57–15	1.3
1861	214–0	41–31	
1864		49–23	
1866	191–15		
1867		81–15	
1870		59–40	1.6
1871	226–58		1.5
1873		86–10	1.3
1876	293–14	43–37	2.1
1879		84–22	4.7
1881	287–12		2.9
1882		102–6	3.0
1885		96–17	3.2
1886	324–0		2.0
1888		94–29	3.5
1891	255–0	54–40	2.7
1894		66–28	4.2
1896	137–134		4.8
1897		68–26	4.8
1900		52–42	4.9
1901	172–79		5.7
1903		38–56	5.6
1906	164–97	53–41	6.1
1909		52–43	7.1
1910	268–0		7.9
1912		62–56	8.4
1915	174–173	65–53	4.3
1918		51–67	5.0
1920	175–174		5.2
1921		68–48	
1924		75–43	5.0

Source: Latin American Historical Elections Database.
Note: Presidential and legislative elections in Chile were often held in different years.

1879 elections witnessed less executive intervention than in previous years in part because the opposition used its influence in the committees of the largest taxpayers to resist the executive's attempts to intervene (Heise González 1982, 67–69; Ponce de León Atria and Fonck Larraín 2017, 181–183; Valenzuela 2012, 63; 1985, 122).[24] Nevertheless, government electoral intervention increased again during the 1880s under presidents Domingo Santa María (1881–1886) and José Manuel Balmaceda (1886–1891) (Donoso 1967, 308; Ponce de León Atria and Fonck Larraín 2017, 183–187; Valenzuela 2012, 63). Santa María and Balmaceda were both Liberal leaders who had been strong proponents of electoral reform when they served in Congress. Balmaceda, for example, had written a well-known political tract calling for electoral freedom in which he declared that there was "no idea more general, more practical, more full of importance than electoral liberty" (Heise González 1982, 74). Once they gained the presidency, however, they aggressively sought to control elections. As president, Santa María proudly declared: "They have called me an interventionist. I am. I belong to the old school and if I intervene [in elections] it is because I want an efficient, disciplined parliament that collaborates with the desires of government to advance the public welfare" (Góngora 1981, 22; Valenzuela 1998, 269).

The government could no longer disqualify opposition voters as easily thanks to the 1874 reform, but it had other tools at its disposal (Valenzuela 2012, 63). The executive and his allies manipulated the lists of the largest taxpayers to maintain control of the electoral authorities, and they also resorted to vote buying and even violence on occasion (Heise González 1982, 71; Valenzuela 1985, 123; Donoso 1967, 313). The high level of executive intervention led the opposition Conservatives to boycott the elections in 1882 in protest, and many Conservative voters stayed away from the polls in 1885 as well (Valenzuela 2012, 63). As a result, voter turnout declined considerably in the 1880s, and government supporters captured a large majority of seats in the legislature. According to Heise González (1982, 65), the government won 102 seats out of 109 seats in the Chamber of Deputies in the 1882 elections, 96 seats out of 115 seats in the 1885 elections, and 94 out of 126 seats in 1888.

The ruling coalition split again under Balmaceda, however, leading a large majority of the legislature to join the opposition. The split stemmed in part from Balmaceda's economic policies. From the outset of his administration, Balmaceda spent massively on public works, including schools, hospitals, government offices, roads, bridges, railways, and docks, which he funded in large part through taxes on the export of nitrates. He created a Ministry of Public Works that by 1890 accounted for more than 30 percent of the government's budget (Collier and Sater 1996, 151). Spending on education also skyrocketed under Balmaceda, tripling between 1886 and 1890. These spending

---

[24] The opposition also used its influence in the committees of largest taxpayers to benefit its own candidates (Heise 1982, 68).

policies alienated fiscal conservatives and members of the financial community (Blakemore 1974, 73–75; Zeitlin 1984).[25]

Balmaceda also managed to antagonize domestic and foreign investors in the nitrate industry through his efforts to extract more resources from them. By 1888, nitrate taxes had risen to 41 percent, up from 27 percent just six years earlier (Zeitlin 1984, 107). Seventy percent of the Chilean nitrate industry was in British hands by 1890 and British investors objected to many of Balmaceda's policies (Blakemore 1974, 22). John North, the British investor and so-called Nitrate King, hired Julio Zegers, a prominent Liberal politician, to defend his interests, and Zegers in turn hired numerous other prominent Liberal deputies and politicians for his legal team. Many of these politicians, like Zegers, subsequently played prominent roles in the opposition to Balmaceda (Blakemore 1974, 126–127; Ramírez Necochea 1969, 74–75). Meanwhile, Antony Gibbs and Son, another prominent British investment firm with nitrate and railway interests, hired Senator Eulogio Altamirano to defend its interests, and Altamirano also ended up leading the opposition to Balmaceda in the legislature (Blakemore 1974, 142–143).

Although foreign and domestic investors, especially those with ties to the nitrate industry, helped mobilize congressional opposition to Balmaceda, the president's authoritarian tendencies also played an important role in his undoing. Significant opposition to Balmaceda first emerged when he tried to impose his minister of finance and public works, Enrique Salvador Sanfuentes, as his successor. Balmaceda ultimately backed down, but many members of the legislature did not trust him to refrain from further electoral manipulation. Opponents of Balmaceda accused him of trying to organize his own party and they believed that he was using the dramatic increase in state spending to build a political patronage machine (Blakemore 1974, 174).

The growing opposition led Balmaceda to lose his majority in both the Chamber of Deputies and the Senate in late 1889, the first time this had happened to a president in Chilean history. By November 1889, Balmaceda controlled no more than 45 of the 123 seats in the two chambers of the legislature (Encina 1952, 178–179; Heise González 1982, 90; Terrie 2014, 188–189). The opposition included Conservatives, Nationals, Radicals, independent Liberals, and even some disaffected government Liberals. Balmaceda responded to the growing dissent by clamping down on the opposition and seeking to circumvent the legislature. These measures simply aggravated the discontent, however, causing more politicians, including many so-called government Liberals, to abandon him.

---

[25] There is a significant historical debate over the causes of the elite split under the Balmaceda administration and the ensuing 1891 civil war. Some scholars emphasize Balmaceda's authoritarian tendencies as the principal cause (Blakemore 1974; Amunátegui Solar 1946; Encina 1952), whereas others focus on his economic policies, which alienated both foreign and domestic economic interests (Ramírez Necochea 1969; Vitale 1975; Zeitlin 1984). There is plenty of evidence to suggest that both factors played a role.

To rein in Balmaceda, the opposition renewed its push for democratic reform. During its long post-1873 reign in the opposition, the Conservative Party had become the staunchest congressional proponent of democratic reform. The Conservatives initially made little headway with their reform proposals, but when the Balmaceda administration lost its majority in the Chamber of Deputies, the Conservative Senator Manuel José Irarrázaval was emboldened to try again.[26] In a speech in the Senate on October 28, 1889, he noted that his previous reform proposal had been rejected, but "the political change that has since occurred in the Chamber [of Deputies] has encouraged me to propose it again to the Senate."[27] According to Irarrázaval, the committees of largest taxpayers that supervised the elections were too easily manipulated by the government, and it was therefore necessary to entrust the electoral system to autonomous municipalities (Cifuentes 1936b, 282).[28] He and others therefore proposed an electoral reform as well as a law creating autonomous municipalities.

The Balmaceda administration briefly flirted with the possibility of negotiating a reform with the Conservatives because it hoped to persuade them to join the government. This effort failed, however, and the government then sought to block the reform proposals (Blakemore 1974, 160–161; Encina 1952, 205–208; Terrie 2014, 192). The minister of justice and public education argued that "intervention by the Government in electoral proceedings cannot be cured through laws, and that only time, education, and self-sacrifice would correct it."[29] Government Liberals also objected to provisions that would make intendants and governors unpaid positions, thereby reducing executive influence over them (Terrie 2014, 192; Salas Edwards 1914, 234–235).[30] The Balmaceda administration proposed its own constitutional reforms, but these measures were rejected by the opposition because they did nothing to weaken presidential powers or reduce executive control over elections (Blakemore 1974, 162–163; Terrie 2014, 192).

By contrast, the other opposition parties quickly threw themselves behind the reform proposals of the Conservatives. In a Senate speech, the Radical Senator Manuel Recabarren voiced his approval of the reforms, although he noted that "it should not be forgotten that when [the Conservative Party]

---

[26] Irarrázaval, a wealthy landowner, had spent years studying electoral and municipal reform, traveling to the United States as well as Europe to study foreign models of government (Cifuentes 1936b, 280–282; Encina 1952, 198–199).

[27] *Boletín de Sesiones de la Cámara de Senadores*, Extraordinary Session 5, October 28, 1889, p. 78.

[28] See also Irarrázaval's long speech to the Senate in *Boletín de Sesiones de la Cámara de Senadores*, Extraordinary Session 7, November 4, 1889, pp. 105–113.

[29] *Boletín de Sesiones de la Cámara de Senadores*, Extraordinary Session 27, December 16, 1889, p. 343.

[30] See, for example, Deputy Fernando Cabrera Gacitúa's speech opposing these measures in *Boletín de Sesiones de la Cámara de Diputados*, Ordinary Session 22, July 8, 1890, pp. 344–345.

was in power, it rejected [similar reforms] when the Liberal Party asked for them."³¹ The opposition elected Irarrázaval as head of the joint committee that was to elaborate the reform, while at the same time excluding government Liberals from the subcommittee that they created to establish the bases of the reform (Salas Edwards 1914, 234). In short order, the committee wrote up a draft of the reform and submitted the proposal to the legislature with the support of all of the opposition members on the committee (Terrie 2014, 193; Cifuentes 1936b, 286). The pro-government Liberals opposed the reforms and refused to sign the committee's report, but they could not block the proposed measures since they represented a minority of the committee (Salas Edwards 1914, 234). The Balmaceda administration then sought to stall the reforms by refusing to call an extraordinary session of Congress to discuss the committee's proposals. Nevertheless, when the legislature reconvened in June 1890 for its ordinary session, it quickly approved the electoral reform law, which was promulgated on August 21, 1890 (Encina 1952, 277).

The 1890 electoral reform law contained a large number of provisions, the most important of which were the measures that helped establish ballot secrecy. According to Valenzuela (1998, 275–76), the law "made a great effort to assure the secret vote," even going so far as to include a drawing that indicated where the voters should wait, where the voting desks and tables should be placed, and how the desks where voters would cast their ballots should be constructed. The law specified that voters would cast their ballots at isolated desks that would provide total privacy (any windows in the room had to be covered). Article 55 stipulated that the desks would contain ballots for all the candidates on white paper of uniform size, although citizens were also allowed to bring their own ballots (Anguita 1912, 128–129). Voters were supposed to place their ballots in white envelopes, which were provided by the electoral authorities, and then return to the main voting table where they would place their ballots in the ballot box.

The 1890 reform clearly had an important democratizing effect since the competitiveness of elections in Chile increased dramatically in the wake of its enactment and candidates supported by the government began to lose much more often. In spite of this reform, however, the secrecy of the vote was not always rigorously enforced in rural areas where agricultural tenant workers (*inquilinos*) were in thrall to the traditional landowning elites.³²

---

³¹ *Boletín de Sesiones de la Cámara de Senadores*, Extraordinary Session 35, January 8, 1890, p. 476.
³² Some scholars have suggested that Chile did not truly establish the secrecy of the vote until the government introduced the single state-provided Australian ballot in 1958 (Baland and Robinson 2008; Scully 1992, 134–135). Indeed, Hellinger (1978) and Baland and Robinson (2008) show that after the passage of this reform support for right-wing parties decreased significantly in areas where agricultural tenant workers represented a larger share of the population, presumably because the landowning elites could no longer influence their tenants' votes. Nevertheless, the decline in *inquilino* support for right-wing parties after 1958 also presumably stemmed from the rise of the Christian Democratic Party and the rural organizing efforts that it and the left-wing parties undertook during this period.

The 1890 law also ensured greater representation for minority parties by extending the cumulative voting procedure to the elections of senators, presidential electors, and municipal councilors, which had previously used the complete-list system. To ensure fair vote counting, the 1890 reform also specified that the opening of the ballot boxes and the counting of the votes would take place in the presence of representatives of the candidates. It also eliminated the voter registration cards that enabled the executive's agents to disqualify opposition voters and control the votes of some state employees (Heise González 1982, 91; Valenzuela 1998, 275).[33] In addition, under the new law, voters would no longer have to reregister to vote every three years – voter registration would last indefinitely.

Whereas the electoral reform bill was signed into law in 1890, the municipal autonomy law stalled in the legislature because of the growing conflict between the president and the Congress. Executive–legislative relations steadily deteriorated over the course of 1890. The legislature repeatedly censured government ministers, but Balmaceda refused to remove them and instead sought to dissolve the legislature. Government agents also attacked a meeting of Conservatives in Santiago, and soldiers and police violently repressed a wave of strikes throughout the country.[34] In late December 1890, the congressional opposition drew up a statement, signed by nineteen senators and seventy deputies, that declared Balmaceda unfit to continue in office (Blakemore 1974, 191). When the legislature refused to approve a budget for the administration, Balmaceda decreed on January 4, 1891 that the previous year's budget as well as other essential laws would be renewed.

In the wake of Balmaceda's decree, the opposition rebelled with the support of the Chilean navy and its leader, Admiral Jorge Montt. On January 7, 1891, the navy sailed its warships out of Valparaíso with the leaders of the opposition aboard, including the president of the Chamber of Deputies, and the vice-president of the Senate. Other members of the opposition went into hiding in Santiago. The army remained loyal to Balmaceda and government agents brutally repressed the opposition and shut down the opposition media. The navy, however, blockaded Chile's ports and gained control of northern Chile and its nitrate revenues, which the opposition used to purchase arms abroad and assemble an army of its own. Emil Körner, the head of the German military mission in Chile, joined the side of the congressionalist opposition and helped train and direct their troops. After several months of fighting, the opposition army defeated Balmaceda's troops in two bloody battles in August 1891 that produced more than 7,000 casualties (Somma 2011, 374). When the opposition army entered Santiago, Balmaceda sought asylum in the Argentine embassy

---

[33] Previously, national guard and police commanders as well as some government officials had collected the voter registration cards from their subordinates, returning them on election day when they would go to vote in a bloc (Valenzuela 1996, 244).

[34] The strikes were largely unrelated to the congressional opposition to Balmaceda.

where he committed suicide on September 19, 1891, the day after his term officially ended.

With the end of the Chilean Civil War, Congress quickly approved the municipal autonomy law, and it was promulgated on December 22, 1891. The law stripped control of the municipalities from the central government, creating Assemblies of Electors (composed of all eligible voters within each municipality) that were responsible for electing municipal officials as well as for approving municipal budget, taxation, and financing agreements (Valenzuela 1977, 193). Perhaps most importantly, the law gave the municipalities control of the electoral process, including registering voters, composing the polling officials, and administering the elections on election day.

Thus, pressure from increasingly strong opposition parties, combined with a split within the ruling coalition, enabled the enactment of important democratic reforms in 1890–1891. The opposition allied with ruling party dissidents to push through these reforms despite the resistance of the government.

ELECTIONS AND DEMOCRACY IN CHILE AFTER 1891

The electoral and municipal reforms of 1890–1891 helped democratize the Chilean political system. In the wake of the reforms, the executive lost control of the electoral process. Chilean presidents could no longer impose their successors, nor could they unilaterally determine the makeup of Congress. The minister of interior ceased to compose official lists of candidates and to intervene extensively in elections (Valenzuela 1996, 249; Heise González 1982, 93). According to Remmer (1977, 210): "Whereas the intervention of the executive had previously deprived elections of all their meaning, their outcome was now largely determined by the number of votes counted." Similarly, Valenzuela (1998, 268–269) argues that in the wake of the 1890 electoral reform, "the Chilean political regime began to meet the minimum requirements of a democracy with incomplete suffrage."

Between 1891 and 1924, a period which was dubbed the Parliamentary Republic, the legislature dominated the executive branch. During this period, cabinet members were responsible to the parliament and were frequently removed at the legislature's request.[35] Because the legislature was divided, presidents struggled to cobble together the alliances necessary to approve legislation. Five parties – the Conservative Party, the Liberal Party, the Radical Party, the National Party, and the Liberal Democratic Party – usually had representation in the legislature, and no party typically held a majority of seats. As a result, the parties formed alliances: One pact centered on the Liberals and was dubbed the Liberal Alliance; the other pact revolved around the

---

[35] Between December 1891 and September 1924, the Ministry of the Interior switched hands almost 100 times and the average cabinet lasted only four or five months (Remmer 1984, 63).

Conservatives and was called the Conservative Coalition.[36] The composition of these alliances changed frequently, and they were often based more on political opportunity than on ideology.

Competition in elections was typically intense. The first elections that took place after the Chilean civil war, the general elections of October 1891, were not competitive at the presidential level, given the existence of a consensus candidate: Admiral Jorge Montt. Nor were they free and fair since the former supporters of Balmaceda were excluded.[37] Beginning in 1894, however, supporters of Balmaceda were reintegrated into politics – they formed the Liberal Democratic Party – and elections became much more competitive and democratic. For example, in the 1894 elections, four out of the five cabinet ministers who ran for legislative posts were defeated, and the government accepted the outcome (Heise González 1982, 107). As Table 5.2 indicates, in the 1896 presidential elections, only three electoral votes separated the top two finishers, and in 1915 and 1920, the winner prevailed by a single vote. Of equal importance, alternation in power became common during this period. In 1901, Germán Riesco, who represented the Liberal Alliance, was elected president even though the Conservative Coalition was the incumbent government.[38] Similarly, in 1915, the Liberal president, Ramón Barros Luco, passed the presidential sash to the candidate of the Conservative Coalition, Juan Luis Sanfuentes; and in 1920 Sanfuentes handed over power to the candidate of the Liberal Alliance, Arturo Alessandri.

To be sure, Chile did not become a full democracy during this period. Some electoral abuses continued, although these abuses tended to be perpetrated by local officials and agents of the parties rather than the central government (Remmer 1977, 210–211). Parties bought votes, stacked the registries full of their supporters, and sought to disqualify voters of other parties (Ponce de León Atria 2014, 6–7; Ponce de León Atria and Fonck Larraín 2017). The municipalities controlled the voter registry and the electoral process so the parties depended in large part on their influence with local officials in order to obtain favorable outcomes (Ponce de León Atria 2014, 6–7; Valenzuela 1977, 194). Money came to play an increasingly important role in electoral campaigns.[39] Indeed, a contemporary observer from the United States argued

---

[36] The Conservatives and the Liberals initially represented the two largest parties in the Chamber of Deputies, but they were overtaken by the Radicals in 1918.

[37] Even the 1891 elections demonstrated democratic progress in that the government did not intervene in them extensively. The son of the minister of interior lost his campaign for congress by eighty-seven votes in this election, and the minister declined to overturn the results (Heise 1982, 101).

[38] There was also alternation in power in 1896 since the incumbent president, Admiral Jorge Montt, did not belong to any party.

[39] Remmer (1984, 81–82) estimates that the average amount spent to win a seat in the Senate during this period was 100,000 Chilean pesos, roughly US$30,000, and the average amount to win a seat in the Chamber of Deputies was 10,000 pesos, approximately US$3,000.

that "the most serious danger to Chilean public life arises from the almost universal use of money to influence the result of elections" (Reinsch 1909, 525). Nevertheless, as he acknowledged, this was a problem that plagued Western democracies in general.

Suffrage restrictions also undermined Chilean democracy throughout the early twentieth century. Neither women nor illiterates could vote, and together they represented more than 70 percent of the adult population during this period (Remmer 1984, 83). The Chilean literacy rate rose sharply in the twentieth century, however, climbing from 31.8 percent in 1895, to 50.3 percent in 1920, to 89.8 percent in 1970, which made the literacy requirement less of an obstacle over time (República de Chile 1925, 303; 1970, 40). As a result, voter turnout increased as Table 5.2 indicates, climbing from 3.6 percent of the population in 1888 to a high of 8.5 percent of the population in 1912 (Borón 1971, table 3; Nazer and Rosemblit 2000, 227). In 1914, however, the legislature enacted a reform that required the voter registry to be freshly compiled every nine years, which led to a temporary reduction in voter registration and turnout (Ponce de León Atria 2014, 17; Scully 1992, 66).

Nevertheless, the regime that was established in Chile at the outset of the 1890s was quite democratic by the standards of the time. Moreover, Chile enacted further reforms over the course of the twentieth century that would help deepen democracy. In the late 1920s, for example, the government created new institutions to oversee voter registration and elections, which were staffed by public employees, and these institutions gradually helped reduce electoral manipulation (Ponce de León Atria and Fonck Larraín 2017, 191; Ponce de León Atria 2014, 19–21; Hasbun 2016). Even more importantly, Chile granted suffrage to women in 1949 and to illiterates in 1970, and it improved voting secrecy in 1958 by requiring voters to use a single, government-provided ballot.

As we have seen, the professionalization of the military played an important role in the establishment of this democratic regime by bringing an end to the opposition revolts that had plagued Chile before 1860. Military professionalization did not bring an end to military coups, however. In 1924, the military overthrew the government of Arturo Alessandri, ushering in an era of authoritarianism and instability that did not end until the reelection of Alessandri in 1932. Nevertheless, during the twentieth century, military intervention remained less common in Chile than most of the other South American countries. Indeed, beginning in 1932, Chile enjoyed a long period of democratic rule that was not broken until the 1973 military coup.

The emergence of strong political parties in Chile during the nineteenth century played an important role in the establishment and maintenance of this democratic regime. Strong opposition parties pushed through the democratic reforms that helped establish democracy in the 1890s and they oversaw the implementation of these reforms by monitoring the polls and protesting electoral abuses when they encountered them. The strength of the opposition parties also ensured that they could compete in elections, enabling the opposition to capture large numbers of seats in the legislature and even the presidency on occasion. This gave the opposition a large stake in the democratic system and discouraged it from calling on the military to intervene. Thus, Chile's relatively strong multiparty system undergirded its democratic and highly competitive regime for much of the twentieth century.

THE ORIGINS OF DEMOCRACY IN URUGUAY

Uruguay was slower than Chile to democratize. Indeed, throughout the nineteenth century, it constituted an unstable authoritarian regime that was plagued by controlled elections, frequent opposition revolts, and periodic state repression. During the first couple of decades of the twentieth century, however, Uruguay stabilized and democratized. Opposition revolts came to an end, and the state began to respect civil and political liberties more consistently. Most importantly, in 1918 Uruguay enacted a new constitution that mandated the use of the secret ballot, proportional representation, universal male suffrage, and obligatory voter registration in elections.[40] With the advent of the new constitution, voter turnout rose considerably, electoral manipulation declined, and elections became increasingly competitive.

Democratization in Uruguay was driven by the same developments that helped bring it about in Chile. First, in the late nineteenth and early twentieth century, the Uruguayan state used its growing export revenues to professionalize its military. Although Uruguay was slower than Chile to strengthen its armed forces in part because it did not face pressing external conflicts, by the end of the first decade of the twentieth century it had clearly established a monopoly on violence. Because the opposition could no longer hope to overthrow the government by force, it abandoned the armed struggle and began to push more aggressively for democratic reforms. In the absence of revolts, the government had fewer incentives to engage in state repression.

The development of strong parties also facilitated democratization in Uruguay. As Chapter 4 discussed, two strong parties emerged in Uruguay in the late nineteenth century: the Blanco Party and the Colorado Party. The opposition Blancos used their influence to win seats in the legislature and to promote democratic reform. The catalyst for democratic reform, however, was a split within the ruling Colorado Party. In the wake of this split, dissident Colorados allied with the Blancos, giving them enough votes in the 1917 constitutional convention to approve democratic reforms. As a result, the dominant faction of the Colorado Party negotiated a pact with the Blancos in which they agreed to support the reforms in exchange for concessions.

---

[40] The constitution was approved by a plebiscite in 1917, but it did not take effect until 1918.

REVOLTS AND MILITARY PROFESSIONALIZATION IN URUGUAY

During the nineteenth century, the Uruguayan state had even lower coercive capacity than Chile and was even more prone to revolts. State infrastructure was minimal until the late nineteenth century: The railroad was not built until 1868, and the Uruguayan countryside initially had few decent roads and virtually no bridges (McLaughlin 1973, 97, 111).[41] Moreover, the government had few funds to spend on its military. The bureaucracy was tiny and the state controlled no resources – most state revenue came from customs duties (López-Alves 2000, 54, 226; Rock and López-Alves 2000, 184).

Uruguay formally established a national army in 1830, but initially it existed mostly on paper (López-Alves 2000, 54; Bañales 1970, 292). The problem was not the number of troops, which generally represented a larger percentage of the population than did the Chilean army, but rather their lack of training, discipline, and equipment (Somma 2011, 148–149).[42] During the first half of the nineteenth century, soldiers were often armed with nothing more than knives and spears (López Chirico 1985, 27). Moreover, the rank-and-file soldier typically earned less than a rural peasant, which obliged the Uruguayan military to resort to widespread forced conscription (López Chirico 1985, 27–28; Bañales 1970, 292–293; Somma 2011, 152–153). As a result, the troops typically came from the poorest sectors of the population, had little discipline, and were often thrust into battle without much training. In 1861, the war minister complained that the army was composed mostly of criminals and vagrants (Somma 2011, 149).

To make matters worse, the officer corps was heavily politicized and lacked training. The Colorado Party gained firm control of the army in 1865 when the Colorado General Venancio Flores overthrew the Blanco President Bernardo Berro and purged the army of its remaining Blanco officers and soldiers (Casal 2004, 123). Even before that time, however, officers were promoted based on political connections rather than their expertise. As Moore (1978, 57) puts it: "A sort of spoils system obtained in which the adherents of the president were appointed to and advanced in the military hierarchy, while the military 'favorites' of the outgoing administration were relegated to reserve status." Owing in part to the political appointments, the number of officers in the army reserve grew, which represented a significant drain on the Treasury (Moore 1978, 57; McLaughlin 1973, 102–103). In 1860, the regular army had 9 generals, 126 commanders, 261 officers, and only 895 soldiers (López Chirico 1985, 26; Bañales 1970, 293). There were occasional efforts to improve the training of officers. For example, in 1823, 1843, 1844, and 1858, the government

---

[41] One contemporary source suggested that it cost three times as much to transport a ton of goods from Montevideo to the town of Durazno, which was 113 miles to the north, than it did to ship the goods from London to Montevideo (cited in McLaughlin 1973, 112).

[42] In 1852, the army constituted 1.1 percent of the national population, and even in the late nineteenth century it generally represented at least 0.4 percent of the population (Somma 2011, 151–152).

established military schools for officers, but none of these schools lasted very long or changed the politicized culture of the military (Somma 2011, 149; López Chirico 1985, 211; Ferrer Llul 1975, 43).

The civic guard, which President Manuel Oribe created in 1835, had even less discipline, training, and equipment than the army. Moreover, troops from the civic guard, which became associated with the Blanco Party, sometimes fought against the Colorado-dominated regular army. Indeed, Blanco President Juan Francisco Giró reestablished the civic guard in 1853 specifically to counterbalance the army (Somma 2011, 150; López Chirico 1985, 29–30). A subsequent Blanco president, Bernardo Berro, continued these efforts, enrolling 16,000 troops in the civic guard while slashing the size of the army to 914 troops in 1860 (Bañales 1970, 293; Casal 2001).

Both the Blanco and the Colorado parties also maintained large militias, which drew on members of the army as well as the civic guard. Regional leaders from the party generally controlled these militias and used them to serve their own personal political ambitions. During wartime, the Colorado militias generally fought alongside the Colorado-dominated army, whereas Blanco officers and soldiers often defected from the army and fought with the Blanco militias.

The weakness of the military and the existence of party militias encouraged the opposition to rebel, and the rebels often mobilized thousands of troops (Somma 2011, 123). Not surprisingly, the opposition sometimes prevailed in the revolts or obtained important concessions, which encouraged further rebellions. There were approximately fifty revolts before 1904, including at least thirteen major armed insurgencies (Vanger 1963, 9; Somma 2011, 120; see Table 5.3). Some of the civil wars, especially the Guerra Grande (1839–1851), lasted years, so that Uruguay had more years of war than peace in the nineteenth century. In 1876, José Pedro Varela, an Uruguayan writer and politician, lamented that "it can well be said, without exaggeration, that war is the normal state of the Republic" (cited in Bañales 1970, 294).

The civil wars typically pitted Blancos versus Colorados, although in some instances, such as the 1855, 1875, and 1886 conflicts, different factions within the parties fought each other. The wars stemmed more often from disputes over power than ideology. The Blancos, for example, rebelled several times because the Colorado governments reneged on power-sharing agreements or sought to exclude them from power. During the early nineteenth century, foreign powers, including Argentina, Brazil, France, and Great Britain, intervened frequently in the conflicts, but after 1865, direct foreign intervention in Uruguayan civil wars largely came to an end, although both parties continued to purchase weapons abroad.

The wars had high human and material costs. For example, approximately 1,000 people are estimated to have died in the 1904 civil war, which is a very high death toll for a country that had a population of less than one million in 1900. The economic costs of the civil wars were also quite large. Military spending absorbed a large portion of the government's budget during wartime. Based on

TABLE 5.3 *Major revolts in Uruguay, 1830–1929*

Year	Description of revolt	Type of revolt (outcome)
1832	Supporters of Juan Antonio Lavalleja failed to assassinate President Fructuoso Rivera and were defeated by Rivera's army with support from Argentina.	Military coup (suppressed)
1836	General Rivera rebelled against President Manuel Oribe after he was dismissed as head of the army. The revolt was defeated.	Military coup (suppressed)
1837–1838	Rivera rebelled against President Manuel Oribe and overthrew him with the help of 2,000 men, the French navy, and the Riograndese Republic.	Elite insurrection (took power)
1839–1851	*Guerra Grande*. Oribe and the Blancos rebelled against Rivera and the Colorados and laid siege to Montevideo. Oribe surrendered after lengthy war.	Elite insurrection (suppressed)
1853	The Colorado-led army rebelled against Blanco president Juan Giró and replaced him with a Colorado triumvirate. Blancos then unsuccessfully rebelled.	Military coup (took power)
1855	Dissident Colorados and some Blancos rebelled and seized control of Montevideo. President Venancio Flores resigned and new elections were held.	Elite insurrection (overthrown)
1858	A faction of the Colorado Party revolted against the Fusion government of Gabriel Pereira. The rebels were defeated and their leaders were executed.	Elite insurrection (suppressed)
1863–1865	Colorado General Venancio Flores led a rebel army of 3,000 that overthrew Blanco President Bernardo Berro with assistance of Brazil.	Elite insurrection (took power)
1868	Bernardo Berro and Blancos initiated a rebellion in which Colorado President Flores was killed. In revenge, Colorados killed Berro and many Blancos.	Elite insurrection (suppressed)
1870–1872	Blanco leader Aparicio Saravia rebelled against the Colorado government with 5,000 men. He ultimately signed a peace agreement and obtained concessions.	Elite insurrection (suppressed)
1875	Military officers deposed President José Ellauri after he named Blancos to his cabinet. Pedro Varela took his place.	Military coup (overthrown)
1875	*Tricolor Revolution*. Dissident Colorados revolted with support of some Blancos against the Colorado government of Pedro Varela. They were defeated.	Elite insurrection (suppressed)
1876	Under pressure from his minister of war, President Varela resigned and the minister Colonel Lorenzo Latorre assumed the presidency.	Military coup (took power)
1886	*Principistas* including Colorados and Blancos rebelled with 1,300 men against President Máximo Santos, but they were easily defeated.	Elite insurrection (suppressed)

TABLE 5.3 (*continued*)

Year	Description of revolt	Type of revolt (outcome)
1896	Aparicio Saravia initiated a revolt with 1,000 men but without support of Blanco leadership. They were quickly defeated.	Elite insurrection (suppressed)
1897	Blanco leader Aparicio Saravia rebelled with 3,000 men against Colorado President Juan Idiarte but signed a peace agreement after several battles.	Elite insurrection (suppressed)
1898	Following President Cuesta's decision to shut down Congress, military revolts occurred in February and July, but they were suppressed.	Military coup (suppressed)
1903	Saravia rebelled with 16,000 men when President José Batlle reneged on a peace accord, but war was averted when Batlle compromised.	Elite insurrection (suppressed)
1904	Saravia revolted with 15,000 men against Colorado President José Batlle, but Saravia was killed after several bloody battles and the Blancos surrendered.	Elite insurrection (suppressed)
1910	Some radical Blanco leaders revolted with 2,000 men, but most Blancos did not join the revolt and the Colorado government quickly defeated them.	Elite insurrection (suppressed)

Source: Latin American Revolts Database.

the research of the Uruguayan historian Eduardo Acevedo, the US embassy calculated that the forty-five revolts and one foreign war that Uruguay experienced between 1828 and 1925 had direct costs of $201 million and created public debts of $394 million in current dollars.[43] The wars also depleted the labor force and resulted in great destruction to infrastructure, firms, farms, and ranches.

The frequent revolts also deepened authoritarianism and subverted constitutional rule. According to Panizza (1997, 671), of the twenty-seven presidents who served between independence and 1910, nine were driven from power, two were assassinated, one was seriously wounded, twelve faced major revolts, and only three served out their terms without facing a major armed revolt. The government typically responded to the revolts by arresting members of the opposition, censoring the press, suspending civil and political liberties, and sometimes executing prisoners. Under the 1830 constitution, the president had the right to unilaterally impose measures in response to security threats and presidents used these emergency powers frequently. For example, in February 1833, the government suspended and arrested opposition legislators whom it accused of supporting the rebels (Loveman 1993, 297). In 1844, in the midst of the Guerra Grande, an opposition legislator denounced the president's growing

[43] Dispatch of US Minister to Uruguay, No. 141, May 25, 1906. Microfilm Roll 19, National Archives.

dictatorial powers and his "attacks on liberties and civil rights" (Loveman 1993, 297).

The Uruguayan government undertook some efforts to increase its coercive capacity during the late nineteenth century, but these efforts did not get very far. In contrast to Chile, Uruguay did not face major external conflicts in the late nineteenth century, which would have put greater pressure on it to strengthen its military. Uruguay did participate alongside Argentina and Brazil in the War of the Triple Alliance (1865–1870) against Paraguay, but it was a minor player in this conflict and its experience was a bitter one that undermined the country's military capacity rather than strengthening it (Casal 2004, 119, 138–139). Uruguay sent 1,500 troops to fight in the war but it experienced massive desertions and high casualties: By the end, only 150–250 Uruguayan troops remained and the Oriental Division fought using Paraguayan prisoners of war (Moore 1978, 22; Casal 2004, 119, 126–127).

After the war, Colonel Lorenzo Latorre, who served as minister of war and then as president (1876–1880), built up the country's infrastructure and sought to create a small but effective army that would have a monopoly on violence. He added two new military battalions and purchased modern weaponry, including Krupp artillery and Remington rifles (McLaughlin 1973, 169–170; López Chirico 1985, 33; Moore 1978, 27–28). Latorre also ordered the political chiefs of each department (the largest administrative unit in Uruguay) to confiscate weaponry in their districts and forbade the import of arms by private citizens in order to prevent rebels from gaining access to weapons (Bañales 1970, 296).[44]

Latorre's reforms, however, did not dramatically increase the state's coercive capacity or bring a permanent end to the cycle of revolts. The military continued to be highly politicized and poorly equipped, and Latorre himself enacted significant military cutbacks toward the end of his term in order to reduce the government's financial deficit (McLaughlin 1973, 239; López-Alves 2000, 93). Between 1876 and 1880, the number of active-duty military officers declined from 1,205 to 153, and the number of battalions dropped from eight to four (Rock and López-Alves 2000, 197). President Julio Herrera y Obes, the civilian president who took power in 1890, weakened the army further by retiring numerous officers and cutting the salaries of those who remained (Rock and López-Alves 2000, 198). In addition, the training of officers remained deficient. The government did not create an enduring military academy until 1885 and even this school did not have an immediate impact (Somma 2011, 159; López Chirico 1985, 37).[45]

---

[44] Latorre also provided weapons and funding to departmental political chiefs and promoted the development of rural police forces to deal with rural insecurity (McLaughlin 1973, 220; Moore 1978, 27). He stationed army battalions in the departments, but he moved them frequently to reduce the likelihood that they would conspire against him (McLaughlin 1973, 217).

[45] Prior to 1885, the government commissioned officers without regard to their educational qualifications, but after that year the government increasingly required officers to have military training (Moore 1978, 66).

The opposition Blancos, meanwhile, retained their ability to launch rebellions. In fact, the control that the Blancos gained of some departments beginning in 1872 strengthened them militarily by enabling them to deploy the local police forces and build up their militias. The national government generally refrained from intervening in these departments, and government efforts to reduce the Blancos' control of these departments led to revolts in 1897 and 1904.

It was not until the early twentieth century that Uruguay built up and professionalized its military, bringing an end to the cycle of revolts. The export boom and accompanying economic growth that Uruguay experienced during the late nineteenth and early twentieth century helped finance the military modernization efforts. Exports grew from an annual average of $76.1 million in 1870–1874 to $332.6 million in 1925–1929 (in constant 1980 dollars), and the country's GDP rose from $738 million to $6,398 million (in constant 1990 dollars) during the same period (Bértola and Ocampo 2013, 86, 96). The strong economic growth that Uruguay experienced at the outset of the twentieth century discouraged revolts not only by financing military professionalization but also by increasing the economic costs of war. The price of land and livestock rose sharply during this period, and Blanco ranchers and businessmen gradually became unwilling to risk their increasingly valuable assets and investments by going to war (Vanger 1980, 9–10, 355; Bértola and Ocampo 2013, 107).[46]

President José Batlle y Ordóñez (1903–1907) built up the military largely in response to a major Blanco revolt at the outset of his presidency. During the 1904 rebellion, the Blancos mobilized 10,000 rebel troops, but Batlle mustered militia units and expanded the military to 30,000 troops, including 8,000 regular army soldiers, creating the largest army in the history of Uruguay (Rock and López-Alves 2000, 201; Vanger 1963, 141; Moore 1978, 38). Even more importantly, the government troops were better armed than the rebels. In the run-up to the war, the military had outfitted its soldiers with modern weapons, including Krupp cannons, Maxim machine guns, and Mauser rifles (Somma 2011, 160). During the war, the government acquired 4,000 new Remington rifles, along with a shipment of Colt machine guns (Vanger 1963, 89, 95).[47] In addition, the government had the advantage of controlling the railroads and the telegraphs, which it used to communicate with officers in the field and rapidly transport troops to where they were needed. By the turn of the century, Uruguay had extensive telegraph networks and more than 1,600 kilometers of railroad track, up from 200 in 1876 (Vanger 1963, 142; Somma 2011,

---

[46] As one rancher said: "A law prohibiting revolutions is necessary because if they exist, cures for scabies [and other investments in livestock] are useless" (cited in López Chirico 1985, 39).

[47] The Blanco opposition also purchased weapons during this conflict, including 2,000 rifles, three cannons, and three machine guns, but they had to rely on voluntary contributions to pay for the weapons and then try to sneak them across the border (Vanger 1963, 123, 155).

161–162). The government's numerous military advantages enabled it to win a resounding victory in the 1904 war.[48]

In the wake of this decisive victory, Batlle took a few steps that reduced the likelihood of subsequent rebellions. First, he granted the rebels an amnesty but little else. Past peace agreements had generally awarded significant concessions to the rebels, which encouraged further rebellions, but Batlle was in a much stronger bargaining position than previous presidents, given his decisive victory in the war. Second, Batlle required the immediate and complete disarmament of the rebels. The loss of weaponry meant that the Blancos would have to rearm themselves at great cost to carry out future rebellions. Third, Batlle stripped the Blancos of their control of the departments and abolished the urban military companies, ostensibly departmental prison guards, which had served as the base of the rebel army (Vanger 1963, 170). As a result, the Blancos could no longer use state employees in these departments to build up their militias; nor could they block the army from intervening in these departments to prevent uprisings. Fourth, Batlle maintained an army of 10,000 men, which was twice the size it had prior to the war (Moore 1978, 40). Moreover, the government made contingency plans so that the army could quickly be expanded to 80,000 men in the event of an uprising (Vanger 1980, 296).

Batlle also took steps to professionalize and depoliticize the military. He integrated some Blanco officers back into the army, thereby reducing the partisan nature of the military (Moore 1978, 40). He boosted military pensions and stripped some nonmilitary personnel, such as police officers and militia members, of their military status so as to boost the prestige of the military (Moore 1978, 40–41). Finally, he divided the military into three regional commands and increased the number of military units in order to make it more difficult for officers to coordinate to overthrow the government (Moore 1978, 49; Vanger 1963, 170, 251–252).

The professionalization efforts intensified after the end of Batlle's first term. During Batlle's second administration (1911–1915), the government hired a ten-person French military mission, although its arrival was postponed until after World War I (Moore 1978, 66). The mission, which lasted until World War II, overhauled the military academies and the training of officers along French lines. Tactical manuals were translated verbatim from French military sources and some Uruguayan officers were sent to France for training (López Chirico 1985, 43; Bañales 1970, 301). Uruguay also expanded the number of officers it trained domestically during this period. Between 1920 and 1932, 374 officers graduated from the country's Military School, which was more than had graduated in the three decades from the founding of the school in 1885 until 1919 (Caetano 1994, 79). During this period, the military's budget increased, and it acquired the most up-to-date weaponry from Europe and the

---

[48] In the battle of Tupambaé, for example, the military's machine guns devastated the Blanco cavalry and the rebel troops eventually ran out of ammunition (Vanger 1963, 147).

United States in sufficient quantities to arm 50,000 men (López Chirico 1985, 42). The government also granted the military greater control over spending and promotions, and Congress enacted a series of organic laws that banned patronage appointments in the military and sought to reduce political interference in the armed forces (Moore 1978, 44). The officer corps continued to be mostly Colorado, but no single faction predominated, and Blanco officers gained some ground (López Chirico 1985, 43; Bañales 1970, 302).

The professionalization of the military and the bitter memory of the 1904 war helped bring an end to the opposition revolts that had plagued the country throughout the nineteenth century. Blanco leaders came to realize that they had little chance of defeating the military and so they began to focus exclusively on the electoral route to power. A prominent Blanco, Basilio Muñoz, attempted another uprising in 1910, but the Conservative leadership of the Blanco Party opposed the revolt, as did the country's major economic interests (Vanger 1980, 64–67, 86–91). The rebels, who sought to prevent Batlle from being elected to a second presidential term, hoped that anti-Batlle sectors of the military would join them in revolt, but no such uprising occurred. President Claudio Williman (1907–1911) quickly mobilized 30,000 troops, which easily suppressed the revolt (Vanger 1980, 90–91; Nahum 1987, 17).[49] Aparicio Saravia's sons sought to foment another rebellion in 1911, but they were discouraged by the leadership of the Blancos on the grounds that they could not possibly succeed (Vanger 1980, 151–152). By 1917, Muñoz, the erstwhile rebel, had also become convinced that armed rebellion would be futile and for that reason persuaded the Blancos to sign a pact with the Colorados that year on the new constitution (Vanger 2010, 232).

Thus, in Uruguay, as in Chile, the gradual strengthening of the coercive capacity of the state helped bring an end to the frequent revolts that had created unstable authoritarian rule in the nineteenth century. The process took longer in Uruguay because the state had fewer resources and it did not face the type of external wars that had stimulated rapid military professionalization in Chile in the late nineteenth century. Nevertheless, by the early twentieth century, the Uruguayan state had acquired a clear monopoly on violence, which led the opposition Blancos to abandon the armed struggle and increasingly focus on the electoral path to power.

THE RISE OF PARTIES AND DEMOCRACY IN URUGUAY

Political parties played a crucial role in the emergence of democracy in Uruguay, as in Chile. Over the course of the nineteenth century, Uruguay developed parties with strong organizations and widespread and enduring ties to the

---

[49] To discourage revolts, Williman also helped push through a law stipulating that rebels would be punished with fifteen to eighteen months in prison (Bañales 1970, 298–299).

electorate. Uruguayan parties arose based on a territorial cleavage, rather than a religious or ideological cleavage. Whereas urban areas, especially the country's capital, Montevideo, became the base of the Colorado Party, the countryside came to constitute the stronghold of the Blanco Party.

Nevertheless, Uruguay's small size and the territorial concentration of its population enabled both parties to gradually develop support and an organizational presence throughout the country. Uruguay was by far the smallest South American country in the nineteenth century, with only 68,000 square miles of territory. By 1908, 50 percent of the population lived in urban areas with Montevideo alone containing 30 percent of the total (Instituto Nacional de Estadística 2021; Nahum 2007, 35). The country had no major geographic obstacles and possessed an extensive coastline that facilitated domestic as well as international travel. Uruguay also benefited from the early introduction of the railroads and the telegraph, which linked together different areas. By 1900, the country already had 1,074 miles of railroad track and 4,500 miles of telegraph lines, which gave it the highest ratio of track and lines to territory on the continent (Summerhill 2006, 302; Banks and Wilson 2014).

The two parties originated in a lengthy civil war, the Great War, which racked Uruguay from 1839 to 1851. During this conflict, followers of the former president, General Fructuoso Rivera, came to be known as Colorados because they wore a red emblem to distinguish themselves from followers of Rivera's successor, General Manuel Oribe, who wore a white emblem and became known as Blancos. Rivera's forces occupied Montevideo in 1838 and managed to hold it throughout the civil war, but the Blancos controlled the countryside and laid siege to the capital. By the time the civil war ended in 1851, strong partisan identities had developed on both sides based in part on geography (McLaughlin 1973, 34; Pivel Devoto 1942). Over time, each party made inroads in the other party's bastions, but territorial cleavages continued to structure the support of each party.[50]

After the Great War came to an end in 1851, efforts to move beyond the partisan divide failed to prosper. During the 1850s, several fusion governments arose that included members of both parties, but these administrations did not significantly weaken partisan ties (Zum Felde 1985, 189–193; Castellanos and Pérez 1981, 16–26). Subsequently, a few military presidents, such as General Lorenzo Latorre (1876–1880), General Máximo Santos (1882–1886), and General Máximo Tajes (1886–1890), also included some Blancos in their cabinets, but all of these presidents belonged to the Colorado Party and their administrations were Colorado-dominated (McLaughlin 1973, 211–222, 264–266; López-Alves 2000, 71).

---

[50] The parties did not differ significantly in terms of ideology during the nineteenth century. Both parties, for example, were largely supportive of free trade and secularization (Somma 2011, 169–170; López-Alves 2000, 56).

The intermittent wars between Blancos and Colorados during the nineteenth century contributed to the development of strong partisan ties by fostering intense antagonisms. The civil wars took a toll not just on the direct participants in the conflicts but also on their friends and family members as well as civilians located in conflict zones. Both sides committed atrocities, including the slaughter of civilians and the execution of prisoners, which deepened antagonisms and hardened partisan loyalties. Referring to the mid-nineteenth century, Zum Felde (1985, 198) wrote: "All the creole families of Montevideo have a father, a brother, or a son in the armies; and the Blancos or the Colorados have killed a son or a brother in many of these families: All have deaths to avenge. The pain, blood, and hate are felt in their own flesh." These partisan loyalties were passed down across generations and tales of the heroism of their leaders and the treachery of the enemy infused popular culture. Not surprisingly, it became rare for people to change parties.

In addition to fighting wars, the parties competed regularly in elections, which also contributed to the construction of party organizations and identities.[51] The parties engaged in numerous activities during electoral periods, including selecting candidates, carrying out propaganda and voter registration campaigns, printing and distributing ballots, and seeking to boost turnout by holding election banquets and transporting voters to the polls. In nonelectoral periods, the parties would sometimes hold conventions to define their platforms, craft their organizational structures and regulations, and select their leadership.[52]

The two parties first developed meaningful organizations in the mid-nineteenth century. In 1854, Blanco leaders formed an executive committee, which created "a Society named the Blanco Party" and identified the responsibilities and desired characteristics of its members (Corbo 2016, 104–106). Subsequently, the leaders of the Blanco Party began to establish clubs to engage in debates and electoral activities, such as the National Club and the Youth Club (Fernández and Machín 2017, 144). Under the auspices of the National Club, the Blancos wrote their first comprehensive party program in 1872 (Lindahl 1962, 246–247; Hierro López 2015, 161–162). In 1887, the Blanco Party held a national convention that selected its national leadership and established departmental and sectional committees (Pivel Devoto 1943,

---

[51] Until 1918, Uruguay held direct elections for the Chamber of Representatives every three years, but indirect elections for the Senate every two years and the presidency every four years. The president, who had a mandate of four years without the possibility of immediate reelection, was elected by the two chambers of the legislature meeting together. The entirety of the lower chamber was renewed every three years, whereas only one-third of the Senate was elected every two years – senators had six-year terms.

[52] The departmental and sectional organizations typically chose the participants in the conventions who usually numbered in the hundreds (Lindahl 1962, 40–42, 230–233). After the parties split in the 1910s and 1920s, the different factions typically held their own conventions and elected their own leaders.

292). At this convention, the party also formally adopted the name of the National Party, although many people continued to refer to it as the Blanco Party (Corbo 2016, 199–202).

The Colorado Party was somewhat slower to develop and did not craft its first party program until 1907 (Lindahl 1962, 246–247). Beginning in the 1860s, Colorado leaders sought to establish a party that was organized from below and had numerous local clubs, but they initially made progress only in Montevideo. Batlle renewed these efforts during the 1890s, building a territorially based party with elected leaders and clubs that represented the different sections of each department (Hierro López 2015, 169–170). Under his leadership, the Colorado Party became a strong, programmatically oriented organization with a permanent nationwide structure that the Blancos felt pressure to imitate.

By the early twentieth century, both parties had established permanent national organizations that had branches or clubs in all the departmental capitals as well as in the judicial sections of cities and sometimes in rural areas as well. Each department and section had its own party officials who were responsible for organizing party activities in that area. In addition, the two parties had affiliated newspapers, which they used to propagandize. These newspapers often represented different tendencies within the parties. For example, the Colorado Party had *El Día*, which was Batlle's paper, as well as *La Mañana*, whereas the Blancos had *El Nacional*, *El Plata*, and *El País* (Fernández and Machín 2017, 227–244).

Party financing came mostly from party members: Wealthy members made monthly contributions and at times funded a newspaper as well. Members who held an elected position were expected to contribute a portion of their salary to the party.[53] The parties also frequently used state resources and personnel to aid their campaigns, and departmental political chiefs typically took charge of political campaigns in their constituencies (Vanger 1963, 175).

Both the Blancos and the Colorados proved extraordinarily durable, dominating elections and controlling the vast majority of political positions for most of the nineteenth and early twentieth centuries. Third parties occasionally emerged during the nineteenth century, such as the *principista* parties, or parties of principles, which called for an end to violence and the enactment of democratic reforms (Castellanos and Pérez 1981, 38–39; Somma 2012, 19–22). The first of the *principista* parties, the Liberal Union, arose in 1855, but the movement reached its peak with the founding of the Radical Party in 1872 and its successor, the Constitutional Party, in 1880. These parties drew support from educated professionals in Montevideo, but they never gained much of a following elsewhere.[54] By the early twentieth century, the *principista* parties

---

[53] For example, in the early twentieth century, the Blanco Party required its members to contribute up to twenty pesos per month to the party (Vanger 1963, 191). The Batllistas even collected fees from ordinary civil servants who belonged to the party (Lindahl 1962, 244).

[54] The Constitutional Party won a few seats in the 1880s and 1890s.

had disappeared, and most of their members had returned to the Blancos or the Colorados (McLaughlin 1973, 277; López-Alves 2000, 57). Other parties, such as the Socialist Party, the Uruguayan Communist Party, and the Civic Union, a party with close ties to the Catholic Church, sprang up in the early twentieth century, but none of them won more than 5 percent of the vote.

Electoral data from nineteenth-century Uruguay are fragmentary, but the data that do exist suggest that both the Colorados and the Blancos had ample support across various departments. Diez de Medina (1994, 193) reports that in 1872 there were 2,494 people who were registered as Colorados and 1,188 registered as Blancos in Montevideo; there were 293 registered Colorados and 88 registered Blancos in Colonia; and 1,146 registered Colorados and 491 registered Blancos in Rocha. The 1887 legislative elections resulted in a lopsided victory for the ruling Colorados, which won two-thirds of the vote thanks in part to electoral manipulation. Nevertheless, the Blancos still managed to win at least one-quarter of the vote in fifteen out of the nineteen departments and it finished first in two of them (Pivel Devoto 1943, 362). The two parties together won 94 percent of the valid vote in 1887, although the Blancos competed in alliance with the Constitutional Party in a few departments. As Table 5.4 indicates, the two parties continued to win an overwhelming share of the vote in the early twentieth century, although the differences between the two parties narrowed somewhat.

The Blancos and the Colorados split on numerous occasions, but none of these ruptures became permanent. During the nineteenth century, the main division in each party was between idealists and personalists. The idealists supported democratic reform and compromise with the other party, whereas the personalists typically backed strong one-party leadership and advocated taking a hard line against the opposing party, even if that meant war or repression. The personalists were often allied with rural leaders and had their main base in the countryside, whereas the core supporters of the idealists were urban professionals. The divisions within parties led to intraparty warfare on a few occasions, such as in 1875 and 1886, but mostly the two factions coexisted uneasily with each other. At times, the idealists in the two parties cooperated with each other, as in the 1873 presidential elections, but partisan loyalties made such cooperation difficult (McLaughlin 1973, 146). Some of the idealists left the two main parties, at least temporarily, to join *principista* parties.[55]

Initially, the Blancos and the Colorados traded control of the government, but in 1865 Venancio Flores overthrew Blanco President Bernardo Berro and established Colorado rule, which would last until 1958. Although the two parties had relatively similar levels of support, Colorado governments intervened in elections in the late nineteenth century to ensure they prevailed.[56] Until the 1870s, the president had influence over the departmental mayors who controlled

---

[55] Factionalism continued in the twentieth century, and the electoral law of 1910 made it worse by enabling factions to run separate lists in elections while still counting their votes for their party.
[56] The Blancos also committed infractions in the departments that they controlled.

TABLE 5.4 *Presidential and legislative elections in Uruguay, 1900–1929*

Election	Colorado votes (% of valid vote)	Blanco votes (% of valid vote)	Valid votes	Valid votes/ population (%)
1901 legislative elections	15,268 (55.0)	12,516 (45.0)	27,784	2.9
1905 legislative elections	27,163 (61.3)	16,645 (37.6)	44,292	4.3
1907 legislative elections	28,202 (63.5)	13,355 (30.1)	44,385	4.3
1910 legislative elections	26,787 (86.8)	Abstained	30,878	2.8
1913 legislative elections	38,011 (69.2)	14,792 (26.9)	54,949	4.2
1917 legislative elections	66,170 (51.5)	61,245 (47.7)	128,388	9.5
1919 legislative elections	98,602 (51.4)	85,982 (44.9)	191,677	15.0
1922 presidential elections	123,076 (50.4)	117,901 (48.3)	244,156	17.8
1925 legislative elections	134,617 (49.6)	127,207 (46.9)	271,468	16.9
1926 presidential elections	141,581 (48.9)	140,055 (48.4)	289,255	18.9
1928 legislative elections	144,070 (48.2)	145,159 (48.5)	299,017	18.5

Source: Latin America Historical Elections Database.
NB: Data for the Colorados and Blancos refer to the votes for all factions of these parties. There are minor discrepancies in the vote totals reported by the different sources.

the electoral registry.[57] Control of the registry enabled the government to purge opposition supporters and to register government supporters multiple times under different names or to allow them to vote even when they were not eligible (Somma 2012, 28). In addition, the president appointed the political chiefs who presided over each department.[58] The political chiefs and their employees, including the local police, could intimidate the opposition, block access to the voting centers, and even suspend the elections (McLaughlin 1973, 39). If necessary, the electoral authorities could even commit fraud, although Somma (2012, 27–28) suggests that fraud was not widespread.

Governmental electoral manipulation was also facilitated by the fact that only a small fraction of the adult population was eligible to vote, and turnout

---

[57] The mayors were popularly elected but many of them owed their election to the support of the president. The position of departmental mayor was eliminated in 1878 (Somma 2012, 9).
[58] The president and his advisers also typically picked the legislative candidates of the ruling party who were therefore beholden to the executive (McLaughlin 1973, 38). Nevertheless, the legislature was not always compliant.

tended to be quite low. State employees represented a large share of the electorate and the executive branch wielded influence over them.[59] Government bureaucrats often instructed their employees how to vote and because the vote was oral and public, it was possible to monitor compliance.

Suffrage rights were relatively broad during the independence and immediate post-independence period, but the 1830 constitution restricted the suffrage considerably. The 1830 constitution, which was not replaced until 1918, disenfranchised women, servants, day laborers, soldiers, drunks, vagrants, criminals, morally and physically incompetent individuals, and people under twenty years of age (eighteen if married). The constitution also denied suffrage to illiterates, but this measure only applied to people who came of age after 1840 on the grounds that many of the men who had participated in the wars for independence did not know how to read or write but should not be prevented from voting (Diez de Medina 1994, 76).[60] The voting restrictions were not always enforced, but they presumably deterred many people from voting, as did the fact that the results were largely predetermined. In addition, opposition parties at times encouraged abstention to protest electoral manipulation. As a result, voter turnout in Uruguay typically represented less than two percent of the total population during the nineteenth century. In some elections, turnout was particularly low. The Uruguayan newspaper *La Tribuna* reported that the 1868 legislative elections were "very peaceful – nobody came" (cited in McLaughlin 1973, 38).[61]

The Blancos often called for democratic reforms during the nineteenth century, but these measures were typically blocked or watered down by the Colorados who controlled the legislature. For example, in 1876 and 1884 the Blanco leader, Justino Jiménez de Aréchaga, proposed various reforms that included the expansion of the franchise, obligatory voting, direct elections, minority representation, and the secret ballot, but the Colorado Party stymied these proposals, although many of them were subsequently taken up in the 1918 constitution (González 1991, 143–145, 163–171). Subsequent reforms proposed by Blanco legislators, Carlos Berro and Martín Aguirre, in 1889 and 1894 also failed to advance in the face of opposition from Colorado legislators (González 1991, 179, 211–212).

Colorado governments did enact some democratic reforms but only measures that did not threaten their electoral dominance. As part of an 1897 peace agreement, President Juan Lindolfo Cuestas pushed through an electoral reform in 1898 that guaranteed minority representation in the legislature and municipal councils (González 1991, 233–234; McLaughlin 1973, 267–269).

---

[59] In 1916, the Uruguayan government had approximately 18,663 civilian employees, most of whom could be counted on to support the president – public employees were believed to represent approximately 15 percent of the electorate at the time (Vanger 2010, 125–126). Some scholars have suggested that they constituted as much as 40 percent of the electorate in earlier decades (Caetano 2015, 99).

[60] According to Somma (2012, 8), 30 percent of the population of Montevideo worked in one of the proscribed occupations in 1882, and 45 percent of the adult population was illiterate.

[61] In the Department of Cerro Largo, no voters showed up at all for the 1868 elections so the political chief, along with the police force, selected the winners (McLaughlin 1973, 38).

Whereas previously Uruguay had used the complete-list system in which all seats had been awarded to whichever party finished first in each department, under the new incomplete-list system the first-place party in each department would receive two-thirds of the seats in that department and the runner-up would receive one-third of the seats. The Cuestas administration also enacted a law stipulating that being able to sign your own name would be considered sufficient proof of literacy for purposes of voting and that only people with authenticated written contracts would be classified as day laborers or domestic servants (González 1991, 229). These stipulations weakened the bans on voting by illiterates, day laborers, and servants since even illiterates could frequently sign their name and servants and day laborers did not typically have written contracts (Vanger 1963, 305). Nevertheless, none of these reforms brought an end to government electoral intervention.

Because elections were neither free nor fair, the Blancos at times refused to participate in them, calling for abstention in the 1854, 1867, 1872, and 1890 elections (Somma 2012, 20). In addition, Blancos sought to take advantage of the government's military weakness by carrying out uprisings. Although they did not succeed in taking power via these revolts during the late nineteenth century, the Blancos often obtained concessions in exchange for laying down their arms.

The most important of these concessions were power-sharing agreements that gave the Blancos political control of certain departments, typically units in which most people supported the Blanco Party. The first power-sharing agreement brought an end to the prolonged Revolution of the Spears (1870–1872). Under this pact, the Colorado government agreed to appoint Blancos as the political chiefs of four departments. The administrations that followed largely upheld the terms of this pact, but in the 1880s Colorado governments began to renege on the agreement, leading the Blancos to revolt again in 1896 and 1897.[62] In 1897 a new pact was signed, giving the Blancos control of six departments, although by this time the total number of departments in Uruguay had grown to nineteen.

The power-sharing agreements increased the political influence of the Blancos. Because the political chiefs could easily manipulate elections in their departments, Blancos were able to win the legislative seats as well as other government posts in these departments (López-Alves 2000, 86). This gave the Blancos significant legislative representation. For example, the four departments awarded to the Blancos in the pact of 1872 provided them with four senators and twelve representatives in a legislature that had a total of thirteen senators and forty-two representatives (McLaughlin 1973, 88). Nevertheless, the power-sharing agreements did little to advance democracy in Uruguay, but

---

[62] In 1882, for example, President Máximo Santos declined to appoint a Blanco as political chief of the Department of San José (McLaughlin 1973, 265). Moreover, in 1893 the government passed a new electoral law that sought to prevent the Blanco political chiefs from controlling elections in their departments (Weinstein 1975, 52).

instead institutionalized authoritarian rule by the parties in the departments that they controlled.

The power-sharing agreements came to an end after the Blancos' resounding defeat in the 1904 civil war, and the Colorados reasserted their dominance. After the war, the victorious president, José Batlle y Ordóñez, named his allies, all but two of whom were Colorados, as political chiefs in all of the departments (Vanger 1963, 175). Batlle also pushed through political reforms that helped the Colorado Party to expand their majority in the legislature.[63] Although the Blancos continued to call for democratic reforms during the early twentieth century, they did not control enough seats to enact the reforms on their own.[64] As a result, Uruguay remained firmly under authoritarian rule at the end of the first decade of the twentieth century.

THE SPLIT IN THE RULING PARTY AND DEMOCRATIC REFORM

During the second decade of the twentieth century, a split occurred within the ruling Colorado Party that would help bring democracy to Uruguay. The principal catalyst of the split was Batlle's proposal to create a collegial executive – a body composed of nine people that would replace the president – which dissidents within the ruling party viewed as a way for him to maintain his influence after his second presidential term ended. The roots of the split ran much deeper than that, however. Batlle's social and economic reforms had antagonized conservative sectors of the Colorado Party, which were tied to wealthy business and agricultural interests. The conservative sectors of the Colorado Party, together with the Blancos, gained a majority in the 1917 constitutional convention, and they embraced democratic reforms partly to weaken Batlle's wing of the Colorado Party.

During his first term as president (1903–1907), Batlle proposed a number of social and economic reforms, but these measures encountered opposition and it was not until after his reelection that his reform project picked up steam. In his second term (1911–1915), Batlle dramatically expanded the role of the state and reduced the role of foreign capital in the Uruguayan economy, nationalizing banks, establishing state-owned railroads, and creating state monopolies in insurance and electrical production. He also expanded public education, pushed for a greater separation of church and state, and enacted the divorce law that he had proposed during his first term. In addition, he proposed a variety of laws to benefit workers, although many of these measures were not passed until after his second term was over. These reforms included the establishment

---

[63] Subsequent presidents made greater efforts to appease the Blancos. President Claudio Williman (1907–1911), for example, adjusted the number of representatives elected in each department in a manner that favored the Blancos and dropped the electoral threshold to win seats to one-quarter of the total vote (McLaughlin 1973, 273–274; Weinstein 1975, 56).

[64] From 1898–1913, the Blancos won an average of 22 percent of the seats in the lower chamber.

of an eight-hour workday and a six-day workweek, restrictions on child labor, occupational safety regulations, old-age pensions, and severance payments for laid-off workers (Nahum 1987, 28–34). These measures were part of Batlle's plan to win labor support and to ensure that "those who would be Socialists elsewhere should be Colorados in Uruguay" (Vanger 2010: 177).

Batlle's most controversial measures, however, were his proposed constitutional reforms, especially his proposal to create a collegial executive. Batlle argued that the collegial executive would prevent presidents from transforming themselves into dictators, but he also sought to ensure that the Colorado Party dominated the collegial executive. According to Battle's proposal, all nine members of the collegial executive would initially belong to the majority party and only one member would be replaced each year.

Batlle's reform project, especially the collegial executive, met fierce resistance not only from the Blancos but also from various sectors of the Colorado Party. Opponents of the collegial executive viewed it as nothing more than a plan for Batlle to maintain his power after he left the presidency in 1915. The opposition newspaper *El Siglo* wrote that the collegial executive was Batlle's plan for "perpetual domination" and that it would lead to "eighteen years of Batlle as president" of the collegial executive (Vanger 1980, 213–214). Wealthy business and landed interests as well as the Catholic Church feared that Batlle sought to hold on to power in order to deepen his social and economic reforms, many of which they opposed (Castellanos and Pérez 1981, 212; Nahum 1987, 61–62; Vanger 1980, 218–219).

The opposition within the Colorado Party was led by Pedro Manini, a former disciple of Batlle who had served as his minister of interior from 1911 to 1912. Manini, who was elected to the Senate in early 1913, rounded up eleven Colorado senators who opposed the collegial executive and persuaded them to sign a statement in which they declared that they would approve the laws necessary for the election of the National Constitutional Convention (CNC), "only if they offer new and ample electoral guarantees and with the understanding that the election [of the CNC] will take place during the year 1914" (Giudici 1928, 447–448; see also Nahum 1987, 61–62; Vanger 1980, 223). The Colorado senators, who represented a majority of the Senate, sought the electoral safeguards in order to prevent Batlle from controlling the elections, which they hoped to delay so that it took place during the last year of his term when he would be politically weaker (Vanger 1980, 221).

Batlle supporters triumphed in the November 1914 Senate elections, however, and as a result the anti-collegialists lost their majority in the Senate. The Batllistas then used their control of both chambers to enact a law governing elections to the constitutional convention, but to win support from the opposition they included several democratic provisions in this law. First, they mandated the use of the secret ballot for the first time in the country's history. Second, voter registration was to be mandatory for all adult male citizens, including illiterates, although they would not be obliged to vote. Third, registered voters would be fingerprinted to ensure that they were who they claimed to be and to prevent people from registering twice. Fourth and finally, the CNC election law provided for some minority representation, but in a way that ensured that the majority party would dominate. In each department, the party or list that finished first would receive two-thirds of the seats and the remaining third would be divided up among the other parties using proportional representation (Vanger 2010, 29).[65]

The Blancos had long demanded some of these reforms, such as the secret ballot and proportional representation, but the Colorados had blocked them because they feared the reforms might weaken their stranglehold on power. In this case, however, Batlle and the Colorados were willing to make concessions because they needed to convince the Blancos and the dissident Colorados to participate in the elections for the constitutional convention in order to provide legitimacy for the new constitution (Giudici 1928, 470–471; Vanger 1980, 180).

Although the Blancos threatened to abstain from the elections to the constitutional convention, in the end they decided to participate, in part because of these electoral guarantees. Nationalist leaders believed that they had no real alternative to contesting the elections and that they had a real chance of defeating Batlle. As one senior Blanco leader, Aureliano Rodríguez Laretta, put it: "Although revolution would be the best and most efficient means, we cannot employ it … We have to choose political means. It could be possible for us to win the great battle in the Constituent Assembly" (Vanger 2010, 37–38). The Blancos tried to forge an electoral alliance with the dissident Colorados, but the differences between the two groups were too great. Instead, both sides ran on independent tickets.

To improve their chances, the Blancos undertook a massive voter registration drive and demanded that the government extend the registration period and create more registration centers, which it agreed to do so as not to give the Blancos an excuse to abstain from the elections (Vanger 2010, 48). By the time the registration period ended, 150,225 people had been added to the voter registration rolls, of which 110,911 were literate and 39,314 were illiterate (Vanger 2010, 52). This brought the total number of registered voters to 223,020, which was triple the number of voters registered previously (Castellanos and Pérez 1981, 213).[66]

The 1916 constitutional convention elections were the cleanest in Uruguay up to that date (Nahum 1987, 70). Voter turnout on election day, July 30,

---

[65] Despite these provisions, the Blancos and the dissident Colorados voted against the bill because of their opposition to the collegial executive. As the Nationalist leader Martín C. Martínez said in a speech to the Chamber of Deputies: "Our divergence with the majority of the Chamber is not over this or that point of the law on elections to the constitutional convention, as important as those might be. Our absolute divergence is over the very core of the question: over the convenience or inconvenience of constitutional reform." See Uruguay, *Diario de Sesiones de la Cámara de Representantes*, August 19, 1915, Extraordinary Session 5: 72.

[66] The Colorados also registered voters aggressively so that registered Colorados outnumbered registered Blancos by 129,745 to 93,275 (Barrán and Nahum 1987, 143).

1916, broke all previous records, equaling 10 percent of the population and 64 percent of registered voters (Castellanos and Pérez 1981, 213).[67] Nevertheless, turnout was significantly higher among Blancos than among Colorados: 72 percent of registered Blancos turned out to vote as opposed to 56 percent of registered Colorados (Barrán and Nahum 1987, 143; Moraes 2010, 107, 109). This may have been partly because Batlle had urged Colorados who opposed the collegial executive to abstain from voting, rather than vote for the opposition.

The outcome was a historic defeat for Batlle's wing of the Colorado Party, which won 41.2 percent of the valid vote, placing it a distant second. The Blancos captured 46.4 percent of the valid vote, and the anti-collegialist wing of the Colorado Party won another 9.9 percent of the valid vote. As a result, the Blancos and anti-collegialist Colorados gained a majority in the constitutional convention, controlling 127 seats to the Batllistas' 85 seats (Vanger 2010, 137).

The Batllistas lost in part because of the split since the two wings of the Colorado Party together captured a majority of the vote. Indeed, Batlle blamed the defeat on the split and on lower than expected voter turnout among the Colorados (Vanger 2010, 144). In addition, many of Battle's proposed reforms were unpopular, especially among the elites. Business and ranching interests helped fund the Blancos' campaign, and the Rural Federation, which represented rural interests, issued a statement exhorting rural workers "to show up at the urns to vote for the anti-collegialist candidates, whatever their party doctrine" (Barrán and Nahum 1987, 18). The Catholic Church opposed his secularization measures, and the highest-ranking church leader in Montevideo urged parishioners to vote for candidates who were against separating church and state (Barrán and Nahum 1987, 17–18; Vanger 2010, 121).

The Batllistas were also hurt by the democratic provisions in the electoral law. The extension of the vote to illiterates helped the Blancos because most illiterates lived in rural areas, which were their strongholds (Barrán and Nahum 1987, 50). Indeed, the departments of the interior accounted for 89.9 percent of the illiterates who registered to vote in the 1916 elections (Barrán and Nahum 1987, 50). The extension of the vote to illiterates and the compulsory voter registration provision also meant that public employees, whose support the governing Colorados could typically count on, represented a smaller portion of the electorate. Whereas previously public employees had represented approximately 15 percent of the electorate, in the elections for the constitutional convention they represented only 5 percent of the electorate (Vanger 2010, 126). Most importantly, however, the establishment of the secret ballot made it difficult for the government to compel public employees and others to support the governing party since the government could no longer monitor how they voted.

---

[67] Some 146,632 people voted in the elections, which was almost three times as many people as in the 1913 legislative elections (Caetano 1999, 418).

The Split in the Ruling Party and Democratic Reform

In the wake of the elections, the new Colorado President Feliciano Viera announced a pause in the reforms and shook up his cabinet, bringing in three or four anti-collegialists, including a Blanco leader. Viera's efforts to reconcile with the Blancos and dissident Colorados failed, however, and the anti-collegialist Colorados, who were dubbed Riveristas, announced that they would run in alliance with the Blancos in the January 1917 legislative elections. The Blancos and the Riveristas agreed upon a joint platform, calling for reduced taxes and the use of the secret ballot and proportional representation in future elections.

Many Batllistas were so convinced they had been hurt by the democratic provisions in the law used to elect the constitutional convention that a month before the 1917 legislative elections, they used their legislative majorities to pass a new electoral law that eliminated the secret ballot, banned illiterates from voting, and eliminated proportional representation in the allocation of legislative seats. The new electoral law also expanded the number of legislative seats, adding seats in populous departments, such as Montevideo, which favored the Batllistas (Vázquez Romero and Reyes Abadie 1979, 224–226). Not surprisingly, the Batllistas fared much better in the 1917 legislative elections than they had in the 1916 elections to the constitutional convention, finishing first with 49.3 percent of the total vote. The Blancos, meanwhile, won 25 percent of the vote on their own, and 22.7 percent in alliance with the Riveristas, while the Riveristas won an additional 2.5 percent of the vote running on their own.[68] The Blancos blamed their loss on fraud and government intervention as well as the absence of a secret ballot (Maiztegui Casas 2005, 191–193; Vanger 2010, 194–196, 200). The ban on the voting of illiterates also presumably hurt the Blancos since turnout fell by 17,264 votes compared to the 1916 elections (Bottinelli, Giménez, and Marius 2012, 63, 73). In addition, the changes in the rules governing the allocation of seats gave the Batllistas a boost. Under the new rules, the Batllistas won sixty-seven seats in the legislature to fifty-six for the opposition, whereas under the old rules the Batllistas would have held only a six-seat majority (Vanger 2010, 200).

Although the Batllistas retained control of the legislature, the Blancos and the Riveristas together held a majority of seats in the constitutional convention. Nevertheless, any constitution they devised would need to be ratified by the electorate in a popular referendum. The likelihood that the referendum would be approved, however, was enhanced by the fact that the legislation setting up the constitutional convention stipulated that the referendum would use the secret ballot and that illiterates would be allowed to vote – the same rules that had helped the Blancos and the Riveristas triumph in the elections for the constitutional convention.

The main goal of the Blancos and Riveristas was to approve constitutional reforms that would weaken the Colorados' control over elections and provide

---

[68] The Blancos and the Riveristas ended up running separate tickets in some departments in the interior where interparty hostility made a joint ticket difficult (Vanger 2010, 192–193).

the opposition with greater political representation.[69] In March 1917, the Constitutional Committee of the CNC, which was controlled by Blancos and Riveristas, submitted its reform proposal to the convention, stating:

> Representative democratic regimes rest on three solid foundations: the liberty of voters; the equality of citizens; [and] the representation in the assemblies of the country of the various forces of opinion according to their numerical strength. For the liberty of voters, we establish the secret vote. With universal suffrage, we proclaim the equality of citizens. But neither liberty nor equality is enough to assure a representative regime ... Proportional representation is the only system that realizes this work of justice.[70]

The committee proposed including language in the constitution stating that males above eighteen years of age would be eligible to vote and that elections would use the secret vote and integral proportional representation. It also called for obligatory voter registration and for the police and military to abstain from involvement in electoral affairs so that the government could not use them to intimidate voters. Finally, the proposal stipulated that all electoral authorities would be chosen using the aforementioned electoral methods and that, until these requirements came into force, elections would use the electoral provisions set forth in the law on the elections to the CNC.[71]

The assembly quickly approved many of the recommendations of the committee, including universal male suffrage, the secret vote, proportional representation, and obligatory voter registration. Most of the proposals of the Blancos and the Riveristas received support from the Socialist Party and the Catholic Civic Unión party, both of which held two seats in the CNC. Some of these measures, such as the secret vote and proportional representation, even passed unanimously because Batllistas boycotted the CNC to obstruct the proceedings.[72] The Blancos and the Riveristas together controlled 127 of the 218 seats in the assembly, which was enough votes to maintain a quorum only if nearly all their members attended.

Not all the democratic reforms discussed were approved. Although the Committee on the Constitution endorsed obligatory voter registration, a narrow majority of the committee rejected making voting compulsory. Proponents

---

[69] According to the Blanco leader, Aureliano Rodríguez Larreta, "it was agreed in the Constitutional Committee that the only reforms that should be formulated must be useful ones, the necessary ones, but not original ones that would raise resistance, not only in the minds of delegates, but in the people" (Vanger 2010, 207).

[70] Uruguay, *Diario de Sesiones de la Convención Nacional Constituyente*, March 21, 1917, Ordinary Session 24, pp. 164–165.

[71] Uruguay, *Diario de Sesiones de la Convención Nacional Constituyente*, March 21, 1917, Ordinary Session 24, pp. 166–167.

[72] Uruguay, *Diario de Sesiones de la Convención Nacional Constituyente*, March 30, 1917, Ordinary Session 28, p. 246; Uruguay, *Diario de Sesiones de la Convención Nacional Constituyente*, April 18, 1917, Ordinary Session, p. 323.

The Split in the Ruling Party and Democratic Reform 169

of obligatory voting argued that it was necessary to increase turnout and to ensure that the government did not block opposition supporters from voting.[73] Other delegates, however, maintained that obligatory voting would undermine the freedom of the voter, and they pointed out that the Blancos had frequently abstained from elections in the past. The Blanco leader, Aureliano Rodríguez Larreta, argued that "abstention is a precious right of citizens ... that right should never be renounced, because abstention is a political weapon of primary force that has been used by the parties of this country, and it may be, unfortunately, that we have to use it tomorrow."[74] Although supporters of obligatory voting claimed to represent a majority of the CNC, they ultimately did not have enough votes to enact it.

Female suffrage was also hotly debated on the floor of the CNC, after having been rejected in the committee by a large majority. Women's groups submitted letters to the CNC calling for women's rights,[75] and the Socialist delegation proposed that the constitution recognize all people as citizens, rather than just men.[76] The Socialist delegation's proposal was attacked by members of the other parties, however. The Colorado delegate Rogelio Mendiondo, for example, stated that "the role of women is not in politics, Mr. President, the role of women is in the home."[77] Juan José Segundo, a Blanco delegate, argued that "the fact of going to vote gives certain liberties to women, gives them a [dangerous] character."[78]

In the end, the Socialists and other proponents of female suffrage lacked the votes to include it in the constitution. To make matters worse, in its last days, the CNC voted to include a provision in the new constitution that stipulated that female suffrage in national or municipal elections could only be approved

---

[73] The Blanco delegate Washington Beltrán argued that "the secret vote loses importance if we don't establish the obligatory vote. The government [and others] ... can force [their employees], if they have suspicious or contrary ideas, to abstain from the elections if suffrage is not obligatory." See Uruguay, *Diario de Sesiones de la Convención Nacional Constituyente*, April 11, 1917, Ordinary Session 29, p. 259.

[74] Uruguay, *Diario de Sesiones de la Convención Nacional Constituyente*, April 13, 1917, Ordinary Session 30, p. 286.

[75] The National Council of Women of Uruguay, for example, submitted a signed letter stating its desire that women obtain "full possession of political and civil rights, because it considers that only through their free exercise could women demonstrate their powers and develop their activities without obstacles." See Uruguay, *Diario de Sesiones de la Convención Nacional Constituyente*, April 25, 1917, Ordinary Session 35, pp. 356–357.

[76] The Socialist delegate, Celestino Mibelli, noted that there were numerous countries that granted women political rights and he argued that since scientists had shown that men and women did not differ in terms of their brains, "there was no motive for banning women, for preventing them from obtaining the same rights as men." See Uruguay, *Diario de Sesiones de la Convención Nacional Constituyente*, April 23, 1917, Ordinary Session 34, p. 345.

[77] Uruguay, *Diario de Sesiones de la Convención Nacional Constituyente*, April 27, 1917, Ordinary Session 36, p. 388.

[78] Uruguay, *Diario de Sesiones de la Convención Nacional Constituyente*, April 23, 1917, Ordinary Session 34, p. 346.

by a vote of two-thirds of the total members of both chambers of the legislature. The Socialist delegate Celestino Mibelli objected vigorously, arguing:

Currently, the Chamber can ... authorize female suffrage by a simple majority vote. By contrast, according to the amendment that is proposed, in the future it could only be conceded by a much larger quorum. This is, as can be seen, a reactionary proposal, which is contrary to all that is occurring in the world where the rights of women are winning step by step.[79]

Despite his protestations, the CNC enacted this provision. As a result, women did not gain the right to vote until 1932, when both chambers of the legislature approved the relevant legislation, and they did not exercise the vote until 1938.[80]

While these discussions were underway, two Batllista deputies, Juan Buero and Eugenio Martínez Thedy, submitted a bill to the legislature that significantly reduced the likelihood that the Blancos and Riveristas could gain approval of their proposed constitutional reforms. The bill specified that the constitution had to be approved by a majority of registered voters and not just a majority of those who voted (Vázquez Romero and Reyes Abadie 1979, 228). In the elections to the constitutional convention, 63.4 percent of the people in the Civic Registry had voted, but only 37.3 percent of them had voted for the Blancos and Riveristas. Thus, it would be practically impossible for the Blancos and Riveristas to reach the 50 percent threshold specified in the bill unless the Batllistas approved the reforms as well.

The Blancos and Riveristas denounced the bill and the CNC approved a resolution stating that they would not "accept the intervention of any authority that aimed to modify the legal standing" of the constituent assembly (Vázquez Romero and Reyes Abadie 1979, 228).[81] There was little the Blancos and Riveristas could do to block the bill, however, since the Batllistas controlled both chambers of the legislature.[82] The Chamber of Deputies quickly approved the bill on a 59-38 vote, and the bill then moved to the Senate where the Committee on Legislation recommended enactment of the law (Vanger 2010, 223).[83]

---

[79] Many proponents of female suffrage argued that the 1830 constitution did not proscribe female suffrage because masculine nouns were often used to refer to women as well as men. Thus, they maintained that female suffrage could be enacted through an ordinary law under the 1830 constitution. Others contested this interpretation, however. See Uruguay *Diario de Sesiones de la Convención Nacional Constituyente*, July 2, 1917, Ordinary Session 56, pp. 86–87.

[80] The CNC also had lengthy debates over how long foreigners would need to reside in Uruguay before they would become citizens (they opted for three years), and whether all state employees should be banned from electoral activities other than voting (they opted just to ban the military and the police).

[81] One of the Blanco deputies, Washington Beltrán, called it "a coup by the State against the Constitutional Convention" (Vanger 2010, 221). Angered by his criticisms of the bill, Martínez Thedy challenged Beltrán to a duel with sabers, in which Martínez Thedy was wounded.

[82] The legislature would also decide on the bill's constitutionality since Uruguay did not have judicial review (Vanger 2010, 222).

[83] Uruguay, *Diario de Sesiones de la Cámara del Senado*, April 28, 1917, Ordinary Session 20: 219.

The Split in the Ruling Party and Democratic Reform

With their proposed constitution in jeopardy, the Blancos were forced to negotiate. In April 1917, the two sides formed a committee consisting of four Blancos and four Batllistas, which hashed out a compromise in secret negotiations.[84] The Blancos agreed to accept the separation of church and state but insisted that the Catholic Church be allowed to hold on to its valuable properties. The Blancos also agreed to a significantly modified version of the collegial executive: The new constitution would create a nine-member National Administration Council that would control most ministries, but the president would continue to exist and would control the ministries of war, interior, and foreign affairs. The council would be composed of six members of the majority party and three members of the minority party. The first president and the first council would be elected by the legislature in 1919 to serve four-year terms, which guaranteed Batllista dominance of these posts until 1923 since the Colorados controlled the legislature that would elect them. Subsequent presidents and councils would be elected directly by the people.

The Batllistas also made some important concessions, which helped establish democracy in Uruguay. They agreed to include provisions in the new constitution mandating the use of the secret ballot and proportional representation in elections, along with universal male suffrage and obligatory voter registration. Under the new constitution, the police and the military would not be allowed to take part in political activities, although they were eligible to vote. Another stipulation held that presidents could not be reelected until eight years had elapsed since their previous presidency. The Blancos demanded this provision to prevent Batlle from running for reelection in 1919, which he had repeatedly threatened to do.[85]

The vast majority of delegates at the convention supported the pact, but the Riveristas, who had been excluded from the negotiations, bitterly opposed it. The Riverista leader, Juan Campisteguy, resigned as president of the constitutional convention in protest, and the Blanco leader, Alfredo Vásquez Acevedo, took his place. The convention approved the new constitution in October 1917, and the following month the electorate enacted it in a referendum. The Blancos and the Colorados, and even the Socialists, supported the ratification of the constitution, but the Riverista Party and the Civic Union called on their members to abstain (Vanger 2010, 255 and 259). As a result, voter turnout was significantly lower than in the previous two elections, but the constitution passed easily, with 95 percent of the vote.

---

[84] The Batllistas refused to accept the participation of the Riveristas in this committee.

[85] The pact also contained some secret side agreements. One agreement gave the Blancos the right to veto two of the Colorados' candidates for the National Administration Council, which they pledged not to exercise unless Batlle was nominated. In addition, the Colorados pledged not to enact the bill that would have required that the new constitution be approved by a majority of the people listed in the Civic Registry (Vanger 2010, 229).

Although the constitution became law in 1918, enabling legislation needed to be enacted before some of its provisions, including the secret ballot, were implemented. Some sectors of the Colorado Party sought to delay the enabling legislation until after the 1919 elections in order to maintain control of these elections.[86] In one acerbic 1918 exchange in the legislature, Blanco deputies denounced the Colorados for delaying the secret vote for tactical reasons:

"Why doesn't [the Colorado Party] want to implant the secret vote for the elections in November?" The Blanco Deputy Eduardo Ferrería asked.
"So as not to lose them." His co-partisan, Aureliano Rodriguez Larreta, responded.
"We, the Nationalists, are supporters of the secret vote." Ferrería later declared.
"And you will stop being [supporters] when you convince yourselves that the secret vote doesn't serve to get what you want." The Colorado Deputy Francisco Bruno replied.[87]

The Colorados succeeded in delaying the implementation of the secret ballot for six years but, in the end, Congress passed the necessary legislation (Vanger 2010, 261).

THE EMERGENCE OF A STRONG DEMOCRACY IN URUGUAY

With the enactment of the 1918 constitution, Uruguay established a democracy that would rank among the strongest in Latin America in the decades that followed. In its wake, voter turnout expanded dramatically thanks mostly to the extension of voting rights to illiterates and the establishment of obligatory voter registration.[88] As Table 5.4 indicates, in the 1919 legislative elections, the first elections to be held under the new constitution, 191,677 people cast ballots, a 49 percent increase from the 1917 legislative elections. Turnout continued to increase in the years that followed, climbing to 299,017 voters in 1928. By 1928, voters represented 18.5 percent of the population, as opposed to only 4.2 percent in 1913 and 9.5 percent in 1917.[89]

---

[86] Many Colorados openly acknowledged their opposition to the secret ballot, which they viewed as something that had been forced upon them. As the Colorado Deputy César Rossi explained, the secret vote was enacted in "a pact in which each side had to cede something. Otherwise, you can be sure that the Colorado majority would not have accepted the inclusion [in the constitution] of the secret vote, which we consider contrary, above all in principle, to the fundamentals of a true democracy" Uruguay, *Diario de Sesiones de la Cámara de Representantes*, July 8, 1918, Ordinary Session 61: 781.

[87] Uruguay, *Diario de Sesiones de la Cámara de Representantes*, July 8, 1918, Ordinary Session 61: 701–702.

[88] The establishment of the secret ballot and proportional representation may also have helped boost turnout by increasing trust in elections and reducing fraud and intimidation.

[89] Voters represented an even larger percentage of the eligible population: In 1925 and 1926 an estimated 82 percent of the native male population above eighteen years of age turned up at the polls (Caetano 1994, 91).

The Emergence of a Strong Democracy in Uruguay

Under the new constitution, electoral competition became much more intense. The Colorados continued to win most national elections and they controlled the presidency until 1959, but they typically triumphed by razor-thin margins, and they even lost some important elections, such as the 1925 elections to the National Administrative Council and the 1928 legislative elections. Between 1919 and 1928, the winning party in presidential and legislative elections won by an average of only 2.4 percentage points. By contrast, the winner had triumphed by an average of 29.7 percentage points in legislative elections that took place between 1901 and 1917. The government's ability to control elections declined considerably thanks in part to the establishment of the secret ballot and the prohibition on state interference in elections. The establishment of universal male suffrage and obligatory voter registration also presumably helped increase competition since the opposition Blancos were stronger in rural departments where the illiteracy rate was high and voter turnout was traditionally low.

To be sure, Uruguay did not become a full democracy until the late 1930s when women acquired the vote.[90] Moreover, some voter fraud, intimidation, and vote buying continued to take place throughout the early twentieth century. Nevertheless, Uruguayan elections after 1918 were relatively free and fair, and represented a dramatic improvement over previous contests (Chasquetti and Buquet 2004; Caetano 1994, 69–70; Lindahl 1962; Nahum 1987, 98). A January 3, 1923 editorial in the *Montevideo Times* (Jan. 3, 1923) by a British sympathizer of the Blancos reported that: "The elections took place on November 26th, in perfect order everywhere, and with fewer complaints than usual as to underhanded or fraudulent practices. In fact – though the electoral laws are still open to improvement – they may be described as the fairest elections this Republic has yet known."[91]

Further reforms were introduced over the course of the 1920s and early 1930s that helped strengthen Uruguayan democracy. In 1924, for example, the government enacted a law that created a nine-member National Electoral Court, along with a National Electoral Office and departmental electoral boards, that would oversee the electoral registry and supervise the voting process (Souza 2016). All the major parties oversaw these electoral organizations and assigned delegates to them, which helped ensure that they acted in a balanced fashion. In addition, a 1925 law required soldiers to stay in the barracks during elections and prevented authorities from intervening at the voting tables or from jailing voters until twenty-four hours after the election had ended (Nahum 1987, 99–100).

As we have seen, the professionalization of the military helped set Uruguay on a democratic path in the early twentieth century by bringing an end to opposition revolts. Military professionalization did not, however, bring an

---

[90] In 1932, the legislature established female suffrage, although women did not vote in national elections until 1938 (Caetano 1999, 420; Castillo 2022).
[91] The editorial was included in a diplomatic dispatch by J. Webb Benton, the chargé d'affaires ad interim of the US Legation in Montevideo on January 4, 1923 (Box 8442 National Archives).

end to military intervention. Indeed, the military participated in or permitted coups in 1933, 1942, and 1973 that brought a temporary end to democracy. Nevertheless, the military intervened in politics less in Uruguay than elsewhere in the region and until 1973 avoided ruling directly. As a result, Uruguay experienced more years of democracy over the course of the twentieth century than any other Latin American country.

Uruguay's strong two-party system helped discourage coups and buttress the country's emerging democracy. The strength of the country's parties ensured not only that elections were closely contested, but also that the opposition consistently had significant representation in government institutions, which it used to monitor elections, contest electoral irregularities, and shape policy. The Colorados held the presidency until 1958, but the Blancos typically controlled at least 40 percent of the country's legislature and a majority of the country's departmental governments (Bottinelli, Giménez, and Marius 2012; Nohlen 2005b).[92] The opposition Blancos therefore had a stake in the system, which ensured their commitment to democratic rule and discouraged them from calling on the military to intervene.

CONCLUSION

The development of professional militaries and strong opposition parties, along with splits within the ruling party, helped lead to the emergence of relatively strong democracies in Chile and Uruguay at the outset of the twentieth century. The professionalization of the military gave the state a monopoly on violence, bringing an end to opposition revolts in both countries. As a result, state repression declined, and the opposition began to focus on the electoral path to power. Although the military continued to intervene occasionally in politics in both Chile and Uruguay, it did so less than in other South American countries.

The emergence of strong parties in both countries helped ensure that elections were competitive and that the opposition could monitor the electoral contests and protest irregularities. Thanks in large part to its party organizations and linkages to the electorate, the opposition gained a significant presence in the legislature and other state institutions in both countries. This gave it a stake in democracy and discouraged it from promoting military coups. Of equal importance, the opposition's legislative presence enabled it to promote democratic reforms.

The opposition did not typically hold sufficient seats to enact democratic reforms, but splits within the ruling parties of both countries led ruling party dissidents to ally with the opposition, giving them control of the legislature in Chile and the constituent convention in Uruguay. In the wake of such splits, the opposition pushed through sweeping electoral reforms, which helped bring democracy to Chile and Uruguay.

---

[92] The Blancos also typically held three or four seats on the nine-member National Administrative Council, which was even more powerful than the president (Lindahl 1962, 351).

6

The Roots of Weak Democracies
Argentina and Colombia

Argentina and Colombia, like Chile and Uruguay, democratized in the early twentieth century and for similar reasons. Argentina and Colombia were both plagued by revolts in the nineteenth century, which undermined constitutional rule and provoked state repression. In the 1880s, however, Argentina began to take important steps to professionalize its military, as did Colombia a couple of decades later. These measures made it increasingly difficult for the opposition to prevail in a revolt and, as a result, the opposition in both countries abandoned the armed struggle by the early twentieth century and began to focus on the electoral path to power. In the absence of armed rebellions, the governments of both countries began to respect civil and political liberties more consistently.

The emergence of strong parties in Argentina and Colombia during the late nineteenth and early twentieth century also helped lead to democratization. The opposition parties pushed aggressively for democratic reforms that would level the electoral playing field. The ruling parties used their control of the legislature to block the reform proposals, but in the early twentieth century these parties split, and a faction sided with the opposition to enact major democratic reforms. In the wake of the reforms, both countries experienced lengthy episodes of democratic rule for the first time.

Nevertheless, the democracies that arose in Argentina and Colombia proved to be weaker than those in Chile and Uruguay, although this only became apparent after 1929. The shortcomings of parties in Argentina and the military in Colombia contributed to the failings of their democracies. In Argentina only one strong party emerged, the UCR. This party played an important role in the democratization process while it was in the opposition, but once the Radicals took power, the country lacked a strong opposition party to protest electoral infractions and promote further democratization. Moreover, because the opposition did not have a strong party, it could not effectively compete with or restrain the ruling party, which ultimately led some opposition leaders to encourage the military to intervene. This occurred in 1930 as well as in later years, albeit under somewhat varying circumstances.

Colombia, by contrast, gave birth to two strong parties during the nineteenth century, but its military was considerably weaker than that of Argentina. Although the professionalization of the military in the early twentieth century deterred opposition revolts by making it difficult for the opposition to overthrow the central government, the state did not gain a monopoly on violence across the large, geographically fragmented country. As a result, opposition groups increasingly resorted to violence at the local level as the twentieth century wore on, thereby undermining democratic rule.

REVOLTS AND MILITARY PROFESSIONALIZATION IN ARGENTINA

For much of the nineteenth century, the Argentine military was weak, and the state lacked a monopoly on the use of violence. The country fought a lengthy war of independence with Spain (1810–1818) during which territories that had formerly belonged to the Vice Royalty of Río de la Plata, including Upper Peru (Bolivia), Paraguay, and Uruguay, broke off to form separate nations. The rest of what is now Argentina fragmented into self-governing provinces, which were loosely allied. During the first half of the nineteenth century, Argentina had no central government; nor did it have a national military that was capable of unifying the nation. The provinces as well as local leaders had their own militias, which often fought among themselves (Álvarez 1987; Casal 2001). Much of the fighting was between Unitarists who favored a strong central government and Federalists who represented regional interests and sought a high degree of provincial autonomy.

Juan Manuel de Rosas, a wealthy landowner who became governor of the province of Buenos Aires in 1829, undertook efforts to impose stability and centralize control. Buenos Aires was wealthier than the other provinces, and Rosas used these resources to extend his influence to other provinces and to build up a large coercive apparatus, including an army, a militia, a police force, and a paramilitary organization, known as the *mazorca* (Gelman and Lanteri 2010, 82–83).[1] The government imported some weapons, but also manufactured primitive rifles, cannons, swords, and gunpowder (Lynch 2006, 61). Nevertheless, Rosas lacked a professional military. He replaced experienced army officers with loyalists, and he relied on poorly armed and trained troops who were pressed into service (Lynch 2006, 88). To maintain order, Rosas also sought out the assistance of militias and friendly indigenous groups, but he was never able to establish a monopoly on violence, facing frequent internal and external conflicts (Gelman and Lanteri 2010, 86). Between 1829 and

---

[1] Military expenditures accounted for 81 percent of government expenditures in Buenos Aires in 1841, not counting debt payments (Garavaglia 2003, 155).

1852, there were fifteen years of war and only eight years of peace (Míguez 2003, 18).

Argentina did not become unified until after Rosas was overthrown in 1852 by Justo José Urquiza, the governor of the Province of Entre Rios. Under Urquiza's leadership, the Argentine Confederation in 1853 adopted its first successful constitution, which was ratified by all the provinces except for Buenos Aires. The refusal of Buenos Aires to join the confederation led to continued conflict, and in 1859, Urquiza invaded Buenos Aires and defeated its provincial militia at the Battle of Cepeda. Two years later, however, the two sides clashed again at the Battle of Pavón, and this time the provincial militia of Buenos Aires prevailed, due in large part to its purchase of rifles from Europe. The victory of Buenos Aires enabled its governor, Bartolomé Mitre, to dictate the terms of the province's incorporation into the federation, and in 1862, he became the first president of a unified Argentine Republic.

The unification of Argentina did not bring an end to revolts, however, in large part because the federal military remained relatively weak and nonprofessional. According to one estimate, between 1862 and 1868 alone, there were 107 revolts and 90 battles in which 4,728 people died (Oszlak 1997, 107). As Table 6.1 indicates, the most common type of revolt involved regional leaders who resisted the control of the federal authorities and/or sought to overthrow provincial governments. Another type of rebellion stemmed from the discontent of the opposition with defeats in elections characterized by fraud and manipulation. For example, supporters of Bartolomé Mitre rebelled unsuccessfully after Nicolás Avellaneda was declared the winner of the 1874 presidential elections. Similarly, backers of Carlos Tejedor, who was the governor of Buenos Aires, revolted after Julio A. Roca was declared the winner of the 1880 elections.

The frequent rebellions not only cost numerous lives and disrupted the economy but they also deepened authoritarian rule. In response to revolts, Argentina's leaders often assumed emergency powers and clamped down on the opposition. State repression was particularly severe under Rosas, and it peaked during periods when his regime faced serious domestic and external threats (Lynch 2006, 95–119). Bartolomé Mitre, who was president from 1862 to 1868, also engaged in state repression in response to rebellions. According to the liberal politician Carlos D'Amico:

[T]here wasn't a single day in those six long years [of the Mitre administration] in which there wasn't a state of siege in some corner of the Republic or in all of them ... Mitre governed like a despot, suppressing all liberties ... When it wasn't the Paraguayan War, it was civil wars that spilled torrents of Argentine blood. (Cited in Camogli 2009, 247)

Subsequent presidents also clamped down on the opposition in response to revolts (Loveman 1993, 288–289). When supporters of Mitre rebelled after he lost the 1874 elections, President Domingo Sarmiento declared a state of siege and censored the press. The Radical Party revolts of the 1890s met with a similar response: The 1892 elections, for example, took place under a state

TABLE 6.1 *Major revolts in Argentina, 1852–1929*

Year	Description of revolt	Type of revolt (outcome)
1851–1852	General Justo Urquiza, Governor Juan M. Rosas' military commander, revolted with 25,000 men and defeated Rosas at the Battle of Caseros.	Military coup (took power)
1852–1853	Buenos Aires rebelled with 8,000 men and declared independence, leading to a failed siege by Argentine Confederation troops under Urquiza.	Elite insurrection (stalemate)
1859	Buenos Aires rebelled in response to a law declaring that it must join the Argentine Confederation, but Urquiza defeated the rebellion.	Elite insurrection (suppressed)
1860–1861	Unitarian rebels assassinated the governor of San Juan and placed an ally in power, but Colonel Juan Sáa and federal troops overthrew him.	Elite insurrection (suppressed)
1861	Buenos Aires rebelled and its forces of 15,000 men led by General Mitre defeated the Argentine Confederation at the Battle of Pavón.	Elite insurrection (took power)
1863	Federalists led by "El Chacho" Peñaloza revolted against Liberal dominance but were defeated by government troops.	Elite insurrection (suppressed)
1866–1867	Federalists revolted with 3,000 men and briefly overthrew Liberal governors of western provinces, but were defeated by government forces.	Elite insurrection (suppressed)
1867–1868	Colonel Patricio Rodríguez and 2,000 *gauchos* overthrew the governor of Santa Fe, but the revolt was quickly suppressed by federal troops.	Elite insurrection (suppressed)
1870–1871	Federalist leader Ricardo López Jordán revolted with 12,000 men and seized Entre Rios, but was defeated by government forces.	Elite insurrection (suppressed)
1873	Federalist leader Ricardo López Jordán revolted in Entre Rios with 9,000 men, but was defeated by government troops.	Elite insurrection (suppressed)
1874	8,000 supporters of Bartolomé Mitre rebelled in La Rioja and Buenos Aires after he lost the 1874 election, but government troops defeated the rebels.	Elite insurrection (suppressed)
1880	9,000 supporters of Carlos Tejedor, the governor of Buenos Aires, rebelled after he lost the elections, but government troops defeated the rebels.	Elite insurrection (suppressed)
1890	The Civic Union movement rebelled in Buenos Aires with support from 2,000 men, but government troops defeated the rebels.	Elite insurrection (suppressed)
1893	UCR rebelled with over 6,000 men in Buenos Aires, Santa Fe, San Luis, Corrientes, and Tucumán, but government troops defeated the rebels.	Elite insurrection (suppressed)
1905	UCR rebelled in Buenos Aires, Córdoba, Entre Rios, Mendoza, and Santa Fe. Government troops defeated the rebels.	Elite insurrection (suppressed)

Source: Latin American Revolts Database.

of siege in which the government arrested opposition politicians or sent them into exile.

In the 1880s, however, the government began to professionalize the military, which gave the state a monopoly on violence for the first time. By the end of the decade, the regional leaders and the indigenous population had been subjugated, and the government had extended its influence throughout the national territory. When President Roca completed his first term in office in 1886, he proudly declared that the country had not suffered a single rebellion, civil war, or indigenous attack under his administration (Rock 2002, 106–107). Revolts remained scarce in the years that followed. There was only one major revolt in the 1880s, two in the 1890s, one in the first decade of the 1900s, and none in the 1910s and 1920s. The number of revolts declined not just because rebels reasoned that they had little chance of prevailing but also because the military's acquisition of ever more lethal weaponry increased the potential costs of rebellion. These costs were clearly demonstrated in the 1880 rebellion, which was significantly deadlier than previous uprisings.[2]

Foreign conflicts helped spur the strengthening and professionalization of the military. The War of the Triple Alliance (1864–1870) led Argentina to acquire additional weaponry and expand the size of its armed forces, which more than doubled in the war (López-Alves 2000, 190–191). Nevertheless, the Argentine military's poor performance in the war persuaded the Argentine government that the military needed upgrading, which it pursued in the years that followed (Nunn 1983, 45–46; Sabato 2010, 134). Argentina's often tense rivalries with Brazil and Chile also contributed to the development of its armed forces. During the late nineteenth century, the Argentine government became profoundly concerned about Chile's military buildup and the two countries nearly went to war. The conflict led the Argentine military to engage in heavy spending on European weaponry and warships beginning in the 1890s (Rock 2002, 174; Resende-Santos 2007, 224–228).

The expansion of the army and the acquisition of foreign weaponry and training was expensive, but Argentina was able to afford these expenditures in large part because of the tremendous export growth it enjoyed during the late nineteenth and early twentieth century. From 1870 to 1913, Argentina's exports increased by 6.3 percent annually and its GDP grew at a rate of 5.8 percent per year, the fastest in South America during this period (Bértola and Ocampo 2013, 86, 97). The economic growth led to a massive flow of resources to the Argentine state, a third of which was channeled to the armed forces. Argentina's expenditures on the army rose from approximately eight million pesos in 1891 to twenty million pesos in 1897 and remained relatively elevated during the first two decades of the twentieth century (Potash 1969, 6; Resende-Santos 2007, 197).

---

[2] Malamud (2000c, 33–34, 47–48) argues that during the nineteenth century the cost of revolution in Argentina was generally low since casualties tended to be modest and the rebels generally received amnesties, but these costs rose towards the end of the nineteenth century.

The rapid development of the Argentine economy during this period financed infrastructure development, which also increased the coercive capacity of the state (Oszlak 1997, 109; Lewis 2002, 165–166). The railways expanded dramatically in Argentina during the late nineteenth and early twentieth century, which allowed the military to rapidly transport troops from one end of the country to the other. In 1870, Argentina had only 455 miles of railway lines, but by 1900 it had 16,292 miles of track and by 1930 it had 23,687 miles (Summerhill 2006, 302). The telegraph, meanwhile, grew from 800 miles of lines in 1870 to 27,100 miles in 1900, enabling the military to quickly communicate with units in the field and coordinate strategies (Banks and Wilson 2014). A French diplomat reporting on the defeat of the regional leader Ricardo López Jordán in 1876 commented that, "with the railroads and the telegraphs, the era of the caudillos has come to an end. This time only five hundred men were needed for just ten days to defeat an insurrection that earlier would have taken the regular army more than a year" (cited in Rock 2002, 68).[3]

Even more importantly, the Roca administration undertook various reforms in the 1880s that helped professionalize the military and ensure that it had a monopoly on violence. In the wake of the 1880 conflict with the Buenos Aires militia, Roca passed a law banning provincial military forces (Sabato 2010, 137). These provincial forces, which significantly outnumbered the national army, had frequently been used in rebellions against the national government (Gallo 1986, 379).[4] The Roca administration also introduced the general staff organization of the military in 1884, although this had existed in a rudimentary way since 1861 (Nunn 1983, 47). In addition, the Argentine government improved the military training of its officers. President Domingo Sarmiento had created a Military College (1869) and a Naval School (1870), and Roca followed up by establishing a School for Noncommissioned Officers (1884) and a Military Engineering School (1886). Roca also issued new rules establishing meritocratic criteria for officer recruitment and promotion (Bragoni 2010, 155). As a result, in the late nineteenth century, military officers began to disengage from politics (Sabato 2010, 131–132).

Foreign training and equipment played an important role in strengthening and professionalizing the Argentine military. In the 1860s and 1870s, the government had purchased Remington repeating rifles from the United States, and they proved so effective at squashing rebellions that various governors successfully petitioned Roca, who was then the minister of war, to supply them with

---

[3] Sarmiento noted that the military's suppression of revolts "confirmed a common fact that is forgotten by the rebels: that is, steam [railways] and the telegraph go faster than the horses ridden by the caudillos" (cited in Oszlak 1997, 179).

[4] Under Roca, the national guard was dissolved and integrated into the army as a reserve force, boosting its numbers by 65,000 men (Nunn 1983, 48).

the weapons in the late 1870s (Rock 2002, 90).⁵ Prior to the 1870s, Argentina had mostly used French artillery and firearms, and had modeled its armed services on the French military. Some Argentine officers also trained in France as well as other European countries (Dick 2014, 77). After France's defeat in the Franco-Prussian War of 1870–1871, Argentina, like Chile, turned its eyes toward Germany. Argentina had begun to purchase German military equipment, such as Krupp field artillery, during the War of the Triple Alliance, and by the 1890s Germany was the exclusive supplier to its land forces (Resende-Santos 2007, 198).

During the 1870s and 1880s, Argentina began to study German military organization and hire individual German military advisers, and in 1899, it contracted a German mission. Argentina did not go as far as Chile in emulating the German military, however, in part because of resistance from some Argentine officers, including General Pablo Riccheri who became minister of war. The German mission in Argentina was much smaller than the one in Chile: It initially consisted of only five German officers, although it was later expanded to eight (Resende-Santos 2007, 194–196).⁶ Nevertheless, the German mission, which lasted until the outbreak of World War I, strengthened the Argentine armed forces considerably. As part of this mission, the Argentine government made further arms purchases, upgrading to more recent models of Mauser rifles and Krupp artillery: The Argentine government also gained permission to redesign and manufacture the Mauser rifle (Resende-Santos 2007, 199). Germany remained the exclusive supplier of military equipment to Argentine land forces until World War I (Resende-Santos 2007, 199; Schiff 1972, 453–454).

At the advice of the mission, the Argentine government expanded the size of the military, modeling its conscription system on that of Germany. A 1901 law (amended in 1905) created universal military service, although it also allowed conscripts to buy their way out (Nunn 1983, 128–129). This law led to a dramatic increase in the size of the army. In the first year alone, it incorporated 68,000 men, and by 1910 Argentina could field a standing force of 250,000 men (Resende-Santos 2007, 201–202). Argentina also copied the organization of the German armed forces, which consisted of a first-line army, reserves, a national guard, and a territorial guard. Similarly, it modeled the curriculum of its Superior War School on Germany's war academy, and employed various German officers as instructors. Moreover, numerous Argentine officers were sent to Germany for training. Potash (1969, 4) estimates that somewhere between 150 and 175 officers trained there before World War I. Under German prodding, the Argentine military also adopted more stringent standards for promotions and required that commissioned officers graduate from

---

⁵ Foreign arms could also be used by rebel troops to deadly effect, as in the 1862 Battle of Pavón, but rebels typically had a harder time obtaining these weapons, especially after Roca dissolved the provincial militias.
⁶ Approximately thirty German officers served in Argentina from 1900 to 1914 (Schiff 1972, 444).

the Military College (Resende-Santos 2007, 203–206). The German mission for a time even gained influence over the promotion of officers to senior ranks (Schiff 1972, 444).

All these measures helped create a stronger and better-trained military. The reforms, the weapons, and the training that the Argentines received increased state coercive capacity, helping bring an end to the outsider revolts that had plagued Argentina. By the end of the nineteenth century, the opposition had little prospect of taking power through armed struggle.

THE EMERGENCE OF THE UCR

Political parties arose in Argentina in the mid-nineteenth century, but the first strong party in the country, the UCR, did not emerge until the 1890s. The UCR quickly built a powerful organization and developed widespread ties to the electorate, especially in the federal capital and province of Buenos Aires. The UCR aggressively denounced electoral corruption and helped put democratic reform on the agenda, but it also initially participated in armed revolts.

As Chapter 4 discussed, strong parties were slower to arise in Argentina than in Chile and Uruguay in part because the population was dispersed. Most of the parties that emerged in Argentina during the nineteenth century were based in the city of Buenos Aires, which had a dense population that was easier to mobilize, but these parties failed to extend their reach to the provinces. According to Alonso (2000, 79), before the 1890s "party organization had been sporadic, inconsistent, and informal." The parties of this period were active only during elections and lacked developed organizations and ideologies. They rarely published party platforms or manifestos, although they typically had affiliated newspapers that disseminated their messages (Míguez 2013; Remmer 1984, 31). Abraham Konig, a Chilean politician and diplomat who traveled to Argentina in 1890, observed that: "In the Argentine Republic, there are no parties with organized ideas ... voters groups themselves around one man, not around a party label represented by a man" (cited in Remmer 1984, 31).

During the 1830s and 1840s, there was little political space for the emergence of independent parties. In Buenos Aires, Governor Juan Manuel de Rosas used state repression to install what became known as a regime of unanimity in which his preferred candidates won elections by enormous margins (Sabato and Ternavasio 2011; Ternavasio 2002).[7] After the downfall of Rosas in 1852, there was greater electoral competition and respect for civil and political liberties, but elections continued to be plagued by fraud and intimidation

---

[7] Rosas made up the lists of candidates, distributed the ballots, and ensured that they won by an overwhelmingly margin. As a result, the legislature consisted of a homogenous group of supporters of Rosas (Ternavasio 2002, 206–214; Zimmermann 2009, 13).

(Sabato 2001a, 10–12; Alonso 2007, 5–6). Incipient parties did emerge during this period, but they were highly personalistic and undisciplined organizations that failed to establish strong ties to the electorate. The parties signed up candidates, registered voters, and mobilized supporters to come to the polls, but they were inactive between elections (Sabato 2001a, 73–78).

During the 1880s, electoral competition began to wane, and a single party, the National Autonomist Party (PAN), came to dominate, winning all of the presidential elections as well as a majority of the seats in both chambers of the legislature for several decades (Alonso 2010, 13).[8] The PAN, which was officially founded in 1881, had emerged in the early 1870s when a coalition of provincial politicians formed a League of Governors to support the presidential candidacy of Nicolás Avellaneda. General Julio A. Roca quickly became the most important figure within the PAN: he served two terms as president (1880–1886 and 1898–1904) and played a key role in the presidential succession process during the late nineteenth and early twentieth century. As Roca and others recognized, governors controlled the elections through their influence over the prefects, justices of the peace, and chiefs of police, so the key to electoral success was to win the support of the governors.[9] In order to do so, presidents distributed revenue, land, and credit to the provinces and made the political appointments that the governors preferred (Alonso 2000, 30–31). In addition, the 1853 constitution gave presidents the right to intervene in the provinces, which they used to get rid of or undermine recalcitrant governors on forty separate occasions between 1880 and 1916 (Botana 2012, 104–112).

Although the PAN ruled Argentina for three decades, it never developed into a strong party. Indeed, it was only a loose alliance of politicians without a disciplined or centralized organization (Alonso 2000, 34; Castro 2012, 22; Alonso 2010, 13). The PAN made little effort to organize mass support or develop a loyal membership (Alonso 2000, 34–38; Remmer 1984, 30). It possessed no program or standing bureaucracy, and its provincial branches had considerable autonomy (López 2001a, 72; Remmer 1984, 31; Alonso 2000, 34–38; 2010, 13; Rock 2002, 166). According to *La Prensa*, the PAN was only "a body of clients ... subject to the orders of the master at the top" (cited in Rock 2002, 166). Loyalty was in short supply within the organization and the president had to engage in constant negotiations in order to maintain the support of the governors and legislators (Alonso 2010, 31–32; Castro 2012, 22–24).

The PAN faced relatively little competition until the emergence of the UCR in the 1890s. The UCR was the first Argentine party to build a strong organization, and it initially did so with private rather than public resources since,

---

[8] Election-day violence declined beginning in the 1880s, but the government continued to intervene in elections (Alonso 1996, 193–194; Botana 2012, 142–152; Alonso 2000, 29–30).
[9] As a newspaper at the time reported: "The justices elect the governor and the governor elects the justices" (cited in Rock 2002, 78).

unlike the PAN, it did not control state offices during its first two decades (Alonso 2000, 162; Remmer 1984, 104; Rock 2002, 144). The UCR created a permanent structure that included precinct-level committees in the major cities around the country and it developed a large and loyal following, which retained its partisan identification even during the late 1890s and early 1900s when the party was inactive. The party not only brought its supporters to the polls, it also mobilized them for rallies and armed uprisings, all of which put pressure on the government to respond to its demands.

Several factors enabled the UCR to develop into a strong party. First, it successfully exploited the center–periphery cleavage that structured Argentine politics during the nineteenth century. The UCR, and its predecessor, the Civic Union, brought together Buenos Aires elites who were frustrated with the dominance of the country by the PAN, a party that was controlled by provincial elites. Indeed, the main leaders of the UCR, such as Leandro Além, Bernardo de Irigoyen, and Hipólito Yrigoyen, came from the federal capital or the province of Buenos Aires. The UCR catered to interests of Buenos Aires. For example, it supported free trade, which disadvantaged many provinces but benefited the federal capital, which had the only port in the country (Alonso 2000, 210). Unlike many previous parties, however, the UCR successfully organized in the province of Buenos Aires as well as the federal capital, which together represented more than 40 percent of the country's population in the 1890s. The UCR could thus gain significant representation in the legislature with support in these two districts alone, although it subsequently built support in other provinces as well.

Second, the UCR developed a broadly appealing message focused on the corruption of the existing political system in Argentina (Alonso 2000, 108–109; Rock 1975, 50–51). Alonso (2000, 105) argues that the party was essentially backward-looking, seeking to restore the system of the 1860s and 1870s before the PAN monopolized politics. The party did not develop any major reform proposals during its time in the opposition, but it relentlessly denounced government electoral manipulation and called for clean elections.[10] These appeals struck a chord with the many people that were disenchanted with the existing political system and the PAN. Indeed, the UCR developed its provincial networks in part by reaching out to local elites that had been marginalized under the PAN (Rock 2002, 162). The UCR's overwhelming focus on electoral corruption enabled it to bring together groups with very different interests that were disenchanted with the PAN, including students and freethinkers as well

---

[10] During the early 1890s, the UCR did propose an amendment to the electoral law that sought to reduce fraud in the electoral registries and simplify voting on election days (Alonso 2000, 166; López 2005a, 190–191). This minor proposal passed, but it failed to significantly reduce fraud. Subsequently, a legislator from the UCR, along with another opposition deputy, proposed a more sweeping reform that included obligatory voting, but the ruling party blocked this measure (López 2005a, 192–193).

The Emergence of the UCR

as pro-clerical groups.[11] It also benefited from the fact that, by the early 1890s, other parties that might have competed with the UCR for the opposition vote had been profoundly weakened or absorbed by the PAN (Alonso 2000, 27–28).

Third, the UCR's principled intransigence also contributed to its popularity. Unlike other parties, the UCR in the 1890s and early 1900s refused to compromise or forge political pacts. Whereas other parties, such as the Autonomist Party and the National Civic Union, undermined their popularity and opposition credentials by forging alliances with the PAN and participating in the government, the UCR resolutely refused to do so. Indeed, beginning in the late 1890s, the UCR vowed it would not even participate in elections until it was certain that they would be fair. This intransigence helped it capture the support of many of those people who had become disillusioned with parties. The UCR's participation in armed uprisings in 1890, 1893, and 1905 also attracted some followers. According to Alonso (2000, 10), "the Radicals' defense of the use of violence became the party's distinguishing feature, producing the most enduring division between the UCR and the other political parties." Many Argentines came to admire the party's steadfastness and the willingness of its leaders to fight for their ideals.

The UCR first emerged in 1890 as the result of a split within the Civic Union movement, which had risen up in protest against the government of Miguel Juárez Celman. The Civic Union had begun as a movement of Buenos Aires students, but it quickly incorporated diverse sectors of the opposition, including political elites, such as Leandro Alem, Bernardo de Irigoyen, and Bartolomé Mitre.[12] The members of the Civic Union had a variety of grievances but most prominent among them were the president's authoritarian governing style and the severe economic crisis that had afflicted Argentina beginning in 1890. The Civic Union also won support among sectors of the army who were dissatisfied with Juárez Celman and his tendency to promote his friends within the military. In July 1890, the Civic Union revolted with the support of its allies in the military. The rebels, who consisted of approximately 1,000 soldiers and 300 civilians, seized an arsenal in the city of Buenos Aires, but they quickly ran out of ammunition and were outnumbered by the army troops that remained loyal to the government. The rebels surrendered after four days of fighting and a toll of some 800–1,000 casualties (Alonso 2000, 56–66; Duncan 1981, 331–332).

A few days after the rebellion, Juárez Celman resigned under pressure from his erstwhile ally Roca who organized the legislature against him.[13]

---

[11] In its 1915 party manifesto, the UCR defended its lack of a developed platform by arguing that "the only preoccupation of this great party is strict compliance with the sanctity of the vote" (cited in Rock 1975, 51).

[12] The main base of the Civic Union was in Buenos Aires where it had sixty clubs, but it also established clubs in Córdoba, Corrientes, Mendoza, Rio Cuarto, Salta, San Luis, Santa Fe, and Tucumán (Remmer 1984, 32).

[13] Juárez Celman had alienated Roca and others with his domineering style. He also made the mistake of fleeing Buenos Aires at the outset of the rebellion.

Roca then forged an alliance with Mitre to run in a coalition in the 1892 presidential elections. The pact between Mitre and Roca split the Civic Union. The sectors of the Civic Union that opposed the alliance, including Leandro Alem, the president of the movement, and his nephew, Hipólito Yrigoyen, broke off and formed the UCR.[14] The UCR declined to compete in the 1892 presidential elections, arguing that the PAN had corrupted the country's institutions and that electoral fraud made such elections illegitimate. Shortly before the elections, the government discovered evidence that the Radicals were planning another uprising, and it responded by declaring a state of siege and arresting some of the leaders of the party. Although the government temporarily lifted the state of siege on election day, the Radicals nevertheless abstained from the elections.

As soon as the leaders of the UCR were released from prison, they began to plot another revolt, which came to fruition in July 1893 when civilian uprisings involving thousands of participants took place simultaneously in the provinces of Santa Fe, San Luis, and Buenos Aires. A second wave of uprisings, which involved some military troops, occurred in August and September 1893 in additional provinces, including Corrientes and Tucumán.[15] Some of these insurrections, including the ones in Buenos Aires and Santa Fe, temporarily overthrew the provincial governments, leading to Radical takeovers. The armed forces mostly remained loyal to the government, however, and by late 1893 it had suppressed the revolts. In the aftermath, the government severely repressed the UCR, jailing many of its leaders, censoring its newspapers, banning public demonstrations, and maintaining a state of siege throughout 1894 (Alonso 2000, 135–136).

In the wake of the failed insurrections, the UCR opted to abandon the armed struggle and participate in elections, and this strategy paid dividends. In 1894, it won elections to the provincial legislature, national legislature, and governorship in the province of Buenos Aires, and it also registered some electoral successes in the federal capital, Mendoza, and La Rioja (Rock 2002, 161).[16] By 1895, the Radicals controlled sixteen out of the eighty-six seats in the lower chamber, along with one seat in the Senate (Alonso 2000, 165).

After 1896, however, the party entered into crisis largely because of internal divisions and the death of the leader of the party, Leandro Alem, who committed suicide in July 1896 after a period of declining health. His death led to a battle for control of the party between the executive committee of the

---

[14] Only twenty of the original sixty members of the Civic Union organizing committee in the capital joined the UCR (Alonso 2000, 93).

[15] The revolt in Buenos Aires was the largest, involving an estimated 6,000 men and taking place in eighty of the eighty-two departments in the province (Alonso 2000, 125; Del Mazo 1957, 82–85).

[16] The party was similarly successful in the federal capital, where it consistently won more than 40 percent of the vote between 1892 and 1896 (Alonso 2000, 155 and 159).

party, which was dominated by leaders from the federal capital, and Hipólito Yrigoyen, who had developed a strong and well-organized branch of the party in the province of Buenos Aires. The executive committee sought to forge an alliance with Mitre's National Civic Union, but Yrigoyen opposed such a move since it would weaken his control of the UCR (Federici 2005, 89). The struggle led the party to split in two, and by the end of 1898 it had dissolved (Alonso 2000, 197–198).

Nevertheless, the UCR's disbandment proved only temporary. In 1903, Yrigoyen began to reconstruct the party, drawing mainly on those members who had remained loyal to him during the party's split. In addition to reopening the Buenos Aires branch, he opened party clubs in Córdoba, Santa Fe, Mendoza, and Entre Rios, reestablishing his links to the provinces (Rock 1975, 48). The relaunch of the party in early 1903 drew a crowd of 50,000 people, demonstrating the Radicals' enduring strength (Alonso 2000, 201; Del Mazo 1957, 113).

Rather than participate in elections, Yrigoyen opted to plan another revolt, this one involving a group of junior army officers. In February 1905, these officers rose up in Buenos Aires and several other provinces and managed to take Vice-President José Figueroa Alcorta hostage. The uprisings received little popular support, however. Senior officers remained loyal to the government and the military quickly suppressed the revolt, which *La Nación* referred to at the time as a "parody of a sedition" (cited in Rock 2002, 193). In the wake of this failed rebellion, the UCR essentially abandoned the armed struggle, although Yrigoyen would occasionally hint at the possibility of future revolts (Yablon 2003, 250).

The failure of the rebellion only briefly interrupted the restructuring of the UCR, however. Yrigoyen and other Radical leaders quickly received an amnesty and deepened their efforts to reorganize the party. By 1906, the party was once again the most popular organization in the federal capital (Yablon 2003, 249). UCR committees were set up not only in the federal capital but in all of the provincial capitals and more than 200 other municipalities between 1906 and 1908 (Remmer 1984, 90; Del Mazo 1957, 123). The UCR continued to abstain from elections after 1905, however, vowing that it would not participate until honest elections could be guaranteed.[17]

Thus, between 1890 and 1910, the UCR grew into a powerful party that relentlessly pushed for free and fair elections. The Radicals were not able to take power during this period either through elections or revolts, but by denouncing the elections as corrupt and refusing to participate in them, the Radicals put pressure on the government to carry out reform. Indeed, as we shall see, one of the reasons that the government enacted democratic reform in 1912 was to persuade the UCR to participate.

---

[17] The party's repeated refrain was "the only program of the UCR is the restoration of the constitution and freedom of suffrage" (Snow 1965, 30).

THE SPLIT WITHIN THE RULING PARTY AND DEMOCRATIC REFORM

Although the emergence of the UCR put democratic reform on the table, it was a split within the ruling party that made enactment of the reform possible. The split dated to 1890, but it grew worse in the early 1900s when Carlos Pellegrini, the second most powerful figure in the PAN, broke with General Roca, the party's dominant leader. The split with Pellegrini undermined Roca's control over the presidential succession process and led in 1910 to the election of a reformist president, Roque Sáenz Peña, who pushed through a sweeping electoral reform in 1912.

The PAN first experienced a major split in the wake of the downfall of President Miguel Juárez Celman, when a number of the former president's supporters formed a group known as the Modernists. With the support of elites from the littoral provinces, including Buenos Aires, Entre Ríos, and Santa Fe, the Modernists sought to nominate Roque Sáenz Peña, who had served in Juárez Celman's cabinet, as the presidential candidate of the PAN in 1892 (Alonso 2010, 280–281; 2000, 90–91). To block his candidacy, Roca engineered the nomination and election of Roque's father, Luis Sáenz Peña, who was viewed as a more malleable figure. The Modernists subsequently disintegrated, while Roca recaptured the presidency in 1898.

The split between Roca and Pellegrini built upon this earlier division but did not occur until 1901 when Pellegrini, who was then an influential senator, proposed a plan that would have stretched out Argentina's annual debt service payments, but at the cost of increasing the country's debt (Richmond 1989, 131–133; Castro 2012, 53–55, 62–69; Waddell 2005, 128–134). Opposition newspapers denounced the plan and students carried out violent protests against it, leading Roca to withdraw his support for it. In response, Pellegrini broke with Roca and thereafter became one of the most prominent supporters of democratic reform (Rock 2002, 177; Waddell 2005, 135–140).[18]

Pellegrini had expected to be chosen as the PAN's presidential candidate in 1904, but after the rupture, Roca was determined to block his candidacy. Neither Roca nor Pellegrini had the power to impose his own preferences, however. As a result, they agreed to hold a Convention of Notables in which the PAN's presidential candidate would be selected (Castro 2012, 118–124). At this convention, Roca successfully maneuvered to have Manuel Quintana, who was not even a member of the PAN, nominated as the party's presidential candidate in order to block the nomination of Pellegrini (Sciarrotta 2005, 144–148; Richmond 1989, 133; Waddell 2005, 137–138).[19] Quintana then

---

[18] Prior to the rupture, Pellegrini had not been a consistent supporter of electoral reform, arguing that electoral practices would improve over time (Waddell 2005, 139; Rock 2002, 177).

[19] That Roca agreed to support the nomination of Quintana, a traditional rival, shows how much the split had weakened him and how determined he was to prevent the nomination of Pellegrini.

insisted on nominating José Figueroa Alcorta, a former Modernist, as his vice-presidential candidate (Sciarrotta 2005, 147–148; Castro 2012, 136–137).

Quintana was elected president in 1904, but he died only sixteen months after he took office, leaving Figueroa Alcorta in power. Under Figueroa Alcorta, the split within the PAN deepened. The new president sought to dismantle Roca's bases of support, intervening in the provinces and channeling government spending in ways that undermined the allies of Roca and bolstered his own supporters (Sciarrotta 2005, 151–152; Rock 2002, 16).[20] Roca fought back, using his ties to provincial governors and his influence in the legislature to block some of the president's policies. This led Figueroa Alcorta to briefly shut down the legislature in January 1908 and to intervene extensively in the elections that year in order to win a narrow majority in the Chamber of Deputies for the first time (Rock 2002, 199–200; López 2005b, 225–226).[21]

Figueroa Alcorta's success in weakening Roca paved the way for the election of a reformist candidate in 1910. For opponents of Roca, Roque Sáenz Peña was an obvious choice, given his long history of opposition to the former president.[22] In 1909, various Buenos Aires elites who were united by their opposition to Roca formed a new party, National Union, to promote Sáenz Peña's candidacy for president (Rock 2002, 202–203; Castro 2012, 278–79). The Figueroa Alcorta administration, several provincial governors, and many local-level political bosses also provided important support, although the president never explicitly endorsed Sáenz Peña (Rock 2002, 203; Castro 2012, 249–250).

Sáenz Peña's election quickly came to be seen as inevitable. The Radicals called on their supporters to abstain from the elections on the grounds of the "impossibility of the guaranteed and honorable exercise of the suffrage" (López 2005b, 234). The Mitristas nominated Guillermo Udaondo as their presidential candidate, but they, too, called for abstention shortly before the elections because of governmental control of the proceedings. Supporters of Roca did not even put forward a candidate. As a result, on election day in March 1910, Sáenz Peña won an overwhelming victory.

After taking office, Sáenz Peña quickly followed up on his campaign promises to reduce electoral fraud and manipulation by introducing a pair of laws

---

[20] Figueroa Alcorta also sought the support of the Radicals, but Yrigoyen refused to join his coalition unless he enacted reforms that guaranteed clean elections, which the president declined to do (Remmer 1984, 91, 247; Castro 2012, 238–239; Sciarrotta 2005, 157–158).

[21] Figueroa Alcorta fell short of a majority in the Senate whose members were elected by the provincial legislatures in which Roca still had considerable influence (Sciarrotta 2005, 156; Castro 2012, 237–238; Botana 2012, 184–185; Rock 2002, 198–199).

[22] Sáenz Peña's hostility to Roca dated at least to the 1880s when he served in the government of Juárez Celman, but it deepened over time. In 1897, Sáenz Peña led a group of members of the PAN who sought unsuccessfully to block the reelection of Roca as president, and after Pellegrini's death in 1906, Sáenz Peña became the head of the reformist wing of the PAN (López 2005b, 218–221). As one of Sáenz Peña's political allies put it, his candidacy represented "a symbol against Roca and the oligarchies" (Cited in Castro 2012, 255).

that sought to create a new electoral registry based on the military registration system (Sáenz Peña 1915, 100). Among other things, the new laws created an enrollment card that citizens would use to prove their identity. The legislature approved these laws in mid-1911, but not without some changes and delays caused by supporters of Roca and others (López 2005b, 241–245).

Sáenz Peña introduced a more sweeping electoral reform bill in August 1911. The proposed electoral law had numerous elements, but the provisions establishing obligatory suffrage, the secret ballot, and the incomplete-list electoral system received the most attention.[23] Article 1, following in the Argentine tradition, granted the right to vote to all male citizens, native born or naturalized, above the age of eighteen, with a few exceptions, including clergymen, soldiers, police officers, prisoners, criminals, the insane, and deaf mutes who did not know how to write. Articles 6 and 7 made voting obligatory, although exceptions were made for senior citizens and judges and their assistants who had to be in their offices during the hours of the election. Articles 41, 42, and 45 specified that the room where voters cast their ballots should not have windows or more than one functioning door, which would be shut to ensure that each voter was alone while casting his ballot. Voters would place their ballots in an envelope provided by the electoral authorities and then deposit them in the urn, before leaving the room. Article 44 mandated the use of the incomplete list for the election of national deputies. Under this system, two-thirds of the seats in each district would be awarded to the party list that finished first in the elections and one-third to the runner-up.

Sáenz Peña introduced the reform partly to woo the UCR. After his election in 1910, Sáenz Peña met twice with Yrigoyen to try to negotiate an agreement for the Radicals to participate in elections. Yrigoyen, however, rejected Sáenz Peña's offer to join his government, stating that "the Radical Party is not looking for ministries. It is only asking for guarantees to vote freely at the polls" (Cárcano 1986, 142; Cárcano 1943, 302). Nevertheless, Yrigoyen pledged to end the UCR's policy of abstention if the government would guarantee that elections would be free and fair, declaring: "The Radical Party [UCR] resorts to Revolution because it finds the electoral path closed ... if the government gives us guarantees, we will show up at the polls" (Cárcano 1943, 298). Although Sáenz Peña and Yrigoyen did not sign a formal agreement at these meetings, both of them made verbal commitments that they ultimately honored. Indeed, after the enactment of the reforms, the UCR ended its electoral boycott.

The negotiations clearly indicate Sáenz Peña's desire to persuade the Radicals to participate in elections and his willingness to use the electoral reform to do so. Nevertheless, the role that the UCR played in the reforms should not be exaggerated. Although Yrigoyen subsequently argued that many of the ideas

---

[23] See *Diario de Sesiones de la Cámara de Diputados*, Ordinary Session 10, August 11, 1911, pp. 807–818.

Split within the Ruling Party and Democratic Reform

for the reform were his own and that he persuaded Sáenz Peña to go along with them, this account is contradicted by the recollections of other participants as well as notes from the meetings (Cantón 1973, 95–99; Cárcano 1986, 142–143; Cárcano 1943, 296–304; López 2005c, 256–257).[24] Sáenz Peña had long called for free elections and he made electoral reform the centerpiece of his 1910 presidential campaign. In August 1909, for example, he gave a speech calling for electoral reform and specifically for the secret and obligatory vote, stating that the latter "has counted at all times on all my sympathy" (López 2005b, 228). Sáenz Peña even demanded that his vice-presidential candidate be someone who shared his concern for electoral reform (López 2005b: 232).[25]

Sáenz Peña and his allies proposed the reform not just to encourage the Radicals to end their electoral boycotts but, equally importantly, to put an end to the electoral fraud and manipulation that had enabled Roca and his allies to dominate the Argentine political system (Castro 2012, 300–304; Hora 2001, 145; Scherlis and López 2005, 572). In presenting the reform to Congress, the president declared that it would "guarantee the liberty and the purity of the suffrage, removing it from the influence of local interests and passions, which were not always well motivated."[26] In a letter to a close friend and political ally in January 1908, Sáenz Peña depicted the reform as a machine composed of two pistons: one that ended fraud and cleaned up the polls and another that pushed citizens to vote, adding that "only in this way can we attenuate the team of professional politicians that Roca has left us" (Cited in Castro 2012, 300). In a September 1908 letter to another friend, Sáenz Peña argued that ending Roca's electoral control and establishing free suffrage would not only destroy the existing regime but also return to power a sector of the elite that had been ostracized by Roca (cited in Castro 2012, 255–256).

Sáenz Peña believed that each component of the proposed reform would contribute to the renovation of the political system in a different way. Obligatory

---

[24] Sáenz Peña did not agree to all of Yrigoyen's demands. Yrigoyen asked the president to intervene in the provinces to guarantee free elections there, but Sáenz Peña refused. Sáenz Peña also declined Yrigoyen's request to enact a stricter form of proportional representation rather than the incomplete list (Devoto, Ferrari, and Melón 1997, 176; Cantón 1973, 96).

[25] Some scholars have argued that the reform was aimed at dissuading the Radicals from carrying out revolts, but this seems unlikely. Sáenz Peña did not seem very concerned about the threat of another Radical uprising, and Radical leaders do not appear to have seriously considered one, given the disastrous failure of the 1905 rebellion (Castro 2012, 301–303; Hora 2001, 142–143; Cárcano 1943, 292–293; Devoto 1996, 96–97). In fact, Sáenz Peña suggested that the prevailing political stability made the electoral reform feasible, arguing in his electoral manifesto that "defensive governments cannot be reformers" (Castro 2012, 301; Devoto 1996, 97). Nor is it accurate to view the reform as an effort to incorporate the middle classes, as some scholars have argued, given that the UCR did not represent the middle classes at the time (Alonso 2000, 8; Scherlis and López 2005, 567; Míguez 2012, 15–16; Gallo and Sigal 1963, 213–216). For further discussion of these points, see Madrid (2019b).

[26] See *Diario de Sesiones de la Cámara de Diputados*, Ordinary Session 10, August 11, 1911, p. 807.

voting would help restore the legitimacy of the system by boosting voter turnout and ending abstentionism, but it would also prevent small groups from controlling the government (Sáenz Peña 1915, 104). The secret ballot, meanwhile, would reduce vote buying and enable free elections. In one speech, he likened vote buying to purchasing an invisible ring: "One does not buy what one cannot see" (Sáenz Peña 1915, 477). Sáenz Peña (1915, 45) supported the incomplete list because it guaranteed the representation of minorities, which he thought was essential to fair elections and good government. His minister of the interior also maintained that the incomplete list would make elections fairer by guaranteeing representation to the losing parties, who were the main victims of electoral manipulation.[27]

The initial prospects for the reform were unclear, given that legislators from the PAN had generally blocked or watered down prior electoral reform proposals.[28] The government had enacted a reform in 1902 that mandated the use of single-member districts to elect federal deputies, but PAN legislators resisted efforts to establish the secret ballot as part of this reform (Botana 2012, 212–213; Castro 2012, 92–100; Malamud 2000a, 111, 116–117; de Privitellio 2006).[29] Moreover, in 1905, PAN legislators, over the objections of the opposition, eliminated the single-member districts, reinstating the complete-list electoral system that they believed facilitated their control of the legislature (Castro 2012, 158–159; Sciarrotta 2005, 150; López 2005a, 207–208). By 1910, however, the elements in the PAN that had traditionally blocked electoral reform were considerably weaker than they had been just a few years earlier. In addition, Sáenz Peña was a relatively popular president who was committed to reform.

The Sáenz Peña administration sought to get the reform approved rapidly so that it could be applied to the March 1912 legislative elections. Nevertheless, the proposal met considerable opposition in the legislature, particularly from traditional politicians who feared that it would undermine their political machines. In the Chamber of Deputies, Roquistas led by Julio A. Roca Jr., the son of the former president, headed the opposition to the reform (López 2005c, 279; Heaps-Nelson 1978, 10). In the Senate, the opposition was led by Benito Villanueva, a traditional ally of Roca and the former leader of the PAN in the federal capital, along with two former governors: Ignacio Irigoyen

---

[27] See *Diario de Sesiones de la Cámara de Diputados*, Extraordinary Session 5, November 8, 1911, pp. 150–151.

[28] In 1893, President Luis Sáenz Peña, in response to pressure from his son, had proposed a major electoral reform, but the ruling party blocked it (López 2005a, 184–188). In 1905, PAN legislators similarly shot down an attempt to establish the secret ballot (Castro 2012, 158; López 2005a, 208–210).

[29] The 1902 reform also created a permanent electoral registry and a civic document to be used to vote. The Roca administration proposed this reform to try to restore its popularity and the legitimacy of the political system (Castro 2012, 80–81, 92; de Privitellio 2006; Malamud 2000a, 105–106).

of Buenos Aires and Pedro A. Echagüe of Santa Fe (López 2005c, 280). Much of the opposition to the reform came from the more densely populated littoral provinces, especially the province of Buenos Aires, because they had the most developed political machines (Heaps-Nelson 1978, 18). The incumbent governor of Buenos Aires, General José Inocencio Arias, gave mixed signals on his position toward the reform, but many of the deputies from the province voted against key aspects of the reform proposal.[30]

Many of Sáenz Peña's own allies were initially opposed to, or at least unenthusiastic, about the reform proposal (López 2005c, 288–289; Devoto 1996, 106–107). As one deputy acknowledged to the newspaper *Crónica*, legislators did not want to enact any reform that might jeopardize their chances at reelection or antagonize their governors or political bosses:

Crónica: "And for what reform proposal will you vote?"
Deputy: "For the one that secures my reelection."
Crónica: "And which is that?"
Deputy: "The one that is promoted by the people who have the most influence over my governor."[31]

In order to get the reform approved, Sáenz Peña had to aggressively lobby members of his own National Union who ended up providing most of the support for the reform (Devoto 1996, 106–107; Castro 2012, 318; Cárcano 1986, 167; Heaps-Nelson 1978, 23). The number of deputies inclined to vote for the incomplete list did not exceed twelve at the beginning of November 1911, but by the end of the month Sáenz Peña had won the support of fifty of them (Botana 2012, 265). One legislator commented that: "I believe that an Argentine deputy would resist a proposition from Cleopatra, but I don't know if he could resist a proposition from the Argentine president" (cited in Botana 2012, 265). The president's allies even delayed approval of the budget in the lower chamber to put pressure on legislators to pass the reform (Devoto 1996, 107).[32]

The reform proposal first went to the Committee on Constitutional Affairs of the Chamber of Deputies, which approved the reform project on September 29, 1911, but eliminated Article 44, which mandated the use of the incomplete-list electoral system for elections to the lower chamber. On the floor of the Chamber of Deputies, however, supporters of the incomplete list restored it to the bill, winning a roll-call vote by the narrow margin of 49–32.[33]

---

[30] See "El Block Bonaerense: Contra la Ley Electoral," *La Razón*, November 27, 1911; and "La Lista Incompleta," *La Gaceta de Buenos Aires*, October 24, 1911.
[31] "En la Presidencia," *Crónica*, November 3, 1911.
[32] Of the deputies elected in 1910 when Sáenz Peña's National Union swept to power, thirty-five ended up supporting the reform and only eleven opposed it. By contrast, only fifteen deputies elected in 1908 voted for the reform, while twenty-three opposed it (López 2005c, 284–285). A somewhat similar pattern held in the Senate (Heaps-Nelson 1978, 23).
[33] *Diario de Sesiones de la Cámara de Diputados*, November 24, 1911, p. 338. See also Heaps-Nelson (1978, 18) for an analysis of who supported and who opposed the incomplete list.

They also won a subsequent vote to mandate the use of the incomplete list for elections to select senators from the federal capital as well as electors for the president and vice-president.[34] The discussion of the secret ballot was, surprisingly, less contentious, passing by a margin of forty-three votes.[35] However, reform opponents rejected the obligatory voting provision by a 34–32 vote.[36] Roca Jr. criticized the obligatory voting proposal on the grounds that it was "a leap into the darkness" since few countries had adopted it.[37]

Once the reform had cleared the Chamber of Deputies, it went to the Senate where the president had fewer allies. Here as well, the articles on the secret ballot received little attention – most of the debate focused on the provisions establishing obligatory voting and the incomplete list. Some senators criticized the obligatory voting proposal on the grounds that it eliminated the right to abstain and had not been widely implemented, but supporters of the obligatory vote easily prevailed on a roll-call vote with thirteen members in favor and six opposed.[38] More senators opposed the incomplete list, but in the end, its supporters narrowly prevailed on a 10–9 vote.[39] The Senate version of the reform then returned to the Chamber of Deputies, which approved the reform bill, including the obligatory voting provision, with only one minor modification.[40] The reform bill, Law 8871, became law on February 10, 1912.

The author carried out a statistical analysis of legislator support for the 1912 reform in the Chamber of Deputies, using a roll-call vote on the incomplete-list provision as well as López's (2005c, 280–283) classification of deputies as reformists, undecided, or anti-reformists (Madrid 2019b). This analysis found that deputies elected in 1910, which was used as a proxy for membership in Sáenz Peña's National Union, were significantly more likely to support the reform than other legislators.[41] Legislators who hailed from districts where the UCR was strong were also more likely to support the reform, although the relationship was weaker and less consistent. By contrast, legislators were not statistically more likely to support the reform if they came from districts where the urbanization rate was higher, industrial production was greater, strikes were more numerous, and the urban working or middle classes represented a larger share of the electorate. This quantitative analysis therefore provides

---

[34] *Diario de Sesiones de la Cámara de Diputados*, December 15, 1911, pp. 613–614.
[35] *Diario de Sesiones de la Cámara de Diputados*, December 13, 1911, pp. 582–583.
[36] *Diario de Sesiones de la Cámara de Diputados*, December 1, 1911, p. 538.
[37] *Diario de Sesiones de la Cámara de Diputados*, November 29, 1911, p. 501.
[38] *Diario de Sesiones de la Cámara de Senadores*, February 3, 1912, pp. 345–347.
[39] See the roll-call vote in *Diario de Sesiones de la Cámara de Senadores*, February 3, 1912, p. 351.
[40] *Diario de Sesiones de la Cámara de Senadores*, February 10, 1912, pp. 382–383.
[41] It is reasonable to assume that most legislators elected in 1910 were members of the National Union, given that party's dominance of the 1910 elections and the fact that the elections used the complete-list system, which awarded all legislative seats in a district to whichever party or list finished first. By contrast, legislators elected in 1908 are assumed not to be members of the National Union since this party did not even exist then.

support for the idea that ruling party dissidents, and to a lesser extent UCR pressure, helped bring about the reform.

Thus, a split within the PAN led to the rise of a dissident faction that promoted reform partly to persuade the opposition Radicals to participate in elections, but also to renovate a corrupt political system that had long excluded them from power. Instead of proposing electoral reform, Sáenz Peña, like Figueroa Alcorta, could have used his control of the presidency to intervene in provinces and elections to weaken Roca and his allies. Yet any such effort might well have proven temporary. Once Sáenz Peña left office, the provincial networks of political bosses could have reassembled under the leadership of Roca or some other leader as they had in the past. By contrast, electoral reform seemed to offer a more permanent solution to the political corruption that Roca embodied. Indeed, in a 1908 letter to an ally, Sáenz Peña cautioned that "destroying Roca with his regime and its phalanxes is not an end but rather a means to redeem and rehabilitate the country" (cited in Castro 2012, 234).

ELECTIONS AND DEMOCRACY IN ARGENTINA AFTER 1912

The 1912 electoral reforms brought democracy to Argentina, although it was not until 1916 that a democratically elected president took office. The establishment of obligatory voting led to a dramatic increase in voter turnout, as did the decision of the UCR to abandon its policy of abstention. Whereas in the 1910 legislative elections 21 percent of registered voters had voted, in the 1912 legislative elections 68.5 percent of registered voters cast ballots (Cantón 1973, 45). During the next eighteen years, turnout would fluctuate somewhat, but in all cases it would remain significantly above the pre-1912 levels (Jones, Lauga, and León-Roesch 2005, 80–82, 108–109; Ministerio del Interior 2008, 59–69). As Table 6.2 indicates, voter turnout as a percent of the overall population also rose dramatically, increasing from 2.8 percent in 1910 to 9.2 percent in 1916 and 13.4 percent in 1928.

In the wake of the 1912 reforms, official intervention in elections declined markedly, particularly in urban areas, and elections became relatively free and fair.[42] The secret ballot discouraged vote buying and made it more difficult for political bosses to compel voters to support certain candidates. The adoption of the incomplete-list electoral system ensured that opposition parties gained legislative representation even in those districts where they did not come out on top. As a result, the opposition's share of legislative seats rose dramatically. The Radicals, for example, won 20 percent of the legislative seats up for election in 1912, 32 percent in 1914, and 42 percent in 1916. Even more importantly, Yrigoyen and the Radicals captured the presidency in 1916, winning 46.8 percent of the popular vote and a narrow majority of the votes in electoral

---

[42] Victorino de la Plaza, who became president after Sáenz Peña's death, described himself as "the first president of Argentina who does not know the name of [his] successor" (Rock 2002, 213).

TABLE 6.2 *Presidential elections in Argentina, 1854–1928*

Year	Winner (party)	Winner's share of electoral votes (%)	Runner-up's share of electoral votes (%)	Popular votes cast (% of total pop.)
1854	Justo José de Urquiza (Federal)	86	7	6,400 (1)
1860	Santiago Derqui (Federal)	58	36	12,800 (1)
1862	Bartolomé Mitre (Liberal)	85	0	14,000 (1)
1868	Domingo Sarmiento (independent)	51	17	16,900 (1)
1874	Nicolas Avellaneda (PAN)	64	35	25,800 (1.2)
1880	Julio A. Roca (PAN)	68	31	52,800 (2.0)
1886	Miguel Juárez Celman (PAN)	72	14	61,900 (2.0)
1892	Luis Sáenz Peña (PAN)	91	2	77,200 (2.0)
1898	Julio A. Roca (PAN)	73	13	89,200 (2.0)
1904	Manuel Quintana (PAN)	80	11	143,000 (2.5)
1910	Roque Sáenz Peña (National Union)	88	1	199,000 (2.8)
1916	Hipólito Yrigoyen (UCR)	51	35	745,825 (9.2)
1922	Marcelo de Alvear (UCR)	63	16	876,354 (9.5)
1928	Hipólito Yrigoyen (UCR)	65	19	1,461,605 (13.4)

Source: Latin American Historical Elections Database.

college. Conservatives, however, continued to control the Senate as well as most governorships (Remmer 1984, 93; Rock 1975, 96–97).

Between 1916 and 1930, the Radicals consolidated their dominance, winning regular victories in both presidential and legislative elections. A Radical leader, Marcelo de Alvear, succeeded Yrigoyen in 1922, winning 49 percent of the valid popular vote and 63 percent of the electoral college. Then in 1928, Yrigoyen returned to the helm, winning a resounding victory with 62 percent of the popular vote and 65 percent of the electoral college. The Radicals also dominated legislative elections during this period. After 1922, the UCR split, but the various Radical factions together still typically won a majority of the seats in the lower chamber.

The Radicals dominated elections throughout this period in large part because they built a strong national organization with branches located throughout the country. In addition, once in office, the UCR developed a strong patronage network that delivered goods to its supporters. The middle classes and the children of immigrants, in particular, flocked to the party drawn by the lure of patronage and the Radicals' criticisms of the traditional political elites (Cornblit 1975, 621–622; Rock 1975, 110–114; Walter 1978, 599–602; Alonso 2000, 202–203). Moreover, the other parties were generally poorly organized and strong in only a few areas, such as the Socialists and the Liga del Sur. The conservatives also suffered from divisions. Indeed, the votes for the various conservative forces actually outnumbered the votes for the Radicals in 1912, 1914, and 1916, but they were split between many parties (Cornblit 1975, 636). Various conservative leaders, including Sáenz Peña (1915, 531), urged the conservatives to unite, but their leaders could not overcome their personal differences, focusing their efforts on overcoming their conservative rivals rather than defeating the Radicals (Castro 2012, 321–322).

In power, the Radicals were guilty of some of the same misdeeds as their predecessors. Yrigoyen concentrated power and frequently intervened in the provinces to replace opposition governments or those controlled by dissident Radicals. The federal government ousted provincial governments on twenty separate occasions between 1916 and 1921, and these interventions lasted on average eleven months (Remmer 1984, 100). The Yrigoyen administration also sometimes interfered in elections, but the central means that the Radicals used to win elections was organization and patronage rather than fraud and intervention. Bartolucci and Taroncher (1994, 183) argue that "fraud in its broadest characteristics was eradicated [with the reform] ... the cases of fraud [that remained] were the product of the isolated actions of lower-level leaders, in contrast to the systematic planning that was evident in the previous political period."

Yrigoyen's personalistic policies gradually led to a split within the party between supporters of Yrigoyen and his opponents, who were dubbed the Antipersonalists (Alemán and Saiegh 2014; Smith 1974). This split broke open during the Alvear administration when the new president sought to weaken Yrigoyen's influence. Although Yrigoyen managed to recapture the presidency in 1928, by that time he was seventy-six years old and no longer at the height of his powers. Moreover, the onset of the Great Depression in 1930 forced the Yrigoyen administration to cut jobs and spending, which undermined the party's support. Unemployment rose, exports fell, and foreign financing disappeared, which prompted landowners, industrialists, and commercial interests as well as workers and employees to abandon the government. Students began to organize violent demonstrations against the government, and in September 1930, the military stepped in, overthrowing the government.[43] The country would not experience another lengthy period of democracy until the 1980s.

---

[43] Yrigoyen's interference in military promotions and his use of the armed forces to intervene in the provinces had gradually alienated many military officers.

Various scholars have argued that Argentina's failure to develop a strong conservative party undermined democracy in the country by encouraging conservatives to call for military intervention, rather than dislodging governments through the ballot box (Gibson 1996; Di Tella 1971–1972; Middlebrook 2000a). Without a strong conservative party to protect them, these scholars suggest, elites resorted to extra-constitutional means to defend their interests. The problem, however, was not just that Argentina failed to develop a strong conservative party but also that only one strong party arose in the country, in contrast to Chile, Colombia, and Uruguay.[44] Without a strong opposition party to constrain them, ruling parties at times abused their governing powers. In the absence of a strong opposition party, ruling parties could not easily be dislodged via elections, encouraging the opposition to call on the military to intervene. This is what occurred in 1930 and it led to the breakdown of democracy in Argentina (Alemán and Saiegh 2014, 851–853; Mainwaring and Pérez-Liñán 2013, 131–132). Similar processes would take place in subsequent years.

Nevertheless, between 1916 and 1930, Argentina represented a democratic pioneer in Latin America and a model for much of the world. Argentina did not become fully democratic during this period since women could not vote and some electoral manipulation continued, but elections were relatively free and fair, electoral participation was high, and alternation in power could and did occur. Although this vibrant democracy came to an end in 1930, many of the democratic innovations of this period, including obligatory voting and the secret ballot, continued to be used in Argentine elections in the decades that followed.

THE ORIGINS OF DEMOCRACY IN COLOMBIA

Colombia democratized at approximately the same time as Argentina and for very similar reasons. Like Argentina, Colombia was plagued by opposition revolts during the nineteenth century, which undermined constitutional rule and provoked state repression. At the outset of the twentieth century, however, Colombia professionalized its military, which deterred the opposition from carrying out further revolts and led it to focus on the electoral path to power.

Parties played a central role in the emergence of democracy in Colombia. As Chapter 4 discussed, two powerful parties, the Liberal Party and the Conservative Party, arose during the nineteenth century. From 1886 until 1930, the Liberal Party was in the opposition, and it advocated democratic reforms. The ruling Conservative Party resisted the reforms, but in the early 1900s Conservative dissidents broke with their party and allied with some Liberals to form the Republican Union. The members of the Republican Union then pushed the democratic reforms through the constituent assembly in 1910.

---

[44] The UCR largely defended elite interests during its tenure in government. For example, it enacted liberal economic policies and opposed labor activism.

The reforms strengthened horizontal accountability, guaranteed minority representation, and expanded the suffrage. In the decades that followed, most elections were relatively free and fair, and the opposition respected the results. Colombia did not become a full democracy in the early twentieth century because some electoral abuses continued and some restrictions on the franchise remained. Moreover, the military was not able to establish a monopoly on violence throughout the entire country, which encouraged regional rebellions that undermined democracy. Nevertheless, the 1910 constitutional reforms represented a watershed in Colombia's democratic development.

THE COLOMBIAN MILITARY AND REVOLTS

The Colombian state had a weak military and low coercive capacity throughout most of the nineteenth century. When the independence struggle ended in 1825, the new nation of Gran Colombia, which included present-day Colombia, Ecuador, and Venezuela, had a large military composed of some 25,000–30,000 men (Safford and Palacios 2002, 111). The armed forces, which absorbed three-quarters of the government's revenues, were dominated by Venezuelans whose interference in politics created resentment among the elites of Bogotá.[45] These anti-military attitudes persisted among the civilian elites even after the secession of Venezuela in 1830, and led Congress to slash the military's budget and limit the number of troops to 3,300 men (Bushnell 1993, 87).

In the decades that followed, the Colombian government kept the military small in part because the country was poor and lacked the resources to invest in the armed forces. In 1870, Colombian exports were less than one-third those of Chile and less than one-fifth those of Argentina, even though Colombia was a much more populous nation (Bértola and Ocampo 2013, 56, 59). According to data from Bolt et al. (2018), Colombia's GDP per capita in 1870 was the third lowest in South America of those for which there are data.

In addition, Colombia had no pressing external security threats during the nineteenth century that required a military buildup. Colombia had border disputes with its neighbors, but it did not fight any foreign wars during the nineteenth century, aside from brief conflicts with Ecuador and Peru that were resolved in Colombia's favor without it having to mobilize troops on a national scale (Esquivel Triana 2010, 159). Nor did it face powerful rivals. Most of Colombia's neighbors – Costa Rica, Ecuador, Peru, and Venezuela – had relatively small and weak militaries in the nineteenth century, and Brazil's much larger armed forces were stretched thin and based far from its border with Colombia. Although Colombia faced numerous internal revolts during the nineteenth century, many civilian elites viewed the military more as a threat than as a reliable ally in suppressing these rebellions.

---

[45] This resentment was exacerbated by the fact that many of the Venezuelan military officers, unlike the Colombian elites, were of African descent.

The size of the Colombian army fluctuated over time but until the 1880s it never exceeded 4,000 men (Payne 1968, 120; López-Alves 2000, 138). The Liberal governments of the 1850s–1870s were particularly frugal, slashing the army to under 2,000 men, a level below that of most other South American nations. The federal constitution of 1863 sought to delegate military responsibilities to the states, calling on each state to organize its own army. As a result, between 1863 and 1875 the army accounted for only 12 percent of the federal budget. William Scruggs, the US minister to Colombia, reported in 1875 that "[t]he National Army is merely nominal. Indeed, it can scarcely be said to exist" (Delpar 1981, 87–88).

The troops, moreover, were poorly paid, trained, and equipped. Soldiers frequently went into battle armed only with clubs, spears, and machetes – rifles had to be shared among various combatants (Tirado Mejía 1976, 54–57). The wages of the troops were often well below what they could obtain in other types of labor, and as a result, the soldiers tended to come from the poorest and least educated families (Deas 2002b, 90; Maingot 1967, 103–104, 115–118). In 1882, the Colombian government reported that less than one-third of the troops could read (Deas 2002b, 92). The government forcibly recruited troops, especially during wartime, and the soldiers frequently resisted combat and deserted in high numbers (Somma 2011, 233–234; Jurado Jurado 2005).

Military officers also lacked training. In 1848, President Tomás Cipriano de Mosquera founded a military college, but it closed in 1854 (Safford and Palacios 2002, 236). Efforts in 1861, 1883, 1891, and 1896 to create schools that would train officers and professionalize the armed forces also failed (Atehortúa Cruz and Vélez 1994, 25; Maingot 1967, 120–121). Officers typically owed their positions to political connections rather than military expertise, and during civil wars the military would divide along party lines (Delpar 1981, 87; López-Alves 2000, 135–137).

The weakness of the military encouraged frequent rebellions throughout the nineteenth century, as Table 6.3 indicates. Between 1830 and 1899, Colombia experienced fifteen major revolts as well as dozens of minor ones.[46] Colombia's vast size and rugged terrain also encouraged revolts by making them difficult to suppress. Even after the loss of Ecuador and Venezuela, Colombia spanned more than 1.1 million square kilometers (twice the size of France), and the country was extremely mountainous.[47] The military therefore could not easily transport troops or communicate with them in the field.[48] As a result,

---

[46] According López-Alves (2000, 118), Colombia suffered more than fifty local rebellions during the nineteenth century.

[47] During the nineteenth century, a trip from Medellín to Bogota could take 20–30 days, even though the two cities are only 260 miles apart (Somma 2011, 220).

[48] The introduction of the railroad and steamships during the late nineteenth century improved the situation, but they only covered a small area of the country. Telegraph lines spread more widely, but these lines were frequently out of service. A contemporary joke was that telegraph delays were so common that a man sent his wife in the provinces a wire saying that "by the time you read this, I will be in your arms" (Safford and Palacios 2002, 255).

TABLE 6.3 *Major revolts in Colombia, 1830–1929*

Year	Description of revolt	Type of revolt (outcome)
1830	General Rafael Urdaneta overthrew President Joaquín Mosquera who had appointed liberals to high positions.	Military coup (took power)
1831	Liberals José María Obando and José Hilario López rebelled and overthrew Urdaneta.	Elite insurrection (took power)
1839–1842	War of the Supremes. Radical Liberals rebelled against President José Ignacio de Márquez, but they were defeated. 3,400 deaths.	Elite insurrection (suppressed)
1851	Conservatives rebelled against Liberal President José Hilario López, but the revolt was suppressed. 1,000 deaths.	Elite insurrection (suppressed)
1854	General José María Melo overthrew Liberal President José María Obando in a coup.	Military coup (took power)
1854	Constitutionalist Liberals and Conservatives assembled 11,000 rebels and defeated General Melo. 4,000 deaths.	Elite insurrection (took power)
1859–1862	Tomás Cipriano de Mosquera overthrew Conservative President Mariano Ospina with help from Liberals. 6,000 deaths.	Elite insurrection (took power)
1865	Conservatives revolted in various states, but they were suppressed by the military.	Elite insurrection (suppressed)
1867	Military officers with aid of Radical Liberals and Conservatives overthrew President Mosquera after he closed Congress.	Military coup (took power)
1875	Conservatives and Radicals joined forces to overthrow the Liberal governor of Magdalena.	Elite insurrection (took power)
1876–1877	War of the Parish Priests. Conservatives rebelled against liberal President Santiago Pérez, but they were defeated. 9,000 deaths.	Elite insurrection (suppressed)
1884	Radical Liberals rebelled against the governor of Santander but were defeated.	Elite insurrection (suppressed)
1884–1885	Radical Liberals rebelled against President Rafael Núñez, but they were defeated. 3,000 deaths.	Elite insurrection (suppressed)
1893	Artisans rioted in response to a newspaper article criticizing them as immoral. The riot was suppressed with 40–45 people killed.	Popular uprising (suppressed)
1895	Liberals rebelled against Conservative President Miguel Antonio Caro, but the revolt was suppressed. 2,000 deaths.	Elite insurrection (suppressed)
1899–1902	War of a Thousand Days. Liberals revolted against Conservative President Manuel Antonio San Clemente but lost. 100,000 deaths.	Elite insurrection (suppressed)
1900	Historical Conservatives carried out a coup that replaced the ailing President San Clemente with his vice-president.	Military coup (took power)

Source: Latin American Revolts Database.

internal wars sometimes dragged on for months and even years: The War of the Supremes (1839–1842), for example, lasted twenty-seven months; and the War of a Thousand Days spanned thirty-nine months (Patiño Villa 2010, 98–99). Both sides relied on the assistance of party militias, which typically did much of the fighting (López-Alves 2000, 137; Maingot 1967, 103).

The government prevailed in most civil wars in part because it typically had superior weaponry. For example, during the War of a Thousand Days, the rebels had only 20,000 firearms as opposed to the 200,000 belonging to the government (Jaramillo 1986, 74). Nevertheless, in some cases, the government was obliged to grant concessions, such as amnesties or policy reforms, to persuade the rebels to surrender, which encouraged the opposition to mount further rebellions. Moreover, in a number of cases, the rebels triumphed: Revolts toppled presidents in 1830, 1831, 1854, 1859, and 1867.[49] Armed revolts, in fact, represented a more promising path to power than elections in nineteenth-century Colombia, given that the latter only twice led to alternations in the party in power (Bushnell 1992, 19).

The nineteenth-century revolts typically pitted Liberals against Conservatives, although intraparty struggles also occurred at times. Occasionally, Liberals and Conservatives would fight on the same side, but as partisan identities developed, the conflicts increasingly broke down along party lines. Electoral fraud, political exclusion, and unconstitutional seizures of power often served as the catalysts for civil wars, but many of the conflicts were rooted in differences the two parties had with regard to the Catholic Church.[50] Liberal reforms that sought to curtail the influence of the Church met intense resistance from Conservatives who received material as well as symbolic support from the clergy.[51] The War of the Supremes, for example, began when President José Ignacio de Márquez ordered the closure of all monasteries with fewer than eight members, whereas the War of the Parish Priests was triggered by a Liberal decree restricting religious education in the public schools.

Rebel leaders mobilized their supporters through a variety of methods. Landlords pressured peasants to fight in the rebel armies or promised them financial rewards, such as a share of the war booty (Somma 2011, 203–216). Both sides also recruited volunteers by pledging to enact policies that would benefit them and by demonizing the other side. Liberal leaders, for example, motivated Afro-Colombians to fight in some of the early conflicts by promising

---

[49] In 1830 and 1854, military leaders overthrew the government, but forces representing the erstwhile political leaders rebelled and recaptured power.

[50] Other factors, including economic and social cleavages, regionalism, and personal political ambition, also contributed to the conflicts (Safford 2000; Earle 2000b).

[51] Uribe-Castro (2019) found that the expropriation of Church assets in the late nineteenth century reduced municipal-level violence in Colombia by weakening the Church and making it a less attractive ally.

them emancipation. Conservatives responded by appealing to racial and class-based fears, as in this 1861 speech by President Mariano Ospina:

> Do you believe that ignorant blacks from Cauca, that these outlaws, dangerous men from the villages, that these men who formed the rebels' army are interested in philosophical questions about the form of government? No, this is a stupid belief. The motives of the masses surrounding the rebels' army are none other than your property and hatred for your race. (Cited in Rojas de Ferro 1995, 218)

Over time, the rebels managed to assemble larger and larger armies, thanks in part to the growing strength of partisan identities in Colombia. In the mid-century conflicts, the rebel armies consisted of only 3,000–4,000 troops, but they mobilized 15,000 soldiers in the 1876–1877 War of the Parish Priests, and tens of thousands of troops in the 1899–1902 War of a Thousand Days (Somma 2011, 203–204).[52]

The rebellions deepened authoritarianism in Colombia. When the rebels overthrew presidents or local-level leaders, they subverted constitutional rule. Even where the rebels did not prevail, however, they still undermined democracy by provoking state repression. Governments often responded to revolts by shutting down opposition newspapers and imprisoning, exiling, or even executing members of the opposition. During the War of the Supremes, for example, both sides executed prisoners, sometimes by firing squad and other times with lances (Safford and Palacios 2002, 222). In addition, the government at times forced citizens to provide loans to finance the war efforts or seized properties belonging to supporters of the rebels (López-Alves 2000, 121). Although some of these repressive measures only lasted as long as the rebellions, others endured. The 1884–1885 civil war, for example, gave birth to the long-lasting 1886 constitution, which granted the president the right to a declare a state of siege in case of foreign war or civil commotion, a measure that presidents frequently invoked (Park 1985, 265).[53]

The revolts also had high human costs. According to McGreevey (1971, 88), the civil wars that occurred between 1830 to 1899 led to 33,300 deaths, and this does not include most of the fatalities in the War of a Thousand Days (1899–1902). Moreover, the lethality of these conflicts went up over time. Whereas the civil wars prior to 1860 led to no more 4,000 deaths each, the revolution of 1860 caused 6,000 deaths, the War of the Parish Priests led to 9,000 deaths, and the War of a Thousand Days led to an estimated 100,000 deaths (Patiño Villa 2010, 98–99). Some of the increase in fatalities was due to the introduction of more sophisticated weaponry into Colombia. During the 1876–1877 war, for example, the Liberal Government of Aquileo Parra

---

[52] Women and children also fought in the rebel armies (Jaramillo 1986, 60–63).

[53] The 1853 and 1863 constitutions in Colombia had not provided for states of exception – they were the only Spanish American constitutions during the nineteenth century to lack this provision (Loveman 1993, 161).

acquired 5,500 Remington rifles and eight artillery pieces, while the rebels obtained 3,000 rifles (Somma 2011, 236). Whereas a traditional rifle could fire one shot per minute, a Remington could fire six per minute and a machine gun could fire dozens.

The economic costs of the rebellions were also high. In 1882 one Independent Liberal newspaper described the ravages of war as follows:

> Every two years we have a war or feel the effects of one. When blood is not shed, or forced loans are not exacted, or property is not confiscated, there is at the very least profound agitation affecting even the lowest levels of society; business is paralyzed, industries decay, and capital flees to where it can find better guarantees – that is, in four or six months of agitation we destroy the good we have done in the previous two years. (Cited in Delpar 1981, 98)

Holguín (1976, 83–84) estimated that nine national civil wars cost the government 31.5 million Colombian pesos and fourteen local wars cost 5.6 million Colombian pesos, counting only the money that the Treasury allocated for the wars. McGreevey (1971, 176) calculated that the soldiers who died in the wars would have earned $822 million in US dollars over their lifetimes. Neither of these figures, however, come close to representing the true economic costs since they do not include the disruption of business, the deterrence of investment, and the destruction of property.

The high costs of these wars led President Rafael Núñez, who dominated Colombia from 1880 until his death in 1894, to seek to create a military capable of bringing an end to the revolts. In 1885 when a rebellion broke out, he reached an agreement with the Conservatives to create a national reserve army composed of Conservative volunteers (Atehortúa Cruz and Vélez 1994, 31; Delpar 1981, 130; Safford and Palacios 2002, 245). The following year, Núñez enacted a new constitution that brought an end to the federalist system established in 1863 and declared that the central government alone had the power to import, manufacture, and possess arms and munitions of war. The Núñez administration also purchased 5,000 Gras rifles from France and significantly increased the number of troops. By 1888, the army had more than 6,200 troops, up from fewer than 1,500 men in the 1870s.

Nevertheless, Núñez did little to professionalize the military. In fact, he deepened its politicization by purging Liberals from the officer corps (Esquivel Triana 2010, 242–243). Efforts to improve the training of officers by creating military schools proved short lived, and the military continued to rely heavily on poorly trained and forcibly recruited troops (Soifer 2015, 230). Moreover, after the brief expansion of the army in the 1880s, the number of troops began to decline again (López-Alves 2000, 138–139). The continued weakness of the military became evident when it struggled to defeat the rebels in the War of a Thousand Days.

It was not until after the War of a Thousand Days that the government took major steps to professionalize the military. The export growth that Colombia experienced in the late nineteenth and early twentieth century helped finance military modernization and other state-building efforts. Between 1870 and 1913, exports grew by 5.4 percent above inflation annually, one of the fastest rates in Latin America (Bértola and Ocampo 2013, 100). Although the economy had suffered during the War of a Thousand Days, under the administration of General Rafael Reyes (1904–1909) it began a rapid recovery, as foreign aid and international loans poured into the country (Lemaitre 2002, 255–256).

The military's poor performance in the war and the painful loss of Panama in the aftermath led to the emergence of a small group of military reformers in the Reyes regime (Studer 1975, 52–54). These reformers sought to professionalize and depoliticize the military, converting it into a national institution (Bergquist 1978, 225–226; Atehortúa Cruz 2009, 22).[54] To help with the overhaul of the military, the government hired a Chilean mission in 1907 and it was followed by three more Chilean missions, which lasted until 1915 (Atehortúa Cruz 2009, 22–30; Arancibia Clavel 2002). None of these missions was large, but they exercised considerable influence, particularly at the outset.

One of the government's first steps was to enact Law 17 of 1907, which aimed to establish rational and meritocratic criteria for advancement within the military and deal with the huge number of officers who had received promotions in the war (Cardona 2008, 85–88; Atehortúa Cruz and Vélez 1994, 62). The following year, Reyes issued Decree 1313, which required that officers take certain courses in order to be promoted (Cardona 2008, 90). In addition, the Reyes administration, with the assistance of Chilean officers, established several institutions to train military officers: the Army Cadet School, the Naval School, and the Superior War College (Arancibia Clavel 2002, 385–386; Atehortúa Cruz and Vélez 1994, 60–63; Cardona 2008, 88–91). By 1914, the Army Cadet School had 110 students and the Superior War College had accepted thirty-six students (Cardona 2008, 89–90).

To cut military expenditures and create a better-trained and more professional force, the government reduced the size of the army, which had ballooned to 50,000 soldiers in the war, to 5,000 troops. Congress also prohibited the forced recruitment of soldiers in 1909. Nevertheless, Reyes' efforts to establish obligatory military service and to ban the use of payments to avoid military service largely failed (Arancibia Clavel 2002, 399; Cardona 2008, 97). As a result, soldiers continued to be drawn largely from the poorest sectors of Colombian society (Cardona 2008, 98).

The Reyes regime sought to ensure that the military had a monopoly on the use of force by initiating a program to collect the weapons Colombians had stockpiled during the War of a Thousand Days and earlier. By 1909, this program had collected 65,505 guns and 1,138,649 bullets (Bergquist 1978, 225; Esquivel Triana 2010, 265; Atehortúa Cruz 2009, 21). Reyes also created

---

[54] Although Reyes was a Conservative, he brought Liberals into his cabinet and sought to reduce partisan hostilities.

some new departments and broke up existing ones to weaken regional power centers, appease some local groups, and reduce the likelihood of rebellion (Bergquist 1978, 226). Finally, the Reyes regime increased the state's ability to respond to rebellions by building up Colombia's transportation and communications infrastructure. By 1910, Colombia had 614 miles of railroad track and 10,600 miles of telegraph lines, up from 409 miles of track and 6,500 miles of lines in 1903 (Banks and Wilson 2014).

Many of the military reforms proposed by the missions generated resistance from officers who resented Chilean interference and sought to protect their traditional prerogatives. Moreover, politicians continued to try to intervene in military promotions. Reyes himself provoked the ire of the Chilean mission by promoting his personal friends to key posts, rather than the graduates of the army School of Cadets (Abel 1987, 60). Nevertheless, overall, Reyes was a strong supporter of the reforms and helped ensure their implementation.

The government of Carlos Restrepo (1910–1914) continued with the professionalization efforts, albeit somewhat more tepidly (Maingot 1967, 192–196). The Restrepo administration modernized the weaponry of the military, expanded the training of officers, strictly implemented the regulations governing the promotion of officers, and avoided using the military to intervene in elections (Esquivel Triana 2010, 269–73; Pinzón de Lewin 1994, 62–67; Abel 1987, 61–62). Restrepo also sought to deny troops the right to vote to ensure that they did not get involved in elections, although he failed to get this measure approved by Congress.

The professionalization efforts clearly improved the coercive capacity of the Colombian state during the early twentieth century, which helped deter revolts. Indeed, there were no major revolts in Colombia during the first few decades of the twentieth century.[55] The Liberal Party engaged in some small local uprisings during the early twentieth century, but eschewed major rebellions, in part because of the bitter memories of the disastrous War of a Thousand Days, and also because it recognized that it had little chance of prevailing in battle (Maingot 1967, 158, 165–166). Instead, Liberals focused on the electoral path to power, competing in elections and pushing for further democratic reforms. Some elements of the Liberal Party did advocate rebellion in the wake of the party's defeat in the 1922 elections in which there were compelling allegations of widespread fraud. However, General Benjamín Herrera, the defeated presidential candidate in 1922, refused to pursue a costly armed struggle that he did not believe his party could win.

The professionalization efforts also helped change the culture of the military. In the wake of the reforms, the military largely ceased to intervene in elections, although the police continued to be used in support of whichever party happened to be in power locally (Deas 1996, 174–175; Posada-Carbó 1997, 269; Pinzón de Lewin 1994, 62–92). Increasingly, the military saw its role as

---

[55] There was a major labor strike in 1928, which the military bloodily repressed.

to guarantee that the elections were held in an orderly fashion, rather than to support one side or another, and local authorities often called on the military to keep the peace at election time. Conservative officers continued to dominate the military throughout the early twentieth century, but these officers largely abstained from politics (Abel 1987, 62; Bushnell 1993, 157). Indeed, when a Liberal candidate was elected president in 1930, the military did not seek to intervene to block him from taking office.

Military professionalization did not go as far in Colombia as it did in the Southern Cone, however. Indeed, the return of Conservative administrations in 1914 brought an end to the military professionalization efforts because many Conservatives were unenthusiastic about measures that sought to undermine their control of the armed forces. In 1914, the government initiated the fourth and final Chilean mission, but it only had one officer to begin with, and this officer resigned in 1915 when the minister of war stripped him of his powers to appoint the officers teaching in the Military School (Arancibia Clavel 2002, 435–438). Once the Chilean mission came to an end, the military training programs deteriorated as the old guard officers reasserted control (Maingot 1967, 198–200). After a failed attempt to hire a German mission, the Colombian government enlisted a Swiss training mission in 1924. The Swiss, however, encountered many of the same obstacles that had obstructed the Chileans, and they ended their mission in 1928 without having made significant progress (Atehortúa Cruz 2009, ch. 5).

As a result, the Colombian military remained considerably weaker than its Argentine and Chilean counterparts. Between 1909 and 1922, the army fluctuated between 5,000 and 6,000 troops, which was below that of many of its neighbors (Abel 1987, 62; Atehortúa Cruz 2009, 124–125). The military budget also declined, dropping to a low of 7.6 percent of the total budget in 1923 (Atehortúa Cruz 2009, 116). Military salaries were low, the equipment was deficient, and the training of officers and troops was rudimentary throughout this period (Atehortúa Cruz 2009, 137; Maingot 1967, 200–208). The relative weakness of the Colombian military, combined with the ruggedness of the country's terrain, made it difficult for the government to establish a monopoly on violence and led to a renewal of revolts during the mid-twentieth century. This violence undermined the country's democracy in the long run. Nevertheless, the reformed military proved more than capable of suppressing the modest threats to the internal order that arose during the early twentieth century, which paved the way for the initial emergence of democracy in Colombia (Atehortúa Cruz and Vélez 1994, 97–110; Abel 1974, 209; Atehortúa Cruz 2009, 173–185).

THE RISE OF STRONG PARTIES IN COLOMBIA

The emergence of two strong parties in Colombia during the nineteenth century also helped lead to democratization. The Conservative and Liberal parties did not formally emerge until the late 1840s, although some scholars have traced the origins of the parties to an earlier rift between the two independence leaders, Simón Bolívar and Francisco de Paula Santander (Bushnell 1993, 65; Delpar 1981, 3–4; Safford and Palacios 2002, 134–143). Over the course of the nineteenth century, the two parties developed strong organizations that had a presence throughout the country (Posada-Carbó 2012, 27; Delpar 1981, 177, 183, 191). The Conservatives first held a national party convention in 1879 at which they drew up a party constitution, named a party leader, designated an official newspaper, and created a complex party organization that would endure for years (Delpar 1981, 127). Similarly, in 1880 the Liberal Party formed a National Central Committee and encouraged the creation of state-level and municipal-level committees (Delpar 1981, 126).

Many of the organizations were initially impermanent. For example, the provincial electoral committees that each party formed to support candidates typically disappeared after the elections. Nevertheless, elections were held frequently in Colombia, so these organizations were usually soon revived. In addition, both parties had some organizations, such as newspapers, schools, and associations of artisans, that operated on a semi-permanent basis. The newspapers waged propaganda campaigns, the schools trained future leaders, and the associations of artisans helped mobilize workers to participate in elections as well as armed conflicts.

Both parties gradually developed strong ties to the electorate and enjoyed diverse, multiclass support, although their constituencies varied somewhat. The Liberal Party, for example, had greater support among the Afro-Colombian population, no doubt partly because of its advocacy of emancipation (Bushnell 1993, 106–107; Sanders 2004, 139–142; Delpar 1981, 18–25). Artisans also mostly supported the Liberals, at least initially, but the Conservatives sought their support as well (Sowell 1992, 48–49; Sanders 2004; Delpar 1981, 28–31). Democratic societies, which consisted mostly of artisans, sprang up throughout Colombia beginning in the late 1840s, and these societies developed close ties to the Liberal Party (Sowell 1992; Sanders 2004, 66–69). Conservatives founded similar mass organizations, such as the Popular Society for Mutual Instruction and the Christian Fraternity in Bogotá (Safford and Palacios 2002, 201; Posada-Carbó 2012, 18).

Each party had its regional strongholds, although neither party was dominated by leaders or supporters from a particular region. For example, in the 1856 elections, the Conservative Party fared best in Antioquia, Cundinamarca, and Boyacá, whereas the Liberal Party performed better in Santander as well as in the coastal states of Bolívar and Magdalena. Some scholars have suggested that Conservatives were stronger in the cities that were major administrative centers under colonial rule, while Liberals tended to hail from towns that were marginal during the colonial period, but there are important exceptions to this general pattern (Safford and Palacios 2002, 152).

During the nineteenth century, the two parties were led by and largely catered to elites. Conservatives tended to have more distinguished social origins, but the leaders of the parties did not differ significantly in terms of their occupations (Delpar 1981, 56–58; Safford and Palacios 2002, 152–153; Safford 1972, 356–365; Bushnell 1993). Nor did the two parties advocate systematically different economic policies: They both mostly supported liberal policies such as free trade (Delpar 1981, 58; Safford and Palacios 2002, 155–156; López-Alves 2000, 123). At various moments, the parties took different positions on political issues, such as federalism and democratic rights, but their positions on these issues tended to vary depending on whether they were in power. Whereas the opposition typically promoted federalism and democratic rights, the ruling party usually resisted these measures.

The most important and consistent difference between the two parties was with regard to the Catholic Church, which the Conservatives strongly supported (Bushnell 1993, 110–111; Safford and Palacios 2002, 156). Conservatives sought to identify their party with the Church and to play up the religious dimension of their conflict with the Liberals. In an 1852 letter, Mariano Ospina, a founder of the Conservative Party, discussed the various banners that the party could use to rally supporters and discarded them all except for Catholicism, which he referred to as: "the only Conservative banner that is alive" (cited in Posada-Carbó 2012, 19).

The Catholic Church was, perhaps, stronger in Colombia than in any other Latin American country, and it did not hesitate to use its influence to support the Conservative Party (Mecham 1966, 115).[56] The Church helped select the party's candidates and formed organizations to support it in elections (Abel 1987, 34). Priests often denounced the Liberal Party and its candidates from the pulpit and the Church even excommunicated some Liberal politicians. For example, in 1897, the Bishop of Pasto told the priests in his parish to teach "the faithful that they cannot vote for Liberals without offending God" (Posada-Carbó 2012, 29).

Whereas Conservatives thought of the Catholic Church as a force for moral and social order, Liberals viewed it as an obstacle to freedom, enlightenment, and economic growth, and pushed for the separation of church and state. Liberals attacked the Church for intervening in politics. A commission of the Liberal-dominated constitutional convention of 1863 noted the "influence of the clergy over the ignorant populations" and reported that the clergy intervened "openly and imprudently" in electoral affairs (Posada-Carbó 2012, 22). The Liberal Party also enacted measures seeking to curtail Church intervention in elections: The 1863 constitution, for example, denied clergymen the right to vote and to hold office.[57]

While in power, Liberals also implemented a broad range of secularizing reforms that sought to reduce the influence of the Church. The Liberal government of José Hilario López (1849–1853) expelled the Jesuits from Colombia

---

[56] Although many Colombians had strong religious beliefs, it is difficult to know how much influence the Church had over the electorate (Posada-Carbó 2012, 3, 12; Deas 1996, 166–167).

[57] On average, priests occupied five (out of twenty-five) positions in the senate and two (out of sixty) positions in the lower chamber from the 1830s through the 1850s (Posada-Carbó 2012, 20).

and passed laws that made the Church financially dependent on provincial legislatures, gave municipal councils a role in choosing priests, and deprived priests of the right to be tried in ecclesiastical courts. Conservatives rebelled in protest in 1851, but their revolt was quickly suppressed. López then enacted a new constitution that provided for freedom of religion and passed laws separating church and state – he also exiled the archbishop of Bogotá when he refused to cooperate with some of the new policies. A second wave of Liberal reforms took place in the early 1860s during the presidency of Tomás Cipriano de Mosquera. Shortly after taking power, Mosquera asserted state control of the Catholic Church, expelled the Jesuits who had returned to Colombia in the late 1850s, and expropriated most Church assets. When the archbishop of Bogotá and other Church leaders protested, Mosquera imprisoned them, and declared that any religious communities that resisted would be abolished. The Pope responded by excommunicating Mosquera.

Another intense religious conflict occurred in the 1870s when the Liberals passed legislation making primary education free, compulsory, and secular (Bushnell 1993, 129; Shaw Jr. 1941, 598). In 1876, Conservatives revolted with the support of many Church leaders. In the wake of the revolt, the Liberals expelled four bishops as well as all clergymen who had taken up arms and it sought to impose further restraints on the Church to prevent future rebellions. In 1877, Congress also passed laws that abrogated the annual payments made to the Church for expropriated property and stipulated that clergymen could be convicted of violating the law if they incited civil disobedience through their sermons or publications. All these conflicts widened the divide between Liberals and Conservatives and strengthened partisan identities.

Beginning in the 1880s, religious conflict dissipated somewhat, although the Church continued to intervene in elections on behalf of the Conservative Party. The independent Liberal leader Rafael Núñez, who became president in 1880, sought to mollify Conservatives, resuming payments to the Church for expropriated property and repealing the 1877 laws that restricted the actions of the clergy. In 1886, Núñez created his own party, the National Party, and brought Conservatives into his government, ushering in an era of Conservative rule that would last until 1930. Under his leadership, Colombia reached a Concordat with the Vatican, and enacted a new constitution that declared Roman Catholicism to be the state religion and called for public education to be carried out in accordance with Catholic principles. Liberals, meanwhile, moderated their anti-clericalism, partly in order to build their ties to Conservative dissidents who opposed Núñez (Delpar 1980, 290–291).

Nevertheless, partisan identities had taken hold in much of the population by the time the religious divide between Liberals and Conservatives softened in the late nineteenth century. These identities had been strengthened by the violent conflicts that ravaged Colombia for much of the nineteenth century. Experiences of war created not only strong emotional attachments to one's own party but also powerful antipathies toward the other side.

Ernst Rothlisberger, a Swiss professor who lived in Colombia during the revolution of 1885, claimed that: "The majority do not fight in one party or another out of conviction but because they must avenge some atrocity. This fellow's father was killed, that one's brother was impressed, the mother and sisters of another were abused; in the next revolution they will avenge these offenses" (cited in Delpar 1981, 40–41). Executions of prisoners, which occurred in many of the wars, contributed to party polarization, enraging the friends, families, and co-partisans of the victims (Safford and Palacios 2002, 150).

The two parties proved extraordinarily durable, retaining their dominance throughout the nineteenth and twentieth centuries. The relative balance between the two parties contributed to their endurance since neither party was able to permanently dominate or destroy the other (Bushnell 1993, 117). Control of government shifted over time because of military victories as well as electoral triumphs and changes in party alignments. Whereas Conservatives dominated between 1841–1849, 1855–1861, and 1886–1930, Liberals controlled the presidency from 1849–1855 and 1861–1885. Both parties, however, managed to retain their core supporters even when they were in opposition. Indeed, the parties were typically more united when they were in the opposition than when they controlled the government.

The parties underwent frequent splits, which were caused by internal differences over policy as well as competition for leadership. The Liberals were particularly prone to splits, suffering major schisms in 1854, 1866–1867, and 1875–1878, which led Liberal candidates to run against each other in elections (Delpar 1981, 90–93; Posada-Carbó 2012, 27). At times, the splits resulted in the formation of new parties, such as the National Party or the Republican Union, but the new parties did not create enduring loyalties. Most of the people who joined the new parties eventually returned to the Liberal or Conservative fold (Delpar 1981, 58–59).

The strong partisan ties of each party meant that many elections were competitive despite the efforts of government officials to manipulate and control them. In four presidential elections – 1836, 1840, 1856, and 1875 – the winner won by less than 10 percent of the vote, and in 1836 and 1848 the opposition candidate prevailed. The average margin of victory in presidential elections in Colombia was the smallest in South America during the nineteenth century. Legislative elections were often similarly competitive, and the opposition party typically won some legislative seats, although there were a few periods, such as between 1886 and 1904, when the opposition was almost entirely excluded from the legislature. The opposition also usually held some state and municipal offices. In 1853, for example, the Conservatives captured nearly as many provincial governorships as did the ruling Liberal faction (Safford and Palacios 2002, 210). Even during the periods of Liberal dominance during the 1860s and 1870s, the Conservatives typically controlled the states of Antioquia and Tolima (Bushnell 1993, 129–130). Similarly, the Radical Liberals held power in some states during the period of Conservative dominance in the late nineteenth century (Bushnell 1993, 142).

Although Colombian elections in the nineteenth century were often competitive, they were not democratic. For most of the nineteenth century, only a relatively small percentage of the population could vote, and turnout was relatively low. The early constitutions of Gran Colombia (1820, 1821, and 1830) and Nueva Granada (1832 and 1843) granted suffrage only to free males who met certain income or property requirements and were not in dependency relationships (Bushnell 1963, 19; Posada-Carbó 2012). The early constitutions also imposed literacy requirements but repeatedly postponed them until 1850 (Posada-Carbó 2012, 15).

The liberal 1853 constitution briefly established universal male suffrage, which led to a dramatic increase in voter turnout: 8.6 percent of the population voted in 1856, as Table 6.4 indicates (Bushnell 1971, 241–242). Nevertheless, the expansion of voting rights in Colombia was short lived. The 1863 Constitution of Ríonegro federalized Colombia, allowing each state to set its own suffrage requirements, and five out of the nine states enacted literacy or income requirements in its wake (Bushnell 1971, 238; Posada-Carbó 2000b, 216; Bushnell 1984, 45). In 1886, a new constitution restricted the franchise for the entire nation, granting suffrage rights only to male citizens of twenty-one years of age who had a profession or means of subsistence, who were literate, and who met certain income or property requirements (República de Colombia, Registraduría del Estado Civil 2017).[58] As a result, voter turnout dropped considerably: Valid voters constituted an average of 3 percent of the total population in the twelve elections for which there are data from 1860–1883 (Bushnell 1971, 1984). Although voter turnout began to climb again in the 1870s, it did not approach the levels it had attained in 1856 under universal male suffrage (Bushnell 1971; Delpar 1981, 108; Bushnell 1984; Posada-Carbó 2012, 24).

To make matters worse, fraud and intimidation were widespread in elections during the nineteenth century, especially after 1863. The forms of fraud were numerous and took place at all stages of the electoral process. Electoral registries were frequently robbed or purged, and ballot boxes were often stuffed or stolen. Some people voted numerous times, while other eligible voters were not allowed to vote at all. The property or literacy requirements were often selectively applied to the opposition: In 1897, for example, government officials in the state of Tolima disqualified Liberals on the grounds that they could not spell words such as "particularísimamente" (Bergquist 1978, 96). Fraud often marred the process of counting the ballots as well: "He who does the counting elects" was a popular saying during the nineteenth century (Posada-Carbó 2012, 30; Pinzón de Lewin 1994, 34).

---

[58] Colombia retained universal male suffrage in departmental and municipal elections after 1886 (Posada-Carbó 2000b, 211, 217).

TABLE 6.4 *Presidential elections in Colombia, 1819–1930*

Year	Winner of election	Party of winner	Winner's % of the vote	Valid votes as a % of total population
1819	Simón Bolívar	None	100	
1821	Simón Bolívar	None	84.7	
1825	Simón Bolívar	None	95.7	
1830	Joaquín Mosquera	None	31.3	
1832	Francisco de Paula Santander	None	75.3	
1833	Francisco de Paula Santander	None	80.1	
1836	José Ignacio de Márquez	Conservative	38.6	
1840	Pedro Alcántara Herrán	Conservative	36.9	
1844	Tomás Cipriano de Mosquera	Conservative	45.8	
1849	José Hilario López	Liberal	43.2	
1852	José María Obando	Liberal	78.8	
1856	Mariano Ospina Rodríguez	Conservative	46.2	8.6
1860	Julio Arboleda	Conservative	73.2	3.0
1863	Tomás Cipriano de Mosquera	Liberal	78.7	
1864	Manuel Murillo Toro	Liberal	43.7	1.8
1865	Tomás Cipriano de Mosquera	Liberal	67.0	1.9
1867	Santos Gutiérrez	Liberal	45.3	2.6
1869	Eustorgio Salgar Moreno	Liberal	53.1	2.8
1871	Manuel Murillo Toro	Liberal	57.5	3.2
1873	Santiago Pérez	Liberal	72.5	3.9
1875	Aquileo Parra	Liberal	23.9	4.9
1877	Julián Trujillo	Liberal	99.8	1.3
1879	Rafael Núñez	Liberal	90.4	2.2
1881	Francisco Javier Zaldúa	Liberal	85.6	2.6
1883	Rafael Núñez	Liberal	69.0	5.9
1885	Rafael Núñez	National	100.0	
1891	Rafael Núñez	National	79.7	
1897	Manuel Antonio Sanclemente	National	78.5	
1904	Rafael Reyes	Conservative	43.9	
1909	Ramón González Valencia	Conservative	59.5	
1910	Carlos E. Restrepo	Republican Union	53.5	
1914	José Vicente Concha	Conservative	89.1	6.2
1918	Marco Fidel Suárez	Conservative	54.0	6.7
1922	Pedro Nel Ospina	Conservative	61.7	10.2
1926	Miguel Abadía Méndez	Conservative	99.9	5.1
1930	Enrique Olaya Herrera	Liberal	44.9	11.1

Source: Latin American Historical Elections Database.
Notes: The data from 1819–1832 as well as 1863, 1886, and 1909–1910 represent the vote in Congress or in a constituent assembly; the data from 1833–1852 and 1891–1904 represent the vote of the electoral college; and the data from 1856–1860, 1864–1883, and 1914–1930 represent the results of the popular vote.

All sides engaged in electoral manipulation, since local authorities controlled the electoral process and no party ever had a monopoly on power across all states or levels of government. Governors were quite powerful in Colombia, but they had no official role in setting up the electoral boards that oversaw elections, which prevented them from dominating the electoral process (Posada-Carbó 1997, 265).[59] Until 1888, municipal councils and assemblies typically appointed the local electoral authorities and there was no national electoral authority, which meant that whoever controlled the local authorities was in a position to manipulate the elections. Even after 1888, control of elections was decentralized since state assemblies gained responsibility for appointing the electoral authorities.[60]

Nevertheless, whichever party controlled the national government had important resources at its disposal, such as the military, which it could use to influence outcomes. Officers often marched their troops to the polls and instructed them how to vote, even forcibly recruiting civilians to swell their numbers.[61] The votes of the troops could potentially determine the results of elections, given the relatively small size of the Colombian electorate in most of the nineteenth century.[62] In addition, the military as well as the police influenced elections by intimidating opposition voters. The government often stationed troops at the polls to block opposition voters from voting and it sometimes circulated rumors that the troops would be impressing civilians in order to frighten off potential opposition voters (Deas 1996, 173). In some cases, the military even helped overthrow recalcitrant opposition governments in states and municipalities. Carlos Holguín, a Conservative politician, noted that during the period of Radical Liberal rule every presidential election "implied the necessity of overthrowing local governments" (cited in Posada-Carbó 1995, 11).

The opposition responded to government electoral manipulation in various ways. In some cases, frustration with government electoral manipulation led the opposition to abstain from elections or to engage in revolts. These strategies, however, usually provoked state repression and cost the opposition an opportunity to win representation in the legislature and other offices. In other cases, the opposition engaged in tit-for-tat strategies, participating in elections but engaging in the same electoral hijinks that it often criticized. The opposition was particularly likely to employ this latter strategy in those areas of the country it controlled.

---

[59] The Colombian states were referred to as provinces, departments, and states at different periods in the nineteenth century, and their executives were referred to as presidents or governors.

[60] State assemblies were also responsible for scrutinizing and certifying the electoral returns (Delpar 1981, 108).

[61] Not all soldiers were eligible to vote, however; nor could they always be counted on to vote for the ruling party (Deas 1996, 172; Posada-Carbó 1997, 268).

[62] The Liberal politician Salvador Camacho Roldán calculated that the troops constituted about one-eighth of the votes in the state of Cundinamarca and swayed the outcome of the elections in Bogotá (Delpar 1981, 107).

At the same time, the opposition frequently called for democratic reforms that would reduce government electoral intervention, guarantee civil and political liberties, and ensure the opposition some political representation. According to Mazzuca and Robinson (2009, 294), "starting in 1891, every Liberal convention, program, and manifesto demanded electoral reform, together with the abolition of the Ley de Caballos," the harsh 1888 law restricting the media. But the opposition Liberals lacked the influence in the legislature necessary to enact these reforms. In the late nineteenth century, the Liberals typically held only one seat in the lower chamber and none in the Senate. Thus, it was not until splits occurred within the ruling Conservative Party that major democratic reforms could be enacted.

SPLITS WITHIN THE RULING PARTY

The Conservative Party underwent a couple of important splits in the late nineteenth and early twentieth century, which helped lead to democratization. The party first divided in the early 1890s as a result of disenchantment with the policies pursued by the Nationalist-Conservative government of Rafael Núñez and his vice-president and successor, Miguel Antonio Caro. Conservative dissidents, who became known as Historical Conservatives, opposed many of the economic policies of the Núñez and Caro administrations as well as their repressive laws and the political exclusion of the Liberals (Bergquist 1978, 36–41). In 1891, Historical Conservatives proposed their own presidential candidate, Marceliano Vélez, whom Liberal leaders instructed their co-partisans to support. Nevertheless, the incumbent Núñez controlled the electoral machinery and he easily defeated Vélez amid widespread abstention and charges of fraud and intimidation (Bergquist 1978, 41–42; Delpar 1981, 150–151; Park 1985, 275–276).

The split within the Conservative Party deepened once Caro took over the government. Caro's refusal to modify the government's policies led to a Liberal revolt in 1895, which the Conservatives easily suppressed. To the disappointment of the Liberals, the Historical Conservatives sided with the government during the rebellion, although they did try unsuccessfully to negotiate a peace settlement involving constitutional reforms (Bergquist 1978, 48–49). In the years that followed, the Caro administration continued to resist major reforms, leading Historical Conservatives to publish an 1896 manifesto entitled "Motives of Dissidence," which outlined their objections to the government's policies.

In the 1897 presidential elections, the Nationalist-Conservatives once again prevailed thanks in part to electoral fraud. Although the Liberal candidate, José Miguel Samper, triumphed in Bogotá where elections were conducted fairly, the governors intervened in the provinces to ensure the victory of Manuel Antonio Sanclemente, the Nationalist-Conservative candidate (Bergquist 1978, 74; Delpar 1981, 168–169). In the wake of the election, the Historical Conservatives continued to promote their program of political and economic reform, which included measures to restore civil liberties and guarantee minority representation and honest elections. The Liberals supported these proposed reforms, with their leader Rafael Uribe Uribe arguing in Congress in 1898 that they were the only means to ensure peace in Colombia:

> Colombia's biggest problem is that of peace. The problem can only be solved in one way: by giving justice to the Liberal Party. And that justice can only be achieved by approving the proposed reforms ... Give us the freedom to make public and defend our rights with the vote, the quill, and our lips; otherwise, nobody in the world will have enough power to silence the barrels of our rifles. (Cited in Mazzuca and Robinson 2009, 295)

Although the legislature approved some of the Historical Conservative's proposals, including a repeal of the restrictive media law, the Nationalist-Conservatives controlled the Senate and, under the instructions of President Sanclemente, they blocked the electoral reform (Bergquist 1978, 77–80; Delpar 1981, 176; Mazzuca and Robinson 2009, 296).

Much as Uribe Uribe predicted, the Liberal Party took up arms shortly after the electoral reform proposal ran aground. The directorate of the party was reluctant to go to war, but the failure of the reforms, along with the country's deteriorating economic and fiscal situation, set off revolts in a few provinces in October 1899, which quickly spread throughout the country. The Historical Conservatives sided with the government in the War of a Thousand Days but pushed unsuccessfully for a peaceful resolution of the conflict, engaging in repeated dialogue with Liberal leaders. Frustration with the continued bloodshed led the Historical Conservatives to carry out a coup in July 1900 that brought the vice-president, José Manuel Marroquín, to power. Although Marroquín brought many Historical Conservatives into his government, he obstinately refused to make concessions to the Liberals and instead engaged in harsh repression (Bergquist 1978, 151–153). As a result, the war dragged on until 1903.

The final peace treaty did not make any major political concessions to the Liberals but only stated that the government would consider the reform proposals that had been discussed in Congress in 1898 (Mazzuca and Robinson 2009, 298). Nevertheless, as soon as the war ended, some liberalization took place (Bergquist 1978, 196). The hardline minister of war, Aristides Fernández, resigned under pressure in 1903. The Marroquín administration then lifted the state of siege and replaced Fernández's authoritarian press decree with the more liberal press law of 1898. The government also repealed the decree that gave the executive the right to name all the members of the Electoral Council.

In the 1904 presidential elections, Historical Conservatives supported General Rafael Reyes, who ran against Joaquín F. Vélez, the candidate of the Nationalist-Conservative faction. Reyes emerged victorious in an extremely close election that was marred by fraud and took months to be resolved (Bergquist 1978, 222–223; Covo 2013). Reyes won in part because he enjoyed the support of Liberals as well as Historical Conservatives, but also because President Marroquín reportedly withdrew his support for the candidacy of Vélez once the latter announced that he would launch an investigation into the secession of Panama (Bergquist 1978, 222–223). In the aftermath of the war, Panamanians had rebelled with the support of the United States and achieved their independence, which angered many Colombians.

As we have seen, to deter future rebellions, Reyes sought to strengthen the coercive capacity of the state by professionalizing the military, collecting weaponry left over from the war, and developing state infrastructure. In addition, Reyes forged an alliance with Uribe Uribe and appointed Liberals to his cabinet and to other positions in the executive branch (Bergquist 1978, 226). Reyes also shut down Congress and convened a constituent assembly in which Liberals comprised one-third of the members (Mazzuca and Robinson 2009, 299; Rios Peñaloza 1991).[63]

The constituent assembly quickly passed a constitutional amendment that called for guaranteed minority representation in all government legislative bodies (Colombia 1906, 63). A subsequent act, Law Number 42, mandated the use of the incomplete list to achieve minority representation (Colombia 1906, 273–274; Mazzuca and Robinson 2009, 300). Under the incomplete list, two-thirds of the seats were to be reserved for the party that finished first in the elections in each district and one-third for the runner-up. Previously, Colombia had used the complete list in which all seats went to the party that finished first in each district.

Although Reyes ended the political exclusion of Liberals, he governed in an authoritarian manner. Not only did Reyes shut down Congress and declare a state of siege in 1905, but he declined to reopen the legislature, governing instead through the compliant constituent assembly, which rubber stamped his decrees (Rios Peñaloza 1991; Duque Daza 2011, 195). The constituent assembly granted Reyes extraordinary powers in economic and fiscal matters as well as a ten-year term, rather than the six-year term to which he had been elected (Bushnell 1993, 158; Bergquist 1978, 228–229). In addition, Reyes exiled or imprisoned many of his foes, including both Liberals and Conservatives, and he replaced all of the existing members of the Supreme Court (Barbosa 2015; Cajas Sarria 2013, 457–458).

Reyes' economic policies and his dictatorial ways prompted another split within the Conservative Party that ultimately led to his downfall. Many Historical Conservatives as well as Liberals quickly became disenchanted with his regime and some of them began to participate in plots against him as early as 1904 (Bergquist 1978, 229). The catalyst of Reyes' downfall, however, was an agreement that the government signed with the United States in 1909 recognizing Panamanian independence in exchange for an indemnity and the future

---

[63] One Liberal and two Conservatives – one from each of the two main Conservative factions – represented each department in the assembly.

use of the canal. This agreement triggered a wave of student-led protests and led dissident Conservatives and Liberals to form a new party, the Republican Union, which won a large share of seats in the May 1909 congressional elections (Bergquist 1978, 245).[64] Shortly thereafter, Reyes resigned and fled Colombia, and the legislature subsequently chose General Ramón González Valencia to serve out Reyes' original six-year term as president.[65]

The new president convoked popular elections for a new constituent assembly in February 1910 (Duque Daza 2011, 196). The Republican Union won a majority of seats in the constituent assembly, and it elected Carlos Restrepo, a Conservative leader of the Republican Union, as Colombia's new president by a vote of 23–18 (Bergquist 1978, 252–253; Rodríguez Piñeres 1956, 269). Under the leadership of the Republican Union, the constituent assembly enacted a broad array of constitutional reforms that laid the groundwork for a more democratic Colombia. Liberals played a central role in the constitutional assembly, especially Nicolás Esguerra who was one of the founders of the Republican Union and was the main architect of the constitutional reforms (Mazzuca and Robinson 2009, 302).

The constitutional reforms (Articles 25–34) strengthened horizontal accountability and weakened the power of the president in an effort to prevent a return to the personalistic rule of the Reyes and Núñez administrations (Bergquist 1978; Acuña Rodríguez 2017, 107–108; Duque Daza 2011, 200–209; Melo 1989). Article 25 reduced the presidential term from six to four years and Article 28 banned the immediate reelection of the president (República de Colombia 1939, 7–8). Under the reformed constitution, the president would no longer have the power to select the magistrates of the Supreme Court and the Superior Tribunals, although the president retained the right to name ministers, governors, and mayors and the power to veto laws (Duque Daza 2011, 205–206). Article 41 gave the Supreme Court the responsibility of "guarding the integrity of the constitution" and of ruling on the constitutionality of laws and decrees, which any citizen was allowed to challenge (República de Colombia 1939, 10; Cajas Sarria 2013, 459). The reformed constitution stipulated that Congress was to meet every year and it was given new responsibilities, including electing the members of the Supreme Court and choosing the designates who would replace presidents in the event of their resignation, leave-taking, or demise (República de Colombia 1939, 6). Congress also gained the right to censure members of the executive branch as well as Supreme Court Justices (Article 20).[66]

---

[64] Although the Republican Union dominated the Chamber of Representatives, supporters of Reyes still controlled the Senate in 1909 (Melo 1989, 220).
[65] González Valencia, a Historical Conservative, had been elected as vice president in 1904, but was removed by Reyes in 1905 (Bergquist 1978, 248).
[66] The president also retained the right to declare a state of siege in the event of a foreign war or an internal uprising, but any emergency decrees enacted would cease to have an effect once the

The constituent assembly also made changes to the country's electoral laws. It modestly reduced suffrage restrictions, decreasing the income and property requirements necessary to vote. Article 44 stipulated that only male citizens who knew how to read and write or had an annual income of 300 Colombian pesos or property worth at least 1,000 pesos would be able to vote in elections to the presidency and lower chamber of the legislature.[67] Perhaps most importantly, the assembly guaranteed the representation of minority parties, although it left it to ordinary law to determine which system would be used to award seats.[68]

Thus, a split within the ruling Conservative Party led to the emergence of a dissident coalition, the Republican Union, which enacted important constitutional reforms that helped bring democracy to Colombia. The constitutional reforms of 1910 strengthened horizontal accountability, reduced restrictions on the franchise, and guaranteed minority party representation. To be sure the reforms had some deficiencies: They lacked a bill of rights, they maintained some suffrage restrictions, and they did not do enough to combat voter fraud (Duque Daza 2011, 206; Acuña Rodríguez 2017). Nevertheless, they represented an important step forward in the struggle for democracy in Colombia.

THE EMERGENCE OF DEMOCRACY IN COLOMBIA

In the aftermath of the constitutional reforms and the professionalization of the military, Colombia began to have relatively peaceful and free and fair elections. During the ensuing four decades, elections took place in relative calm and all sides accepted the results (Bergquist 1978, 247). As Bergquist (1978, 247) has argued: "The unstable politics of the previous century, the politics of fundamental ideological contention and partisan exclusiveness, of chronic civil war and ephemeral constitutions, was succeeded after 1910 by a new era of remarkable political stability." Colombian governments began to consistently respect constitutional procedures and allow the exercise of civil and political liberties, declining to repress opposition leaders or overturn opposition electoral victories. The political opposition, meanwhile, eschewed armed revolts, focusing on winning power at the ballot box. In the words of Safford and Palacios (2002, 266), "civil war was delegitimized as a form of political competition."

Bipartisanship became the norm after 1910. Minority parties not only won a significant share of seats in the legislature, they also formed alliances with the

---

war or uprising had ended. Moreover, Article 29 stipulated that the president would be held "responsible for acts or omissions that violate the Constitution and its laws" (República de Colombia 1939, 8).

[67] The Senate continued to be elected indirectly by Electoral Councils whose members were chosen by the Departmental Assemblies (República de Colombia 1939, 10).

[68] In 1916 the legislature enacted an electoral code mandating the use of the incomplete list, the system that had been in use since 1905 (Mazzuca and Robinson 2009, 303).

ruling parties and held ministerial positions. President Restrepo (1910–1914), for example, resisted pressure from Conservatives to exclude the Liberals, naming three Liberals as well as various Conservatives to his cabinet (Rodríguez Piñeres 1956, 284–296). In defending his bipartisanship, Restrepo remarked: "I have been a Conservative, but in the post that has been awarded to me I cannot work as a member of any political entity. From the Presidency, I will see Colombians only as compatriots whose rights I must protect equally" (Rodríguez Piñeres 1956, 278). Most subsequent administrations also practiced bipartisanship. Conservative President José Vicente Concha (1914–1918) forged an alliance with the Liberal faction led by Rafael Uribe Uribe and included various Liberals in his cabinet. The Conservative administration of Marco Fidel Suárez (1918–1921) similarly governed through a bipartisan cabinet, as did the Liberal administration of Enrique Olaya Herrera (1930–1934) (Bergquist 1978, 256–257).

With armed uprisings largely a thing of past, elections became the focal point of political contestation and voter turnout rose sharply. The number of votes cast nearly tripled in the two decades after 1914, rising from 337,597 in 1914 to 942,009 in 1934 (Jaramillo and Franco-Cuervo 2005, 307). Approximately 28 percent of adult males voted in the 1914 elections, 30 percent voted in the 1918 elections, and 48 percent in 1922 (Posada-Carbó 1997, 260). Opposition parties sometimes abstained from elections after 1910. For example, the opposition refused to participate in the 1926, 1934, 1938, and 1949 presidential elections on the grounds that they would not be fair (Safford and Palacios 2002, 267). Nevertheless, even when opposition parties abstained from the presidential elections, they typically participated in legislative and local elections.

Although Colombia retained some income and literacy restrictions in national elections, these restrictions became less meaningful over time because a growing proportion of people met the requirements. Posada-Carbó (1997, 258–259) reports that by the turn of the century many working-class people already earned more than the required sum owing to inflation. Fewer people met the literacy requirement initially, but the literacy rate grew rapidly in Colombia during the twentieth century, increasing from 34 percent in 1900 to 51.9 percent in 1930, 69.6 percent in 1960, and 89.7 percent in 1990 (Thorp 1998, 354). Moreover, the literacy requirements could often be satisfied by merely signing one's name, and the income and literacy restrictions did not apply to elections for municipal councils and departmental assemblies.

Some fraud and intimidation in elections continued to take place after 1910. The 1922 elections, in which a Conservative candidate, General Pedro Nel Ospina, defeated a Liberal candidate, General Benjamín Herrera, was notoriously fraudulent, and in its wake the Liberal Party published a 422-page document documenting the fraud.[69] A recent study found that in 508

---

[69] The Conservative government published a report disputing many of the Liberals' claims.

out of the 755 municipalities, the reported vote totals exceeded the authors' estimates of the maximum potential franchise, which they based on the 1918 Colombian census (Chaves, Fergusson, and Robinson 2015, 125). Some fraud and intimidation also took place at the local level in other post-1910 elections.[70]

Nevertheless, fraud and intimidation in elections generally declined after 1910, and electoral violence became much less common. The executive branch lost much of its influence over the electoral authorities, which made it difficult to control elections. Law 80 of 1910 gave Congress the right to appoint the members of the Great Electoral Council, which supervised the electoral process. The Great Electoral Council chose the members of the Departmental Electoral Councils, which in turn elected the members of the electoral boards of each district (República de Colombia 1939, 105; República de Colombia, Registraduría del Estado Civil 1988, 31–32). The Electoral Juries of each municipality, meanwhile, were elected at the local level using the incomplete-list system, which ensured that minorities had representation (República de Colombia 1939, 105–106; Posada-Carbó 1997, 266). Thus, local electoral authorities were largely independent from the president as well as the governors, and no single party could control them (Posada-Carbó 1997, 265–266).

As a result, candidates supported by the government often failed to win. There were numerous cases in which incumbents were defeated in local elections after 1910, and the opposition won control of local governments (Posada-Carbó 1997, 262–263 and 275). Turnover also occurred at the national level. For example, the candidate of the incumbent Republican Union party lost badly in the 1914 presidential elections. Similarly, Conservatives lost the 1930 presidential elections even though they held the presidency at the time.

Throughout the early twentieth century, the opposition pushed for further reforms to reduce fraud and government intervention and to gain greater representation for minority parties. There were more than ten electoral reforms discussed in Congress between 1910 and 1930, many of them proposed by Liberals (Posada-Carbó 2000b, 218; Montoya 1938, 31–57). These measures sought to strengthen the secret ballot, create an identity card for voters, reorganize the electoral authorities, and establish obligatory voting and proportional representation, among other goals. Some of these measures passed. Liberals, for example, helped enact legislation in 1920 to prevent Conservatives from presenting two lists of candidates in order to try to win the seats set aside for the minority as well as those of the majority (Mazzuca and Robinson 2009, 315). Thanks to a split in the Conservative Party, Liberals also managed to pass a law in 1929 mandating a form of proportional representation known as the quotient rule, which provided representation to minority parties based on their share of

---

[70] In 1918, for example, a violent uprising took place in Santa Marta because of allegations of electoral fraud – it left two people dead and two wounded (Posada-Carbó 1997, 268). Similar incidents took place in 1916, 1922, and 1923 (Posada-Carbó 1995, 9).

the vote (Mazzuca and Robinson 2009, 313–314; Montoya 1938, 61–64). The same law created an identity card that citizens would need in order to vote, although this proved ineffective (Mayorga García 2010; Montoya 1938).[71]

The existence of a strong opposition party thus helped bolster democracy in Colombia after 1910. The Liberal Party's strength and large presence in the legislature – Liberals generally held one-third of the legislative seats – meant that it only had to win support from a fraction of Conservatives to enact reforms. In addition, the party's national presence helped it monitor and denounce local-level fraud and intimidation.

The Liberal Party's strength and organization, along with a split within the ruling Conservative Party, also enabled the Liberals to win the presidency in 1930, thus consolidating the country's transition to democracy. Once the Conservatives moved into the opposition, they, too, played an important democratizing role. They monitored and protested electoral abuses and helped restrain the more authoritarian impulses of the governing Liberals. In addition, the strength of parties in Colombia reduced the temptation of the opposition to call on the military to intervene since it could gain power and exercise influence via elections.

The professionalization of the military also aided Colombian democracy after 1910. As we have seen, the strengthening of the armed forces in the first decade of the twentieth century, along with the memory of the bloody War of a Thousand Days, discouraged the opposition from taking up arms. The coercive capacity of the state was considerably lower in Colombia than in Argentina or Chile, however, and the Colombian state never exercised a monopoly on violence throughout the country. As a result, the Colombian military could not suppress the widespread fighting between Conservatives and Liberals that broke out in the late 1940s and lasted through the 1950s, a period known as *La Violencia*. This brutal fighting, which caused an estimated 200,000 deaths, led to the breakdown of democracy and military discipline in Colombia during this period. The Colombian armed forces also struggled to defeat the guerrilla forces that emerged beginning in the 1960s, which further undermined the country's democracy.

Nevertheless, during the first three decades of the twentieth century, the Colombian military proved capable of maintaining internal peace, which encouraged the opposition to focus on the electoral path to power. Although Conservative officers dominated the military in the early twentieth century, the armed forces largely stayed out of politics. The generals allowed the Republican Union to take power in 1910, and the opposition Liberals to do so in 1930. In this way, the Colombian military paved the way for the initial emergence of democracy in the country.

---

[71] Liberals also repeatedly proposed laws to prevent the military from voting on the grounds that officers and troops typically voted for incumbents – they finally passed such a law in 1930 (Pinzón de Lewin 1994, 65–66, 84–85, 100–101; Posada-Carbó 1997, 269).

Conclusion

CONCLUSION

Thus, Argentina and Colombia democratized in the early twentieth century for many of the same reasons that Chile and Uruguay did. The professionalization of the military helped lead to democratization by bringing an end to the revolts that had plagued both sets of countries in the nineteenth century. Once armed struggle was foreclosed, opposition parties began to focus on the electoral path to power, pushing for democratic reforms that would level the electoral playing field. Argentina and Colombia, like Chile and Uruguay, had developed strong opposition parties in the late nineteenth and early twentieth century and these parties used their influence to promote reform. The opposition parties could not enact reforms on their own, owing to resistance from the ruling party, but splits within the ruling party led to the emergence of dissident factions that pushed through the reforms.

The democracies that arose in Argentina and Colombia were weaker than in Chile and Uruguay, however. In Argentina, democracy was destabilized by the fact that only one strong party arose: the UCR. This party supported democratic reform when it was in the opposition, but once it took power, there was no strong opposition party in Argentina to contest elections, protest electoral abuses, and promote further reform. Moreover, because the opposition had no chance of defeating the ruling party on its own, it repeatedly called on the military to intervene.

By contrast, the main destabilizing factor in Colombia was the continued weakness of the armed forces. Although the professionalization of the military made it impossible for the opposition to overthrow the central government, it did not obtain a monopoly on violence throughout Colombia. Partly as a result, there was a resurgence of local-level violence between Conservatives and Liberals at mid-century that undermined Colombian democracy.

Despite these problems, the reforms that Argentina and Colombia implemented at the outset of the twentieth century proved important. Although neither country developed a strong democracy, Argentines and Colombians would continue to struggle to maintain the democratic principles and institutions that were first established in the early twentieth century.

7

The Roots of Stable Authoritarianism
Brazil, Peru, and Venezuela

Brazil, Peru, and Venezuela traveled a very different political route than did Argentina, Chile, Colombia, and Uruguay in the early twentieth century, but they began at somewhat similar places. Authoritarian rule was the norm in all seven countries throughout the nineteenth century as governments intervened regularly in elections to ensure that their favored candidates won. Nevertheless, it was an unstable form of authoritarianism. Both sets of countries had weak militaries during most of the nineteenth century, which led to frequent internal revolts that overthrew elected presidents and provoked intermittent state repression. All seven countries, however, took important steps to strengthen and professionalize their militaries in the late nineteenth or early twentieth century, which resulted in a sharp decline in the frequency of revolts. In Argentina, Chile, Colombia, and Uruguay, strong opposition parties emerged in the late nineteenth century or early twentieth century, and these parties helped bring about democracy. By contrast, in Brazil, Peru, and Venezuela, parties remained weak, and, as a result, these countries became relatively stable authoritarian regimes.

The absence of strong parties impeded democratization in Brazil, Peru, and Venezuela in several ways. First, the weakness of parties meant that the opposition had little chance of winning elections. Opposition parties had neither the organizational strength, nor the partisan attachments necessary to overcome government electoral manipulation. Second, opposition party weakness made it difficult for the opposition to enact meaningful democratic reforms since it typically held few seats in the legislature and the ruling party consistently blocked proposed reforms. Third, the weakness of the opposition parties encouraged them to abstain from elections and seek to foment coups. Because they were too weak to defeat the ruling party in elections or overthrow it in an armed revolt, opposition parties often called on the military to intervene, which only deepened authoritarian rule. Fourth and finally, the weakness of both opposition and ruling parties allowed presidents to concentrate authority and, at times, extend their hold on power. As a result, in some cases, power became highly personalized.

Although all three countries had authoritarian regimes, there were important differences among them. Venezuela developed the most stable authoritarian regime during the early twentieth century. The Venezuelan dictators, Cipriano Castro and Juan Vicente Gómez, strengthened and modernized the military, but they also stocked it with officers from their home state of Táchira to ensure its loyalty. In addition, they developed a network of spies and used repression to eliminate any potential threats to their regime. The opposition might have been able to resist this repression had it been organized in strong parties, but Venezuela had only weak parties at the outset of the twentieth century, and none of these parties had the organization or partisan attachments necessary to survive in a hostile climate. Neither Castro nor Gómez tolerated dissent, establishing exclusionary authoritarian regimes that manipulated elections and brutally repressed opposition parties and politicians. Both leaders also sought to concentrate authority and rule indefinitely, and therefore declined to invest in a ruling party that might constrain them.

Peru also developed a relatively stable authoritarian regime during the early twentieth century, although it experienced brief periods of instability in the 1910s. During the nineteenth century, Peru was plagued by frequent opposition revolts, but the professionalization of the military at the turn of the century largely brought an end to these outsider revolts. Nevertheless, Peru failed to democratize and continued to experience occasional coup attempts. As in Venezuela, opposition parties in Peru were too weak to resist government electoral manipulation or push through democratic reforms; nor could they prevent the country's presidents from concentrating power and seeking to extend their tenure in office. Because the opposition could not defeat the ruling party at the ballot box or on the field of battle, it at times called on the military to overthrow the regime. A couple of these coup attempts were successful in part because the Peruvian government had less control of the military than did its Venezuelan counterpart.

Brazil, like Peru and Venezuela, developed a relatively stable authoritarian regime, but it did so earlier and in a different manner than its South American neighbors. Brazil remained an empire after independence, which enabled a degree of political continuity and stability. Although Brazil experienced frequent revolts during the first couple of decades after independence, the revolts largely came to an end in the mid-nineteenth century with the accession of Emperor Pedro II and the gradual strengthening of the country's armed forces. In 1889, the Brazilian military overthrew the emperor and created a republic, but the country did not democratize in large part because parties remained weak. Throughout the early twentieth century, Brazilian presidents and their allies intervened regularly in elections to ensure that their preferred candidates won, which opposition parties were powerless to prevent. Brazilian presidents did not concentrate power or seek to extend their terms like their counterparts in Peru and Venezuela, but neither did they permit free or fair elections. Since they could neither compete in elections nor enact democratic reforms, some members of the opposition called on military officers to intervene, which only led to increased state repression.

THE MILITARY AND REVOLTS IN VENEZUELA

During the wars of independence, Venezuela witnessed the most intense fighting in Spanish America, and afterwards, the regional leaders who had participated in the combat maintained control of their forces and weaponry (López-Alves 2000, 196; Guardia Rolando and Olivieri Pacheco 2016, 14–19). Little effort was initially made to centralize the means of violence in the hands of the state. Governments relied upon the regional leaders and their private militias to fend off revolts, but these same leaders often turned against the government. Even in the late nineteenth century, the national military existed more on paper than in reality – the regional leaders continued to control most troops (Irwin and Micett 2008, 141). As a result, revolts remained common throughout the nineteenth century.

The Venezuelan government established a central army after independence as well as a navy and a national militia, but these organizations remained weak and underfunded throughout the nineteenth century in large part due to anti-military sentiments, budget constraints, and resistance from regional powerbrokers. The troops typically numbered fewer than 2,500 men during the nineteenth century, which was woefully inadequate for a country the size of Venezuela (Gilmore 1964, 140–141, 148). During periods of civil war, the army often swelled. For example, in 1846, the number of troops grew from 1,155 to 11,085 men, before declining to approximately 2,000 active-duty men in 1848 (Irwin and Micett 2008, 105–108, 116). Soldiers were conscripted and they were poorly paid, fed, and housed, which undermined their discipline (Arráiz 1991, 146–149; Scheina 2003, 236). In addition, the soldiers were poorly equipped. The cavalry continued to use the lance as its main weapon until the late nineteenth century, and it was not until the 1860s that the army gained access to percussion-capped muskets and modern ordnance (Scheina 2003, 236). As late as 1878, rebels wielding machetes managed to defeat the military, which was lightly armed with poor quality rifles (Arráiz 1991, 157).

Officers and troops typically received only rudimentary training. The government established military schools, including the Military Academy of Mathematics and the Nautical School, but they were in a deplorable condition for much of the nineteenth century and educated relatively few students (Irwin and Micett 2008, 95–99, 118–119; Gilmore 1964, 130–131). Officers received military titles based on political considerations or as a reward for their service, rather than merit. As a result, officers at times outnumbered soldiers (Scheina 2003, 248).

The national militia, which in theory consisted of all able-bodied men between 18 and 40–45 years of age, served as a large reserve force for the army. In the late 1830s and 1840s, the militia had over 60,000 men (Irwin and Micett 2008, 93–94). The militia was responsible for keeping internal order, but the government had a hard time arming and mobilizing it.[1] Moreover, states and regional leaders controlled their local militia units and sometimes sent them to fight against the government. During the 1870s, the administration of Antonio Guzmán Blanco tried to limit the power of the militia units by ordering government weapons returned and by banning the import and sale of weapons, but these efforts did not significantly undermine the regional leaders' ability to wage war (Gilmore 1964, 44–45, 119).

The low coercive capacity of the state encouraged frequent rebellions. As Table 7.1 indicates, LARD records twenty-three major revolts between 1830 and 1929, but the total number of rebellions was even higher. According to Arráiz (1991, 29–32), between 1830 and 1903, Venezuela had 166 rebellions. War was so common in Venezuela that the entire nineteenth century had only sixteen years of peace, averaging twelve acts of war per year (Tarver and Frederick 2005, 74).

The revolts had enormous human and material costs. Arraiz (1991, 175–176) calculates that the revolts cost the government about 25 percent of the revenues of the national treasury between 1830 and 1903, and this does not include the indirect costs, which were probably more than twice that amount. According to his estimates, approximately 300,000 people died in the fighting, and the conflicts may have indirectly led to the deaths of one million people (Arráiz 1991, 174).

The revolts deepened authoritarianism in Venezuela. Governments were overthrown on eleven occasions during the nineteenth century, thereby undermining constitutional rule. The revolts also led governments to arrest members of the opposition, clamp down on civil and political liberties, seize property, and engage in widespread repression. For example, during the Federalist War, Páez suspended the 1858 Constitution, revoked the liberal press laws, and gave his authorization to provincial governors to arrest anyone who published anti-government views (Loveman 1993, 154).

At the outset of the twentieth century, however, the Venezuelan government strengthened and modernized its military, which dramatically reduced the frequency of revolts. The strengthening of the military was made possible in large part by Venezuela's growing exports, which increased at an annual rate of 5.2 percent above inflation between 1870–1929, one of the fastest rates in the region (Bértola and Ocampo 2013, 100). The economy grew particularly quickly in the early twentieth century thanks in large part to the country's booming oil production.

---

[1] Militia members were responsible for providing their own uniforms, weapons, and ammunition (Gilmore 1964, 112).

TABLE 7.1 *Major revolts in Venezuela, 1830–1930*

Year	Description of revolt	Type of revolt (outcome)
1831	Regional leaders, including José Tadeo Monagas, revolted against President José A. Páez and the 1830 constitution. They surrendered in exchange for an amnesty.	Elite insurrection (suppressed)
1835–1836	*Revolución de las Reformas.* Military rebels overthrew President Vargas, but the minister of war, General Páez, assembled an army and defeated the rebels.	Military coup (took power)
1837	Colonel Francisco Farfán and the military garrison at Guayana rebelled in support of General Mariño. Páez's army defeated the 800-man rebel army.	Military coup (suppressed)
1846–1847	Liberal supporters of Antonio Leocadio Guzmán rebelled after he lost the fraudulent 1846 presidential election. The rebellion was eventually suppressed.	Elite insurrection (suppressed)
1848–1849	Páez revolted after President Monagas broke off an alliance with him and organized an attack on Congress. Liberal troops of Monagas defeated the rebels.	Elite insurrection (suppressed)
1853	Supporters of Páez revolted in various parts of Venezuela and assembled rebel armies numbering in the thousands, but the government suppressed the revolts.	Elite insurrection (suppressed)
1854	General Juan Bautista Rodriguez revolted in favor of Páez with 2,600 troops, but they were defeated by the government's 4,000-man army.	Military coup (suppressed)
1858	*The March Revolution.* With the support of Liberals and Conservatives, Julián Castro overthrew President Monagas when he dictated a new constitution.	Elite insurrection (took power)
1859	Manuel Vicente de las Casas, the military commander of Caracas, overthrew President Castro in a coup. Pedro Gual became president.	Military coup (took power)
1859–1863	*The Federal War.* Federalist regional leaders (Liberals) revolted and defeated the government in long guerrilla war. Juan Falcón became president. 20,000 deaths.	Elite insurrection (took power)
1861	José Echezuria, the commander of the Caracas garrison, led a coup against President Gual. Conservative military officers named Páez as president.	Military coup (took power)
1867–1868	*The Blue Revolution.* Former Liberal José Tadeo Monagas allied with various Conservative regional leaders and overthrew the government. 1,000 deaths.	Elite insurrection (took power)
1869	General Venancio Pulgar, the president and military chief of Zulia, revolted and declared independence. He raised an army of 6,000 men but they mutinied.	Military coup (suppressed)
1869–1872	*April Revolution.* The Liberal regional leader Antonio Guzmán Blanco financed a 6,000-man army that overthrew President Monagas. Guzmán Blanco became president.	Elite insurrection (took power)

TABLE 7.1 (*continued*)

Year	Description of revolt	Type of revolt (outcome)
1874	José Antonio Pulido, the minister of war, revolted in Barcelona and León Colima, a state president, revolted in Coro. They were both defeated.	Military coup (suppressed)
1878–1879	*The Vindicating Revolution.* Guzmán Blanco organized an army of 10,000 men and overthrew President Gregorio Valera. Guzmán Blanco became president.	Elite insurrection (took power)
1880	General José Pío Rebolledo and his garrison rebelled in Ciudad Bolivar with allied groups elsewhere. Guzmán Blanco sent 12,000 troops to suppress them.	Military coup (suppressed)
1892	*The Legalist Revolution.* General Joaquín Crespo overthrew President Raimundo Andueza Palacio to prevent him from extending his term. 4,000 deaths.	Elite insurrection (took power)
1898	*The Queipa Revolution.* General José Manuel Hernández rebelled in response to electoral fraud and assembled 16,000 men but was defeated.	Elite insurrection (suppressed)
1899	*The Restorative Revolution.* General Cipriano Castro overthrew the government with a rebel army of 10,000 men. 2,100 deaths.	Elite insurrection (took power)
1899–1900	General José Manuel Hernández, the minister of development, raised a rebel army of 2,000 men and revolted. He was defeated.	Elite insurrection (suppressed)
1901	Venezuelan General Carlos Rangel Garbiras invaded Táchira with an army of 4,000 Colombians and Venezuelan exiles, but his invasion was quickly defeated.	Elite insurrection (suppressed)
1901–1903	*The Liberating Revolution.* Various regional leaders rebelled with the support of foreign creditors. The government defeated the rebels after a prolonged war. 4,000 deaths.	Elite insurrection (suppressed)
1908	General Juan Vicente Gómez overthrew President Cipriano Castro in a nonviolent coup while Castro was in Europe for medical treatment.	Military coup (took power)

Source: Latin American Revolts Database.

Although the military modernization efforts were partly aimed at defending the government from internal rebellions, they also responded in part to external threats, which worsened significantly under President Cipriano Castro (1899–1908). In addition to its long-standing conflict with Colombia, Venezuela had a boundary dispute with Britain, which nearly led to war in 1895. Moreover, in 1902–1903, Britain, Germany, and Italy blockaded Venezuela in response to Castro's refusal to pay its foreign debts or compensate citizens of those countries for their losses. Venezuela's foreign relations improved under Juan

Vicente Gómez who succeeded Castro in 1908, but Gómez's domestic opponents repeatedly sought foreign support to topple him (McBeth 2008, 4–6).

President Castro took the first important steps to strengthen the military, while at the same time seeking to collect the weapons that were in private hands in order to weaken the ability of regional leaders to carry out revolts (Quintero 2009, 85–92). Castro tripled the size of the army and improved the troops' pay and equipment, purchasing Mauser rifles, Krupp artillery, and Hotchkiss machine guns (Scheina 2003, 248; Straka 2005, 103; Schaposnik 1985, 20). In 1901 alone, the military budget doubled, reaching 47 percent of the government's total budget (Quintero 2009, 95). Castro also sought to improve the training of officers, establishing a military academy in 1903, although it did not begin to function until 1910 (Blutstein et al. 1985, 247–248; Schaposnik 1985, 18–20). In addition, he created a general staff to run the military and he published a new military code that established stricter rules governing the promotion of officers (Schaposnik 1985, 20). Finally, he recruited large numbers of officers and troops from his home state of Táchira (Scheina 2003, 248). According to Norman Hutchinson, the US minister to Venezuela, Castro "treated [the army] better than it has ever been treated before, especially the rank and file, and he takes good care who his officers are" (cited in Scheina 2003, 248).

Efforts to strengthen the military accelerated during the reign of General Juan Vicente Gómez, who overthrew Castro in 1908 in a nonviolent coup. Gómez opened the military academy that had been decreed by Castro, and he appointed a Chilean colonel, Samuel McGill, to oversee military reform (McBeth 2008, 31–32; Schaposnik 1985, 20). McGill initially sought to remake the Venezuelan military along the lines of the Prussian army, although after World War I, the country began to copy the French model. Under his leadership, Venezuela established new military schools to train naval officers, pilots, engineers, and noncommissioned officers, among others (Schaposnik 1985, 20–21; Ziems 1979). Using the country's growing petroleum revenues, the Gómez administration expanded the army to 8,000 men, boosted and regularized the troops' pay, established military pensions, and purchased weaponry (Blutstein et al. 1985, 248; Schaposnik 1985, 20–25). The government also created frontier garrisons and military roadways to ensure that the army could be deployed quickly to suppress revolts and invasions.

The military was not Gómez's only coercive arm, however. He also developed a secret police force known as *La Sagrada* (The Sacred), which was composed mostly of people from Gómez's home state of Táchira (Ziems 1979, 166–167). *La Sagrada* functioned as a virtual army of occupation, spying on and harassing the opposition. During Gómez's tenure they imprisoned tens of thousands of opponents of the regime, and tortured and executed many of them (Tarver and Frederick 2005, 80).

Gómez also took important steps to undermine the regional leaders. He asked foreign nations to block the export of weapons to private citizens in Venezuela, and he restricted the amount of weapons available to the state presidents, ensuring that the armories remained under his control (McBeth 2008, 6, 79–80). In 1919, he also abolished the state militias, which had often helped regional leaders overthrow the government (Blutstein et al. 1985, 248). In 1922, he prohibited private citizens from owning weapons and sought to collect those weapons that were already in private hands (Schaposnik 1985, 21).

Under Castro and Gómez, the state finally gained a monopoly on violence and Venezuela's long era of rebellions came to an end. The last major rebellion in Venezuela occurred in 1901–1903 when Castro's troops, under the command of Gómez, defeated the rebels after prolonged fighting. Although elements in the military and a few opposition leaders attempted insurrections during the three decades that followed, the government quickly suppressed these revolts (McBeth 2008).

WEAK PARTIES AND AUTHORITARIANISM IN VENEZUELA

The strengthening of the military in Venezuela did not lead to democratization in large part because Venezuelan parties remained weak at the outset of the twentieth century. Various groupings that were commonly referred to as parties had emerged in the first half of the nineteenth century, but they represented little more than the personal followings of individual politicians (Pérez 1996, 49). The Conservative Party, for example, consisted of a loose grouping surrounding the Venezuelan independence leader, José Antonio Páez, which governed Venezuela in the immediate post-independence period (Lombardi 1982, 179; Pérez 1996, 51).[2] The Liberal Party, meanwhile, revolved around its founder, Antonio Leocadio Guzmán.[3]

Although the Conservative and the Liberal parties endured for many decades, both remained personalistic institutions without permanent organizations (Gilmore 1964, 25, 27, 56; Pérez 1996, 49). Páez dominated the Conservative Party, throughout its existence, whereas Guzmán and his son, Antonio Guzmán Blanco, controlled the Liberal Party for much of the nineteenth century. The two parties fragmented frequently along personalistic lines. The Conservatives, for instance, split in the late 1850s between supporters of Páez, who were referred to as dictatorials, and adherents of Pedro Gual and Manuel Felipe Tovar, who were called constitutionalists (Tarver and Frederick 2005, 67–68). Similarly, in the 1860s, the faction of the Liberals that supported José Gregorio Monagas and José Tadeo Monagas became known as

---

[2] The Conservative Party did not adopt this name initially, running in the 1840 elections as the Party of Constitution, Peace and Order, but its members were commonly referred to as Conservatives or, disparagingly, as the Oligarchy or Goths (Butler 1972, 38, 45).
[3] Many historians date the founding of the Liberal Party to 1840 when Guzmán and others established a newspaper, El Venezolano, which they used to attack the Conservative government (Butler 1972, 47–48).

the Blue Liberals, while the group that supported Guzmán Blanco were called the Yellow Liberals (Pérez 1996, 61–62).[4]

The two parties did not have consistent ideological differences, but each party frequently criticized the policies and platforms of the other (Tarver and Frederick 2005, 64; Gil Fortoul 1956, 364–365; Rey 2015, 62). Indeed, Guzmán famously said, "if our opponents had declared in favor of federalism, we would have declared in favor of centralism" (Tinker Salas 2015, 42). Both parties often took antagonistic positions vis-à-vis the Catholic Church, although their hostility toward the Church varied over time. Each party's economic policies and positions on democratic reforms also changed over time, depending in part on whether it was in power. When it was in the opposition, the Liberal Party, for example, denounced the economic program and electoral manipulation of the Conservatives, but it carried out many of the same policies when it came to power (Butler 1972, chs. 2–3; Pérez 1996).

Both parties represented the elites and some leaders, such as the Monagas brothers, moved between them. Under Antonio Leocadio Guzmán, the Liberal Party obtained a lot of backing from artisans and other members of the working classes, which frightened the Conservatives as well as some Liberal elites (Butler 1972, 58–60, 64–65, 71–75, 77–78; Lombardi 1982, 180–181). The Liberal Party also initially presented itself as the party of agriculture and drew more support from agricultural interests.

Nevertheless, neither party established meaningful organizations or strong roots in Venezuelan society, which contributed to their fragility. The Conservative Party fell apart in the 1860s after the Federal War (Pérez 1996, 61; Tarver and Frederick 2005, 68). The Liberal Party was also weakened by the war, but it survived in various forms until the early twentieth century when it disintegrated with the rise of the dictatorships of Cipriano Castro and Juan Vicente Gómez.

The weakness of parties in Venezuela undermined the prospects for democracy in two main ways. First, the weakness of opposition parties meant that they could neither defeat the government at the ballot box nor resist government electoral manipulation. Venezuela held regular elections throughout the nineteenth and early twentieth century, but these elections were mostly uncompetitive, and sometimes uncontested, because of the disorganization of the opposition. Second, the weakness of both opposition and ruling parties meant that presidents could concentrate power and seek to extend their term in office. As a result, Venezuelan politics during the late nineteenth and early twentieth century was characterized by a very high degree of personalism.

In the early nineteenth century, when the Conservative and Liberal parties first emerged and maintained a degree of parity, Venezuelan elections were at times competitive. In the 1834 presidential elections, a liberal opposition

---

[4] The first split within the Liberal Party occurred in the 1846 elections when different factions supported four different candidates (Butler 1972, 76–86; Pérez 1996, 53).

candidate, José Antonio Vargas, even triumphed over the conservative candidate favored by the incumbent, although Vargas was quickly overthrown (Gabaldón 1986; Posada-Carbó 1999). The 1846 presidential elections, in which General José Tadeo Monagas narrowly defeated General Bartolomé Salom, was also highly competitive. According to Deas (2012, 14), "the run-up to the election of 1846 was an unprecedented campaign, and more intense popular mobilization than had been seen in Venezuela, or perhaps any South American country at that time." Even the 1842 and 1850 elections had a degree of competition, although Navas Blanco (1993, 64–65) characterizes these as controlled elections in which the incumbent imposed his successor.

By contrast, after the disintegration of the Conservative Party, presidential elections in Venezuela had little, if any, competition, as the incumbent intervened extensively to ensure his own reelection or to impose his successor. Whereas the winner won 67 percent of the vote on average in presidential elections during the first half of the nineteenth century, he won 92 percent of the vote in the second half of the nineteenth century. In many presidential elections during the late nineteenth century, the official candidate won by a share of the vote that was so large as to strain belief. Joaquín Crespo, for example, was reported to have won 349,447 of the 350,450 valid votes cast in 1893 (Botello 2009, 61; Sanoja Hernández 1998, 12). Many elections in the late nineteenth century were not even contested, and where competition did exist, as in 1868 and 1876, it generally occurred among members of the same party or even the same family. In 1868, for example, the winning candidate, José Tadeo Monagas, who was eighty-four years old and somewhat reluctant to run, competed against his son and his nephew. Monagas won a plurality of the votes but died before he could take office, leading Congress to elect his son to take his place (Mendoza 2016; Rodríguez 1997).[5]

The one major democratic advance that occurred in the late nineteenth century was the establishment of universal male suffrage. The 1857 constitution abolished all property and income restrictions on the franchise, and although it imposed a literacy restriction, it suspended this requirement until 1880 (Bushnell 1972). The 1858 constitution then eliminated the literacy restriction altogether, granting suffrage to all male citizens above the age of twenty (Bushnell 1972, 203–205; Urdaneta García 2007, 120, 123–124). The enactment of universal male suffrage led to a dramatic increase in voter turnout in Venezuela: Valid votes rose from 4.7 percent of the population in 1846 to 9.6 percent in 1868 and 15.1 percent in 1893. Nevertheless, the expansion of suffrage did not lead to an improvement in the fairness of the elections.

---

[5] The 1876 election was a close contest between General Francisco Linares and General Hermenegildo Zavarce, both of whom belonged to the Liberal Party. The incumbent president, Antonio Guzmán Blanco, officially remained neutral in this election, but he was reported to have favored Linares who won narrowly (Floyd 1982, 134–146; Franceschi 2019, 139; García Ponce 2009, 443).

Throughout the nineteenth century, Venezuelan politics was characterized by a high degree of personalism, which was made possible in large part by the weakness of parties. Presidents concentrated authority, manipulated elections, and extended their terms at the expense of rivals within their own party as well as in the opposition. For example, the Monagas brothers, José Tadeo and José Gregorio, dominated Venezuelan politics for a dozen years, taking turns in the presidency and practicing the "shameless manipulation and corruption" of elections (Deas 2012, 19). During this period, they switched parties, expanded the powers of the president, purged the legislature of their opponents, declared all gubernatorial and congressional offices vacant, and revised the constitution to allow presidential reelection (Butler 1972, 86–90, 191–193; Lombardi 1982, 182–183; Floyd 1982, 15). Their time in power only came to an end in 1858 when Conservatives and Liberals joined forces to overthrow them.

Another lengthy experience with personalistic rule began a decade later after Antonio Guzmán Blanco, the son of the founder of the Liberal Party, seized power in the 1869 April Revolution. Guzmán Blanco, who referred to himself as the "Illustrious American," ruled Venezuela for most of the next eighteen years. During this period, he refounded the Liberal Party, renaming it the Great Yellow Liberal Party, but he declined to provide it with organization or independent leadership (Bautista Urbaneja and Magallanes 1997; Magallanes 1973, 134–136; Pérez 1996, 61–62).[6] As president, Guzmán Blanco centralized power and tightly controlled elections. In the 1872 elections, he was reported to have won 239,691 of the 239,709 votes cast (Bushnell 1997, 203; Franceschi 2019, 137). Guzmán Blanco also made changes to the electoral system that severely compromised the country's elections. In 1874, for example, he modified the constitution to require signed public votes, which were easier for the government authorities to monitor.

Guzmán Blanco briefly left power in 1876, but he returned to Venezuela in 1879, assembling a 10,000-man rebel army, which overthrew the government. The following year, a new Congress elected Guzmán Blanco as president, without any opposition, and granted him extraordinary powers (Pino Iturrieta 1997). Congress also drafted a new constitution that suppressed popular elections, which enabled Guzmán Blanco to be reelected unanimously as president by Congress in 1882 and 1886, before he departed to Europe for the final time in 1887.

Personalistic rule in Venezuela continued in the early twentieth century under the dictatorial regimes of Cipriano Castro and Juan Vicente Gómez. Castro seized power in 1899 at the head of a rebel army from the Andean state of Táchira. He faced various revolts at the outset of his regime, but he managed to defeat them all thanks in part to the loyalty of his Andean comrades-in-arms.

---

[6] Magallanes (1973, 134) writes: "In truth this was no longer the binding party of all liberals, but rather of those who servilely followed the lucky caudillo. This was not even the party of government but rather the party of Guzmán Blanco. It was his directions that were the only that should be followed both in the government and in the party."

Castro initially governed with a cabinet composed largely of Liberal politicians and regional leaders, but he gradually replaced them with Andean allies (Viloria Vera 2009, 96). He founded his own party, the Restorative Liberal Party, to take the place of the existing parties, but it was a personalistic vehicle that lacked organizational structure (Magallanes 1973, 208–209). Castro's main base of support was the military, which he built up to strengthen his grasp on power, using it to repress any individuals or groups that posed a threat to him. Castro, like Guzmán Blanco, used indirect elections to maintain his hold on power, creating a system in which the secrecy of the vote was severely restricted and municipal councils and state legislatures played the lead role in presidential elections (Lott 1956, 427; Arráiz Luca 2012, 51–52). This system ensured Castro's uncontested election as president in 1901 and again in 1904, after he amended the constitution to run for another six-year term.

In 1908, however, Castro's second-in-command, General Juan Vicente Gómez, seized power when the president was on a trip to Europe, prohibiting him from returning to the country. Gómez ruled the country in dictatorial fashion until his death in 1935, although at times he exercised power through puppet presidents while remaining commander-in-chief of the Venezuelan armed forces. Although many Liberal politicians supported him at the outset and he initially brought some Liberals into his regime, Gómez quickly turned against the traditional political elites, excluding them from his cabinet and exiling, imprisoning, and even killing those who dared oppose him (McBeth 2008, 24–27, 30–31, 63, 318). Gómez and his advisers believed that there was no need for political parties and he sought to "unite Venezuelans without distinction of parties" (McBeth 2008, 372; Rey 2015, 63–64). He revised the constitution to require that the president be elected by the National Congress, which was chosen in a two-stage system controlled by the president and the interior minister (McBeth 2008, 32–33; Velásquez 1997). This enabled Gómez and his puppets to be elected unanimously in 1910, 1915, 1922, and 1929 (Gómez 2009). The existing parties, which were too weak to resist his iron rule, disappeared altogether.

Thus, the strength of the military and the weakness of parties created stable authoritarian rule in Venezuela. The modernization of the military at the outset of the twentieth century brought an end to the revolts that had plagued Venezuela throughout the nineteenth century, but opposition parties were too weak and unorganized to contest elections or enact democratic reforms. Under Castro and Gómez, the existing parties disintegrated as the two dictators imposed a highly repressive and personalistic form of authoritarianism.

THE MILITARY AND REVOLTS IN PERU

Peru also failed to democratize during the nineteenth and early twentieth century. For much of the nineteenth century, Peru had a relatively small and nonprofessional military, which encouraged opposition revolts. In the 1830s, for example, the army was fixed at 2,950 troops, and in 1872, it was set at 4,000 men, which was quite small for a country the size of Peru (Hidalgo Morey et al. 2005, 108, 158, 188). The army expanded during and immediately before the War of the Pacific (1879–1883), but in the aftermath of the war the size of the army was fixed at 3,000 men (Hidalgo Morey et al. 2005, 364). Even during wartime, Peru struggled to mobilize more than 8,000 troops (Soifer 2015, 210).

The organization and training of the military was quite deficient (Hidalgo Morey et al. 2005, 357–360). The Peruvian military lacked a general staff and many types of military specialists, such as engineers, throughout most of the nineteenth century (Scheina 2003, 377; Hidalgo Morey et al. 2005, 358). What training officers and the troops received was rudimentary. Various Peruvian governments established military schools over the course of the nineteenth century, but these schools generally did not remain open for long (Muñoz 1932, 7–24; Reano 2002, 53–55). According to Nunn (1983, 54), "military training was in a sorry state," even at the end of the nineteenth century. Officers were typically promoted or discharged based on their political connections rather than their abilities or experience. Presidents frequently purged the military after rebellions and sought to stack it with their supporters. Partly as a result, the military tended to be quite top heavy. As late as 1900, there were ninety-three officers for every 100 soldiers (Villanueva 1971, 35). Officers typically came from the elite or the middle class and were of European or mixed descent, but soldiers came from the poorest sectors of the population, especially the indigenous peasantry, and many of them were illiterate (Nunn 1983, 54–55). Many of the troops were forcibly impressed, although the constitution explicitly prohibited conscription (Mücke 2004, 174–175).

Military spending represented a large share of the government's budget (45 percent in 1900), but most funds went to retired officers, invalids, and war survivors, rather than to purchase weaponry or to pay active-duty officers and troops (Villanueva 1971, 35). Officer salaries were quite low, which reduced the appeal of the profession for many. In 1900, a military general earned the same as he had twenty-seven years earlier, which was less than a bishop, a prefect, or the director of a government ministry (Villanueva 1971, 17–18, 48). The equipment of the Peruvian military was also typically shoddy despite periodic efforts to upgrade it. During the War of the Pacific, for example, the Peruvians had equipment that was clearly inferior to that of the Chileans and they lacked modern field artillery (Scheina 2003, 377).

In addition to the regular military, Peru had civilian militias and the line between the two was often blurry. Militia members were sometimes incorporated into the army, particularly during and after rebellions (Sobrevilla Perea 2012, 162; Reano 2002, 57). In some cases, the militias guarded the government against internal and external threats. President Manuel Pardo, for example, sought to build up the national guard in the 1870s as a counterbalance to the military, stacking it with his own supporters from the Civil Party (Hidalgo

Morey et al. 2005, 185). In many cases, however, the militias undermined state security by participating in rebellions against the central government.

The weakness of the military encouraged frequent revolts. Between 1830 and 1900, Peru experienced nineteen major rebellions and numerous minor ones. See Table 7.2. Many of the revolts were quite violent, and eight of them involved more than 1,000 battlefield deaths. Opposition leaders headed most of the revolts: Ten of the nineteen major revolts were insurrections by opposition elites, seven were military rebellions, and two were popular uprisings. Defecting military units or national guardsmen often participated in the opposition revolts, however. For example, in 1894–1895, Nicolás Piérola, the head of the opposition Partido Demócrata, returned from exile in Chile and raised an army of 5,000 troops by taking in civilian volunteers and militia members.

TABLE 7.2 *Major revolts in Peru, 1830–1929*

Year	Description of revolts	Type of revolt (outcome)
1834	General Pedro Bermúdez led an unsuccessful military revolt against the liberal president, General Luis José de Orbegoso, after Bermúdez lost the election.	Military coup (suppressed)
1835	The Callao garrison revolted against President Orbegoso and General Felipe Salaverry took control of the rebellion and declared himself chief of state.	Military coup (took power)
1835–1836	Orbegoso joined forces with the president of Bolivia, Andrés de Santa Cruz, and defeated Salaverry and his ally, former president Agustín Gamarra.	Elite insurrection (took power)
1836–1839	Chile and Argentina along with Peruvian dissidents defeated the Peru–Bolivian Confederation, and Agustín Gamarra became president of Peru.	Elite insurrection (took power)
1842	General Juan Crisostomo Torrico, who was the head of the Army of the North, carried out a coup overthrowing President Manuel Menéndez.	Military coup (took power)
1842	General Francisco de Vidal, who was the constitutional successor of Menéndez, rose up with the Army of the South and defeated Torrico.	Military coup (took power)
1843	General Manuel Ignacio de Vivanco, who was minister of war, carried out a rebellion and overthrew General Vidal.	Military coup (took power)
1843–1844	*The Constitutional Revolution*. Rebels under General Ramón Castilla defeated the troops of Manuel Vivanco and restored Manuel Menéndez to the presidency.	Elite insurrection (took power)
1844	Domingo Elias, the prefect of Lima, rebelled and named himself political-military chief of the Republic while President Vivanco was in the south.	Elite insurrection (took power)

(*continued*)

TABLE 7.2 (continued)

Year	Description of revolts	Type of revolt (outcome)
1854	*Liberal Revolution of 1854.* Liberals led by General Ramón Castilla overthrew the government of José Rufino Echenique and wrote a new constitution.	Elite insurrection (took power)
1856–1858	Conservatives led by Manuel Ignacio de Vivanco rebelled against the liberal Constitution of 1856. They were defeated by Castilla in a lengthy civil war.	Elite insurrection (suppressed)
1865	Colonel Mariano Prado and allies overthrew President Juan Antonio Pezet when he signed an unfavorable treaty with Spain. Prado became president.	Military coup (took power)
1867	*Civil War of 1867.* General Pedro Diez Canseco and Colonel José Balta overthrew President Mariano Prado, and Diez Canseco became president.	Elite insurrection (took power)
1870	Over 1,000 Chinese workers in Pativilca revolted against the deplorable working conditions in the plantations. The rebellion was brutally suppressed.	Popular uprising (suppressed)
1872	General Tomás Gutiérrez, the defense minister, and his brothers seized power, but they were overthrown after four days and lynched.	Military coup (suppressed)
1879	Nicolás de Piérola overthrew President Mariano Prado when he left for Europe to seek loans during the War of the Pacific.	Elite insurrection (took power)
1884–1885	General Andrés Cáceres rebelled against President Miguel Iglesias who had been put in power by Chile. Cáceres became president.	Military coup (took power)
1885	Indigenous population rebelled against the reimposition of a poll tax and treatment of leaders. They were brutally repressed.	Popular uprising (suppressed)
1894–1895	Nicolás de Piérola overthrew President Cáceres after he arranged his own fraudulent reelection. Piérola became president.	Elite insurrection (took power)
1914	Military Chief of Staff Colonel Oscar Benavides overthrew President Guillermo Billinghurst after he dismissed him. Benavides became president.	Military coup (took power)
1919	Augusto Leguia, a presidential candidate, seized power with the help of the police and some military officers because he feared he would be denied victory.	Elite insurrection (took power)
1923–1924	Indigenous peasants in Puno rebelled against local authorities, but the revolt was brutally repressed by local authorities and the army with 2,000 deaths.	Popular uprising (suppressed)

Source: Latin American Revolts Database.

The frequent revolts hindered the prospects for democracy in Peru. Many of the rebellions succeeded: On fourteen occasions in the nineteenth century, rebels overthrew the government and installed a new president by force. For example, in 1895, Piérola's volunteer troops defeated the regular army in a bloody battle and occupied Lima, sending the existing president, Andrés Avelino Cáceres, into exile. These forcible seizures of power undermined constitutional rule and encouraged further revolts. The revolts also deepened authoritarianism by provoking state repression and the abrogation of civil and political liberties. Peruvian constitutions typically provided the government with the right to suspend constitutional guarantees in the event of internal or external threats, and presidents did not hesitate to declare a state of emergency in response to revolts. The 1839 constitution, for example, gave the president almost unlimited authority to suspend constitutional rights, and Article 59 of the 1860 constitution, which was in place until 1920, allowed for the suspension of constitutional guarantees when "the Fatherland is in danger" (Loveman 1993, 220, 229–230).

At the end of the nineteenth century, however, Peru took major steps to professionalize its military, which largely brought an end to the opposition revolts. Peru sought to professionalize its military in part to discourage domestic insurrections but also to deal with external threats (Nunn 1983, 64–65). The Peruvian military was particularly concerned about Chile, which had defeated and taken land from Peru during the War of the Pacific. When Chile strengthened and professionalized its armed forces in the 1880s and 1890s, Peru felt compelled to respond.

Peru's military professionalization efforts were made possible by the rapid growth in exports registered in the late nineteenth and early twentieth century, which dramatically increased government revenue. Between 1895 and 1899, Peruvian exports tripled and government revenues doubled, and they continued to increase in the first few decades of the twentieth century (Villanueva 1978, 80). Indeed, between 1913 and 1929, exports grew by an annual average of 12.4 percent in real terms, the second highest rate in Latin America (Bértola and Ocampo 2013, 100).

The professionalization efforts began during the second administration of Nicolás Piérola (1895–1899). After taking power in 1895, Piérola dismissed and retired many of those officers who had remained loyal to the former president and reduced the army's size and share of the national budget (Klarén 1986, 601). Piérola then brought in a French mission to professionalize the military. The French mission helped draft important legislation, including a military legal code, an obligatory military service law, an organizational and administrative code, and regulations on promotions, military pay, pensions, and retirement (Nunn 1983, 114–116; Hidalgo Morey et al. 2005, 349–352). Under the compulsory military service law, which took effect in 1898, the size of the Peruvian military more than tripled in ten years (Klarén 1986, 601). The French mission also promoted the acquisition of French weapons and oversaw the creation of munitions factories within Peru (Loveman 1999, 86).

With the assistance of the French mission, the government improved the training of military officers. It revived the Military School at Chorrillos in 1898 and required all officers to attend it, and in 1904, it opened the Superior War College, which trained upper-ranking officers (Nunn 1983, 116–120). Between 1896 and 1914, thirty-three French officers taught in the various military schools in Peru, creating a cadre of Peruvian officers who were imbued with French military doctrine (Nunn 1983, 117). Although the French mission came to an end with the outbreak of World War I, it started up again after the war. From 1919 to 1925, twenty-four more French officers came to Peru, and ten more came between 1925 and 1940, although after 1922 they came as individuals rather than as part of a mission (Nunn 1983, 198–199). By 1930, more than a quarter of high-ranking Peruvian military officers had graduated from the Superior War Academy (Loveman 1999, 86).

The French mission encountered various problems, including resource shortages, political interference, the lack of prior preparation of the officers and the troops, and frequent administrative changes within the Peruvian high command (Nunn 1983, 121–122; Loveman 1999, 86–88). Politicians continued to interfere with promotions, raises, and assignments, and nationalists both inside and outside the military resented the French and accused them of peddling French weaponry to serve their own interests (Nunn 1983, 201).[7] In spite of these problems, however, the French mission made a great deal of progress, transforming the Peruvian military in important ways (Hidalgo Morey et al. 2005, 344–352; Loveman 1999, 86; Villanueva 1971, 64). Indeed, Nunn (1983, 120) suggests that the Peruvian officers the French mission trained were the equal of the Chilean officers in terms of the scientific and technical knowledge and clearly superior to the Argentines or the Brazilians.

As a result of the strengthening of the Peruvian military, the number of outsider revolts declined dramatically. Once the armed forces became professionalized, opposition forces had little chance of defeating the military and so they largely desisted from launching their own revolts. Those revolts that the opposition did attempt either failed to get off the ground or were quickly suppressed. For example, in 1909, Nicolás de Piérola's brother and sons, along with approximately twenty-five militants of the opposition Partido Demócrata, staged a violent kidnapping of President Augusto Leguía in 1909, but the military quickly suppressed this uprising. Augusto Durand, the leader of the Liberal Party, similarly engaged in a variety of unsuccessful revolutionary plots during the early twentieth century (Pike 1969, 186–187; Peralta 2005, 87). As we shall see, a more successful opposition strategy was to try to persuade the military to intervene. Indeed, the only successful revolts in Peru during the early twentieth century involved the direct participation of the military.

---

[7] Officers criticized President Augusto Leguía (1908–1912 and 1919–1930), in particular, for meddling with the military and seeking to coopt it (Nunn 1983, 277).

WEAK PARTIES AND AUTHORITARIANISM IN PERU

Although the professionalization of the military largely brought an end to outsider revolts, it did not lead to democracy in large part because Peru continued to have weak parties. With the partial exception of the Civil Party, the parties that arose in Peru in the nineteenth century tended to be personalistic and relatively short lived.[8] Indeed, none of them lasted beyond the 1930s. The parties had little in the way of organizational structures and few formal members: One prominent politician of that time observed that "the total membership of any given political party in Peru could easily fit into one railroad coach" (cited in Stein 1980, 25). Nor were the parties particularly ideological. According to Victor Andrés Belaunde, Peruvian political parties of this period were "inconsistent and ephemeral personal groupings" (cited in Klarén 2000, 214).

Electoral clubs emerged in Peru in the mid-nineteenth century, but the first real party, the Civil Party, did not arise until the 1870s.[9] Manuel Pardo, a prominent businessman and the first civilian president of Peru, founded the party, which was then known as the Society of Electoral Independence, to support his successful presidential candidacy in 1872. Pardo developed a large national network of supporting organizations in this campaign, but it was not until the late 1870s, when he went into exile, that the party institutionalized to a degree and acquired a relatively disciplined contingent in the legislature (Mücke 2004, 64).[10] The party never developed a strong national organization, however. It did not have formal members during this period, nor did it develop a clear platform, bureaucratic rules, or any permanent organizations aside from an executive committee and its parliamentary contingent (Mücke 2004, 200–201). Moreover, the party weakened considerably beginning in the 1880s.

The other political parties that arose in Peru during this period were even more personalistic and weakly organized than the Civil Party. According to Klarén (2000, 214): "Three of Peru's early political parties were entirely based on personal loyalties to an individual caudillo." These parties were: the Constitutional Party of General Andrés Avelino Cáceres, which was founded in 1884; the Democrat Party, which was created by Nicolas de Piérola in 1884; and the Liberal Party of Augusto Durand, which was formed in 1900. The three parties lacked organization, ideologies, and internal discipline, not to mention a second generation of leaders (Pike 1969, 218). Although the parties lasted until the 1920s, they operated on the margins of power during the twentieth century and did not long survive the deaths of their founders.

---

[8] The first strong party to arise in Peru, the American Popular Revolutionary Alliance (APRA), was not founded until 1930.
[9] On the electoral clubs, see Forment (2003) and Loayza (2005).
[10] According to Mücke (2004, 202), the party "was organized along extremely modern lines compared with Latin American and European parties" of that period.

The weakness of parties in Peru meant that the opposition could not typically compete with government-sponsored candidates or resist government manipulation of elections during the nineteenth century. Both the government and the opposition bought the support of local notables, legislators, electors, voters, and party combatants, but the government typically had more money to spend, given its access to state coffers (Mücke 2004, 99–100; 2001, 331–332). Local government authorities also controlled the electoral registries, which they could use to disqualify opposition voters (Mücke 2004, 83). In addition, Peruvian governments frequently used the police and the military to prevent opposition supporters from voting by intervening in the battles for the control of the public squares and other locations where elections were conducted. According to Aljovín de Losada (2014, 62), these battles were so violent that elections in the postwar period at times resembled civil wars. A Lima newspaper reported that the government's candidate, Mariano Prado, won the 1876 presidential elections "because his partisans were armed with modern Winchester carbines, whereas [the opposition's] supporters were equipped only with revolvers" (Pike 1969, 139).

During the nineteenth century, an opposition candidate did win the presidency twice. In 1833, a constitutional convention elected an opposition liberal, General Luis Jose de Orbegoso, in large part because the opposition was united and the incumbent and his preferred candidate were unpopular (Basadre 1968, 62). Similarly, in 1872, Manuel Pardo prevailed over the candidates supported by the incumbent thanks in part to the use of his considerable personal resources in his campaign. Nevertheless, these were exceptions to the general rule of government control. Many nineteenth-century elections were not even contested since the opposition was sometimes barred from competing or opted to abstain rather than participate in an election that they had no chance of winning. Only fourteen of the twenty-one presidential elections in Peru during the nineteenth century had more than one candidate, and only five of the twenty-one presidential elections were competitive (meaning that the winner won less than 70 percent of the valid vote). On average, the winner captured 83.9 percent of the presidential vote during the nineteenth century and the average margin of victory was 72.1 percentage points.

The weakness of parties in nineteenth-century Peru enabled presidents to concentrate power and act in undemocratic ways. The legislature at times resisted the president, but it had limited authority and it was fairly common during the nineteenth century for presidents to shut down Congress altogether (Sobrevilla Perea 2017, 226). In 1858, for example, President Ramón Castilla closed a recalcitrant legislature, silenced independent newspapers, and exiled many of his opponents in order to elect a more pliant assembly, which drafted a constitution that was to his liking (Pike 1969, 108). After the death of President Remigio Morales Bermúdez in 1894, a former president, Andrés Cáceres, engineered a nonviolent coup to elevate the second vice-president, Justiniano Borgoño, to the presidency instead of the constitutionally mandated first vice-president whom Cáceres did not trust. Once in office, Borgoño assured Cáceres' reelection as president in 1894, arresting any opposition leaders who might have gotten in the way (Klarén 2000, 201; Pike 1969, 156–157).

Although opposition parties called for democratic reforms and curbs on the power of the executive, they generally did not have the legislative votes to enact such measures on their own. The ruling party typically controlled a majority of the seats in the legislature, and members of the ruling party generally obeyed the dictates of the president. Even the Civil Party, the best organized party in Peru in the nineteenth century, was largely dominated by its leader, Manuel Pardo, during his tenure as president.

Peru did take some steps toward democracy in the early twentieth century. Piérola's seizure of power in 1895 ushered in a period that became known as the Aristocratic Republic (1895–1914), during which electoral violence declined. Congress played an increasingly important role in politics during this period, and it often opposed executive initiatives. The legislature, for example, rejected presidential budgets in 1901, 1903, 1911, 1914, and 1917, and blocked a number of other major presidential initiatives during this period (Klarén 2000, 216).[11] In addition, Piérola enacted a new electoral law in 1896 that reinstituted municipal elections, mandated a direct popular vote in presidential elections, and established minority representation in legislative elections (Peralta 2005, 77–78; Aguilar Gil 2002, 11; Pike 1969, 173).

The 1896 electoral reform, however, represented a step backward for Peruvian democracy in that it restricted the suffrage. As Chapter 2 discussed, Peru had universal male suffrage from 1828 to 1834 and 1855 to 1856, and it maintained relatively broad suffrage rights during most of the late nineteenth century because the 1856 and 1860 constitutions enfranchised anyone who satisfied *either* the economic *or* the literacy requirements, which many Peruvians did in the mid-nineteenth century (Mücke 2004, 82; Peloso 1996, 195). The 1896 reform, however, made literacy a prerequisite for voting, which disenfranchised hundreds of thousands of, mostly indigenous, people since only 24.3 percent of Peruvians were literate in 1900 (Thorp 1998, 354). The disenfranchisement of large sectors of the population was intentional. The Senate Commission that approved this reform argued that "it was not in the interest of the Nation that many participate in elections, but rather that those who participate do so well" (Cited in Klarén 2000, 206).[12] In the wake of the reform, voter turnout fell dramatically. In the 1890 presidential elections, valid votes had represented 12 percent of the population, but this figure declined to 1.6 percent in 1899. Voter turnout inched upward in the first two decades

---

[11] Ministerial turnover was also quite high during this period. According to Klarén (2000, 215–216), between 1886 and 1919, there were fifty-seven ministers of justice, sixty-four ministers of war, sixty-five ministers of finance, and seventy ministers of government.

[12] Piérola justified the reform by arguing that "the least illustrious citizens" were subject to electoral manipulation (Peralta 2005, 78).

of the twentieth century, but it still averaged only 3.2 percent in presidential elections during this period.

The 1896 law also created a National Electoral Board to supervise elections, which helped bring an end to some undemocratic practices, such as the battles over the electoral tables and congressional certification of elections (Peralta 2005, 79; Aguilar Gil 2002, 11). Nevertheless, the electoral reform did not establish the secret ballot, which enabled the government to monitor how state employees and others voted (Pike 1969, 173). This allowed the government to intimidate voters and to disqualify supporters of the opposition. Although reforms were enacted to the electoral law in 1908, 1912, and 1915, they did little to address the restrictions on the franchise or government electoral manipulation (Peralta 2005, 89).

Perhaps most importantly, the weakness of parties in Peru enabled the executive to ignore or manipulate the electoral authorities and to run roughshod over the opposition. After coming to power in 1895, Piérola forged a coalition between his party, the Democrat Party, and the Civil Party. This alliance easily won the elections that year since Piérola controlled the electoral authorities and the Constitutional Party was banned from participating (Peralta 2005, 77).[13] In the 1899 elections, Piérola shut down the National Electoral Board and intervened to ensure that his handpicked successor, Eduardo López de Romaña, won the elections, which the Constitutional Party and some other candidates boycotted in protest (Pike 1969, 175; Aguilar Gil 2002, 25; Peralta 2005, 81). Soon after taking office, however, López de Romaña had a falling out with Piérola and allied with the Civil Party, which gradually gained control of the key ministries in his government as well as the majority of the seats on the reopened National Electoral Board.[14] The Civil Party used its control of the government and the electoral authorities to dominate elections over the next ten years, committing a variety of electoral abuses (Klarén 2000, 203; Stein 1980, 28; Aguilar Gil 2002, 23, 28, 32).[15] Some of the violations were particularly egregious. For example, President Augusto Leguía dissolved the National Electoral Board in the run-up to the 1911 legislative elections and then intervened extensively to ensure that the government won a majority of the races (Peralta 2005, 92; Aguilar Gil 2002, 34).

In response, opposition parties often abstained from presidential elections, and sometimes municipal and legislative elections as well. The Democrat Party, for example, declined to compete in the 1903, 1904, and 1908 presidential

---

[13] Observers commented that Piérola was both a participant in and judge of this election since he presided over the legislative committees that certified the new members of the chambers (Peralta 2005, 77).

[14] By law, Congress appointed four members of the board, the judiciary named four members, and the executive chose one, but the ruling party typically controlled these institutions, which enabled it to determine the appointments (Pike 1969, 173; Chiaramonti 2000, 255).

[15] The Constitutional Party allied with the Civil Party for some of this period.

elections. Only four of the nine presidential elections that took place during the Aristocratic Republic period were contested. Moreover, only two of the nine presidential elections during this period were competitive: the 1912 and the 1919 elections. The winning presidential candidates captured 82.6 percent of the vote on average and triumphed by an average margin of 77.4 percentage points during this period.

With few other alternatives at its disposal, the opposition sometimes urged the military to intervene to overthrow governments it opposed. These coups only served to entrench authoritarian rule, however. The first coup of the Aristocratic Republic took place in 1914 when President Guillermo Billinghurst was overthrown. Billinghurst, a populist former mayor of Lima, had become president in 1912 with the support of a broad coalition of opposition parties, which included a large dissident faction of the Civil Party. The Leguía administration supported the official Civil Party candidate, Antero Aspíllaga, who appeared headed toward victory, but Billinghurst's working-class supporters called a strike and disrupted the election in Lima by attacking polling places and chasing off the electoral authorities (Stein 1980, 33; Gerlach 1973, 17–18). Since the number of ballots cast did not reach the requisite one-third of eligible voters, the election was declared constitutionally invalid and it fell to Congress to choose the winner (Peralta 2005, 94; Aguilar Gil 2002, 38). President Leguía's supporters in Congress then agreed to vote to confirm Billinghurst as president in exchange for Leguía's brother being elected as the first vice-president (Klarén 2000, 223–224; Blanchard 1977, 258).

Billinghurst never developed a good working relationship with the existing parties, however. He tried to bypass them by enacting his budget and labor legislation by decree, and he reportedly even planned to dissolve Congress and hold new elections to gain a more compliant body (Blanchard 1977, 267–269; Gerlach 1973, 31–32). Instead of relying on parties, Billinghurst sought to build up his base of support among the workers, intervening in strikes and calling for the enactment of new labor laws. He mobilized workers to intervene in elections and attack opposition newspapers and leaders (Blanchard 1977, 264–265; Gerlach 1973, 28–31). Opposition leaders, including the Liberal leader Augusto Durand and right-wing Civilista leaders, Jorge and Manuel Prado, objected strenuously to Billinghurst's policies and authoritarian inclinations, and began to seek the support of the military to overthrow him (Pike 1969, 200–201; Blanchard 1977, 267–270; Gerlach 1973, 39–42). They managed to obtain the backing of key military officers, including the army chief of staff, Colonel Oscar Benavides, who were disgruntled with Billinghurst in part because of military cutbacks and rumors that the president was going to arm his supporters (Blanchard 1977, 270–271; Gerlach 1973, 45–47). When Billinghurst got word of these plots in February 1914, he dismissed Benavides who responded by mobilizing the Lima garrison against the president. After a two-hour gun battle at the presidential palace that led to 50–60 deaths, the military rebels seized Billinghurst and sent him into exile (Gerlach 1973, 51–54).

The return to civilian rule in 1915 did not bring about democracy, however, in part because parties remained weak and divided. The ruling Civil Party split into four main factions that warred with each other, and public support for the party ebbed (Stein 1980, 36–37). President José Pardo, who was elected in 1915, governed in the same personalistic and arbitrary manner that previous presidents had, intervening in elections to help his preferred candidates (Klarén 2000, 235; Peralta 2005, 98–99; Stein 1980, 36). As Pardo's term came to an end in 1919, two main candidates emerged to succeed him: the former president and ex-Civilista, Augusto Leguía; and Antero Aspíllaga, the conservative leader of the Independent Civil Party who had lost to Billinghurst in 1912. Pardo supported Aspíllaga, and the government intervened to help him, closing an opposition newspaper, falsifying electoral registries and votes, and intimidating the opposition (Peralta 2005, 99–100). The main branch of the Civil Party, along with the Constitutional Party, the Liberal Party, and even the Socialist Party, rallied around Leguía, however, as did students, labor unions, and middle-class organizations (Pike 1969, 214; Gerlach 1973, 116–117).

According to the official returns, Leguía won by a large margin, capturing 122,736 votes to Aspíllaga's 64,936, but Aspíllaga refused to accept his loss, arguing that there was widespread fraud, particularly in rural areas. Although most observers suggest that the government had committed more electoral abuses than Leguía's supporters, the Supreme Court issued a series of decisions favoring Aspíllaga (Peralta 2005, 99–100; Klarén 2000, 238). Aspíllaga and Pardo insisted that Congress decide the winner of the elections, but Leguía refused to accept this, given that he did not control a majority of votes in the legislature (Gerlach 1973, 118–119). Instead, Leguía sought out the support of the military and the police to overthrow Pardo. In July 1919, some army and naval officers revolted and a contingent of ninety police officers under the command of an army colonel took over the presidential palace, with the assistance of some rebellious palace guards (Gerlach 1973, 122–127). Leguía then assumed power, sending Pardo into exile.[16]

Once in power, Leguía quickly moved to concentrate his power and undermine the opposition, establishing a personalist dictatorship that would last for eleven years. He dissolved Congress and called new legislative elections, which enabled him to gain control of the legislature. The legislature then drafted a new constitution that helped consolidate Leguia's control, enabling him to appoint provisional municipal officials and suspend municipal elections and provincial councils (Peralta 2005, 102–103; Pike 1969, 220–221; Stein 1980, 47). At the same time, Leguía jailed and exiled independent journalists and harassed or shut down newspapers that were critical of him, even turning one opposition paper, *La Prensa*, into a government mouthpiece (Pike 1969, 224–225; Peralta 2005, 103). He also suppressed student protests and enacted

---

[16] The armed forces generally supported the coup, as did the political parties, with the notable exception of the Independent Civil Party and the Democrat Party (Gerlach 1973, 125–127).

an educational reform that enabled him to get rid of university professors who were his political opponents (Pike 1969, 223–223). Although Leguía initially tolerated the labor unions, some of which had supported him in the 1919 elections, by 1923 he had turned against them, and in 1927 he banned all union activities and arrested the most prominent labor leaders, forcing them underground (Stein 1980, 78). Leguía twice revised the constitution to make it possible for him to run for reelection in 1924 and again in 1929. In both elections, he ran unopposed and his supporters triumphed in the legislative elections, gaining firm control of both chambers of Congress (Peralta 2005, 105–107).

The weakness of the existing parties made it possible for Leguía to concentrate power and act in authoritarian ways. According to Stein (1980, 38), by 1919, all of the major parties in Peru were near collapse: "They resembled the imposing colonial houses still owned by many of their most prominent members; impressive façades that hid aging structures beset by internal decay." Leguía weakened them further, exiling or imprisoning their leaders, breaking up party meetings, and encouraging mobs to attack opposition newspapers and politicians (Stein 1980, 41).[17] The Civil Party and the Liberal Party bore the brunt of the attacks.[18] Shortly after taking office, Leguía announced that the exiled former president, José Pardo, had organized a movement to carry out a coup and he arrested a number of leaders of the party, along with various army and police officers (Gerlach 1973, 143–144). Pro-Leguía mobs then assaulted two newspapers that were critical of the new president, and when Augusto Durand, the publisher of one of those newspapers, protested, he was sent into exile. Durand later returned to Peru but was arrested and died in prison under mysterious circumstances, which led to the demise of the Liberal Party. Leguía also persecuted new political movements, such as the APRA, whose leader, Víctor Raúl Haya de la Torre, was exiled in 1923. Other parties, such as the Constitutional Party and the Democrat Party, cooperated with Leguía, but they had little influence over him and they, too, dissolved in short order.

Leguía founded his own personalistic party, the PDR, in 1920, but he had no interest in building a strong party organization (Pike 1969, 218). The PDR's leadership was stacked overwhelmingly with friends and family members of Leguía, and it had no ideology to speak of, existing only to serve the interests of the president (Stein 1980, 47). As a result, it failed to constrain the president in any meaningful way.

The most significant resistance to Leguía came from the military itself. The Leguía administration experienced several military insurrections, plus at least five military conspiracies that never reached fruition, during its first five years

---

[17] Pike (1969, 218) writes that Leguía "only applied the *coup de grâce* to organizations that were already moribund."

[18] As Klarén (2000, 242) puts it, Leguía "unleashed a systematic campaign of repression to dismantle the [Civil Party] and force its leaders into exile."

in power (Gerlach 1973, 175). Some of these plots and uprisings involved members of the political opposition, but they were led by military officers and involved active-duty troops. None of these plots gained many adherents or posed a serious threat to the regime.[19] In 1930, however, the strong economic growth that had boosted the president's popularity came to an end, leading to a dramatic increase in unemployment and sharp cuts in government spending. The economic crisis helped prompt a military uprising in Arequipa led by Major Luis M. Sánchez Cerro. The military rebellion quickly spread throughout the country, leading to the overthrow of Leguía who by this time was deeply unpopular. This coup, too, failed to bring democracy to Peru, however.

Thus, the weakness of parties in Peru undermined the prospects for democracy in Peru even after the professionalization of the military brought an end to outsider revolts. Weak opposition parties could not compete effectively in elections, nor could they push through democratic reforms or prevent presidents from concentrating power and manipulating the political and electoral system. Consequently, the opposition frequently abstained from elections and sometimes encouraged the military to intervene. The result was a relatively stable authoritarian regime during the first three decades of the twentieth century, albeit one that experienced a brief period of political instability in the 1910s brought on by military coups.

THE MILITARY AND REVOLTS IN BRAZIL

Brazil also had a relatively stable authoritarian regime for much of the late nineteenth and early twentieth century. Unlike its Spanish-American neighbors, Brazil enjoyed considerable political continuity after independence. The prince regent, Dom Pedro I, who was the son of the Portuguese emperor, led the country's independence movement, and after declaring its independence in 1822, Brazil remained an empire. Nine years later, Dom Pedro I abdicated in favor of his son, Dom Pedro II, but because Dom Pedro II was only five years old at the time, Brazil was governed through elected regents until 1840 when the Brazilian parliament declared him to be of age to rule. Dom Pedro II then governed Brazil until he was overthrown by the military in 1889.

The Brazilian military was relatively weak in the decades following independence. A scarcity of tax revenue constrained military spending and local powerholders opposed the creation of a strong army partly on the grounds

---

[19] To retain the support of the military, Leguía boosted officer salaries, doubled the military budget, and increased the size of the army from 4,000 to 7,422 men between 1919 and 1927 (Gerlach 1973, 146–147). He also transferred officers and troops he did not trust to distant regions and expanded the national guard and the police to help resist revolts, establishing a battalion armed with machine guns to protect the presidential palace (Gerlach 1973, 145–148, 157–159).

that it might reduce their autonomy (Beattie 2001, 32). Before 1865, the size of the army fluctuated between 12,000 and 25,000 men, which was small given the country's size (McBeth 1987, 126). To make matters worse, the military was poorly armed. The army had muskets and artillery, but the lance was often the dominant battlefield weapon in the early nineteenth century (Scheina 2003, 151).

The troops, who came overwhelmingly from the poorest sectors of the population, lacked training and discipline. The state forcibly recruited many soldiers – between 1850 and 1861, 57 percent of the army's troops were impressed – and the conditions in which they served were poor (Beattie 2001, 294). As a result, many troops deserted. The navy, for example, experienced 6,568 desertions between 1836 and 1884 – in some years, 10 percent of its sailors left (Beattie 2001, 192).

The officer class was also woefully inadequate. The country established a military academy in 1810, but it operated sporadically and attendance was not required (Dudley 1978; Nunn 1972, 57). Most officers lacked a military education and owed their positions to personal or political connections rather than merit. Many officers also initially lacked combat experience because the Brazilian independence struggle had only limited fighting.

The initial weakness of the Brazilian military encouraged frequent revolts. As Table 7.3 indicates, Brazil suffered a dozen major revolts between 1831 and 1852. These revolts had a variety of causes and aims, but they were made possible by the Brazilian state's lack of coercive capacity. Although some of the rebellions were motivated by liberal or republican sentiments, they did not bring about democratization. Instead, the revolts provoked a great deal of violence and state repression, costing tens of thousands of lives. None of these rebellions ever seriously threatened to topple the central government, but the weak Brazilian military had a difficult time suppressing many of them. The national guard, which was developed as a counterweight to the military and grew to include 200,000 men by the 1830s, played an important role in combating some of the regional revolts (Schneider 1993, 41; Scheina 2003, 150). The national guard was even more poorly trained and armed than the military, however. Moreover, national guard troops sometimes joined in the rebellions, fighting against the imperial army (Johnson 1964, 183–184). Members of the army also sometimes participated in the rebellions (Beattie 2001, 33; Kraay 1992).

Beginning in the 1850s, the Brazilian government took some steps to professionalize the military. New military schools were opened in Porto Alegre, São Paulo, and Rio de Janeiro, although instruction continued to be irregular (Nunn 1983, 57–58). Legislation was passed that sought to depoliticize military promotions and gave priority to officers with seniority and degrees (Schneider 1993, 50; Beattie 2001, 36; Castro 2001). Middle-income groups began to enter the military in larger numbers, and favoritism and corruption declined (Beattie 2001, 36).

TABLE 7.3 *Major revolts in Brazil, 1830–1929*

Year	Description of revolt	Type of revolt (outcome)
1831	Military sided with popular revolt critical of the emperor and against the Portuguese. Pedro I abdicated in favor of his five-year old son.	Military coup (abdication)
1831	Anti-Portuguese riots continued in some states after the abdication of Pedro I and some called for reform. Some elements of the military joined in. 130 deaths.	Popular uprising (suppressed)
1832	More than 500 Conservatives (*caramuros*) carried out an uprising in Rio de Janeiro to restore Pedro I to the throne, but it was quickly suppressed.	Elite insurrection (suppressed)
1832–1835	*War of the Cabanos*. A popular revolt in some northern provinces that called for the return of Pedro I and the end of the regency. It was suppressed.	Popular uprising (suppressed)
1835–1840	*War of the Cabanagem*. The poor of Grão-Pará rebelled. Rebel army grew to 25,000 before it was suppressed. 30,000–40,000 deaths.	Popular uprising (suppressed)
1835	A slave revolt in Salvador, Bahia was brutally suppressed, leading to the deaths of hundreds of slaves. This was the largest slave revolt in Brazilian history.	Popular uprising (suppressed)
1835–1845	*War of the Farrapos*. Landowners in Rio Grande do Sul rebelled against taxes with support of Liberals and Uruguay but were defeated. 3,000–10,000 deaths.	Elite insurrection (suppressed)
1837–1838	*Sabinada*. A popular revolt in Salvador that included military and elite elements and grew to 5,000 rebels. The rebels were suppressed. 1,200 deaths.	Popular uprising (suppressed)
1838–1841	*Balaiada*. Liberals (*bentevis*) revolted and assembled an army of 11,000 soldiers, including many slaves, before they were defeated. 30,000 deaths.	Popular uprising (suppressed)
1842	*Liberal Revolutions of 1842*. Liberals rebelled in São Paulo, Rio de Janeiro, and Minas Gerais against Conservative control but were quickly defeated.	Elite insurrection (suppressed)
1848	*Praiera Revolution*. Liberals in Pernambuco revolted against Conservative dominance. The rebels numbered 2,800 but were suppressed. 815 total deaths.	Elite insurrection (suppressed)
1851–1852	*The War of the Wasps*. A popular rebellion against the decrees calling for a general census and civil registry. The government suspended the decrees.	Popular uprising (policy revoked)
1889	The military overthrew the emperor and declared Brazil a republic. The coup was nonviolent, but pro-Monarchist reactions led to more than 100 casualties.	Military coup (took power)
1891	The navy under Admiral Cústodio de Mello revolted after President Fonseca declared martial law. Fonseca resigned, leading the vice-president to take over.	Military coup (resignation)

TABLE 7.3 (*continued*)

Year	Description of revolt	Type of revolt (outcome)
1892	General Antonio Maria Coelho, the former provincial president, declared the Transatlantic Republic of Mato Grosso. The revolt was suppressed.	Elite insurrection (suppressed)
1893–1894	*Naval Revolt of 1893–1894*. Admiral Mello unsuccessfully revolted with support of navy after President Floriano Peixoto sought to stay in power. 10,000 deaths.	Military coup (suppressed)
1893–1895	*The Federalist Riograndense Revolution*. Federalists revolted in Rio Grande do Sul with support of Argentina and Uruguay but were suppressed. 10,000 deaths.	Elite insurrection (suppressed)
1896–1897	*The War of the Canudos*. A religious community in rural Bahia revolted but were defeated by the federal military. 30,000 deaths.	Popular uprising (suppressed)
1910	*Revolt of the Lash*. 2,000 navy sailors mutinied in Rio de Janeiro in response to whippings. A few officers were killed then the sailors surrendered.	Military mutiny (suppressed)
1912–1916	*The War of the Contestados*. Land disputes prompted a popular uprising led by a monk on the southern frontier. It was suppressed. 6,000–9,000 deaths.	Popular uprising (suppressed)
1922	Junior officers rebelled in Rio in response to the arrest of General Hermes da Fonseca. A few units joined the revolt, but it was suppressed. 18 deaths.	Military coup (suppressed)
1924–1927	Junior officers rebelled and sought to overthrow President Bernardes. They were defeated but some continued a march through the backlands. 1,000 deaths.	Military coup (suppressed)

Source: Latin American Revolts Database.

The bloody Paraguayan War of 1865–1870 led to the further strengthening of the military. Brazil created special battalions called Volunteers of the Fatherland to fight in the war, and the Brazilian army swelled to more than 50,000 men (Scheina 2003, 317; Loveman 1999, 51; Beattie 2001, 39–41). Ultimately, Brazil deployed more than 110,000 men in the war, including national guard troops and many freed slaves (Beattie 2001, 38–41). Brazil also invested heavily in modern weaponry during the war, purchasing ironclad ships, artillery, and repeating rifles (Scheina 2003, 318; Loveman 1999, 51). Nevertheless, Brazil and its allies struggled to defeat the much smaller forces of Paraguay, and suffered an estimated 100,000 casualties (Scheina 2003, 331).

The poor performance of the army in this war led Brazilian officers to push the government to further modernize the military, but the emperor and allied elites were reluctant to invest heavily in the armed forces (Nunn 1972, 31;

Dudley 1978, 59–61). Some reform measures were enacted in 1873–1874. The government overhauled the military curriculum, created provincial police forces, and established a military conscription lottery to replace the existing system of impressment (Schneider 1993, 55; Beattie 1999, 857). Yet implementation of the latter system was delayed until 1916, and regional divisions continued to bedevil the army, which barely kept pace with the evolution of doctrine, strategy, and tactics (Nunn 1983, 58–59; Mendes 2010). A politician in the 1880s quipped that the army was "more apt, by its organization, background and education, for police service than for duties of war" (Graham 1990, 63). In addition, the size of the army steadily declined in the wake of the war, dropping to 19,000 in 1871 and 13,000 in 1889 (Nunn 1983, 61). To make matters worse, promotions were slow and military pay and budgets stagnated in the postwar period (Dudley 1975, 45). In 1887, army officers had gone thirty-five years without an increase in their base pay, and the military budget was the same from 1870 to 1880 as it had been in 1857 (Dudley 1975, 56–57; Schneider 1993, 57).

Frustration with military salaries, budgets, and promotions as well as the lack of reform helped lead the military to overthrow the emperor in 1889, establishing the First Republic. Internal divisions, including revolts by the navy between 1891–1894, spurred the military to yield the presidency to an elected civilian leader in 1894, but while in power, the military boosted the pay and promotions of officers and opened some new military schools (Beattie 1999, 862; McCann 2004, 79–80; Johnson 1964, 193; Hahner 1969). Nevertheless, at the end of the century, the military curriculum was still woefully out of date (McCann 2004, 90, 93–94). A 1907 report by the minister of war, Hermes da Fonseca, concluded that the army was "deficient in personnel, war materiel, organization and command" (McCann 2004, 97). As McCann (2004, 70) puts it, Brazilian generals were "not prepared to lead, [and] the soldiers were likewise unfit to follow."

It was not until the early twentieth century that Brazil took major steps to professionalize the military, although even then they proceeded slowly and haphazardly. Brazil's military professionalization efforts of the early twentieth century were driven in part by concern about the growing military buildup in Argentina (McCann 2004, 100; Resende-Santos 2007, 246, 286–294), but they were made possible by the strong economic growth Brazil experienced in the early twentieth century. Between 1913 and 1929 alone, exports increased by 7.8 percent annually in real terms and the economy grew at an annual rate of 4.2 percent (Bértola and Ocampo 2013, 100). The export revenues helped fund the expansion and strengthening of the armed forces.

Germany played an important role in the initial professionalization efforts. Brazil sent thirty-four junior officers to be trained in Germany between 1906 and 1910, and it purchased several hundred thousand Mauser rifles as well as Krupp cannons from the Germans (McCann 1984, 746; Nunn 1972, 35; Resende-Santos 2007, 252–253). The military professionalization efforts, however, met resistance from within the military as well as from powerful state political elites who opposed strengthening the coercive powers of the federal government (Resende-Santos 2007, 275–276). Military officers, for example, blocked an effort to hire a full-scale German mission both for nationalistic reasons and concerns about how it would affect their own standing (Resende-Santos 2007, 261–262; Grauer 2015, 294–295).

World War I brought an end to military cooperation with Germany, but after the war Brazil commissioned a French mission, which ultimately had greater success in professionalizing the military. The French mission, which lasted from 1920 to 1940 and numbered around thirty officers annually, took over the training of military officers, establishing new schools and overhauling the curriculum of existing ones. Under their auspices, Brazil passed a law in 1934 that established strict meritocratic criteria for military promotions (Resende-Santos 2007, 272). Brazil also gradually expanded the size of the military, which grew from 30,000 men in 1920 to 50,000 in 1930 and 93,000 in 1940 (McCann 2004, 176). Brazilian arms purchases, however, remained relatively modest, as budget considerations forced the military to abandon some planned acquisitions (Resende-Santos 2007, 268). Moreover, it took time for the impact of the French mission on the training of officers and troops to take effect.

The gradual modernization of the military brought down the frequency of rebellions in Brazil. The number of revolts dropped precipitously beginning in the 1850s, although this decline probably stemmed more from Emperor Pedro II's popularity and governing skills than the strength of the military. Revolts ticked up again after the overthrow of the emperor in 1889, but most of these revolts were military uprisings. As Table 7.3 indicates, major military coups or mutinies took place in 1891, 1892, 1893, 1910, 1922, and 1924. The revolts of the early 1890s reflected a struggle for power that occurred in the wake of the overthrow of the emperor, but the military revolts of the 1920s stemmed from the rise of a group of reformist junior officers, known as *tenentes*, who wanted sweeping military and political changes (Alexander 1956; Wirth 1964). Opposition parties and politicians at times encouraged these coup attempts since they had little possibility of dislodging the government through elections.

A few major outsider revolts also occurred during this period, including the Federalist Riograndense Rebellion of 1893–1895, the War of the Canudos of 1896–1897, and the War of the Contestados of 1912–1916. These revolts, like the rebellions of the early nineteenth century, had a variety of causes, but they took advantage of the vast size and rugged nature of Brazil's territory, the federalist structure of the country, and the continued weakness of the Brazilian state and the military (Resende-Santos 2007, 275). Even in the early twentieth century, the Brazilian state barely penetrated the interior. Many areas lacked roads, bridges, telegraph lines, and electricity, which made it difficult for the military to suppress the rebellions. In the War of the Contestados, for example, 20,000 poorly armed and untrained rebels held off the Brazilian army for years in a remote area of southern Brazil (Diacon 1995). These internal wars not only cost thousands of lives, they also prompted authoritarian measures by the government.

The most politically consequential revolt, however, took place in 1930 when the political opposition managed to topple the government. The revolt occurred after the opposition candidate, Getulio Vargas, denounced the widespread fraud in the 1930 presidential election. Vargas and his allies managed to mobilize discontented military officers as well as members of the state militias, policemen, firemen, and irregular forces throughout much of Brazil (Wirth 1964, 168). State militias represented a particularly important source of troops for the rebels since some of these state militias were larger and better armed than the federal military garrisons. The military leadership initially opposed this rebellion and over several weeks the federal military fought a series of battles with the rebels (McCann 2004). As the rebels gathered strength, however, the military leadership switched sides, asking the president to step down and recognizing Vargas as the new president.

In the years that followed, the military gradually strengthened its coercive capacity, which led opposition groups to abandon the armed struggle. The last major opposition revolt occurred in 1932, when opposition groups in São Paulo revolted against Vargas with the support of state militias and police, along with some rebellious army troops. Although the rebels managed to assemble an army of 40,000 troops, more than half of them were civilian volunteers and they were a poor match for the army's 75,000 troops, which suppressed the rebellion after a few months of fighting (Schneider 1993, 124). In the wake of this rebellion, the military for the first time in its history gained a monopoly on force throughout the country (McCann 2004, 331). Although elements within the military continued to engage in periodic uprisings and coup attempts, the opposition began to increasingly focus on the electoral path to power.

Thus, the gradual strengthening of the Brazilian military during the late nineteenth and early twentieth century slowly brought an end to the outsider revolts that had plagued Brazil during the early nineteenth century. Although Brazil did not professionalize its military as rapidly or as thoroughly as Argentina and Chile, it nevertheless gradually obtained a monopoly on violence, which helped bring about a degree of political stability.[20]

WEAK PARTIES AND AUTHORITARIAN RULE IN BRAZIL

Military professionalization and the decline of outsider revolts did not bring democracy to Brazil. Government electoral intervention and military coup attempts persisted throughout the late nineteenth and early twentieth century in large part because of the weakness of parties in Brazil.

---

[20] In 1917, Edwin Morgan (1978, 65) of the US mission in Rio de Janeiro reported that "[i]n esprit, technical knowledge and general efficiency [the Brazilian military] is inferior to similar organizations in Argentina and Chile and would be at a disadvantage in a trial of strength."

As Chapter 4 discussed, Brazil failed to develop strong parties in the nineteenth century and early twentieth century. The Conservative Party and the Liberal Party dominated Brazilian politics for most of the nineteenth century, but neither of these parties developed significant organizational structures, consistent political positions, or enduring partisan loyalties.[21] The Conservatives never even developed a written party program and the Liberal Party did not formulate one until the late nineteenth century (Carvalho 1974, 426; Motta 1971, 2–3; Needell 2001).

The two parties arose during the 1830s and rotated in power until 1889, except for a brief period between 1853 and 1868 when they governed jointly.[22] The parties had relatively similar social bases, in that both were led by and represented the landowning elites, but the Liberal Party had more professionals among its leaders, whereas the Conservative Party had more government bureaucrats (Carvalho 1974, 440–442). Although they often disagreed, neither party had stable ideologies (Costa 1989, 198; Graham 1990, 169–175, 181).[23] Both Conservatives and Liberals criticized the emperor and demanded democracy when they were out of power but did little to reform the system that benefited them once they were in power (Graham 1990, 97).

Personalistic and patronage-based ties, rather than ideological or programmatic linkages, undergirded the party system. Neither party developed a strong territorial organization, depending instead on local political bosses (*coroneis*) to turn out the votes at the local level (Barman 1988; Nunes Leal 1977; Graham 1990). These local bosses focused on patronage and they would typically side with the governing party in order to gain access to resources (Barman 1988, 226; Graham 1990, 156–159). Factionalism was pervasive in both parties, and party loyalty and discipline were sorely lacking – politicians switched parties as well as policy positions at their convenience (Barman 1988, 228–229; Graham 1989, 145; 1990, 161). According to Graham (1990, 181): "Party labels were put on and taken off almost as easily as a set of clothes."

The weakness of parties meant that the opposition could not compete in elections since they had neither the organization nor the partisan attachments required to prevail under adverse circumstances. Whoever was in power controlled elections through patronage, fraud, and intimidation. The cabinet appointed and could remove provincial presidents and judges, both of whom held great sway over the electoral process (Graham 1990, 81–85; Carvalho 2012, 15). The cabinet also named the leaders of the military,

---

[21] The two parties did not begin to use the names Conservative and Liberal parties until the 1840s and 1850s (Barman 1988, 224; Needell 2001, 275–276, 305).

[22] This alliance was initially called the conciliation cabinet and subsequently became known as the Progressive League or the Progressive Party (Carvalho 1974, 424–425; Costa 1986, 172).

[23] The Conservatives typically claimed to represent the interests of the monarchy, order, and centralized power, whereas the Liberals frequently took up the banner of individual rights and the decentralization of power (Barman 1988, 224–225; Carvalho 1974, 426–427). Their positions often shifted when they were in office, however.

the police, and the national guard, all of which could be used to intimidate voters, especially given that the vote was not secret (Graham 1990, 85–93; Carvalho 2012, 15).

The governing party invariably won the vast majority of seats in the legislature. Liberals, for example, captured only one of the 110 seats elected in 1849 when the Conservatives were in control, but the Liberals won all 122 seats in 1878, when they were the ruling party (Carvalho 2012, 12–14; Porto 1989, 134–135).[24] As a member of the cabinet noted in an 1852 letter to a friend: "We defeated them completely because we're in the government; if they were in the government, they would have won completely ... That is the system" (cited in Graham 1990, 80).

Nevertheless, the opposition could come to power if the emperor desired it, since he had extensive powers, including the right to suspend judges, to name and dismiss ministers, to dissolve the Chamber of Deputies, and to choose senators-for-life from lists of three candidates nominated by provincial electors (Schneider 1993, 45). On eleven occasions during the nineteenth century, the emperor dissolved the cabinet and called new elections for the Chamber of Deputies. The emperor alternated between the two main parties for diverse reasons, including to get rid of unpopular governments and to enact policy reforms. These interventions were hardly democratic, however, since the emperor used authoritarian methods to ensure that the party he favored won. Nevertheless, the emperor's interventions ensured some degree of alternation in government. Indeed, between 1840 and 1889, Conservatives governed for twenty-six years and Liberals ruled for over thirteen years, whereas the two parties governed jointly in an alliance for almost ten years (Carvalho 1974, 434).

The opposition frequently called for democratic reforms, but they did not have the legislative strength to enact the measures themselves. To pass reforms they needed the support of the emperor and at least some members of the ruling party. Although electoral reforms were enacted in 1842, 1846, 1855, 1860, and 1875, they were mostly minor measures that failed to bring an end to government manipulation of the electoral system. As Costa (1989, 173) argues, the electoral reforms of this period did not touch the sources of patronage or address the economic inequalities that undergirded the political system, nor did it guarantee the independence of electors. The 1855 reform did ban public employees from running for elected positions in their jurisdictions, which reduced the number of government officials in the legislature (Carvalho 2012, 10–13; Graham 1989, 147). This reform also created single-member districts for electing federal legislators, which enabled the opposition to win more seats, but in 1860 this system was replaced with districts that elected three members by simple majority (Carvalho 2012, 13). In 1875, the government made further changes, introducing an incomplete-list system, which was supposed

---

[24] By contrast, legislative seats were divided more evenly in election years when the two parties governed jointly, such as 1857 and 1861.

to grant one-third of the seats to the opposition, but it failed to prevent the Liberals from winning all the seats in the 1878 elections (Carvalho 2012, 14; Graham 1990, 76).

The most important electoral reform was enacted in 1881, but it had, at best, a mixed effect on democracy in Brazil. The 1881 reform created direct parliamentary elections, which reduced government electoral control and helped increase opposition representation in the legislature (Carvalho 1974, 456; Costa 1989, 195–196). At the same time, however, the 1881 reform restricted the suffrage by imposing a literacy requirement for the first time, and by requiring written documents to prove that voters met the existing income requirements.[25] These restrictions dramatically reduced voter registration and turnout in Brazil. In the 1870s, approximately 10 percent of the total population had been eligible to vote, which was one of the highest rates in Latin America, but this dropped to 1.2 percent in 1881, before recovering to 6.7 percent in 1894. Voter turnout, meanwhile, declined from 8.6 percent in 1872 to 0.8 percent in 1881 and 1886, before rising to 2.3 percent in 1894.

The opposition revolted on a few occasions in the early nineteenth century to protest the unfairness of elections and the lack of democracy. In 1842, for example, liberals rebelled in São Paulo, Minas Gerais, and Rio de Janeiro partly in response to efforts by Conservatives to consolidate their dominance by appointing police delegates to the electoral boards that supervised voting (Graham 1990, 53; Bethell and Carvalho 1989, 81–83; Bento and Giorgis 2016, 171–176). Similarly, in 1848 Liberals in Pernambuco revolted against Conservative efforts to dismantle their political base – the Liberals called for federalism, free and universal suffrage, and the elimination of the emperor's moderating powers, among other demands (Bethell and Carvalho 1989, 104–105; Bento and Giorgis 2016, 179–183). As we have seen, however, the gradual strengthening of the military in the late nineteenth century discouraged opposition revolts. Moreover, Pedro II dissuaded the opposition from revolting by allowing both the Conservatives and Liberals to govern at different times, giving both parties a stake in the existing system (Graham 1990, 78).

Nevertheless, opposition discontent with the authoritarian political system grew steadily over time, helping lead to the overthrow of the emperor. In the 1870s, Republican parties, which opposed the monarchy and called for representative government and federalism, emerged in some states. Most Republican leaders adopted a gradual, democratic approach to achieving their goals, but some of them conspired with the military to topple the emperor and declare Brazil a republic in 1889 (Costa 1989, 206–212). Military leaders initially governed Brazil in the aftermath of the coup, but the military was divided and soon handed power back to civilian leaders. In 1894, Brazil elected Prudente de Morais of the Paulista Republican Party as its first civilian president.

---

[25] The Saraiva Law of 1881 did lower the voting age to twenty-one and granted the suffrage to former slaves, non-Catholics, and naturalized citizens (Bethell 2000).

The overthrow of the empire did not bring democracy to Brazil, in part because parties continued to be weak during the First Republic (1889–1930). After the fall of the empire, the Liberal and Conservative parties disappeared, but no strong national parties emerged to replace them. Some states, such as São Paulo and Minas Gerais, developed strong state-level Republican parties, which routinely delivered a large share of the state vote for their candidates, but they had a minimal presence outside of their home states (Love 1970, 13; 1980; Wirth 1977).[26] Although there were periodic attempts to create a national party based on coalitions of state parties, none of these national parties lasted more than a few years (Love 1970, 15). In 1910, for example, Rio Grande do Sul and some northeastern states created the Conservative Republican Party, but it failed to develop a meaningful organization, common platform, or national following and it rapidly declined after 1916 (Fausto 1989, 292; Schneider 1993, 92–93). Another party, the Democratic Party, arose in 1926 and built support within the middle classes with its calls for democratic reform, but it failed to move beyond its base in São Paulo and dissolved in 1934 (Fausto 1989, 297–298).

As a result of their organizational weakness, the opposition usually could not compete effectively in elections since opposition candidates and parties typically lacked the resources and partisan ties to overcome the electoral disadvantages they faced. Presidential elections were held regularly every four years beginning in 1894, but the presidential races rarely had serious competition. Indeed, between 1894 and 1930, the winning presidential candidate captured an average of 82 percent of the vote. The Republican parties of the two largest states, São Paulo and Minas Gerais, generally traded control of the presidency in what became known as the *café com leite* alliance.[27] Leaders of the Paulista Republican Party won the presidency six times during the First Republic, whereas representatives of the Mineiro Republican Party held it three times (Fausto 1989, 272). The Republican parties of these two states would usually reach an accord on who their joint presidential candidate should be and the other states would typically fall into line. This meant there was little competition in the presidential race since the governors and the ruling parties could deliver the votes in their states. In 1910 and 1930, however, São Paulo and Minas Gerais failed to come to an agreement on a candidate, which prompted competitive races in those years as some states sided with São Paulo and others with Minas Gerais. The 1922 presidential election was also competitive, but in this case, São Paulo and Minas Gerais did reach an agreement on a candidate. However, an unprecedented coalition of almost all the other states supported another candidate who lost in a competitive race that year.

---

[26] The presidential and gubernatorial candidates of the Paulista Republican Party, for example, typically won at least 90 percent of the state's vote (Love 1980, 143).

[27] São Paulo was a large producer of coffee, whereas Minas Gerais was a large producer of milk.

Even when they were competitive, the elections were not free and fair. Governors and ruling parties used their control of patronage and the electoral authorities to favor the candidates they supported, so whichever side controlled a particular state would typically dominate elections there.[28] According to Schneider (1993, 92), governors used "electoral corruption that bordered on the absurd, rather than being merely abusive." Ruling parties had influence over all stages of the electoral process. They typically controlled the voter registration process, which enabled them to distribute voter identification cards only to their supporters (Ricci and Zulini 2016, 254). Parties used patronage and clientelism to buy votes and thugs to intimidate the opposition. They also sought to control the committees that oversaw the voting process on election day so they could "count votes their way" (Ricci and Zulini 2016, 256; Nicolau 2012, 68–69). Fraud was a last resort, but it, too, was used, especially where the ruling parties did not have complete control over the electoral authorities (Ricci and Zulini 2016, 247–248; Telarolli 1982).

The opposition pushed for democratic reforms, including the secret ballot, but it lacked the legislative votes to enact significant measures. The opposition candidate Rui Barbosa, for example, made democratic principles and the adoption of the secret ballot a central part of his platform in the 1910 presidential campaign, but to little effect (Fausto 1989, 294; Telarolli 1982, 68–69).[29] During the First Republic, the government typically controlled at least two-thirds of the seats in the lower chamber and a similar proportion in the Senate, which made it impossible for the opposition to enact legislation without the support of members of the ruling party.[30] As a result, there were no major changes in the voting process during the First Republic (Nicolau 2012, 66). The government did pass an electoral reform in 1916, which shifted the responsibility of registering voters to state judges, but this simply led parties to focus on gaining influence over the judges (Ricci and Zulini 2016, 253). The 1916 reform also shifted the electoral scrutiny process to the capital of each state, instead of the capital of each district, but this gave the governor more influence over the process (Ricci and Zulini 2016, 263).

Because the opposition could not capture the presidency through elections, it sometimes urged the military to intervene. The opposition, for

---

[28] This system became known as the politics of the governors because of the crucial role that governors played. The heads of the states were officially called presidents, but I use the term governor to avoid confusion.

[29] The 1892 electoral law stipulated that the process of voting was to be secret, but it did little to ensure ballot secrecy (Nicolau 2012, 67–68; Telarolli 1982, 66–67). It was not until 1932 that Brazil established the secret ballot.

[30] The Chamber of Deputies occasionally refused to recognize the election of opposition legislators, but as Ricci and Zulini (2012, 508) have shown this was a relatively rare occurrence – the legislature only overturned 8.7 percent of the election certificates approved by the local election boards between 1894 and 1930 and most of these so-called beheadings took place when duplicate certificates were issued.

example, initially refused to accept its loss in the 1922 presidential elections and demanded that the military step in. Field Marshall Hermes da Fonseca, the head of the Military Club, supported the opposition candidate and called for a Tribunal of Honor to verify the results instead of the Chamber of Deputies. Fonseca also sent a threatening telegram to federal garrisons in the state of Pernambuco advocating passive resistance to the government, which led to his arrest for insubordination (McCann 2004, 262–263). In the wake of his arrest, some junior officers carried out a revolt at Fort Copabacana in Rio de Janeiro. Although this revolt was quickly suppressed, it inspired another larger revolt by reformist junior officers in 1924 that culminated in a 15,000-mile rebel march through Brazil that lasted three years. The rebels, who were led by Captain Luis Carlos Prestes, demanded a series of reforms, including the adoption of the secret ballot.

The most important opposition revolt, however, occurred in the wake of the 1930 presidential election. As noted, the opposition candidate, Getulio Vargas, and his supporters denounced the election as fraudulent and refused to accept their defeat.[31] Indeed, there was extensive evidence of fraud by both sides. Shortly after the election, Vargas' running mate, João Pessoa, who was the governor of the state of Paraíba, was murdered. Although his killing was unrelated to the election, it triggered a revolt. The rebels initially received the support of some reformist junior officers as well as the state militia of Rio Grande do Sul where Vargas was the governor, but others quickly joined the cause, enabling the rebels to seize areas of the northeast as well as Minas Gerais. Senior military officers in Rio de Janeiro then deposed the president, but their efforts to maintain power themselves failed in the face of the growing rebel opposition and they agreed to allow Vargas to assume power, which he did in November 1930. Democracy failed to emerge in the years that followed, however, as Vargas gradually consolidated his control of the country.

Thus, Brazil remained an authoritarian regime throughout the nineteenth and early twentieth century in part because of the weakness of the country's parties. Opposition parties were not strong enough to compete in elections, to resist government electoral manipulation, or to enact meaningful democratic reform. Instead, members of the opposition at times resorted to revolts or urged the military to intervene on their behalf. The modernization of the country's armed forces in the late nineteenth century discouraged opposition revolts and created a more stable authoritarian regime, but the military itself began to intervene increasingly in politics beginning in 1889, at times undermining the relative stability of the country's authoritarian system.

---

[31] In this election, Vargas had the support of Rio Grande do Sul, which he governed, as well as Minas Gerais, which was angry that the president had nominated a politician from São Paulo as the official candidate in 1930 when it would normally be the turn of Minas Gerais.

CONCLUSION

Brazil, Peru, and Venezuela had similar regime trajectories during the nineteenth and early twentieth century in large part because they all strengthened their militaries considerably over time. All three countries were plagued by frequent revolts in the nineteenth century, which sometimes toppled governments and often provoked state repression. The professionalization of the countries' armed forces in the late nineteenth and early twentieth century helped reduce the frequency of these revolts, leading to the establishment of relatively stable authoritarian regimes. Parties remained weak in all three countries, however, which impeded the emergence of democracy. Opposition parties did not have the organizational strength or partisan ties necessary to win elections or democratize the countries' electoral systems. Nor could they always prevent presidents from concentrating authority or extending their hold on power. Instead, the opposition often abstained from elections and sometimes called on the military to intervene. As a result, in 1930, the three countries were still firmly under authoritarian rule.

Although the regime trajectories of Brazil, Peru, and Venezuela were similar in some ways during the nineteenth and early twentieth century, they also had important differences. For most of the nineteenth century, Brazil had an emperor, and it took steps to professionalize its military at an earlier stage than did Peru or Venezuela. As a result, Brazil enjoyed greater political stability than Peru or Venezuela during the late nineteenth century. Although Peru and Venezuela professionalized their militaries and developed relatively stable authoritarian regimes in the early twentieth century, their regimes took a different form than in Brazil. Personalistic regimes emerged in Venezuela and, subsequently, in Peru that rewrote constitutions, concentrated authority, and extended the president's hold on power. By contrast in Brazil, presidents largely respected constitutional rule, leaving office after their terms expired. Thus, authoritarian rule in Brazil during the early twentieth century was less dictatorial and exclusionary than it was in Peru or Venezuela.

8

The Roots of Unstable Authoritarianism
Bolivia, Ecuador, and Paraguay

Bolivia, Ecuador, and Paraguay had relatively unstable authoritarian regimes throughout the late nineteenth and early twentieth century. Like their South American neighbors, these three countries were plagued by internal rebellions during the nineteenth century, which were encouraged by the weakness of their armed forces. Although they sought to strengthen and professionalize their militaries at the beginning of the twentieth century, they made much less progress than other South American countries. Bolivia, Ecuador, and Paraguay were relatively small and poor nations that could not easily afford to build modern, professional armies that would provide them with a monopoly on violence. As a result, they continued to suffer from frequent revolts during the early twentieth century, which provoked state repression and undermined constitutional rule.

The weakness of parties in Bolivia, Ecuador, and, to a lesser extent, Paraguay also hindered their prospects of democratization. Parties arose in all three countries in the late nineteenth century, but they remained highly personalistic and factionalized institutions with only minimal organizational structures well into the twentieth century. The weakness of parties enabled presidents to concentrate authority, undermine rivals, and extend their hold on power. Opposition parties, in particular, were too weak to restrain the president, compete in elections, or enact democratic reforms that would have leveled the electoral playing field. Instead, opposition parties often boycotted national elections and sometimes sought power via armed revolt. These revolts undermined the prospects for democracy since they provoked government repression and civil strife. Moreover, opposition parties that took power through force tended to rule by force, intervening in elections and repressing their opponents, just as their predecessors had done.

Although Bolivia, Ecuador, and Paraguay all had unstable authoritarian regimes during the late nineteenth and early twentieth centuries, they differed in important ways. Bolivia, for example, took greater steps to professionalize its military than did the other two countries. Although these efforts ultimately failed, they helped Bolivia enjoy a modicum of political stability during the first two decades of the twentieth century. Paraguay, by contrast, enjoyed political stability in the early nineteenth century thanks to the powerful coercive apparatus it developed. The Paraguayan armed forces were destroyed in the War of the Triple Alliance (1864–1870), however, which led to a wave of revolts in the country that continued into the early twentieth century. Paraguay developed stronger parties than either Bolivia or Ecuador in the early twentieth century, but the weakness of the Paraguayan military undermined any sustained move toward democracy since the opposition continued to seek power via armed revolt. As a result, all three countries ended the third decade of the twentieth century still under authoritarian rule.

THE MILITARY AND REVOLTS IN BOLIVIA

During the nineteenth century, Bolivia's army was relatively small, often numbering fewer than 2,000 men. Indeed, for much of the nineteenth century, the personal militias of regional leaders outnumbered the regular army's troops (Shesko 2012, 36). The army would typically swell in size when Bolivia faced a major war or rebellion, then decline rapidly after the conflict came to an end. The military, for example, rose to as many as 4,500 men during the War of the Confederation (1836–1839), then descended to fewer than 2,000 men after the Battle of Ingavi in 1841, and fell to only 500 men in 1865 (Scheina 2003, 263; Díaz Arguedas 1971, 26). It expanded again in the run-up to the War of the Pacific, then shrank afterwards, remaining at approximately 1,000 troops for the rest of the nineteenth century (Díaz Arguedas 1971, 28, 71).

The military was also quite top heavy. In 1841, for example, Bolivia had one general for every 102 soldiers and one officer for every six soldiers (Scheina 2003, 263). Even during the 1890s, it was common for commissioned officers to represent more than 10 percent of the army, with noncommissioned officers accounting for another 25 percent (Dunkerley 2003, 71).

Discipline tended to be poor among the troops. Soldiers were typically recruited by force and drawn overwhelmingly from the poor, although tribute-paying indigenous people were often exempted. The military paid the troops poorly and, at times, treated them quite brutally. During the late 1870s and 1880s, soldiers earned sixteen bolivianos per month, whereas a captain earned seventy-four bolivianos and a colonel made 225 per month (Dunkerley 2003, 70). The harsh conditions, brutal discipline, poor pay, lengthy term of service (5–8 years), and requirements of the harvest led to frequent desertions. Even in the 1880s, it was common for the desertion rate to approach 75 percent (Dunkerley 2003, 22).

Neither officers nor troops had much training. The military education system was rudimentary at best during the nineteenth century and military schools were often closed (Díaz Arguedas 1971, 76–77, 115–117). The government granted promotions based on personal and political connections, rather than on education or experience (Díaz Arguedas 1971, 26–27). Presidents sought to gain control of the military by promoting those officials who they believed would be loyal to them personally. Changes in the presidency thus often led to wholesale purges of the officer corps. Officers and troops also moved back and forth frequently between the army and the country's various militias.

The Bolivian army had limited access to modern military materiel, and the weaponry it did have frequently broke down and could not easily be repaired. Often only the premier battalions, such as the Colorado Battalion, had modern equipment such as repeating rifles – other troops had to make do with antiquated weaponry (Díaz Arguedas 1971, 28). The Bolivian military was also short on artillery: During the War of the Pacific, it had only two old Krupp cannons (Díaz Arguedas 1971, 28; Dunkerley 2003, 48).

The weakness and lack of professionalization of the military encouraged frequent revolts. According to LARD, Bolivia had thirty-seven major revolts between 1830 and 1899, more than any other South American country (see Table 8.1).[1] Major revolts took place in forty of the seventy years during this period. Some of the revolts were quite violent: Six revolts, for example, involved deaths of more than 1,000 people. Opposition leaders typically spearheaded the rebellions: Twenty-one of the revolts were insurrections by opposition elites, ten were military coups, and six were popular uprisings. Nevertheless, the opposition elites who led the revolts were often former military officers, and active military units sometimes joined the rebellions.

The revolts undermined constitutional rule and hindered the prospects for democracy. Thirteen of the rebellions during this period overthrew the president, which was more than any other South American country except Peru. Even those revolts that failed to overthrow the government deepened authoritarian rule by provoking state repression. Bolivian constitutions typically provided the president with the right to exercise emergency powers and suspend constitutional guarantees in the event of revolts. An extreme example was the 1843 constitution, which declared that in cases of internal commotion or external danger, the president could take "whatever security measures he deems convenient" without regard to congressional review or the rights of Bolivian citizens (Loveman 1993, 244). Presidents, frequently, took advantage of these provisions, declaring states of siege, suspending constitutional guarantees, shutting down independent newspapers, and arresting, exiling, and even executing members of the opposition. In response to an 1857 rebellion in Cochabamba, Bolivian president Jorge Córdova called on his troops to kill the

---

[1] If minor rebellions are counted, the number of revolts was much higher. According to Aranzaes (1918), there were 185 revolts, mutinies, and coups or coup attempts in Bolivia between 1826 and 1903. Scheina (2003, 268), meanwhile, counts at least sixty rebellions.

TABLE 8.1 *Major revolts in Bolivia, 1830–1929*

Year	Description of revolt	Type of revolt (outcome)
1839	General José Miguel de Velasco seized power, repudiating the authority of President Andres de Santa Cruz.	Military coup (took power)
1839	José Ballivián gained control of three battalions and one squadron and declared himself president, but his troops were defeated.	Elite insurrection (suppressed)
1841	General Sebastian Agreda seized power from President Velasco whom he deported to Argentina.	Military coup (took power)
1841	José Miguel de Velasco invaded with 1,200 men, but the government defeated them. Subsequent pro-Velasco revolts were also vanquished.	Elite insurrection (suppressed)
1841	José Ballivián revolted and seized power and then defeated a Peruvian invasion.	Elite insurrection (took power)
1847–1848	José Miguel de Velasco and his supporters rebelled and eventually overthrew the government. Velasco became president.	Elite insurrection (took power)
1847–1848	Manuel Belzú and his supporters rebelled. He allied with Velasco and became minister of war when they overthrew the government.	Elite insurrection (took power)
1848	Minister of War Belzú rebelled and defeated President José Miguel de Velasco in the Battle of Yamparaez. Belzú became president.	Military coup (took power)
1849	José Ballivián rebelled against President Belzú but was defeated when the citizens of La Paz rose up against him.	Elite insurrection (suppressed)
1849	José Miguel de Velasco and José María Linares invaded from Argentina with 2,000 men, but Belzú defeated them.	Elite insurrection (suppressed)
1853	Velasco and Linares invaded again from Argentina with 2,000 men, but Belzú suppressed the revolts.	Elite insurrection (suppressed)
1854	Colonel José María de Achá revolted with his military regiments, but he was defeated by forces loyal to President Belzú.	Military coup (suppressed)
1855	A series of revolts in favor of José María Linares broke out, but they were quickly suppressed by forces loyal to President Jorge Córdova.	Elite insurrection (suppressed)
1857	José María Linares and his supporters rebelled against President Jorge Córdova who fled into exile. Linares became president.	Elite insurrection (took power)
1860	José Martínez initiated a revolt in Santa Cruz and organized an army of 600 men, but they were quickly defeated by the government.	Elite insurrection (suppressed)

(*continued*)

TABLE 8.1 (*continued*)

Year	Description of revolt	Type of revolt (outcome)
1861	Minister of War Achá carried out a coup overthrowing President Linares. Congress then elected Achá president.	Military coup (took power)
1861	At the instigation of Ruperto Fernández, revolts were initiated in La Paz and Sucre, but the rebellions were suppressed by President Achá.	Elite insurrection (suppressed)
1862	Mariano Torrelio and others rebelled in support of Belzú with 1,500 men. Forces loyal to President Achá defeated the rebels.	Elite insurrection (suppressed)
1862	General Gregorio Pérez rebelled with support of regiments he commanded in Oruro and La Paz. President Achá defeated the rebels.	Military coup (suppressed)
1864	General Mariano Melgarejo carried out a coup, taking President Achá prisoner and proclaiming himself president.	Military coup (took power)
1865	Belzú returned from exile and conquered La Paz. President Melgarejo marched from Oruro and defeated and killed Belzú.	Elite insurrection (suppressed)
1865	Various revolts broke out calling for the restoration of the constitution, but the government of Melgarejo suppressed them.	Elite insurrection (suppressed)
1868	Revolts in favor of constitutional rule broke out, but President Melgarejo suppressed them.	Elite insurrection (suppressed)
1869	More than 5,000 indigenous people rebelled and occupied land in Tiquina, but the uprising was brutally suppressed. 600 deaths.	Popular uprising (suppressed)
1870	Thousands of indigenous people rebelled over land rights in rural La Paz, but they were brutally repressed. 2,000 deaths.	Popular uprising (suppressed)
1870–1871	Opposition forces rebelled and overthrew Melgarejo after extended fighting and 1,087 deaths. Agustín Morales became president.	Elite insurrection (took power)
1874–1875	Revolts in support of Quintín Quevedo broke out and included 2,500 rebels, but they were defeated by forces loyal to President Frías.	Elite insurrection (suppressed)
1876	General Hilarión Daza, who was head of the 1st Battalion, carried out a coup against President Frías and Congress proclaimed him president.	Military coup (took power)
1878–1879	The military command overthrew President Daza in a bloodless coup. General Narciso Campero became president.	Military coup (took power)
1880	Colonel Uladislao Silva, the inspector general of the army, mobilized his battalions against President Aniceto Arce, but protests led him to flee.	Military coup (suppressed)

TABLE 8.1 (*continued*)

Year	Description of revolt	Type of revolt (outcome)
1886	More than 3,000 indigenous people in Omasuyos revolted over land claims, but the rebellion was repressed after one month.	Popular uprising (suppressed)
1888	3,000 indigenous people revolted in Sacasaca over land issues, but they were repressed. 50 deaths.	Popular uprising (suppressed)
1888	Colonel Eliodoro Camacho and the Loa Battalion rebelled against President Arce with 800 men. Arce's forces defeated them.	Military coup (suppressed)
1890	Liberals carried out several simultaneous revolts against President Arce, but they were all defeated rather easily.	Elite insurrection (suppressed)
1891	Several thousand Chiriguano indigenous people revolted in Santa Cruz, but they were brutally repressed with about 1,000 killed.	Popular uprising (suppressed)
1892	Indigenous people in Tiwanaku and elsewhere in La Paz rebelled over land rights. They were repressed.	Popular uprising (suppressed)
1898–1899	Liberals rebelled with support of indigenous people and overthrew the Conservative government. Colonel José Pando became president.	Elite insurrection (took power)
1920	Bautista Saavedra, with the support of some officers, overthrew the government in a nearly bloodless revolt. Saavedra became president.	Elite insurrection (took power)
1921	Thousands of indigenous people rebelled in Jesús de Machaca and Yungas. The government repressed the rebellion and killed hundreds.	Popular uprising (suppressed)
1924	A separatist anti-government revolution erupted in Santa Cruz with 2,000 rebels. The government easily defeated this revolt.	Elite insurrection (suppressed)
1927	5,000 indigenous people rose up in Chayanta in a rebellion that spread to more than 100,000 people. The government quelled the rebellions.	Popular uprising (suppressed)

Source: Latin American Revolts Database.

residents without pity, promising his soldiers "all the booty of the city" including the young girls (Arguedas 1975, 199–200; Loveman 1993, 247–248).

Beginning in the early 1900s, the Bolivian government took steps to professionalize its military to deal with external threats as well as internal ones. During the late nineteenth and early twentieth century, Bolivia lost more than 600,000 square kilometers of land to Brazil and Chile, and it continued to have territorial conflicts with these countries as well as Paraguay (Shesko 2012, 49). Moreover, Bolivia's neighbors, especially Argentina, Chile, and Peru, had taken major steps to strengthen their militaries, which provided the Bolivian government with ample motive to invest in its own armed forces. The export boom of the late nineteenth and early twentieth century helped pay for the military professionalization efforts, although Bolivia continued to be much poorer than its neighbors. According to estimates by Federico and Tena-Junguito (2016), Bolivia's total exports rose from $5.7 million in 1870 to $14.0 million in 1900 and $46.8 million in 1929.[2]

As part of the professionalization efforts, the military retired 317 active-duty officers between 1899 and 1901 and began to train and recruit new ones with the assistance of foreign officers (Dunkerley 2003, 128). The government reopened the War Academy and the Military College and it established a new school for noncommissioned officers in 1900 (Díaz Arguedas 1971, 76–77, 115, 145). In 1905, the first French military mission arrived in Bolivia led by Colonel Jacques Sever and staffed by four other French officers (Díaz Arguedas 1971, 642–643; Dunkerley 2003, 126–128).[3] Sever was given the rank of brigadier general and served as chief of staff of the Bolivian military from 1906 to 1909 (Shesko 2012, 47). The French mission immediately undertook the task of reforming the curriculum of all three military schools along French lines and sent officers to train in France, Germany, Chile, and Argentina (Dunkerley 2003, 129). It also began to import significant amounts of weaponry from France, including a shipment of Schneider-Creusot cannons (Bieber 1994, 96, 99). In addition, the French mission reorganized the general staff and helped implement a new system of officer ranks with age limits (Díaz Arguedas 1971, 642–643; Shesko 2012, 42; Dunkerley 2003, 127–129). Perhaps most importantly, the French mission helped draft an obligatory military service law, which was enacted in 1907. This law, which governed military conscription in Bolivia for a half century, required all Bolivian men from age eighteen to forty-nine to perform military service, with relatively few exemptions (Shesko 2012, 42).

In 1909, however, the Bolivian military decided not to renew the contract of the French mission, replacing it with a much larger German mission in 1911 (Shesko 2012, 58). Major Hans Kundt headed the new mission, which also included three captains, one lieutenant, and thirteen sergeants (Shesko 2012, 58–59). Although the German mission came to an end in 1914 with the outbreak of World War I, German officers returned after the war and continued to train the Bolivian military into the 1930s.[4] Indeed, between 1900 and 1935,

---

[2] Tin production took off in the late nineteenth century: By 1900, tin accounted for 41 percent of Bolivia's exports, and by 1921–1925 it represented 70.5 percent (Volk 1975, 29).

[3] As Bieber (1994, 87) points out, the French delegation was not a military mission in the strict sense of the term because the officers were privately contracted, but it is commonly referred to as such owing to its size.

[4] The German officers that returned to Bolivia after World War I came under private contracts and did not represent a German mission per se. Under the treaty of Versailles, Germany was forbidden from sending foreign military missions after the war and the government discouraged the activities of Kundt and other German officers in Bolivia. Kundt, however, became a Bolivian citizen in 1920 and ignored the warnings of German diplomats to refrain from involvement in the military affairs of the country (Bieber 1994, 91–92).

Bolivia had more German instructors than any other Latin American country except Argentina and Chile (Bieber 1994, 86). The German mission overhauled the training of the Bolivian military, focusing mostly on noncommissioned officers and soldiers. The number of officers declined, but officer salaries went up, which helped strengthen the officer corps (Dunkerley 2003, 131–132). In the 1920s, Kundt also reorganized the command structure of the military, creating new divisions (Díaz Arguedas 1971, 647). At the advice of the German mission, Bolivia bought large quantities of German weapons, spending five million marks on German military equipment from 1911–1913 alone (Bieber 1994, 97; Shesko 2012, 59). The Bolivian military gradually diversified its acquisitions, however, and Germany ceased to be its most important source of military equipment beginning in 1927 (Bieber 1994, 101).

The foreign military missions in Bolivia did not have the transformative impact that they had in some other countries. According to Díaz Arguedas (1971, 643), the French mission came to a premature end without achieving many of its aims or bringing much new to the Bolivian military. Dunkerley (2003, 128–129) suggests that it was "predictable that four [French] officers could not generate big changes, especially without the support of all of the establishment." The German mission reportedly had more of an impact, especially during its initial years (Díaz Arguedas 1971, 644, 648; Dunkerley 2003, 131). Nevertheless, it too encountered significant obstacles, including poorly educated and undisciplined soldiers and resistance from Bolivian officers who opposed the reforms and accused the missions of profiting unfairly at the expense of the Bolivian government.[5] Indeed, more than 150 officers signed a petition in 1926 that called for the government to prevent the return of Kundt to the country (Klein 1969b, 173). Opposition politicians, especially the Liberals, also bitterly criticized Kundt's involvement in politics and sought to resist the reforms.

Despite the professionalization efforts, the Bolivian military did not acquire a monopoly on violence in the early twentieth century. The number of revolts declined in the early twentieth century. Aside from a minor Conservative uprising in 1903, there were no revolts of significance during the first couple of decades of the twentieth century (Dunkerley 2003, 119). Yet in the 1920s, revolts began to occur again. Most of these rebellions were indigenous uprisings, but the Bolivian government also experienced major opposition revolts in 1920 and 1924. Revolts continued to take place frequently in the decades that followed, and some of them succeeded in toppling the government. These revolts subverted the rule of law, provoked state repression, and undermined the country's prospects for democracy.

The failure of the foreign missions to transform the Bolivian military became clear during the Chaco War, which Bolivia fought with Paraguay between 1932 and 1935. The Bolivian armed forces performed dismally in this war,

---

[5] Some Bolivian officers also preferred the French mission to the German one.

losing more than 50,000 men and 240,000 square kilometers of territory to a much smaller neighbor (Bieber 1994, 105).[6] According to Bieber (1994, 105), "if all of [Bolivia's military] investment had made sense, the war with Paraguay would have demonstrated it." The Chaco War further weakened the Bolivian military, destroying its morale and discipline and paving the way for more revolts in the decades that followed, including the Bolivian revolution of 1952.

WEAK PARTIES AND AUTHORITARIAN RULE IN BOLIVIA

The weakness of Bolivian parties also obstructed the emergence of democracy during the early twentieth century. Bolivian parties during this period were personalistic institutions, which had little in the way of ideology or organization. The parties were prone to splits and defections, and none of them developed an enduring following. Of the many parties that appeared in Bolivia in the late nineteenth or early twentieth century, only the Liberal Party lasted more than a few decades, and even it never held power after 1920.

For most of the nineteenth century, Bolivia had only loose electoral clubs and personalist electoral vehicles. Toward the end of the War in the Pacific (1879–1883), however, two main groups emerged that formed the basis of parties: the pacificists and the war hawks. Whereas the pacifists, who were led by southern elites, formed the Conservative Party, the war hawks, who came mostly from La Paz, Oruro, and Cochabamba, established the Liberal Party (Dunkerley 2003, 54–56; Irurozqui 1997, 404–405; Klein 1969b, 15, 19–21). The division over the war quickly faded, however, and the two parties ended up with relatively few ideological differences since they both represented the elites and sought to maintain the existing social and economic system. Conservatives were closer to the Catholic Church and Liberals embraced some of the standard postulates of nineteenth-century liberalism, but both parties relied more on personalistic than ideological linkages to the electorate (Dunkerley 2003, 61–62; Irurozqui 2000, 399–400; Klein 1969b, 22; Lora 1987, 95–97). As Bolivian president Bautista Saavedra wrote: "The [Conservative] Party has not been a conservative party, just like the so-called Liberal Party has not been a purely liberal grouping. In Bolivia, allegiances to people, to caudillos, more than principles, are what have determined the formation of political parties" (cited in Irurozqui 1997, 400).

The Conservative Party initially dominated, governing from 1884 to 1899, a period that became known as the Conservative oligarchy.[7] The party's initial electoral victories stemmed not from its organization or strong ties to the electorate but rather from the willingness of its wealthy leaders, such as the silver

---

[6] General Kundt presided over the most devastating defeats in this war and was relieved of his command as a result.

[7] The Conservative Party, which emerged from an 1884 alliance of the Democrat Party and the Constitutional Party, was sometimes known as the Constitutional Party or the National Party.

magnates Aniceto Arce and Gregorio Pacheco, to spend large sums to win elections (Dunkerley 2003, 58; Irurozqui 2000, 242).[8] Conservative victories were also facilitated by the fact that Bolivia restricted the franchise to literate male citizens above twenty-one years of age, which limited the number of votes they had to buy to win elections. During the nineteenth century, the number of votes cast in Bolivia never constituted more than 2.6 percent of the population.

Once the Conservative Party took office, it used its powers to ensure that it held on to the presidency and won a majority in Congress. Local-level authorities, especially the prefects, controlled the voting process during the nineteenth century, but the central government had a great deal of influence over these officials (Klein 1969b, 23). To help government-supported candidates, local authorities detained opposition leaders, purged the voter registries of opposition supporters, and blocked the access of opposition voters to the voting tables, while allowing government supporters to vote multiple times (Demélas 2003, 470). A popular saying at the time was "the prefect who doesn't win elections is not a prefect" (cited in Dunkerley 2003, 140).

The Liberal Party, which was the main opposition party during the period of Conservative dominance, did not have the organizational strength to resist the government's electoral manipulation. Nor did it have the resources to engage in electoral intervention on the same scale as the ruling party since it did not control as many local-level authorities or have equivalent access to state coffers. Like the Conservative Party, the Liberal Party was fragmented, personalistic, and weakly organized. The party had close ties to the armed forces, which provided its main leaders, but the army officers lacked the financial resources of the Conservative leaders. In the 1884 election, for example, Liberals spent only a third as much as each of the two Conservative candidates (Irurozqui 2000, 242).[9]

The Liberals complained frequently about the unfairness of the elections and called for reforms, but the only electoral reforms enacted during this period were relatively minor measures (Irurozqui 2000, 143, 173–174).[10] Although the Liberals typically had representation in the legislature, they did not control enough seats to pass major democratic reforms on their own.[11] The Liberals' lack of party discipline also impeded reform. For example, in 1888,

---

[8] Dunkerley (2003, 58) reports that Pacheco spent 3.5 million pesos and Arce another 3 million pesos on the 1884 campaign. The funds went to buy votes as well as pay for publicity and electoral agents (Klein 1969b, 21).

[9] The Conservatives also controlled more newspapers than the Liberals. In 1884, supporters of Pacheco had at least twenty-five newspapers, supporters of Arce had twenty-one, and the Liberals had eighteen (Irurozqui 2000, 241).

[10] Congress did debate a major electoral reform in 1883 that would have shifted the electoral system to proportional representation, but this reform proposal failed to win majority support (Irurozqui 2000, 143).

[11] The Liberals, for example, won thirty seats in congress, about two-fifths of the total, in 1884 (Irurozqui 2000, 237; Klein 1969b, 23).

their leader, General Eliodoro Camacho, presented legislation declaring that year's presidential elections to be null and void, but he failed to get support for it from many of the Liberals in the legislature (Irurozqui 2000, 249).

In response to government electoral interference, the Liberals sometimes abstained from elections. In 1892, for example, the Liberals boycotted the elections in various provinces, accusing the government of intimidating voters, attacking Liberal clubs, supplying false documents, liberating prisoners to allow them to vote, and cancelling the registrations of opposition supporters (Irurozqui 2000, 254–255). At other times, the Liberals resorted to uprisings, but these revolts deepened authoritarian rule since the Conservative governments typically reacted to them with repression. In the wake of the 1888 rebellion, for example, President Arce declared a state of siege, exiled prominent Liberal leaders, asserted his party's control over the legislature, and purged and even executed some rebellious officers (Dunkerley 2003, 65; Irurozqui 2000, 250). Similarly, after reports of planned Liberal uprisings in 1892, the government declared a state of siege, imprisoning and exiling Liberal leaders and expelling their members from Congress (Dunkerley 2003, 66–67; Irurozqui 2000, 256; Klein 1969b, 27).

The first major Liberal revolt occurred in September 1888 after Camacho lost the presidential elections to Arce amid allegations of widespread fraud (Aranzaes 1918, 330–333; Demélas 2003, 457; Dunkerley 2003, 65–66; Irurozqui 2000, 250). Liberals, with the support of some renegade troops, seized the presidential palace in Sucre, declaring Camacho to be president. President Arce escaped, disguised as a monk, and went to Cochabamba, where he assembled a force of 1,000 men, which defeated the rebels (Aranzaes 1918, 330–333; Dunkerley 2003, 65–66). Another major Liberal rebellion occurred in 1890 when General Camacho, who had been exiled to Peru in the aftermath of the previous revolt, returned to Bolivia with some insurgents (Aranzaes 1918, 334–335). Liberals then rose up in various provinces, but the government managed to suppress these revolts (Aranzaes 1918, 335–337; Dunkerley 2003, 66).

The Liberals did not take power until the end of the century when Colonel José M. Pando spearheaded a successful revolt. The Liberals rebelled partly in response to a government decision to make Sucre the permanent capital of the country, which antagonized the citizens of La Paz.[12] The Bolivian military's small size, poor training, and lack of equipment contributed to its defeat, as did the fact that the Liberals were able to win the support of numerous indigenous communities. In addition, at the outset of the conflict, President Severo Fernández Alonso dismissed officers and troops that had ties to La Paz because of concerns about their loyalty, which reduced the size of the Bolivian military by approximately one-third (Shesko 2012, 39).

---

[12] A worldwide decline in silver prices had also provoked a destabilizing economic crisis that undermined the government of Severo Fernández Alonso (Dunkerley 2003, 89–90).

Once in power, the Liberals abandoned many of the ideological stances they had taken as an opposition party, including support for federalism, democratic reform, and individual rights. Instead, they engaged in the same electoral abuses that they had decried when they were in the opposition (Klein 1969b, 37, 40). In the 1904 elections, for example, President Pando intervened to support the election of Ismael Montes despite his pledge of noninterference. The opposition accused the government of blocking the registration of opposition supporters and preventing the exercise of the secret ballot, among other infractions (Irurozqui 2000, 267).

Opposition parties, however, were too weak to defeat the Liberals or resist electoral manipulation. The Conservatives had failed to build a strong party organization during their period in power and they gradually disintegrated after being overthrown (Dunkerley 2003, 60; Irurozqui 2000, 243; Klein 1969b, 23). Some Conservatives joined or allied with the ruling Liberals, while others ran as independents or retired from political life altogether (Shesko 2012, 175). The Conservatives presented presidential candidates in 1904 and 1909, but they won relatively few votes, and the party soon disappeared (Irurozqui 2000, 268, 275–276).[13]

New opposition parties arose from within the Liberal Party, but these parties were also too weak to compete with the Liberals or prevent electoral manipulation. The party's first major split came shortly after they took power when the so-called Puritan Liberals broke from the party and ran their own presidential candidate in 1904. The Puritans criticized the government for its intervention in elections as well as the Liberals' other departures from their traditional principles. Montes, however, easily won the 1904 elections with 76 percent of the vote, and in the years that followed, he gradually asserted his control of the Liberal Party. He resisted building a strong party organization, which enabled him to control party nominations and win a second presidential term in 1913. The Puritans, meanwhile, disintegrated.

A more consequential split occurred in 1914 when various prominent Liberals, including Bautista Saavedra and Daniel Salamanca, broke with Montes during his second term as president and formed the Republican Party. The government responded to this new threat with harsh repression, declaring a state of siege, exiling forty opposition leaders, and shutting down thirteen newspapers. The new party denounced the repression and called for "free elections, an independent parliament and a judiciary free from executive influence," but the Republicans did not have the power to resist the measures or to enact democratic reforms (Klein 1969b, 48–49; Chávez Zamorano, Paredes Zárate, and Velasco Agular 2007, 278–280). Nor did the Republican Party have the organization or the following necessary to win elections in the face of electoral intervention by the government. Although the Republicans achieved some

---

[13] Dunkerley (2003, 136) suggests that the Conservative Party was virtually extinct by 1905.

successes in municipal elections, their performance in national elections was disappointing. In the 1917 presidential elections, the Republican candidate, José M. Escalier, won only 8,904 votes, which was 11 percent of the total votes cast (Irurozqui 2000, 299; Chávez Zamorano, Paredes Zárate, and Velasco Agular 2007, 284).[14] According to various reports, the Liberals ensured their victory with their usual mix of vote buying, fraud, and intimidation, even organizing a paramilitary force, called the White Guard, to harass the opposition (Dunkerley 2003, 144; Irurozqui 2000, 298; Shesko 2012, 180).[15]

In the wake of these losses and the burning of an opposition newspaper's headquarters by a Liberal mob, the Republicans declared they would abstain from the 1920 elections (Dunkerley 2003, 144; Klein 1969b, 57).[16] At the same time, some Republicans began to plot to overthrow the Liberal government, which had been weakened by internal splits. The Republican leader Bautista Saavedra had been in contact with military officers since 1918, but he initially received little support from them for his plans (Dunkerley 2003, 145–146; Shesko 2012, 188–189). In July 1920, however, some key army colonels and junior officers joined the conspiracy and carried out a successful revolt, installing Saavedra in the presidential palace with little bloodshed.

The Republican seizure of power did not bring democracy to Bolivia. Instead, Saavedra and his allies practiced the same electoral manipulation they had denounced when they were in the opposition. Saavedra also consolidated power by creating his own military organization, the Republican Guard, establishing his own party newspaper, and building up a personal following, especially among urban workers (Klein 1969b, 65). The Saavedra administration did enact electoral reforms in 1920 and 1924 that overhauled the electoral registries, created citizen commissions to oversee the elections, and established minority representation through the incomplete list, but these measures failed to bring an end to government electoral intervention (Chávez Zamorano, Paredes Zárate, and Velasco Agular 2007, 298–311; Irurozqui 2000, 312–313; Whitehead 1981, 316).

Opposition parties remained too weak and fragmented to resist government electoral manipulation. Saavedra's main rivals within the Republicans Party, José María Escalier and Daniel Salamanca, quickly became disenchanted with his government and founded the Genuine Republican Party in July 1921, but the new party lacked organization and a social base. Moreover, the opposition was divided between the Genuine Republicans and the Liberals. The opposition grew somewhat stronger over time thanks to defections from the

---

[14] In 1916, only three Republicans were elected to the Chamber of Deputies and none to the Senate, and in 1918 the Republicans only won ten seats in congress (Klein 1969b, 52, 54).

[15] Elections during this period were relatively violent with both sides organizing clubs to try to take control of the squares where elections were held (Klein 1969b, 50–51; Dunkerley 2003, 140).

[16] The decision to abstain, however, was not supported by Salamanca and the Republican Party committees of Oruro and Potosí (Irurozqui 2000, 304).

ruling party, and it even briefly captured control of Congress in late 1922, but Saavedra responded by dissolving the legislature and calling for new elections in May 1923 (Dunkerley 2003, 160; Klein 1969b, 82–83). Saavedra's determination to intervene in these elections and his decision to exile many Genuine Republican leaders led most of the opposition to abstain from these elections and, as a result, the ruling party gained firm control of the legislature (Dunkerley 2003, 180; Klein 1969b, 83).

The inability of the opposition to compete electorally in the face of Saavedra's authoritarian maneuvers led it to encourage the military to overthrow the president (Dunkerley 2003, 155; Shesko 2012, 198). The first such attempt came shortly after Saavedra was sworn in as president in January 1921, when one of the leaders of the July 1920 coup rebelled. Another military mutiny occurred in March 1921, which was quickly followed by a popular rebellion of 3,000 indigenous peasants in Jesús de Machaca (Dunkerley 2003, 167–168; Shesko 2012, 200–203). Further plots and revolts took place in the years that followed. In February 1924, for example, the opposition torched the barracks of the Republican Guard and a Liberal general staged a rebellion in Yacuiba on the frontier (Dunkerley 2003, 165; Shesko 2012, 212). Even more threatening, in July 1924 Genuine Republican leaders enlisted the support of five army colonels and mounted a major secessionist rebellion in Santa Cruz (Dunkerley 2003, 165–166; Shesko 2012, 212).

Saavedra responded to all of these revolts with further repression (Dunkerley 2003, 159). As a result, Bolivia was under a state of emergency for 890 days during Saavedra's four-year term, as opposed to only 222 days during the previous twenty-one years of Liberal rule (Klein 1969b, 84). Saavedra also brought back the German General Hans Kundt as chief of staff of the armed forces in February 1921, and Kundt began to weed out opponents of the government from the military and erect a network of spies to detect any conspiracies within it (Bieber 1994, 88–89; Loveman and Davies Jr. 1978, 57; Dunkerley 2003, 162–164, 194). In addition, the president slashed the size and budget of the army, while building up his Republican Guard so that it was a larger, better paid, and better equipped force (Dunkerley 2003, 160–161; Shesko 2012, 208). Although these measures did not bring an end to the revolts, they helped the president complete his term.

Toward the end of his term, Saavedra sought to extend his mandate, but even his own party refused to go along, which led him to turn to a largely unknown loyalist, José Gabino Villanueva, to run as his successor. Thanks in part to the government's electoral interference, Villanueva won the May 1925 election easily, earning 45,826 votes to 8,252 votes for Daniel Salamanca, the candidate of the Genuine Republicans (Irurozqui 2000, 317). After the election, however, Villanueva began to demonstrate some political independence, leading Saavedra to call out the troops in La Paz to pressure the legislature to nullify the election on the grounds of a technicality. Congress agreed to hold new elections in December 1925, but Saavedra's own party obliged him to accept

Hernando Siles as the party's presidential candidate, even though Siles was a rival whom Saavedra had exiled in 1923 (Dunkerley 2003, 171; Klein 1969b, 85–86). Under pressure from Saavedra, Siles agreed to sign a document pledging to respect party discipline and to allow Saavedra's brother to run as the party's vice-presidential candidate (Klein 1969b, 85). The opposition abstained from the December 1925 elections because of concerns about electoral manipulation, which enabled Siles to win unopposed (Irurozqui 2000, 318).

Once in office, Siles moved to consolidate his power, employing the same authoritarian measures as his predecessors. The Siles administration, for example, harassed the opposition, maintained a state of siege for most of his tenure, and intervened in elections regularly to ensure the ruling party's dominance (Klein 1969b, 95, 107).[17] To strengthen his hold on power, Siles also dismantled Saavedra's Republican Guard and staffed the military with his supporters, such as General Kundt and Colonel David Toro (Klein 1969b, 88; Dunkerley 2003, 172–173). Siles formed his own party, which became known as the Nationalist Party, but he kept it weak and largely under his control. In addition, he sent Vice-President Abdón Saavedra on a diplomatic tour and then encouraged demonstrations to prevent him from returning.

The opposition parties initially cooperated with the Siles administration, but they quickly became disaffected with the president's authoritarian ways. The weakness and fragmentation of the opposition parties, however, made it impossible for them to resist government electoral intervention or enact reforms.[18] Instead, the opposition mostly abstained from elections and began to plot to overthrow the government (Dunkerley 2003, 177; Klein 1969b, 107). Siles claimed in 1927 that there had already been fourteen attempts on his life (Dunkerley 2003, 177). The government responded to these plots and protests with repression, imposing a state of siege, shutting down opposition newspapers, and exiling opposition leaders, including Ismail Montes (Klein 1969b, 95, 107). When an indigenous rebellion began in Chayanta, Potosí in 1927 and grew to include more than 100,000 people around the country, the government responded with even harsher repression, leading to the deaths or imprisonment of hundreds of indigenous people (Shesko 2012, 215).

With the support of General Kundt and Colonel Toro, Siles managed to retain the backing of the military for most of his tenure. As his term came to an end, however, Siles called for a constituent assembly with the aim of revising the constitution to permit him to stay in power. Siles then resigned and handed power over to a council of ministers, which called for elections for this constituent assembly to be held in June 1930 (Klein 1969b, 109). This move

---

[17] Thanks to electoral manipulation, the Nationalist Party won twenty-one of thirty-four congressional seats and four of seven senate seats in the May 1927 elections – it also won a majority in the 1929 congressional and municipal elections (Dunkerley 2003, 186; Klein 1969b, 95, 107).

[18] One faction of the Republican Party, the so-called Government Republicans, supported Siles for most of his tenure (Klein 1969b, 109).

immediately prompted riots and protests as well as an armed rebellion by forty leftists who invaded from Argentina (Klein 1969b, 109). Opposition parties and politicians, along with military dissidents, also accelerated their plotting against the regime (Klein 1969b, 109). On June 25, a violent revolt broke out in various cities, and the rebels, who included armed students as well as military officers and cadets, seized power after three days of fighting. Siles, along with Kundt and Toro, fled into exile. The military coup did not bring democracy to Bolivia, however. Indeed, Bolivia continued to be plagued by political instability and authoritarianism in the years that followed.

Thus, the weakness of the military and parties hindered democratization in Bolivia during the nineteenth and early twentieth century. The military's weakness led to frequent revolts throughout the nineteenth century, which prompted authoritarian clampdowns. Efforts in the early twentieth century to strengthen the military brought a temporary end to revolts, but they resurged beginning in the 1920s, which further undermined the rule of law. The weakness of opposition parties, meanwhile, made it difficult for them to compete in elections, resist government electoral manipulation, and enact democratic reforms. Instead, opposition parties often boycotted elections and/or sought to overthrow the government by force. Even where these revolts were successful, they did not lead to democratization, however, since opposition parties that took power via force tended to use the same tactics as their predecessors to maintain themselves in power.

THE MILITARY AND REBELLIONS IN ECUADOR

During the nineteenth and early twentieth century, Ecuador, like Bolivia, was an unstable authoritarian regime. The government regularly manipulated elections, the country's military was weak, and the state barely penetrated many areas of the geographically fragmented country. As a result, the opposition frequently sought power via armed revolts and sometimes managed to overthrow the government.

Ecuador in the nineteenth century was a relatively poor country, which could not afford to arm and maintain a large modern military. According to data from the Maddison Project, Ecuador's GDP per capita in the late nineteenth century was the lowest in South America (there are no data on GDP for Bolivia and Paraguay during this period), ranking significantly below Colombia and Peru (Bolt et al. 2018). Ecuador had extensive foreign debts left over from the wars of independence, but it could not afford to pay them, which foreclosed its access to foreign loans. Moreover, the country's tax collection system was woefully inadequate (Rodríguez 1985, 53–55, 73–75).

Military spending initially represented more than 50 percent of the state's budget, but the government reduced it, and by the late nineteenth century it typically constituted less than 30 percent (Rodríguez 1985, 223–224). The military cutbacks meant that the troops often had shortages of weaponry and those weapons they did have were poorly maintained (Quintero López and Silva 1991, 82). There were also efforts to reduce the number of officers since officer pay constituted the bulk of military expenditures (Quintero López and Silva 1991, 82). President Diego Noboa cut 163 officers from the force in the early 1850s because of fiscal pressures (Spindler 1987, 44).

In addition, Ecuadorian governments pared down the number of troops. In the wake of independence from Gran Colombia, the military had 1,300 soldiers, many of them from Colombia or Venezuela, but by order of Congress the size of the army fell to under 1,000 in 1847 (Arancibia Clavel 2002, 158–159; Ayala Mora 2011, 172). As late as 1894, the army had only 1,777 troops (Martínez Bucheli 2017, 16). Soldiers were recruited primarily from the poorest sectors, often by force, and were only paid intermittently (Scheina 2003, 141). As a result, military discipline was poor and mutinies were common (Van Aken 1989, 47–48, 55, 287). In the words of one historian, soldiers of this period were "hungry, naked, and immoral" (cited in Van Aken 1989, 54).

Some Ecuadorian politicians sought to keep the army small, not just because of fiscal concerns but also because of fears of excessive military influence and intervention (Van Aken 1989, 46–47). These concerns led Congress to ban military men from serving as legislators and even from voting at times (Van Aken 1989, 57, 100). They also led the government to create a national guard in the 1830s to serve as a counterweight to the military. By 1858, the national guard consisted of more than 18,000 troops, although they tended to be poorly trained and equipped and did not operate with any regularity (Ayala Mora 2011, 116–121, 182).[19]

Throughout the nineteenth century, promotions in the military were based mostly on political affiliations and personal connections, rather than education or experience. Numerous presidents sought to restructure the military and ensure its loyalty by elevating officers who belonged to their political party or faction, while removing or marginalizing those from other parties or factions (Bravo, Macías Núñez, and Aguilar Echeverría 2005, 8–9). Rebel victories in civil wars typically led to wholesale purges of the military.

There were periodic efforts to professionalize the military but none of them prospered. A Military College was opened in 1838, but it only had a few students and shut down in 1845 (Arancibia Clavel 2002, 159; Romero y Cordero 1991, 147–154; Van Aken 1989, 109, 129, 307–308). In the 1860s, President Gabriel García Moreno sought unsuccessfully to find foreign military officers to help professionalize the country's military; when this effort failed, in part because of a lack of funds, he imported some weaponry and created a

---

[19] All Ecuadorian males between sixteen and sixty were required to register for the national guard, but indigenous people and slaves were exempted because the government was reluctant to arm and train them (Ayala Mora 2011, 117). In 1861, García Moreno enacted a new law regulating the national guard, while cutting the size of the military and imposing stricter discipline on it (Henderson 2008, 150–151; Romero y Cordero 1991, 269–270; Spindler 1987, 64).

school for military cadets (Henderson 2008, 150–151). The military academy was closed after his death in 1875, however, and did not reopen until 1892 (Lauderbaugh 2012, 65; Arancibia Clavel 2002, 159). The irregular functioning of military academies meant that even upper-level officers often lacked a military education (Arancibia Clavel 2002, 161).

The lack of resources, politicization, and frequent disruption of the military prevented it from developing into a strong national institution in the nineteenth century. This, in turn, made it difficult for the government to defend itself against external or internal threats. As a result, Ecuador lost the brief wars or skirmishes it fought against Colombia and Peru during the late nineteenth and early twentieth century. These losses further debilitated the country's armed forces.

The weakness of the military encouraged frequent internal revolts. As Table 8.2 indicates, between 1830 and 1899, Ecuador suffered more than a dozen major revolts and countless small rebellions. The revolts, which sometimes dragged on for months or even years, typically pitted Liberals against Conservatives but sometimes involved fighting between different factions of the same party. Opposition leaders, many of whom had military backgrounds, typically commanded the rebel troops, who consisted of members of civilian militias, the police, and paramilitary forces as well as soldiers or regiments that defected from the regular army or had formerly served in it. Foreign countries, especially Colombia and Peru, sometimes helped finance or arm the rebels, and often provided an embarkment point for invasions.

The revolts undermined the prospects for democracy in Ecuador. Owing to the relative weakness of the Ecuadorian military, the opposition sometimes triumphed in these revolts. Indeed, on eight occasions between 1830 and 1899, the opposition overthrew the government and took power via armed rebellion, thus subverting constitutional rule. The revolts also typically provoked state repression. Ecuadorian constitutions gave the president emergency powers in the event of "internal commotion" and presidents used these powers frequently (Loveman 1993).[20] President Antonio Borrero, for example, declared a state of siege for four months in 1876 in the wake of an insurrection (Loveman 1993, 197). At times, presidents went beyond what was permitted by the constitution. President Vicente Rocafuerte established a policy of executing captured rebel officers without trial and exiling all rebels who surrendered without fighting (Van Aken 1989, 98). García Moreno also executed rebel leaders and sought to weed out potentially rebellious officers with whippings and banishments (Van Aken 1989, 269).

After the 1895 Liberal Revolution, the new president, Eloy Alfaro, took more significant steps to professionalize the military and to acquire a monopoly on the use of force. In 1899, the Alfaro government issued a decree requiring

---

[20] Gabriel García Moreno's 1869 constitution enabled the government to suspend virtually all individual rights in case of internal strife (Loveman 1993, 195).

TABLE 8.2 *Major revolts in Ecuador, 1830–1930*

Year	Description of revolt	Type of revolt (outcome)
1830–1832	*Secession from Gran Colombia.* General Juan José Flores, the governor of Ecuador, sides with secessionists in Quito. Flores becomes president.	Military coup (took power)
1833–1834	*War of the Chihuahuas.* Liberals led by Vicente Rocafuerte rebelled with support of the navy. They were defeated, but Rocafuerte was promised the presidency. 900 deaths.	Elite insurrection (suppressed)
1834–1835	Ecuadorian exiles led by José Felix Valdivieso and General Isidoro Barriga invaded Ecuador, but the government crushed 2,000 rebels at the Battle of Miñaruca.	Elite insurrection (suppressed)
1845	*March Revolution.* Guayaquil-based Liberals rebelled and defeated the government army. Vicente Ramón Roca, a Conservative, became president.	Elite insurrection (took power)
1850	Liberal General José María Urbina pushed out President Manuel Ascásubi. Diego Noboa became president in a peaceful transition.	Military coup (took power)
1851	General José María Urbina and other Liberal generals overthrew President Noboa. General Urbina became president.	Military coup (took power)
1852	General Juan José Flores invaded from Peru with a small flotilla and 700 men. The rebels attacked Guayaquil, but they were driven off by the army.	Elite insurrection (suppressed)
1859–1860	Conservatives rebelled in Quito. After an extended civil war and shifts in power, Conservative Gabriel García Moreno became president.	Elite insurrection (took power)
1869	Gabriel García Moreno organized a coup to overthrow President Javier Espinosa and prevent free elections. García Moreno became president.	Military coup (took power)
1871	Fernando Daquilema led an indigenous rebellion in Riobamba that was suppressed by well-armed government troops.	Popular uprising (suppressed)
1876	General Ignacio Veintemilla, the military commander of Guayaquil, rebelled and took power with the support of Liberals, overthrowing President Borrero. 1,000 deaths.	Military coup (took power)
1877	Conservatives led by General Manuel Santiago Yépez rebelled but were defeated by the government after twenty hours of fighting.	Elite insurrection (suppressed)
1882–1883	*War of the Restoration.* Liberals and Conservatives overthrew General Veintemilla after he declared himself dictator. They elected a Conservative president, José Caamaño.	Elite insurrection (took power)

TABLE 8.2 *(continued)*

Year	Description of revolt	Type of revolt (outcome)
1886–1887	Eloy Alfaro and his Liberal supporters attempted to overthrow President Caamaño in various uprisings, but they were defeated.	Elite insurrection (suppressed)
1895	Eloy Alfaro and Liberals overthrew Conservatives with indigenous support. Alfaro became president. 1,000 deaths.	Elite insurrection (took power)
1896	Conservatives revolted at various locations and seized the town of Cuenca, but the government suppressed the rebellions.	Elite insurrection (suppressed)
1898–1899	Conservatives revolted at numerous locations. At the Battle of Sanancajas, the government defeated 1,300 rebels. 437 deaths.	Elite insurrection (suppressed)
1906	The Campaign of Twenty Days. Military garrisons revolted and overthrew President Lizardo Garcia and restored Eloy Alfaro to the presidency. 1,000 casualties.	Military coup (took power)
1911	The president-elect Emilio Estrada led a popular revolt after Eloy Alfaro sought to block him from taking power. Alfaro went into exile, and Estrada became president.	Elite insurrection (took power)
1911–1912	War of the Generals. Eloy Alfaro, Flavio Alfaro, and Pedro Montero revolted against the government. They were defeated in bloody fighting and subsequently killed by a mob.	Elite insurrection (suppressed)
1913–1916	Colonel Carlos Concha Torres, a supporter of Alfaro, launched a lengthy guerrilla uprising in Esmeraldas. It petered out after he was captured.	Elite insurrection (suppressed)
1914	Colonel Carlos Andrade and his brothers invaded Ecuador from Colombia with an army of 600 rebels, but they were defeated by the government.	Elite insurrection (suppressed)
1924	Jacinto Jijón y Caamaño led a Conservative revolt of 1,000 men in response to fraud in the 1924 presidential election. They were defeated with forty-nine killed.	Elite insurrection (suppressed)
1925	July Revolution. Junior military officers overthrew the government of Gonzalo Córdova and established a provisional military/civilian junta.	Military coup (took power)

Source: Latin American Revolts Database.

that people turn in any state-owned weapons or munitions that were in their possession (Moncayo Gallegos 1995, 152). That same year, the Ecuadorian military sent some officers to enroll in a military academy in Chile, and it also hired a Chilean military mission to train officers in Ecuador (Arancibia Clavel

2002, 190–196). At the instigation of the Chilean mission, the government created a few new schools, including a military preparatory school, a war academy, and a school for noncommissioned officers, and they sought to model the training in these schools along Prussian lines. These schools, which did not charge tuition and admitted students based on merit, attracted many officers from the middle classes (Moncayo Gallegos 1995, 152–154; Fitch 1977, 17).

The efforts at professionalization continued in subsequent administrations. The Chilean mission trained officers in Ecuador until 1916, and the Ecuadorian military continued to send officers to study in Chile until 1928, dispatching approximately 100 Ecuadorian officers there (Arancibia Clavel 2002, 212, 261–266). In addition, Chile sold a variety of military equipment to Ecuador, including rapid-fire artillery, torpedoes, submarine mines, and radiotelegraphic equipment, and Ecuador began to purchase sophisticated weaponry from France and Germany as well (Arancibia Clavel 2002, 212). With the assistance of the Chilean mission, the government of General Leonidas Plaza (1901–1905) also drew up a new Organic Law of the Military regulating the entire functioning of the Ecuadorian military including promotions, retirement, and salaries – this law remained in force until 1923 (Arancibia Clavel 2002, 200). The new regulations prohibited battlefield promotions, banned solders from joining parties or electoral clubs, established military pensions, and made military service obligatory (Moncayo Gallegos 1995, 155; Fitch 1977, 15).

The professionalization efforts were financed in part by the export boom that Ecuador experienced in the late nineteenth and early twentieth century. Exports grew at an annual rate of 5.6 percent between 1870 and 1929, one of the higher rates in South America (Bértola and Ocampo 2013, 86). The export growth made it possible to pay for a sharp increase in military spending at the end of the nineteenth century. Military expenditures rose to 42 percent of all government spending in 1899 and 1900, up from 24.9 percent in 1893 (Rodríguez 1985, 224). Nevertheless, Ecuador remained a poor country, which could scarcely afford extensive investments in the military. Indeed, in 1900, GDP per capita was still only $594 (Bolt et al. 2018). Not surprisingly, military expenditures as a percentage of total expenditures declined sharply in 1902 and remained low in the years that followed (Rodríguez 1985, 224–225). The government gradually reduced the size of the standing army and reduced officer pay, causing military salaries to fall behind those of civilian employees (Fitch 1977, 16).

The professionalization efforts failed to transform the Ecuadorian military. Indeed, the Ecuadorian army remained highly politicized in the first few decades of the twentieth century, and senior Ecuadorian officers continued to be promoted, demoted, and discharged based on their personal and political affiliations (Fitch 1977, 16). Romero y Cordero (1991, 380–383) suggests that the long-term influence of the Chilean mission was relatively superficial, and even Arancibia Clavel (2002, 267) acknowledges that the Chilean efforts took a while to bear fruit. The Chileans encountered a great deal of resistance to their efforts to reshape the Ecuadorian military. Some Ecuadorian officers opposed the Chilean mission for nationalistic reasons or because it threatened their interests. The Head of the Chilean Legation in 1906 complained that the Ecuadorian soldiers were not accustomed to working as much as the Chileans demanded, but he also acknowledged that the Chilean officers at times behaved badly and lacked sensitivity (Arancibia Clavel 2002, 206–208).

As a result, the Ecuadorian military remained relatively weak and could not bring an end to revolts. The opposition continued to carry out numerous rebellions during the first two decades of the twentieth century, and some of these revolts were successful. Rebels overthrew the government in 1906 and 1911, and nearly did so again in the bloody 1911–1912 civil war. The military also had a very difficult time suppressing a guerrilla rebellion that ravaged the province of Esmeraldas from 1913 to 1916, and some blamed the Chilean mission for not teaching tactics that were appropriate for jungle warfare (Macías Núñez 2012, 43–44). The continued revolts not only created political instability but they also prompted state repression. Eloy Alfaro, for example, created an informal secret police, known as *garroteros* (thugs), to ferret out insubordination and intimidate the opposition (Loveman 1993, 201; Lauderbaugh 2012, 89, 91–92).

Beginning in the 1920s, however, the cycle of opposition rebellions began to come to an end. Although there were a few opposition revolts after 1916, the military easily and rapidly crushed these rebellions (Rodríguez 1985, 37). The gradual strengthening of the armed forces, which continued with the arrival of an Italian mission in 1922, helped bring an end to these revolts by reducing the likelihood that the opposition could prevail. In addition, improvements in state capacity and infrastructure, such as the railroads, made it easier for the government to mobilize troops quickly, transport them where they were needed, and communicate with them in the field. Finally, the memories of the bloody civil war of 1911–1912 helped dissuade the opposition from launching further insurrections. In this war, both sides had highly lethal modern weapons, including repeating rifles and machine guns, that left an estimated 3,000 people dead in one month of fighting in January 1912 (Rodríguez 1985, 49). The slaughter, which culminated in the mob lynching of opposition leaders, including Eloy Alfaro, shocked and horrified many Ecuadorians, thus reducing the appeal of the armed struggle.

WEAK PARTIES AND AUTHORITARIAN RULE IN ECUADOR

Although the professionalization of the military eventually brought an end to opposition revolts, it did not bring democracy to Ecuador. Ecuador remained firmly under authoritarian rule during the early twentieth century in large part because of the weakness of the country's parties. Throughout the nineteenth and early twentieth century, opposition parties were too weak to overcome government electoral manipulation or enact democratic reforms. Instead, the opposition often boycotted elections and/or resorted to violent uprisings.

For most of the nineteenth century, Ecuador lacked parties altogether. Personalist leaders dominated Ecuadorian politics during this period, and these leaders tended to eschew party building, preferring to concentrate power in their persons rather than diffuse it through parties and institutions. Gabriel García Moreno, for example, strengthened the powers of the executive and reformed Ecuador's electoral laws to consolidate his hold on power (Henderson 2008, 57–60; Spindler 1987, 58–59). His 1869 constitution extended the presidential term to six years, permitted presidential reelection, and allowed presidents to appoint mayors and governors and to declare a state of siege without consulting Congress (Lauderbaugh 2012, 64). Although García Moreno and other personalist leaders, such as Juan José Flores, held power for a long time, their movements disintegrated as soon as the leaders died since they lacked organizational structures.

Although leaders during the nineteenth century often came to power via armed revolts, they typically sought to legitimize their rule through elections.[21] Ecuadorian governments thus held elections regularly but intervened in these elections to ensure that their preferred candidates won. According to Van Aken (1989, 140), "intimidation of voters and candidates, violation of the secrecy of voting, and improper manipulation of electoral assemblies were among the methods used by the government to maintain control." Until 1860, the franchise was limited to literate Ecuadorian males who met certain economic requirements. This significantly reduced the size of the electorate – less than 0.5 percent of the population voted in 1830 – which made it easier for the government to control elections (Quintero López and Silva 1991, 100).

The opposition often protested government electoral manipulation, but its lack of organization and close linkages to the electorate made it difficult to overcome government intervention and compete in elections. Nor did the opposition control enough seats in the legislature to enact democratic reforms.[22] Between independence and 1874, opposition candidates won only 23 percent of the vote in presidential elections on average, and the margin between the victor and the runner-up averaged 60 percent. In no presidential election during this period did an opposition candidate win. Although the opposition did occasionally take power via armed rebellion, once they came to power, they typically resorted to the same electoral manipulation that they had decried previously while in the opposition.

Parties first emerged in Ecuador during the 1880s and they gradually developed constituencies and basic organizational structures (Rodríguez 1985, 45; McDonald and Ruhl 1989, 309; Ayala Mora 1989, 12–18; 1982). Two of the

---

[21] Many of these leaders described themselves or were described by others as conservatives or liberals, but they predated the founding of the Conservative and Liberal parties.

[22] The opposition did achieve occasional victories, such as when it managed to persuade the legislature, which was dominated by pro-government members, to annul the fraudulent elections in Cuenca in 1840, but these victories tended to be short lived (Van Aken 1989, 141).

parties – the Conservative Party and the Liberal Party – proved enduring, surviving into the twenty-first century. The parties were led by and represented elites, but they drew increasing support from the masses over time and they had distinctive ideologies and bases of support. The Conservative Party, which had its main base in the highlands, advocated strong church–state ties and relied heavily on the organizational support of the Catholic Church. The Liberal Party, which was stronger on the coast, pushed for the secularization of the state and enjoyed the backing of the Masonry. A third party, the Progressive Party, arose from a split within the Conservative Party in the 1880s and sought to carve out a middle path, but it disintegrated after it lost power in 1895.

The emergence of parties initially helped bring about greater electoral competition. Legislative elections were hotly contested during the late 1880s and early 1890s, and the legislature was divided relatively evenly between Conservatives and Liberals and/or Progressives (Quintero López and Silva 1991, 209). Presidential elections were also at times vigorously contested. In 1883 a constituent assembly that had thirty-five conservatives and twenty-seven liberals had to go through multiple rounds of voting before electing the Conservative leader, José María Caamaño, as interim president (Spindler 1987, 117–118). The assembly then drafted a new constitution that represented a democratic advance in that it mandated direct presidential elections. As a result, the elections in 1888 and 1892 took place via popular vote. Although the 1888 election was a lopsided contest, the 1892 elections represented the most vigorously contested election to date, with Dr. Luis Cordero, the candidate of the governing Progressives, prevailing over the candidate of the Conservatives with 58 percent of the vote.

Even in the late nineteenth century, however, most elections continued to be marred by government manipulation, which the opposition was powerless to prevent. For example, the government shut down Liberal newspapers and harassed Liberal leaders in the run-up to the 1883 constituent assembly elections (Spindler 1987, 150). Similarly, President Caamaño intervened extensively in the 1888 elections, using fraud as well as violence to ensure the victory of his brother-in-law, Dr. Antonio Flores of the Progressive Party, with 96 percent of the vote. One newspaper reported that "there were more gun shots than votes" in this election (Ayala Mora 1982, 191–192). Flores, who had been serving as a diplomat in Europe during the campaign, offered to resign when he found out about the extent of the electoral abuses, but Congress rejected his resignation (Spindler 1987, 126). Four years later, the Conservative opposition accused the Flores administration of fraud in the closely contested 1892 election, although the evidence in this case is not entirely clear (Ayala Mora 1982, 194–196; Reyes 1982, 183; Spindler 1987, 137–138).

The opposition, meanwhile, continued to carry out revolts throughout most of this period, taking advantage of the relative weakness of the military. Conservatives rebelled unsuccessfully against the liberal General Ignacio Veintemilla in 1877, and then joined forces with disaffected liberals in

1882–1883 to oust Veintemilla in the War of Restoration. The most persistent rebel was the Liberal leader Eloy Alfaro, who led more than a dozen revolts against the government beginning in the 1860s before finally overthrowing the Cordero administration in the 1895 Liberal Revolution. These revolts prompted further state repression, including the exile, imprisonment, and even execution of opposition leaders (Spindler 1987, 155).

Once in power, Alfaro engaged in the same types of electoral abuses and repressive activities that he had protested while in the opposition. He jailed and exiled his opponents and used his secret police to harass the media and leaders of the opposition (Spindler 1987, 195; Lauderbaugh 2012, 89). Alfaro convened elections for a constituent assembly, but he banned the clergy from participating, leading the Conservative Party to boycott the elections (Spindler 1987, 169–170; Ayala Mora 1994, 112–114). As a result, Alfaro's supporters won the vast majority of the seats in the constituent assembly and promptly elected him interim and then constitutional president. Subsequent elections that Alfaro presided over, such as the 1901 and 1906 presidential elections, were also rigged. In the 1901 election, Alfaro picked his right-hand man, General Leonidas Plaza, as the party's presidential nominee, and Plaza then won with 88 percent of the vote in an election that the Conservatives denounced as fraudulent (Ayala Mora 1994, 131). In the 1906 elections to the National Assembly, the government again intervened to ensure that supporters of Alfaro won. The assembly then overwhelmingly elected Alfaro for a second term, even though the new constitution called for direct elections (Spindler 1987, 197-198).

Opposition parties protested the electoral abuses and repression, but they were too weak to prevent or overcome them. The Progressive Party fell apart after the Liberal Revolution of 1895, and while the Conservative Party held together, it did not have the organizational strength or partisan ties to compete on a tilted playing field. It abstained from presidential elections until 1912 and fared poorly in the elections it participated in thereafter. During the Liberal era, the main electoral competition came from within the Liberal Party, but even it was quite muted. In the twenty years of Liberal dominance (1895–1924), the winning presidential candidate won by an average of 93.6 percent of the vote.

Because the military remained weak, the opposition during the Liberal era continued to focus to a large extent on the armed struggle. Conservatives, for example, carried out major revolts in 1896 and 1898–1899, but neither of these were successful. More threatening were the revolts from within the Liberal Party. Soon after nominating Plaza as his successor in 1901, Alfaro broke with his erstwhile ally and sought to force his resignation before Congress could confirm his election. Plaza refused to resign, however, and used his influence in the military and Congress to prevail over Alfaro who was then marginalized from power.[23] Plaza engineered the election of his successor, Lizardo García,

---

[23] Under Plaza, state repression declined, although electoral manipulation continued.

in 1905, but García had scarcely taken office when Alfaro overthrew him in a brief but bloody revolt. Alfaro managed to serve out most of his second term as president despite various plots and revolts against him, and nominated his old friend, Emilio Estrada, to succeed him in 1911. Shortly after Estrada's election, however, Alfaro again regretted his choice and sought to persuade Estrada to withdraw. When Estrada refused, Alfaro convened a session of Congress to annul the election, but he was again unsuccessful. Supporters of Estrada in the military then rose up and overthrew Alfaro, enabling Estrada to be sworn in as president. The violence did not end there, however. In late 1911, Estrada died of heart and kidney disease, leading Eloy Alfaro, along with his nephew, General Flavio Alfaro, and General Pedro Montero to initiate a revolt. General Plaza, however, took command of the government troops and defeated the three generals in a bloody one-month war. In the wake of their surrender, a mob seized and lynched the rebel leaders, desecrating and burning their bodies.

In the wake of Alfaro's death, the Ecuadorian political situation stabilized somewhat. General Plaza was elected to a second term as president in September 1912, and with the support of the military and a coastal-based economic elite known as The Ring, he dominated Ecuadorian politics for the next dozen years. Ecuador held regular elections throughout this period, but Plaza and his cronies determined the winners. According to Rodríguez (1985, 45): "From 1912 to 1924 liberal governments perfected the techniques of political control ... The authorities employed violence and intimidation only in the countryside ... If it appeared that the government's candidate would not win, the police or military would be ordered to stuff the ballot boxes." During this period, opposition parties remained too weak to overcome government electoral manipulation, and they often withdrew prematurely or boycotted elections altogether.

The opposition continued to carry out occasional revolts after Alfaro's death, but they did so less frequently and with less success than in the past, owing to the gradual modernization of the military. Carlos Concha Torres, a supporter of Alfaro, launched a guerrilla insurgency in Esmeraldas that lasted from 1913 to 1916, but it never posed a serious threat to the government. Conservatives carried out rebellions in 1912, 1914, and 1924, but none of these revolts prospered.

Beginning in the 1920s, coups represented a much greater threat to the Ecuadorian government than did opposition revolts. Indeed, as the military grew stronger and acquired a corporate identity and monopoly on violence, it became increasingly tempted to take power for itself. In 1925, junior officers overthrew the government and created a provisional military junta as part of the so-called Julian Revolution, bringing an end to the era of Liberal dominance. The military handed power to a civilian dictator the following year, but it would return to power again and again over the course of the twentieth century, and, in some instances, the military stayed in power for years. The opposition played a role in many of these coups, encouraging the military to intervene to topple governments that it opposed. In 1932, for example, the Quito military garrison rebelled with the support of the opposition after Congress blocked the Conservative leader Neptalí Bonifaz from taking power in the wake of his victory in the 1931 presidential election.

Thus, the weakness of parties and the military undermined the prospects for democracy in Ecuador throughout the late nineteenth and early twentieth century. Opposition parties lacked the organization and partisan ties to compete effectively in elections, enact democratic reforms, or resist government electoral manipulation. Instead, they mostly focused on seizing power by force, taking advantage of the relative weakness of the military. The slow professionalization of the Ecuadorian military eventually brought an end to opposition revolts, but it took longer in Ecuador than in most other South American countries. As a result, Ecuador continued to have a relatively unstable authoritarian regime during the early twentieth century.

PARAGUAY

Paraguay pursued a somewhat different path from Bolivia and Ecuador for much of the nineteenth century, but it wound up in a similar place, transitioning from a stable to an unstable authoritarian regime beginning in 1870. During the first sixty years after independence, Paraguay suffered from harsh but stable dictatorships that built up the country's coercive apparatus and used it to repress all dissent. The War of the Triple Alliance (1864–1870), however, destroyed the country's repressive apparatus and, in its wake, Paraguay enacted a liberal constitution that established universal male suffrage, created a bicameral legislature, restricted presidential reelection, guaranteed civil liberties, and declared all citizens to be equal (Lewis 1993, 16; Abente 1989; González de Oleaga 2000). Democracy failed to emerge in Paraguay during the late nineteenth or early twentieth century, however. Because of the weakness of the country's military, the opposition often abstained from elections and sought to overthrow the government by force. A number of these uprisings proved successful, but even when the opposition took power it failed to democratize. Instead, it used the same authoritarian tactics to hang on to power that it had decried when it was in the opposition. Although Paraguayan parties began to develop strong ties to the electorate during the early twentieth century, party organization remained feeble, and the opposition continued to focus on the armed path to power.

PARAGUAYAN MILITARY AND REVOLTS

For much of the nineteenth century, Paraguay enjoyed significantly greater stability than did most other countries in the region. The country's leaders centralized power and built a strong coercive apparatus, which enabled them to avoid the frequent rebellions that plagued other South American countries during this period. In the wake of independence, José Gaspar Rodríguez da

Francia, who became known as the Supreme Dictator and governed from 1814 until he died in 1840, created a repressive and highly personalistic dictatorship. He strengthened and co-opted the military in order to prevent internal rebellions and defend the country from its larger and more powerful neighbors.[24] Between 1816 and 1820, the military grew from 842 soldiers to a high of 1,793 troops, in a country that had a population estimated at only 120,000 at the at the beginning of the nineteenth century (Williams 1979, 13; White 1978, 87).[25] Francia imported significant amounts of weapons and built factories to manufacture weapons, ammunition, and ships, causing military expenditures to take up 80 percent of the government's total budget (White 1978, 87, 102–104, 143–144, 181–186). To ensure that the military was not used against him, Francia created an army battalion that was placed directly under his command, giving him control of half of the country's troops and munitions (White 1978, 54). He also named his followers to the most important commands, rotated officers throughout the country so they could not easily conspire against him, ensured that no officer commanded enough troops to be a real threat, and kept the best troops in Asunción where they could defend him (Williams 1979, 60–61; 1975, 85). Finally, the dictator developed a large network of spies and imprisoned, tortured, and executed his suspected enemies (White 1978, 88–92; Hanratty and Meditz 1988, 20). His jails were full of political prisoners, many of whom hailed from the elite. One former prisoner testified that: "We were six hundred prisoners in that jail in 1840, and scarcely a third were murderers and thieves. Four hundred or more men belonged to the most decent and cultured class of the country" (cited in White 1978, 92).

After Francia's death in 1840, Carlos Antonio López quickly rose to power. López's rule was just as personalistic and repressive as Francia's, and he also invested significantly in the country's armed forces.[26] He brought in foreign officers, such as the Hungarian Lieutenant Colonel Francisco Wisner, to modernize and train the army (Williams 1979, 179; 1977, 237–243). López also imported large quantities of weapons and expanded the domestic arms industry and railroads with the help of foreign assistance (Williams 1979, 110–111; Hanratty and Meditz 1988, 24). By 1858, the country's industries were producing cannons, ammunition, ships, and naval equipment (Williams 1979, 183). To assist in the maintenance of internal order, López also created a police force and a national guard, although both of these institutions remained quite small (Williams 1979, 123–124).

---

[24] Williams (1975, 73–76) argues that the militarization of Paraguay dates back to the colonial era when the Crown kept a large militia in the country to fend off hostile indigenous people, slave raids from Brazil, and fear of Portuguese expansionism.
[25] Francia maintained a great deal of secrecy about the military and encouraged exaggerations about its size in order to deter foreign invasions (White 1978, 150–151).
[26] López's policies differed from Francia's in that he invested more in education and infrastructure and opened the country to foreign trade and influence.

Upon López's death in 1862, his son, Francisco Solano López (1862–1870), took control of the country and accelerated the military buildup, expanding the army to 30,000 troops in 1864, including thirty infantry regiments, twenty-three cavalry regiments, and four artillery regiments (Hanratty and Meditz 1988, 205). Although the Paraguayan military was not professionalized – its officers and troops, for example, typically lacked training – the Paraguayan military was quite large and strong by regional standards.

The investments in the military, along with the state repression, discouraged revolts. Paraguay also managed to avoid becoming involved in foreign conflicts until Solano López became president. In response to a Brazilian invasion of Uruguay that helped overthrow an allied government, Solano López invaded Brazil and then sent forces into Argentina, triggering a war against all three countries. Paraguay quickly mobilized 75,000 soldiers to fight in this war, which represented approximately half of the male population of military age (Cooney 2004, 31–32). Although the Paraguayan military fought valiantly, the allied blockade impeded its access to foreign weapons and ammunition, and it eventually succumbed. According to one estimate, Paraguay lost about two-thirds of its total population in the war (Whigham and Potthast 1999, 185). By the time the war ended, the country's economy was in ruins and the Paraguayan army had been reduced to a few hundred poorly armed troops.

The destruction of the Paraguayan military and the death of Solano López ushered in a period of instability in Paraguay that lasted until the mid-twentieth century. Owing to the devastation of the Paraguayan economy, there was little money to devote to the military after the war (Hanratty and Meditz 1988, 206). In 1881, Paraguay had an army of only 57 officers and 550 men, and eleven years later the army still had only 600 men (Warren 1985, 31–32). In 1893, the British minister remarked that "Paraguay, owing to her unfortunate circumstances, pecuniary and other, need scarcely be taken into account at present. She has but one small gunboat, and no army to speak of worthy of the name" (cited in Warren 1985, 32). The troops, which were conscripted, generally came from the poorest sectors of the population and they lacked discipline and training. Soldiers typically considered military service a prison sentence (Gatti Cardozo 1990, 32–33; Warren 1949, 32–33). In 1898, Paraguay created a national guard to counterbalance the army, but few men joined (Warren 1985, 32; Bareiro Spaini 2008, 76; Lewis 1993, 88).

The military was not only small and poorly trained in the late nineteenth and early twentieth century, it was also factionalized. Soldiers were loyal to individual leaders not to the military as an institution. Officers were promoted based on their political connections and affiliations rather than merit. Often when a new party or faction came to power, it sought to dismantle and rebuild the military to strengthen its co-partisans, as the Liberals did when they assumed the presidency in 1904 (Gatti Cardozo 1990, 32). As late as the 1920s, Paraguay still lacked anything resembling a professional army because of decades of political manipulation of promotions and assignments (Lewis 1993, 133). For most of this period, Paraguay had no real military schools, and officers typically had little, if any, training, although a few were sent abroad for their education (Gatti Cardozo 1990, 32–33; Bareiro Spaini 2008, 75; Warren 1949, 33). In addition, the Paraguayan military lacked modern equipment. The government acquired 10,000 rifles in 1905, but these deteriorated quickly and many were lost in uprisings (Riart 1990, 37). According to Riart (1990, 46), "the state of the armed forces in the middle of 1924 was truly disastrous."

Given the weakness and factionalization of the military, it is not surprising that revolts were frequent in Paraguay throughout the late nineteenth and early twentieth century. As Table 8.3 indicates, at least twenty-two major revolts took place between 1870 and 1922, along with a host of conspiracies and minor uprisings. Some of the rebellions devolved into civil wars with prolonged and extensive fighting: This was the case, for example, in 1873–1874, 1904, 1911–1912, and 1922–1923. Military officers typically participated in or led the revolts, but they sought power for themselves and their factions or parties, rather than for the military per se. Sometimes they were not even serving in the military at the time of the revolt.[27] Argentina and Brazil, which occupied Paraguay until 1876 and continued to intervene in the country afterwards, encouraged many of these rebellions as they jockeyed to maintain their influence in the country.

The revolts often prompted state repression, which deepened authoritarian rule in Paraguay. In 1891, for example, Liberals carried out a revolt after Colorado soldiers and thugs stole ballot boxes, attacked Liberals, and prevented them from voting in many areas (Warren 1985, 81–83; Lewis 1993, 71). The government quickly suppressed this revolt, declared a state of siege, and arrested 150 Liberal sympathizers, including the editors of opposition papers (Lewis 1993, 74; Warren 1985, 83).

Nevertheless, owing to the weakness of the military, many of the rebellions were successful, which subverted constitutional rule. Rebels overthrew the government in 1874, 1880, 1894, 1902, 1904, 1905, 1908, and four times in 1911–1912. By contrast, the opposition never won a presidential election during this period and typically did not even contest them. Thus, armed struggle was clearly the most promising path to power for the opposition in Paraguay during the late nineteenth and early twentieth century.

Beginning in the 1920s, Paraguay undertook some concerted efforts to strengthen and professionalize the military. Growing tensions with Bolivia

---

[27] Most of the important politicians in Paraguay during the late nineteenth and early twentieth century had a military background.

TABLE 8.3 *Major revolts in Paraguay, 1830–1929*

Year	Description of revolt	Type of revolt (Outcome)
1841	An infantry unit overthrew the junta that governed after José Gaspar de Francia's death. Sergeant Ramón Dure presided over the triumvirate that took charge.	Military coup (took power)
1841	A junior officer, Mariano Roque Alonso, led a military overthrow of Dure. Carlos Antonio Lopez, a lawyer, became one of two governing consuls and assumed control.	Military coup (took power)
1873–1874	A rebel army of 4,000 men supported by Argentina and Brazil defeated the government of Salvador Jovellanos. General Bernardino Caballero became president.	Elite insurrection (took power)
1874	Major José Dolores Molas rebelled with General Caballero's former troops, but he was defeated when Brazilian troops intervened to save the government.	Elite insurrection (suppressed)
1877	Juansilvano Godoi and Major Jose Dolores Molas assassinated the president, Juan Bautista Gill, but their attempt to take power in a revolt was crushed.	Elite insurrection (suppressed)
1879	Juansilvano Godoi and Nicanor Godoi invaded Paraguay with 500 men, but the Paraguayan military sent 2,000 men to suppress the invasion.	Elite insurrection (suppressed)
1880	After President Bareiro's death, the military arrested the vice-president on orders of the war minister. Interior Minister Bernardino Caballero took over as president.	Military coup (took power)
1891	Major Eduardo Vera and Liberal Party leaders revolted but the government suppressed the rebellion. Vera was killed and 150 Liberals were jailed.	Elite insurrection (suppressed)
1894	General Egusquiza overthrew President González in a nonviolent coup with the support of Brazil and many Colorado leaders. The vice-president took over until the elections.	Military coup (took power)
1902	Colonel Juan A. Escurra, the war minister, overthrew President Aceval in a nonviolent coup with the support of Caballero and Colorado leaders. The vice-president took over.	Military coup (took power)
1904	Benigno Ferreira, with the support of Liberals and some Colorados, defeated President Escurra in a civil war after several months of fighting.	Elite insurrection (took power)
1905	General Ferreira and Chief of Police Garcia overthrew President Gaona in a nonviolent coup. Cecilio Báez, the finance minister, became president.	Military coup (took power)

TABLE 8.3 (*continued*)

Year	Description of revolt	Type of revolt (Outcome)
1908	Radicals allied with Major Albino Jara and Lieutenant Colonel Escobar revolted and overthrew President Benigno Ferreira after two days of fighting.	Military coup (took power)
1909	Colorados and Cívicos led by Colonel Gill and supported by Caballero and Ferreira invaded from Argentina but were quickly defeated.	Elite insurrection (suppressed)
1911	Colonel Jara rebelled when the Minister of Interior Riquelme tried to arrest him. Most military and police units supported the revolt, which overthrew the government.	Military coup (took power)
1911	Radical Liberals led by Adolfo Riquelme revolted but were defeated by the Jara government after several battles.	Elite insurrection (suppressed)
1911	Interior Minister Cipriano Ibañez participated in a nonviolent coup that overthrew President Jara and replaced him with the leader of the Radicals, Liberato Marcial Rojas.	Military coup (took power)
1911	Colorados led by Police Chief Romero Pereira overthrew President Rojas and named Pedro Peña as the new president.	Military coup (took power)
1911–1912	Radical Liberals led by Eduardo Schaerer invaded from Argentina and overthrew the government after much fighting. 5,000 casualties.	Elite insurrection (took power)
1912	Colonel Jara led a rebellion of Liberal Cívicos and Colorados against the government. It was suppressed after fierce fighting.	Elite insurrection (suppressed)
1914	Liberal Cívicos carried out a revolt led by Colonel Manuel J. Duarte and Gómez Freire Esteves. The government bombarded their position and they surrendered.	Elite insurrection (suppressed)
1918	General Patricio Escobar rebelled after the president refused to sanction an officer that he accused of insulting him. The rebellion was quickly suppressed.	Military coup (suppressed)
1922–1923	*Civil war of 1922–1923.* Colonel Adolfo Chirife and the Schaeristas rebelled and almost overthrew the government but were defeated after prolonged fighting.	Elite insurrection (suppressed)

Source: Latin American Revolts Database.

over the Chaco region provided the main impetus for the investments in the military, but an export boom helped fund the professionalization efforts – Paraguayan exports rose from $11.5 million in 1910–1914 to $76.2 million in 1925–1929 in constant 1980 dollars (Bértola and Ocampo 2013, 86).[28] In response to Bolivian incursions into disputed territory in the Chaco desert, President Eligio Ayala (1923–1928) reorganized the general staff command, purchased European weapons, and began to build forts and run telegraph lines to the Chaco (Lewis 1993, 142; Riart 1990, 45, 54–61; Bareiro Spaini 2008, 77). In 1925, the government hired a French military mission, and subsequently it recruited an Argentine mission, although the latter pulled out in 1932 when Paraguay went to war with Bolivia (Bareiro Spaini 2008, 76–77). During this period, the government also created various military academies, including the Military School (1915), an Aviation School (1923), a school for officers in the military reserve (1924), a Higher War College (1931), and a school for noncommissioned officers (1932) (Bareiro Spaini 2008, 76–77; Gatti Cardozo 1990, 33; Sosa 2004, 102–103).

These reforms gradually strengthened the military, helping it defeat Bolivia in the Chaco War (1932–1935), the longest and bloodiest international war in Latin America during the twentieth century. The strengthening and professionalization of the military also led to a reduction in the number of outsider revolts. Nevertheless, the Paraguayan military remained relatively politicized. Widespread disenchantment with the treatment of the soldiers and the condition of the military led to a revolt by soldiers that overthrew the Liberal government in 1936. Subsequent years saw further coups and coup attempts. It was not until the 1950s when General Alfredo Stroessner seized power and strengthened Colorado Party control of the military that the cycle of coups and rebellions in Paraguay came to an end.

PARTIES AND AUTHORITARIAN RULE IN PARAGUAY

Parties arose relatively late in Paraguay but developed more quickly than in most other countries in the region. By the early twentieth century, Paraguayan parties had already begun to forge relatively strong ties to the electorate. Nevertheless, the parties had little in the way of organizational structures, and they were plagued by internal divisions, which made it difficult to compete for power on the national level or enact democratic reforms. Although the opposition usually contested legislative elections after 1869, it typically abstained from presidential elections and often sought power via armed revolt, seeking to take advantage of the weakness of the military.

Prior to 1870, Paraguay had a highly repressive political environment that was not conducive to the emergence of parties. In the aftermath of the war, however, political clubs arose to compete in elections and these political clubs gradually evolved into political parties. Paraguay's small size and lack

---

[28] Paraguay had the second lowest level of per capita exports in the region in 1910–1914, after Ecuador, but by 1925–1929 it ranked in the middle of the pack in the region (Bértola and Ocampo 2013, 86).

of geographical fragmentation facilitated the development of the parties. The country lost half of its land and, perhaps, two-thirds of its population in the War of the Triple Alliance. In 1887, the country had a population of only 329,000 people and a territory of 253,000 square kilometers (Kleinpenning 1992, 477). More importantly, three-quarters of its inhabitants were concentrated in the central zone, a relatively small and flat area surrounding the capital (Lewis 1993, 32; Kleinpenning 1992, 476–477).

Nevertheless, Paraguay did not have the kinds of social cleavages that were conducive to the development of parties during this period. By the late nineteenth century, Paraguay was a relatively homogenous *mestizo* nation without significant religious or territorial divisions (Lewis 1993, 6; 1986, 489).[29] Although the Catholic Church had been strong in Paraguay during the colonial era, the dictators that governed Paraguay until 1870 systematically co-opted, persecuted, and undermined it, and most of the country's clergy died in the War of the Triple Alliance. As a result, by the late nineteenth century, the Paraguayan Church was, perhaps, the weakest in South America and could hardly serve as the basis for a strong party (Mecham 1934, 244). Paraguayan governments implemented some secularization policies in the late nineteenth and early twentieth century, but these measures never became a major source of division within the political arena in part because of the weakness of the Church (Mecham 1966, 196).

The main two parties, the Colorado Party and the Liberal Party, did not take different positions on religious issues, nor did they represent distinct ideologies (Nichols 1970; Hicks 1971, 92; 1967, 275; Warren 1985, 94; Lewis 1993, 18). Both parties largely embraced the liberal ideas then prevalent among the dominant economic classes of Paraguay, although their enthusiasm for such principles waned when they conflicted with their political or economic interests. The Liberals, for example, protested governmental corruption and electoral abuses when they were in the opposition, but they committed the same types of abuses after taking power in 1904.

Parties in Paraguay initially sprang from government–opposition divisions (Warren 1985, 72–73; Lewis 1993, 62–67; Abente 1989, 535).[30] A variety of wealthy elites established the predecessor of the Liberal Party, the Democratic Center, in July 1887 in part because they had grown critical of governmental repression and corruption and of the sale of Paraguayan land to foreigners (Lewis 1993, 62–67). In response, supporters of the government, led by

---

[29] As Lewis (1993, 6) notes, "the usual bases for ideological conflict – class, race, language, and regionalism – are absent" in Paraguay.

[30] Pro-Colorado politicians and scholars subsequently sought to trace the parties to divisions stemming from the War of the Triple Alliance, arguing that the founding members of the Colorado Party were supporters of President Francisco Solano López in this war, and the founding members of the Liberal Party had fought with Argentina and Brazil against López. In fact, more of the founding members of the Colorado Party had fought against López than had the founding Liberals (Lewis 1993, 64–66; Chartrain 2013, 198–200).

General Bernardino Caballero, formed the National Republican Association, which became known as the Colorado Party, that same year.

From the outset, both parties enjoyed the support of many elites. At least 128 men attended the Democratic Center's founding assembly and 106 men participated in the founding of the Colorado Party (Lewis 1993, 63–64; Warren 1985, 73). The relative balance of forces helped contribute to the endurance of the two parties. Although both parties represented elites, their leadership varied slightly. Whereas the Colorado Party had more high-ranking generals, landowners, and traditional families in its ranks, the Liberal Party had more junior officers, professionals, and businessmen (Chartrain 2013, 200–201; Lewis 1993, 63–66; Warren 1985, 69–70; Hicks 1971, 92).

The two parties gradually developed strong personalist and patronage-based linkages to the masses thanks in large part to the influence and resources of their founding members (Caballero Aquino and Livieres Banks 1993, 50; Hicks 1971, 92; Nichols 1970, 29–31).[31] The 1870 constitution, which mandated universal male suffrage, encouraged the parties to reach out to the masses (Abente 2021, 131).[32] Moreover, peasants depended heavily on merchants for food, credit, and transportation, creating ties that the patrons exploited for political purposes (Abente 1989: 537). Party elites also used state resources to build up a base of loyal followers, and each party controlled the government for long periods of time, which gave it access to patronage. The Colorados and their precursors held the presidency from 1882 to 1904 and the Liberals controlled it from 1904 to 1936. Moreover, each party typically had representation in the legislature and held some public offices even when it did not control the government, which ensured that it maintained some access to state resources.

The Colorado and Liberal parties did not develop strong organizations in the late nineteenth or early twentieth century, however. Lewis (1993, 124) argues that the "parties in 1922 were not much different than they had been in 1887," remaining loose alliances of political chiefs and local notables. The parties' links to the electorate also took time to develop. During the early twentieth century, most voters had ties to individual leaders rather than to a party per se. Nor were the parties particularly cohesive. To the contrary, both parties frequently split into factions, although these ruptures generally proved temporary.

---

[31] Over the course of the twentieth century, the vast majority of Paraguayans came to identify strongly with one party or the other, and people rarely switched parties since the parties represented a social identity and an economic resource as well as a political attachment. Family members typically all belonged to the same party and party affiliations were passed down from generation to generation (Nichols 1970, 47–48). Parties also became the source of jobs, credit, medical and legal aid, and a variety of other services – they even served a social function, sponsoring community activities (Nichols 1970, 32, 100; Hicks 1967, 276).

[32] According to Nichols (1970, 30), the influence of these original founders persisted into the late twentieth century – the areas of Colorado and Liberal strength in the 1960s corresponded to the redoubts of the nineteenth-century regional leaders who supported each party.

Parties and Authoritarian Rule in Paraguay

The absence of strong party organizations made it difficult for the opposition to compete in elections, which took place on an uneven playing field. The government generally permitted opposition parties and newspapers to function, but it engaged in a variety of authoritarian tactics to ensure its preferred candidates won (Warren 1985, 54, 65–66).[33] According to Warren (1985, 36), during the late nineteenth century: "The entire electoral process, from registration of voters to recording the voice votes was permeated by fraud ... Troops and police armed with pistols, rifles, and swords; thugs armed with machetes and knives; and election officials blind to the planned terror around them, made voting an act of heroism for members of the opposition." During the era of Colorado Party dominance, the opposition Liberals abstained from presidential elections because they knew they had little chance of winning. At times, the Liberals nominated candidates, but they typically withdrew once it became apparent that they could not win. In 1890, Liberals sought to negotiate a consensus slate with the Colorado Party in the presidential election, but when this failed, they boycotted the election (Lewis 1993, 69–70; Warren 1985, 75–78). In 1894 and 1898, the Liberals were too divided to agree on a presidential candidate, and in 1902 a military coup prompted them to again abstain from the presidential elections (Lewis 1993, 75–79, 84–87; Warren 1985, 90–92, 99–105).

By contrast, the Liberals usually participated in legislative elections, and they often won seats in their strongholds. For example, in their electoral debut in 1887, the Liberals won eleven out of the twenty-six seats in the legislature (Warren 1985, 72). Subsequently, however, the Colorado government clamped down on the Liberals and their share of the legislature declined to less than 20 percent of the seats. In the December 1888 legislative elections, Minister of Interior Juan A. Meza dispatched mounted police to all polling places in Asunción to prevent Liberals from registering to vote, leaving a toll of four dead, thirty-seven wounded, and sixty-eight people arrested (Lewis 1993, 69; Warren 1985, 75).[34] In 1891, the Liberals managed to elect two senators and three deputies in spite of government repression and the theft of ballot boxes, but the Colorado-dominated Congress refused to seat them (Warren 1985, 81; Lewis 1993, 71). Given the relative weakness of the Liberal Party, however, there was little it could do to resist these abuses.

To have a chance at winning seats, the Liberals at times sought to ally with moderate Colorados.[35] Indeed, a moderate faction of the Liberals known as the Civic Liberals so often allied with moderate Colorados during the 1890s that

---

[33] The opposition committed electoral abuses as well, but these tended to be less widespread because the opposition had fewer resources at its disposal. See Warren (1985, 72).

[34] Similarly, in 1890, the mayor of Asunción sent soldiers and employees with machetes to block Liberals from registering (Warren 1985, 76).

[35] Within the Colorado Party, the military leaders tended to take a harder line on the opposition and commit more electoral abuses than did the civilian leaders.

they became a virtual third party (Warren 1985, 84). Presidents Juan Bautista Egusquiza (1894–1898) and Eduardo Aceval (1898–1902) cooperated with the moderate Liberals, even bringing some of them into their cabinets and allowing them to gain control of the Supreme Court (Lewis 1993, 80–83, 87–89; Warren 1985, 95, 102, 109). In 1895, Egusquiza presided over legislative elections that were reputed to be relatively free and fair, leading to the election of two Liberal senators and four Liberal deputies (Warren 1985, 95). Nevertheless, at times, such as in 1901, the Colorados reneged on their commitments to support Liberal candidates (Lewis 1993, 89). Moreover, the cooperation between the governing Colorados and the Liberals did not last long since the hardline wing of the Colorado Party gained control of the government in a 1902 military coup.

The Liberals sometimes resorted to revolts to protest electoral abuses and seek to capture power. In 1891, for example, Liberals carried out a major rebellion in response to the government's electoral abuses that year. This revolt failed, but there were constant rumors of Liberal plots against the government in the years that followed (Warren 1985, 98–99). Nevertheless, it was not until 1904 that the Liberals carried out a major revolt again. The 1904 Liberal rebellion was successful in part because of the weakness of the military, but also because it received support, including weapons, from the Argentine government and financing from many businessmen and landowners who had turned against the regime because of its corruption and incompetence (Lewis 1993, 95; Warren 1980, 375; 1985, 125).[36] The revolt, which was led by the Liberal former general Benigno Ferreira, began with an invasion of a few hundred rebels from Argentina, but it quickly attracted numerous volunteers, uniting Radical and Civic Liberals as well as some disaffected Colorados (Lewis 1993, 95–96).[37] In the wake of the rebel victory, Juan B. Gaona, one of the rebels' main financial backers, became president and General Ferreira became the new minister of war. The army was dissolved and reorganized under Liberal command and the rebel troops were integrated into its ranks (Lewis 1993, 97–98; Warren 1980, 381; 1985, 132–133).

The triumph of the Liberals in 1904 did not bring democracy to Paraguay, however. Nor did it end the rebellions that had plagued the country since 1870. In the years that followed, the Liberals intervened extensively in elections, just as the Colorados had when they were in power. The Colorado Party, like the Liberal Party, was too weak to overcome government electoral intervention and responded by boycotting elections.[38] Colorados, for example, abstained from legislative elections in 1904 and 1906, and they did not field a candidate

---

[36] Juan B. Gaono, the president of the Banco Mercantil, raised $30,000 from wealthy merchants and landowners to support the revolt (Warren 1980, 380).

[37] By the end, the rebel armies numbered 6,000 people (Warren 1980, 382).

[38] Some moderate Colorados joined the Civic Liberals in the wake of the 1904 revolution (Lewis 1993, 98).

in the presidential elections until 1928 (Lewis 1993, 97–98, 101; Warren 1980, 381; 1985, 132–133). Instead, the Colorados frequently plotted against the government and carried out occasional revolts, often in collaboration with disgruntled Liberals. In 1909, for example, Colorados and Civic Liberals invaded from Argentina, but the government quickly defeated the revolt (Lewis 1993, 108–109). Colorados briefly overthrew the Liberal government in 1912, but this was the only time they managed to come to power during the lengthy Liberal era (1904–1936).

The biggest threat to Liberal governments came from within the party. Throughout most of this era, the Liberal Party was divided between the moderate Civic Liberals and the Radical Liberals, both of which sought power via coups and rebellions as well as elections. The Civic Liberals initially held the upper hand, controlling the presidency as well as a majority of the cabinet, the party directorate, and both houses of Congress, but they lacked a popular base and none of their leaders enjoyed a large following (Lewis 1993, 98, 103).[39] In 1908, the Radical Liberal faction led by Major Albino Jara overthrew Ferreira in a violent coup. The years that followed saw numerous rebellions, including major civil wars in 1911–1912 and 1922–1923, as Radical Liberals, Civic Liberals, and Colorados vied for power. Radical Liberals managed to hang on to power for most of the two decades that followed, but no Liberal president completed his presidential term until 1916 and only two did during the entire period of Liberal rule.

The Liberals enacted some electoral reforms in an effort to persuade the opposition to desist from revolts and participate in elections, but none of these reforms brought an end to government electoral intervention (Del Valle 1951, 90–91; Bordon 1962, 75–78). As the Liberal president Eusebio Ayala remarked in 1922: "No law is capable of assuring the purity of suffrage when politicians seek to falsify it" (Bordon 1962, 84). Perhaps the most important changes took place under President Manuel Franco, who governed from 1916 to 1919 and demonstrated a greater commitment to democracy than his predecessors. During his administration, the government first overhauled the voter registration system, which led to an increase in the number of registered voters from 77,715 in 1913 to 95,259 in 1917 (Franco 1917, 9). Subsequently, it passed Law 323 of 1918, which established the secret ballot, prohibited the stationing of troops and crowds near the voting tables, and created an incomplete-list electoral system that guaranteed representation for minority parties. During the Franco administration, the opposition competed in some elections and fared reasonably well. In 1917, for example, the opposition Colorados won 46 percent of the vote in Asunción in an election in which allegations of fraud were limited (Abente 1989, 534). In 1919, the Colorados won a total of 26 percent of the vote in the 1st, 2nd, 4th, 5th, and

---

[39] According to Lewis (1993, 102), the Civic Liberals were a party of notables.

6th districts, and in 1921, they captured 31 percent of the vote in the 1st, 2nd, and 3rd districts (Chartrain 2013, 230–231; Gondra 1921, 10–11; Franco 1919, 8–9).[40] President Franco died of a heart attack in 1919, however, and relations between the government and the opposition deteriorated in the years that followed. The low point came with the bloody civil war of 1922–1923, in which disaffected Liberals and Colorados sought unsuccessfully to overthrow the Radical Liberal government.

In the wake of the 1922–1923 civil war, the Liberals patched up their differences somewhat, but the opposition Colorados remained divided about whether to participate in elections or not. In 1923 and 1924, the Colorados voted to abstain from the elections in part because they thought existing laws did not offer them sufficient guarantees (Chartrain 2013, 235–237). In 1927, however, the collaborationist wing of the Colorados helped negotiate an electoral reform and it then participated in the legislative elections of 1927 to test the government's goodwill (Bordon 1962, 78). The Colorados won 25 percent of the legislative seats that year, which helped persuade them to participate for the first time in the presidential elections the following year. According to various sources, the 1928 presidential elections, which took place without violence, were relatively free and fair (Abente 1989, 534; Caballero Aquino and Livieres Banks 1993, 24; Cardozo 1956, 12; Chartrain 2013, 237–238; Lewis 1993, 143). As to be expected, José P. Guggiari, the candidate of the governing Liberal Party, was declared the winner, with 68 percent of the valid vote, but the defeated Colorado Party candidate accepted the outcome.

The rapprochement did not last long, however. Once in office, the Guggiari administration violently repressed student protests and harassed the opposition, arresting and exiling the Colorado leaders who refused to collaborate with his regime. The Colorados were too weak and divided to respond, and instead returned to their traditional policy of abstaining from elections. The opposition, which included both Colorados and disaffected Liberals, sought military support for a coup in 1930, but the plot was stymied (Lewis 1993, 150). As a result, the Liberal regime persisted, albeit shakily, until 1936 when discontented military officers overthrew the government in the wake of the country's victory in the Chaco War (1932–1935).

Thus, Paraguay struggled with political instability throughout the late nineteenth and early twentieth century. Although Paraguay's two main parties began to develop strong ties to the electorate in the early twentieth century, opposition parties did not have the strength or organization to resist the government's efforts to manipulate elections. The government was slow to strengthen the military, however, which encouraged the opposition to seek power, at times successfully, via armed revolts during the early twentieth century.

---

[40] Electoral returns for the other districts are missing.

Conclusion

CONCLUSION

Throughout the late nineteenth and early twentieth century, Bolivia, Ecuador, and Paraguay constituted unstable authoritarian regimes, enduring frequent opposition rebellions and military coups. Some of these revolts succeeded, thus subverting constitutional rule, but even when they failed, they typically led to authoritarian clampdowns that undermined the prospects of democratization. The weakness of the armed forces in the three countries encouraged frequent revolts since the militaries could not easily suppress uprisings. Although Bolivia, Ecuador, and Paraguay took steps to professionalize their armed forces in the early twentieth century, their professionalization efforts were relatively modest and slow to take effect in part because the countries lacked the funds to make major military investments. As a result, their militaries did not achieve a monopoly on force until the mid-twentieth century.

The weakness of political parties also contributed to authoritarian rule and political instability in Bolivia, Ecuador, and Paraguay during the late nineteenth and early twentieth century. Although parties in Paraguay developed stronger partisan ties than they did in Bolivia and Ecuador in the early twentieth century, even in Paraguay parties were weakly organized and highly factionalized. Weak parties could not prevent executives from concentrating authority and extending their hold on power. Nor could they compete in elections, resist government electoral manipulation, or enact democratic reforms. Instead, the opposition often chose to boycott national elections and at times sought to overthrow the government by force. As a result, these countries continued to be plagued by instability and authoritarian rule well into the twentieth century.

Conclusion

Contributions and Implications

This study represents the first comprehensive analysis of the origins of democracy in South America, the region of the world that for much of the twentieth century had the largest number of democracies after Europe. The central theoretical contribution of this book is to provide an original explanation for why democracy arose in some South American countries and not others during the early twentieth century. In so doing, the book also explains why some South American countries developed strong militaries and parties during the late nineteenth or early twentieth century.

The book shows that three main developments – the professionalization of the military, the rise of strong opposition parties, and ruling party splits – contributed to the emergence of democracy in the region. Military professionalization boosted the *incentives* for the opposition to abandon the armed struggle and focus on the electoral path to power. The rise of strong parties enhanced the *capacity* of the opposition to enact, implement, and enforce democratic reforms. And ruling party splits created the *opportunity* for the opposition and ruling party dissidents to enact democratic reforms that leveled the electoral playing field.

During the nineteenth century, the relative weakness of the armed forces in South America encouraged opposition forces to seek to overthrow governments by force, especially since they had little chance of prevailing in elections. These revolts undermined the rule of law and led governments to clamp down on the opposition, which deepened authoritarian rule. At the end of the nineteenth century, however, South American governments began to use their growing export revenues to strengthen and professionalize their militaries, which gave them a monopoly on violence for the first time. As a result, the opposition abandoned the armed struggle in most countries in the region during the early twentieth century and increasingly focused on elections.

The rise of strong opposition parties also played a central role in the emergence of democracy in the region. Opposition parties supported democratic reform to improve their chances of winning elections, but they were more likely to be able to enact reforms if they had powerful organizations and deep roots in the electorate. Strong opposition parties typically held more seats in the legislature, which could provide the votes to enact reforms. They could also put more pressure on the government to support reform. In addition, strong opposition parties could contest electoral abuses in a systematic manner and mount sustained electoral challenges to the ruling party despite continued government electoral manipulation. Where opposition parties were weak, the opposition was more likely to abstain from elections, to seek power through armed uprisings, or to call on the military to intervene, all of which had negative implications for democracy in the region.

Strong opposition parties tended to arise in countries where religious or territorial cleavages were intense and relatively balanced. If conservative supporters of the Catholic Church and liberal critics of it were relatively similar in terms of their size and the amount of resources they controlled, strong parties based on this cleavage were more likely to emerge and endure. Strong parties could also arise if the population was closely divided between the center and periphery. Where one side of a cleavage dominated the other, however, competition tended to take place within the cleavage, which contributed to personalism and undermined party development. In addition, strong parties were more likely to arise in countries where the population was geographically concentrated, which made it easier for politicians to campaign throughout the country and for parties to develop nationwide organizations and electorates. By contrast, it was extremely difficult to build strong national parties in geographically fragmented countries owing to regional divides and the lack of communication and transportation infrastructure in the nineteenth century.

Even strong opposition parties could not typically enact democratic reforms on their own, given that they almost never held a majority in the legislature during this period. Splits within the ruling party, however, provided the opportunity to enact the reforms. These splits occurred frequently in the nineteenth and early twentieth century and were typically caused by internal leadership struggles and/or policy differences. In the wake of splits, ruling party dissidents sometimes forged alliances with the opposition to push through democratic reforms to undermine the ruling party's ability to control elections. Ruling party dissidents often supported democratic reforms for the same reason opposition party legislators did – that is, to level the electoral playing field and increase their chances of winning elections and holding office.

Chile and Uruguay had the strongest democracies in the early twentieth century in part because they developed strong parties and professional militaries that enjoyed a monopoly on the use of force. The existence of two or more strong parties was conducive to electoral competition and meant there was always at least one strong party in the opposition that was committed to the electoral path to power and could promote democracy. Weaker democracies arose where there was only one strong party (Argentina) or where the military was not powerful enough to establish a monopoly on violence nationwide (Colombia). Once the strong party took power in Argentina, the country lacked a powerful opposition party, which undermined electoral competition and democratic stability in the long run. In Colombia, the professionalization of the military in the early twentieth century led the opposition to abandon the armed struggle, but the continuing weakness of the armed forces generated periodic outbreaks of regional violence, which destabilized the country's democracy.

Relatively stable authoritarian regimes arose in those countries, namely Brazil, Peru, and Venezuela, that developed strong militaries but continued to have weak parties in the early twentieth century. In these countries, the strength of the military was typically sufficient to deter opposition revolts. Opposition parties in these countries, however, were too weak to push through democratic reforms or to compete in elections on an uneven playing field. Instead, the opposition often abstained from presidential elections or presented only token opposition. In some cases, opposition leaders even called on the military to intervene, which led to occasional coup attempts in these countries, such as those that occurred in Peru in 1914 and 1919.

By contrast, those countries that continued to have weak militaries in the early twentieth century remained unstable authoritarian regimes, regardless of the strength of their parties. These countries, specifically Bolivia, Ecuador, and Paraguay, continued to be plagued by revolts and some of these rebellions even overthrew their leaders. Given government control of elections, opposition leaders in these countries viewed armed rebellion as their most effective means of taking power and so they frequently resorted to it. Indeed, as Chapter 3 showed, the number of outsider revolts and executive overthrows in Bolivia, Ecuador, and Paraguay substantially exceeded those in the other South American countries during the first three decades of the twentieth century.

IMPLICATIONS FOR POST-1929 POLITICS

The emergence of democracy in South America during the early twentieth century had important consequences for politics in the region in subsequent decades. Many of the democratic reforms adopted in the early twentieth century proved to be sticky. Countries that adopted the secret ballot prior to 1930 generally maintained it in later years, and efforts were frequently made to better enforce it, such as by requiring the electoral authorities to furnish voters with a single ballot on which all the parties and candidates were listed, rather than having parties provide their own ballots. South American countries that shifted to electoral systems that provided for representation of minority parties, such as the incomplete list or proportional representation, generally continued to provide for minority representation in the years that followed, although countries frequently made adjustments to the precise formula they used to achieve it.[1] Finally, South American countries that granted new suffrage rights in the early twentieth century almost always maintained these rights going forward. In fact, over the course of the twentieth century, virtually all Latin American countries steadily expanded suffrage rights, enfranchising women and illiterates, among other groups.

Why did many of these democratic reforms prove sticky? To begin with, some of the reforms were enshrined in constitutions, which required supermajority votes to amend. However, a more important factor was that many of the democratic reforms created vested interests. Newly enfranchised citizens opposed efforts to deprive them of the suffrage, and politicians who were elected under one set of rules typically preferred to maintain those rules. Moreover, the prolonged democratic experiences that some South American countries enjoyed during the early twentieth century led to the development of democratic norms among the citizenry. This made it risky for vote-seeking politicians to overturn the democratic reforms. International norms also increasingly favored democracy as the twentieth century wore on, and countries that departed from these norms faced disapproval and even sanctions from the international community. In short, the democratic laws often represented a bright line that was difficult to cross without provoking considerable attention and resistance.

In addition, some of the factors that favored democracy before 1930 continued to facilitate it in the decades that followed. Strong militaries, for example, discouraged the opposition from carrying out revolts in most South American countries post-1929, which helped stabilize democratic regimes. By contrast, countries with weak militaries, such as Bolivia, Ecuador, and Paraguay, were subject to frequent revolts post-1929, which overthrew governments and undermined the likelihood of democratization.

Even more importantly, strong parties, especially powerful *opposition* parties, contributed to the preservation and strengthening of democracy in the long run. Strong parties fostered electoral competition, which was sometimes absent in countries with weak parties. Because they could typically compete in elections, strong opposition parties had fewer incentives than weak ones to revolt or to call on the military to overthrow the president. Strong opposition parties were also typically in a better position to promote further democratic reforms and to resist efforts by the president or ruling party to engage in democratic backsliding. These parties often controlled enough seats in the legislature and other institutions to pose a significant obstacle to presidential initiatives to concentrate power and undermine democracy. Well-organized opposition parties were also in a better position to carefully monitor the registration and voting process. Indeed, strong opposition parties usually had the organization and geographical reach to place their members on the committees that oversaw

---

[1] In the late twentieth century, some Latin American countries established mixed systems that combined proportional representation and single-member districts.

TABLE C.1 *Democracy in South America, post-1929*

Country	Number of years of democracy, 1930–2010 (BMR)	Number of years of democracy, 1930–2010 (MBP)	Mean Polity2 score 1930–2015 (Polity)	Mean Polyarchy score 1930–2022 (V-Dem)
Argentina	39	43	0.01	0.493
Chile	60	62	3.14	0.528
Colombia	64	72	5.62	0.410
Uruguay	61	66	4.43	0.673
Mean of democratic pioneers	56	60.8	3.3	0.526
Bolivia	30	38	0.87	0.372
Brazil	44	44	1.34	0.460
Ecuador	44	52	2.88	0.448
Paraguay	8	22	-2.57	0.301
Peru	31	48	2.41	0.418
Venezuela	46	52	3.02	0.439
Mean of democratic laggards	33.8	42.7	1.33	0.406

Sources: Boix, Miller, and Rosato (2013); Mainwaring, Brinks, and Pérez-Liñán (2001); Mainwaring and Pérez-Liñán (2013); Center for Systemic Peace (2012); Coppedge et al. (2023).

voter registration and the casting and counting of ballots throughout the country. In addition, strong opposition parties could use their political influence and capacity to mount popular protests to object to fraudulent elections and to demand a return to democracy in the event of a military coup or some unconstitutional seizure of power.

As Table C.1 indicates, the countries that established democracy before 1930 (Argentina, Chile, Colombia, and Uruguay) on average experienced significantly more years of democracy post-1929 than the other South American countries. This is true whether we measure democracy using the dichotomous BMR index (Boix, Miller, and Rosato 2013) or the trichotomous MBP index (Mainwaring, Brinks, and Pérez-Liñán 2001).[2] Post-1929, the democratic pioneers have also registered significantly higher mean scores than the democratic laggards on two prominent democracy indexes: Polity II and V-Dem's Polyarchy index. A series of t-tests indicate that the differences between the democratic pioneers and democratic laggards is highly statistically significant (at the 0.0001 level) for all four measures of democracy post-1929.

Nevertheless, the degree of democracy and path dependence post-1929 should not be exaggerated. None of the democratic pioneers were entirely stable after 1929. They all experienced democratic breakdowns, some of which lasted a long time. Chile, for example, was under military rule from 1973 to 1989;

---

[2] I count as democratic the years that Mainwaring, Brinks, and Pérez-Liñán code as semi-democratic.

Colombia was under authoritarian rule from 1953 to 1957; and Uruguay had a military-backed government from 1973 to 1984. Of the democratic pioneers, however, Argentina suffered the most frequent breakdowns during this period. Indeed, between 1930 and 1982, Argentina experienced thirty-six years of authoritarian rule and only fifteen years of democracy, according to Mainwaring and Pérez-Liñán (2013, 67). According to both Boix, Miller, and Rosato and Mainwaring, Brinks, and Pérez-Liñán, Argentina had fewer years of democracy after 1929 than most of the democratic laggards. Similarly, as Table C.1 indicates, Colombia scored lower on V-Dem's Polyarchy index than most of the democratic laggards during this period. As I have argued, the democratic shortcomings of Argentina and Colombia post-1929 stemmed from the fact that Argentina had only one strong party and Colombia lacked a military capable of maintaining a monopoly on violence throughout the country.

The big problem for most South American democracies post-1929 was military coups. As Chapter 3 discussed, the strengthening and professionalization of the military dramatically reduced outsider revolts, but it did not bring an end to insider revolts, such as military coups. Indeed, many of the countries with relatively strong militaries, such as Argentina, Brazil, Peru, and Venezuela, experienced numerous military coups post-1929. Countries with strong parties, such as Colombia, Chile, and Uruguay, suffered fewer coups post-1929, presumably because strong opposition parties could take power through elections in these countries and thus were less likely to call on the military to intervene. Nevertheless, even these countries were not entirely invulnerable to military interventions, and in some cases even strong opposition parties called on the military to intervene.

Post-1929 political outcomes, such as coups, were shaped by numerous factors. The rise of strong labor movements and populist governments, for example, sometimes provoked coups and political instability (Collier 1999; O'Donnell 1973; Collier and Collier 1991). International factors also clearly played a more important role in post-1929 political developments in South America than they did in previous decades. For example, the international economic crisis of the 1930s destabilized governments in the region and helped set off a wave of coups. Cold War tensions also led to numerous coups and guerrilla rebellions, as the United States and Soviet Union struggled for influence in the region.

In sum, the strength of the military and parties continued to matter after 1929, but they were only two of the many factors that influenced post-1929 political outcomes. Many of the democratic reforms that were adopted in the first decades of the twentieth century proved sticky, but they did not prevent military coups or other interruptions of democratic rule. Although the countries that democratized in the early twentieth century on average enjoyed more years of democracy post-1929 than other South American countries, only Chile and Uruguay stood head and shoulders above the rest of the pack.

EMPIRICAL AND CONCEPTUAL CONTRIBUTIONS

In addition to developing original theoretical arguments, this study makes some empirical and conceptual contributions. One important empirical contribution of the book is the development of a database on all revolts in South America from 1830 to 1929. LARD includes many more revolts and contains much more information about each revolt than existing conflict databases that cover this period.[3] Chapter 3, which discusses this data set, also presents an original typology that identifies four different types of revolts based on whether the rebel leaders came from inside or outside the state apparatus (insider vs. outsider revolts) and whether these leaders hailed from the elites or the masses. It shows that outsider revolts, especially elite insurrections, were by far the most common type of revolt during the nineteenth century, but these types of revolts declined precipitously during the early twentieth century, which paved the way for the emergence of democracy in the region. By contrast, insider revolts, such as coups, remained relatively frequent in many South American countries for most of the twentieth century, which had negative consequences for democracy.

Another important empirical contribution of this book is the development of a database on historical elections in South America. LAHED, which was discussed in Chapter 2, covers all presidential elections during the nineteenth and early twentieth century, containing many more elections and much more information than existing data sets that cover this period. It provides data on the election results, the competitiveness and fairness of the elections, and voter turnout, among other variables. The database enables me to make a comprehensive assessment of the quality of elections in South America during the nineteenth and early twentieth century and to weigh in on the scholarly debate about the nature of regimes in this period.

As Chapter 2 discusses, the traditional view was that elections in nineteenth-century Latin America were a sham perpetrated by deeply authoritarian regimes, but in recent decades revisionist historians have argued that there were many democratic institutions and practices during this period. My analysis suggests that both sides are correct in many respects. As the revisionist historians have argued, numerous elections in South America in the nineteenth century were competitive and some were even relatively free and fair. Moreover, some South American countries established relatively broad suffrage rights during the nineteenth century, and in a few cases even adopted virtually universal male suffrage. Nevertheless, as the traditional view has stressed, government electoral manipulation undermined the vast majority of elections in nineteenth-century South America. More than two-thirds of presidential elections were not competitive and approximately one-third of them were not even contested. Most South American countries maintained

---

[3] LARD is a joint project with Luis L. Schenoni, Guillermo Kreiman, and Paola Galano Toro.

economic or literacy restrictions on the franchise, but even where they did not, voter turnout tended to be relatively low. On average, the level of voter turnout and the degree of competitiveness of elections was significantly lower in South America than it was in Europe, North America, and the Antipodes during the nineteenth century.

LAHED also enables me to identify when and where democracy first arose in South America, which is another key empirical contribution of the book. I define the emergence of democracy as the first ten-year period of uninterrupted democratic rule to distinguish it from what I call ephemeral democratization, which refers to fleeting democratic openings that do not have a significant, long-term impact. Although a few relatively free and fair elections took place in the region during the nineteenth century, the presidents who won these elections were either quickly overthrown or themselves undermined democracy by manipulating subsequent elections and/or clamping down on the opposition. As a result, these early democratic episodes failed to have an enduring impact. In the early twentieth century, however, some South American countries, specifically Argentina, Chile, Colombia, and Uruguay, began to hold relatively inclusive, competitive, and free and fair elections on a regular basis. Opposition parties typically participated in these elections and accepted the results, and governments began to respect civil and political liberties more consistently. To be sure, these countries did not become full democracies during this period since some electoral abuses continued and certain suffrage restrictions remained. Nevertheless, these four South American countries took major steps toward democracy that would have significant long-term benefits.

IMPLICATIONS FOR THEORIES OF DEMOCRATIZATION

The findings of this study have important implications for theories of democratization. One important theoretical implication of this book is that strong militaries may be conducive to democratization. The military is not usually thought of as a democratizing force owing to its participation in coups and repression. To the contrary, much of the literature has suggested that military weakness, rather than military strength, may lead to democratization. From this perspective, governments democratize when they believe that their military is too weak to suppress the opposition or that the costs of doing so are too high.

As the South American cases have shown, however, weak militaries often have negative consequences for democracy. Where the military is weak, the opposition will be tempted to try to seize power via armed revolt, which will undermine the rule of law and typically provoke state repression. Where the military is strong, by contrast, the opposition will have greater incentives to focus on the electoral path to power. Under these circumstances, the opposition may push for democratic reforms to level the electoral playing field and provide it with a greater chance of winning elections. Thus, the strengthening or professionalization of the military may help lead to democracy, as it did in South America during the early twentieth century.

The route taken by the democratic pioneers in South America is not the only path to democracy, however. Countries in Latin America and elsewhere have also arrived at democracy via the conflict-settlement route. Indeed, many scholars have argued that some Central American countries, such as El Salvador, Guatemala, and Nicaragua, took this path to democracy in the late twentieth century. Nevertheless, there are reasons to believe that conflict-settlement democratization may be less common than has been surmised. To begin with, the prolonged civil wars that are conducive to conflict-settlement democratization are relatively rare.[4] Lengthy civil wars have always been uncommon, but the gradual strengthening of state coercive capacity in many parts of the world have made them even rarer since governments with strong militaries are able to deter or quickly suppress most uprisings. As we have seen, the strengthening and professionalization of the armed forces in South America at the outset of the twentieth century led to a dramatic decline in revolts in that region. Even in nineteenth-century South America, however, prolonged civil wars were not that common since most revolts either toppled the government quickly or were defeated in short order.

Although lengthy civil wars have continued to take place in less developed regions of the world where state coercive capacity is low, these civil wars have rarely led to democratization. Several factors discourage the settlement of prolonged civil wars through democratization. First, informational deficits often mean that neither side in a conflict knows that it has little chance of defeating the other. Each side, for example, may overstate its own capabilities and underestimate the military strength of the other. Second, neither side can necessarily trust the other to comply with the terms of an agreement. The rebels, for example, may be concerned that if they demobilize, it will be difficult to take up arms again if the government reneges on its side of the bargain. Third, the expected costs of a democratic settlement often outweigh the expected benefits even when the conflict has stalemated. Opposition rebels may be unwilling to give up control of resources they extract from rebel-held areas in exchange for the mere possibility of winning elected positions in the future. Similarly, the ruling party may be reluctant to grant major concessions to the rebels if the rebellion is limited to isolated provinces and does not significantly undermine the economy or the government's hold on power.

---

[4] The conflict-settlement path to democratization is more likely to take place in countries that have prolonged civil wars in part because the duration of the war provides evidence that neither side can defeat the other. Conflict-settlement democratization is also more likely to occur in conflicts that are subject to international arbitration since international actors can help provide assurances that neither side will renege on the agreement. Finally, democratization through conflict settlement should be more likely where the conflict is significantly undermining the economy and where the rebels do not benefit significantly from the continuance of the conflict.

By contrast, the democratization path I describe here does not rely on the existence of a mutually recognized stalemate or a mutually beneficial and enforceable agreement. Rather, it depends on the opposition's recognition that government forces have the military capacity to easily suppress any rebellion. It therefore is more likely to occur in the wake of failed revolts or civil wars, but not in the middle of them. Revolts that have led to the resounding defeat of the opposition are particularly conducive to this type of democratization since they will make the opposition less likely to rebel again. Not surprisingly, the opposition suffered devastating defeats in revolts or civil wars that occurred in Argentina, Colombia, and Uruguay, shortly before these countries democratized.

None of this is to suggest that strengthening or professionalizing the military will inevitably lead to democratization. The military rarely uses its power to promote democratization and it frequently does not support democracy at all. Although a state monopoly on violence is conducive for democratization, it does not guarantee it will take place. Other developments, such as ruling party splits and the emergence of strong opposition parties, are necessary for democracy to come to fruition.

Another significant implication of this study is that opposition parties play a key role in the establishment and maintenance of democracy. With a few exceptions, the existing literature has not emphasized the democratizing role of opposition parties, focusing instead on ruling or conservative parties.[5] Strong conservative parties are said to reduce the likelihood of coups and ensure the stability of democracy by safeguarding the interest of elites (Gibson 1996; Middlebrook 2000b; Ziblatt 2017). Strong ruling parties, meanwhile, may serve as an instrument of horizontal accountability, preventing the president from concentrating power and undermining democracy (Rhodes-Purdy and Madrid 2020).

Although strong ruling parties and/or conservative parties may help maintain democratic stability, they do not have clear incentives to establish it in the first place. Some studies have suggested that strong ruling parties may be more supportive of democracy than weak ruling parties because they are more likely to prevail in democratic elections, but this does not explain why they would want to hold democratic elections at all (Riedl et al. 2020; Slater and Wong 2013). Democratizing measures, such as the adoption of the secret ballot, the creation of independent electoral authorities, or bans on police and military involvement in elections, typically undermine the control that ruling parties exercise over elections. As a result, ruling parties will usually oppose these measures, as they did in South America during the nineteenth and early twentieth century. Where ruling parties have supported democratization, it has typically been because they have faced strong international or societal pressures

---

[5] For an exception, see LeBas (2011).

to democratize, not because the ruling parties themselves stood to benefit from democracy.

Ruling parties and conservative parties do have incentives to extend the suffrage in some instances. As some scholars have shown, ruling parties have eliminated suffrage restrictions to win support from newly enfranchised groups, such as women (Collier 1999; Przeworski 2009a; Teele 2018). In some cases, conservative ruling parties have extended the franchise because they have believed that the rural peasantry would vote for conservative local elites (Bendix 1969; Rokkan 1970). Nevertheless, these arguments apply principally to democratic polities where ruling parties face stiff electoral competition from the opposition and thus have incentives to seek the support of new constituencies. In electoral authoritarian regimes, ruling parties typically do not need the support of new constituencies to win elections because they can rely on fraud and intimidation, among other tactics. Moreover, suffrage expansion measures pose risks to ruling parties since they will bring new voters with uncertain loyalties to the polls.[6] These new voters will reduce the electoral weight of captive constituencies, such as state employees, that many ruling parties have used to dominate elections in electoral authoritarian regimes. Finally, suffrage expansion measures make it more difficult to disqualify opposition supporters through the selective enforcement of restrictions on the franchise. As a result, ruling parties in electoral authoritarian regimes usually have incentives to oppose suffrage expansion measures as well as other types of democratic reforms.[7]

By contrast, opposition parties in electoral authoritarian regimes have clear incentives to support democratic reforms since they tend to strengthen the opposition or level the electoral playing field. The adoption of the incomplete list or proportional representation typically increases the number of legislative seats held by opposition parties. Reforms such as the secret ballot and bans on police and military involvement in elections make it more difficult for the government to intimidate and sanction opposition voters. The elimination of suffrage restrictions and the creation of independent electoral authorities reduce the government's control of elections and make it harder to bar opposition supporters from the polls. As we have seen, opposition parties tended to promote all these measures in South America during the late nineteenth and early twentieth century, and strong opposition parties were more likely than weak ones to have possessed the capacity to enact and implement the reforms.

---

[6] These risks were particularly high in Latin America during the nineteenth and early twentieth century since there were no public opinion surveys that could provide information on how newly enfranchised groups were likely to vote.

[7] As Chapter 1 discussed, ruling parties may have incentives to enact democratic reforms if they do not control the electoral authorities. In Argentina and Colombia, for example, ruling party dissidents gained control of the national government, but the traditional ruling party elites continued to control the electoral authorities. Democratic reform thus represented a means of preventing the traditional elites from continuing to manipulate elections.

I would not expect opposition parties to play an important democratizing role in all types of authoritarian regimes, however. In exclusionary authoritarian regimes, opposition parties may be banned from elections and the legislature, giving them few incentives to push for electoral reform and little possibility of enacting it. By contrast, in electoral authoritarian regimes, the opposition is generally allowed to compete in elections and participate in the legislature, providing it with ample incentives and opportunities to push for electoral reform. Nevertheless, even in electoral authoritarian regimes, opposition parties may focus largely on the armed struggle if they view that as a more promising path to power.[8] Thus, the coercive capacity of the state also helps shape whether opposition parties promote democratic reform.

A third important theoretical implication of this study is that divisions within the ruling party can play a key role in the democratization process. The democratization literature has long argued that splits within the authoritarian regime may trigger transitions to democracy (O'Donnell and Schmitter 1986; Przeworski 1992). Indeed, O'Donnell and Schmitter (1986, 19) argued long ago that "there is no transition whose beginning is not the consequence – direct or indirect – of important divisions within the authoritarian regime itself." These studies, however, focused to a large extent on how divisions between hard-liners and soft-liners within authoritarian regimes shaped negotiations with the opposition on the terms of the democratic transition. Because these studies focused on exclusionary authoritarian regimes, such as military regimes, rather than electoral authoritarian regimes, they paid little attention to how the divisions shaped the electoral incentives of some members of the ruling party.

This study argues that in electoral authoritarian regimes internal splits can realign the incentives of some members of the ruling party and affect the balance of power in the legislature. In the wake of splits, ruling party dissidents often come to fear that the dominant sector of the ruling party will use its control of elections to defeat them. As a result, these dissidents have incentives to ally, at least temporarily, with the opposition to enact democratic reforms and level the electoral playing field. In this way, they hope to maintain their access to power. By contrast, in exclusionary authoritarian regimes where elections are absent or uncontested, ruling party dissidents would not have the same incentives, but such regimes have been much less common than electoral authoritarian regimes in recent decades.

A final theoretical implication of the arguments made in this book is that development increases the likelihood of democratization, but not just in the ways that modernization theory has suggested. Modernization theory has posited that economic development helps bring about democracy by fostering more democratic values among the population and by changing the class structure

---

[8] Opposition parties may also impede democratization or contribute to its breakdown if elites view the demands of opposition parties as too extreme.

of society, strengthening groups that support democracy and weakening those that do not. By contrast, this study argues that economic development helps lead to democratization largely by strengthening the military and parties. The export boom of the late nineteenth and early twentieth century helped finance the professionalization of the military in many South American countries. It also helped pay for the improvements in transportation and communications infrastructure that facilitated the development of national parties. These alternative mechanisms may well be the main avenue through which development brings about democracy in pre-industrial regimes.

FUTURE RESEARCH AGENDA

This book has left some important areas for future research. To begin with, future studies will need to explore to what extent the arguments presented in this book can explain the emergence of democracy in other parts of the world. An obvious place to begin would be in Mexico and Central America since this region has much in common with South America. At first glance, it would appear that the factors that shaped the prospects for democracy in South America also played a role in Mesoamerica. Mexico and Central America had relatively weak militaries during the nineteenth and early twentieth century, and this led to frequent opposition revolts, which toppled governments, subverted constitutional rule, and provoked state repression (Holden 2004). The feebleness of parties in the region, meanwhile, hindered opposition efforts to contest elections and enact democratic reforms during this period.

Among the countries of Mesoamerica, only Costa Rica took major democratizing steps prior to 1930, enacting important electoral reforms in the 1920s, which led to an extended period of democracy. The opposition Agricultural Party, which held 49 percent cent of the seats in the legislature at the time, was the driving force behind the reforms, proposing measures in 1925 that aimed to weaken the government's control of elections by establishing the secret ballot, adopting a permanent civic registry of voters, and creating an electoral tribunal to oversee elections (Lehoucq and Molina 2002, 119–122, 131–135).[9] Legislators from the ruling coalition initially resisted the opposition's reform proposal, but when the president embraced it, they grudgingly went along, although they passed a number of amendments designed to cripple the reform. According to Lehoucq and Molina (2002, 123–124), the president, Ricardo Jiménez, embraced the proposed reforms largely to burnish his reputation as a reformer, and because the reforms did not affect his electoral possibilities since he could not run for immediate reelection in any event. A couple of years later, President Jiménez pushed through additional measures that strengthened

---

[9] The opposition also initially proposed extending suffrage to women, but this measure was blocked because legislators feared the uncertainty that such a dramatic expansion in the number of eligible voters would bring (Lehoucq 2000, 466).

the secrecy of the ballot and weakened the government's control of elections. Although ruling party legislators continued to resist reform, divisions within the ruling coalition made it difficult for ruling party legislators to present united resistance to the reform proposals.

Thus, it appears that the theoretical framework developed here can help explain the emergence of democracy in Costa Rica in the 1920s as well as the high levels of political instability, repression, and authoritarianism that existed in most of Mesoamerica during the nineteenth and early twentieth century. Of course, other factors presumably shaped democratic development in the region as well. Existing explanations for the emergence of democracy (or the lack thereof) in Central America have emphasized a variety of factors, including institutional configurations, political culture, agrarian structure, interclass alliances, and variation in the types and consequences of liberal reforms that countries of the region enacted in the nineteenth century (Mahoney 2001; Cruz 2005; Lehoucq and Molina 2002; Yashar 1997). These explanations may well be complementary to the arguments developed here, but I leave it to future studies to assess the relative weight of different variables in the origins of democracy in this and other regions.

Future research should also attempt to provide a more rigorous assessment of the degree to which the variables emphasized here can explain post-1929 political developments in South America and elsewhere. This book has suggested that strong parties and militaries not only helped bring about democratization in the early twentieth century but also facilitated democratic development post-1929. As we have seen, those countries that developed strong parties, such as Chile, Colombia, and Uruguay, tended to have fewer coups than those countries with weak parties, presumably in part because strong opposition parties had fewer incentives to encourage the military to intervene. Strong parties also fostered electoral competition. Those Latin American countries with at least two strong parties tended to have more closely contested elections than those countries with weak parties or only one strong party. Finally, the existence of strong parties, especially strong opposition parties, facilitated the enactment of further democratizing reforms. Indeed, opposition parties continued to promote a variety of democratic reforms throughout the twentieth century, gradually improving the functioning of democracy in the region.

The strengthening and professionalization of the military in South American countries at the outset of the twentieth century also had some long-term benefits, dramatically reducing the outsider revolts that had plagued these countries in the nineteenth century. The decline in outsider revolts, in turn, strengthened the rule of law and helped reduce state repression in the region. A few South American countries, such as Bolivia, Ecuador, and Paraguay, continued to experience outsider revolts in the early twentieth century, as did the Central American countries, but these countries were small and poor nations that were slow to strengthen and professionalize their militaries.

There was a resurgence of outsider revolts in Latin America beginning in the late 1950s as guerrilla movements arose that sought to carry out left-wing revolutions. The guerrilla movements grew strongest in countries with relatively weak and unprofessional armed forces, and they even succeeded in taking power in Cuba and Nicaragua, which had particularly feckless militaries. By contrast, in countries where the military was relatively powerful, such as Brazil and the Southern Cone countries, the guerrillas never managed to control any territory or pose a serious threat to the government.

The guerrilla revolts of the late twentieth century provoked vicious state repression and helped lead to the installation of highly exclusionary authoritarian regimes during this period. The military played a central role in the repression, and the most repressive regimes of this period were military regimes, although democratic governments also engaged in repression. The strength and level of professionalization of the armed forces appears to be inversely related to the degree of repression in Latin America, however. The greatest repression, especially on a per capita basis, occurred in those countries where the guerrillas were the strongest, especially Cuba and the Central American countries, which were generally countries with relatively weak militaries. Nevertheless, even strong and professional militaries participated in repression during this period.

Future research should explore the relationship between democracy, state repression, and military strength more systematically. It should also examine the role played by party strength in the deepening of democracy around the world. Although military professionalization and the rise of strong parties clearly contributed to the democratization of South America during the early twentieth century, we still have much to learn about how these variables affected democratic development in other time periods and parts of the world.

References

Abel, Christopher. 1974. "The Conservative Party in Colombia, 1930–53." PhD diss., History, Oxford University.
Abel, Christopher. 1987. *Política, Iglesia y Partidos en Colombia: 1886–1953*. Bogotá: Universidad Nacional de Colombia.
Abente, Diego. 1989. "The Liberal Republic and the Failure of Democracy." *The Americas* 45 (4): 525–546.
Abente, Diego. 2021. "The Case of the Traditional Parties in Paraguay." In *Diminished Parties: Democratic Representation in Contemporary Latin America*, edited by Juan Pablo Luna, Rafael Piñeiro Rodríguez, Fernando Rosenblatt, and Gabriel Vommaro, 129–150. New York: Cambridge University Press.
Acemoglu, Daron, Simon Johnson, James A. Robinson, and Pierre Yared. 2008. "Income and Democracy." *American Economic Review* 98 (3): 808–842.
Acemoglu, Daron, Simon Johnson, James A. Robinson, and Pierre Yared. 2009. "Reevaluating the Modernization Hypothesis." *Journal of Monetary Economics* 56: 1043–1058.
Acemoglu, Daron, and James A. Robinson. 2006. *Economic Origins of Dictatorship and Democracy*. New York: Cambridge University Press.
Acuña Rodríguez, Olga Yanet. 2017. "The 1910 Colombian Constitutional Reform and the Electoral System (1910–1914)." *Historia y Memoria* 14: 97–126.
Aguilar Gil, Roisida. 2002. Las Elecciones de Hace un Siglo: La Junta Electoral Nacional de 1896–1912. In *Documentos de Trabajo*. Lima: Oficina Nacional de Procesos Electorales.
Aguilar Rivera, José Antonio, Eduardo Posada-Carbó, and Eduardo Zimmermann. 2022. "Democracy in Spanish America: The Early Adoption of Universal Male Suffrage, 1810–1853." *Past and Present* 256 (1): 165–202.
Aidt, Toke, and Raphael Franck. 2014. "Workers of the World, Unite! Franchise Extensions and the Threat of Revolution in Europe, 1820–1938." *European Economic Review* (72): 52–75.
Aidt, Toke, and Raphael Franck. 2015. "Democratization under the Threat of Revolution." *Econometrica* 83 (2): 505–547.

Albertus, Michael, and Victor Menaldo. 2012. "Coercive Capacity and the Prospects for Democratization." *Comparative Politics* 44 (2): 151–169.
Aldrich, John. 1995. *Why Parties?* Chicago: University of Chicago Press.
Alemán, Eduardo, and Sebastián Saiegh. 2014. "Political Realignment and Democratic Breakdown in Argentina, 1916-1930." *Party Politics* 20 (6): 849–863.
Alexander, Robert J. 1956. "Brazilian 'Tenentismo'." *The Hispanic American Historical Review* 36 (2): 229–242.
Aljovín de Losada, Cristóbal. 2014. "Elecciones y Oficiales del Ejército: Peru 1827–1896." *Journal of Iberian and Latin American Research* 20 (1): 50–65.
Alonso, Paula. 1996. "Voting in Buenos Aires, Argentina, before 1912." In *Elections before Democracy: The History of Elections in Latin America and Europe*, edited by Eduardo Posada-Carbó, 181–199. London: Macmillan Press.
Alonso, Paula. 2000. *Between Revolution and the Ballot Box: The Origins of the Radical Party in the 1890s*. New York: Cambridge University Press.
Alonso, Paula. 2007. "Ideological Tensions in the Foundational Decade of 'Modern Argentina': The Political Debates of the 1880s." *Hispanic American Historical Review* 87 (1): 3–41.
Alonso, Paula. 2010. *Jardines Secretos, Legitimaciones Públicas: El Partido Autonomista Nacional y la Política Argentina de Fines del Siglo XIX*. Buenos Aires: Edhasa.
Álvarez, Juan. 1987. *Las Guerras Civiles Argentinas*. 8th ed. Buenos Aires: Editorial Universitaria de Buenos Aires.
Amunátegui Solar, Domingo. 1946. *La Democracia en Chile: Teatro Político, 1810–1910*. Santiago: Universidad de Chile.
Andersen, David, and Jonathan Doucette. 2022. "State First? A Disaggregation and Empirical Interrogation." *British Journal of Political Science* (52): 408–415.
Andersen, David, Jorgen Moller, Lasse Lykke Rorbaek, and Svend-Erik Skaaning. 2014. "State Capacity and Political Regime Stability." *Democratization* 21 (7): 1305–1325.
Andrews, George Reid. 2004. *Afro-Latin America, 1800–2000*. New York: Oxford University Press.
Angrist, Joshua D., and Jörn-Steffen Pischke. 2009. *Mostly Harmless Econometrics*. Princeton: Princeton University Press.
Anguita, Ricardo. 1912. *Leyes Promulgadas en Chile, Desde 1810 Hasta el 1 de Junio de 1912*. Vol. 3. Santiago: Imprenta Nacional.
Annino, Antonio, ed. 1995. *Historia de las Elecciones en Iberoamerica, Siglo XIX*. Mexico City: Fondo de Cultura Económica.
Anonymous. 1878. "Orijen de las Funciones Electorales de los Mayores Contribuyentes." *Revista Chilena* XII: 311–315.
Ansell, Ben W., and David J. Samuels. 2014. *Inequality and Democratization: An Elite-Competition Approach*. New York: Cambridge University Press.
Arancibia Clavel, Patricia, ed. 2007. *El Ejército de los Chilenos, 1540–1920*. Santiago: Editorial Biblioteca Americana.
Arancibia Clavel, Roberto. 2002. *La Influencia del Ejército Chileno en América Latina, 1900–1950*. Santiago: Centro de Estudios e Investigaciones Militares.
Aranzaes, Nicanor. 1918. *Las Revoluciones de Bolivia*. La Paz: Casa Editora Talleres Gráficos "La Prensa."
Arguedas, Alcides. 1975. *Historia General de Bolivia*. La Paz: Gisbert & Cia.
Arráiz, Antonio. 1991. *Los Días de la Ira: Las Guerras Civiles en Venezuela, 1830–1903*. Valencia: Vadell Hermanos Editores.

Arráiz Luca, Rafael. 2012. *Las Constituciones de Venezuela, 1811–1999*. Caracas: Editorial Alfa.

Atehortúa Cruz, Adolfo León. 2009. *Construcción del EjércitoNacional en Colombia, 1907–1930*. Medellín: La Carreta Editores.

Atehortúa Cruz, Adolfo León, and Humberto Vélez. 1994. *Estado y Fuerzas Armadas en Colombia (1886–1953)*. Bogotá: Tercer Mundo Editores.

Ayala Mora, Enrique. 1982. *Lucha Política y Origen de los Partidos en Ecuador*. Quito: Corporación Editona Nacional.

Ayala Mora, Enrique. 1989. *Los Partidos Políticos en el Ecuador: Síntesis Histórica*. Quito: Ediciones La Tierra.

Ayala Mora, Enrique. 1994. *Historia de la Revolución Liberal Ecuatoriana*. Quito: Corporación Editora Nacional.

Ayala Mora, Enrique. 2011. *Ecuador del Siglo XIX: Estado Nacional, Ejército, Iglesia y Municipio*. Quito: Corporación Editora Nacional.

Baland, Jean-Marie, and James A. Robinson. 2008. "Land and Power: Theory and Evidence from Chile." *American Economic Review* 98 (5): 1737–1765.

Bañales, Carlos 1970. "Las Fuerzas Armada en la Crisis Uruguaya." In *El Papel Político y Social de las Fuerzas Armadas en América Latina*, edited by Virgilio Rafael Beltrán, 289–329. Caracas: Monte Avila Editores.

Banks, Arthur S., and Kenneth Wilson. 2014. Cross-National Time-Series Data Archive. Edited by Databanks International.

Barbosa, Francisco. 2015. "Las Cinco Grandes Crisis de la Justicia en la Historia de Colombia." *El Tiempo*, March 20. Accessed November 22, 2017. www.eltiempo.com/archivo/documento/CMS-15430396.

Bareiro Spaini, Luis N. 2008. *Las Fuerzas Armadas y su Profesionalidad: Realidad y Perspectivas*. Asunción: Intercontinental Editora.

Barman, Roderick J. 1988. *Brazil: The Forging of a Nation, 1798–1852*. Stanford: Stanford University Press.

Barrán, Jose P., and Benjamín Nahum. 1987. *Batlle, los Estancieros y el Imperio Británico: La Derrota del Batllismo, 1916*. Vol. 8. Montevideo: Ediciones de la Banda Oriental.

Bartolini, Stefano. 2000. *The Political Mobilization of the European Left, 1860–1980: The Class Cleavage*. New York: Cambridge University Press.

Bartolini, Stefano, and Peter Mair. 1990. *Identity, Competition, and Electoral Availability: The Stabilisation of European Electorates, 1885–1985*. New York: Cambridge University Press.

Bartolucci, Mónica, and Miguel Angel Taroncher. 1994. "Cambios y Continuidades en las Prácticas Político-Electorales en la Provincia de Buenos Aires: 1913–1922." In *La Construcción de las Democracias Rioplatenses*, edited by Fernando J. Devoto and Marcela Ferrari, 169–187. Buenos Aires: Editorial Biblios.

Basadre, Jorge. 1968. *Historia de la República del Peru, 1822–1933*. Vol. 2. Lima: Editorial Universitaria.

Bautista Urbaneja, Diego, and Manuel Vicente Magallanes. 1997. "Partidos políticos." In *Diccionario de Historia de Venezuela*. Caracas: Fundación Empresas Polar. https://bibliofep.fundacionempresaspolar.org/dhv/entradas/p/partidos-politicos/.

Beattie, Peter M. 1999. "Conscription versus Penal Servitude: Army Reform's Influence on the Brazilian State's Management of Social Control, 1870–1930." *Journal of Social History* 32 (4): 847–878.

Beattie, Peter M. 2001. *The Tribute of Blood: Army, Honor, Race, and Nation in Brazil, 1864–1945.* Durham: Duke University Press.
Bell, Curtis. 2016. "Coup d'État and Democracy." *Comparative Political Studies* 49 (9): 1167–1200. https://doi.org/10.1177/0010414015621081.
Bendix, Reinhard. 1969. *Nation-Building and Citizenship.* New York: Anchor Books.
Bento, Claudio Moreira, and Luiz Ernani Caminha Giorgis. 2016. *Brasil: Lutas Internas, 1500–1916.* Rio de Janeiro: Federação de Academias de História Militar Terrestre do Brasil.
Bergquist, Charles W. 1978. *Coffee and Conflict in Colombia, 1886–1910.* Durham: Duke University Press.
Bértola, Luis, and José Antonio Ocampo. 2013. *The Economic Development of Latin America since Independence.* New York: Oxford University Press.
Bethell, Leslie. 2000. "Politics in Brazil: From Elections without Democracy to Democracy without Citizenship." *Daedalus* 129 (2): 1–27.
Bethell, Leslie, and José Murilo de Carvalho. 1989. "1822–1850." In *Brazil: Empire and Republic, 1822–1930*, edited by Leslie Bethell, 45–112. New York: Cambridge University Press.
Bieber, Leon E. 1994. "La Política Militar Alemana en Bolivia, 1900–1935." *Latin American Research Review* 29 (1): 85–106.
Blakemore, Harold. 1974. *British Nitrates and Chilean Politics, 1886–1896: Balmaceda and North.* London: The Athlone Press.
Blanchard, Peter. 1977. "A Populist Precursor: Guillermo Billinghurst." *Journal of Latin American Studies* 9 (2): 251–273.
Blattman, Christopher, and Edward Miguel. 2020. "Civil War." *Journal of Economic Literature* 48 (1): 3–57. doi:10.1257/jel.48.1.3.
Blaydes, Lisa. 2011. *Elections and Distributive Politics in Mubarak's Egypt.* New York: Cambridge University Press.
Blutstein, Howard I., David J. Edwards, Kathryn Therese Johnston, David S. McMoriss, and James D. Rudolph. 1985. *Venezuela: A Country Study.* Washington: Government Printing Office.
Boix, Carles. 2003. *Democracy and Redistribution.* New York: Cambridge University Press.
Boix, Carles. 2007. "The Emergence of Parties and Party Systems." In *The Oxford Handbook of Comparative Politics*, edited by Carles Boix and Susan Stokes, 499–521. New York: Oxford University Press.
Boix, Carles, Michael K. Miller, and Sebastián Rosato. 2013. "A Complete Data Set of Political Regimes, 1800–2007." *Comparative Political Studies* 46 (12): 1523–1554.
Boix, Carles, and Susan Stokes. 2003. "Endogenous Democratization." *World Politics* 55: 517–549.
Bolt, Jutta, Robert Inklaar, Herman de Jong, and Jan Luiten van Zanden. 2018. "Rebasing 'Maddison': New Income Comparisons and the Shape of Long-Run Economic Development." *Maddison Project Working Paper* 10.
Bordón, Arturo. 1962. *Verdades del Barquero.* Asunción: El Gráfico.
Bormann, Nils-Christian, Lars-Erik Cederman, and Manuel Vogt. 2017. "Language, Religion, and Ethnic Civil War." *Journal of Conflict Resolution* 61 (4): 744–771. https://doi.org/10.1177/0022002715600755.
Borón, Atilio A. 1971. La Evolución del Régimen Electoral y Sus Efectos en la Representación de los Intereses Populares: El Caso de Chile. In *Estudios ELACP* 24: Santiago: Escuela Latinoamericana de Ciencia Política y Administración Pública.

Botana, Natalio R. 2012. *El Orden Conservador: La Política Argentina Entre 1880 y 1916*. Buenos Aires: Edhasa.
Botello, Oldman. 2009. "Joaquín Crespo." In *Tierra Nuestra: 1498–2009*, edited by Heraclio Atencio Bello. Vol. 2, 41–68. Caracas: Fundación Venezuela Positiva.
Bottinelli, Oscar Alberto, Wilfredo Giménez, and Jorge Luis Marius. 2012. *Enciclopedia Electoral del Uruguay, 1900–2010*. Montevideo: Instituto Factum.
Bragoni, Beatriz. 2010. "Milicias, Ejército y Construcción del Orden Liberal en la Argentina del Siglo XIX." In *La Construcción de la Nación Argentina: El Rol de las Fuerzas Armadas*, edited by Oscar Moreno, 141–157. Buenos Aires: Ministerio de Defensa.
Brancati, Dawn. 2014. "Democratic Authoritarianism: Origins and Effects." *Annual Review of Political Science* 17: 313–326.
Bravo, Kléver Antonio, Edison Macías Núñez, and Marisol Aguilar Echeverría. 2005. *Breve Historia del Ejército Ecuatoriano*. Quito: Centro de Estudios Históricos.
Brinks, Daniel, and Michael Coppedge. 2006. "Diffusion Is No Illusion: Neighbor Emulation in the Third Wave of Democracy" *Comparative Political Studies* 39 (4): 463–489.
Brownlee, Jason. 2007. *Authoritarianism in an Age of Democratization*. New York: Cambridge University Press.
Bushnell, David. 1963. "El Sufragio en la Argentina y en Colombia Hasta 1853." *Revista del Instituto de Historia del Derecho* 19: 11–29.
Bushnell, David. 1971. "Voter Participation in the Colombian Election of 1856." *The Hispanic American Historical Review* 51 (2): 237–249.
Bushnell, David. 1972. "La Evolución del Derecho de Sufragio en Venezuela." *Boletín Histórico* 29: 189–206.
Bushnell, David. 1984. "Las Elecciones Presidenciales, 1863–1883." *Revista de Extensión Cultural* 18: 44–50.
Bushnell, David. 1992. "Politics and Violence in Nineteenth-Century Colombia." In *Violence in Colombia: The Contemporary Crisis in Historical Perspective*, edited by Charles W. Bergquist, Ricardo Peñaranda and Gonzalo Sánchez, 11–30. Wilmington: Scholarly Resources.
Bushnell, David. 1993. *Colombia: A Nation in Spite of Itself*. Berkeley: University of California Press.
Bushnell, David. 1997. "Elecciones." In *Diccionario de Historia de Venezuela*, edited by Manuel Rodríguez Campos, 201–208. Caracas: Fundación Polar.
Bushnell, David, and Neill Macaulay. 1994. *The Emergence of Latin America in the 19th Century*. 2nd ed. New York: Oxford University Press.
Butler, Robert Wayne. 1972. "The Origins of the Liberal Party in Venezuela: 1830–1848." PhD diss., History, The University of Texas.
Caballero Aquino, Ricardo, and Lorenzo Livieres Banks. 1993. *Los Partidos Políticos en América Latina: El Sistema Político Paraguayo*. Buenos Aires: Konrad Adenauer Stiftung.
Caetano, Gerardo. 1994. "La Articulación Electoral del Sistema Político Uruguayo (1919–1933)." In *La Construcción de las Democracias Rioplatenses*, edited by Fernando J. Devoto and Marcela Ferrari, 69–104. Buenos Aires: Editorial Biblos.
Caetano, Gerardo. 1999. "Ciudadanía Política e Integración Social en el Uruguay, 1900–1933." In *Ciudadanía Política y Formación de las Naciones*, edited by Hilda Sabato, 405–427. Mexico City: Fondo de Cultura Económica.

Caetano, Gerardo. 2015. *La República Batllista*. 5th ed. Vol. 1. Montevideo: Ediciones de la Banda Oriental.
Cajas Sarria, Mario Alberto. 2013. "La Corte Suprema de Justicia de Colombia, 1886–1910." *Historia Constitucional* 14: 425–465.
Camogli, Pablo. 2009. *Batallas Entre Hermanos: Todos los Combates de las Guerras Civiles Argentinas*. Buenos Aires: Aguilar.
Cantón, Dario. 1973. *Elecciones y Partidos Políticos en la Argentina: Historia, Interpretación y Balance, 1910–1966*. Buenos Aires: Siglo Veintiuno Argentina Editores.
Capello, Ernesto. 2006. "Imaging Old Quito." *City* 10 (2): 125–147.
Capoccia, Giovanni, and Daniel Ziblatt. 2010. "The Historical Turn in Democratization Studies: A New Research Agenda for Europe and Beyond." *Comparative Political Studies* 43 (8/9): 931–968.
Caramani, Daniele. 2004. *The Nationalization of Politics: The Formation of National Electorates and Party Systems in Western Europe*. New York: Cambridge University Press.
Cárcano, Miguel Angel. 1986. *Sáenz Peña: La Revolución por los Comicios*. Buenos Aires: Hyspamérica.
Cárcano, Ramón J. 1943. *Mis Primeros 80 Años*. Buenos Aires: Editorial Sudamericana.
Cardona, Christopher Michael. 2008. "Politicians, Soldiers, and Cops: Colombia's *La Violencia* in Comparative Perspective." PhD diss., Political Science, University of California.
Cardozo, Efraím. 1956. *23 de Octubre: Una Página de Historia Contemporánea del Paraguay*. Buenos Aires: Editorial Guayra.
Carvalho, José Murilo de. 1974. "Elites and State-Building in Imperial Brazil." PhD diss., Political Science, Stanford University.
Carvalho, José Murilo de. 2012. "Elections and Politics in Nineteenth-Century Brazil." In *Elections and the Origins of Democracy in the Americas, 1770s–1880s*, edited by Eduardo Posada-Carbó and J. Samuel Valenzuela. Unpublished manuscript.
Casal, Juan Manuel. 2001. "The Military Aristocracy of the Rio de la Plata: Monarchy, Republic, and Military Institutions in Argentina and Uruguay, 1806–1865." PhD diss., History, University of Iowa.
Casal, Juan Manuel. 2004. "Uruguay and the Paraguayan War: The Military Dimension." In *I Die with My Country: Perspectives on the Paraguayan War, 1864–1870*, edited by Hendrik Kraay and Thomas L. Whigham, 119–139. Lincoln: University of Nebraska Press.
Castellanos, Alfredo, and Romeo Pérez. 1981. *El Pluralismo: Examen de Experiencia Uruguaya (1830–1918)*. Vol. 1. Montevideo: CLAEH.
Castellucci, Aldin Armong Silva. 2014. "Muitos Votantes e Poucos Eleitores: A Difícil Conquista da Cidadania Operária no Brasil Império (Salvador, 1850–1881)." *Varia Historia* 30 (52): 183–206.
Castillo, Isabel. 2022. "Motivation Alignment, Historical Cleavages, and Women's Suffrage in Latin America." *Perspectives on Politics* 21 (1): 78-93. doi:10.1017/S1537592722000147.
Castro, Celso. 2001. "The Army as a Modernizing Actor in Brazil, 1870–1930." In *The Soldier and the State in South America: Essays in Civil-Military Relations*, edited by Patricio Silva, 53–70. London: Palgrave Macmillan.
Castro, Martín O. 2012. *El Ocaso de la República Oligárquica: Poder, Política y Reforma Electoral, 1898–1912*. Buenos Aires: Edhasa.

Cederman, Lars-Erik, and Luc Girardin. 2007. "Beyond Fractionalization: Mapping Ethnicity onto Nationalist Insurgencies." *American Political Science Review* 101 (1): 173–185. doi:10.1017/S0003055407070086.
Cederman, Lars-Erik, and Manuel Vogt. 2017. "Dynamics and Logics of Civil War." *Journal of Conflict Resolution* 61 (9): 1992–2016. https://doi.org/10.1177/0022002717721385.
Centeno, Miguel Angel. 2002. *Blood and Debt: War and the Nation-State in Latin America*. University Park: Pennsylvania State University Press.
Centeno, Miguel Angel, and Agustín E. Ferraro, eds. 2013. *State and Nation Making in Latin America and Spain: Republics of the Possible*. New York: Cambridge University Press.
Center for Systemic Peace. 2012. "Polity IV." Center for Systemic Peace, accessed 2012. www.systemicpeace.org/polity/polity4.htm.
Chartrain, François. 2013. *La Iglesia y los Partidos en la Vida Política del Paraguay Desde la Independencia*. Asunción: Centro de Estudios Antropológicos de la Universidad Católica.
Chasquetti, Daniel, and Daniel Buquet. 2004. "La Democracia en Uruguay: Una Partidocracia de Consenso." *Política* 42: 221–247.
Chaves, Isaías, Leopoldo Fergusson, and James A. Robinson. 2015. "He Who Counts Elects: Economic Elites, Political Elites, and Electoral Fraud." *Economics & Politics* 27 (1): 124–159.
Chávez Zamorano, Omar, Ramiro Paredes Zárate, and Wilma Velasco Aguilar. 2007. *La Autonomía Electoral: Historia Política e Institucional del Sistema Electoral Boliviano (1825–2006)*. La Paz: Konrad Adenauer Stiftung.
Chhibber, Pradeep, and Ken Kollman. 2004. *The Formation of National Party Systems: Federalism and Party Competition in Canada, Great Britain, India, and the United States*. Princeton: Princeton University Press.
Chiaramonti, Gabriella. 2000. "Construir el Centro, Redefinir al Ciudadano: Restricción del Sufragio y Reforma Electoral en el Perú de Finales del Siglo XIX." In *Legitimidad, Representación y Alternancia en España y América Latina: Las Reformas Electorales, 1880–1930*, edited by Carlos Malamud, 230–259. Mexico City: El Colegio de México.
Cifuentes, Abdón. 1936a. *Memorias*. Vol. 1. Santiago: Editorial Nascimento.
Cifuentes, Abdón. 1936b. *Memorias*. Vol. 2. Santiago: Editorial Nascimento.
Clodfelter, Michael. 2017. *Warfare and Armed Conflicts: A Statistical Encyclopedia of Casualty and Other Figures, 1492–2015*. Jefferson: McFarland & Co.
Coatsworth, John H. 1998. "Economic and Institutional Trajectories in Nineteenth-Century Latin America." In *Latin America and the World Economy since 1800*, edited by John H. Coatsworth, and Alan M. Taylor, 23–54. Cambridge: Harvard University Press.
Collier, Ruth Berins. 1999. *Paths Toward Democracy: The Working Class and Elites in Western Europe and Latin America*. New York: Cambridge University Press.
Collier, Ruth Berins, and David Collier. 1991. *Shaping the Political Arena*. Princeton: Princeton University Press.
Collier, Simon. 2003. *Chile: The Making of a Republic, 1830–1865*. New York: Cambridge University Press.
Collier, Simon, and William F. Sater. 1996. *A History of Chile, 1808–1994*. New York: Cambridge University Press.

Colombia, República de. 1906. *Constitución Política de Colombia: Actos Legislativos que la Reforman y Leyes de 1905*. Bogotá: Imprenta Nacional.

Converse, Philip. 1969. "Of Time and Partisan Stability." *Comparative Political Studies* 2 (2): 139–171.

Cooney, Jerry W. 2004. "Economy and Manpower: Paraguay at War, 1864–69." In *I Die with My Country: Perspectives on the Paraguayan War, 1864–1870*, edited by Hendrik Kraay and Thomas L. Whigham, 23–43. Lincoln: University of Nebraska Press.

Coppedge, Michael. 2012. *Democratization and Research Methods*. New York: Cambridge University Press.

Coppedge, Michael et al., 2020. V-Dem Data Set – Version 10. Varieties of Democracy (V-Dem) Project.

Coppedge, Michael et al., 2022a. *V-Dem Codebook v12*. Gothenburg: Varieties of Democracy (V-Dem) Project.

Coppedge, Michael et al., 2022b. V-Dem Data Set – Version 12. Varieties of Democracy (V-Dem) Project.

Coppedge, Michael et al., 2023. V-Dem Data Set – Version 13. Varieties of Democracy (V-Dem) Project.

Coppedge, Michael et al., 2024a. *V-Dem Codebook v14*. Gothenburg: Varieties of Democracy (V-Dem) Project.

Coppedge, Michael et al., 2024b. V-Dem Data Set – Version 14. Varieties of Democracy (V-Dem) Project.

Corbo, Daniel J. 2016. *El Origen del Partido Nacional*. Montevideo: Ediciones de la Plaza.

Cornblit, Oscar. 1975. "La Opción Conservadora en la República Argentina." *Desarrollo Económico* 14 (56): 599–639.

Correlates of War Project. 2020. National Material Capabilities. Version 5. https://correlatesofwar.org/data-sets/national-material-capabilities/

Costa, Emília Viotti da. 1986. "Brazil: The Age of Reform, 1870–1889." In *The Cambridge History of Latin America*, edited by Leslie Bethell, 725–778. New York: Cambridge University Press.

Costa, Emília Viotti da. 1989. "1870–1889." In *Brazil: Empire and Republic, 1822–1930*, edited by Leslie Bethell, 161–213. New York: Cambridge University Press.

Covo, Adelina. 2013. *El Chocorazo: El Fraude de Reyes en 1904*. Bogotá: Grupo Editorial Ibáñez.

Cruz, Consuelo. 2005. *Political Culture and Institutional Development in Costa Rica and Nicaragua: World Making in the Tropics*. New York: Cambridge University Press.

Dahl, Robert A. 1971. *Polyarchy: Participation and Opposition*. New Haven: Yale University Press.

de Privitellio, Luciano. 2006. "Representación Política, Orden y Progreso: La Reforma Electoral de 1902." *Política y Gestión* 9: 1–30.

de Tocqueville, Alexis. [1835] 1945. *Democracy in America*. New York: Knopf.

Deas, Malcolm. 1996. "The Role of the Church, the Army and the Police in Colombian Elections." In *Elections before Democracy: The History of Elections in Europe and Latin America*, edited by Eduardo Posada-Carbó, 163–180. London: Institute for Latin American Studies.

Deas, Malcolm. 2002a. "The Man on Foot: Conscription and the Nation-State in Nineteenth-Century Latin America." In *Studies in the Formation of the Nation State in Latin America*, edited by James Dunkerley, 77–93. London: Institute of Latin American Studies.

Deas, Malcolm. 2012. "Venezuelan Elections, 1830–1900." In *Elections and the Origins of Democracy in the Americas, 1770s–1880s*, edited by Eduardo Posada-Carbó and J. Samuel Valenzuela. Unpublished manuscript.

del Águila Peralta, Alicia. 2013. *La Ciudadania Corporativa: Política, Constituciones y Sufragio en el Perú (1821–1896)*. Lima: Instituto de Estudios Peruanos.

Del Mazo, Gabriel. 1957. *El Radicalismo: Ensayo Sobre su Historia y Doctrina*. Buenos Aires: Ediciones Gure.

Del Valle, Florentino. 1951. *Cartilla Política: Proceso Político del Paraguay, 1870–1950*. Buenos Aires: Talleres Gráficos Lucania.

Delpar, Helen. 1980. "Colombian Liberalism and the Roman Catholic Church, 1863–1886." *Journal of Church and State* 22 (2): 271–293.

Delpar, Helen. 1981. *Red against Blue: The Liberal Party in Colombian Politics: 1863–1899*. Tuscaloosa: University of Alabama Press.

Demélas, Marie-Danielle. 2003. *La Invención Política: Bolivia, Ecuador y Perú en el Siglo XIX*. Lima: Instituto Frances de Estudios Andinos.

Devoto, Fernando J. 1996. "De Nuevo el Acontecimiento: Roque Sáenz Peña, la Reforma Electoral y el Momento Político de 1912." *Boletín del Instituto de Historia Argentina y Americana "Dr. Emilio Ravignani"* 3 (14): 93–113.

Devoto, Fernando J., Marcela Ferrari, and Julio Melón. 1997. "The Peaceful Transformation? Changes and Continuities in Argentinian Political Practices, 1910–22." In *Political Culture, Social Movements and Democratic Transitions in South America in the 20th Century*, edited by Fernando J. Devoto and Torcuato S. Di Tella, 167–191. Milan: Fondazione Giangiacomo Feltrinelli Milano.

Di Tella, Torcuato S. 1971–72. "La Búsqueda de la Fórmula Política Argentina." *Desarrollo Económico* (2): 317–325.

Diacon, Todd. 1995. "Bringing the Countryside Back In: A Case Study of Military Intervention as State Building." *Journal of Latin American Studies* 27 (3): 569–592.

Díaz Arguedas, Julio. 1971. *Historia del Ejército de Bolivia, 1825–1932*. La Paz: Editorial Don Bosco.

Dick, Enrique. 2014. *La Professionalización en el Ejército Argentino, 1899–1914*. Buenos Aires: Academia Nacional de la Historia.

Diez de Medina, Alvaro. 1994. *El Voto que el Alma Pronuncia: Historia Electoral del Uruguay*. Montevideo: Fundación de Cultura Universitaria.

Dinas, Elias. 2014. "Does Choice Bring Loyalty? Electoral Participation and the Development of Party Identification." *American Journal of Political Science* 58 (2): 449–465.

Dix, Robert H. 1992. "Democratization and the Institutionalization of Latin American Political Parties." *Comparative Political Studies* 24 (4): 488–511.

Donoso, Ricardo. 1967. *Las Ideas Políticas en Chile*. Santiago: Editorial Universitaria.

Drake, Paul. 2009. *Between Tyranny and Anarchy: A History of Democracy in Latin America, 1800–2006*. Stanford: Stanford University Press.

Dudley, William S. 1975. "Institutional Sources of Officer Discontent in the Brazilian Army, 1870–1889." *The Hispanic American Historical Review* 55 (1): 44–65.

Dudley, William S. 1978. "Professionalization of the Brazilian Military in the Late Nineteenth Century." In *The Politics of Antipolitics: The Military in Latin America*, edited by Brian Loveman and Thomas Davies Jr., 58–64. Lincoln: University of Nebraska Press.

Duncan, William Timothy. 1981. "Government by Audacity: Politics and the Argentine Economy, 1885–1892." PhD diss., Economic History, University of Melbourne.

Dunkerley, James. 2003. *Orígenes del Poder Militar: Bolivia, 1879–1935*. La Paz: Plural Editores.
Duque Daza, Javier. 2011. "La Reforma Constitucional de 1910: Constantes Institucionales, Consensos y Nuevas Reglas." *Papel Político* 16 (1): 185–212.
Durán Bernales, Florencio. 1958. *El Partido Radical*. Santiago: Editorial Nascimento.
Duverger, Maurice. 1972. *Political Parties*. London: University Paperbacks.
Earle, Rebecca. 2000a. "Introduction." In *Rumours of Wars: Civil Conflict in Nineteenth-Century Latin America*, edited by Rebecca Earle, 1–5. London: Institute of Latin American Studies.
Earle, Rebecca. 2000b. "The War of the Supremes: Border Conflict, Religious Crusade or Simply Politics by Other Means." In *Rumours of War: Civil Conflict in Nineteenth-Century Latin America*, edited by Rebecca Earle, 119–134. London: Institute of Latin American Studies.
Encina, Francisco A. 1949. *Historia de Chile: Desde la Prehistoria Hasta 1891*. Vol. 13. Santiago: Editorial Nascimento.
Encina, Francisco A. 1950. *Historia de Chile: Desde la Prehistoria Hasta 1891*. Vol. 14. Santiago: Editorial Nascimento.
Encina, Francisco A. 1952. *La Presidencia de Balmaceda*. Vol. 1. Santiago: Editorial Nascimento.
Engerman, Stanley L., and Kenneth Sokoloff. 2012. *Economic Development in the Americas since 1500: Endowments and Institutions*. New York: Cambridge University Press.
Epstein, Leon D. 1980. *Political Parties in Western Democracies*. New Brunswick: Transaction Books.
Esquivel Triana, Ricardo. 2010. *Neutralidad y Orden: Política Exterior y Militar en Colombia, 1886–1918*. Bogotá: Pontificia Universidad Javeriana.
Esteban, Joan, Laura Mayoral, and Debraj Ray. 2012. "Ethnicity and Conflict: An Empirical Study." *American Economic Review* 102 (4): 1310–1342. doi:10.1257/aer.102.4.1310.
Estelle Méndez, Patricio. 1970. "El Club de la Reforma de 1868–1871: Notas para el Estudio de una Combinación Política en el Siglo XIX." *Revista Historia* 9: 111–135.
Fausto, Boris. 1989. "Society and Politics." In *Brazil: Empire and Republic, 1822–1930*, edited by Leslie Bethell, 257–307. New York: Cambridge University Press.
Fearon, James D. 2004. "Why Do Some Civil Wars Last So Much Longer than Others?." *Journal of Peace Research* 41 (3): 275–301. https://doi.org/10.1177/0022343304043770.
Fearon, James D. 2010. "Governance and Civil War Onset." *World Development Report 2011 Background Paper*.
Fearon, James D., and David D. Laitin. 2003. "Ethnicity, Insurgency, and Civil War." *American Political Science Review* 97 (1): 75–90. doi:10.1017/S0003055403000534.
Federici, Mario F. 2005. "Sistema Político y Crisis de la UCR a Fines del Siglo XIX." In *De la República Oligárquica a la República Democrática: Estudio Sobre la Reforma Política de Roque Sáenz Peña*, edited by Mario Justo López, 69–118. Buenos Aires: Ediciones Lumiere.
Federico, Giovanni, and Antonio Tena-Junguito. 2016. "World Trade, 1800–1938: A New Data Set." *European Historical Economics Society, Working Paper* (93).
Fernández Abara, Joaquín. 2017. "Las Guerras Civiles en Chile." In *Historia Política de Chile, 1810–2010*, edited by Iván Jaksic and Juan Luis Ossa Santa Cruz, 53–82. Santiago: Fondo de Cultura Económica.

Fernández, Nelson, and Hugo Machín. 2017. *Una Democracia Única: Historia de los Partidos Políticos y las Elecciones del Uruguay*. Montevideo: Editorial Fin de Siglo.
Ferrer Llul, Francisco. 1975. *Sinopsis Gráfica de la Historia Militar del Uruguay*. Montevideo: Barreiro y Ramos Editores.
Fitch, John Samuel. 1977. *The Military Coup d'Etat as a Political Process: Ecuador, 1948–1966*. Baltimore: The Johns Hopkins University Press.
Fitch, John Samuel. 1998. *The Armed Forces and Democracy in Latin America*. Baltimore: The Johns Hopkins University Press.
Fitzgibbon, Russell H. 1957. "The Party Potpourri in Latin America." *The Western Political Quarterly* 10 (1): 3–22.
Floyd, Mary Bernice. 1982. "Antonio Guzmán Blanco: The Dynamics of Septenio Politics." PhD diss., Indiana University.
Forment, Carlos A. 2003. *Democracy in Latin America, 1760–1900: Civic Selfhood and Public Life in Mexico and Peru*. Vol. 1. Chicago: University of Chicago Press.
Forte, Riccardo. 2002. "Incertidumbre y Determinación: Transición Liberal y Construcción del Poder Coactivo del Estado en México y Argentina (ca. 1855–1880)." *Anuario de Historia Regional y de las Fronteras* 7 (1): 213–244.
Franceschi, Napoleón. 2019. *Caudillos y Caudillismo en la Historia de Venezuela*. Caracas: Universidad Metropolitana Publicaciones Arbitradas.
Franco, Manuel. 1917. *Mensaje del Presidente de la República del Paraguay: Dr. Don Manuel Franco*. Asunción: Talleres Gráficos del Estado.
Franco, Manuel. 1919. *Mensaje del Presidente de la República del Paraguay: Dr. Don Manuel Franco*. Asunción: Talleres Gráficos del Estado.
Gabaldón, Eleonora. 1986. *Las Elecciones Presidenciales de 1835: La Elección del Dr. José María Vargas*. Caracas: Academia Nacional de la Historia.
Galdama, Luis. 1964. *A History of Chile*. New York: Russell & Russell.
Gallo, Ezequiel. 1986. "Argentina: Society and Politics, 1880–1916." In *The Cambridge History of Latin America*, edited by Leslie Bethell, 359–391. New York: Cambridge University Press.
Gallo, Ezequiel, and Silvia Sigal. 1963. "La Formación de los Partidos Contemporáneos: La Unión Cívica Radical (1890–1916)." *Desarrollo Económico* 3 (1–2): 173–230.
Gallup, John Luke, Alejandro Gaviria, and Eduardo Lora. 2003. *Is Geography Destiny? Lessons from Latin America*. Washington: Inter-American Development Bank.
Gandhi, Jennifer. 2008. *Political Institutions under Dictatorship*. New York: Cambridge University Press.
Gandhi, Jennifer, and Ellen Lust-Okar. 2009. "Elections under Authoritarianism." *Annual Review of Political Science* 12: 403–422.
Garavaglia, Juan Carlos. 2003. "Ejército y Milicia: Los Campesinos Bonaerenses y el Peso de las Exigencias Militares, 1810–1860." *Anuario IEHS* 18: 153–187.
García Bryce, Iñigo. 2004. *Crafting the Republic: Lima's Artisans and Nation Building in Peru, 1821–1879*. Albuquerque: University of New Mexico Press.
García Covarrubias, Jaime. 1990. *El Partido Radical y la Clase Media: La Relación de Intereses Entre 1888 y 1938*. Santiago: Editorial Andrés Bello.
García Molina, Fernando. 2010. *La Prehistoria del Poder Militar en la Argentina: La Professionalización, el Modelo Alemán y la Decadencia del Régimen Oligárquico*. Buenos Aires: Eudeba.

García Ponce, Antonio. 2009. "Antonio Guzmán Blanco." In *Tierra Nuestra: 1498–2009*, edited by Heraclio Atencio Bello. Vol 1, 419–450. Caracas: Fundación Venezuela Positiva.

Gatti Cardozo, Gustavo. 1990. *El Papel Político de los Militares en el Paraguay, 1870–1990*. Vol. 35. Asunción: Biblioteca de Estudios Paraguayos.

Gazmuri, Cristián. 2002. "Las Revoluciones Europeas de 1848 y su Influencia en la Historia Política de Chile." In *The European Revolution of 1848 and the Americas*, edited by Guy Thomson, 158–190. London: Institute of Latin American Studies.

Gazmuri, Cristián. 2019. *El "48" Chileno: Igualitarios, Radicales, Reformistas, Masones y Bomberos*. Santiago: RiL Editores.

Geddes, Barbara, Joseph G. Wright, and Erica Frantz. 2018. *How Dictatorships Work*. New York: Cambridge University Press.

Gelman, Jorge, and Sol Lanteri. 2010. "El Sistema Militar de Rosas y la Confederación Argentina (1829–1852)." In *La Construcción de la Nación Argentina: El Rol de las Fuerzas Armadas*, edited by Oscar Moreno, 81–98. Buenos Aires: Ministerio de Defensa.

Gerlach, Allen. 1973. "Civil-Military Relations in Peru, 1914–1945." PhD diss., History, The University of New Mexico.

Gerring, John. 2007. *Case Study Research: Principles and Practices*. New York: Cambridge University Press.

Gerring, John, and Brendan Apfeld. 2018. Global Democracy for Europeans: A Demographic Study. In *Working Paper*. Gothenburg: The Varieties of Democracy Institute.

Gerring, John, Brendan Apfeld, Tore Wig, and Andreas Tollefsen. 2022. *The Deep Roots of Modern Democracy*. New York: Cambridge University Press.

Gibson, Edward. 1996. *Class and Conservative Parties: Argentina in Comparative Perspective*. Baltimore: The Johns Hopkins University Press.

Gil Fortoul, José. 1942. *Historia Constitucional de Venezuela*. Vol. 2. Caracas: Editorial Las Novedades.

Gil Fortoul, José. 1956. *El Hombre y la Historia. Obras Completas*. Vol. 4. Caracas: Ministerio de Educación.

Gilmore, Robert L. 1964. *Caudillism and Militarism in Venezuela, 1810–1910*. Athens: Ohio University Press.

Giudici, Roberto R. 1928. *Batlle y el Batllismo*. Montevideo: Imprenta Nacional Colorada.

Gleditsch, Kristian Skrede, and Michael D. Ward. 2006. "Diffusion and the International Context of Democratization." *International Organization* 60 (4): 911–933.

Gómez, Carlos Alarico. 2009. "Juan Vicente Gómez." In *Tierra Nuestra: 1498–2009*, edited by Heraclio Atencio Bello. Vol 1, 103–134. Caracas: Fundación Venezuela Positiva.

Gondra, Manuel. 1921. *Mensaje del Presidente de la República del Paraguay*. Asunción: Imprenta Nacional.

Góngora, Mario. 1981. *Ensayo Histórico Sobre la Noción de Estado en Chile en los Siglos XIX y XX*. Santiago: Ediciones La Ciudad.

González de Oleaga, Marisa. 2000. "El Problema de la Legitimidad: Valores e Intereses en la Ampliación del Sufragio en Paraguay Liberal." In *Legitimidad, Representación y Alternancia en España y América Latina: Las Reformas Electorales, 1880–1930*, edited by Carlos Malamud, 182–207. Mexico City: Fondo de Cultura Económica.

González, Rodolfo. 1991. *Legislación Electoral del Uruguay*. Vol. 1. Montevideo: Centro de Estudios para la Democracia Uruguaya.

Gootenberg, Paul. 1991. "Population and Ethnicity in Early Republican Peru: Some Revisions." *Latin American Research Review* 26 (3): 109–157.
Gopnik, Adam. 2019. "Diderot Dicta." *The New Yorker*, March 4, 54–60.
Graham, Richard. 1989. "1850–1870." In *Brazil: Empire and Republic, 1822–1930*, edited by Leslie Bethell, 113–160. New York: Cambridge University Press.
Graham, Richard. 1990. *Patronage and Politics in Nineteenth-Century Brazil*. Stanford: Stanford University Press.
Grauer, Ryan. 2015. "Moderating Diffusion: Military Bureaucratic Politics and the Implementation of German Doctrine in South America, 1885–1914." *World Politics* 67 (2): 268–312.
Guardia Rolando, Inés, and Giannina Olivieri Pacheco. 2016. *Estudio de las Relaciones Civiles Militares en Venezuela Desde el Siglo XIX Hasta Nuestros Días*. Caracas: Universidad Católica Andrés Bello.
Guerra, François-Xavier. 1994. "The Spanish-American Tradition of Representation and its European Roots." *Journal of Latin American Studies* 26: 1–35.
Guilisasti Tagle, Sergio. 1964. *Partidos Políticos Chilenos*. Santiago: Editorial Nascimento.
Hahner, June. 1969. "The Brazilian Armed Forces and the Overthrow of the Monarchy: Another Perspective." *The Americas* 26 (2): 171–182.
Hanratty, Dennis M., and Sandra W. Meditz, eds. 1988. *Paraguay: A Country Study*. Washington: Library of Congress.
Harbers, Imke. 2010. "Decentralization and the Development of Nationalized Party Systems in New Democracies: Evidence from Latin America." *Comparative Political Studies* 43 (5): 606–627.
Hariri, Jacob Gerner. 2012. "The Autocratic Legacy of Early Statehood." *American Political Science Review* 106 (3): 471–494.
Hariri, Jacob Gerner, and Asger Mose Wingender. 2023. "Jumping the Gun: How Dictators Got Ahead of Their Subjects." *The Economic Journal* 133 (650): 728–760.
Hasbun, Cristóbal. 2016. "TRICEL: Historia, Legislación Comparada y Revisión de sus Funciones." *Debates de Política Pública* (16): 1–30.
Heaps-Nelson, George. 1978. "La Aprobación de la Ley Sáenz Peña." *Revista de Historia* 7: 9–26.
Hegre, Håvard, Tanja Ellingsen, Scott Gates, and Nils Petter Gleditsch. 2001. "Toward a Democratic Civil Peace? Democracy, Political Change and Civil War, 1816–1992." *American Political Science Review* 95 (1): 33–48. doi:10.1017/S0003055401000119.
Heise González, Julio. 1974. *Historia de Chile: El Período Parlamentario, 1861–1925*. Vol. 1. Santiago: Editorial Andrés Bello.
Heise González, Julio. 1978. *Años de Formación y Aprendizaje Político, 1810–1833*. Santiago: Editorial Universitaria.
Heise González, Julio. 1982. *Historia de Chile: El Periodo Parlamentario, 1861–1925*. Vol. 2. Santiago: Editorial Universitaria.
Hellinger, Daniel. 1978. "Electoral Change in the Chilean Countryside: The Presidential Elections of 1958 and 1970." *The Western Political Quarterly* 31 (2): 253–278.
Henderson, Peter V. N. 2008. *Gabriel García Moreno and Conservative State Formation in the Andes*. Austin: University of Texas Press.
Hendrix, Cullen S. 2010. "Measuring State Capacity: Theoretical and Empirical Implications for the Study of Civil Conflict." *Journal of Peace Research* 47 (3): 191–208. https://doi.org/10.1177/0022343310361838.

Hensel, Paul R. 1994. "One Thing Leads to Another: Recurrent Militarized Disputes in Latin America, 1816–1986." *Journal of Peace Research* 31 (3): 281–297. https://doi.org/10.1177/0022343394031003004.

Hicks, Frederic. 1967. "Politics, Power, and the Role of the Village Priest in Paraguay." *Journal of Interamerican Studies and World Affairs* 9 (2): 273–282.

Hicks, Frederic. 1971. "Interpersonal Relationships and Caudillismo in Paraguay." *Journal of Interamerican Studies and World Affairs* 13 (1): 89–111.

Hidalgo Morey, Teodoro, Lourdes Medina Montoya, Guillermo Sánchez Ortíz, and Manuel Gálvez Ríos. 2005. *Historia General del Ejército del Perú: El Ejército en la República, Siglo XIX*. Vol. 5. Lima: Comisión Permanente de Historia del Ejército del Perú.

Hierro López, Luis A. 2015. *Las Raíces Coloradas: Fundamentos del Partido de Don Pepe Batlle*. Montevideo: Ediciones de la Banda Oriental.

Hillmon Jr., Tommie. 1963. "A History of the Armed Forces of Chile from Independence to 1920." PhD diss., History, Syracuse University.

Holden, Robert H. 2004. *Armies without Nations: Public Violence and State Formation in Central America, 1821–1960*. New York: Oxford University Press.

Holguín, Jorge. 1976. "Desde Cerca: Asuntos Colombianos." In *Aspectos Sociales de las Guerras Civiles en Colombia*, edited by Alvaro Tirado Mejía, 83–86. Bogotá: Instituto Colombiano de Cultura.

Holsti, Kalevi J. 1996. *The State, War, and the State of War*. New York: Cambridge University Press.

Hora, Roy. 2001. *The Landowners of the Argentine Pampas: A Social and Political History, 1860–1945*. New York: Oxford University Press.

Horowitz, Donald L. 1985. *Ethnic Groups in Conflict*. Berkeley: University of California Press.

Huntington, Samuel P. 1957. *The Soldier and the State: The Theory and Politics of Civil-Military Relations*. Cambridge: Belknap/Harvard.

Huntington, Samuel P. 1968. *Political Order in Changing Societies*. New Haven: Yale University Press.

Ibarra Rueda, Héctor. 2013. "Why Factions Matter: A Theory of Party Dominance at the Sub-National Level." PhD diss., Government, University of Texas at Austin.

Instituto Nacional de Estadística. 2021. "Población en el País Según Departamento, Censos de Población años 1852, 1860, 1908, 1963, 1975, 1985, 1996, 2004 (Fase 1) y 2011." Instituto Nacional de Estadística. www.ine.gub.uy/web/guest/censos-1852-2011.

Irurozqui, Marta. 1997. "Political Leadership and Popular Consent: Party Strategies in Bolivia, 1880–1899." *The Americas* 53 (3): 395–423.

Irurozqui, Marta. 2000. *A Bala, Piedra y Palo: La Construcción de la Ciudadanía Política en Bolivia, 1826–1952*. Sevilla: Diputación de Sevilla.

Irwin, Domingo, and Ingrid Micett. 2008. *Caudillos, Militares y Poder: Una Historia del Pretorianismo en Venezuela*. Caracas: Universidad Católica Andrés Bello.

Jaramillo, Carlos Eduardo. 1986. "La Guerra de los Mil Dias: Aspectos Estructurales de la Organización Guerrillera." In *Pasado y Presente de la Violencia en Colombia*, edited by Gonzalo Sánchez and Ricardo Peñaranda, 47–86. Bogotá: Fondo Editorial CEREC.

Jaramillo, Juan, and Beatriz Franco-Cuervo. 2005. "Colombia." In *Elections in the Americas*, edited by Dieter Nohlen, 295–364. New York: Oxford University Press.

Johnson, John J. 1964. *The Military and Society in Latin America*. Stanford: Stanford University Press.

Jones, Mark P., Martín Lauga, and Marta León-Roesch. 2005. "Argentina." In *Elections in the Americas*, edited by Dieter Nohlen, 59–122. New York: Oxford University Press.
Jones, Mark P., and Scott Mainwaring. 2003. "The Nationalization of Parties and Party Systems." *Party Politics* 9 (2): 139–166.
Jurado Jurado, Juan Carlos. 2005. "Soldados, Pobres y Reclutas en las Guerras Civiles Colombianas." In *Ganarse el Cielo Defendiendo la Religión: Guerras Civiles en Colombia, 1840–1902*, edited by Luis Ortíz Mesa, 211–235. Bogotá: Universidad Nacional de Colombia.
Kallsen, Osvaldo. 1983. *Historia del Paraguay Contemporáneo*. Asunción: Imprenta Modelo.
Kalyvas, Stathis N. 1996. *The Rise of Christian Democracy in Europe*. Ithaca, NY: Cornell University Press.
Klarén, Peter F. 1986. "The Origins of Modern Peru, 1880–1930." In *The Cambridge History of Latin America*, edited by Leslie Bethell, 587–640. New York: Cambridge University Press.
Klarén, Peter F. 2000. *Peru: Society and Nationhood in the Andes*. New York: Oxford University Press.
Klein, Herbert S. 1969a. "The Colored Freedmen in Brazilian Slave Society." *Journal of Social History* 3 (1): 30–52.
Klein, Herbert S. 1969b. *Parties and Political Change in Bolivia, 1880–1952*. New York: Cambridge University Press.
Klein, Herbert S. 1995. "A Participação Política no Brasil do Século XIX: Os Votantes de São Paulo em 1880." *Dados – Revista de Ciências Sociais* 38 (3): 527–544.
Kleinpenning, Jan M. G. 1992. *Rural Paraguay, 1870–1932*. Amsterdam: Centro de Estudios y Documentación Latinoamericanos.
Kleinpenning, Jan M. G. 2002. "Strong Reservations about 'New Insights into the Demographics of the Paraguayan War'." *Latin American Research Review* 37 (3): 137–142.
Kraay, Hendrik. 1992. "As Terrifying as Unexpected: The Bahian Sabinada, 1837–1838." *The Hispanic American Historical Review* 72 (4): 501–527.
Kurtz, Marcus J. 2013. *Latin American State Building in Comparative Perspective: Social Foundations of Institutional Order*. New York: Cambridge University Press.
Langston, Joy. 2002. "Breaking Out Is Hard to Do: Exit, Voice, and Loyalty in Mexico's One-Party Hegemonic Regime." *Latin American Politics and Society* 44 (3): 61–88.
LaPalombara, Joseph, and Myron Weiner. 1966. "The Origin and Development of Political Parties." In *Political Parties and Political Development*, edited by Joseph LaPalombara and Myron Weiner, 3–42. Princeton: Princeton University Press.
Lauderbaugh, George. 2012. *The History of Ecuador*. Santa Barbara: Greenwood.
LeBas, Adrienne. 2011. *From Protest to Parties: Party-Building and Democratization in Africa*. New York: Oxford University Press.
Lehoucq, Fabrice. 2000. "Institutionalizing Democracy: Constraint and Ambition in the Politics of Electoral Reform." *Comparative Politics* 32 (4): 459–477.
Lehoucq, Fabrice, and Iván Molina. 2002. *Stuffing the Ballot Box: Fraud, Electoral Reform, and Democratization in Costa Rica*. New York: Cambridge University Press.
Lemaitre, Eduardo. 2002. *Rafael Reyes: Caudillo, Aventurero y Dictador*. Bogotá: Intermedio Editores.

Levitsky, Steven. 2003. *Transforming Labor-Based Parties in Latin America*. New York: Cambridge University Press.
Levitsky, Steven, James Loxton, and Brandon Van Dyck. 2016. "Introduction: Challenges of Party-Building in Latin America." In *Challenges of Party-Building in Latin America*, edited by Steven Levitsky, James Loxton, Brandon Van Dyck and Jorge I. Domínguez, 1–48. New York: Cambridge University Press.
Levitsky, Steven, and Lucan A. Way. 2010. *Competitive Authoritarianism: Hybrid Regimes after the Cold War*. New York: Cambridge University Press.
Lewis, Colin. 2002. "The Political Economy of State-Making: The Argentine, 1852–1955." In *Studies in the Formation of the Nation State in Latin America*, edited by James Dunkerley, 161–188. London: Institute for Latin American Studies.
Lewis, Paul H. 1986. "Paraguay from the War of the Triple Alliance to the Chaco War, 1870–1932." In *The Cambridge History of Latin America*, edited by Leslie Bethell, 475–496. New York: Cambridge University Press.
Lewis, Paul H. 1993. *Political Parties and Generations in Paraguay's Liberal Era, 1869–1940*. Chapel Hill: University of North Carolina Press.
Lieuwen, Edwin. 1961. *Arms and Politics in Latin America*. New York: Praeger.
Ligon, Steven R. 2002. "The Character of Border Conflict: Latin American Border Conflicts, 1830–1995." PhD diss., The Catholic University of America.
Lindahl, Goran G. 1962. *Uruguay's New Path: A Study in Politics during the First Colegiado, 1919–33*. Stockholm: Library and Institute of Ibero-American Studies.
Lindberg, Staffan I. 2006. *Democracy and Elections in Africa*. Baltimore: The Johns Hopkins University Press.
Lindberg, Staffan I., ed. 2009. *Democratization by Elections: A New Mode of Transition*. Baltimore: The Johns Hopkins University Press.
Lipset, Seymour Martin. 1983. *Political Man: The Social Bases of Politics*. New York: William Heinemann Ltd.
Lipset, Seymour Martin, and Stein Rokkan. 1967. "Cleavage Structures, Party Systems, and Voter Alignments." In *Party Systems and Voter Alignments: Cross-National Perspectives*, edited by Seymour Martin Lipset and Stein Rokkan, 1–64. New York: The Free Press.
Loayza, Alex. 2005. "El Club Progresista y la Coyuntura Electoral de 1849–1851." In *Historia de las Elecciones en el Perú: Estudios Sobre el Gobierno Representativo*, edited by Cristóbal Aljovín de Losada and Sinesio López, 395–424. Lima: Instituto de Estudios Peruanos.
Lombardi, John V. 1982. *Venezuela: The Search for Order, The Dream of Progress*. New York: Oxford University Press.
López-Alves, Fernando. 2000. *State Formation and Democracy in Latin America, 1810–1900*. Durham: Duke University Press.
López Chirico, Selva. 1985. *Estado y Fuerzas Armadas en el Uruguay*. Montevideo: Ediciones de la Banda Oriental.
López, Mario Justo. 2001a. *Entre la Hegemonía y el Pluralismo: Evolución del Sistema de Partidos Políticos Argentinos*. Buenos Aires: Lumiere.
López, Mario Justo. 2001b. "Pluralismo de Provincias, 1852–1879." In *Entre la Hegemonía y el Pluralismo: Evolución del Sistema de Partidos Políticos en la Argentina*, edited by Mario Justo López, 37–65. Buenos Aires: Ediciones Lumiere.
López, Mario Justo. 2005a. "Antecedentes de la Reforma Electoral, 1893–1910." In *De la República Oligárquica a la República Democrática: Estudio Sobre la Reforma*

Política de Roque Sáenz Peña, edited by Mario Justo López, 183–216. Buenos Aires: Ediciones Lumiere.

López, Mario Justo. 2005b. "La Elección de Roque Sáenz Peña y la Estrategia de la Reforma Electoral." In *De la República Oligárquica a la República Democrática: Estudio Sobre la Reforma Política de Roque Sáenz Peña*, edited by Mario Justo López, 216–252. Buenos Aires: Lumiere.

López, Mario Justo. 2005c. "La Nueva Ley Electoral." In *De la República Oligárquica a la República Democrática: Estudio Sobre la Reforma Política de Roque Sáenz Peña*, edited by Mario Justo López, 253–316. Buenos Aires: Lumiere.

Lora, Guillermo. 1987. *Historia de los Partidos Políticos en Bolivia*. La Paz: Ediciones La Colmena.

Lott, Leo B. 1956. "Executive Power in Venezuela." *The American Political Science Review* 50 (2): 422–441.

Love, Joseph L. 1970. "Political Participation in Brazil, 1881–1969." *Luso-Brazilian Review* 7 (2): 3–24.

Love, Joseph L. 1980. *São Paulo in the Brazilian Federation, 1889–1937*. Stanford: Stanford University Press.

Loveman, Brian. 1993. *The Constitution of Tyranny: Regimes of Exception in Spanish America*. Pittsburgh: University of Pittsburgh Press.

Loveman, Brian. 1999. *For la Patria: Politics and the Armed Forces in Latin America*. Wilmington: Scholarly Resources.

Loveman, Brian, and Thomas Davies Jr., eds. 1978. *The Politics of Antipolitics: The Military in Latin America*. Lincoln: University of Nebraska Press.

Lupu, Noam, and Susan Stokes. 2010. "Democracy, Interrupted: Regime Change and Partisanship in Twentieth-Century Argentina." *Electoral Studies* 29 (2010): 91–104.

Lynch, John. 2006. *Argentine Caudillo: Juan Manuel de Rosas*. Lanham: Scholarly Resources.

Lynch, John. 2012. *New Worlds: A Religious History of Latin America*. New Haven: Yale University Press.

Macías Núñez, Edison. 2012. *Misiones Militares Extranjeras y su Aporte a la Profesionalización del Ejército Ecuatoriano*. Quito: Centro de Estudios Históricos del Ejército.

Madrid, Raúl L. 2019a. "Opposition Parties and the Origins of Democracy in Latin America." *Comparative Politics* 51 (2): 1–19.

Madrid, Raúl L. 2019b. "The Partisan Path to Democracy: Argentina in Comparative Perspective." *Comparative Political Studies* 52 (10): 1535–1569.

Madrid, Raúl L. and Luis L. Schenoni. 2023/2024. "Reining in Rebellion: The Decline of Political Violence in South America, 1830–1929." *International Security* 48 (3): 129–167.

Magallanes, Manuel Vicente. 1973. *Los Partidos Políticos en la Evolución Histórica Venezolana*. Caracas: Editorial Mediterraneo.

Magaloni, Beatriz. 2008. *Voting for Autocracy: Hegemonic Party Survival and Its Demise in Mexico*. New York: Cambridge University Press.

Mahoney, James. 2001. *The Legacies of Liberalism: Path Dependence and Political Regimes in Central America*. Baltimore: The Johns Hopkins University Press.

Mahoney, James. 2003. "Long-Run Development and the Legacy of Colonialism in Spanish America." *American Journal of Sociology* 109 (1): 50–106.

Mahoney, James, and Dietrich Rueschemeyer. 2003. "Comparative Historical Analysis: Achievements and Agendas." In *Comparative Historical Analysis in the Social Sciences*, edited by James Mahoney and Dietrich Rueschemeyer, 3–38. New York: Cambridge University Press.

Maingot, Anthony P. 1967. "Colombia: Civil-Military Relations in a Political Culture of Conflict." PhD diss., History, University of Florida.

Mainwaring, Scott. 2018. "Party System Institutionalization in Contemporary Latin America." In *Party Systems in Latin America*, edited by Scott Mainwaring, 34–70. New York: Cambridge University Press.

Mainwaring, Scott, Daniel Brinks, and Aníbal Pérez-Liñán. 2001. "Classifying Political Regimes in Latin America, 1945–1999." *Studies in Comparative International Development* 36 (1): 37–65.

Mainwaring, Scott, and Aníbal Pérez-Liñán. 2003. "Level of Development and Democracy: Latin American Exceptionalism, 1945–1996." *Comparative Political Studies* 36 (9): 1031–1067.

Mainwaring, Scott, and Aníbal Pérez-Liñán. 2013. *Democracies and Dictatorships in Latin America: Emergence, Survival, and Fall*. New York: Cambridge University Press.

Mainwaring, Scott, and Timothy R. Scully. 1995. "Conclusion: Parties and Democracy in Latin America – Different Patterns, Common Challenges." In *Building Democratic Institutions: Party Systems in Latin America*, edited by Scott Mainwaring and Timothy R. Scully, 459–474. Stanford: Stanford University Press.

Mainwaring, Scott, and Timothy Scully. 2003. *Christian Democracy in Latin America: Electoral Competition and Regime Conflicts*. Stanford, CA: Stanford University Press.

Mainwaring, Scott, and Mariano Torcal. 2003. "The Political Recrafting of the Social Bases of Party Competition: Chile, 1973–1995." *British Journal of Political Science* 33: 55–84.

Maiztegui Casas, Lincoln R. 2005. *Orientales: Una Historia Política del Uruguay*. Vol. 2. Montevideo: Editorial Planeta.

Malamud, Carlos. 2000a. "La Efímera Reforma Electoral de 1902 en Argentina." In *Legitimidad, Representación y Alternancia en España y América Latina: Las Reformas Electorales (1880–1930)*, edited by Carlos Malamud, 103–129. Mexico City: Fondo de Cultura Económica.

Malamud, Carlos, ed. 2000b. *Legitimidad, Representación y Alternancia en España y América Latina: Las Reformas Electorales (1880–1930)*. Mexico City: Fondo de Cultura Económica.

Malamud, Carlos. 2000c. "The Origins of Revolution in Nineteenth-Century Argentina." In *Rumours of War: Civil Conflict in Nineteenth-Century Latin America*, edited by Rebecca Earle, 29–48. London: Institute of Latin American Studies.

Maldonado, Carlos. 2019. "El Ejército Chileno en el Siglo XIX: Génesis Histórica del 'Ideal Heroico', 1810–1885." CEME Archivo Chile, accessed September 17. www.archivochile.com/Poder_Dominante/ffaa_y_orden/Sobre/PDffaasobre0015.pdf.

Mares, David. 2001. *Violent Peace: Militarized Interstate Bargaining in Latin America*. New York: Columbia University Press.

Mares, Isabela. 2015. *From Open Secrets to Secret Voting: Democratic Electoral Reforms and Voter Autonomy*. New York: Cambridge University Press.

Markoff, John. 1996. *Waves of Democracy*. Thousand Oaks, CA: Pine Forge Press.

Marshall, Monty G., Ted Robert Gurr, and Keith Jaggers. 2016. *Polity IV Project: Dataset Users' Manual*. Vienna, VA: Center for Systemic Peace.

Martínez Bucheli, Jorge Fernando. 2017. "La Primera Misión Militar Chilena y su Influencia en el Ejército Ecuatoriano, 1899–1905." Master's thesis, Historia, Universidad Andina Simón Bolívar.

Mayorga García, Fernando. 2010. "La Primera Cédula de Ciudadanía en Colombia (1929–1952) o el Fracaso de una Institución." *Revista Chilena de Historia del Derecho* 220 (2): 955–986.

Mazzuca, Sebastián. 2021. *Latecomer State Formation: Political Geography and Capacity Failure in Latin America*. New Haven: Yale University Press.

Mazzuca, Sebastián, and Gerardo L. Munck. 2014. "State or Democracy First? Alternative Perspectives on the State-Democracy Nexus." *Democratization* 21 (7): 1221–1243.

Mazzuca, Sebastián, and James A. Robinson. 2009. "Political Conflict and Power Sharing in the Origins of Modern Colombia." *Hispanic American Historical Review* 89 (2): 285–321.

McBeth, Brian S. 2008. *Dictatorship and Politics: Intrigue, Betrayal, and Survival in Venezuela, 1908–1935*. Notre Dame: University of Notre Dame Press.

McBeth, Michael C. 1987. "Brazilian Generals, 1822–1865: A Statistical Study of their Careers." *The Americas* 44 (2): 125–141.

McCann, Frank D. 1984. "The Formative Period of Twentieth-Century Brazilian Army Thought, 1900–1922." *The Hispanic American Historical Review* 64 (4): 737–765. https://doi.org/10.1215/00182168-64.4.737.

McCann, Frank D. 2004. *Soldiers of the Pátria: A History of the Brazilian Army, 1889–1937*. Stanford: Stanford University Press.

McDonald, Ronald H., and J. Mark Ruhl. 1989. *Party Politics and Elections in Latin America*. Boulder: Westview Press.

McEvoy, Carmen. 1994. "Estampillas y Votos: El Rol Del Correo Político en una Campaña Electoral Decimonónica." *Histórica* 18 (1): 95–134.

McGreevey, William Paul. 1971. *An Economic History of Colombia, 1845–1930*. Cambridge: Harvard University Press.

McLaughlin, Doris Brandenburg. 1973. "From Batlle to Batlle: Uruguay in the Late Nineteenth Century." PhD diss., History, University of Michigan.

Mecham, J. Lloyd. 1934. *Church and State in Latin America*. 1st ed. Chapel Hill: University of North Carolina Press.

Mecham, J. Lloyd. 1966. *Church and State in Latin America*. 2nd ed. Chapel Hill: University of North Carolina Press.

Melo, Jorge Orlando. 1989. "De Carlos E. Restrepo a Marco Fidel Suárez: Republicanismo y Gobiernos Conservadores." In *Nueva Historia de Colombia*, edited by Alvaro Tirado Mejía, 215–242. Bogotá: Planeta Colombiana Editorial.

Mendes, Fábio Faria. 2010. *Recrutamento Militar e Construção do Estado no Brasil Imperial*. Belo Horizonte: Argumentum Editora.

Mendoza, Alexandra. 2016. "La Revolución Azul: Última Escena Política de José Tadeo Monagas (1867–1868)." *Tiempo y Espacio* 35 (66): 23–44.

Middlebrook, Kevin J. 2000a. "Introduction: Conservative Parties, Elite Representation, and Democracy in Latin America." In *Conservative Parties, the Right, and Democracy in Latin America*, edited by Kevin Middlebrook, 1–50. Baltimore: The Johns Hopkins University Press.

Middlebrook, Kevin J., ed. 2000b. *Conservative Parties, the Right and Democracy in Latin America*. Baltimore: The Johns Hopkins University Press.

Míguez, Eduardo José. 2003. "Guerra y Orden Social en los Orígenes de la Nación Argentina, 1810–1880." *Anuario IEHS* 18: 17–38.

Míguez, Eduardo José. 2012. "Reforma Electoral y Longue Durée." *Estudios Sociales* 43: 11–28.

Míguez, Eduardo José. 2013. "Política y Partidos en la Organización Nacional." In *Actores e Identidades en la Construcción del Estado Nacional*, edited by Ana Laura Lanteri, 171–210. Buenos Aires: Editorial Teseo.

Miller, Michael K. 2013. "Democratic Pieces: Autocratic Elections and Democratic Development since 1815." *British Journal of Political Science* 45: 501–530.

Miller, Michael K. 2021. *Shock to the System: Coups, Elections, and War on the Road to Democratization*. Princeton: Princeton University Press.

Ministerio del Interior, Subsecretaría de Asuntos Políticos y Electorales. 2008. *Historia Electoral Argentina, 1912–2007*. Buenos Aires: Ministerio del Interior.

Moncayo Gallegos, Paco. 1995. *Fuerzas Armadas y Sociedad*. Quito: Corporación Editora Nacional.

Montoya, Hernán. 1938. *La Cédula y el Sufragio*. Bogotá: Imprenta Nacional.

Moore, Barrington. 1966. *Social Origins of Dictatorship and Democracy: Lord and Peasant in the Making of the Modern World*. Boston: Beacon Press.

Moore, Richard Kinney. 1978. "Soldiers, Politicians, and Reaction: The Etiology of Military Rule in Uruguay." PhD diss., History, The University of Arizona.

Moraes, Juan Andrés. 2010. "Party Competition and Political Representation in Uruguay." PhD diss., Political Science, University of Notre Dame.

Morgan, Edwin. 1978. "Selected Documents on Military Professionalization in Brazil." In *The Politics of Antipolitics: The Military in Latin America*, edited by Brian Loveman and Thomas Davies Jr., 65–71. Lincoln: University of Nebraska press.

Morse, Richard M. 1974. "Trends and Patterns of Latin American Urbanization, 1750–1920." *Comparative Studies in Society and History* 16 (4): 416–447.

Motta, Paulo Roberto. 1971. *Movimentos Partidarios no Brasil*. Rio de Janeiro: Fundação Getulio Vargas.

Mücke, Ulrich. 2001. "Elections and Political Participation in Nineteeth-Century Peru: The 1871–72 Presidential Campaign." *Journal of Latin American Studies* 33 (2): 311–346.

Mücke, Ulrich. 2004. *Political Culture in Nineteenth-Century Peru: The Rise of the Partido Civil*. Pittsburgh: The University of Pittsburgh Press.

Muñoz, Alfredo. 1932. *Las Escuelas Militares del Peru*. Lima: Imprenta de la Escuela Militar.

Nahum, Benjamín. 1987. *Historia Uruguay: La Época Batllista, 1905–1930*. Vol. 6. Montevideo: Ediciones de la Banda Oriental.

Nahum, Benjamín. 2007. *Estadísticas Históricas del Uruguay, 1900–1950*. Vol. 1. Montevideo: Universidad de la República.

Navas Blanco, Alberto. 1993. *Las Elecciones Presidenciales en Venezuela del Siglo XIX, 1830–1854*. Caracas: Fuentes Para la Historia Republicana de Venezuela.

Nazer, Ricardo, and Jaime Rosemblit. 2000. "Electores, Sufragio Y Democracia en Chile: Una Mirada Historica." *Mapocho* 48: 215–228.

Needell, Jeffrey D. 2001. "Party Formation and State-Making: The Conservative Party and the Reconstruction of the Brazilian State, 1831–1840." *Hispanic American Historical Review* 81 (2): 259–308.

Nichols, Byron Albert. 1970. "The Role and Function of Political Parties in Paraguay." PhD diss., Political Science, The Johns Hopkins University.

Nicolau, Jairo. 2012. *Eleições no Brasil: Do Império aos Dias Atuais*. Rio de Janeiro: Zahar.

Nohlen, Dieter, ed. 2005a. *Elections in the Americas*. New York: Oxford University Press.

Nohlen, Dieter. 2005b. "Uruguay." In *Elections in the Americas: A Data Handbook*, edited by Dieter Nohlen, 487–534. New York: Oxford University Press.

Nunes Leal, Victor. 1977. *Coronelismo: The Municipality and Representative Government in Brazil*. New York: Cambridge University Press.

Nunn, Frederick M. 1972. "Military Professionalism and Professional Militarism in Brazil, 1870–1970." *Journal of Latin American Studies* 4 (1): 29–54. doi:10.1017/S0022216X0000167X.

Nunn, Frederick M. 1976. *The Military in Chilean History: Essays on Civil-Military Relations, 1810–1973*. Albuquerque: University of New Mexico Press.

Nunn, Frederick M. 1983. *Yesterday's Soldiers: European Military Professionalism in South America, 1890–1940*. Lincoln: University of Nebraska Press.

O'Donnell, Guillermo A. 1973. *Modernization and Bureaucratic-Authoritarianism: Studies in South American Politics*. Berkeley: Institute for International Studies, University of California.

O'Donnell, Guillermo A., and Philippe C. Schmitter. 1986. *Transitions from Authoritarian Rule: Tentative Conclusions about Uncertain Democracies*. Baltimore: The Johns Hopkins University Press.

Obando Camino, Iván Mauricio. 2017. "Rotación y Reelección de Diputados Bajo la Constitución de 1833." *Atenea* 516: 69–85.

Oficina Central de Estadística. 1885. *Sexto Censo Jeneral de la Población de Chile*. Valparaíso: Imprenta de La Patria.

Ossa Santa Cruz, Juan Luis. 2014. "The Army of the Andes: Chilean and Rioplantense Politics in an Age of Military Organisation, 1814–1817." *Journal of Latin American Studies* 46: 29–58.

Oszlak, Oscar. 1997. *La Formación del Estado Argentino*. Buenos Aires: Editorial Planeta.

Palma Zuñiga, Luis. 1967. *Historia del Partido Radical*. Santiago: Editorial Andrés Bello.

Palmer, Glenn, Roseanne W. McManus, Vito D'Orazio, Michael R. Kenwick, Mikaela Karstens, Chase Bloch, Nick Dietrich, Kayla Kahn, Kellan Ritter, and Michael J. Soules. 2022. "The MID5 Dataset, 2011–2014: Procedures, Coding Rules, and Description." *Conflict Management and Peace Science* 39 (4): 470–482. https://doi.org/10.1177/0738894221995743.

Panizza, Francisco. 1997. "Late Institutionalisation and Early Modernisation: The Emergence of Uruguay's Liberal Democratic Political Order." *Journal of Latin American Studies* 29 (3): 667–691.

Park, James William. 1985. *Rafael Núñez and the Politics of Colombian Regionalism, 1863–1886*. Baton Rouge: Louisiana State University Press.

Patiño Villa, Carlos Alberto. 2010. *Guerra y Construcción del Estado en Colombia, 1810–2010*. Bogotá: Universidad Militar Nueva Granada.

Payne, James L. 1968. *Patterns of Conflict in Colombia*. New Haven: Yale University Press.

Peloso, Vincent C. 1996. "Liberals, Electoral Reform, and the Popular Vote in Mid-Nineteenth-Century Peru." In *Liberals, Politics and Power: State Formation in Nineteenth-Century Latin America*, edited by Vincent C. Peloso and Barbara A. Tenenbaum, 186–211. Athens: University of Georgia Press.

Peralta, Victor. 2005. "Los Vicios del Voto: El Proceso Electoral en el Perú, 1895–1929." In *Historia de las Elecciones en el Perú: Estudios Sobre el Gobierno Representativo*, edited by Cristóbal Aljovín de Losada and Sinesio López, 75–107. Lima: Instituto de Estudios Peruanos.

Pérez-Liñán, Aníbal, and Scott Mainwaring. 2013. "Regime Legacies and Levels of Democracy in Latin America." *Comparative Politics* 45 (4): 379–397.

Pérez, Samuel. 1996. *Los Partido Políticos en Venezuela I: Sistema de Partidos y Partidos Históricos*. 1st ed. Caracas: Fundación Centro Gumilla.

Persson, Torsten, and Guido Tabellini. 2009. "Democratic Capital: The Nexus of Political and Economic Change." *American Economic Journal: Macroeconomics* 1 (2): 88–126.

Philip, George. 1985. *The Military in South American Politics*. Dover: Croom Helm.

Pike, Fredrick B. 1969. *The Modern History of Peru*. New York: Frederick A. Praeger.

Pino Iturrieta, Elías. 1997. "Gobiernos de Antonio Guzmán Blanco." In *Diccionario de Historia de Venezuela*, edited by Manuel Rodríguez Campos. Caracas: Fundación Empresas Polar. https://bibliofep.fundacionempresaspolar.org/dhv/entradas/g/guzman-blanco-antonio-gobiernos-de/

Pinzón de Lewin, Patricia. 1994. *El Ejército y las Elecciones: Ensayo Histórico*. Bogotá: CEREC.

Pivel Devoto, Juan E. 1942. *Historia de los Partidos Políticos en el Uruguay*. Vol. 1. Montevideo: Universidad de la República Oriental del Uruguay.

Pivel Devoto, Juan E. 1943. *Historia de los Partidos Políticos en el Uruguay*. Vol. 2. Montevideo: Universidad de la República Oriental del Uruguay.

Ponce de León Atria, Macarena. 2014. "La Construcción Electoral del Poder Político en Chile, 1891–1925: El Fraude Como Práctica de Representación." Seminario de Historia Electoral del Instituto José María Luis Mora, Mexico City, December 10.

Ponce de León Atria, Macarena, and Antonia Fonck Larraín. 2017. "Election through Complaint and Controversy for Political Power in Chile, 1874–1925." *Parliaments, Estates and Representation* 37 (2): 176–192.

Porto, Walter Costa. 1989. *O Voto no Brasil: Da Colônia a Quinta República*. Brasília: Gráfica do Senado Federal.

Posada-Carbó, Eduardo. 1995. "Civilizar las Urnas: Conflicto y Control en las Elecciones Colombianas, 1830–1930." *Boletín Cultural y Bibliográfico* 32 (39): 3–25.

Posada-Carbó, Eduardo. 1996a. "Elections before Democracy: Some Considerations on Electoral History from a Comparative Approach." In *Elections before Democracy: The History of Elections in Europe and Latin America*, edited by Eduardo Posada-Carbó, 1–15. London: ILAS, University of London.

Posada-Carbó, Eduardo, ed. 1996b. *Elections before Democracy: The History of Elections in Europe and Latin America*. London: ILAS, University of London.

Posada-Carbó, Eduardo. 1997. "Limits of Power: Elections under the Conservative Hegemony in Colombia, 1886–1930." *Hispanic American Historical Review* 77 (2): 245–279.

Posada-Carbó, Eduardo. 1999. "Alternancia y República: Elecciones en la Nueva Granada y Venezuela, 1835–1837." In *Ciudadanía Política y Formación de las*

Naciones, edited by Hilda Sabato, 162–180. Mexico City: Fondo de Cultura Económica.

Posada-Carbó, Eduardo. 2000a. "Electoral Juggling: A Comparative History of the Corruption of Suffrage in Latin America, 1830–1930." *Journal of Latin American Studies* 32 (3): 611–644.

Posada-Carbó, Eduardo. 2000b. "Fraude al Sufragio: La Reforma Electoral en Colombia, 1830–1930." In *Legitimidad, Representación y Alternancia en España y América Latina: Las Reformas Electorales (1880–1930)*, edited by Carlos Malamud, 208–229. Mexico City: Fondo de Cultura Económica.

Posada-Carbó, Eduardo. 2003. "New Granada and the European Revolutions of 1948." In *The European Revolutions of 1848 and the Americas*, edited by Guy Thomson, 217–240. London: Institute of Latin American Studies.

Posada-Carbó, Eduardo. 2010. "Newspapers, Politics, and Elections in Colombia, 1830–1930." *The Historical Journal* 53 (4): 939–962.

Posada-Carbó, Eduardo. 2012. The Catholic Church, Elections and Democracy in Colombia, 1830–1930. In *Kellogg Working Paper* 387, Kellogg Institute, University of Notre Dame.

Posada-Carbó, Eduardo. 2018. "Democracy." Encyclopedia.com, Last Modified May 18, 2018, accessed July 25. www.encyclopedia.com/social-sciences-and-law/political-science-and-government/political-science-terms-and-concepts/democracy.

Posada-Carbó, Eduardo. 2012. "Elections and the Origins of Democracy in Colombia, 1808–1886." In *Elections and the Origins of Democracy in the Americas, 1770s–1880s*, edited by Eduardo Posada-Carbó and J. Samuel Valenzuela. Unpublished manuscript.

Posada-Carbó, Eduardo, and J. Samuel Valenzuela, eds. 2012. *Elections and the Origins of Democracy in the Americas, 1770–1880s*. Unpublished manuscript.

Potash, Robert A. 1969. *The Army and Politics in Argentina, 1928–1945*. Stanford: Stanford University Press.

Powell, Jonathan. 2012. "Determinants of the Attempting and Outcome of Coups d'État." *Journal of Conflict Resolution* 56 (6): 1017–1040. https://doi.org/10.1177/0022002712445732.

Powell, Jonathan, and Clayton L. Thyne. 2011. "Global Instances of Coups from 1950 to 2010: A New Dataset." *Journal of Peace Research* 48 (2): 249–259. https://doi.org/10.1177/0022343310397436.

Przeworski, Adam. 1992. "The Games of Transition." In *Issues in Democratic Consolidation*, edited by Scott Mainwaring, Guillermo A. O'Donnell, and J. Samuel Valenzuela, 105–152. South Bend: University of Notre Dame Press.

Przeworski, Adam. 2009a. "Conquered or Granted? A History of Suffrage Extensions." *British Journal of Political Science* 39 (2): 291–321.

Przeworski, Adam. 2009b. "The Mechanics of Regime Instability in Latin America." *Journal of Politics in Latin America* 1 (1): 5–36.

Przeworski, Adam. 2011. "Divided We Stand? Democracy as a Method of Processing Conflicts: The 2020 Johan Skytte Prize Lecture." *Scandinavian Political Studies* 34 (2): 168–182.

Przeworski, Adam. 2013. *Political Institutions and Political Events Data Set*. New York University. https://sites.google.com/a/nyu.edu/adam-przeworski/home/data

Przeworski, Adam, and Fernando Limongi. 1997. "Modernization: Theories and Facts." *World Politics* 49 (2): 155–183.

Przeworski, Adam, Gonzalo Rivero, and Tianyang Xi. 2015. "Elections as a Conflict Processing Mechanism." *European Journal of Political Economy* 39 (C): 235–248.
Przeworski, Adam, and Henry Teune. 1970. *The Logic of Comparative Social Inquiry*. New York: Wiley.
Quintero, Inés. 2009. *El Ocaso de una Estirpe*. Caracas: Editorial Alfa.
Quintero López, Rafael, and Erika Silva. 1991. *Ecuador: Una Nación en Ciernes*. Vol. 1. Quito: FLACSO.
Rabinovich, Alejandro M., and Natalia Sobrevilla Perea. 2019. "Regular and Irregular Forces in Conflict: Nineteenth Century Insurgencies in South America." *Small Wars and Insurgencies* 30 (4–5): 775–796. https://doi.org/10.1080/09592231 8.2019.1638538.
Rabushka, Alvin, and Kenneth Shepsle. 1972. *Politics in Plural Societies*. Columbus: Merrill Publishing.
Ramírez Jr., Gilberto. 1987. "The Reform of the Argentine Army." PhD diss., History, University of Texas at Austin.
Ramírez Necochea, Hernán. 1969. *Balmaceda y la Contrarrevolución de 1891*. Santiago: Editorial Universitaria.
Ramírez Necochea, Hernán. 1984. *Las Fuerzas Armadas y la Política en Chile, 1810–1970*. Mexico City: Casa de Chile en Mexico.
Ramírez Necochea, Hernán. 1985. *Fuerzas Armadas y Política en Chile, 1810–1970*. Havana: Casa de las Américas.
Reano, Mariella. 2002. "The Origin of Peruvian Professional Militarism." MA thesis, Louisiana State University.
Reber, Vera Blinn. 2002. "Comment on 'The Paraguayan Rosetta Stone'." *Latin American Research Review* 37 (3): 129–136.
República de Colombia, Registraduría del Estado Civil. 1988. *Historia Electoral Colombiana*. Bogotá: La Registraduría.
República de Colombia, Registraduría del Estado Civil. 2017. "Historia del Voto en Colombia." accessed November 1. www.registraduria.gov.co/-Historia-del-voto-en-Colombia-.html.
Reinsch, Paul S. 1909. "Parliamentary Government in Chile." *American Political Science Review* 3 (4): 507–538.
Remmer, Karen L. 1977. "The Timing, Pace and Sequence of Political Change in Chile, 1891–1925." *The Hispanic American Historical Review* 57 (2): 205–230.
Remmer, Karen L. 1984. *Party Competition in Argentina and Chile: Political Recruitment and Public Policy, 1890–1930*. Lincoln: University of Nebraska Press.
República de Bolivia. 1900. *Censo General de la Población de la República de Bolivia*. Vol. 2. La Paz: Oficina Nacional de Inmigración, Estadística y Propaganda Geográfica.
República de Chile. 1863. *Anuario Estadístico*. Santiago: Oficina Central de Estadística.
República de Chile. 1871. *Anuario Estadístico*. Vol. 11. Santiago: Imprenta Nacional.
República de Chile. 1879. *Anuario Estadístico*. Santiago: Imprenta Nacional.
República de Chile. 1882. *Anuario Estadístico*. Santiago: Imprenta Nacional.
República de Chile. 1907. *VIII Censo General de la República de Chile: Levantado el 28 de Noviembre de 1907*. Santiago: Sociedad, Imprenta Litografía Universo.
República de Chile. 1925. *Censo de Población de la República de Chile de 1920*. Santiago: Dirección General de Estadística.
República de Chile. 1970. *XIV Censo de Población y III de Vivienda*. Santiago: Instituto Nacional de Estadística.

República de Colombia. 1939. *Actos Legislativos y Leyes de Colombia Expedidos por la Asamblea Nacional de 1910.* Bogotá: Imprenta Nacional.
Resende-Santos, João. 2007. *Neorealism, States, and the Modern Mass Army.* New York: Cambridge University Press.
Rey, Juan Carlos. 2015. *El Sistema de Partidos Venezolano, 1830–1999.* Caracas: Editorial Jurídica Venezolana.
Reyes, Oscar Efrén. 1982. *Breve Historia General del Ecuador.* 14th ed. Vol. 2–3. Quito.
Rhodes-Purdy, Matthew, and Raúl L. Madrid. 2020. "The Perils of Personalism." *Democratization* 27 (2): 321–339.
Riart, Gustavo Adolfo. 1990. *El Partido Liberal y el Ejército.* Asunción: Archivo del Liberalismo.
Ribeiro, José Iran. 2011. "O Fortalecimento do Estado Imperial a Través do Recrutamento Militar no Contexto da Guerra dos Farrapos." *Revista Brasileira da História* 31 (62): 251–271. https://doi.org/10.1590/S0102-01882011000200014.
Ricci, Paolo, and Jaqueline Porto Zulini. 2012. "Beheading, Rule Manipulation and Fraud: The Approval of Election Results in Brazil, 1894–1930." *Journal of Latin American Studies* 44 (3): 495–521.
Ricci, Paolo, and Jaqueline Porto Zulini. 2016. "The Meaning of Electoral Fraud in Oligarchic Regimes: Lessons from the Brazilian Case (1899–1930)." *Journal of Latin American Studies* 49: 243–268.
Richmond, Douglas W. 1989. *Carlos Pellegrini and the Crisis of the Argentine Elites, 1880–1916.* New York: Praeger Publishers.
Riedl, Rachel Beatty, Dan Slater, Joseph Wong, and Daniel Ziblatt. 2020. "Authoritarian-Led Democratization." *Annual Review of Political Science* 23: 315–332.
Ríos Peñaloza, Gilma. 1991. "Las Constituyentes de 1905 y 1910." *Revista Credencial Historia* 13. www.banrepcultural.org/biblioteca-virtual/credencial-historia/numero-13/las-constituyentes-de-1905-y-1910
Rock, David. 1975. *Politics in Argentina, 1890–1930: The Rise and Fall of Radicalism.* New York: Cambridge University Press.
Rock, David. 2002. *State Building and Political Movements in Argentina, 1860–1916.* Stanford: Stanford University Press.
Rock, David, and Fernando López-Alves. 2000. "State-Building and Political Systems in Nineteenth-Century Argentina and Uruguay." *Past and Present* 167: 176–202.
Rodríguez-Franco, Diana. 2016. "Internal Wars, Taxation, and State Building." *American Sociological Review* 81 (1): 190–213.
Rodríguez, Jeannette. 1997. "Elecciones Presidenciales en la República de Venezuela (1868)." *Ensayos Históricos: Anuario del Instituto de Estudios Hispanoamericanos* 9: 121–138.
Rodríguez, Linda Alexander. 1985. *The Search for Public Policy: Regional Politics and Government Finances in Ecuador, 1830–1940.* Berkeley: University of California Press.
Rodríguez, Linda Alexander. 1994. "Introduction." In *Rank and Privilege: The Military and Society in Latin America*, edited by Linda Alexander Rodríguez, ix–xxii. Wilmington: Scholarly Resources.
Rodríguez Piñeres, Eduardo. 1956. *Hechos y Comentarios: Nova et Vetera.* Bogotá: Editorial Sucre.
Roessler, Philip. 2011. "The Enemy Within: Personal Rule, Coups, and Civil War in Africa." *World Politics* 63 (2): 300–346. doi:10.1017/S0043887111000049.

Rojas de Ferro, Cristina. 1995. "Identity Formation, Violence, and the Nation-State in Nineteenth-Century Colombia." *Alternatives: Global, Local, Political* 20 (2): 195–224.

Rokkan, Stein. 1970. *Citizens, Elections, Parties: Approaches to the Comparative Study of the Processes of Development.* New York: David McKay Company.

Romero y Cordero, Remigio. 1991. *El Ejército en Cien Años de Vida Republicana, 1830–1930.* Quito: Centro de Estudios Históricos del Ejército.

Rouquié, Alain. 1987. *The Military and the State in Latin America.* Berkeley: University of California Press.

Rueschemeyer, Dietrich, Evelyne Huber Stephens, and John D. Stephens. 1992. *Capitalist Development and Democracy.* Chicago: University of Chicago Press.

Rustow, Dankwart A. 1970. "Transitions to Democracy: Toward a Dynamic Model." *Comparative Politics* 2 (3): 337–363.

Sabato, Hilda. 2001a. *The Many and the Few: Political Participation in Republican Buenos Aires.* Stanford: Stanford University Press.

Sabato, Hilda. 2001b. "On Political Citizenship in Nineteenth-Century Latin America." *The American Historical Review* 106 (4): 1290–1315.

Sabato, Hilda. 2010. "¿Quién Controla el Poder Militar? Disputas en Torno a la Formación del Estado en el Siglo XIX." In *La Construcción de la Nación Argentina: El Rol de las Fuerzas Armadas*, edited by Oscar Moreno, 125–140. Buenos Aires: Ministerio de Defensa.

Sabato, Hilda. 2018. *Republics of the New World: The Revolutionary Political Experiment in 19th-Century Latin America.* Princeton: Princeton University Press.

Sabato, Hilda, and Elías Palti. 1990. "¿Quién Votaba en Buenos Aires?: Práctica y Teoría del Sufragio: 1850–1880." *Desarrollo Económico* 30 (119): 395–424.

Sabato, Hilda, and Marcela Ternavasio. 2011. "El Voto en la República: Historia del Sufragio en el Siglo XIX." In *Historia de las Elecciones en la Argentina, 1805–2011*, edited by Marcela Ternavasio, 17–134. Buenos Aires: Editorial El Ateneo.

Sáenz Peña, Roque. 1915. *Escritos y Discursos.* Vol. 2. Buenos Aires: Casa Jacobo Peuser.

Safford, Frank. 1972. "Social Aspects of Politics in Nineteenth-Century Spanish America: New Granada, 1825–1850." *Journal of Social History* 5 (3): 344–370.

Safford, Frank. 1974. "Bases of Political Alignment in Early Republican Spanish America." In *New Approaches to Latin American History*, edited by Richard Graham and Peter H. Smith, 71–111. Austin: University of Texas Press.

Safford, Frank. 1992. "The Problem of Political Order in Early Republican Spanish America." *Journal of Latin American Studies* 24: 83–97. doi:10.1017/S0022216X00023798.

Safford, Frank. 2000. "Reflections on the Internal Wars in Nineteenth-Century Latin America." In *Rumours of Wars: Civil Conflict in Nineteenth-Century Latin America*, edited by Rebecca Earle, 6–28. London: Institute of Latin American Studies.

Safford, Frank, and Marco Palacios. 2002. *Colombia: Fragmented Land, Divided Society.* New York: Oxford University Press.

Salas Edwards, Ricardo. 1914. *Balmaceda y el Parlamentarismo en Chile: Un Estudio de Psicología Política Chilena.* Santiago: Sociedad Imprenta y Litografía Universo.

Sanders, James E. 2004. *Contentious Republicans: Popular Politics, Race, and Class in Nineteenth-Century Colombia.* Durham: Duke University Press.

Sanoja Hernández, Jesús. 1998. *Historia Electoral de Venezuela, 1810–1998.* Caracas: Los Libros de El Nacional.

Sater, William F., and Holger H. Herwig. 1999. *The Grand Illusion: The Prussianization of the Chilean Army*. Lincoln: University of Nebraska Press.
Saylor, Ryan. 2014. *State Building in Boom Times: Commodities and Coalitions in Latin America and Africa*. New York: Oxford University Press.
Schaposnik, Eduardo C. 1985. *La Democratización de las Fuerzas Armadas Venezolanas*. Caracas: Instituto de Investigaciones Sociales.
Schattschneider, Elmer E. 1942. *Party Government*. New York: Holt, Rinehart, and Winston.
Schedler, Andreas. 2009. "The Contingent Power of Authoritarian Elections." In *Democratization by Elections: A New Mode of Transition*, edited by Staffan I. Lindberg, 291–313. Baltimore: The Johns Hopkins University Press.
Schedler, Andreas. 2013. *The Politics of Uncertainty: Sustaining and Subverting Electoral Authoritarianism*. New York: Oxford University Press.
Scheina, Robert L. 2003. *Latin America's Wars: The Age of the Caudillo, 1791–1899*. Washington: Brassey's.
Schenoni, Luis L. 2020. "Bringing War Back In: Victory and State Formation in Nineteenth-Century Latin America." PhD diss., Political Science, University of Notre Dame.
Schenoni, Luis L. 2021. "Bringing War Back In: Victory and State Formation in Latin America." *American Journal of Political Science* 65 (2): 405–421. https://doi.org/10.1111/ajps.12552.
Schenoni, Luis L. 2024. *Bringing War Back In: Victory, Defeat, and the State in Nineteenth-Century Latin America*. New York: Cambridge University Press.
Scherlis, Gerardo, and Mario Justo López. 2005. "¿De la República Oligárquica a la República Democrática?" In *De la República Oligárquica a la República Democrática*, edited by Mario Justo López, 553–607. Buenos Aires: Lumiere.
Schiff, Warren. 1972. "The Influence of the German Armed Forces and War Industry on Argentina, 1880–1914." *The Hispanic American Historical Review* 52 (3): 436–455. https://doi.org/10.1215/00182168-52.3.436.
Schlesinger, Joseph A. 1991. *Political Parties and the Winning of Office*. Ann Arbor: University of Michigan Press.
Schneider, Ronald. 1993. *Order and Progress: A Political History of Brazil*. Boulder: Westview Press.
Schumpeter, Joseph A. 2008 [1942]. *Capitalism, Socialism and Democracy*. 3rd ed. New York: Harper Perennial.
Sciarrotta, Fernando J. 2005. "Las Presidencias de Manuel Quintana y de José Figueroa Alcorta." In *De la República Oligárquica a la República Democrática*, edited by Mario Justo López, 143–181. Buenos Aires: Lumiere.
Scully, Timothy R. 1992. *Rethinking the Center: Party Politics in the Nineteenth and Twentieth Century Chile*. Stanford: Stanford University Press.
Seymour, Charles, and Donald P. Frary. 1919. *How the World Votes: The Story of Democratic Development in Elections*. Springfield: C.A. Nichols.
Shaw Jr., Carey. 1941. "Church and State in Colombia as Observed by American Diplomats, 1834–1906." *The Hispanic American Historical Review* 21 (4): 577–613.
Shesko, Elizabeth. 2012. "Conscript Nation: Negotiating Authority and Belonging in the Bolivian Barracks, 1900–1950." PhD diss., History, Duke University.
Sidel, John T. 2008. "Social Origins of Dictatorship and Democracy Revisited: Colonial State and Chinese Immigrant in the Making of Modern Southeast Asia." *Comparative Politics* 40 (2): 127–147.

Simpser, Alberto. 2013. *Why Governments and Parties Manipulate Elections: Theory, Practice, and Implications*. New York: Cambridge University Press.

Skocpol, Theda. 1979. *States and Social Revolutions*. New York: Cambridge University Press.

Slantchev, Branislav L. 2003. "The Principle of Convergence in Wartime Negotiations." *American Political Science Review* 97 (4): 621–632.

Slater, Dan. 2010. *Ordering Power: Contentious Politics and Authoritarian Leviathans in Southeast Asia*. New York: Cambridge University Press.

Slater, Dan, and Joseph Wong. 2013. "The Strength to Concede: Ruling Parties and Democratization in Developmental Asia." *Perspectives on Politics* 11 (3): 717–733.

Smith, Peter H. 1974. *Argentina and the Failure of Democracy: Conflict among Political Elites, 1904–1955*. Madison: University of Wisconsin Press.

Snow, Peter G. 1963. "The Radical Parties of Chile and Argentina." PhD diss., Political Science, University of Virginia.

Snow, Peter G. 1965. *Argentine Radicalism: The History and Doctrine of the Radical Civic Union*. Iowa City: University of Iowa Press.

Sobrevilla Perea, Natalia. 2002. "The Influence of the European 1848 Revolutions in Peru." In *The European Revolutions of 1848 and the Americas*, edited by Guy Thomson, 191–216. London: Institute of Latin American Studies.

Sobrevilla Perea, Natalia. 2012. "Ciudadanos en Armas: El Ejército y la Creación del Estado, Perú 1821–1861." In *Las Fuerzas de Guerra en la Construcción del Estado: América Latina, Siglo XIX*, edited by Juan Carlos Garavaglia, Juan Pro Ruiz and Eduardo Zimmermann, 161–182. Rosario: Prohistoria Ediciones.

Sobrevilla Perea, Natalia. 2017. "Power of the Law or Power of the Sword: The Conflictive Relationship between the Executive and the Legislative in Nineteenth-Century Peru." *Parliaments, Estates and Representation* 37 (2): 220–234.

Soifer, Hillel David. 2015. *State Building in Latin America*. New York: Cambridge University Press.

Somma, Nicolás M. 2011. "When the Powerful Rebel: Armed Insurgency in 19th Century Latin America." PhD diss., Sociology, University of Notre Dame.

Somma, Nicolás M. 2012. "Elections and the Origins of Democracy in Nineteenth-Century Uruguay." In *Elections and the Origins of Democracy in the Americas, 1770s-1880s*, edited by Eduardo Posada-Carbó and J. Samuel Valenzuela. Unpublished manuscript.

Sosa, Eduardo Ramón. 2004. *Defensa Nacional: Períodos y Reformas de las Fuerzas Armadas*. Asunción: AGR Servicios Gráficos.

Souza, Alexandre de Oliveira Bazilio de. 2016. "Antes de la Corte Electoral: Judicatura y Elecciones en Uruguay (1825–1924)." *Claves. Revista de Historia* (2): 199–225.

Sowell, David. 1992. *The Early Colombian Labor Movement: Artisans and Politics in Bogotá, 1832–1919*. Philadelphia: Temple University Press.

Spindler, Frank MacDonald. 1987. *Nineteenth Century Ecuador: An Historical Introduction*. Fairfax: George Mason University Press.

Stein, Steve. 1980. *Populism in Peru: The Emergence of the Masses and the Politics of Social Control*. Madison: University of Wisconsin Press.

Stepan, Alfred. 1973. "The New Professionalism of Internal Warfare and Military Role Expansion." In *Authoritarian Brazil: Origins, Policies, and Future*, edited by Alfred Stepan, 47–65. New Haven: Yale University Press.

Straka, Tomás. 2005. "Guiados por Bolívar: López Contreras, Bolivarianismo y Pretorianismo en Venezuela." In *Militares y Poder en Venezuela*, edited by Domingo Irwin and Frédérique Langue, 99–138. Caracas: Universidad Católica Andrés Bello.

Studer, Robert William. 1975. "The Colombian Army: Political Aspects of its Role." PhD diss., Political Science, University of Southern California.

Summerhill, William R. 2006. "The Development of Infrastructure." In *The Cambridge Economic History of Latin America*, edited by Victor Bulmer-Thomas, John H. Coatsworth and Roberto Cortés Conde, Vol. 2. 293-326. New York: Cambridge University Press.

Svolik, Milan W. 2012. *The Politics of Authoritarian Rule*. New York: Cambridge University Press.

Tarver, H. Micheal, and Julia C. Frederick. 2005. *The History of Venezuela*. Westport: Greenwood Press.

Teele, Dawn Langan. 2018. *Forging the Franchise: The Political Origins of the Women's Vote*. Princeton: Princeton University Press.

Telarolli, Rodolpho. 1982. *Eleições e Fraudes Eleitorais na República Velha*. São Paulo: Editora Brasilense.

Ternavasio, Marcela. 2002. *La Revolución del Voto: Política y Elecciones en Buenos Aires, 1810-1852*. Buenos Aires: Siglo XXI.

Terrie, P. Larkin. 2014. "State Building and Political Regimes: The Nineteenth-Century Origins of Liberal Democracy in Latin America." PhD diss., Political Science, Northwestern University.

Thelen, Kathleen, and James Mahoney. 2015. "Comparative-Historical Analysis in Contemporary Political Science." In *Advances in Comparative-Historical Analysis*, edited by James Mahoney and Kathleen Thelen, 3-36. New York: Cambridge University Press.

Thies, Cameron. 2005. "War, Rivalry, and State Building in Latin America." *American Journal of Political Science* 49 (3): 451-465.

Thorp, Rosemary. 1998. *Progress, Poverty and Exclusion: An Economic History of Latin America in the 20th Century*. Washington: Inter-American Development Bank.

Tilly, Charles. 1975. "Reflections on the History of European State-Making." In *The Formation of National States in Western Europe*, edited by Charles Tilly, 3–83. Princeton: Princeton University Press.

Tinker Salas, Miguel. 2015. *Venezuela: What Everyone Needs to Know*. New York: Oxford University Press.

Tirado Mejía, Alvaro. 1976. *Aspectos Sociales de las Guerras Civiles en Colombia*. Bogotá: Instituto Colombiano de Cultura.

Toronto, Nathan W. 2017. "Why Professionalize? Economic Modernization and Military Professionalism." *Foreign Policy Analysis* 13 (4): 854-875.

Tuesta Soldevilla, Fernando. 2001. *Perú Político en Cifras: 1821-2001*. 3rd ed. Lima: Friedrich Ebert Stiftung.

Urdaneta García, Argenis Saúl. 2007. "Elecciones y Democracia Liberal: Período 1830-1858." *Memoria Política* 11: 79-126.

Uribe-Castro, Mateo 2019. "Expropriation of Church Wealth and Political Conflict in 19th Century Colombia." *Explorations in Economic History* 73: 1012-1071.

Urzúa Valenzuela, Germán. 1968. *Los Partidos Políticos Chilenos*. Santiago: Editorial Jurídica de Chile.

Urzúa Valenzuela, Germán. 1992. *Historia Política de Chile y Su Evolución Electoral, Desde 1810 a 1992*. Santiago: Editorial Jurídica de Chile.
Valenzuela, Arturo. 1977. *Political Brokers in Chile: Local Government in a Centralized Polity*. Durham: Duke University Press.
Valenzuela, Arturo, and J. Samuel Valenzuela. 1983. "The Origins of Democracy: Theoretical Reflections on the Chilean Case." *Estudios Públicos* 12: 1–32.
Valenzuela, J. Samuel. 1985. *Democratización vía Reforma: La Expansión del Sufragio en Chile*. Buenos Aires: IDES.
Valenzuela, J. Samuel. 1996. "Building Aspects of Democracy before Democracy: Electoral Practices in Nineteenth Century Chile." In *The History of Elections in Europe and Latin America*, edited by Eduardo Posada-Carbó, 223–257. London: Palgrave Macmillan.
Valenzuela, J. Samuel. 1998. "La Ley Electoral de 1890 y la Democratización del Régimen Político Chileno." *Estudios Políticos* 71: 265–296.
Valenzuela, J. Samuel. 2000. "The Politics of Religion in a Catholic Country: Republican Democracy, Cristianismo Social and the Conservative Party in Chile, 1850–1925." In *The Politics of Religion in an Age of Revival: Studies in Nineteenth-Century Europe and Latin America*, edited by Austin Ivereigh, 188–223. London: Institute of Latin American Studies.
Valenzuela, J. Samuel. 2001. "Class Relations and Democratization: A Reassessment of Barrington Moore's Model." In *The Other Mirror: Grand Theory through the Lens of Latin America*, edited by Miguel Angel Centeno and Fernando López-Alves, 240–286. Princeton: Princeton University Press.
Valenzuela, J. Samuel. 2012. From Town Assemblies to Representative Democracy: The Building of Electoral Institutions in Nineteenth-Century Chile. In *Kellogg Working Paper*. Notre Dame: Kellogg Institute.
Van Aken, Mark J. 1989. *King of the Night: Juan José Flores and Ecuador, 1824–1864*. Berkeley: University of California Press.
Vanger, Milton I. 1963. *José Batlle y Ordoñez of Uruguay: The Creator of his Times, 1902–1907*. Cambridge: Harvard University Press.
Vanger, Milton I. 1980. *The Model Country: José Batlle y Ordoñez of Uruguay, 1907–1915*. Hanover: The University Press of New England.
Vanger, Milton I. 2010. *Uruguay's José Batlle y Ordoñez: The Determined Visionary, 1915–1917*. Boulder: Lynne Rienner.
Vanhanen, Tatu. 2000. "A New Dataset for Measuring Democracy, 1810–1998." *Journal of Peace Research* 37 (2): 251–265.
Varas, Augusto. 2017. "Los Militares y la Política en Chile: 1810–2015." In *Historia Política de Chile, 1810–2010*, edited by Iván Jaksic and Juan Luis Ossa Santa Cruz, 83–115. Santiago: Fondo de Cultura Económica Chile.
Vázquez Romero, Andrés, and Washington Reyes Abadie. 1979. *Crónica General del Uruguay: El Uruguay del Siglo XX*. Vol. 4. Montevideo: Ediciones de la Banda Oriental.
Velásquez, Ramón J. 1997. "Gobierno de Juan Vicente Gómez." In *Diccionario de Historia de Venezuela*. Caracas: Fundación Empresas Polar. https://bibliofep.fundacionempresaspolar.org/dhv/entradas/g/gomez-juan-vicente-gobierno-de/
Villanueva, Victor. 1971. *Cien Años del Ejército Peruano: Frustraciones y Cambios*. Lima: Editorial Juan Mejía Baca.
Villanueva, Victor. 1978. "Military Professionalization in Peru." In *The Politics of Antipolitics: The Military in Latin America*, edited by Brian Loveman and Thomas Davies Jr., 79–85. Lincoln: University of Nebraska Press.

Viloria Vera, Enrique. 2009. "Cipriano Castro." In *Tierra Nuestra: 1498–2009*, edited by Heraclio Atencio Bello, Vol. 2. 85–102. Caracas: Fundación Venezuela Positiva.
Vitale, Luis. 1975. *Interpretación Marxista de la Historia de Chile*. Vol. 4. Frankfurt: University of Frankfurt.
Volk, Steven S. 1975. "Class, Union, Party: The Development of a Revolutionary Union Movement in Bolivia (1905–1952)." *Science & Society* 39 (1): 26–43.
Waddell, Jorge E. 2005. "La Ruptura Roca-Pellegrini y la División del PAN." In *De la República Oligárquica a la República Democrática*, edited by Mario Justo López, 119–142. Buenos Aires: Lumiere.
Wagner, R. Harrison. 2000. "Bargaining and War." *American Journal of Political Science* (3): 469–484.
Walter, Richard J. 1977. *The Socialist Party of Argentina, 1890–1930*. Austin: Institute of Latin American Studies.
Walter, Richard J. 1978. "Elections in the City of Buenos Aires during the First Yrigoyen Administration: Social Class and Political Preferences." *The Hispanic American Historical Review* 58 (4): 595–624.
Warren, Harris Gaylord. 1949. *Paraguay: An Informal History*. Norman: University of Oklahoma Press.
Warren, Harris Gaylord. 1980. "The Paraguayan Revolution of 1904." *The Americas* 36: 365–380.
Warren, Harris Gaylord. 1985. *Rebirth of the Paraguayan Republic: The First Colorado Era, 1878–1904*. Pittsburgh: University of Pittsburgh Press.
Weber, Max. 1946. "Politics as a Vocation." In *From Max Weber: Essays in Sociology*, edited by Hans H. Gerth, and C. Wright Mills, 77–128. New York: Oxford University.
Weinstein, Martin. 1975. *Uruguay: The Politics of Failure*. Westport: Greenwood Press.
Wejnert, Barbara. 2014. *Diffusion of Democracy: The Past and Future of Global Democracy*. New York: Cambridge University Press.
Wesson, Robert, ed. 1986. *The Latin American Military Institution*. New York: Praeger.
Weyland, Kurt. 2014. *Making Waves: Democratic Contention in Europe and Latin America since the Revolutions of 1848*. New York: Cambridge University Press.
Whigham, Thomas L. 2002. *The Paraguayan War*. Lincoln: University of Nebraska Press.
Whigham, Thomas L., and Barbara Potthast. 1999. "The Paraguayan Rosetta Stone: New Insights into the Demographics of the Paraguayan War, 1864–1870." *Latin American Research Review* 34 (1): 174–186. doi:10.1017/S0023879100024341.
White, Richard Alan. 1978. *Paraguay's Autonomous Revolution, 1810–1840*. Albuquerque: University of New Mexico Press.
Whitehead, Laurence. 1981. "Miners as Voters: The Electoral Process in Bolivia's Mining Camps." *Journal of Latin American Studies* 13 (2): 313–346.
Williams, John Hoyt. 1975. "From the Barrel of a Gun: Some Notes on Dr. Francia and Paraguayan Militarism." *Proceedings of the American Philosophical Society* 119 (1): 73–86.
Williams, John Hoyt. 1977. "Foreign Tecnicos and the Modernization of Paraguay, 1840–1870." *Journal of Interamerican Studies and World Affairs* 19 (2): 233–257.
Williams, John Hoyt. 1979. *The Rise and Fall of the Paraguayan Republic, 1800–1870*. Austin: Institute of Latin American Studies.
Wirth, John D. 1964. "Tenentismo in the Brazilian Revolution of 1930." *The Hispanic American Historical Review* 44 (2): 161–179.

Wirth, John D. 1977. *Minas Gerais in the Brazilian Federation: 1889–1937*. Stanford: Stanford University Press.
Wood, Elizabeth. 2003. *Insurgent Collective Action and Civil War in El Salvador*. New York: Cambridge University Press.
Wood, James A. 2011. *The Society of Equality: Popular Republicanism and Democracy in Santiago de Chile, 1818–1851*. Albuquerque: University of New Mexico.
Yablon, Ariel Sergio. 2003. "Patronage, Corruption, and Political Culture in Buenos Aires, Argentina, 1880–1916." PhD diss., History, University of Illinois.
Yashar, Deborah J. 1997. *Demanding Democracy: Reform and Reaction in Costa Rica and Guatemala*. Stanford: Stanford University Press.
Zeitlin, Maurice. 1984. *The Civil Wars in Chile*. Princeton: Princeton University Press.
Ziblatt, Daniel. 2017. *Conservative Parties and the Birth of Democracy*. New York: Cambridge University Press.
Ziems, Angel. 1979. *El Gomecismo y la Formación del Ejército Nacional*. Caracas: Editorial Ateneo de Caracas.
Zimmermann, Eduardo. 2009. Elections and the Origins of an Argentine Democratic Tradition, 1810–1880. In *Kellogg Institute Working Paper*. Kellogg Institute, University of Notre Dame
Zum Felde, Alberto. 1985. *Proceso Histórico del Uruguay*. 10th ed. Montevideo: Arca Editorial.

Index

Aceval, Eduardo, 297–298
Acevedo, Eduardo, 149–151
actor-based theories, for democratization, 44
Aguirre, Martín, 161
Além, Leandro, 185–186
Alessandri, Arturo, 145, 146
Alfaro, Eloy, 279–282, 283, 286–287
Alfaro, Flavio, 287
Altamirano, Eulogio, 140
Arce, Aniceto, 270–271
Argentina
  Battle of Pavón, 177, 181
  democracy in, 69
    after 1912, 195–198
    transformation of, 1
  elections in
    free and fair, 66
    incomplete lists and, 190, 192, 193–194
    legislative, 194
    after 1912, 195–198
    obligatory voting in, 191–192
    presidential, 196
  geographic fragmentation of, 35
  military coups in, 6
  military missions in, 181
  military professionalization in, 27, 40–41, 176–182
    government expenditures for, 176
    military schools and training, 181–182
  militias in, 84–85
  National Autonomist Party, 183–186, 188–195
  opposition revolts in, 22
  political parties in
    personalistic, 183, 197
    splits in ruling parties, 188–195
    strong, 103
  Radical Civic Union party, 36, 69, 92, 182–187, 195–197, 198
    manifesto for, 185
    split within, 188–195
  revolts in, 77, 176–182
  suffrage rights in, 59
  unification of, 177
  war of independence for, 176
  War of the Triple Alliance and, 25, 26, 85, 86, 89, 179
  weak democracies in, 175–176
  weak military in, 19–20
Arias, José Inocencio, 192–193
armies. *See* mass armies; militias
Army of the Andes, 124
Arteaga Conspiracy, 126–127
Aspíllaga, Antero, 245, 246–248
authoritarian regimes, authoritarianism and
  armed revolts and, 20
  in Bolivia, 5
    as unstable, 262–263
  in Brazil, 225–226, 254–260
  in Colombia, 203, 217–218
  in Ecuador, 5, 283–288
    as unstable, 262–263
  electoral, 9, 23
  in Paraguay, 5
    as unstable, 262–263

349

authoritarian regimes (cont.)
  in Peru, 241–248
  stable authoritarian regimes, 5, 42
  transitional, 39
  unstable, 38–39, 262–263
  in Uruguay, 151–152
  in Venezuela, 231–235
  revolts as influence on, 227
Avellaneda, Nicolás, 177, 183
Ayala, Eligio, 294
Ayala, Eusebio, 299

balanced cleavages, 37–38, 115
ballots. *See* secret ballots
Balmaceda, José Manuel, 132, 136, 137–141, 143–144
Barbosa, Rui, 259
Barros Luco, Ramón, 145
Batlle y Ordóñez, José, 153–155, 163–172
Battle of Loncomilla, 127
Battle of Pavón, 177, 181
Bautista Egusquiza, Juan, 297–298
Belaunde, Victor Andrés, 241
bellicist approach, to state building, 24–25
Beltrán, Washington, 169
Belzú, Manuel, 74
Benavides, Oscar, 245
Berro, Bernardo, 148, 149, 159
Berro, Carlos, 161
Billinghurst, Guillermo, 42, 245
Blanco Party (Uruguay), 41, 84–85, 147, 148, 155–163, 171, 173
  membership requirements for, 158
  National Club, 157–158
Bolívar, Simón, 208
Bolivia
  authoritarian regimes in, 5, 270–277
  Chaco War, 269–270
  democracy
    obstacles to, 277
  electoral fraud in, 69–70
  export boom in, 267–268
  geography of, 34
  military in, 263–270
    foreign involvement in, 268–269
    professionalization of, 267–269
    strength of, 94
    training of, 263–264, 268
  mutinies in, 275
  political parties in
    Conservative Party, 270–274
    Liberal Party, 270–274
    opposition parties, 274–275
    personalistic, 270
    weak, 103–104, 270–277
  revolts in, 263–270
    opposition, 1
  War of the Confederation, 263
  War of the Pacific and, 25, 85, 86, 129, 239
    origins of, 87
Bonifaz, Neptalí, 287–288
booms. *See* export booms
Borgoño, Justiniano, 242–243
Brazil
  authoritarianism in, 254–260
    stable regimes in, 5, 42, 225–226
  Catholic Church in, 37
  coercive capacity in, 254
  colonial history of, 248
  democratic reforms in, 256–257
  elections in, 23
  electoral reforms, 257
    presidential, 258, 259–260
  Federalist Riograndense Rebellion, 253–254
  First Republic in, 258, 259
  military in, 248–254
    German role in, 252–253
    professionalization of, 249–253
    weak, 248–249
  militias in, 84–85
  Minas Gerais state, 258–259
  political parties in
    Conservative, 254–260
    Liberal, 254–260
    Mineiro Republican Party, 258–259
    Paulista Republican Party, 258–259
    personalistic, 255
    weak, 104–105, 254–260
  revolts, 248–254
    outsider, 1, 253–254
  São Paulo state, 258–259
  War of the Canudos, 253–254
  War of the Contestados, 253–254
  War of the Triple Alliance and, 25, 26, 85, 86, 89, 179, 251
Buero, Juan, 170
Bulnes, Manuel, 126, 127

Caamaño, José María, 285
Cáceres, Andrés Avelino, 239, 241, 242–243
Cádiz Constitution. *See* 1812 Constitution (Cádiz Constitution)
Camacho, Eliodoro, 271–272
Campisteguy, Juan, 171

Index

351

Caro, Miguel Antonio, 215
Castilla, Ramón, 242–243
Castro, Cipriano, 42, 105, 225, 230–231, 232, 234–235
Catherine the Great, 29
Catholic Church
  in Brazil, 37
  in Chile, 4, 37
  in Colombia, 4, 37, 209
  in Latin America, 37
  in Paraguay, 37, 295
  regional strength of, 37
  strong political parties influenced by, 113–114
  in Uruguay, 37, 166, 171
  in Venezuela, 37
Chaco War, 269–270, 294
Chile
  Arteaga Conspiracy, 126–127
  Battle of Loncomilla, 127
  Catholic Church in, 4, 37
  Chincha Islands War and, 129
  civil wars in, 124, 126–127, 144
  coercive capacity in, 85
  Conservative Party in, 131–134, 136, 144–145
  Conspiracy of the Daggers, 126–127
  democratic reforms in, 33, 146
    opposition parties and, 136–139
  democratization in, 68, 130–144
    breakdown of, 68
    elections as part of (after 1891), 144–147
    geographic factors for, 19
    military professionalization as influence on, 146
    strong political parties' role in, 146–147
    transformation of, 1, 10
  elections in, 134–136
    campaign costs, 145
    competition in, 145
    democratization and (after 1891), 144–147
    electoral reform, 142
    government intervention in, 137–139
    legislative, 138
    opposition parties' role in, 135–137
    presidential, 138
    voter participation, 134–135, 137
    voting secrecy in, 142
  geographic fragmentation of, 35
  Liberal Democratic Party in, 144–145
  Liberal Party in Chile, 31, 131–134, 136, 144–145
  Mapuche indigenous population in, 124, 134
  military professionalization in, 25, 27, 40–41, 124–130
    Army of the Andes and, 124
    export boom and, 129
    international assistance for, 129
    international conflicts as influence on, 129
  militias in, 84
  mutinies in, 124
  National Party in, 131–134, 144–145
  political parties in, 130–144
    democratization influenced by, 146–147
    opposition parties, 32, 40, 136–139
    personalistic, 130–131, 133
    religious conflict and, 130–131
  Radical Party in, 36, 131–134, 144–145
  revolts in, 77, 124–130
    opposition, 126, 130
    Society of Equality and, 127
    state repression as response to, 128
    weak military and, 126
  strong political parties in, 102
    democratization influenced by, 146–147
  suffrage restrictions in, 146
  territorial cleavages in, 112
  War of the Pacific and, 25, 85, 86, 129, 239
  origins of, 87
  weak military in, 19–20, 124
Chincha Islands War, 129
Cifuentes, Abdón, 135–136
Civil Party (Partido Civil) (Peru), 42, 236–237, 241, 243, 244–245, 247
civil wars. *See also specific wars*
  in Chile, 124, 126–127, 144
  in Colombia, 202
  strong political parties and, 109–110
  in Uruguay, 149–151
  Guerra Grande, 151–152, 156
class pressure model, 46–47
cleavages. *See also* regional/territorial cleavages; religious cleavages
  balanced, 37–38, 115
  religious, 98–99, 111, 113–114
  strong political parties influenced by, 35–36, 37–38
  strong political parties influenced by, 35–38, 110–117
  balanced cleavages, 115
  class cleavages, 36, 110, 111–112
  ethnic cleavages, 36, 110

coercive capacity
  in Brazil, 254
  in Chile, 85
  in Colombia, 206
  military strength and, 21–22
  opposition revolts and, 20–21
  in Paraguay, 85
  in Uruguay, 152, 155
  in Venezuela, 227
Colombia, 202, 203
  authoritarianism in, 203, 217–218
  Catholic Church in, 4, 37, 209
  civil wars in, 202
  coercive capacity in, 206
  Conservative Party, 207–215, 221–222
    split within, 215–219
  constitutions in, 203, 212
    reforms of, 218–219
  democracy in, 69
    analysis of, 223
    breakdown of, 68
    historical development of, 219–222
    origins of, 198–199
  democratic reforms in, 1, 41–42, 215
  Ecuadorian-Colombian War, 93
  1853 constitution, 108
  elections in, 211–212
    competition in, 212
    complete-lists and, 217
    electoral reforms and, 219
    fraud in, 202, 212, 220–221
    incomplete lists and, 217, 219
    legislative, 211–212
    presidential, 211–212, 213
  electoral participation in, 61
  geography of, 34
  Liberal Party, 207–215, 220–221
    split within, 215–219
  military professionalization in, 41–42,
    204–205, 206–207, 222
    under Law 17 of 1907, 205
    limits of, 207
    military training as part of, 200, 205
    after War of a Thousand Days, 204–205
  political parties in
    Conservative Party, 207–219, 221–222
    Liberal Party, 207–219, 221–222
    opposition parties, 32, 38, 220, 221–222
    Republican Union in Colombia, 198, 211,
      218, 221
    strong, 103, 207–215
  revolts in, 199–207
    authoritarianism as result of, 203

costs of, 203–204
opposition, 1, 22
suffrage rights in, 59
territorial cleavages in, 112
uprisings in, 220
La Violencia period, 222
War of a Thousand Days, 1, 22, 41, 44, 89,
  202, 203
  military professionalization after,
    204–205
  opposition parties and, 222
War of the Parish Priests, 203
War of the Supremes, 202, 203
weak military in, 19–20, 82–83, 199–207
colonial rule, colonialism and
  in Brazil, 248
  in Latin America, elections in, 23
  in Paraguay, 289
Colorado Party (Paraguay), 295–300
Colorado Party (Uruguay), 147, 148,
  155–163, 171, 172, 173
  democratic reform under, 163–172
  opposition within, 164
  Riveristas faction in, 167–168, 170–171
  split in, 163–172
commodity booms, military professionalization
  influenced by, 26
complete-list, 63
  in Argentine elections, 192, 194
  in Chilean elections, 143
  in Colombian elections, 217
  in Uruguayan elections, 161–162
compulsory military service, 130, 239
Concha, José Vicente, 219–220
Concha Torres, Carlos, 287
conflict-settlement path, to democratization, 310
conservative parties, geography as factor for, 117
Conservative Party (Bolivia), 270–274
Conservative Party (Brazil), 254–260
Conservative Party (Chile), 131–134, 136,
  144–145
Conservative Party (Colombia), 207–219,
  221–222
Conservative Party (Ecuador), 284–286
Conservative Party (Venezuela), 231–233
conservative political parties, 116
  democratic reforms and, 27–28
Conspiracy of the Daggers, 126–127
constitutions. *See specific countries*
Cordero, Luis, 285
Costa Rica
  democracy in, 315
  weak military in, 199

Index

coups
  in Argentina, 6
  during Aristocratic Republic, 245
  definition of, 78
  in Paraguay, 291
  regime outcomes and, 39
Crespo, Joaquín, 233
Cruz, José María de la, 127
Cuestas, Juan Lindolfo, 161–162
cumulative voting, 137, 143

Dahl, Robert A., 19
democratic laggards, 70–72
democratic pioneers, 70–71
democratic reforms. *See* reforms, democratic
democratization, democracy and. *See also*
    weak democracies; *specific countries;*
    specific topics
  actor-based theories, 44
  alternative explanations for, 43–47
  class pressure model and, 46–47
  conceptual approach to, 2–7, 9–12, 308–309
    analysis of, 73, 302–304
  conflict-settlement path to, 310
  in early twentieth century, 68–73
    presidential elections and, 70
  empirical approaches to, 308–309
  ephemeral, 50, 66–67
  European-origin populations as influence
      on, 45
  first wave of, 6, 7
  future implications
    for post-1929 politics, 304–307
    for research, 314–316
  geographic diffusion and, 46
  ideational diffusion and, 46
  Index of Democratization, 53, 72
  indigenous populations as influence on, 45
  measurement of, 9–12
  in Mesoamerica, 314–315
  methodological approach to, 12–16
  modernization theory and, 2, 44
  origins of, 1–2
  past experience with democratic institutions
      as factor in, 45–46
  political parties' role in, 3–4
  Polyarchy Index and, 72
  regime formation and, 7
  research methodology for, 7–9
    databases in, 8–9
    qualitative evidence, 7–8
    quantitative evidence, 7–8
  state-building and, 7

temporal diffusion and, 46
theoretical approaches to, 309–314
direct elections
  electoral competition in, 63–64
  presidential elections, 6
  in Uruguay, 157
Dom Pedro I (Emperor), 248
Dom Pedro II (Emperor), 248
Durand, Augusto, 240, 241, 245

Echagüe, Pedro A., 192–193
Ecuador
  authoritarian rule in, 5, 283–288
  elections in
    fraud in, 69–70
    free and fair, 66
  geographic fragmentation of, 118
  geography of, 34
  independence movement in, 278
  Julian Revolution in, 287–288
  Liberal Revolution in, 279–282, 286
  military in, 277–283
    professionalization of, 43, 278–283
    weak, 93–94, 199
  political parties
    Conservative Party, 284–286
    historical development of, 284–285
    Liberal Party, 284–286
    personalistic, 284
    weak, 104, 283–288
  revolts in, 77, 277–283
    opposition, 1
  suffrage rights for women in, 55–56
Ecuadorian-Colombian War, 93
1812 Constitution (Cádiz Constitution), 23, 55
election fraud. *See* fraud, election
elections, electoral systems and. *See also*
    free and fair elections; presidential
    elections; *specific countries; specific*
    elections
  abuses of, 62–63
  electoral fraud, 28, 29, 49, 62,
      69–70
  intimidation, 28, 29, 49
  under colonial rule, 23
  data sources on, 49
  independent electoral authorities, 28, 29–31
  indirect
    electoral competition in, 63–64
    in LAHED, 53
  Latin American Historical Elections
      Database, 49–50, 51–54, 60, 63
    data sources for, 52, 53–54

elections, electoral systems (cont.)
    historical scope of, 51
    presidential elections in, 51, 52, 53
    secret ballot, 3–4
    theoretical approach to, 48–51
electoral authoritarian regimes, 9, 23
electoral competition, 62–68
    compared to U.S. elections, 64–65
    in direct elections, 63–64
    electoral fraud and, 62
    ephemeral democratization and, 66–67
    free and fair elections and, 66
    in indirect elections, 63–64
    lack of competitiveness, 65
    margin of victory and, 65–66
    voter intimidation and, 28, 29, 49, 62
electoral intimidation, 28, 29, 49, 62
elite insurrections and revolts, 77
    definition of, 78
enslaved populations, suffrage restrictions for, 56
ephemeral democratization, 50
    electoral competition and, 66–67
ephemeral political parties, 122
Escalier, José María, 274–275
Esguerra, Nicolás, 218
Estrada, Emilio, 286–287
ethnic cleavages, 36, 110
executive dominance, 29–30
export booms
    in Bolivia, 267–268
    in Chile, 129
    military professionalization influenced by, 24, 26, 129
    military strength and, 87

Federalist Riograndense Rebellion, 253–254
Federalist War, 227
Fernández, Aristides, 216
Fernández Alonso, Severo, 272
Ferreira, Benigno, 298
Fidel Suárez, Marco, 219–220
Figueroa Alcorta, José, 188–189
Flores, Antonio, 285
Flores, Juan José, 284
Flores, Venancio, 148, 159
Fonseca, Hermes da, 252, 259–260
Francia, José Gaspar Rodríguez da, 288–289
Franco, Manuel, 299
fraud, election, 28, 29, 49, 62
    in Bolivia, 69–70
    in Colombia, 202, 212, 220–221
    in Peru, 69–70
    in Venezuela, 69–70

free and fair elections, 53, 66, 71
    in Argentina, 66
    in Paraguay, 66
    in Peru, 66
    in Uruguay, 162
Freire, Ramón, 126

Gallegos, Rómulo, 105
Gallo, Pedro León, 127
Gaona, Juan B., 298
García, Lizardo, 286–287
García Moreno, Gabriel, 278–279, 284
geographic concentration, 14, 18, 38, 99, 123
geographic diffusion approach, democratization and, 46
geographic fragmentation
    strong political parties and, 34–35, 99, 117–121
    transportation infrastructure and, 119–120
Gibbs, Antony, 140
Giró, Juan Francisco, 149
Gómez, Juan Vicente, 42, 105, 225, 230–231, 232, 234–235
Gual, Pedro, 231–232
Guggiari, José P., 300
Guzmán, Antonio Leocadio, 232
Guzmán Blanco, Antonio, 227, 231–232, 233, 234

Haya de la Torre, Víctor Raúl, 247
Herrera, Benjamín, 90–91, 206
Herrera y Obes, Julio, 152
Holguín, Carlos, 214
Hutchinson, Norman, 230

ideational diffusion approach, democratization and, 46
incomplete list, 304–305, 312
    in Argentine elections, 190, 192, 193–194
    in Bolivian elections, 274
    in Brazilian elections, 256–257
    in Colombian elections, 217, 219
    in Paraguayan elections, 299
    in Uruguayan elections, 161–162
independent electoral authorities, 28, 29–31
Index of Democratization, 53, 72
indigenous populations
    democratization influenced by, 45
    Mapuche, 124
indirect elections
    electoral competition in, 63–64
    in LAHED, 53

Index

insider revolts, 79
insurrections. *See* elite insurrections and revolts
interstate disputes, interstate wars and. *See also specific wars*
  military professionalization after, 24, 25, 27
  war outcomes as influence on, 26
Irarrázaval, Manuel José, 141
Irigoyen, Bernardo de, 184, 185
Irigoyen, Ignacio, 192–193

Jara, Albino, 299
Jiménez, Ricardo, 314–315
Jiménez de Aréchaga, Justino, 161
Juárez Celman, Miguel, 185–186, 188, 189
Julian Revolution, 287–288

Konig, Abraham, 182
Körner, Emil, 87, 129, 130
Kundt, Hans, 268, 269, 276

laggards. *See* democratic laggards
LAHED. *See* Latin American Historical Elections Database (LAHED)
LARD. *See* Latin American Revolts Database (LARD)
Latin America. *See also* Latin American Revolts Database (LARD); *specific countries; specific topics*
  Catholic Church in, 37
  international constitutions as influence in
    1812 Spanish Constitution, 23
    US Constitution, 23
  late twentieth century revolts in, 316
  representative institutions in, 23
  US Constitution as influence in, 23
Latin American Historical Elections Database (LAHED), 49–50, 51–54, 60, 63
  data sources for, 52, 53–54
  historical scope of, 51
  indirect elections in, 53
  presidential elections in, 51, 52, 53
Latin American Revolts Database (LARD), 227, 264
  revolts in
    data sources for, 76–77
    decline of, 79–80
Latorre, Lorenzo, 152, 156
Leguía, Augusto, 42, 104, 240, 244, 246–248
  military support under, 248
  personalistic political party, 247–248
Liberal Democratic Party (Chile), 144–145
liberal movements, 116
  geography as factor for, 117

Liberal Party (Bolivia), 270–274
Liberal Party (Brazil), 254–260
Liberal Party (Chile), 131–134, 136, 144–145
Liberal Party (Colombia), 207–219, 220–221
Liberal Party (Ecuador), 284–286
Liberal Party (Paraguay), 295–300
Liberal Party (Peru), 247
Liberal Party (Venezuela), 231–233, 234
liberal political parties, in Chile, 31
Liberal Rebellion, in Paraguay, 298
Liberal Revolution, in Ecuador, 279–282, 286
Linares, Francisco, 233
López, Carlos Antonio, 289
López, José Hilario, 209–210
López de Romaña, Eduardo, 244
López Jordán, Ricardo, 180

Manini, Pedro, 164
Mapuche indigenous population, in Chile, 124, 134
Márquez, José Ignacio de, 202
Marroquín, José Manuel, 216–217
Martínez, Martín C., 165
Martínez Thedy, Eugenio, 170
mass armies, 22, 24, 75
McGill, Samuel, 230
Mendiondo, Rogelio, 169
Mibelli, Celestino, 169, 170
militaries, strong
  in Bolivia, 94
  coercive capacity and, 21–22
  decline in, 81
  democratization influenced by, 72–73
  in Ecuador, 93–94
  expansion of military and, 88
  export booms and, 87
  military modernization as influence on, 87–88
  military professionalization and, 85–94
    data sources on, 90
    international conflicts and, 86
    monopolies on use of force, 89
    through officer training, 88
    opposition revolts and, 21
    outsider revolts and, 92
    in Paraguay, 85, 93
    popular uprisings and, 91
    regime outcomes, 39
    regime stability and, 91
    revolts as influence on, 81
    state-building and, 87
    through use of foreign weaponry, 88–89
    war outcomes as influence on, 86–87

militaries, weak
　democratization influenced by
　　in Argentina, 19–20
　　in Bolivia, 19
　　in Brazil, 248–249
　　in Chile, 19–20, 124
　　　revolts as result of, 126
　　in Colombia, 19–20, 82–83, 199–207
　　in Costa Rica, 199
　　in Ecuador, 19, 199
　　military expenditures as factor for, 82–83
　　during nineteenth century, 82–85
　　in Paraguay, 19
　　in Peru, 199, 237
　　regime outcomes and, 38–39
　　in Uruguay, 19–20, 149
　　in Venezuela, 199, 231–235
militarized conflicts. *See* civil wars; wars
military. *See also* mass armies; military professionalization; military strength; *specific countries; specific topics*
　in authoritarian regimes, 22–23
　democratization and, 18–24
　　with dominant militaries, 20
　　legitimate use of force in, 18–19
　　literature on, 19
　　military stalemate as influence on, 20
　　state capacity and, 19
military professionalization, 3, 22
　in Argentina, 27, 40–41, 176–182
　　government expenditures for, 176
　　military missions, 181
　　military schools and training, 180, 181–182
　in Bolivia, 267–269
　in Brazil, 249–253
　in Chile, 25, 27, 40–41, 124–130
　　Army of the Andes and, 124
　　export boom and, 129
　　international assistance for, 129
　　international conflicts as influence on, 129
　in Colombia, 41–42, 204–205, 206–207, 222
　　by geographic region, 207
　　under Law 17 of 1907, 205
　　military training as part of, 200, 205
　　after War of a Thousand Days, 204–205
　commodity booms and, 26
　costs of, 26
　democratization influenced by, 44–45, 72–73
　in Ecuador, 279–283
　export booms and, 24, 26

interstate conflicts and, 24, 25, 27
　war outcomes, 26
military strength and, 85–94
　data sources on, 90
　international conflicts and, 86
　opposition rebellions and, 22
origins of, 24–27
in Paraguay, 43, 291–294
in Peru, 239–240
regime outcomes and, 38, 39–43
　with strong military, 39
　unstable authoritarianism and, 38–39
　with weak military, 38–39
revolts and, 74–76, 81–82
state-building and, 24–25
　bellicist approach to, 24–25
in Uruguay, 40–41, 148–155, 173–174
　establishment of national army, 148
in Venezuela, 227–230
War of a Thousand Days and, 44
in wealthy nations, 27
military schools, military training and
　in Argentina, 180, 181–182
　in Bolivia, 263–264, 268
　in Colombia, 200, 205
　in Paraguay, 294
　in Peru, 236
　in Venezuela, 226
military service. *See* compulsory military service
military strength. *See also* militaries, strong; militaries, weak
　in Bolivia, 94
　coercive capacity and, 21–22
　export booms and, 87
　military professionalization and, 85–94
　　data sources on, 90
　　international conflicts and, 86
　opposition revolts and, 21
　outsider revolts and, 92
　in Paraguay, 85, 93
　popular uprisings and, 91
　revolts as influence on, 81
　state-building and, 87
　through weapons accumulation, 88–89
military training. *See* military schools, military training and
militias, 84–85
　in Peru, 236–237
　in Uruguay, 148
　in Venezuela, 227
Mineiro Republican Party, 258–259
Mitre, Bartolomé, 177–179, 185

Index

modernization theory, democratization and, 2, 44
Monagas, José Gregorio, 231–232, 234
Monagas, José Tadeo, 231–233, 234
monopolies, on violence or use of force, 89
Montero, Pedro, 287
Montt, Manuel, 127, 130–131, 143, 145
Morais, Prudente de, 257
Morales Bermúdez, Remigio, 242–243
Mosquera, Tomás Cipriano de, 200, 210
Muñoz, Basilio, 90–91, 155
mutinies
  in Bolivia, 275
  in Chile, 124
  definition of, 78

National Autonomist Party (PAN) (Argentina), 183–186, 188–195
National (civic) guard, 89, 136, 143, 249, 251, 278
National Party (Chile), 131–134, 144–145
National Union Party, 189, 193, 194
New Zealand, democratic transformation in, geographic factors for, 19
North, John, 140
Norway, democratic transformation in, geographic factors for, 19
Núñez, Rafael, 204, 210, 215

obligatory voting and registration, 31, 168–169, 191–192, 194, 195
O'Higgins, Bernardo, 124
Olaya Herrera, Enrique, 219–220
opposition parties
  in Bolivia, 274–275
  in Chile, 32, 40, 135–139
  in Colombia, 32, 38, 220, 221–222
  democratic reforms and, 3–4, 29–32
  democratization influenced by, 3–4, 72–73
  in Peru, 243
  in Uruguay, 32, 38, 164
  use of past conflicts by, 21
opposition revolts
  in Argentina, 22
  in Bolivia, 1
  in Chile, 126, 130
  coercive state capacity and, 20–21
  in Colombia, 22
  military professionalization and, 22
  state military strength and, 21
  in Uruguay, 22
Orbegoso, Luis Jose de, 242
Oribe, Manuel, 149, 156

Ospina, Mariano, 203
Ospina, Pedro Nel, 220–221
outsider revolts, 79
  in Brazil, 253–254
  military strength and, 92
  in Peru, 240

Pacheco, Gregorio, 270–271
Páez, José Antonio, 231–232
PAN. *See* National Autonomist Party (PAN) (Argentina)
Pando, José M., 272–273
Paraguay
  authoritarian regimes in, 5
  Catholic Church in, 37, 295
  Chaco War, 269–270, 294
  coercive capacity in, 85
  coups in, 291
  democracy in
    development of, 288
    political instability and, 300
  elections in
    free and fair, 66
    legislative, 297
    presidential, 297–298
  geographic fragmentation of, 35
  military in, 288–294
    during colonial era, 289
    military academies, 294
    professionalization of, 43, 291–294
    strength of, 85, 93
  militias in, 84
  opposition revolts in, 1
  political parties in, 294–300
    Colorado Party, 295–300
    Liberal Party, 295–300
    partisan identification with, 296
  revolts in, 43, 77, 288–294
    Liberal Rebellion, 298
    state repression from, 291
  uprisings in, 291
  War of the Triple Alliance (Paraguayan War), 25, 26, 85, 86, 89, 93, 179, 251
    democratization influenced by, 288
Pardo, José, 246, 247
Pardo, Manuel, 236–237, 241, 242, 243
Paredes, Manuel Rigoberto, 103–104
Parra, Aquileo, 203–204
Partido Civil (Civil Party) (Peru), 42, 236–237, 241, 243, 244–245, 247
Paulista Republican Party, 258–259
Pedro II (Emperor), 257
Pellegrini, Carlos, 188–189

personalistic political parties, 101, 104, 122
  in Argentina, 183, 198
  in Bolivia, 270
  in Brazil, 255
  in Chile, 130–131, 133
  in Ecuador, 284
  Leguía and, 247–248
  in Peru, 101, 104, 241
  in Venezuela, 231–232, 234–235
Peru
  Aristocratic Republic in, 243
    coups during, 245
  authoritarianism in, 241–248
  constitutions in, 239
  democratic reforms in, 243
  elections in
    electoral reforms, 243–244
    fraud in, 69–70
    free and fair, 66
    legislative, 244–245
    presidential, 244–245
  military in, 235–240
    compulsory service for, 239
    international assistance for, 240
    professionalization of, 239–240
    training for, 236
    weak, 199, 237
  militias in, 236–237
  political parties
    Civil Party, 42, 236–237, 241, 243, 244–245, 247
    Liberal Party, 247
    opposition parties, 243
    personalistic, 101, 104, 241
    weakness of, 104, 241–248
  revolts in, 235–240
    opposition revolts, 1
    outsider, 240
  suffrage rights for males in, 59, 243–244
  War of the Pacific and, 25, 85, 86, 129, 239
Pessoa, João, 260
Piérola, Nicolás, 237, 239, 240, 241, 244–245
Plaza, Leonidas, 282, 286, 287
political parties. *See also* opposition parties; specific countries; specific topics
  attachment to electorate, 210–211, 224, 225, 255–256
  conservative, democratic reforms and, 27–28
  democratic reforms and, 27–34
    conservative parties, 27–28
    opposition parties, 3–4, 29–32
    ruling parties, 28–29, 32–34
  democratization and, 3–4

ephemeral, 122
institutionalization of, 100, 102
linkages, 37, 98, 174, 284
ruling, 28–29, 32–34
weak, 122
political parties, weak, 122
  in Bolivia, 270–277
  in Brazil, 254–260
  in Ecuador, 283–288
  in Peru, 241–248
political party strength, 34–38
  analysis of, 121–122
  in Argentina, 103
  in Bolivia, 103–104
  in Brazil, 104–105
  Catholic Church and, 113–114
  in Chile, 102
    democratization influenced by, 146–147
  in Colombia, 103, 207–215
  conservative parties, 116
    geography as factor for, 117
  data sources on, 101
  definition of, 100
  democratization influenced by, 72–73, 107–108
  in Ecuador, 104
  from 1870–1930, 100–105, 106–107
  factors for, 106–110
  geographic fragmentation in countries and, 34–35, 99, 119, 117–121
  transportation infrastructure and, 119–120
  inter-party civil wars and, 109–110
  liberal movements, 116
    geography as factor for, 117
  origins of, 34
  in Paraguay, 103
  in Peru, 104
  social cleavages as influence on, 35–38, 110–117
    balanced, 115
    economic class cleavages, 36, 110, 111–112
    ethnic cleavages, 36, 110
    religious cleavages, 35–36, 37–38, 98–99, 111, 113–114
    territorial cleavages, 36–37, 98–99, 112–113
  socioeconomic modernization as influence on, 109
  theoretical approach to, 98–100
  in Uruguay, 102, 147
  in Venezuela, 105
  violent conflict and, 109

Index

Polyarchy (Dahl), 19
Polyarchy Index, 72
popular uprisings, 78
  in Colombia, 220
  military strength and, 91
  in Paraguay, 291
Portales, Diego, 126–127
Prado, Jorge, 245
Prado, Manuel, 245
Prado, Mariano, 242
presidential elections
  in Argentina, 196
  in Brazil, 258, 259–260
  in Chile, 138
  in Colombia, 211–212, 213
  as democratic reform, 6
  democratization and, 70
  free and fair, 71
  in Latin American Historical Elections Database, 51, 52, 53
  in Paraguay, 297–298
  in Peru, 244–245
  in Uruguay, 159–160
Prestes, Luis Carlos, 260
Prieto, José Joaquín, 126
principista parties, in Uruguay, 158–159
proportional representation
  democratic reforms and, 28
  in Uruguay, 172

Quintana, Manuel, 188–189

Radical Civic Union party (UCR), in Argentina, 36, 69, 92, 182–187, 195–197, 198
  manifesto for, 185
  split within, 188–195
Radical Party (Chile), 36, 131–134, 144–145
rebellions. *See* revolts, rebellions and
Recabarren, Manuel, 141–142
reforms, democratic
  in Brazil, 256–257
  in Chile, 33, 146
    opposition parties and, 136–139
  in Colombia, 1, 41–42, 215
  direct presidential elections, 6
  expansion of suffrage, 28–29
  incentives for, 312
  packages of complementary measures, 31
  in Peru, 243
  political parties and, 27–34
    conservative parties, 27–28
    opposition parties, 3–4, 29–32
    ruling parties, 28–29, 32–34

proportional representation and, 28
ruling parties and, 28–29
  political splits within, 32–34
secret ballots and, 28
term limits, 6
in third wave of democratization, 31
in Uruguay, 33, 161–162, 173
  under Batlle y Ordóñez, 163–172
  Colorado Party role in, 163–172
regime outcomes
  coups and, 39
  determinants of, 38
    exogenous factors, 38
  military professionalization and, 38, 39–43
    with strong military, 39
    unstable authoritarianism and, 38–39
    with weak military, 38–39
  opposition parties and, 38
  scoring of, 40
regional/territorial cleavages
  strong political parties and, 36–37, 98–99, 112–113
  in Uruguay, 112–113, 156
religious cleavages, 35–36, 37–38, 98–99
representation. *See* proportional representation
representative institutions, in Latin America, 23
Republican Union (Colombia), 198, 211, 218, 221
Restrepo, Carlos, 206, 218, 219–220
revolts, rebellions and. *See also* elite insurrections and revolts; mutinies; opposition revolts; popular uprisings
  in Argentina, 77, 176–182
  in Bolivia, 263–270
    in Latin American Revolts Database, 264
    opposition revolts, 1
  in Brazil, 248–254
    opposition revolts, 1
    outsider revolts, 253–254
  in Chile, 77, 124–130
    opposition revolts, 126, 130
    Society of Equality and, 127
    state repression as response to, 128
    weak military and, 126
  in Colombia, 199–207
    authoritarianism as result of, 203
    costs of, 203–204
    opposition revolts, 1, 22
  conceptual approach to, 74–76
  decline in, 76–82
    from 1830–1929, 77
    factors for, 80–82

revolts, rebellions (cont.)
    in Latin American Revolts Database, 79–80
    military strength as factor in, 81
    state capacity as factor for, 80–81
    democratization as result of, 1
    in Ecuador, 77, 277–283
    opposition revolts, 1
    insider, 79
    in late twentieth century Latin America, 316
    Latin American Revolts Database
        data sources for, 76–77
        decline of revolts in, 79–80
        leadership of, 78–79
        typology of revolts and, 77, 78
        methodological approach to, 75–76
        temporal range in, 76
    military professionalization and, 74–76, 81–82
    military strength influenced by, 81
    negative impacts of, 74–75
    outsider, 79
    in Paraguay, 43, 77, 288–294
        Liberal Rebellion, 298
        state repression from, 291
    in Peru, 235–240
        opposition revolts, 1
        outsider revolts, 240
    statistical analysis of, 94–97
        determinants in, 96
    Tocqueville on, 74
    typology of, 77–78
        by leader types, 77, 78
    in Uruguay, 148–155
    in Venezuela, 226–231
        authoritarianism as result of, 227
        in Latin American Revolts Database, 227
        opposition revolts, 1
Revolution of the Spears, 162
Reyes, Rafael, 204–206, 216–218
Riccheri, Pablo, 181
Riesco, Germán, 145
Rivera, Fructuoso, 156
Roca, Julio A., 177, 179, 180, 183
Roca, Julio A., Jr., 192
Rocafuerte, Vicente, 279
Rodríguez Laretta, Aureliano, 165, 168, 169
Roldán, Salvador Camacho, 214
Rosas, Juan Manuel de, 176–177, 182–183
Rossi, César, 172
Rothlisberger, Ernst, 210–211
ruling political parties, democratic reforms and, 28–29, 32–34

Saavedra, Bautista, 273, 274–275, 276
Sáenz Peña, Luis, 188
Sáenz Peña, Roque, 41, 188–195
La Sagrada police force, in Venezuela, 230
Salamanca, Daniel, 273, 274–275
Salom, Bartolomé, 232–233
Samper, José Miguel, 215–216
Sánchez Cerro, Luis M., 248
Sanclemente, Manuel Antonio, 215–216
Sanfuentes, Enrique Salvador, 140
Sanfuentes, Juan Luis, 145
Santa María, Domingo, 129, 136, 137–139
Santander, Francisco de Paula, 208
Santos, Enrique, 4
Santos, Máximo, 156, 162
Saravia, Aparicio, 155
Sarmiento, Domingo, 177–179, 180
secret ballots, 3–4
    in Chile, 142
    democratic reforms and, 28
    in Uruguay elections, 172
Segundo, Juan José, 169
Sever, Jacques, 268
Siles, Hernando, 275–277
social cleavages. *See* cleavages
Society of Equality, 127
Solano López, Francisco, 290, 295
South America. *See also specific countries; specific topics*
    democracy in
        conceptual approach to, 17–18
        methodological approach to, 17–18
        origins of, 1–2, 17–18
Spain, 1812 Constitution, 23, 55
stable authoritarian regimes, 5, 42, 224–226, 235. *See also* Brazil; Peru; Venezuela
state capacity. *See also* coercive capacity
    revolts influenced by, 80–81
state repression
    in Chile, 128
    in Paraguay, 291
state-building
    costs of, 26
    military professionalization and, 24–25
    bellicist approach to, 24–25
    military strength and, 87
Stroessner, Alfredo, 294
suffrage rights
    in Argentina, 59
    in Chile, 146
    in Colombia, 59
    in democratic reforms, 28–29

Index

in Ecuador, 55–56
electoral participation and, 54–62
  by age, 60
  expansion of, 56–58
  for males, 55, 59
    definition of, 59
  in Peru, 59, 243–244
  restrictions on
    by country, 56–58
    economic, 57–58, 59–60
    for enslaved populations, 56
    literacy, 57–58, 59–60
    for women, 55–56, 146
  universal, 55, 59
  in Uruguay, 161
    for women, 169–170
  in Venezuela, 233
  for women
    in Chile, 146
    in Ecuador, 55–56
    in Uruguay, 169–170
Switzerland, democratic transformation in, geographic factors for, 19

Tajes, Máximo, 156
Tejedor, Carlos, 177
temporal diffusion approach, democratization and, 46
term limits, as democratic reforms, 6
territorial cleavages. *See* regional/territorial cleavages
third wave of democracy, democratic reforms in, 31
Tocqueville, Alexis de, 74
Tornero, Santos, 128
Toro, David, 276
Tovar, Manuel Felipe, 231–232
training, of military. *See* military schools, military training and
transitional authoritarianism, 39

UCR. *See* Radical Civic Union party (UCR), in Argentina
Udaondo, Guillermo, 189
United States (US), electoral competition in South America compared to, 64–65
universal suffrage, 55, 59
unstable authoritarian regimes, 262–263
  military professionalization in, 38–39
Uribe Uribe, Rafael, 216, 217, 219–220
Urquiza, Justo José, 177
Urriola, Pedro, 127

Uruguay, 4
  authoritarianism in, 151–152
  Blanco Party in, 41, 84–85, 147, 148, 155–163, 171, 173
    membership requirements for, 158
    National Club, 157–158
  Catholic Church in, 37, 166, 171
  civil wars in, 149–151
    Guerra Grande, 151–152, 156
  civilian government employees in, 161
  coercive capacity in, 152, 155
  Colorado Party in, 147, 148, 155–163, 171, 172, 173
    democratic reform under, 163–172
    opposition within, 164
    Riveristas faction in, 167–168, 170–171
    split in, 163–172
  democracy in, 68–69, 155–163
    breakdown of, 68
    conceptual approach to, 147
    constitutional support of, 172–174
    proportional representation in, 172
    strong, 172–174
    transformation to, 1
  democratic reforms in, 33, 161–162, 173
    under Batlle y Ordóñez, 163–172
    Colorado Party role in, 163–172
  elections in
    competition in, 157
    direct, 157
    free and fair, 162
    legislative, 160
    presidential, 160
    secret ballots in, 172
    voter participation in, 165–166
  geographic fragmentation of, 35
  military professionalization in, 40–41, 148–155, 173–174
    establishment of national army, 148
  militias in, 149
  political parties in, 155–163
    national organizations for, 157, 158
    opposition parties in, 32, 38, 164
    opposition revolts in, 22
    power-sharing agreements between, 162–163
    principista parties, 158–159
    split in, 163–172
  state infrastructure in, 148
  strong political parties in, 102, 147
  territorial cleavages in, 112–113, 156

Uruguay (cont.)
    War of the Triple Alliance and, 25, 26, 85, 86, 89, 93, 179
    weak military in, 19–20, 149
    revolts in, 148–155
    Revolution of the Spears and, 162
    suffrage rights in, 161
    for women, 169–170
US *See* United States (US), electoral competition in South America compared to

Varela, José Pedro, 149
Vargas, Getulio, 254, 260
Vargas, José Antonio, 232–233
Vásquez Acevedo, Alfredo, 171
Veintemilla, Ignacio, 285–286
Vélez, Joaquín F., 216–217
Vélez, Marceliano, 215
Venezuela
    authoritarian regimes in, 231–235
        revolts as influence on, 227
        stable, 5, 42, 225–226, 235
    Catholic Church in, 37
    coercive capacity in, 227
    elections in, 232–234
        electoral fraud, 69–70
    Federalist War, 227
    military in, 226–231
        professionalization of, 227–230
        training for, 226
        weak, 199, 231–235
    militias in, 227
    political parties in
        Conservative Party, 231–233
        Liberal Party, 231–233, 234
        personalistic, 231–232, 234–235
        strength of, 105
    revolts in, 226–231
        authoritarianism as result of, 227
        in Latin American Revolts Database, 227
        opposition revolts, 1
    La Sagrada police force in, 230
    suffrage rights for males in, 233
Vidaurre, José Antonio, 126–127
Viera, Feliciano, 167
Villaneuva, Benito, 192–193

Villanueva, José Gabino, 275
La Violencia period, in Colombia, 222
voting rights. *See* suffrage rights
voting systems
    complete-list, 217
    cumulative, 137, 143
    incomplete list, 190, 192, 193–194, 217, 219
    obligatory voting, 31, 168–169, 191–192, 194, 195

War of a Thousand Days, 1, 22, 41, 89, 202, 203
    military professionalization after, 44, 204–205
    opposition parties and, 222
War of the Canudos, 253–254
War of the Confederation, 263
War of the Contestados, 253–254
War of the Pacific, 25, 85, 86, 129, 239
    origins of, 87
War of the Parish Priests, 203
War of the Supremes, 202, 203
War of the Triple Alliance (Paraguayan War), 25, 26, 85, 86, 89, 93, 179
    democratization in Paraguay influenced by, 288
wars. *See* civil wars; *specific topics*
Wars of Independence, 82–83
weak democracies. *See also* Argentina; Colombia
    in Argentina, 175–176
    in Colombia, 175–176
weapons
    imports of, 88–89
    military strength through, 88–89
Williman, Claudio, 155, 163
Wisner, Francisco, 85, 289
women, suffrage rights for
    in Chile, 146
    in Ecuador, 55–56
    in Uruguay, 169–170

Yrigoyen, Hipólito, 41, 184, 185–187, 190, 191, 197–198

Zavarce, Hermenegildo, 233
Zegers, Julio, 140

Cambridge Studies in Comparative Politics

OTHER BOOKS IN THE SERIES (*continued from page ii*)

Catherine Boone, *Inequality and Political Cleavage in Africa: Regionalism by Design*
Soledad Artiz Prillaman, *The Patriarchal Political Order: The Making and Unraveling of the Gendered Participation Gap in India*
Charlotte Cavaillé, *Fair Enough?: Support for Redistribution in the Age of Inequality*
Noah L. Nathan, *The Scarce State: Inequality and Political Power in the Hinterland*
Scott de Marchi and Michael Laver, *The Governance Cycle in Parliamentary Democracies: A Computational Social Science Approach*
Egor Lazarev, *State-Building as Lawfare: Custom, Sharia, and State Law in Postwar Chechnya*
Lorenza B. Fontana, *Recognition Politics: Indigenous Rights and Ethnic Conflict in the Andes*
Martha Wilfahrt, *Precolonial Legacies in Postcolonial Politics: Representation and Redistribution in Decentralized West Africa*
Sidney Tarrow, *Power in Movement: Social Movements and Contentious Politics*
Victor C. Shih, *Coalitions of the Weak: Elite Politics in China from Mao's Stratagem to the Rise of Xi*
Torben Iversen and Philipp Rehm, *Big Data and the Welfare State: How the Information Revolution Threatens Social Solidarity*
Eduardo Moncada, *Resisting Extortion: Victims, Criminals and States in Latin America*
Jacob S. Hacker, Alexander Hertel-Fernandez, Paul Pierson, and Kathleen Thelen, *The American Political Economy: Politics, Markets, and Power*
Lily Tsai, *When People want Punishment: Retributive Justice and the Puzzle of Authoritarian Popularity*
Kevin Mazur, *Revolution in Syria: Identity, Networks, and Repression*
Andreas Wiedemann, *Indebted Societies: Credit and Welfare in Rich Democracies*
Antje Ellerman, *The Comparative Politics of Immigration: Policy Choices in Germany, Canada, Switzerland, and the United States*
Michael Albertus, *Property without Rights: Origins and Consequences of the Property Rights Gap*
Ben W. Ansell and Johannes Lindvall, *Inward Conquest: The Political Origins of Modern Public Services*
Yanilda María González, *Authoritarian Police in Democracy: Contested Security in Latin America*
Robert H. Bates, *The Political Economy of Development: A Game Theoretic Approach*
Guillermo Trejo and Sandra Ley, *Votes, Drugs, and Violence: The Political Logic of Criminal Wars in Mexico*
Janet I. Lewis, *How Insurgency Begins: Rebel Group Formation in Uganda and Beyond*
David Szakonyi, *Politics for Profit: Business, Elections, and Policymaking in Russia*
Mai Hassan, *Regime Threats and State Solutions: Bureaucratic Loyalty and Embeddedness in Kenya*
Daniel C. Mattingly, *The Art of Political Control in China*
Adam Michael Auerbach, *Demanding Development: The Politics of Public Goods Provision in India's Urban Slums*
Gwyneth H. McClendon and Rachel Beatty Riedl, *From Pews to Politics in Africa: Religious Sermons and Political Behavior*
David Rueda and Daniel Stegmueller, *Who Wants What? Redistribution Preferences in Comparative Perspective*

Yue Hou, *The Private Sector in Public Office: Selective Property Rights in China*
Thad Dunning et al., *Information, Accountability, and Cumulative Learning: Lessons from Metaketa I*
Ignacio Sánchez-Cuenca, *The Historical Roots of Political Violence: Revolutionary Terrorism in Affluent Countries*
G. Bingham Powell Jr., *Ideological Representation Achieved and Astray: Elections, Institutions, and the Breakdown of Ideological Congruence in Parliamentary Democracies*
Noah L. Nathan, *Electoral Politics and Africa's Urban Transition: Class and Ethnicity in Ghana*
S. Erdem Aytaç and Susan C. Stokes, *Why Bother? Rethinking Participation in Elections and Protests*
Deborah J. Yashar, *Homicidal Ecologies: Illicit Economies and Complicit States in Latin America*
Simeon Nichter, *Votes for Survival: Relational Clientelism in Latin America*
Santiago Anria, *When Movements Become Parties: The Bolivian MAS in Comparative Perspective*
Benjamin Lessing, *Making Peace in Drug Wars: Crackdowns and Cartels in Latin America*
Richard A. Nielsen, *Deadly Clerics: Blocked Ambition and the Paths to Jihad*
Kanchan Chandra, *Why Ethnic Parties Succeed: Patronage and Ethnic Head Counts in India*
Mary E. Gallagher, *Authoritarian Legality in China: Law, Workers, and the State*
Karen Jusko, *Who Speaks for the Poor? Electoral Geography, Party Entry, and Representation*
Alisha C. Holland, *Forbearance as Redistribution: The Politics of Informal Welfare in Latin America*
John D. Huber, *Exclusion by Elections: Inequality, Ethnic Identity, and Democracy*
Laia Balcells, *Rivalry and Revenge: The Politics of Violence during Civil War*
Daniel Ziblatt, *Conservative Parties and the Birth of Democracy*
Gretchen Helmke, *Institutions on the Edge: The Origins and Consequences of Inter-Branch Crises in Latin America*
Ana Arjona, *Rebelocracy: Social Order in the Colombian Civil War*
Rory Truex, *Making Autocracy Work: Representation and Responsiveness in Modern China*
Daniel Corstange, *The Price of a Vote in the Middle East: Clientelism and Communal Politics in Lebanon and Yemen*
Philipp Rehm, *Risk Inequality and Welfare States: Social Policy Preferences, Development, and Dynamics*
Prerna Singh, *How Solidarity Works for Welfare: Subnationalism and Social Development in India*
Alberto Diaz-Cayeros, Federico Estévez, and Beatriz Magaloni, *The Political Logic of Poverty Relief: Electoral Strategies and Social Policy in Mexico*
Sarah Zukerman Daly, *Organized Violence after Civil War: The Geography of Recruitment in Latin America*
Melanie Manion, *Information for Autocrats: Representation in Chinese Local Congresses*
Kate Baldwin, *The Paradox of Traditional Chiefs in Democratic Africa*
Michael Albertus, *Autocracy and Redistribution: The Politics of Land Reform*
Jesse Driscoll, *Warlords and Coalition Politics in Post-Soviet States*
Isabela Mares, *From Open Secrets to Secret Voting: Democratic Electoral Reforms and Voter Autonomy*
Carles Boix, *Political Order and Inequality: Their Foundations and their Consequences for Human Welfare*

Kenneth M. Roberts, *Changing Course in Latin America: Party Systems in the Neoliberal Era*
Yuhua Wang, *Tying the Autocrat's Hand: The Rise of the Rule of Law in China*
Ben W. Ansell and David J. Samuels, *Inequality and Democratization: An Elite-Competition Approach*
Kevin M. Morrison, *Nontaxation and Representation: The Fiscal Foundations of Political Stability*
Tariq Thachil, *Elite Parties, Poor Voters: How Social Services Win Votes in India*
Timothy Hellwig, *Globalization and Mass Politics: Retaining the Room to Maneuver*
Roger Schoenman, *Networks and Institutions in Europe's Emerging Markets*
Kathleen Thelen, *Varieties of Liberalization and the New Politics of Social Solidarity*
Catherine Boone, *Property and Political Order in Africa: Land Rights and the Structure of Politics*
Ken Kollman, *Perils of Centralization: Lessons from Church, State, and Corporation*
Michael Hechter, *Alien Rule*
Susan C. Stokes, Thad Dunning, Marcelo Nazareno, and Valeria Brusco, *Brokers, Voters, and Clientelism: The Puzzle of Distributive Politics*
Ben Ross Schneider, *Hierarchical Capitalism in Latin America: Business, Labor, and the Challenges of Equitable Development*
Richard M. Locke, *The Promise and Limits of Private Power: Promoting Labor Standards in a Global Economy*
Christopher Adolph, *Bankers, Bureaucrats, and Central Bank Politics: The Myth of Neutrality*
Stephen B. Kaplan, *Globalization and Austerity Politics in Latin America*
Edward L. Gibson, *Boundary Control: Subnational Authoritarianism in Federal Democracies*
Andreas Wimmer, *Waves of War: Nationalism, State Formation, and Ethnic Exclusion in the Modern World*
Leonardo R. Arriola, *Multi-Ethnic Coalitions in Africa: Business Financing of Opposition Election Campaigns*
Milan W. Svolik, *The Politics of Authoritarian Rule*
Guillermo Trejo, *Popular Movements in Autocracies: Religion, Repression, and Indigenous Collective Action in Mexico*
Cathie Jo Martin and Duane Swank, *The Political Construction of Business Interests: Coordination, Growth, and Equality*
Pablo Beramendi, *The Political Geography of Inequality: Regions and Redistribution*
Roger D. Petersen, *Western Intervention in the Balkans: The Strategic Use of Emotion in Conflict*
Jane R. Gingrich, *Making Markets in the Welfare State: The Politics of Varying Market Reforms*
Sidney Tarrow, *Power in Movement: Social Movements and Contentious Politics, Revised and Updated Third Edition*
Pepper D. Culpepper, *Quiet Politics and Business Power: Corporate Control in Europe and Japan*
Eric C. C. Chang, Mark Andreas Kayser, Drew A. Linzer, and Ronald Rogowski, *Electoral Systems and the Balance of Consumer-Producer Power*
Karen E. Ferree, *Framing the Race in South Africa: The Political Origins of Racial Census Elections*
Layna Mosley, *Labor Rights and Multinational Production*

Pauline Jones Luong and Erika Weinthal, *Oil is Not a Curse: Ownership Structure and Institutions in Soviet Successor States*
Dan Slater, *Ordering Power: Contentious Politics and Authoritarian Leviathans in Southeast Asia*
Sven Steinmo, *The Evolution of Modern States: Sweden, Japan, and the United States*
Stephen E. Hanson, *Post-Imperial Democracies: Ideology and Party Formation in Third Republic France, Weimar Germany, and Post-Soviet Russia*
Timothy Frye, *Building States and Markets After Communism: The Perils of Polarized Democracy*
Lauren M. MacLean, *Informal Institutions and Citizenship in Rural Africa: Risk and Reciprocity in Ghana and Côte d'Ivoire*
Ben W. Ansell, *From the Ballot to the Blackboard: The Redistributive Political Economy of Education*
Herbert Kitschelt, Kirk A. Hawkins, Juan Pablo Luna, Guillermo Rosas, and Elizabeth J. Zechmeister, *Latin American Party Systems*
James Mahoney, *Colonialism and Postcolonial Development: Spanish America in Comparative Perspective*
Monika Nalepa, *Skeletons in the Closet: Transitional Justice in Post-Communist Europe*
Orit Kedar, *Voting for Policy, Not Parties: How Voters Compensate for Power Sharing*
Maria Victoria Murillo, *Political Competition, Partisanship, and Policy Making in Latin American Public Utilities*
Henry Farrell, *The Political Economy of Trust: Institutions, Interests, and Inter-Firm Cooperation in Italy and Germany*
Andy Baker, *The Market and the Masses in Latin America: Policy Reform and Consumption in Liberalizing Economies*
Mark Hallerberg, Rolf Ranier Strauch, and Jürgen von Hagen, *Fiscal Governance in Europe*
Mark Irving Lichbach and Alan S. Zuckerman, eds., *Comparative Politics: Rationality, Culture, and Structure, 2nd edition*
John M. Carey, *Legislative Voting and Accountability*
Thad Dunning, *Crude Democracy: Natural Resource Wealth and Political Regimes*
Scott Gehlbach, *Representation through Taxation: Revenue, Politics, and Development in Postcommunist States*
Margarita Estevez-Abe, *Welfare and Capitalism in Postwar Japan: Party, Bureaucracy, and Business*
Henry E. Hale, *The Foundations of Ethnic Politics: Separatism of States and Nations in Eurasia and the World*
Bonnie M. Meguid, *Party Competition between Unequals: Strategies and Electoral Fortunes in Western Europe*
Austin Smith et al, *Selected Works of Michael Wallerstein*
Robert H. Bates, *When Things Fell Apart: State Failure in Late-Century Africa*
Lily L. Tsai, *Accountability without Democracy: How Solidary Groups Provide Public Goods in Rural China*
Aníbal Pérez-Liñán, *Presidential Impeachment and the New Political Instability in Latin America*
Daniel Treisman, *The Architecture of Government: Rethinking Political Decentralization*
Christian Davenport, *State Repression and the Domestic Democratic Peace*
Marc Howard Ross, *Cultural Contestation in Ethnic Conflict*
Anna Grzymala-Busse, *Rebuilding Leviathan: Party Competition and State Exploitation in Post-Communist Democracies*

José Antonio Cheibub, *Presidentialism, Parliamentarism, and Democracy*
Jeremy M. Weinstein, *Inside Rebellion: The Politics of Insurgent Violence*
Beatriz Magaloni, *Voting for Autocracy: Hegemonic Party Survival and its Demise in Mexico*
Alberto Diaz-Cayeros, *Federalism, Fiscal Authority, and Centralization in Latin America*
Julia Lynch, *Age in the Welfare State: The Origins of Social Spending on Pensioners, Workers, and Children*
Stathis Kalyvas, *The Logic of Violence in Civil War*
Regina Smyth, *Candidate Strategies and Electoral Competition in the Russian Federation: Democracy without Foundation*
Jason Wittenberg, *Crucibles of Political Loyalty: Church Institutions and Electoral Continuity in Hungary*
Isabela Mares, *Taxation, Wage Bargaining, and Unemployment*
Joshua Tucker, *Regional Economic Voting: Russia, Poland, Hungary, Slovakia and the Czech Republic, 1990–1999*
M. Steven Fish, *Democracy Derailed in Russia: The Failure of Open Politics*
Charles Tilly, *Trust and Rule*
Torben Iversen, *Capitalism, Democracy, and Welfare*
Gretchen Helmke, *Courts Under Constraints: Judges, Generals, and Presidents in Argentina*
Yoshiko Herrera, *Imagined Economies: The Sources of Russian Regionalism*
Michael Bratton, Robert Mattes, and E. Gyimah-Boadi, *Public Opinion, Democracy, and Market Reform in Africa*
Kathleen Thelen, *How Institutions Evolve: The Political Economy of Skills in Germany, Britain, the United States, and Japan*
Joseph Jupille, *Procedural Politics: Issues, Influence, and Institutional Choice in the European Union*
Stephen I. Wilkinson, *Votes and Violence: Electoral Competition and Ethnic Riots in India*
Daniele Caramani, *The Nationalization of Politics: The Formation of National Electorates and Party Systems in Europe*
Kanchan Chandra, *Why Ethnic Parties Succeed: Patronage and Ethnic Headcounts in India*
Catherine Boone, *Political Topographies of the African State: Territorial Authority and Institutional Change*
Junko Kato, *Regressive Taxation and the Welfare State*
Evan Lieberman, *Race and Regionalism in the Politics of Taxation in Brazil and South Africa*
Elisabeth J. Wood, *Insurgent Collective Action and Civil War in El Salvador*
Carles Boix, *Democracy and Redistribution*
Beverly Silver, *Forces of Labor: Workers' Movements and Globalization since 1870*
Lyle Scruggs, *Sustaining Abundance: Environmental Performance in Industrial Democracies*
Layna Mosley, *Global Capital and National Governments*
James Mahoney and Dietrich Rueschemeyer, eds., *Historical Analysis and the Social Sciences*
John D. Huber and Charles R. Shipan, *Deliberate Discretion? The Institutional Foundations of Bureaucratic Autonomy*
Roger D. Petersen, *Understanding Ethnic Violence: Fear, Hatred, and Resentment in Twentieth-Century Eastern Europe*
Lisa Baldez, *Why Women Protest? Women's Movements in Chile*

Fabrice E. Lehoucq and Ivan Molina, *Stuffing the Ballot Box: Fraud, Electoral Reform, and Democratization in Costa Rica*
Pauline Jones Luong, *Institutional Change and Political Continuity in Post-Soviet Central Asia*
Scott Morgenstern and Benito Nacif, eds., *Legislative Politics in Latin America*
Jefferey M. Sellers, *Governing from Below: Urban Regions and the Global Economy*
Anna Grzymala-Busse, *Redeeming the Communist Past: The Regeneration of Communist Parties in East Central Europe*
Robert F. Franzese, *Macroeconomic Policies of Developed Democracies*
Duane Swank, *Global Capital, Political Institutions, and Policy Change in Developed Welfare States*
Mark Beissinger, *Nationalist Mobilization and the Collapse of the Soviet State*
David C. Kang, *Crony Capitalism: Corruption and Capitalism in South Korea and the Philippines*
Amie Kreppel, *The European Parliament and the Supranational Party System*
Simona Piattoni, ed., *Clientelism, Interests, and Democratic Representation*
Joel S. Migdal, *State in Society: Studying How States and Societies Constitute One Another*
Nancy Bermeo, ed., *Unemployment in the New Europe*
Susan C. Stokes, *Mandates and Democracy: Neoliberalism by Surprise in Latin America*
Susan C. Stokes, ed., *Public Support for Market Reforms in New Democracies*
Richard Snyder, *Politics after Neoliberalism: Reregulation in Mexico*
Jeff Goodwin, *No Other Way Out: States and Revolutionary Movements*
Maria Victoria Murillo, *Labor Unions, Partisan Coalitions, and Market Reforms in Latin America*
Stefano Bartolini, *The Political Mobilization of the European Left, 1860–1980: The Class Cleavage*
Ton Notermans, *Money, Markets, and the State: Social Democratic Economic Policies since 1918*
Gerald Easter, *Reconstructing the State: Personal Networks and Elite Identity*
Ruth Berins Collier, *Paths toward Democracy: The Working Class and Elites in Western Europe and South America*
Wolfgang C. Müller and Kaare Strøm, *Policy, Office, or Votes?*
Herbert Kitschelt, Zdenka Mansfeldova, Radek Markowski, and Gabor Toka, *Post-Communist Party Systems*
Herbert Kitschelt, Peter Lange, Gary Marks, and John D. Stephens, eds., *Continuity and Change in Contemporary Capitalism*
Carles Boix, *Political Parties, Growth, and Equality: Conservative and Social Democratic Economic Strategies in the World Economy*
Sidney Tarrow, *Power in Movement: Social Movements and Contentious Politics*, Revised and Updated Fourth Edition
Geoffrey Garrett, *Partisan Politics in the Global Economy*
Anthony W. Marx, *Making Race, Making Nations: A Comparison of South Africa, the United States, and Brazil*
Michael Bratton and Nicolas van de Walle, *Democratic Experiments in Africa: Regime Transitions in Comparative Perspective*
J. Rogers Hollingsworth and Robert Boyer, eds., *Contemporary Capitalism: The Embeddedness of Institutions*
Miriam Golden, *Heroic Defeats: The Politics of Job Loss*
Robert O. Keohane and Helen B. Milner, eds., *Internationalization and Domestic Politics*
Frances Hagopian, *Traditional Politics and Regime Change in Brazil*

David Knoke, Franz Urban Pappi, Jeffrey Broadbent, and Yutaka Tsujinaka, eds., *Comparing Policy Networks*
Doug McAdam, John McCarthy, and Mayer Zald, eds., *Comparative Perspectives on Social Movements*
Donatella della Porta, *Social Movements, Political Violence, and the State*
Roberto Franzosi, *The Puzzle of Strikes: Class and State Strategies in Postwar Italy*
Ashutosh Varshney, *Democracy, Development, and the Countryside*
Marino Regini, *Uncertain Boundaries: The Social and Political Construction of European Economies*
Paul Pierson, *Dismantling the Welfare State? Reagan, Thatcher, and the Politics of Retrenchment*
Theda Skocpol, *Social Revolutions in the Modern World*
Joel S. Migdal, Atul Kohli, and Vivienne Shue, eds., *State Power and Social Forces: Domination and Transformation in the Third World*
Herbert Kitschelt, *The Transformation of European Social Democracy*
Thomas Janoski and Alexander M. Hicks, eds., *The Comparative Political Economy of the Welfare State*
Catherine Boone, *Merchant Capital and the Roots of State Power in Senegal, 1930–1985*
Sven Steinmo, Kathleen Thelen, and Frank Longstreth, eds., *Structuring Politics: Historical Institutionalism in Comparative Analysis*
David D. Laitin, *Language Repertoires and State Construction in Africa*

For EU product safety concerns, contact us at Calle de José Abascal, 56–1°, 28003 Madrid, Spain or eugpsr@cambridge.org.

www.ingramcontent.com/pod-product-compliance
Ingram Content Group UK Ltd.
Pitfield, Milton Keynes, MK11 3LW, UK
UKHW010648050825
461241UK00026B/92